CulturalSubjects

A POPULAR CULTURE READER

Allan J. Gedalof
The University of Western Ontario

Jonathan Boulter
St. Francis Xavier University

Joel Faflak
The University of Western Ontario

Cameron McFarlane
Nipissing University

THOMSON

NELSON

Australia   Canada   Mexico   Singapore   Spain   United Kingdom   United States

THOMSON

————★————

NELSON

Cultural Subjects: A Popular Culture Reader

by Allan J. Gedalof, Jonathan Boulter, Joel Faflak, and Cameron McFarlane

Editorial Director and Publisher:
Evelyn Veitch

Acquisitions Editor:
Pam Duprey

Marketing Manager:
Lisa Rahn

Senior Developmental Editor:
Mike Thompson

Photo Researcher:
Natalie Barrington

Permissions Coordinator:
Indu Ghuman

Production Editor:
Carrie McGregor

Copy Editor and Proofreader:
Rohini Herbert

Indexer:
Jin Tan

Production Coordinator:
Hedy Sellers

Creative Director:
Angela Cluer

Interior Design:
Peter Papayanakis

Interior Design Modifications:
Tammy Gay

Cover Design:
Angela Cluer

Cover Image:
Robin Collyer, "Lichtman's Newstand" (2000, retouched photographic image)

Compositor:
Alicja Jamorski

Printer:
Webcom

COPYRIGHT © 2005 by Nelson, a division of Thomson Canada Limited.

Printed and bound in Canada
1 2 3 4   06 05 04

For more information contact Nelson, 1120 Birchmount Road, Toronto, Ontario, M1K 5G4. Or you can visit our Internet site at http://www.nelson.com

National Library of Canada Cataloguing in Publication Data

Cultural subjects: a popular culture reader/Allan J. Gedalof... [et al.].

Includes bibliographical references and index.

ISBN 0-17-641584–X

1. Popular culture—Textbooks.
I. Gedalof, Allan J.

HM621.C83 2004   306
C2004-902118-4

Table of Contents

A Preface to Instructors

What we have tried to put together in this book is a challenging introductory Cultural Studies reader for Canadian university and college students of popular culture. Most existing readers aimed at introductory courses take a popular culture approach to the study of popular culture and provide short, often critically unsophisticated and theoretically uninformed articles or excerpts largely drawn from the popular media. Generally, these seem more suitable for secondary school media courses or junior college courses where these anthologies are used to give students something they feel comfortable writing and talking about. Other current readers offer much more sophisticated sets of essays suited to the advanced university-level study of popular culture, but, not surprisingly, are ill-suited to students coming to the discipline for the first time, are typically theory-heavy and application-light. As well, they usually take no account of the experience of Canadians who, with varying degrees of pleasure and resistance, negotiate with and consume a culture that both is and is not their own. At the same time, we felt an anthology of readings solely from a Canadian perspective would hardly represent either the general field of cultural studies or Canadian culture within a global economy that circulates both culture and ideas about that culture.

In the material that follows, we have tried to find a reasonable balance among those various challenges. Given that this collection is aimed at postsecondary students new to the field, we have provided a pair of general introductions. The first of these outlines the history and evolution of a cultural studies approach to popular culture, providing various definitions of the field, what it studies, how it stands in relation to its subjects (i.e., the cultural products and phenomena it examines and the subjects who consume them), and how it is situated at the intersection of a variety of disciplines. The second part of the general introduction provides a summary of some of the central branches of theory that inform and drive the discipline. Where necessary, we also introduce key concepts, theories, and approaches useful to the students but not included in the readings that follow.

The general introductions are followed by the readings themselves, 22 articles by international scholars of popular culture from a range of critical, theoretical, and political perspectives. While many of the articles selected are not by Canadian scholars and do not focus specifically on Canadian experience, popular culture being far too global a phenomenon to be artificially restricted in that way, introductions to the readings and to the four sections into which the essays are grouped have been written with Canadian students and their experiences in mind. For each essay, there is a list of suggestions for further reading*, and a glossary of key terms is also provided at the end of the book.

---

*Please note that in the Unit Introductions and the Editors' Introductions, quotations are referenced in one of two ways. For quotations from readings that appear in this text, only the page number is shown in parentheses after the quotation. For quotations from another source, the source's name and accompanying page number are shown in parentheses after the quotation. The sources are listed at the end of each section.

Necessarily, such an anthology will be selective, rather than comprehensive. What we have learned through extensive and much appreciated consultation with our colleagues teaching the proliferating courses in Cultural Studies across this country is that no anthology will satisfy everyone's interests—that the range of subjects and approaches is far too extensive to represent, and the resulting anthology would be dauntingly bulky and prohibitively expensive. Our selection, then, attempts to economically provide students with a number of ways to look at popular culture, with a set of tools they can use to prise open the things and phenomena that make up such a large part of their daily lives, and to give them some good examples of both theoretical and analytical practices upon which they can model their own analyses of popular culture. For those instructors interested in a textbook to supplement this collection of readings, Nelson has also published *Popular Culture: A User's Guide* by Susie O'Brien and Imre Szeman. Nelson has also created a website to accompany *Cultural Subjects,* which offers helpful weblinks and other material: **www.culturalsubjects.nelson.com**.

While we are trying to cover a lot of diverse ground with a relatively small set of essays, we have also tried to give the collection some sort of coherence. To that end, we have taken as a focus for the anthology, as discussed below in the general introduction to the theories of cultural studies, the issue of the "subject" as the privileged object of culture that emerges from the 18th century onward, and as the "subject" that Cultural Studies takes as one of its primary loci: whatever happens in culture, whether through history, politics, economics, sexuality, gender, and so on, eventually affects/accrues to/influences how subjects act and interact within the public sphere—affects their bodies, their minds, their ideological perspectives. By wedding "classic" theory articles to more specific theories and approaches that riff off these by providing more concrete interventions into culture and engaging with its texts and artefacts, we model how subjects use and are used by culture. More specifically, in terms of the volume's methodology, we are offering students a way of thinking through their own positions, behaviours, and assumptions about their places within culture.

A Preface to Students

This anthology is meant to challenge and complicate the ways in which you think about popular culture as a whole way of life, something that you are not only a part of, but that it seems you cannot escape. Indeed, part of the challenge, perhaps the most difficult, arises precisely from the fact that there is hardly a place to stand outside a popular culture that presents itself to us as ideologically natural, as the normal order of things. While the essays that follow are intended to provide models of places you can stand and strategies you can apply to look at culture analytically and critically, the essays themselves may pose another challenge to beginning students of Cultural Studies. Not to put too fine a point on it, the ideas discussed and even the language used in many of these essays can seem difficult, can even seem like a new language. While we have tried to provide a context for understanding the essays in the various introductions and the glossary, you will probably find that you have to read an essay more than once, just as we did and continue to do, before its ideas begin to become clear and you are able to apply and evaluate those ideas in the light of your own extensive experience of popular culture.

This difficulty can be both stimulating and productive: if we rise to it, it challenges us intellectually, gets us to think in more complex and resistant ways about culture, requires us to think through the terms and ideas provided, and thus models how we are meant to think critically about the given terms of culture. For instance, readings in the first section of the book by Baudrillard, Benjamin, and Adorno and Horkheimer can also seem unnecessarily obscure, reflecting a "high" or elite theoretical language that wields the power of its own rigour as a critical weapon, a way of dominating its own debate with its subject(s). "Only those with enough education will understand," the essay seems to say. How this accessibility is granted involves, at least since the 19th century, certain implicit assumptions about class, race, and gender. You, as the current reader of these articles, perhaps in a college or university classroom setting, are often still bound by these assumptions. Are you the child of economically disadvantaged, or racially or culturally persecuted, immigrants striving to get ahead in a more affluent and seemingly more tolerant and inclusive country, such as Canada or the United States? Are your parents "established" Canadian or American citizens whose socioeconomic status affords an upward mobility that, in turn, grants you the opportunity to pursue higher education and thus greater odds for social advancement? To what extent do race, class, and gender factor in the students' ability to understand complex "theoretical" issues as expounded, in the case of Adorno and Horkheimer, for instance, by two white male members of the German-Jewish bourgeoisie? The essay reflects Arnold's earlier 19th-century race-, gender- and class-based ideas of culture, discussed below in the historical introduction to this anthology, as something needed to educate mass culture away from its own popular instincts. Part of this education was to adopt a higher universal standard of taste established by those educated enough to decide what this standard should be. In Arnold's case, this meant white, male, British thinkers who maintained a predominantly Western, Christian, and overtly imperialist vision of how culture would maintain world order.

What similar biases, then, inform the "high" culture still being championed by Adorno and Horkheimer, especially given the brutal racial implications of the Nazi ideology against which they were reacting?

Although Adorno and Horkheimer, to stick with their example, may try to force us to decide between what they see as the polarities of elite and popular culture, we do not have to make such absolute and mutually exclusive choices. Rather, we can take these poles as indicative of counterforces within the sphere of culture itself: high versus low; the emotional versus the intellectual; superiority versus inferiority. That is, we can read the essay within popular culture in the way that Dick Hebdige defines hegemony in another essay in this collection: as a "moving equilibrium" in which there is always a motivation toward homogeneity and the embodiment of subjects through the ideologies of a dominant order of things, on the one hand, countered by the resistances of subjects *as bodies* within the culture of everyday life on the other. The extent to which this site of resistance is itself real or manufactured will be the subject of many of these essays, all of them a part of this anthology's discussion of how subjects come to be and how they come to be embodied in popular culture.

Among the things tracked in this discussion are some that are of particular relevance and importance to students using this anthology. As you will see in the course of this volume, the history of Cultural Studies begins with a strong emphasis on the power and value of "high" or elite culture, and a corresponding fear of and distaste for the mass culture, seen as without or of little value, that increasingly seems to be threatening it and growing more powerful. Over time, the focus of cultural studies shifts to include more analyses of just what it is that constitutes "value" or the ideologically preferred in culture, and how those values got there and got built into us. There is a growing focus on the nature and power of the consumer of culture, on how culture is used and practised. Through that evolution of ideas, it becomes clearer and clearer that we can always have a choice, a degree of agency in the face of culture and in our own determination. Powerful as culture of all sorts seems to be, perhaps tautologically, if we take it to be a whole way of life, we need not be servile in its face. We as subjects have complex positions in complex cultures, and the more we understand about ourselves and our culture, and the relations between us and that culture, the richer life will be in meanings and pleasures, not least among them the new pleasures provided by the play of meaning in the mind.

Just as you are not helpless at the hands of big culture, neither should you be passive in the consumption of the big ideas and well-worked out applications that follow, or our own accounts or analyses of them. As any study of Cultural Studies itself shows, ideas, meanings, and theories are never finally fixed, they are always *being* fixed. In this anthology, we try to give you a good set of tools to do some of that "fixing" of meaning yourself. Remember that you come to this study with vast experience of popular culture, and of experiencing popular culture, that you should consult extensively as you critically read this anthology. What follows will, we hope, act as a set of mirrors that will refract and reflect your own experience in ways that illumine both you and the study of culture itself.

---

*Please note that in the Unit Introductions and the Editors' Introductions, quotations are referenced in one of two ways. For quotations from readings that appear in this text, only the page number is shown in parentheses after the quotation. For quotations from another source, the source's name and accompanying page number are shown in parentheses after the quotation. The sources are listed at the end of each section.

Acknowledgments

We and the publisher would like to thank the following reviewers who took the time to review the manuscript during its development. They include:

Mark Lowes, University of Ottawa

Carol Corbin, University College of Cape Breton

Monique Tschofen, Ryerson University

Dana Morningstar, Fanshawe College

Goran V. Stanivukovic, Saint Mary's University

Brian Patton, King's College

Al Uhryniw, Algonquin College

Iain Barrie, Algonquin College

Glenn Willmott, Queen's University

Dr. E. David Gregory, Athabasca University

Michael Cross, Dalhousie University

Phillip Thurtle, Carleton University

In addition to the pleasures the four of us have had individually in thinking, teaching, and writing about popular culture, we have especially enjoyed the opportunity Thomson Nelson has provided us to work together. Mike Thompson, Pam Duprey, Anne Williams, Carrie McGregor, and Rohini Herbert have been helpful, generous, and sensitive throughout, and we thank them. We are, as always, also grateful to the graduate and undergraduate students over the past several years who continue to teach us why the study of popular culture matters.

Jonathan Boulter: I would like to thank Mitra Foroutan. I also offer thanks to my co-editors, Allan, Joel, and Cameron.

Joel Faflak: I would like to thank the Department of English and Film Studies at Wilfrid Laurier University for their collegiality and support, and Norm, who never lets me down.

Allan Gedalof: Many thanks to my supportive colleagues at the University of Western Ontario, especially Tom Carmichael, Alison Lee, and Brian Wall, and to Monique Mailloux, the final answer to all of my questions.

Cameron McFarlane: As usual, my biggest thanks go to Jennifer O. Venn, Lisa Zeitz, and Nan McFarlane. I also owe a debt of gratitude to my colleagues in English Studies at Nipissing University: Ann-Barbara Graff, Laurie Kruk, Gyllian Phillips, Laura Robinson, and, especially, Lorraine Janzen.

And finally, Jonathan, Cameron, and Joel would like to thank Allan—great teacher, great mentor, great friend. This book would not exist without his initiative and encouragement.

Allan J. Gedalof
Jonathan Boulter
Joel Faflak
Cameron McFarlane

Part I: A General and Historical Overview of Cultural Studies

CULTURAL SUBJECTS

The readings collected in this volume explore a wide range of cultural subjects: Hollywood films, popular music, advertising, tourist destinations, national symbols, Internet activities, and much more—the products and practices that make up our everyday lives, our culture. However, these readings also explore the ways in which we ourselves are cultural subjects, the subjects *of* culture. From a rather innocent point of view, one might say that we are the subjects of culture because culture often seems to be "about" us. We are its topic. One radio station plays "the music *you* want to hear" and another one plays "*your* music at work." Local news programmes broadcast "the stories that are important to *you*" or sometimes simply "*your* stories," and "all the brand names *you* are looking for" can be found at the mall. "*You* deserve a break today," and don't worry: "*you're* in good hands." From this point of view, culture seems like a good arrangement. From a rather cynical point of view, of course, one might point out that even in ordinary usage, the word *subject* has quite another meaning: *servant, slave, captive, dependent.* And try using *subject* as a verb! Suddenly, the picture is not so nice. Perhaps that radio station will play those songs whether you want to hear them or not. Perhaps it will play them over and over until you find that you *do* want to hear them, that everyone wants to hear them. Perhaps that is the plan.

Of course, most of us have a more complex relationship to the culture around us than either of these brief models would suggest, a relationship that is neither one of unthinking, innocent, individual gratification nor one of equally unthinking, enthralled, mass submission. We all know that the music on the radio and the goods at the mall have not been produced for us as individuals; indeed, sometimes we cannot imagine whom they have been produced for. We all know that most of our culture—particularly that part of it made up of the mass entertainment forms normally designated by the term "popular culture"—is a business, not a service, an offering, or a gift. We are not so easily fooled by slogans and catchphrases. Still, this knowledge does not stop us from participating in that culture and from consuming it and enjoying it, however selective we may try to be. It does not stop us from listening to music or from sometimes having a deeply emotional response to particular songs that do seem to speak to us and to our experiences. It does not stop us from being moved by a film. It does not stop us from desiring things at the mall that seem just right for us. We are not necessarily taken in by culture, but we are taken with it. In a strange and complex way, then, we both are and are not the *you* that culture addresses. The nature of our strange and complex position in culture is what the readings collected here take as their subject.

CULTURE, POPULAR CULTURE, AND CULTURAL STUDIES

Popular culture and pornography have at least one thing in common: few people can define either one but everybody knows them when they see them. And some would go one step farther and argue that the two share a second important characteristic—namely, that we should be ashamed of ourselves for experiencing either one.

– Nachbar and Lause, *Popular Culture*

We have just used the words *culture* and *subject* as though their meanings were entirely obvious and self-evident. They are not. As the above quotation indicates, even things that seemingly "everybody knows" can be hard to pin down when it comes to definitions—perhaps especially things that everyone supposedly knows. The second part of this introduction will look at the complexity of the term *subject* in its critical and theoretical use. First, though, we will try to establish working definitions of *culture* and *popular culture*—a task that is more difficult than it sounds. It is unlikely, of course, that any of you has ever been flung into a state of confusion by someone's use of the terms *culture* and *popular culture*. For all their apparent obviousness, however, both terms are notoriously ambiguous when it comes to precise definitions, and scholarly debate continues concerning exactly what they mean. The following discussion, therefore, should not be taken as being in any way exhaustive, much less definitive. Our aim is only to offer you some context and some points to think about and discuss as you work through these essays. It is likely that the more you read, the more you will wish to develop and refine your own definitions of *culture* and *popular culture*; the material presented here, then, is intended to help you get under way, not prescribe your destination. We will also offer a brief description of the place of popular culture in academic study as well as raise some issues of particular concern to Canadian students.

If you look up *culture* in a good dictionary, you will likely be surprised at the range of definitions listed there. As Raymond Williams remarks in *Keywords: A Vocabulary of Culture and Society,* "Culture is one of the two or three most complicated words in the English language" (87). It is complicated because it gets used in different ways by different people in different fields. The word *culture* comes from the Latin *cultura*, which is itself derived from the verb *colere* meaning "to till the soil." We still use *culture* in this sense when we speak of agri*culture* and mean developing the soil to produce crops. Scientists also use *culture* to indicate a process of growth as well as the product of that process. A group of cells, say, grown for an experiment is referred to as a *culture*. And *cultured* pearls are pearls that have been manipulated to develop in a specific way. Culture, in this sense, is a process of tending and transforming, of producing and changing. These definitions may seem to wander wide of the kind of culture we are interested in here, but they do remind us that at its root, the word *culture* implies an active process, a development, rather than a finished, static product or accomplishment as we are sometimes apt to think. Culture is dynamic; it has effects.

In human, social terms, culture is used, variously, to designate the behaviour, customs, and products of a particular society or social subgroup; the pattern of meaning expressed in the symbols, practices, and objects of a particular group; and the pattern of thinking particular to a specific social group or subgroup. According to Raymond Williams, culture is "a whole way of life, material, intellectual and spiritual" (*Culture and*

Society 18). We use *culture* in this sense when we say something like "I'm interested in learning about other cultures" or "Canada is a multicultural society." Yet, these definitions, which are primarily sociological or anthropological, to some, seem too broad. Ministries of Culture, for example, are not in charge of our whole way of life and, when major cities get called "centres of culture," it is for very specific reasons: they have a large number of museums, theatres, galleries, concert halls, and the like. Many people take *culture* to mean pursuits of an intellectual or artistic kind: literature, music, theatre, the visual arts, and scholarship.

Matthew Arnold

This definition of culture just provided above, which we can call the humanistic definition, is the legacy of 19th century poet Matthew Arnold who, in his book *Culture and Anarchy* (1869), defined culture as the "pursuit of our total perfection by means of getting to know, on all matters which most concern us, the best which has been thought or said in the world" (6).

Arnold saw culture—the pursuit of perfection—as an antidote to what he called the "machinery" of the modern, industrialized world. The term "machinery" here is to some extent used metaphorically. Arnold was not concerned with the actual machines of industrial society in and of themselves but with the preoccupations and habits of mind that he felt were consequent on mechanization: an obsession with such material things as railroads, factories, and wealth as the measure of a society's worth, for example, to the exclusion of its spiritual and intellectual development. Culture, famously described by Arnold as "sweetness and light," could redress this imbalance and improve society. Ultimately, Arnold argued for the promotion of culture as a means of promoting a more egalitarian society, a society where all could share in the sweetness and light, but it is not hard to see that his definition of culture is practically the opposite of egalitarian: it is hierarchical—there is the "best" and then there is the rest. And it is elitist: who, for example, gets to decide what is best? Only persons of taste, judgment, and learning, persons *of culture*, can distinguish what is best for the poor, benighted masses.

F.R. Leavis

This latter point was made quite forcefully by the literary critic F. R. Leavis in his well-known monograph *Mass Civilization and Minority Culture* (1930):

> In any period it is upon a very small minority that the discerning appreciation of art and literature depends: it is (apart from cases of the simple and familiar) only a few who are capable of unprompted, first-hand judgment. ... Upon this minority depends our power of profiting by the finest human experience of the past; they keep alive the subtlest and most perishable parts of tradition. Upon them depend the implicit standards that order the finer living of an age, the sense that this is worth more than that, this rather than that is the direction in which to go, that the centre is here rather than there. (1–2)

For Leavis, as for Arnold, culture is something that is relatively static. It can be inserted into a process of dissemination—the education system, for example—but culture itself is relatively fixed. It is the best that *has* been thought; it is a tradition that can change only by perishing if we are not careful. Culture is something to be cherished, preserved, and protected—preserved and protected from its opposite: the anarchy of Arnold's title, the mass civilization of Leavis's. This hierarchical and oppositional understanding of culture has led to the reductive distinction between "high" culture and "low" culture. In this view, "high" culture, or minority culture, to keep Leavis's term, refers to elite productions, such as opera, poetry, and sculpture, conceived of as having timeless and transcendent value. These objects and activities are seen as the province of an elite minority, first, because they often require a substantial amount of money to produce and support them and, second, because it was imagined that they were produced for reasons other than commercial gain. Importantly, it was assumed that only those with the kind of education that wealth and privilege could afford were capable of understanding and appreciating them correctly. "Low" culture, or mass culture, refers to those objects and activities that are not part of the elite culture: such things as popular music, newspapers, and movies, conceived of as empty distractions of no value whatsoever.

While Arnold uses "machinery" more or less metaphorically to mean not just the machines of industrialization but the fixations of the industrial age, Leavis understands culture to be threatened by literally machine-made distractions. Q. D. Leavis, F. R. Leavis's wife, writes in *Fiction and the Reading Public* (1932), "The training of the reader who spends his leisure in cinemas, looking through magazines and newspapers, listening to jazz music, does not merely fail to help him, it prevents him from normal development…, partly by providing him with a set of habits inimical to mental effort" (224). Mass culture, then, is seen as worse than valueless; it is damaging and unhealthy, and its supposed brain-deadening effects render the minority capable of appreciating "real" culture ever smaller and smaller.

Few people would subscribe to this view today, although one does still hear occasional references to "highbrow" and "lowbrow" cultures. No one, however, would distinguish them with the vehemence of Mr. and Mrs. Leavis. For one thing, most scholars now agree that even such elite cultural productions as Shakespeare's *Hamlet* and Verdi's *La Traviata* are not transcendent and timeless; rather, they express the specific values and beliefs of the time and place in which they were created—values that, today, we may neither share nor wish to share. Second, many scholars have also become suspicious of the motives behind a fierce distinction between "high" culture and "low" culture. After all, it must have been very nice for the Leavises to believe that only they and a few others could "truly" understand "real" culture.

According to Herbert Gans, the distinctions between "high" culture and "low" culture are often made for political, rather than aesthetic, reasons. Such distinctions, he suggests, are "about which culture and whose culture should dominate in society…. As such, the mass culture critique is an attack by one element of society against another" (3–4). Finally, there is also a general consensus that if the boundaries between the "high" and the "low" were once distinct, those boundaries are not so clear anymore. When you can see an adaptation of a Jane Austen novel on television or a painting of a soup can in an art gallery, where does "high" end and "low" begin? And what about objects whose status has changed over time? Silent movies, as Lee Harrington and Denise Bielby have noted, "are treated as 'art' films today but were originally created for (and consumed by) a mass audience" (7). That last point about the status of silent films returns us to the idea of culture as a dynamic process, a process that involves considering how and for whom cultural objects are produced as well as how and by whom cultural objects are consumed.

Like *culture*, *popular* is also a complex word with many meanings. It can mean "belonging to the people" or "of the people," the populace. A grassroots political movement, for example, could be called a popular movement. *Popular* can also mean "well liked" as when we say, "Sue is very popular." *Popular* can mean "common" or "prevalent" ("SUVs are popular"), and *popular* can mean "approved" or "well received" ("That was a popular decision"). All of these meanings enter into the various definitions of popular culture, though none completely holds sway. Here are four useful, though very different, ideas of popular culture.

"Of the people": Popular Culture as Folk Culture

Understood as folk culture, "popular culture" refers to those objects and activities that are created by people for themselves and which are passed from generation to generation, usually in small, localized communities. Examples of folk culture would include handicrafts, working songs, tales and legends, and local festivals and customs. For the most part, folk culture tends to be associated with pre-industrialized societies, and many would argue that at least in the West, it does not exist anymore except as a concept or, worse, a gimmick. One can, for example, buy "folk-inspired" objects for home decoration. Even recent "do-it-yourself" trends seem only to emphasize our attachment to the ready-made: some people make their own bread, but they make it, for the most part, in mass-produced breadmakers; some people enjoy making decorative crafts for themselves and for friends, but they tend to buy their supplies at chain stores and to follow the instructions provided in such mass-distributed magazines as *Martha Stewart Living* or *Canadian Living*. A number of scholars, however, have suggested that certain kinds of urban rituals—say, rap music, for example, before it became mainstream—constitute a new kind of folk culture, though the fact that rap *has* gone mainstream makes this a rather ambiguous example.

"Prevalent": Popular Culture as Mass Culture

Understood as mass culture, "popular culture" designates precisely the opposite of folk culture. Mass culture refers to objects and activities that are industrially produced and widely disseminated *via* electronic or mechanical means for commercial purposes. From this point of view, culture is understood less as something that is created and more as something that is manufactured. Examples of mass culture would include television shows, magazines, music videos, and Hollywood films. Whereas the idea of folk culture emphasizes local differences, the idea of mass culture emphasizes the essential sameness of culture everywhere: you could hear the same song or see the same film in Halifax or Honolulu, in Alaska or Australia. Indeed, ideas of mass culture frequently carry the suggestion that one has no choice but to hear the same song or see the same film wherever one happens to be.

The mass entertainment industries are likely what most people think of when they hear the term "popular culture," but understood as mass culture, "popular culture" would designate *all* the mass-produced and reproduced objects of industrial culture: cars, toasters, McDonald's hamburgers, furniture, Tim Horton's coffee, cell phones, frozen vegetables, and clothing from The Gap, as well as television shows and popular songs—the many identical things that surround us. This definition of popular culture also sets a historical limit to its object of study: popular culture begins with the development of the means of mass mechanical and electronic reproduction and distribution in the last half of the 19th century and the beginning of the 20th century.

"Well-Received" or "Well-Liked": Popular Culture as Consumption

The idea of popular culture as consumption is a variation of the concept of mass culture. Understood as consumption, "popular culture" refers not just to the products of an industrial culture but also to the ways in which people use those products—or whether they use them at all. For example, the Hollywood film industry could produce a film, but if no one wanted to see it, if it was a "bomb," it could not really be called popular. Alternatively, consumers may use industrial products in unexpected and unintended ways. The builders and owners of a shopping mall, for example, expect consumers to come to spend their money at the stores; however, teenagers may use the mall only as a place to "hang out" after school, and senior citizens may use the mall as a safe and climate-controlled place to walk for exercise. While the concept of mass culture stresses the power of industries in defining what counts as popular culture, popular culture as consumption insists that consumers play an active and crucial role in the creation of their own culture and in the making of its meanings. In this definition, popular culture becomes meaningful at that point where the consumer and the artefact of culture meet.

"Common": Popular Culture as Everyday Culture

Another way to conceptualize popular culture is to think of it as the objects and activities that make up the everyday life of a group, large or small, and of the meanings that people, even unconsciously, invest in those objects and activities. This idea of popular culture would include mass-produced industrial products and the ways in which people consume them, as well as such things as our ways of speaking, the jobs we do, how we do those jobs, the places we pass time in, the ways we go about dating and forming relationships, how we are educated, who we form alliances with, how we decorate our homes, and so on. Defined this way, as everyday culture, popular culture often eludes our attention because it seems so ordinary, so unexceptional; it is "just what we do." Studying popular culture thus involves defamiliarizing it, making strange what we normally take for granted.

Each of the above definitions has strengths, highlighting different and important aspects of popular culture. No one definition, however, is the "correct" one. In general, those who study popular culture try to take all of these definitions into account (see the various theoretical approaches to popular culture discussed in the second part of this Introduction), though they may prefer or be more interested in one version or vision of popular culture than another as, indeed, may you. But the effort to define popular culture—a phenomenon thought by many to be so obviously self-explanatory as to require no definition—is the first step in taking popular culture seriously as a subject of study.

THE ACADEMIC STUDY OF POPULAR CULTURE

"In what is probably the most wide-reaching transformation of the humanities since literary criticism's rise to power over half a century ago," writes Simon During, "popular culture has become an important object of academic attention" (808). During is correct in his view that popular culture has received and is receiving an increasing amount of academic attention. It is still not always the case, however, that popular culture has an easy place in the academy itself, particularly in times of straitened economic resources when choices need to be made. Even though almost all universities now have pop-culture courses, eyes can still roll at the thought of university-level courses on situation comedies or soap operas or theme parks—and interestingly not just among the "old codgers." Sometimes, students sign up for courses on popular culture thinking that they must be easy because popular culture is not really a "serious" subject. Sometimes, students taking courses on situation comedies, soap operas, or theme parks—and taking them seriously—find themselves defending their choices to family and friends who think they are wasting their time (and money) taking university courses on such matters. After all, the argument goes, you could watch *General Hospital* at home. Frequently, "standards" are mentioned, along with their seemingly inevitable susceptibility to falling. Most people who feel that popular culture has no place in the academy have never heard of the Leavises, but such sentiments are testimony to the legacy of a Leavisite conception of "high" culture that is frequently associated with the university. Naturally, students need help understanding and appreciating Shakespeare or Wagner or Einstein, but sitcoms and comic books are obvious in their meanings, aren't they?

The Birmingham School

Serious academic study of popular culture—what would become Cultural Studies — emerged in the 1950s in the United Kingdom and is most closely associated with the work of three scholars: Richard Hoggart, who founded the Centre for Contemporary Cultural Studies (CCCS, also known as "The Birmingham School") at the University of Birmingham in 1964, Raymond Williams, and E. P. Thompson. Hoggart and Williams both came from working-class backgrounds, attended university as "scholarship boys," and spent part of their teaching careers at adult education institutes—experiences that affected the shape that their cultural studies initially took. Adult education institutes were set up after World War II as part of the postwar reconstruction effort in an attempt to create an informed and well-educated citizenry. Before World War II, most students concluded their formal schooling at age 15 years and entered the workforce; only those from privileged families and the few lucky enough to win scholarships went on to university. The adult education institutes were intended to extend educational opportunities to a broader spectrum of the population.

Both Hoggart and Williams were literary scholars, trained in the Leavisite tradition of elite culture, a tradition to which they would always retain an allegiance; however, their own working-class backgrounds and the backgrounds of their students convinced them that the universities needed to develop a broader, less elitist notion of culture, one that might speak to, rather than ignore or erase, the experience of the vast majority of the population. Hoggart's *The Uses of Literacy* (1957) and Williams's *Culture and Society* (1958) used the methods of literary criticism to validate working-class life and culture as meaningful and worthy of study. They, thus, redefined what could count as culture in the academy by moving the definition of culture away from the humanistic "best that has been thought and said" to the more anthropological definition of culture as "a way of life." Instead of being composed only of what someone had deemed was the "best" or the "greatest," Williams argued, in a famous phrase, that "culture is ordinary." Hoggart and

Williams focused on what they called "authentic" or "organic" working-class life—the pubs, community activities, patterns of language and of family relations, and so on— things they saw as threatened by, on the one hand, an elitist, academic conception of culture and, on the other hand, the postwar influx of American mass culture that seemed to be displacing more traditional pastimes. Stuart Hall, a later director of the Centre for Contemporary Cultural Studies, has suggested that part of Hoggart and Williams's achievement was to apply the methods of literary analysis to "a living culture," rather than to the artefacts of tradition. However, others have noted in their works a distinctly nostalgic element and, in their disparagement of the mass entertainment industries, the lingering traces of their Leavisite training.

Whereas Hoggart and Williams demonstrated that the experience of the working class had been excluded from ideas of culture, E. P. Thompson's *The Making of the English Working Class* (1963) demonstrated that working-class experience had been excluded from ideas of history. By tracing the construction of a specific working-class identity over a given historical period, Thompson showed that all culture, not just elite culture, had a history. Further, Thompson demonstrated that the production of culture takes place on an uneven playing field: there are winners and losers. That is, culture cannot be separated from the systems of power, the systems of dominance and subservience that structure a class-based society, for it is precisely from the conflict and the struggles which these systems create that culture is produced.

The Uses of Literacy, Culture and Society, and *The Making of the English Working Class* established a shape for cultural studies and exerted a powerful influence on subsequent work at the CCCS. The Centre maintained a focus on working-class culture throughout the 1960s and 1970s, in particular on the habits of young, working-class men. Unlike Hoggart or Williams, though, who celebrated an "authentic" or "organic" working-class life, the scholars working at the Birmingham School in this period saw the working class as an increasingly fragmented group and reconceptualized popular culture as a site of resistance to or negotiation with dominant political structures and class hierarchies.

Stuart Hall

This reconceptualization or retheorizing of popular culture led to a broadening of the methodologies used to study it and an increasing interdisciplinarity in those studies. Stuart Hall's seminal "The Television Discourse—Encoding/Decoding" is illustrative. Hall draws on theories and practices from linguistics, semiotics, structuralism, sociology, literary and film studies, as well as Marxist theory and an industrial analysis of the television industry to analyze how the television message is first created, marketed and distributed, and then consumed and used by the members of its audience (see the second part of this Introduction for a discussion of these theoretical approaches). Hall argued that each stage in this process involves a struggle over the creation and reading of meaning and that each stage is "relatively autonomous" from the others, limiting, but not foreclosing, differences in meaning. These differences are largely due to "structural differences of relation and position" between broadcasters and audiences and to "asymmetry between the codes of 'source' and 'receiver'" (125). Hall's analysis suggested that this asymmetry—the fact that television viewers may "decode" meaning in ways other than those in which producers "encode" it— is not a product of misreading or misunderstanding but a potentially political act, in part dependent on the position of the consumer. "Readers" of popular culture may interpret

from within dominant ideology, but they can also reserve the right "to make a more negotiated application" or to read oppositionally. Such a view led Hall to argue that the consumer is not powerless in the face of big culture, as earlier theorists had often concluded.
This emphasis on an active audience produced an increased interest in how subordinate
groups within culture find ways to resist, even thumb their noses at, dominant ideology.

As a result, scholars at the Birmingham school gave a great deal of attention to the
"subcultural styles" of such groups as mods, rockers, punks, and Teds. The clothing, hair-
styles, behaviour, and dance club rituals of these young men were read as signs of symbolic resistance to a dominant, exclusionary social system, a resistance through which a
communal identity was forged. Implicitly, and sometimes explicitly, then, the project of
cultural studies as it developed at the CCCS was to give a voice to disempowered and
marginalized groups within contemporary culture.

Given this last point, it was perhaps inevitable that cultural studies at the Birmingham
School would itself eventually come under fire for its focus on class to the exclusion of gender and race. In a collection of essays called *Women Take Issue* (1978), the Women's Study
Group at the CCCS critiqued not only the overwhelmingly male-oriented bias of what cultural studies took as its subjects but also the way in which it tended to ignore that the
"authentic," "organic," or "resistant" groups it celebrated were structured on the subordination of women. Others pointed out that "culture" at the Birmingham School was
almost exclusively white and did not, therefore, reflect the increasingly multi-racial character of British society or examine the extent to which racism is a powerful force in the
shaping of culture. The importance and necessity of these critiques cannot be underesti-
mated, but they can be seen more as an extension than as a dismissal of the principles
that gave rise to the field of Cultural Studies in the first place: the attempt to define a
broader, more inclusive, less elitist conception of culture and the desire to shift the study
of culture from an appreciation of "great" works to the examination of how culture is
made, by whom it is made, and how it is practised. Today, "Cultural Studies" designates
the study of such diverse topics as cyber culture, African-American culture, lesbian cul-
ture, postcolonial culture, youth culture, Asian-Canadian culture, sport culture, queer
culture, mall culture, "tweenie" culture, feminist culture, gym culture, diaspora cultures,
advertising culture, retirement culture, television culture, global culture, and more.

Characteristics of Cultural Studies

It may, at a glance, seem odd to group the study of so many different things under one
umbrella term, and we certainly would seem to have travelled far from an examination
of "authentic" working-class life; however, all cultural studies today share, for the most
part, three characteristics that have been present from the beginning.

1. *Interdisciplinarity*. Cultural Studies has been described as being an inter- or multi-
   (and even an anti-) disciplinary field of study. What that means is that Cultural
   Studies operates by borrowing theories and methods from a variety of disciplines in
   the social sciences and humanities: anthropology, linguistics, history, literary criticism, philosophy, political science, art history, the history of science, and so on. Many
   would argue that the vitality and validity of Cultural Studies derive from its ability to
   move freely between established disciplines and, thus, address diverse and contentious
   intellectual questions; some, therefore, fear that Cultural Studies will become estab-

lished as a standard, academic discipline and, in consequence, become part of the academic power structure it began by critiquing.

2. **Connectedness**. Cultural Studies has emphasized from its beginning that culture is not something that can be studied separate from its lived social and political contexts. It was this conviction, of course, that inspired the field's initial rejection of the Leavisite notion of transcendent and timeless culture. Culture, in Cultural Studies, is not so much a thing as a set of practices—practices that take place within a specific set of power relations; Cultural Studies attempts to expose those power relationships and the ways in which they shape and influence particular cultural practices.

3. **Engagement**. Cultural Studies is not a value-free or "objective" mode of scholarship; its attempt to understand the structure of power relations that shape culture is a first step in an attempt to change those relations. Cultural Studies aims to be both a field of study and a location of political criticism and intervention and, in this way, follows from Richard Hoggart's belief in founding the Centre for Contemporary Cultural Studies—that the academy needed to "come into an active relation with its age."

Admittedly, not everything that gets called Cultural Studies always has all three of these characteristics. North-American Cultural Studies, for example, has been criticized for its relative indifference to engaged, political activism as an integral part of the Cultural Studies project. But Cultural Studies developed at a different historical moment and under very different conditions in North America than it did in the United Kingdom. For one thing, the British class system, so central to the formation of Cultural Studies there, was not relevant to North-American scholars. Further, Cultural Studies emerged in the North American academy in the 1980s, a time when traditional humanities disciplines where already in turmoil, and Cultural Studies, therefore, did not need to establish itself as specifically revisionist or oppositional. Third, Cultural Studies tended to find a home in Departments of Communications or Departments of Media Studies, and an emphasis on mass-media representations—as opposed to cultural practices—inevitably followed. However, admittedly, scholars were interested in how mass-media representations affect cultural practices. Finally, the influence of postmodern theories (see the theory section of this Introduction) engendered a distrust of both the explicit and implicit Marxism of British Cultural Studies. North-American Cultural Studies, therefore, developed more as a form of textual analysis—*text* being broadly defined—than as an interventionist practice. This distinction, however, can be contested: as you will see, many of the essays collected here characterize analysis—ways of reading popular culture—as an interventionist practice.

A NOTE ON CULTURAL STUDIES IN A CANADIAN CONTEXT

A popular Canadian creation myth has it that when the Fathers of Confederation came together, they decided to build a truly great country by borrowing the best of what their ancestors and neighbours had produced. The country they envisioned would combine French culture, British politics, and American technology. But the plan went wrong, and Canada was left instead with French politics, British technology, and American culture.

– Frank E. Manning

Frank E. Manning's observation is both astute and witty in the way it brings together two popular—though ultimately ambivalent—conceptions of Canada: Canada as a multicultural amalgam and Canada as a country of compromise. In official government documents, newspaper columns, television specials, Bell telephone ads, and elementary school pageants, Canada is represented as a cultural "mosaic." Meant to be understood in often smug contrast to an imagined American "melting pot" of monoculturalism, the metaphor of a Canadian cultural mosaic attempts to define Canada as a friendly, pluralistic, tolerant, multicultural society, in which the diversity of its citizens is celebrated, rather than erased. Even setting aside a consideration of the truth of this image, it still does not take long for the celebration to shade into confusion. What exactly is the mosaic image supposed to mean? Does anyone know what the picture is that all the pieces add up to? What is "Canadian" if it is just bits of this and that? Although the idea of the mosaic sounds nice, it tends to fall apart under scrutiny, and probably more time, ink, and hand wringing have gone into the question of "Canadian identity" than into any other national question.

The idea of Canada as a country of compromise is similarly double edged. On the one hand, it is meant to convey that Canada is a peaceful country, preferring diplomacy to the use of force: *we* did not need a revolution to become a nation. On the other hand, compromise also carries the sense of having to settle for whatever one can get—or keep: well, at least we still have hockey, sort of.

Questions of identity and compromise loom large in the Canadian imagination for obvious reasons: first, efforts to define a trans-Canadian identity—efforts made by English-speaking Canadians, that is—are generally tripped up by their inability to account for Quebec and the First Nations. Second, even the effort to define a distinctly English-speaking Canadian identity must come to terms with the fact that we share our border with the richest, most powerful nation on earth which also happens to be the world's largest producer and exporter of cultural objects. Most of us listen to American music, follow American fashion trends, watch American television shows, read American magazines, and see American movies. We are awash with American mass culture, and it does not end with the entertainment industries. We eat at franchises of American chain restaurants; our cars may be Canadian-made, but they are usually American-designed; and no matter how many maple leaves Wal-Mart puts on its signs, it is still an American chain store. In other words, despite decades of government interventions intended to protect and promote "Canadian culture," most of what makes up "our" culture is American (see the essay by Rutherford in this reader and the section on National Identity in the second part of this Introduction).

The predominance of American cultural products in Canada must necessarily have an effect on the shape of Cultural Studies in this country. However, it would be a mistake to assume—or to lament or fear—that the study of popular culture in Canada inevitably ends up being the study of American popular culture or, at the other extreme, to insist that a "truly" Canadian Cultural Studies project should look only at exclusively Canadian cultural products and practices. Each of these extremes mistakes the aim of Cultural Studies. Canadian Cultural Studies must inevitably look at American *cultural production,* but that is not the same thing as American *popular culture.* Cultural Studies examines how and by whom cultural products and practices are produced *and* how and by whom cultural products and practices are consumed.

The culture these things give rise to is defined neither solely by producers nor solely by consumers. So, if, for example, 10 million Canadians watch CNN every week, it would be fruitless to argue that watching CNN is not part of Canadian popular culture, just as it would be unproductive to assume that those 10 million Canadians do not realize that they are watching an American newscast or that that knowledge does not affect the ways in which they respond to it.

As Canadians, we potentially have a unique perspective on what it means to be cultural subjects, to engage in complex negotiations of identification and difference, because we inhabit a culture that does not entirely inhabit us. We may sing along with American songs, model our style on American celebrities, and identify with the characters in American movies, but when asked "Is there really any difference between Canadians and Americans?" we generally stare at the questioner in stunned disbelief. True, when asked to articulate that difference, we often find ourselves reduced to mumbling something about "health care" and "gun-control laws," not quite able to put our fingers on exactly what that difference is.

Similarly, the ubiquity of American cultural products in Canada makes them so familiar that we rarely consciously think of them *as* American: we do not say, "I'm going to an American movie" or "Let's go for an American burger." They have, to a large extent, become naturalized. Yet frequently, when we are informed that a particular actor, singer, or writer is Canadian, we are surprised, and that surprise registers the fact that, at some level at least, we do not quite feel a part of the culture around us. In some ways, Cultural Studies asks us to be outside and inside of culture at the same time, and that is a feeling Canadians are used to. In *Mondo Canuck: A Canadian Pop Culture Odyssey*, Geoff Pevere and Greig Dymond write that to grow up Canadian is "to grow up with a peculiar certainty of the in-betweeness of things." From that "peculiar certainty"—a kind of uncertain certainty—we can ask the most interesting questions about a variety of cultural subjects.

—CM

REFERENCES AND FURTHER READING

Abelove, Henry et al., eds. *The Lesbian and Gay Studies Reader*. London: Routledge, 1993.

Adorno, Theodor W., and Max Horkheimer. 1947. *The Dialectic of Enlightenment*. London: Verso, 1979.

Arnold, Matthew. *Culture and Anarchy*. Ed. J. Dover Wilson. Cambridge, UK: Cambridge University Press, 1960.

Bhabha, Homi. *The Location of Culture*. London: Routledge, 1994.

During, Simon. "Popular Culture on a Global Scale: A Challenge for Cultural Studies?" *Critical Inquiry* 23 (Summer 1997).

Frow, John. *Cultural Studies and Cultural Value*. Oxford: Clarendon Press, 1995.

Gans, Herbert. *Popular Culture and High Culture: An Analysis and Evaluation of Taste*. New York: Basic, 1974.

Hall, Stuart. "Encoding/Decoding." Rpt. in *Culture, Media, Language*. Ed. Stuart Hall, Dorothy Hobson, Andrew Lowe, and Paul Willis. London: Hutchinson, 1980.

Harrington, C. Lee, and Denise D. Bielby. *Popular Culture: Production and Consumption*. Oxford: Blackwell, 2001.

Hoggart, Richard. *The Uses of Literacy: Aspects of Working-Class Life with Special Reference to Publications and Entertainments*. Harmondsworth: Penguin, 1957.

Hutcheon, Linda. *As Canadian as Possible…Under the Circumstances*. Toronto: Robarts Centre for Canadian Studies, 1988.

Leavis, F. R. *Minority Culture and Mass Civilization*. Cambridge: Minority Press, 1930. Rpt. in Folcroft, CA: Folcroft Press, 1969.

Leavis, Q.D. *Fiction and the Reading Public*. 1932. New York: Russell and Russell, 1965.

Manning, Frank E. "Reversible Resistance: Canadian Popular Culture and the American Other." *The Beaver Bites Back?* Montreal: McGill-Queen's University Press, 1993.

Morley, David, and Kuan-Hsing Chen, eds. *Stuart Hall: Critical Dialogues in Cultural Studies*. London: Routledge, 1996.

Nachbar, Jack, and Kevin Lause, eds. *Popular Culture: An Introductory Text*. Bowling Green, OH: Bowling Green University Press, 1992.

Pevere, Geoff, and Greig Dymond. *Mondo Canuck: A Canadian Pop Culture Odyssey*. Harmondsworth: Prentice-Hall, 1996.

Said, Edward. *Culture and Imperialism*. London: Chatto and Windus, 1993.

Thompson, E.P. *The Making of the English Working Class*. Harmondsworth: Penguin, 1963.

Williams, Raymond. *Culture and Society*. Harmondsworth: Penguin, 1961.

---. *Keywords: A Vocabulary of Culture and Society*. Oxford, UK: Oxford University Press, 1976.

Part II: Cultural Studies Theory

APPROACHING POPULAR CULTURE

This reader assumes that the productions of popular culture can be read as texts that require some kind of decoding, some interpretive intervention, if the complexities of these texts are to be fully appreciated. A cultural and literary critic—such as F.R. Leavis, who hated popular novels—would have found this statement hugely problematic, and it still presents something of a problem to contemporary thinkers for whom popular culture is far too simple to understand and should simply be dismissed. Why analyze the novels of Stephen King or James Patterson when the works of William Shakespeare, Charles Dickens, or Samuel Beckett cry out for more interpretation? What, then, are we to make of the following statement by Stephen King himself: "My works are the literary equivalent to a Big Mac and french fries" (Introduction to *Night Shift*). King suggests that popular culture is cheaply paid for, quickly consumed, and immediately forgotten. Another reading of the statement would note that King uses a metaphor of consumption to describe the reading of his work; that his metaphor equates his literary work with an image of American cultural domination; that inherent, therefore, in both his statement and his work is a politics of cultural domination that simultaneously disparages (it is only a burger) and tacitly praises (billions and billions served) the dissemination of his work.

Our reading of Stephen King's comment suggests a number of things. First, popular culture often offers commentary on its own logic (King has, in fact, issued several statements about his work in prefaces and books). It is part of the responsibility of the reader of popular culture to see how popular cultural texts, often highly self-aware, "read" themselves, ironically, seriously, or otherwise (one thinks here of how often in *The Simpsons* the cartoon reveals to us that it "knows" it is a cartoon, thus foregrounding its complete artifice). Second, popular culture can, indeed, sustain the kinds of analysis that "traditional" literary or cultural texts unquestioningly do. Indeed, it is our claim that popular culture needs to be read, decoded, interpreted, and understood, precisely because it does reveal a great deal about how contemporary culture thinks about itself (what does it mean that we spend our time "reading" Big Macs?). Thus, at some level, we can see the various texts of popular culture as the dream-work of a culture revealing its unconscious impulses, anxieties, and desires. Thus, as in Freud's analysis of dreams, everything in a text carries potential meaning. Perhaps, we could go as far as to suggest, to borrow from cultural critic Roland Barthes, that in a text, "everything has a meaning or nothing has" (Introduction to "The Structural Analysis of Narrative" 89). All of the readings that follow—even, perhaps especially, those hostile to contemporary popular culture—tacitly assume that to ignore the claims of popular culture, to ignore its massive influence on the ways we think and act, is ultimately, and dangerously, to ignore ourselves.

Popular culture invites a plurality of theoretical approaches, some of which this Introduction maps out by offering practical demonstrations of what a theoretical reading of popular texts may look like. Thus, we will see how semiotics, structuralism, poststructuralism, Marxism, feminism, and postmodernism, figure and reconfigure popular texts in terms of their own theoretical requirements; we will see that each approach is valuable for revealing previously unseen aspects of texts, aspects that work to reveal the full complexity of the cultural imagination of contemporary culture.

SEMIOTICS

Semiotics, the study of signs and the various ways in which signs signify or "mean," has a long history. In its oldest usage, the term *semiotics* referred to a branch of medicine, specifically to the diagnosis of illness. Semiotics, thus, is a method of interpreting signs, of diagnosing symptoms. In our view, the term is a crucial point of departure, precisely as it encompasses the notion of both "reading" and "diagnosing" the productions of culture. As it is used in contemporary theory—in, for instance, the work of Roland Barthes (*Elements of Semiology*; *Mythologies*) or Umberto Eco (*A Theory of Semiotics*; *Travels in Hyperreality*)—the term derives its resonance from Ferdinand de Saussure who derived a theory of the relation between the signifier and the signified in his enormously influential series of lectures, *Course in General Linguistics*. The "signifier" is the graphic representation of an idea, termed the "signified": thus, "dog" is the signifier of the idea of "four-legged flea-bitten animal," the signified.

While this idea may not strike us as particularly insightful or even interesting, de Saussure added the idea that there is no natural relation between signifier and signified: there is no reason why "pencil" could not refer to a four-legged flea-bitten animal. Further, Saussure, and others after him, became interested in the idea that if there is no natural relation between the two parts of the linguistic sign, then language becomes somewhat slippery, meaning becomes more ambivalent than absolute. The practical implications of a semiotic reading of culture require that one be aware of how meaning is produced *arbitrarily* (in the truest sense of the word, "to judge") by culture: culture determines how meaning is produced, judges what is meaningful; the reader of culture must be aware of how context determines specific meanings. A related idea, especially in the works of Barthes and Eco, is that the semiotic text is fully charged with an abundance of meaning, meaning awaiting the interpreter. As Barthes writes, and as previously quoted, in a narrative, "Everything has a meaning or nothing has."

A semiotic approach to a narrative, filmic, or televisual text would see the text as a proliferation of signs requiring, first, apprehension *as* a structure of meaning. Second, each individual sign within the larger structure needs to make sense in relation to that totality: semiotics borrows from an older tradition of hermeneutics (or the science of interpretation) that requires the *part* to make sense in relation to the *whole*. Thus, if, as de Saussure suggests, the sign may be ambivalent in itself, the larger structure of meaning is less so. And certainly, filmmakers require their audiences to be attentive to both the proliferation of signs and to the ways signs relate to a larger structure, or structures, of meaning. In James Cameron's two *Terminator* films, for instance, a repeated motif, or sign, is the image of the machine—the foot of a cyborg, the tread of a tank-like vehicle—

crushing something, a skull, a child's toy truck, under its weight. As an image of implacable force and brutality, its meaning is quite clear. What is crucial to notice is the frequency of its use in the films and how Cameron ties the two films together (part to whole) by repeating the motif across the span of the two works: the toy truck that the terminator crushes underfoot in the first film is the same make of truck that pursues both the Terminator and the child in the second. A semiotic reading would register the proliferation of this sign and note, perhaps with pleasure, the ironic reversal occurring in the second film.

This example from Cameron's films demonstrates the practical implications of Barthes' idea that in popular culture, everything has a meaning or nothing has. One of the major schools of semiotics, the so-called "Prague circle"—a group of scholars working in Prague in the 1930s—observed how on theatrical stages, everything had a meaning or potential meaning simply by virtue of being on stage. Describing this phenomenon as the "semiotization of the object," the Prague school observed that art confers meaning onto everything within its boundaries—within the frame of the film shot, on the stage, within the song. An object within the everyday world, a pencil, a sink, does not necessarily mean anything; put that pencil or sink into a film, and it *could* become meaningful. Culture, thus, has an enormous power to convert the everyday into something highly resonant. The task of the semiotician is to trace how this process of conversion from the everyday occurs.

STRUCTURALISM

A central notion in this reader, then, is that all readings of culture, whether they acknowledge it or not, are implicitly semiotic inasmuch as they see texts as structures requiring interpretation. The signs in a film, or a novel, or a television show are signs *intended to be read*. Semiotics, and structuralism, presuppose meaning in meaningful cultural productions. Structuralism, a complex and much-debated term, finds its origins ultimately in the science of the sign, that is, in semiotics. It was, in its origins, part of the discipline of linguistics. As such, structuralism posited a kind of science of language: it looked for regulatory patterns in languages and, as its methods began to be used in other fields (ethnology, poetics, psychoanalysis), for regulatory patterns in all forms of human culture.

A basic premise of structuralism, even and especially as it was applied to ethnology and cultural analysis, is that all cultural practices were structured like a language (the psychoanalyst, Jacques Lacan, went as far as to say the unconscious was itself structured like a language). The structuralist analysis of, say, kinship patterns or classical myths, would see in them an underlying narrative pattern. Claude Lévi-Strauss, the foremost structuralist anthropologist, argued that even the most chaotic, absurd, irrational myth has rules and a latent narrative logic. He writes that what appears to be "unbridled inventiveness" in the myth "presuppose[s] laws which operate at a deeper level…that the human mind appears as determined even in its myth" ("Overture" 7). There are several important implications in these ideas. First, Lévi-Strauss suggests that nothing in a myth, however irrational or illogical, is beyond the scope of structuralist logic; that is to say, as with Barthes's notion of the meaningfulness of narrative, or the Prague circle's notion of the semiotization of the object, cultural productions have an enormous potential for bearing huge significance. When this idea is applied more widely to contemporary cultures, it is possible to suggest that all cultural productions have underlying logics to them even, perhaps, the most puerile (one thinks of *Married with Children,* for instance). The implications of these ideas are crucial. Structuralism's first premise, that narrative laws operate at deeper levels, is, in fact, a liberatory politics of reading; it manages to slip free of a modernist elitism that suggests that only "high" culture is worth interpreting. Second, the logic of myths and, by extension, any cultural production, require "deep" reading in order to uncover the text's full narrative logic. This notion, in turn, confers on the anthropologist, the critic, the reader, a degree of power: she is the one who holds the key to all mythologies.

Roland Barthes

Roland Barthes's *Mythologies,* originally published in France in 1957, is one of the best-known examples of a structuralist analysis of contemporary and popular culture. His premise is that popular culture reveals a great deal about the culture from which it arose when both individual text and its wider cultural context are subjected to the proper kinds of analysis. In this text, Barthes analyzes the logic of wrestling, the iconic face of film star Greta Garbo, the semiology of toys, and the narratives of advertising. Barthes uses the term "myth" to refer to the narratives of popular culture, narratives that confer to us an understanding of the world in which we live. Because Barthes (like Lévi-Strauss) believes that these myths are structured like a language (he is explicit: "Myth is a language" [*Mythologies* 11]), he is able to offer a series of rigorous linguistic and grammatological interpretations of these various aspects of culture. Thus, the placid face of the very modern Garbo reveals a link, a cultural filiation, to the masks of antiquity; Garbo's face becomes a text, even perhaps an intertext (a term that will become important in our discussion of postmodernism below), that is read according to its relation to a wider structure of meaning. The world of wrestling reveals itself to be nothing but a series of archetypal narratives: the battle between Law and transgression, the triumph of Justice over the criminal Other. The various characters of the wrestling world play their roles to the satisfaction of the audience who, like all good and expectant readers, follow the narrative logic of the villain's or hero's actions. Wrestling is like a short story (surely it is not a novel) with recognizable characters and a perfectly predictable plot and dénouement.

Structuralism is no longer fashionable in the academy. Its pretensions to being a science and its rather imperialist claims to be able to reveal the "truth" of various narratives have lessened its claims on the literary and anthropological imaginations. Yet, its influence on the study of popular culture is still felt, if only implicitly. The basic premises of structuralism—that cultural productions have an underlying logic; that the critic holds a degree of interpretive power; that culture is pregnant with meaning—still hold. And certainly, the work of especially Roland Barthes still exerts, and should exert, a degree of influence. His notion that all cultural productions are open to meaning, that everything has the potential for meaning, if placed *within* culture is an important one. As he writes in *Mythologies:* "Everything, then, can be a myth? Yes, I believe this, for the universe is infinitely fertile in suggestions" (109).

POSTSTRUCTURALISM

What Barthes's statement does not consider is how the universe *comes to have meaning* in the first instance. How did the cultural context from which popular culture emerges get there in the first place? How do subjects *make meaning* from the world around them? How does this production differ from other sign systems (those of animals, for instance)? Do the meanings put in place by human subjects reveal essential truths, or do they constitute a complex matrix of meanings that *makes us*? Poststructuralism asks questions about how "truth" got to be there in the first place. The "post" in poststructuralism would thus seem to imply that the premises of structuralism have been superceded. And in some sense, this is true (although the matter is still open for discussion). It is precisely the pretense to the rigours of science and, especially, the claims to the "truth" (of the narrative, of the determined "laws" of the human mind) that spurred on the original theorists of poststructuralism. Because the term itself is much debated (almost as much debated as postmodernism), it is perhaps best to begin with suggesting some of the premises of this, let us call it for now, "school of thought."

At a basic level, poststructuralism is a refinement and radicalization of what is termed a "hermeneutics of suspicion." This term, applied as it is to the works of Freud, Nietzsche, and Marx, suggests that one way of interpreting the world, and the cultural productions of the world, is to read against the grain, to be suspicious of the overt or manifest content of what you see. Freud, of course, uses the distinction between "manifest" and "latent" content in his analysis of dreams: the manifest content, what you remember on waking, is only a portion, a distorted portion of the meaning of the "real" dream. The dream analysis must work to realize the latent or hidden content of the dream text. A hermeneutics of suspicion, thus, takes nothing at face value and, in fact, posits that what appears to be the case is very often not the case at all.

The poststructuralist interpretation of texts begins with these ideas and then, as mentioned, radicalizes them. It is not only that a text may have many levels and that the literal, manifest, level needs to be left behind. For the poststructuralist the text may, in fact, be totally at odds with itself: the manifest content may, in fact, be completely contradicted by the latent content. A text may seem to assert one idea, one ideological premise, but a subterranean aspect of the same text may threaten that logic (or, indeed, support that logic in strange ways). The poststructuralist text, thus, is always already (to use a phrase favoured by such readers as Hans-Georg Gadamer and Jacques Derrida) in perpetual conflict, threatening to founder on the reef of its own conflicted logic.

If a structuralist poetics looked for the "laws" of a text, a poststructuralist reading would seek out ambivalence; if the structuralist interpretation of myth would see a logic to its language, the poststructuralist would see contradictory and irresolvable tensions between languages in the same text. Indeed, although a poststructuralist, such as French philosopher Jacques Derrida, would claim to be going beyond the structuralist logic of de Saussure, he is still bound to de Saussure's fascinating idea that language is an arbitrary system. Applied more widely, this idea would suggest that a degree of arbitrariness inhabits all linguistic—and hence cultural—productions. (The poststructuralist believes, with the structuralist, that a linguistic approach to experience is unavoidable.) One implication of this kind of reading is that nothing in the text is fixed and final: the text is a tissue of pluralities and offers itself to a multiplicity of readings. Some critics of poststructuralism suggest that this kind of reading is, or leads to, a kind of philosophical nihilism, that arbitrariness and ambivalence translate into the idea that nothing means anything. This is a naive misreading of the premises of the work of Derrida and others (one thinks of Paul de Man and J. Hillis Miller's readings of literature; of Maurice Blanchot's readings of philosophy and culture; of Gilles Deleuze's readings of psychoanalysis). Derrida's texts, actually microscopically close, brilliant readings of the tradition and history of philosophy, suggest a deep commitment to meaning, a deep commitment to exposing the many tortuous, yet exquisitely beautiful, avenues of thought inhabiting philosophical texts.

Différance

Poststructuralism has been closely identified with the work of Jacques Derrida who, since the publication of *Of Grammatology* (1967) has redefined what constitutes philosophical practice. Several key concepts emerge from Derrida's work, but perhaps the most important is the notion of *différance*. The term is a conflation of two concepts: the idea of "difference" and the verb "to differ." Working from (and against) de Saussure, Derrida argues that meaning is constructed out of a network of difference: words mean certain things because they do not mean something else. "Cat" means what it does insofar as it does not mean "dog." More importantly, meaning for Derrida is always deferred, always endlessly "put off." If language is a differential network, but a network of close relations (the word "cat" needs the word "dog" in order to mean fully), meaning is always potentially there and always potentially elsewhere, always pointing to yet more words (which, in turn, point to more words).

Poststructuralist literary critic J. Hillis Miller is fond of demonstrating that individual words, in their histories, etymologies, and usages, shift meanings over time and may, in fact, contain contradictory definitions. His famous reading of the word "host" in his essay "The Critic as Host," demonstrating as it does that the word has antithetical meanings built into its etymology (guest, stranger, enemy), is an illustration that texts, even at the microscopic level of individual words, can be at interpretive odds with themselves. How does one decide which root meaning to emphasize? Who, or what, regulates meaning? In any context, the word "host" will always shimmer with its plurality of meanings; indeed, its energy derives precisely from the fact that contradiction strains against the boundary of the word. A poststructuralist reading would suggest that language—and language systems, such as novels, films, television shows—are constructed around a series of inevitable and *necessary* antitheses; the meaning of the text is found in how that text negotiates, sometimes painfully, that structure of contradiction and ambivalence.

Poststructuralism, thus, attends to the primary complications of texts, reads texts against themselves, looks not to come to singular conclusions about meaning, but listens for the endless potential for deferred meaning. As such, poststructuralism emphasizes that reading is a *process* in which meaning is placed in (contested) dialogue with meaning. This has the practical effect of suggesting that a film, for example, will never exhaust its meaning; this, in turn, perhaps explains why readings of, for instance, *Blade Runner* or *Alien* continue 20 years after they appeared. Not content to allow a film to present itself as a unified and stable entity, a poststructuralist reading would demonstrate how a film works against what may appear to be its first premises. For example, in 1930, Alfred Hitchcock directed *Murder,* his third sound feature. The film, a fairly straightforward whodunit, concerns a woman on trial for murder; a juror, convinced of her innocence, sets out to win her freedom and, inevitably, her love by unmasking the real killer. It is clear, as Donald Spoto suggests in his reading of the film, that the film's energies derive from its differential desires and drives. It wishes, on the level of story, to be a straightforward whodunit, but the camera work and directing suggest that Hitchcock is more interested in pursuing a homosexual subtext: the killer, one of many "effeminate" villains in Hitchcock, is played with languorous campiness by Esme Percy. The villainy of the killer is clearly a result of both his "perverse" sexuality and his racial origins (it turns out he is part African-American, part Native American). The film, clearly more interested in the minutiae of perversity and the horrors of miscegenation, wanders away from its primary agenda into an area that threatens to turn it into quite another film altogether. Instead of seeing this tension as perhaps an indication of Hitchcock's boredom with the story, we can see that the film is properly "about" the conflict and relation between "normal" heterosexual love (the innocent heroine; the manly hero) and "perversity": it is possible that, at some level, the film is exploring how each aspect of this opposition, in fact, requires the other to make sense of itself: innocent heterosexuality "needs" perverse homosexuality to make sense of itself precisely *as* innocent heterosexuality. The film, however, does not resolve these questions and tensions. It remains a film seemingly divided against itself, two films in one. How do we decide which narrative line to follow? Do we conflate both? Where is our authority as readers in such a case?

MARXISM

Poststructuralism reads texts as a matrix of meanings that, like the market economy of capitalism, fluctuate, change, and frequently contradict one another as part of a *textual economy* determined both by the text itself and those who interpret it. A Marxist reading of popular culture analyzes the matrixes of social relations and material forces that determine how subjects make and are made by popular culture, specifically by considering the economics of capitalism itself as an essential component *of* this textual economy. In this way, Marxism expands upon what seem to be the more purely linguistic concerns of poststructuralism, although this appearance misses the fact that, by asking us not to take for granted how texts *mean,* poststructuralism implicitly asks us to consider language's sociopolitical character. Karl Marx himself was not a critic of language or texts, *per se,* but he does ask us to critique the kinds of authority guaranteed by the power of language throughout history. Our general sketch of Marxist and post-Marxist readings of popular culture below builds on our previous discussion of poststructuralism's hermeneutics of suspicion. This is done by way of establishing the general critical tools within which to situate a variety of other approaches to popular culture, such as feminism, informed by poststructuralism and Marxism.

Marx famously called religion the "opium of the masses," by which he meant religion's Word-based authority to govern people's lives—or more to the point for Marx, to opiate subjects against recognizing oppressive economic, social, and political effects perpetrated in religion's name. One can think of Marx questioning religion's Word in the way that Derrida deconstructs the *logos.* The Word or *logos* asserts the divine power of words over things, the signifier over the signified. In Genesis, God gives Adam the power to name things in "His" creation, just as God created the world from chaos. Words assert a *human* and *rational* authority, separating us from animals and, thus, from our baser natures. We move from infancy to childhood partly by acquiring language, which helps us become properly functioning social beings. How *well* we acquire language skills marks how well we advance educationally, which, in turn, guarantees how we advance economically and socially. Language determines texts and textuality, but it also determines the power relations that bind the world around us. Think of the Canadian Charter of Rights and Freedoms, the United States Constitution, the Bible, the Koran, the Talmud, to name only a few documents that govern how we think. When we take these documents' authority as *natural* or *given*, Marx would argue, we remain blind to the politics they generate, to how they determine our actions and interactions as social subjects.

Marx's works, frequently co-authored with Friedrich Engels, address society under industrial capitalism as the site of class struggle. The economic and political inequalities created by this struggle would, Marx hypothesized, be overcome through political revolution and the creation of a more equitable socialism that benefited society *en masse,* rather than merely its social elites. World history since Marx has shown capitalism to be a rather more resilient structure for global order than Marx had hoped. Yet, one can argue that the lasting *critical* power of Marxist theory has more than made up for this theory's shortcomings in political practice. Indeed, paradoxically, this theory's greatest effectiveness comes with its ongoing social and cultural critique of capitalism. And, it might even be argued, this effectiveness can be gauged no more tellingly than in the study of popular culture as perhaps the most expressive symptom of capitalism's pre-eminence in global culture. That popular culture is, in one of its salient definitions, also *mass* culture—a culture for and of the masses—makes it an obvious choice of Marxist analysis.

The focus of Marx's theory is mid-19th century European society in the Industrial Age, particularly the relationship between the ruling class, or *bourgeoisie,* which controlled industrialism's capitalistic economy, and the working class or *proletariat,* whose labour kept this economy's production processes running. How industrial social relations differed from those of earlier orders indicated to Marx the even broader epochal shift from agrarian to urban life. Whereas slaves were indentured to their masters in an earlier slave society or peasants were subservient to their lords in later feudal society, the *proletariat* was subordinate to a middle class which owned the means of, and thus profits from, industrial production. Barely distinguished from the tools of production they used, workers were dehumanized and alienated, both from themselves and others, enslaved by a system that profited from their labour but allowed them few of its economic, psychological, or social payoffs. For Marx, although this subordination was less obviously effected by force, as in slave or feudal societies, it was, paradoxically, no less deterministic or coercive. It, thus, led Marx to undertake a scientific analysis of the social relations generated by capitalism in order to *demystify* how capitalism could so effectively mystify its subjects about the real conditions of their lives.

Base and Superstructure

Marx divides the industrial social order into base and superstructure. The base consists of forces of production (e.g., the factory, its technologies, its workers) and the socio-economic relations generated by these forces. The superstructure is defined by the institutions and their ideologies as they are determined by the base, including the types of consciousness produced by the superstructure's social influence. In short, the superstructure expresses the ideological ends of the base's economic means and, in turn, provides an intellectual justification for those who own these means. In *The German Ideology* Marx and Engels write that "The ideas of the ruling class are in every epoch the ruling ideas, i.e., the class which is the ruling *material* force in society is at the same time its ruling *intellectual* force" (67).

More derivative forms of Marxism argue that the base determines the superstructure so that ideology is always reducible to the material reality of economic subsistence. So, when we hear such an ad slogan as "Just Do It," we are meant to think of the Third World factory worker whose labour is being exploited to make a pair of Nike running shoes, which cost more than the worker's monthly salary. This person cannot "Do As Much" as the person who buys the shoes. However, both base and superstructure are also inflected by such issues as race, politics, sexuality, gender, and geographical and cultural location, to name only a few, which may or may not be related to economics but which, nonetheless, condition relations in both the base and the superstructure. That is, less reductive forms of Marxism consider how base and superstructure exist in a dynamic, rather than binary, relationship to one another, the economics of capitalism being only one factor in determining this larger sociocultural economy of relations.

Overdetermination

We can, thus, say that base and superstructure are *over*determined strata within Marx's model and that the entire model itself is overdetermined by the tensions between them. The idea of overdetermination recalls Freud's dreamwork as well as the relationship between consciousness and the unconscious. For the purposes of studying popular culture, overdetermination means that any sign or social system functions at both manifest and latent levels, as a matrix of both determining and contradictory forces. Behind a text's manifest terms (for instance, a pair of Nike runners or the advertisement and attendant ideology that sell them), there is a latent scene of production, both economic and cultural. Usually, this "other" story is set aside, reduced, or simplified in order to construct the text's manifest meaning (Jeffrey Auerbach's decodings of a magazine ad in this reader represents this kind of analysis).

For popular culture and its subjects, meaning manifests itself in the superstructural play of ideologies. But these ideologies are both real and imaginary at once. The post-Marxist theorist Louis Althusser, drawing on both psychoanalytic and Marxist ideas, demystifies ideology as the invisible yet overdetermined intellectual glue cementing social relations in the public sphere. For Althusser, ideology defines how we think of ourselves as subjects amid the real conditions of existence, how we interpret those conditions for ourselves. This is to say that ideology is necessarily imaginary because it evokes how we *imagine* the world to be and our place in it. Think of the power of the religious right in North American politics or the political fractiousness caused by religious beliefs on the world stage. Religion is powerful in these cases because it asks that we accept its moral doctrines as common sense. That is, it asks that we remain unconscious of its power as ideological effects. Ideology is effective, Althusser argues, because it functions unconsciously (his revision of Marx's idea of religion's sedative quality) by mystifying us into accepting its terms as natural or given.

Ideology, thus, catches us in the network of ideas and social relations it generates. It defines and interprets us *as* subjects. Althusser calls this process *interpellation.* In his famous example, we do not name ideology; *it* calls to *us,* as when a police officer hails someone on the street by calling out, "Hey there!" This call, Althusser argues, marks us as a subject within the officer's authority (or, rather, the authority for which he speaks and by which *he* is named). Because the call startles the subject, he obeys it in the first instance before thinking to question this authority. This automatic response, before consciousness or personal agency, evokes how ideology names us as subjects within its power before we have time to resist. We are not entirely dupes of what Althusser calls Ideological State Apparatuses (ISAs)—government, church, school, medicine, the law, and so on— through which ideology exerts its power. But we are first "subjected" by them before we bring this process of subjection to consciousness, maybe to accept, maybe to resist, its terms. "Just Do It," for instance, calls us to be certain kinds of subjects. Its archetypal character empowers a universal situation: there is only ("Just") one situation in which one is called upon to perform ("Do") a necessary and vital function ("It"). But "It" is an indefinite pronoun, a nameless entity that stands in for a more concrete (or "real") noun, a signifier standing in for a signified, the identity of which we cannot know. "It" points to a meaningless or at least superficial popular culture—the "French fries" syndrome described by Stephen King. But "It" is clearly potent in spite of—even because of—its meaninglessness. Behind the slogan's pop cultural text lies another scene of meaning and action which the slogan glosses over in the name of naming us and, thus, supposedly empowering us to accept its terms. What scene or story? A global conglomerate that wants to profit from our complacency in believing what it is selling us? That exploits its workers, who, nonetheless, yearn for its privileges? That wants to help us transform our personal lives and make us better citizens and, thus, make the world a better place to live in? Is the network of social relations generated by capitalism a benign or toxic one? We need to consider which of these options are more credible than others. *But,* we need to consider *all* of them and, thus, attend to the complex ways in which base and superstructure are intertwined to form a heterogeneous social and cultural economy of relations. In these relations different aspects of the world around us, read as part of a vast and ongoing textual or semiotic sphere of potential meanings, mean different things for different people at different times. A Marxist reading asks us to demystify the ideological terms assumed by pop culture texts, to interpret and critique the offstage as well as onstage meanings of their ideological performances.

FEMINISM

Just as there are reductive Marxisms, there are reductive feminisms, such as the Marxist feminism that argues that we need to understand women solely in terms of how capitalism has exploited them. This idea is by no means false, but it limits the broader analytical power of feminism as a critique of ideology in practice, of how ideology has affected the material existences not only of women but of all groups frequently marginalized within culture. One powerful site of this marginalization is the distinction of the "feminine" from the "masculine"; this difference, particularly, marks a whole array of economic, political, and social practices which seek to naturalize or normalize relations between the genders, including definitions of sexual identities. In this section, we will discuss feminism specifically, but by way of gesturing toward how a feminist methodology, read in light of both poststructuralist and Marxist methodologies, can be extended to considerations of race, ethnicity, and nationality in studies of popular culture.

A questioning of the diminished role of women in society goes back at least to Mary Wollstonecraft's *A Vindication of the Rights of Woman* (1792), written in the wake of the French Revolution, when the rights of men were on everyone's mind (Wollstonecraft's earlier text was, in fact, *A Vindication of the Rights of Men* [1790]). That she spoke of "men" signifies their existence as autonomous individuals. That she then spoke of "woman," however, suggests that she was "inventing" a new species, which was precisely her point: in many ways, women had not previously "existed" because political and social ideologies (although she would not have used the term "ideology") either did not acknowledge their equity with men or took their existence for granted and, thus, worse, did not *need* to acknowledge their existence. While one risks oversimplifying the case, one can safely assume that women were treated as passive, submissive creatures of feeling and emotion or as mere reproductive entities. Conversely, men were rational, emotionally controlled, and their reproductive capacity figured through an ability to think imaginatively and, thus, actively to harness their own inherent creativity toward constructive social action. In short, women were biological creatures; men were social agents.

This body/mind, female/male split resulted in a series of binaries that informed later Victorian conceptions of the "separate spheres." Here, women controlled the domestic sphere as "domestic goddesses," paradigms of virtue glorified for their role in the moral and spiritual education of their children. Men ruled the public sphere, ready to educate their sons (not daughters) for civic action once their wives had instilled in them the proprieties of individual character. Only with the suffrage movements of the late 19th and early 20th centuries in the United States, the United Kingdom, and elsewhere did the long process of emancipating what Simone de Beauvoir in 1949 called *le deuxième sexe*—"the second sex"—from its lower status in the social hierarchy really take shape. Only with what is called the Second Wave of Feminism in the 1960s and 1970s, however, was this emancipation brought to social fulfillment, although we can argue that the emancipation, such a long time coming, still has a long way to go.

Why has society been—why is it still—troubled by the question of "woman"? Simply in terms of numbers, it makes sense that women are equal to men. Why throughout history, then, has so much power accrued to men? Brute force? Greater intelligence? Maybe the former; certainly *not* the latter. The better question is: what systems of thought have been constructed to justify a masculine (and thus masculinist) superiority? Why do wage disparities still exist between the genders in our post-industrial age? Why are women, more often than not, still treated as "homemakers" in television or magazine ads? Why have women's bodies always been more overtly sexualized than men's in a whole range of media?

Gender Roles

Providing answers to these questions involves questioning gender and sexual stereotypes, which asks, in turn, that we consider the artificially constructed nature of gender and sex. As Judith Butler argues, "the substantive effect of gender is performatively produced and compelled by the regulatory practices of gender coherence. . . . There is no gender identity behind the expressions of gender; that identity is performatively constituted by the very 'expressions' that are said to be its results" (*Gender Trouble* 24–25). Butler is drawing upon the idea of subjectivity as a social construction, a critical distinction in gender studies that also informs a broad array of issues within the broader field of Cultural Studies. Human biology—being born with a penis or vagina—is separate from the issue of how we get constructed—conceived, idealized, and/or marginalized—as masculine or feminine subjects. Sex is merely an accident of procreation, Butler suggests, and is deterministic only insofar as we initially have no say in the matter.

What is arguably more deterministic are the gender roles society assigns us (baby boys are dressed in blue, baby girls in pink; girls play with "dolls," boys with "action figures"). Ideas about masculinity and femininity, that is, are social codes or identities delegated to us with rather startling regularity. We perform or act out these regulations without necessarily understanding that they are "constructed" rather than "essential" (like interpellation in Althusser). Ideologies *about* sex, and the differences they distinguish, give gender its "coherence," its air of common sense; they express, assign, and regulate masculine and feminine attributes of subjects, rather than possess any intrinsic or essential value.

Sexuality

The same can be said of concepts of sexuality. Michel Foucault, Butler, and others have explored how since the 19th century, we have understood heterosexuality as "normal" by distinguishing it from the pathology of homosexuality. Adrienne Rich calls this a "compulsory heterosexuality." As Foucault argues in *The History of Sexuality*, it is not a matter of sexuality *per se*, which for him remains radically uninterpretable, but of the discourses mobilized by culture to talk *about* sexuality and, thus, to define it as a certain type of knowledge. Paraphrasing Foucault, O'Brien and Szeman define discourses as "whole systems of thought, speech, and knowledge-*production* that structure institutional and social practices"(177).

Discourses mobilize a social power that does not accrue specifically to a dominant group so much as it "circulates continuously throughout society, concentrating in different places at different historical moments and constituting particular meanings and identities as it does so" (O'Brien and Szeman 177). Nonetheless, this power, in the moments it coheres, produces the monolithic or eternal appearance of itself in this coherence. One such example of this coherence is hetero*normativity*, which privileges male–female relations—and the male factor within these relations—as the social norm over gay, lesbian, or other transgendered distinctions. Indeed, society names these distinctions in order to mark differences from the norm as a way of distracting us from the norm's tenuous status in the first instance. Ongoing federal debates in Canada and abroad about same-sex marriages evoke the kinds of stereotypes confronted when one has to think outside the box of what Eve Sedgewick, writing after Rich, calls an "obligatory heterosexuality." How this heterosexuality is made to seem indispensable to social coherence, making us imagine that chaos would otherwise ensue, is one central consideration of Queer Studies, a relatively new area of Cultural Studies.

The question that needs to be asked, Butler suggests, is this: who gets to say that one gender, one set of gender relations, or one version of sexuality is better than another?

Obviously, someone has to be the culprit. Those who believe that God made woman from Adam's side hold to one version of the story that critics of religious ideology would hold to be ultra-essentialist. Butler's analysis is telling and subtle on this point. As we suggested above, that gender or sex categories have to be repeated—that the Biblical story is reinvoked to defend the social virtues of heterosexuality—means that they are in trouble from the beginning. The logic here is simple. On the one hand, repeating something means affirming the truth of its existence in the first instance, not unlike the signifier assuring us of the reality of the signified to which it corresponds. A repetition of an idea, like the repetition of certain patterns of music or phrases of thought in a politician's speech, suggests consistency, continuity, and assurance that the idea has intrinsic value. Arnold Schwarzenegger kept talking about "terminating" California's budget problems by way of assuring Californians that the *idea* of a solution was as valuable as any solution itself. God created the world in His own image, and that image reassured Him that he had the right idea (and why is it always "Him"—and with a capital "H"?). On the other hand, to repeat something is intrinsically to admit that it might not be right in the first instance. If it *was,* why repeat it? Between the original and its copy emerges a certain anxiety about the repetition, a lingering doubt about its efficacy.

Gender codes work this way. They reinforce their coherence by repeating themselves over and over, except that the repetition itself simultaneously demonstrates that they are constructed, not essential. But for Butler, this repetition also offers a political solution by pointing to gender's performative nature: we *perform* various roles within the social sphere that assigns these roles to us. This means that gender can be *re*-performed, however, that we can rewrite gender or sex codes on our own terms. We never escape these codes' determining matrix. Butler is clear on this point: in a world where the biologies of our bodies are as much socially and culturally as well as biologically determined, there is no ultimate position outside of these codes from which to speak (the articles in this reader's final section perform variations on this theme). Here, a poststructuralist sensibility re-enters our discussion: to exist as human beings is to exist in the realm of "the human" as a construct of humanity itself, gender and sexuality being only two, albeit powerful, constructions informing how we think of this humanity. For a feminist analysis, this means that women can rewrite their existences on their own terms, although Butler offers a powerful critique of feminism itself. For if feminism deconstructs for women the prison house of their own biology, which has for so long been the site of their exploitation, to reclaim women's bodies as powerful material forces in their own right risks *re*-essentializing womanhood. To avoid this trap, we can recognize that re-drawing the effaced identities of women is only part of the picture. To rematerialize "woman" is to ignore women's already powerful history, however much men have limited this history. We might ask how women *have* figured in the ideological sphere of things by recovering their past histories (to remember women writers ignored by a male-constructed literary tradition, for instance) and by analyzing how women wrote or spoke their way out of the ideological boxes in which they found (or did not find) themselves. In this reader, duCille and Radway offer both negative and positive versions of this kind of history.

NATION AND NATIONAL IDENTITY

Our approach in the above two sections has been to explain Marxism and feminism less as historically specific critical movements than as critical *methodologies* that, when informed especially by semiotics and poststructuralism, allow us to think through other aspects of and approaches to the study of popular culture. We can see in Marxism and feminism, for instance, how a dominant ideology has defined its "self" by reading the group or groups it subordinates as the "other," be it the working class as the "other" of the *bourgeoisie* or "woman" as the "other" of "man." This division between self and other is a central tenet of psychoanalytical thought (subjects are divided between a conscious self and an unconscious other, or are dependent on others for their definition of selfhood) that borrows from the paradox of Hegel's earlier master/slave dialectic: the master defines himself by virtue of his subordination of the slave as the other. But his power also, thus, depends *on* this subordination so that he is, in turn, the slave's "other." The methodology of this distinction not only helps us think through how individuals define themselves as parts of groups but also how groups define the individuals of which they are constituted.

Exploring the boundary and intersection between self and other, group and individual, informs other approaches to the study of popular culture which have emerged in the past several decades, at first separately but now increasingly as part of the broader interdisciplinary terrain mapped by Cultural Studies. These approaches consider an array of ideologically fraught issues, such as race, ethnicity, and nation. Several articles in this reader contain more specific discussions of these issues. Our present concern, however, is to focus on the issue of nationhood as it defines individuals as parts of larger group identities, race and ethnicity being two particularly powerful ways of effecting this coherence. We are particularly concerned at this juncture to discuss how Canadian culture defines itself against the more powerful hegemony of American cultural dominance. This issue is of central relevance to many of this reader's articles but is more broadly relevant to the idea of the reader itself and to its selection of articles that respect Canadian context and content but that also demonstrate how national identity, Canada's or otherwise, is itself a heterogeneous, often tenuous, and by no means essential concept.

Ideas of nationhood and nationality are used to evoke the broader political coherence of groups as a nation. This coherence produces what Benedict Anderson calls an "imagined community," an imagined communal organization that gives groups a sense of their ideal citizenship but also, in turn, acts as a way of making state power cohere effectively.

Definitions of racial or ethnic identities are often powerful instruments of this organization, although they are also separate objects in the study of how races and ethnicities are frequently essentialized, and subsequently demonized or glorified, by way of marking the identities of individuals and groups to various ideological ends. For instance, although the English nation was absorbed under the multinational umbrella of the British Empire, the notion of an essential "Englishness" still informed the idea of "Britain" as it defined the Empire's core values and beliefs. This British ideology was crucial to the Empire's colonizing project, which worked by a whole series of cultural binaries (again, see Auerbach's article in this reader).

Postcolonialism

Demystifying how various individual and group identities were shaped by this process of colonization, of which British domination forms only one example, is the central preoccupation of postcolonial studies. Postcolonialism rethinks the collective identities of various communities or social groups after the various colonial projects of the 18th and 19th centuries—using the powerful discursive tools of race, ethnicity, and nation as well as class, gender, and sexuality—called these groups into being in the first place. Space does not permit an extended discussion of postcolonialism and its concerns (see Chapter 7 of O'Brien and Szeman's *Popular Culture: A User's Guide*), but we can think of the construction of Canadian nationhood and national identity.

Defining Canada and Canadianness is a complex issue. Unlike America, which broke away from England in 1776, Canada was confederated as a separate nation yet *within* the British Commonwealth. Governed by the metaphor of the multicultural "mosaic," rather than that of the American "melting pot" of national, racial, and ethnic differences, our identity is, thus, a paradoxically negative image of this imperial vision, albeit in the name of tolerance and inclusiveness. A mosaic is marked by its differences as much as its unity. The principal populations of Canada at the time of Confederation were derived from two different colonial powers, France and England. But now, as then, Canada is made up of multiple groups, defined by earlier forms of colonization, who have, either by choice or by force, moved here from different parts of the world. And this diaspora from the outside produced an internal diaspora—the displacement of indigenous populations on our own soil. We can see how defining "Canada" as a monolithic entity becomes a complex and problematic issue in the face of this heterogeneity.

The American Fact

This issue is further complicated by our struggle, seemingly more present than ever, to define ourselves against the United States. American cultural and economic might and proximity makes the United States both our closest ally and a dominant force difficult to resist. When we think of things that define us *as* Canadian—hockey, Molson Canadian beer, the West Edmonton Mall, or Anne of Green Gables, the latter two examples being examined in this reader—more often than not, we find it difficult to stack these icons against the Statue of Liberty, the Empire State Building, or just the sheer impact of American popular culture itself. Moreover, how can a mall, that most generic example of post-industrial society under multinational late capitalism, have a distinctly Canadian identity? How can we say that Niagara Falls, to cite another example discussed in this reader, is a Canadian natural icon when it literally splits as well as unites the two countries? So, while we recognize popular forms of a specifically Canadian identity—Group of Seven paintings, East Coast music, various folk cultures indigenous to each province—we also have to say that the trademark of that most Canadian of icons, the Mountie, was purchased by the Disney corporation. And we need to think of the cultural power of a company like Disney to represent the world back to itself (think how many people, after visiting the Canadian pavilion at EPCOT, imagine that all Canadians dress like either lumberjacks or Mounties).

Szeman and O'Brien argue that "the nation remains viable as an idea . . . because the ideals of political sovereignty and cultural autonomy that it embodies—ideals that many still strive for—don't seem to be attainable in any other form" and that "the framework of nationhood remains a powerful cultural and legal mechanism for securing basic rights to self-determination" (225). However, while the United States seems to control how the cultural map gets drawn and re-drawn and Canada still struggles to define itself as a nation both within and against this process, we need to recognize still further that we all exist as part of an increasingly multinational, global enterprise composed of continually migrating populations and defined by constantly shifting cultural, national, and economic boundaries. Just as it would be reductive to study popular culture purely in terms of its economic base, it would be reductive to say that Internet technology or the global interconnection of financial markets are the sole determinants of this changing landscape. Nor can we say that nations, races, ethnicities, or classes are entirely absorbed or erased within a global community. Instead, we need to ask how these elements are transformed by the demands of globalism *and* continue to exert, in turn, their own particular resistant meanings. Instead, perhaps, we need to think how, like popular culture itself, Canadian identity is, as Linda Hutcheon has argued, postmodern—a country defined by continually asking if it is real or not. And so, perhaps, the condition of being Canadian *is* the postmodern condition that defines so much of popular culture.

POSTMODERNISM

To go back to our earlier point: why didn't Marx's revolution to overthrow capitalism succeed? The question is a vital one to ask, even for those who find Marx's political theories too deterministic themselves. The answer might be the staying power of ideology itself, which is what made Althusser's rethinking of Marx's theory inevitable in the first place. Why is it that various modes of thinking in popular culture—despite popular culture's democratic appeal to the many rather than the few—end up producing an often derivative or normative common sense about who we are and how we should behave as subjects? A postmodernist critique of popular culture helps answer this question.

Perhaps no other term is more contested in contemporary discussion of art, literature, and philosophy than "postmodernism." The term, first making an appearance in the 1870s, has a relatively long history. However, the term began to be used more pointedly in the 1960s and 1970s as a way, perhaps a tentative way, to describe the nature of contemporary cultural productions that seemed qualitatively different from the productions of what had come to be known as the "modernist" period. Another deeply contested term but arguably referring, in art and literature at least, to work produced between 1890 to 1930, "modernism" produced art that was highly self-conscious, celebrated its own difficulty, and strove, as some critics suggest, to separate itself from the masses, from the people, for whom many modernists had undisguised contempt (one thinks of Ezra Pound, W.B. Yeats, and D.H. Lawrence). Postmodernist art, too, is highly self-conscious, highly self-referential: we often find postmodern novels in which the author himself will appear (see John Fowles' *The French Lieutenant's Woman*, for example). The postmodern novel will also stop the flow of narrative to offer commentary on itself, will, in other words, interpret itself *as* a novel. Perhaps the major difference between modernist self-consciousness and postmodernist self-consciousness is that the postmodernist novel is overtly playful, inviting the reader to share in the game: the postmodern novel, in other words, works to incorporate its reader, potentially all readers, rather than speak to an elite few. Think of the difference between *Sex and the City* and *Ferris Bueller's Day Off*. In *Sex and the City,* Carrie, played by Sarah Jessica Parker, provides a voice-over narration that comments authoritatively, if often ironically and cynically, on the activities of the four main characters. In *Ferris Bueller's Day Off,* the central character, played by Matthew Broderick (Parker's real-life husband) frequently addresses the camera directly, thus self-consciously gesturing to the audience that the film is aware of itself as a constructed artifact whose meaning is up for grabs.

One indication that postmodern art seeks to incorporate the masses is the fact that it often uses popular or mass genres: the detective novel is hugely important to postmodern novel writing (one thinks of Peter Ackroyd's *Hawksmoor* and Paul Auster's *New York Trilogy*). John Fowles' novel works simultaneously as a parody of the 19th-century novels (especially Hardy's) and as a contemporary romance. Therefore, postmodernist art has, at its root, the desire to break down the distinctions between "high" and "low" art, between elite culture and popular culture. One of the practical effects of this impulse is that postmodern art and culture are densely semiotic: because postmodernism feels comfortable, indeed responsible for, referring to aspects of high culture and low culture, the texts it produces are massively allusive, containing myriad references to all manner of culture. And because postmodern art will refer to aspects of culture we are all familiar with, the reader comes fully equipped to decode that art. Indeed, Umberto Eco suggests that we are all "instinctive semioticians" because our art, our films especially, are conceived within what he calls a "metasemiotic culture" ("Casablanca: Cult Movies and Intertextual Collage"). Such films as Steven Spielberg's *The Raiders of the Lost Ark* require no real analysis because they are, perhaps, too easily legible. Because *Raiders* is a transparent reworking of television and film serials, because it is a film version of any number of comic book situations, a first viewing of the film is a deeply familiar (and, for some, comforting) experience.

High Culture, Low Culture, and Intertextuality

It is not hard to find examples of the postmodernist impulse to break down the distinctions between high culture and low culture. A single episode of *The Simpsons* in its prime (those episodes produced within the first five years of the show's production) features a blur of quotations from films, contemporary television, contemporary politics, and current events. The show would structure itself, at times quite consciously, as a parody of classic "high" culture. The episode entitled "Rosebud" (March 18, 1993), a brilliant parody of Orson Welles' canonical (1941) film *Citizen Kane,* demonstrates the degree to which *The Simpsons* constructs itself as a tissue of quotations, in this case referring to and, in turn, gently mocking what is for some the most revered modern film. A film such as Ridley Scott's *Blade Runner* is another example of a highly allusive text: its architecture recalls Mayan temples (the headquarters of the Corporation is modelled on the ancient temple structure); the cinematic cityscape recalls Fritz Lang's *Metropolis* (1927); the main character Deckard, with his iconic trench coat and laconic delivery, is a postmodern version of the 1930s hard-boiled detective; the film offers a range of philosophical and literary allusions, from René Descartes (Deckard) to John Milton and William Blake.

One of the effects of this kind of allusive structure is that it calls into question the value of previous cultural productions: *Citizen Kane* is held up to a kind of parodic ridicule, and the sacred aura of the Mayan temple is reduced to a marker of capitalist hegemony. Postmodernism, thus, is a subversive genre; it subverts value as it works to claim its allusive potential and prestige.

The postmodernist impulse toward intertext, parody, and dense allusion raises, for some critics, a number of questions. What are we to make of these allusions? How are we being asked to read them? What, for example, does it actually mean that the cityscape in *Blade Runner* refers to Mayan architecture? Are we to interpret this "sign" as an indication that Los Angeles in 2019 has "returned," perhaps nostalgically, to the ancient sacred past? What, if this is so, would this mean? Moreover, how is an audience equipped to read the very amount of allusion that structures the film, or an episode of *The Simpsons?* Certainly, we cannot register and interpret all allusions, even if we did recognize them all. And precisely because there will be allusions that some readers will not recognize (and others will), does this not suggest the possibility for a kind of elitism that postmodernism seems to wish, at some level, to resist? One of postmodernism's strongest critics, Jean Baudrillard suggests, in fact, that postmodernist culture, precisely because it embraces the potential of everything for meaning, eventually winds up devaluing meaning as a whole. According to Baudrillard, this incorporation of everything for culture leads to what he calls a "transaesthetics of banality": if the idea of the aesthetic is carried over into all aspects of life, he argues, nothing is aesthetic. Postmodernism, in short, works actively to detonate the very *idea* of the aesthetic which in an earlier modernist schema equates with a fundamental, and fundamentally privileged, social and cultural value.

Reassessing Narratives

One possible rejoinder to Baudrillard is the fact, as previously mentioned, that postmodern art works to level out value: by incorporating the cultural value of past productions, it suggests a kind of possibility that culture can be claimed and used—or at least enjoyed—by all. From another perspective, we can read the intertextual, parodic aspects of postmodern culture as a *critique* of the past, as a critique of elitist culture. One of postmodernism's main theorists, Jean-Francois Lyotard, famously defined postmodernism as "incredulity towards metanarratives" in *The Postmodern Condition*. This phrase means, though not simply, that postmodern culture offers itself as a critique of the main values of the past, values that were contained in the stories we told of ourselves in order to consolidate ourselves as a culture. Marxism, Christianity, liberalism, democracy, science, all are metanarratives (large overdetermining stories) that determined our beliefs and actions on smaller scales: we acted, within the logic of the metanarrative of democracy, for instance, according to the belief that power inheres in equality and representation; as such, our actions—or inactions—on an individual scale were determined by that logic, a notion that, perhaps, translates into the idea that a perceived injustice in the political system cannot be fully questioned precisely because "we" have determined it to be so. With the advent of postmodernism, which sees a deep (hermeneutics of) suspicion toward the value of the stories we have told ourselves, these past narratives are held up to the highest scrutiny.

On a cultural level, on the level of film and television, we can see a similar impulse at work: the past productions of art and culture are (1) parodied ruthlessly (think of *The Simpsons'* reading of Tennessee Williams' *Streetcar Named Desire* in the episode "A

Streetcar Named Marge" [October 1, 1992]), or (2) fractured without apparent logic into a pastiche of their former glory. Cultural critic Fredric Jameson, in his massively influential writings on postmodern culture, points to the way in which postmodern film, by incorporating the past into its framework, levels out the legibility, the meaningfulness, of history itself. Pointing to such films as *Body Heat,* which recreates an aesthetic of the 1930s *film noir,* Jameson suggests that postmodernist art seems incapable of focusing on its own present (a literary equivalent is present in postmodern British fiction: such novels as John Fowles' *The French Lieutenant's Woman,* Jeanette Winterson's *The Passion,* Angela Carter's *Nights at the Circus,* or Michel Faber's more recent *The Crimson Petal and the White,* all focus on the past to the seeming exclusion of the present moment). Indeed, it is possible that one way of understanding postmodernist art and postmodernism as a genre of thought, generally, is that it is an attempt to come to terms with the past. Instead of embracing Ezra Pound's modernist slogan "Make it New!" the postmodernist wishes to return nostalgically to the past, perhaps in order to understand more clearly—via critique, parody, or outright destruction—how the present moment may work itself away from the claims of the past. If looked at from this perspective, it is clear that this process is only in its first stage and that the claims to, or fascinations with, the past still exert an uncanny and inexorable power.

POPULAR CULTURE AND CULTURAL POPULISM

A final word needs to be said about the vision of popular culture generated by the various theoretical approaches discussed above. That ideology—like the intellectual power of the ruling class for which it speaks—is imaginary means that its authority is never stable or natural. Postmodernism helps us see that all ideology is essentially postmodernist in this respect. Some might argue that a postmodernist levelling of meaning produces an atmosphere of apoliticism and, worse, cultural chaos (certainly Arnold would make the latter point). Some varieties of post-Marxism would see postmodernism's apparent refusal to make meaningful distinctions as a refusal to make changes in the cultural landscape (although we need to be aware of the irony that these changes also smack of the need for a kind of cultural discrimination that Marx was reacting against in the first place). But we can also see that postmodernism offers a version of culture in which no single meaning is allowed to exert dominance, in which meanings are continually negotiated between the various groups that participate in the social order. The name for this process is *hegemony,* a term elaborated by the neo-Marxist political theorist Antonio Gramsci to express the conflictual and dynamic nature of the social sphere which produces popular culture. In his essay in this reader, Dick Hebdige describes hegemony as a "moving equilibrium" of competing forces through which one group asserts dominance by subordinating others. Like the interdependence of master and slave, this dominance is only so great as the subordination it negotiates with those it subordinates.

This negotiation points to the multiple significations of the "popular." Popular culture is both product and process, both the artifacts or texts produced by industry or technology and the various processes that define their production. Part of this production includes how subjects consume or interpret these texts. *We* make culture popular (or not) through the ways in which we consume it. Cultural Studies has always been divided on this subject.

Many have accused Cultural Studies of both broadening and flattening the cultural landscape to the point where, by considering *all* forms of cultural expression and meaning valid—from Wagner's *Tristan und Isolde*, to *Something About Mary*, to a Hallmark Valentine's card, a prediction about romance in a fortune cookie, or a wedding performed at the edge of Niagara Falls—Cultural Studies makes the discrimination of *any* meanings impossible. This has led, the argument goes, to a dumbing down of scholarly practice that, in turn, evokes a kind of cultural populism in which all of culture is the product of our consumption of it.

The Frankfurt School

A more Marxist criticism bemoans this turn of events described in the previous paragraph because it gives the subject far too much agency and glosses over the always-prevalent ideological designs pop culture has upon us. Founded in 1923, the Frankfurt School (known as the Institute for Social Research), one of the key purveyors of Marxist thought in the 20th century, was an important precursor of the CCCS (described in the history of cultural studies above). Part of its agenda (although the various members of the school held no established doctrine and often disagreed with one another) was to critique the ideological effects of mass culture on society at large. Theodor Adorno and Max Horkheimer, key members of the Frankfurt School, and represented in this volume, privilege high against mass culture in the way that Matthew Arnold does. Where for Arnold culture is a standardizing safeguard against the chaotic pull of the masses or the popular, for Adorno and Horkheimer, however, mass culture exerts this standardizing effect against which elite culture stands for the radically utopian vanguard, transgressing, transcending, or alerting us to the dystopian banalities of this standardization. For Arnold, culture helps protect the box; for Adorno it helps us continually think our way out of or against the box.

Walter Benjamin, often closely associated with the Frankfurt School, reads popular culture differently. For Benjamin, the problem is not with how mass culture is made and disseminated but with how it is consumed, and in this consumption, he sees the possibility of political agency. The technological reproductiveness of mass culture offers the possibility of alternative subjectivities. Rather than being coerced by the fixed standards of the elite, according to Benjamin, the technologies of mechanical reproduction give us tools to release us from this elitist stranglehold, to refashion culture on our own terms, to construct alternative subjectivities. This shift—from an emphasis on how mass production (to use Adorno's term) *individuates* or (to use Althusser's) *interpellates* our subjectivities to a consideration of how our consumption of mass culture can radically revise its given terms—in many ways establishes the competing poles of a later Cultural Studies project. In both cases, the question of agency is important. This concern with agency, and thus with identity, is, as we have seen, a primary focus of feminist critiques of popular culture. DuCille's and Radway's articles in this reader deploy such an analysis, rooted in an exploration of how popular culture figures in the material realities of what Michel de Certeau calls the "practice of everyday life."

Ideological versus Populist Approaches

In the final chapter of *An Introduction to Cultural Theory and Popular Culture*, John Storey address the fundamental tension in Cultural Studies between what one might call its ideological and its populist poles. One holds that popular culture is always ideological or, at the very least, always has an ideological dimension—what Ien Ang, whom Storey cites at this point, calls the "ideology of mass culture" always working to manufacture our identities for us—while the other argues that popular culture resides in how we make *it*. In one view, popular culture is hegemonic, reductive, restrictive, and coercive; in the other, it is decentralized, productive, resistant, and empowering. Earlier cultural critics, such as Adorno and Horkheimer, would speak for the former viewpoint. A more recent critic, such as John Fiske, with whom Storey very much agrees, would speak for the latter, more positivist view by saying that popular culture, which for Fiske means *our readings of* popular culture, is transgressive and liberating—liberating *because* transgressive. This more populist view of pop culture argues that we can get inside its "official" ideologies in order to rewrite them from this space on our own terms. "Buy Nothing Day," a worldwide annual event held the day after the American Thanksgiving, would represent for Fiske the most extreme form of this resistance to, and thus refashioning of, the given terms of mass culture and capitalism. But we need to consider how even this event takes place within the highly predetermined and deterministic environment of capitalism as much as we need to realize that late capitalism and the paradigm of globalism that has emerged from it exist hegemonically. That is to say, to return to Hegel's dialectic between the master and the slave, we need to see, paradoxically, that capitalism exists *because* of its hegemonic dependence upon such an event as "Buy Nothing Day" as sure as "Buy Nothing Day" would be meaningless without the capitalism against which it reacts. Returning to Butler's paradox about identity, we need to ask: can we ever get outside the cultural matrix of things set in motion by capitalism to assume any autonomous mode of subjectivity that is not somehow mediated (media-ted) by capitalism and the popular culture for which it so strongly speaks? Perhaps we need to say that our subjectivities are always situated at the locus of a variety of cultural forces, some transgressive and emancipatory, others deterministic and regulatory.

Perhaps it is impossible to avoid the fact that a postmodern, global culture *is* the culture of our everyday lives, wherein the social sphere of how meanings are generated never privileges any one object of analysis but instead classifies and interprets the multiple meanings generated within a social situation. To ask *how* the situation got there in the first place is to guess that a single origin for popular culture can be found. Postmodernism, via poststructuralism, offers, despite what some might call its nostalgic cynicism or its banal or repetitive meaninglessness, a *critical* politics that releases us from the expectations of meaning that ideological structures have placed on subjects and by which subjects have been "placed." The lesson of postmodernism allows for a degree of play with the "placing" that has already been done, a way of both accepting and rejecting the given. Accepting all of culture as popular culture does not mean that we therefore refuse to make critical discriminations, and making those discriminations does not automatically mark us as elitists appealing to superior bodies of knowledge. We invite you to keep this balancing act in mind as you use the following essays to find your way through popular culture. Happy travelling!

—JB and JF

REFERENCES AND FURTHER READING

Althusser, Louis. *Lenin and Philosophy and Other Essays*. Trans. Ben Brewster. London: New Left, 1971.

Anderson, Benedict. *Imagined Communities*. London: Verso, 1983.

Ang, Ien. *Watching Dallas: Soap Opera and the Melodramatic Imagination*. London: Methuen, 1985.

Barthes, Roland. *Mythologies*. Trans. Annette Lavers. London: Granada, 1973.

---. "Introduction to the Structural Analysis of Narratives." *Image/Music/Text*. Trans. Stephen Heath. New York: The Noonday Press, 1977. 779–124.

Butler, Judith. *The Psychic Life of Power: Theories in Subjection*. Stanford, CA: Stanford University Press, 1997.

---. *Gender Trouble: Feminism and the Subversion of Identity*. London and New York: Routledge, 1993.

Derrida, Jacques. *Dissemination*. Trans. Barbara Johnson. Chicago: Chicago University Press, 1981.

---. *Writing and Difference*. Trans. Alan Bass. London: Routledge, 1978.

Fiske, John. *Understanding Popular Culture*. London and New York: Routledge, 1989.

Foucault, Michel. *The History of Sexuality, Vol. 1: An Introduction*. London: Allen Lane, 1979.

King, Stephen. "Introduction." *Night Shift*. New York: Signet, 1979.

Jameson, Fredric. *Postmodernism, or, The Cultural Logic of Late Capitalism*. Durham, NC: Duke University Press, 1991.

Lacan, Jacques. *Ecrits: A Selection*. Trans. Alan Sheridan. London: Tavistock, 1977.

Leavis, F.R., and Denys Thompson. *Culture and Environment*. Westport, CT: Greenwood, 1977.

Lévi-Strauss, Claude. *Structural Anthropology*. Trans. C. Jacobson, and B.G. Schoepf. New York: Basic Books, 1963.

---. *Tristes Tropiques*. Trans. John and Doreen Weightman. London: Jonathan Cape, 1973.

---. *The Raw and the Cooked*. Trans. John Weightman. Chicago: University of Chicago Press, 1983.

Lyotard, Jean Francois. *The Postmodern Condition: A Report on Knowledge*. Manchester: Manchester University Press, 1986.

Marx, Karl, with Friedrich Engels. *The German Ideology*. Amherst, NY: Prometheus Books, 1998.

McClellan, David, ed. *Karl Marx: Selected Writings*. 2nd ed. New York: Oxford University Press, 2000.

McRobbie, Angela. *Postmodernism and Popular Culture*. London: Routledge, 1994.

O'Brien, Susie, and Imre Szeman. *Popular Culture: A User's Guide*. Toronto: Thomson Nelson, 2004.

Spoto, Donald. *The Dark Side of Genius: The Life of Alfred Hitchcock*. New York: Ballantine, 1983.

Storey, John. *An Introductory Guide to Cultural Theory and Popular Culture*. New York: Prentice Hall/Harvester, 1993.

Unit I — *Cultural Subjects*

1. Andrew Bennett and Nicholas Royle, "Me"
2. Theodor Adorno and Max Horkheimer, "The Culture Industry: Enlightenment as Mass Deception"
3. Dick Hebdige, "From Culture to Hegemony," from *Subculture: The Meaning of Style*
4. Walter Benjamin, "The Work of Art in the Age of Mechanical Reproduction"
5. Marshall McLuhan, "The Gadget Lover: Narcissus as Narcosis," from *Understanding Media: The Extensions of Man*
6. Jean Baudrillard, "The Precession of Simulacra"
7. Paul Rutherford, "Made in America: The Problem of Mass Culture in Canada"
8. Naomi Klein, "Alt.everything: The Youth Market and the Marketing of Cool," from *No Logo*

INTRODUCTION

The eight articles in this section are meant to function as a compressed introduction to some of the central theories, approaches, and practices—most of them discussed in the two general introductions above—that have informed the study of popular culture over the past 50 years or so since Cultural Studies became a recognized and rapidly growing field of scholarly enquiry. As such, these articles serve as the basic groundwork and help provide a theoretical and critical context and vocabulary that prepare readers for a better informed reading of the more specific and applied studies in the remaining three sections of this anthology.

This is not to say that the articles in this section are purely theoretical. One thing you should notice when working your way through this part of the book is that theory always has to work on something, has to be tested to see that it does some work in the world, whether it is an over-arching analysis of the culture industry, as in Adorno and Horkheimer; the photographic or film image in Baudrillard; the work of art in its original form and in a mechanically reproduced form in Benjamin; or Canadianness itself in the Rutherford essay. Since the general introductions as well as those offered for individual readings and the suggestions for further reading provide a variety of contexts for understanding the ideas and approaches of the essays, the task that remains here is to briefly trace a number of major trajectories through the eight essays that will draw attention to the evolution of thinking about some of the central concerns in the study of popular culture. While it is always reductive to generalize about the themes and subjects of complex works without considering the niceties of their specific workings out and applications, it can still be valuable to trace some of the central and broad questions that the study of popular culture asks through these essays.

Some of those central questions are: How is power wielded in culture? Who has it, and how do they gain and maintain it, and to what ends? Who makes and controls meaning, and how is meaning made? What are the criteria of value in popular culture, and who decides? Is there always a struggle over meaning, value, and ideology among the makers, distributors, consumers, and users of the artefacts of popular culture? What can we say about the nature of the subject or of the consumer and user of culture, and the related construction of individual and national identities in the face of industrial and cultural globalization? How do we *use* culture in our daily lives, and what do those practices signify both about us and about culture as a whole way of life?

For the most part, those concerns are clearly enunciated in the essay by Adorno and Horkheimer, where the debate over the value and nature of mass or popular culture—its power over the individual subject, and the nature and power of the subject in the face of that culture—is truly engaged. The picture they paint of a docile and thoughtless mass, undifferentiated except in accidents of external style and alienated from themselves, and of a similarly vacuous and homogeneous culture is hardly a cheerful or flattering one. At the same time, we recognize that their challenge to us and our ideas about ourselves and our culture is serious: while their rhetoric might be extreme, occasioned by their experience of political fascism and a corresponding centralization of power in the culture industry, we know that a great deal of what they say is at least sometimes true. Mass culture *is* a culture of repetition, and its unthinking consumers run the risk of being assembled through a process analogous to the mechanical one used to produce hamburgers, car parts, television serial spin-offs, and film sequels and prequels. In Adorno and Horkheimer's account, an industrialized culture of little or no perceived value is a juggernaut, an unstoppable force, and we accept its artefacts, meanings, and ideologies without resistance.

Adorno and Horkheimer draw a firm line between a high or elite culture—characterized by genuine individuality, originality, complex meanings, and serious values, the culture that Arnold and Leavis championed—and a mass culture of individuation, imitation, and no values, except those that suit an establishment whose chief concern is the perpetuation of its own power and value system. However, Walter Benjamin had already, in 1936, issued a challenge to such thinking that was to have a profound effect on future studies of culture. Faced with the rise of Nazism and his expulsion from the 1930s Germany, Benjamin's response was, in many ways, the opposite of Adorno and Horkheimer's. For him, technologically produced art, especially photography and film, has beneficial effects and alters power relations between us and the work of art. Mechanical reproduction allows the work of art to come to us; we no longer have to visit the shrines of culture where those works are treated as cult objects to be worshipped on their own terms. By stripping the artefact of its aura of uniqueness and authenticity, he argues, our power to read it critically and to assign it value is enhanced. We become active, critical consumers and users of culture; a new context for seeing strips familiarity from the object. Technology, in his account, liberates us from the habitual and transfers power from the work of art, its creator, and its privileged and specialized interpreters to its consumer who becomes the arbiter of meaning and value and, thus, has power in the construction of her own identity.

While Benjamin's somewhat idealistic account of our relation to technology, power, meaning, and value thus stands in marked contrast to Adorno and Horkheimer's in one way, it contrasts with Marshall McLuhan's and Jean Baudrillard's accounts of the effects of technology in other ways. For McLuhan, technology not only does not set us free: it ties us inextricably to itself in a system of interdependency where technology becomes a "natural" part of our environments and, thus, profoundly alters our relations with our culture, environment, and, crucially, our own bodies. Thus, McLuhan posits technology as essentially prosthetic, something outside the body and mind that does the body's and mind's work.

For Baudrillard, the triumph or predominance of the technologically produced images of things, what he calls *simulacra*, is so well established that all we know are representations of things, rather than the things themselves, which makes reality itself an empty and unknowable category. With no grounding in the real against which to measure value or authenticity, there can be no preferred values and no discrimination among values. Thus, there can be no common values, no truly integrated individuals, no real rational exchange, and therefore no real society or community, merely its illusion.

Dick Hebdige, in "From Culture to Hegemony," tries to come to terms with how "subjects" of culture—that changing idea that Bennett and Royle discuss in the opening essay of this collection—can make sense of culture and of their complex relationship with it. Hebdige's essay, extracted from a larger work on the meaning of style in subcultures, in part tries to answer Adorno and Horkheimer's claims that all that differentiates us from one another are the accidental marks of style. For Hebdige, that choice of style marks a way that subordinate groups in culture, or subcultures, can find a place to express opposition to the provisionally dominant or hegemonic. Since the signs of culture can be variously interpreted and can have many meanings (are polysemous)—as has been suggested by Baudrillard, Benjamin, and others (notably by Stuart Hall in "The Television Discourse: Encoding and Decoding")—individuals can use those signs in oppositional ways to construct their own style and identity. Hebdige shifts the grounds of the debate from an analysis of the power of big culture to shape individuals, or to destroy individuality itself, to an interest in what power we have in the ways that we consume that culture, the meanings that we make of it, and the ways we use what culture has provided. For Hebdige and Hall, the way we choose to read is profoundly political, which means that when we read against the grain, we are not misreading but performing a political act by inserting ourselves into the power relations between culture and its users.

Two essays in this section, Bennett and Royle's "Me" and Rutherford's "Made in America: The Problem of Mass Culture in Canada," raise questions about the nature of individual and national identities and about how the "human subject" is formed. Both essays offer rather paradoxical accounts of our status as individual and national subjects. For Bennett and Royle, following the work of Sigmund Freud, Michel Foucault, and Judith Butler, the human subject has self-knowledge and self-control but is also subject to forces beyond her control. We have power, but external forces also act powerfully on us; we have a degree of freedom, but our freedoms are qualified and compromised, and thus, we are constantly negotiating a way through the push me–pull you maze of freedom and subjection. At play here is also another version of the debate over the value and nature of elite and popular culture, where the proponents of the elite culture advocated by Arnold and Leavis believe that the most important product of that elite culture is the fully integrated, well-informed, stable, good citizen who has been formed with all the right values and attitudes, and the vision of the human subject as unstable, incompletely integrated, always negotiating between internal and external forces, that has emerged more recently.

Perhaps not surprisingly, what happens at the microcosmic level of the individual subject in Bennett and Royle's account also happens at the macrocosmic or national level in Rutherford's historically based examination of attempts to safeguard Canadians from the power of American mass culture. It seems that as a nation, the historical forces that created us as a hybrid also led us to a sense of our identity as negotiated, provisional, and open, as a kind of proleptic postmodern nation. In the debate about what it is to be Canadian that swirled around the celebration of our centenary in 1967, what became clearest is not what we are, but what we are not. We are not the melting pot that America is, the crucible that dissolves all into one; we are, as Rutherford argues, always aware of the difference, that the American mass culture so prevalent among us is not our own, just as the culture legacy of English and French colonialism no longer defines us either. In choosing the metaphor of the cultural mosaic as an act of national identity, we have chosen the fact of difference as a central term in our self-definition.

Ironically then, by being aware that the powerful and seductive American culture we consume in such large doses is not our own, that when it calls it does not call our names, we are being interpellated into a sense of Canadianness. We are interpellated as clearly as we might be when we, as Cecily Devereux argues later in this collection, recognize something in *Anne of Green Gables* that speaks "Canadian" to us. Yet, as Devereux points out to us, Anne is hardly our exclusive national property but also circulates as a token of national identity and nationalism in several other countries.

Canadian journalist Naomi Klein's essay that ends this section leaps over the niceties of national difference to consider how the "subjects" we discuss in this anthology are formed and affected in the context of a global corporate culture that hearkens back to Adorno and Horkheimer's Marxist analysis of the culture industry as mass deception. Like Hebdige, she looks at how subcultures in particular are brought within the control of and used by hegemony, and the strategies those subcultures can and sometimes do use to appropriate the dominant culture to their own ends. Klein's essay, interesting and useful in its own right, is also important here because it demonstrates—drawing on Marxist philosophy and analyses, linguistics, semiotics, sociology, cultural anthropology, and the various theoretical approaches outlined in the general introduction above—the degree to which what we might call the "high" and interdisciplinary theory of Cultural Studies now informs even journalistic or popular analyses of popular culture. Perhaps we are now seeing the results of the Birmingham School's announced intention in the 1950s to break down the barriers between elite and popular culture.

Finally, we can note that the questions and issues discussed here play themselves out in all of the essays that follow, and it is crucial to realize that none of these questions is finally answered or settled. Nor are they likely to be. Since both we and culture change—and thus our understanding of culture, of what it is to be human, and of the relations between the two changes—we come to also understand that all meanings are provisional, that there is ample room for all of us to try to provide informed answers to the complex questions about the nature and value of culture and our relations to it.

—AG

REFERENCES AND FURTHER READING

Abelove, Henry et al., eds. *The Lesbian and Gay Studies Reader*. London: Routledge, 1993.

Adorno, Theodor W., and Max Horkheimer. 1947. *The Dialectic of Enlightenment*. London: Verso, 1979.

Anderson, Benedict. *Imagined Communities: Reflections on the Origin and Spread of Nationalism*. London: Verso, 1983.

Bhabha, Homi. *The Location of Culture*. London: Routledge, 1994.

Fiske, John. *Understanding Popular Culture*. London: Routledge, 1989.

Frow, John. *Cultural Studies and Cultural Value*. Oxford: Clarendon Press, 1995.

Hutcheon, Linda. *As Canadian as Possible…Under the Circumstances*. Toronto: Robarts Centre for Canadian Studies, 1988.

Jameson, Fredric. *Postmodernism or the Cultural Logic of Late Capitalism*. Durham, NC: Duke University Press, 1991.

Morley, David, and Kuan-Hsing Chen, eds. *Stuart Hall: Critical Dialogues in Cultural Studies*. London: Routledge, 1996.

O'Brien, Susie, and Imre Szeman. *Popular Culture: A User's Guide*. Toronto: Thomson Nelson, 2004.

Said, Edward. *Culture and Imperialism*. London: Chatto and Windus, 1993.

Andrew Bennett and Nicholas Royle, "Me"

EDITORS' INTRODUCTION

Bennett and Royle's short essay focuses on how language, as in literary texts, is one of the primary determinants of human identity. But literature also questions what it says and, thus, questions the subject *of* meaning, questions the subject *who means* in any meaningful, fixed, or essential sense. If Leavisism follows Arnold's idea of a literary tradition that defends high culture against the chaos of mass or popular culture, Bennett and Royle use literature to critique the "discriminating" or culturally elite subject imagined by this tradition and, thus, to debunk culture, high or otherwise, as a space of stable meanings. They distinguish the terms "person" or "human individual," which evoke autonomy and agency, from "the human subject." Citing the French poststructuralist Michel Foucault, Bennett and Royle note how the subject defined by self-knowledge and self-control is also *subject to* external forces, two senses of the idea of *subjection* explored by Judith Butler:

> Power not only *acts on* a subject but . . . *enacts* the subject into being. As a condition, power precedes the subject. Power loses its appearance of priority, however, when it is wielded by the subject, a situation that gives rise to the reverse perspective that power is the effect of the subject, and that power is what subjects effect. (Butler 14)

For Foucault and Butler, power is a matrix of multiple codes or discourses—cultural, political, economic, sexual, racial, national, educational—out of which the subject emerges, by and to which he is subjected. We control ourselves and our environments and *do not* at the same time.

This ambivalence exposes the illusion of human mastery that has governed thinking about culture since at least the 18th century. Jean-Jacques Rousseau begins *The Social Contract* (1762) by stating, "Man was born free, and he is everywhere in chains." But even for Rousseau this freedom is qualified. Born into the chains of power, we gradually become aware of how they bind us. From this awareness we build relationships to these structures by both accepting and resisting their terms: we find ourselves *in* these structures by finding our way *through* them. We are neither entirely prisoners nor free agents but, rather, negotiators of meaning between these two poles.

Why do we need to grasp that we are not autonomous subjects? Bennet and Royle remind us that different social, economic, political, or cultural situations create different linguistic terms and, thus, different subjects. These differences mean that linguistic meanings are unstable. Descartes's still-influential idea that *cogito ergo sum*—"I think, therefore I am"—locates thinking beings at the top of the food chain. This supremacy of reason has mobilized an army of ideas, values, and ideologies to and by which we have been "subjected." (One first sign of trouble in Rousseau's sentence is that he says "Man" rather than "Woman.") Seeing subjects as decentred and self-divided allows us to critique our assumptions about culture.

This is why psychoanalysis is important to this article. Bennet and Royle refer to the thought and writings of Sigmund Freud, but not necessarily to a reductive Freudianism in which a train = a penis or a subway tunnel = a vagina, and so a fear of riding on subway trains = a fear of sleeping with one's mother. Rather, psychoanalysis teaches us that the subject is never who he *thinks* he is. He is subject to both internal and external forces of which he is not always or *ever* aware—forces that are *unconscious*. Considered thus broadly, the *unconscious* signifies forces, meanings, desires, and drives beyond our control or apprehension. The unconscious reminds us how we *pretend* that other determinants—race, sexuality, nationality, gender, ethnicity, class—are transparent or invisible in order, often blindly, to promote or believe in certain ideologies.

Finally, we can recall Andy Warhol's statement that in a media culture obsessed with celebrity and fame, everyone will be famous for 15 minutes. P.D. Marshall argues that celebrity emerges "from the twinned discourses of modernity: democracy and capitalism" (Marshall 4). We value individual freedom above all else (think of the Canadian Charter of Rights and Freedoms), while we also champion a consumer culture that treats subjects like automatons. Celebrity reflects these "two faces of capitalism—that of defaced value and prized commodity value" (Marshall x). Celebrity suggests how democratic capitalism treats the subject as both authentic and a figure of false value, both idealizing his status and exploiting his exchange value as a fetishized commodity.

—JF

ISSUES TO CONSIDER WHILE READING

1. Bearing in mind Bennet and Royle's discussion of how language assigns our identities for us, you might consider the implications of the still often common practice of women changing their surnames to those of their husbands when they get married. What are, or have been until recently, the different social, political, legal implications and imperatives behind this practice? Are these imperatives the same when a man changes his name? What does it mean when husbands and wives hyphenate their last names?
2. Bennet and Royle's essay suggests that it would be impossible to think of how we come to be subjects without thinking about how we are subjected by various signifying practices in our culture. Are there any ways in which we are ever free from language's definition of our subjectivities?

REFERENCES AND FURTHER READING

Butler, Judith. "Introduction." *The Psychic Life of Power: Theories in Subjection.* Stanford: Stanford University Press, 1997. 1–30.

Foucault, Michel. "The Subject and Power." *Selections: Power.* Ed. James D. Faubion. Trans. Robert Hurley et al. New York: New Press, 2000, 326–48.

Marshall, P.D. *Celebrity and Power: Fame in Contemporary Culture.* Minneapolis: University of Minnesota Press, 1997.

Rousseau, Jean-Jacques. *The Social Contract.* 1762. Trans. and Intro. Maurice Cranston. Harmondsworth, UK: Penguin, 1968.

Taylor, Charles. *Sources of the Self: The Making of the Modern Identity.* Cambridge, Mass.: Harvard University Press, 1989.

Me

Who are we? What am I? What is an 'I'? What does it mean to say 'me'? What is the relationship between an 'I' in a literary text and an 'I' outside it? One of the central ideas of this book is literature's capacity to question, defamiliarize and even transform the sense of who or what we are. In the next few pages we would like to elaborate further on this, by trying to look at the nature of personal identity or 'me' both in broadly historical and theoretical terms and more specifically in terms of what literary texts themselves may suggest on this topic.

In Flannery O'Connor's story 'Revelation' (1961) a woman called Mrs. Turpin has a traumatic and bizarre reaction when a strange girl sitting in a doctor's waiting room tells her: 'Go back to hell where you came from, you old wart hog' (217). Mrs. Turpin is scandalized by this statement and that same evening, back at the farm, by herself, hosing down the pigs, she demands an explanation. Being Christian and superstitious (as well as grotesquely racist and class-prejudiced), Mrs. Turpin regards the girl's words as a message from God:

> 'What do you send me a message like that for?" she said in a fierce voice, barely above a whisper but with the force of a shout in its contrasted fury. "How am I a hog and me both?' (222)

What is striking here is not only the woman's confusion and indignation at the apparently contradictory idea that she might be a human being and an old wart hog at the same time, but also the fact that her 'fury' is expressed in a direct, personal address to God. Mrs. Turpin's sense of outrage becomes outrageous in turn, as her questions addressed to God culminate in a questioning *of* God : 'A final surge of fury shook her and she roared, "Who do you think you are?"' (223) The strangeness of putting this question to God comes from the fact that it is a question that should only be asked of another human. Only humans are supposed to be able to reflect on who they are and at the same time be obliged to take seriously a questioning of their own identity. If the question 'Who do you think you are?' is one that cannot or should not be asked of God, nor is it a question one would normally ask of a wart hog. In this respect it would seem that there is something characteristically human about the question. 'Who do you think you are?' is the question that humans ask of others and try to answer about themselves. As Socrates said, 'The unexamined life is not worth living' (Plato, *Apology,* 38a). And the definition of being human must remain in the form of a questioning: Mrs Turpin's 'final surge of fury' is, in this respect, pitifully, comically human.

At the same time, it could be said that this question ('Who do we think we are?') is most clearly raised and most fully explored in works of literature. This might in fact be another general definition: literature is the space in which questions about the nature of personal identity are most provocatively articulated. In the nineteenth century and earlier in the twentieth century, literary critics used to talk about 'the person' and 'the individual.' In more recent years, however, there has been a tendency to refer to 'the human subject.' This may sound jargonistic but there are good reasons, in fact, for talking about 'the human subject' rather than, say, 'the person' or 'the human individual.' The French poststructuralist Michel Foucault has written: 'There are two meanings of the word "subject": subject to someone else by control and dependence, and tied to one's own identity by a conscience or self-knowledge' (Foucault 1983, 212, cited During 1992, 153). The word 'person,' by contrast, perhaps too easily retains connotations of the 'I' or 'me' as detached from everything, a *free agent*. Likewise, the term 'individual' (etymologically from the Latin *individuus*, 'undivided' or 'not divisible') misleadingly suggests a sense of the 'I' as simply free, as being at one with itself and autonomous or self-ruling. It is this idea of the sovereignty of the 'I' that Freud gestures toward when he speaks of 'His Majesty the ego.'

The usefulness of the term 'subject,' then, is that it encourages a more critical attentiveness to the fact that the 'I' is *not* autonomous, that it does not exist in a sort of vacuum. Rather an 'I' or 'me' is always *subject* to forces and effects both outside itself (environmental, social, cultural, economic, educational, etc.) and 'within' itself (in particular in terms of what is called the unconscious or, in more recent philosophical terms, otherness). We are subjects in the sense of being 'subject to' others 'by control or dependence' (in Foucault's phrase) right from birth and even before: not only are we radically dependent on the father who sires us and the mother who bears us, but also on the environment (ecological, economic, familial, social, etc.) into which we are born, as well as on the multiple forms of authority and government which condition our upbringing. A 'me' born to a single mother in Soweto is not the same kind of 'me' as a 'me' born to a duchess in Kensington, but they are both in their different ways *subjects*. Of course if the Kensington 'me' had been in line for the throne, things would have looked slightly different: in Britain, at least, one is subject not only to the authority of one's parent or parents, one's local authorities, the police and central government, but also—at least on paper—to the Queen (thus one is 'a British subject') and, beyond her (if only nominally), to the Christian God. That, then, is one way in which every 'I' is necessarily and fundamentally a *subject*. Rather differently, being a subject has specifically to do with language. You cannot be an 'I' without having a proper name, and in English-speaking countries you usually acquire a proper name around the time of birth or even before. We are born into language, we are born—more precisely—into patriarchal language, into being identified by a patronym, by a paternal proper name. (Even the mother's maiden name is, of course, a patronym.) We are also endowed with a forename and again this is not something *we* choose, it is something to which we are *subject*—even if, in Britain for example, people do legally have the right to change their names at the age of eighteen. Juliet's complaint is haunting and even tragic precisely because it highlights the way in which we are *subject to* names, even if we wish to ignore or disown them:

Oh Romeo, Romeo, wherefore art thou Romeo?
Deny thy father and refuse thy name;

Or, if thou wilt not, be but sworn my love,
And I'll no longer be a Capulet.

(*Romeo and Juliet*, II, ii, 33–6)

More broadly what is being suggested here is that questions of personal or individual identity are indissociably bound up with language. We may like to suppose that there is some 'me' outside language or that there is some way of thinking about ourselves which involves a non-linguistic 'me.' But the idea of this non-linguistic 'me' must found itself in language. We cannot, in any *meaningful* way, escape the fact that we are *subject to* language.

We can also consider this topic from a historical perspective. The idea of the 'I' or 'me,' in other words, is not unchanging and unchangeable. It is in many respects historically and ideologically determined. The way we think about 'I' today is inevitably different from the way in which 'I' was thought about and defined in, say, seventeenth-century France by René Descartes. The principle of the Cartesian cogito ('I think therefore I am')—that is to say, the model of the *rational subject* which Descartes theorizes in his *Discourse on Method* (1637; 1977)—in many respects continues to govern Western thinking. But there are other ways of thinking, and other ways of thinking about thinking. Earlier in the present century, for example, the German philosopher Martin Heidegger declared: 'Thinking begins only when we have come to know that reason, glorified for centuries, is the most stiffnecked adversary of thought' (Heidegger 1977, 112, cited by Judovitz 1988, 186). Likewise, and more recently, Jacques Derrida has been repeatedly concerned to demonstrate that, as he puts it: 'reason is only one species of thought—which does not mean that thought is "irrational" (Derrida 1983, 16).

But perhaps the most obvious way of illustrating the changes over the past century in thinking about thinking, and in thinking about the model of the rational subject, is in terms of psychoanalysis. Psychoanalysis has changed the way in which we are obliged to think about 'the subject.' In the light of the psychoanalytic theory of the unconscious, the proposition 'cogito ergo sum' ('I think therefore I am') becomes manifestly problematic. I do not, and perhaps strictly speaking never can, know precisely *why* or *how* I think what I think, if only because of the extent to which what I think is necessarily determined by forces and effects of which I am (in many ways thankfully) unaware. In a short essay written as an encyclopaedia entry on 'Psychoanalysis' first published in 1923, Freud suggests that the unconscious is evident not only in dreams but in

> such events as the temporary forgetting of familiar words and names, forgetting to carry out prescribed tasks, everyday slips of the tongue and of the pen, misreadings, losses and mislayings of objects, certain errors, instances of apparently accidental self-injury, and finally habitual movements carried out seemingly without intention or in play, tunes hummed 'thoughtlessly,' and so on. (Freud 1986, 136–7)

The significance of Freud's theory of the unconscious thus consists in the demonstration that the subject who thinks (the subject of 'I think') is composed of forces and effects which are at least in part unconscious. 'I,' let us remind ourselves, is not 'God'—even if it may be *subject to* fantasies of being so.

Psychoanalysis, then, has been a particularly disturbing but valuable discourse in the twentieth century because it has promoted an awareness of the extent to which any 'I' or human subject is *decentred:* I, in other words, can never be simply or precisely who or what I think. What makes this idea disturbing and at the same time valuable is that it involves a dislocation of the notions of human mastery and autonomy of self and introduces instead the humility of recognizing that the human subject is not centred in itself, let alone centred in relation to the surrounding world or solar system. In an essay on 'The Resistances to Psychoanalysis' (1925), Freud talks about the 'emotional' difficulties people have in accepting the ideas of psychoanalysis and draws analogies between this and the theories of Darwin and Copernicus. In the case of psychoanalysis, he says, 'powerful human feelings are hurt by the subject-matter of the theory. Darwin's theory of descent met with the same fate, since it tore down the barrier that had been arrogantly set up between men and beasts.' Freud goes on to suggest that 'the psychoanalytic view of the relation of the conscious ego to an overpowering unconscious was a severe blow to human self-love,' and that, 'as the *psychoanalytical* blow to men's narcissism,' it compares 'with the *biological* blow delivered by the theory of descent and the earlier *cosmological* blow aimed at it by the discovery of Copernicus' (Freud l986, 272–3). In this sense, psychoanalysis complements the Copernican revolution and nineteenth-century evolutionary theory in providing a powerful critique of anthropocentric values and ideas. Psychoanalysis demonstrates in uncomfortably clear terms how the 'arrogance' of anthropocentrism—that is to say, every kind of thinking, including every kind of philosophy and politics, which puts the human at the centre of the earth and solar system, if not of the universe—is both unwarranted and unsustainable.

The Cartesian 'I think therefore I am' can be further considered specifically in relation to language. Language determines the 'I' and the 'I think.' This can be illustrated simply by reflecting on the idea that Descartes's formulation was originally in Latin ('cogito ergo sum'). We anglophone subjects are already adrift in effects of language and translation, but so too was Descartes himself: after all, he wrote not in some form of seventeenth-century French but in a foreign, 'dead' language. Descartes was subject to the scholarly protocols of his own time and the requirement to write (and in some sense presumably think) in Latin.

What is at stake in this logic of being *subject to language* is a conception of language as not simply *instrumental:* language is not simply something that we *use.* Language governs what we (can) say as much as we govern or *use* language. Language is not simply an instrument: we are, unavoidably, *agents* of language. Moreover we are, more precisely perhaps, secret or double agents of language: we do not necessarily know, from one moment to the next, *how* we are being used by language or where it might be leading us. As in the most compelling kind of espionage story, however, this is not a situation we can get out of. As the narrator neatly puts it, in Margaret Atwood's short story 'Giving Birth' (1977): 'These are the only words I have, I'm stuck with them, stuck in them' (225–6). The 'in' is, no doubt, more difficult to reflect on than the 'with,' but it is no less important.

How do these various questions and ideas relate to literary works more generally? First of all let us emphasize that, if literature is concerned with exploring and reflecting on the nature of personal identity, it is also a space of exhilarating, even anarchic openness and imaginative or transformational possibility. Literature might be thought of as being, in Derrida's words, 'the institution which allows one to *say everything,* in *every way*' (Derrida 1992a, 36). In particular there is this astonishing, anarchic freedom in literature: at least in principle, the author of a literary work can be any 'I' he or she wishes to. To put it like this is to imply that the author is an 'I' before or outside the literary work. But who is to say that there is an 'I' anywhere that is not in part *literary*? This rather strange question is a focus of one of the greatest comical literary or philosophical works in the twentieth century, Samuel Beckett's *The Unnamable* (first published in English in 1959). This text is preoccupied with the idea that it is the 'I' itself that is in a sense the unnamable: the 'I' that speaks, or that seems to speak, is never true, never precisely itself, never the same, for example, as the 'I' who has spoken or the 'I' that writes 'I.' *The Unnamable*, then, starts off from the apparently simple but perhaps unfathomable remark, 'I, say I,' and from the paradox that 'I seem to speak, it is not I, about me, it is not about me' (293). Nearly fifty pages later the narrator is still impelled to observe that 'on the subject of me properly so called… so far as I know I have received no information up to date' (338). In Beckett's wonderfully funny, but also dark and unnerving text, the Cartesian-rationalistic 'I think' becomes: 'I only think, if that is the name for this vertiginous panic as of hornets smoked out of their nest, once a certain degree of terror has been exceeded' (353). As with so much of Beckett's writing, this sentence is at once quite straightforward and semantically dense, unsettling, surprisingly resistant to a single interpretation. We might note, for example, the explicit attention to the uncertainties of language ('if that is the name') and of the relationship between terror and thinking. To think about this sentence can induce vertiginous panic and become terrifying. It succinctly illustrates literature's complex and unsettling effects when it comes to thinking about identity and about the 'I' that claims to think.

We could conclude by trying to say a little more about the ways in which, as we suggested earlier, the 'I' or 'me' is in fact historically determined. One very broad but decisive example of this would be the question of the 'I' or 'me' in relation to romantic and postromantic literature. In *Of Grammatology* (1967), Derrida argues that the importance of Jean-Jacques Rousseau's work consists in the fact that he 'starts from a new model of presence: the subject's self-presence within *consciousness* or *feeling*' (Derrida 1976, 98). European romanticism in general might be characterized in terms of this kind of 'new model of presence,' and in particular in terms of a new emphasis on the centrality and importance of the 'I' as a subject who both thinks and feels. This could be exemplified by the fragment often published as the prologue or opening stanza to George Gordon Byron's *Don Juan* (1819–24):

> I would to heaven that I were so much clay,
> As I am blood, bone, marrow, passion, feeling—
> Because at least the past were pass'd away—
> And for the future—(but I write this reeling,
> Having got drunk exceedingly to-day,
> So that I seem to stand upon the ceiling)
> I say—the future is a serious matter—
> And so—for God's sake—hock and soda-water!

The new emphasis on the 'I' in romantic culture is consistently articulated in terms of the polarity or gulf between a subject ('I feel') and an object (the clouds, a skylark, a nightingale). The (impossible) desire for a fusion between subject and object (the idea for example of being, in Matthew Arnold's words, 'in harmony with nature') is one of the most striking characteristics of the work of the English romantic poets. It is clear, for instance, in Keats's 'Ode to a Nightingale,' in which the speaker is eventually compelled to admit to defeat in his attempt to fuse or dissolve into the nightingale's song: the word 'forlorn' is 'like a bell / To toll me back from thee to my sole self.' This emphasis on the 'sole self' broaches the notion of solipsism, that is to say the refusal or inability to believe in the reality of anything outside or beyond the self. The idea of such an isolation of the self has its representatives in classical philosophy and literature, but it is particularly pervasive in nineteenth- and twentieth-century European culture. It is evoked by the pathos, or bathos, of the opening lines of Matthew Arnold's poem, 'To Marguerite—Continued' (1849):

Yes! in the sea of life enisled
With echoing straits between us thrown,
Dotting the shoreless waters wild,
We mortal millions live *alone*.

It is also implicit in the work of Freud, to the extent that psychoanalysis suggests that everything comes down to the power and significance of *projection,* of the qualities, moods or emotions which we *project onto* people and things. Wallace Stevens sums this up when he says:

few people realize on that occasion, which comes to all of us, when we look at the blue sky for the first time, that is to say: not merely see it, but look at it and experience it . . . —few people realize that they are looking at the world of their own thoughts and the world of their own feelings. (Stevens 1951, 65–6)

But as we hope will by now be clear, solipsism is a myth, a delusion or mirage. Solipsism presupposes the idea of something like what Wittgenstein calls a private language (Wittgenstein 1984). There is no such thing as a private language: the phrase 'private language' is an oxymoron. Language is social or, at least, language comes from elsewhere, from others and from otherness in general. Even to say, as a self-avowed solipsist might, 'I do not believe in the reality of living apart from myself,' is to demonstrate a dependence on what is not 'me,' not oneself. It is to demonstrate that one is *subject to* language. As the voice, or one of the voices, in *The Unnamable* puts it: 'I'm made of words, others' words . . .' (390).

Literature, like art more generally, has always been concerned with aspects of what can be called the unconscious or 'not me': it is and has always been centrally concerned with dreams and fantasy, hallucinations and visions, madness, trance, and other kinds of impersonality or absences of self. But we could say that romantic and post-romantic literature has been increasingly sensitive to the role of otherness and increasingly aware of what might be described as our obligations in relation to otherness. Beckett's writing is perhaps only the most philosophically refined recent example of post-romantic literature which is concerned to explore, deflate and transform our understanding of the question, 'Who do we think we are?' In this respect his work might be seen to anticipate and encapsulate much of what is called poststructuralism. Poststructuralism demonstrates that the 'I' or human subject is necessarily *decentred.* It argues against the reductiveness (and even the possibility) of rationalism, in particular through its attention to what is other (though not simply 'irrational') as regards Western 'rational' thinking. And it persistently shows up the presumptuousness of the model of an autonomous, supposedly masterful human being, and thus points beyond 'merely' literary questions, exposing the barbarities of anthropocentrism in general. Some of this may be felt in a faltering, haunting few words from *The Unnamable:*

> if only I knew if I've lived, if I live, if I'll live, that would simplify everything, impossible to find out, that's where you're buggered, I haven't stirred, that's all I know, no, I know something else, it's not I, I always forget that, I resume, you must resume . . . (417)

REFERENCES

Arnold, Matthew. "To Marguerite—Continued." *The Poems of Matthew Arnold.* Ed. Kenneth Allott. London: Longman, 1965.

Atwood, Margaret. "Giving Birth." *Dancing Girls and Other Stories.* London: Virago, 1985.

Beckett, Samuel. *The Unnamable.* London: Calder and Boyars, 1959.

Byron, Lord. *Don Juan.* Ed. L.A. Marchand. Boston: Houghton Mifflin, 1969.

Derrida, Jacques. *Of Grammatology.* Trans. Gayatri Chakravorty Spivak. Baltimore: The Johns Hopkins University Press, 1976.

Derrida, Jacques. "The Principle of Reason: The University in the Eyes of Its Pupils." Trans. Catherine Porter and Edward P. Morris. *Diacritics* 13.2 (1983): 3–20.

---. *Acts of Literature.* Ed. Derek Attridge. London: Routledge, 1992.

Descartes, René. *Discourse on Method and the Meditations.* Trans. F.E. Sutcliffe. Harmondsworth: Penguin, 1977.

During, Simon. *Foucault and Literature: Towards a Genealogy of Writing.* London: Routledge, 1992.

Freud, Sigmund. "Psychoanalysis." 1923. *Pelican Freud Library,* vol. 15. Trans. James Strachey. Harmondsworth: Penguin, 1986.

---. "The Resistance to Psychoanalysis." (1925). *The Standard Edition of the Complete Psychological Works of Sigmund Freud.* 24 vols. Trans. J. Strachey. London: Hogarth Press and the Institute of Psychoanalysis, 1974.

Judovitz, Dalia. *Subjectivity and Representation in Descartes: The Origins of Modernity.* Cambridge: Cambridge University Press, 1988.

Keats, John. "Ode to a Nightingale." *The Poems of John Keats.* Ed. Jack Stillinger. London: Heinemann, 1978.

O'Connor, Flannery. "Revelation." *The Secret Self: Short Stories by Women.* Ed. Hermione Lee. London: Everyman, 1991.

Plato. *The Collected Dialogues of Plato, Including the Letters.* Ed. Edith Hamilton and Huntington Cairns. New Jersey: Princeton University Press, 1961.

Shakespeare, William. *Romeo and Juliet. The Riverside Shakespeare.* Boston: Houghton Mifflin, 1974.

Stevens, Wallace. *The Necessary Angel: Essays on Reality and the Imagination.* New York: Alfred A. Knopf, 1951.

Wittgenstein, Ludwig. *Philosophical Investigations.* Oxford: Blackwell, 1984.

2 | Theodor Adorno and Max Horkheimer, "The Culture Industry: Enlightenment as Mass Deception"

EDITORS' INTRODUCTION

Theodor Adorno and Max Horkheimer's seminal critique of the culture industry and the popular culture it produces was written in the 1940s. Products of the Frankfurt School, the authors share a post-Marxist concern to analyze within the products and processes of 20th-century culture the ideologies by which state power binds subjects together within a coherent public sphere, albeit frequently against subjects' individual interests and concerns. The authors had sought refuge in the United States from the Third Reich's state domination of cultural production, which exerted a deadening and deadly conformity.

The 1936 Nazi political rallies at Nuremberg, documented in Leni Reifenstal's film *The Triumph of the Will* epitomize this conformity. Using light, music, and the frenzied patriotism of Hitler's speeches, these rallies were delirious displays of propaganda choreographing thousands of military and civilian subjects. This mass hysteria materialized state power in the bodies of its subjects by transforming them into a deluded and docile body politic. These were also *aesthetic* spectacles that appealed to the senses and passions as a way of masking the horrific racism of Nazi ideology. In terms of visceral effect, they were not entirely unlike the games in the ancient Roman Coliseum as depicted in Ridley Scott's 2001 film *Gladiator,* although in 1930s Germany the entertainment was purged of bloody persecution, which was meant to play "offscreen." An entertained people can be distracted from thinking about the lack of political process. Democratic consensus was instead manufactured by a leadership interested only in displaying brute power as a way of hiding this power's brutalizing effects.

The rallies offered a chilling example of "popular" culture as a monolithic sphere in which people are absorbed by, rather than interact with, the terms of their everyday life. This is why Adorno and Horkheimer turned to the United States as an example of democratic self-expression unfettered by state control. They found Hollywood. Hollywood made movies the way Henry Ford made automobiles (a useful parallel to think of when reading the essay). The intrinsic aesthetic value of films was subservient to the demands of standardization and profitability. Films no longer pretended to be art; they were interchangeable and disposable manufactured products. Culture was not born of creativity; it assembled its products as part of an industry that reflected the "absolute power of capitalism" and its "technological rationale," what Adorno and Horkheimer call "the rationale of domination itself" (55). This process was fundamentally economic and profit-driven, and it relied on efficiency, administration, uniformity, and rationality. Indeed, the essay's opening section focuses on how the culture industry, via capitalism and technology, "now impresses the same stamp on everything" (54), rather than creating the "cultural chaos" warned against already in the 19th century by Matthew Arnold.

This conformity extended most ominously to individuals, whom the culture industry classifies the way the Enlightenment classified plants and animals in the 18th century: as *types,* rather than authentic human beings. Like any other industry, the culture industry *creates* its consumers by making them desire, and thus identifies them through, the products it wants them to consume. Individuals are commodities to be manufactured, "unfailingly reproduced in every product" (58). Or in one of the essay's final distinctions, the culture industry "individuates" its subjects at the expense of their unique or authentic "individuality." In short, it perpetrates a vicious circle in which subjects consume themselves (this cycle of cultural cannibalism is the subject of such horror films as George Romero's 1978 *Dawn of the Dead*).

The essay's longer second section focuses primarily on how the culture industry creates the illusion of difference and agency among its consumers through style. The authors write: "The whole world is made to pass through the filter of the culture industry." Employing the powerful technology of mechanical reproduction made possible by the moving image and sound recording, a movie is, thus, indistinguishable from real life (this idea of a virtual verisimilitude is behind Jean Baudrillard's idea of simulation). This immediate reality creates a type of automatic spectacle that absorbs the viewer's imagination and judgment within the film's visual and aural language (think of the overpoweringly sublime technology of recent films, such as *Independence Day* or *X-Men*). Viewers have no choice but to buy into a film's style wholesale.

For instance, if we adopt Brad Pitt's clothing in *Fight Club,* we are also adopting the social character of an anarchist. Indeed, in the culture industry's sphere of superficial distinctions outlined by the authors, a messy hairstyle and transgressive morality are the same thing. This closed system allows for invention, but only as a diversion from style's gold standard. This explains the essay's rather illogical example of jazz improvisation, which the authors read as a form of cultural forgery (not unlike digital sampling), rather than individual expression. Style, then, means aesthetic regularity, rather than individuality, a mode of domination that stamps bodies with the impression of culture's sameness. Style is, thus, the antithesis of style, holding out personal transformation as a false promise. If style in high art marks the struggle for self-expression, "the necessary failure of the passionate striving for identity" (60), mass culture turns real struggle into the feigned reality of crisis easily overcome. It offers, for instance, love as mere romance (boy gets girl, boy loses girl, boy gets girl back): it repeats this triumph as the spectacle of an ideal forever reachable yet never attainable (think of the likelihood of living out Julia Roberts' Cinderella fantasy in *Pretty Woman*). In short, whereas high art offers the possibility of transformation for its subjects, the culture industry offers the illusion of its attainment.

For Adorno and Horkheimer, then, Hollywood evokes a mode of thought control not unlike Hitler's totalitarianism (one might think here of Busby Berkeley's *Goldiggers of 1933*, which choreographs the dancers' beautiful white bodies according to a lockstep precision not unlike that of the Nuremberg rallies). "The might of industrial society," they argue, "is lodged in men's minds" (57) but treats their capacity for independent thought and action as a mere illusion. The essay's final section drives this point home in chilling fashion by arguing that the individual in capitalist society is "tolerated only so long as his complete identification with the generality is unquestioned" (62). "What is individual is no more than the generality's power to stamp the accidental detail so firmly that it is accepted as such" (63), which means that even changeability and spontaneity are always already anticipated and orchestrated by the culture industry. The individual with rights and privileges, herself a recent invention of the Enlightenment, interferes with more than she facilitates industrial and technological progress. Human nature can be a messy thing to control. But if individuality is where society and its subjects are flawed, and moreover unable to see these defects, the culture industry exploits this fragility by turning enlightenment into deception—or, rather, by masking deception *as* enlightenment, as the essay's subtitle suggests.

Adorno and Horkheimer offer a powerfully seductive and even apocalyptic account of a culture obsessed with entertainment, mass production, and conformity. Given current popular culture, which blurs the line between politics and entertainment in network news or between everyday life and the television screen in "reality" TV, the essay seems increasingly prophetic, rather than outdated. There are, however, limitations. The essay was written at a time when the vertically integrated studio system and its five major studios (Metro-Goldwyn-Mayer, Twentieth-Century Fox, Warner Brothers, Paramount, and Universal) exerted almost total control over film production and distribution. By the 1950s, this system was in decline due to the rise of television. Over time, the film industry, like TV, evolved according to a more diversified, competitive economic interaction between a variety of groups: producers, advertisers, talent agents, distributors, and so on (although the horizontal corporate network of late capitalism at the dawn of the 21st century has come to seem no less monolithic than the power dynamic of the hierarchical model in Adorno and Horkheimer's critique). The authors are also ambivalent about high culture. On the one hand, the essay suggests that Matthew Arnold's Victorian idea of the best that has been thought or written in world history is a "common denominator" that "already contains in embryo that schematization and process of cataloguing and classification" (60) which make culture more administrative than creative. On the other hand, it implicitly values high culture as a standard of excellence that reflects vital civil values. Even if mass culture leads to standardization, rather than chaos, it is still a bad thing. And finally, the authors do not consider popular culture as a *process* as well as *product,* a social sphere in which subjects interact to "decode" cultural artifacts (to borrow Stuart Hall's term) in ways that resist how they have been "encoded" by the culture industry. The essay is effective in its polemical desire to re-exercise a political agency atrophied by cultural conformity. But it fails to see how the "popular" in popular culture means that human subjects might embody themselves differently—might use their bodies and minds differently. While the culture industry might want to turn us into Pavlov's dogs, we are not only the stereotypes of its docile citizenry.

The essay's limitations are as instructive as its strengths. Rather than decide between the two poles, one can take them as indicative of counterforces being waged within the sphere of culture itself: high versus low; the emotional versus the intellectual; superiority versus inferiority. We can, that is, read the essay within popular culture in the way that Dick Hebdige defines hegemony: as a "moving equilibrium" in which there is always a motivation toward homogeneity and the embodiment of subjects through the ideologies of a dominant order of things on the one hand, countered by the resistances of subjects *as bodies* within the culture of everyday life on the other. The extent to which this site of resistance is itself real or manufactured will be the subject of many of the essays following Adorno and Horkheimer's, which continues this anthology's discussion of how subjects come to be and how they come to be embodied in popular culture.

—JF

ISSUES TO CONSIDER WHILE READING

1. Adorno and Horkheimer's essay offers a vision of subjects as mere dupes of the culture industry. In what ways is this vision too limited for our understanding of 21st century cultural subjects? In what ways is it accurate? You might want to think of this question in relation to the Naomi Klein excerpt in this volume.
2. When defining the culture industry, Adorno and Horkheimer are thinking of the kind of "vertically integrated" model of industrial or economic organization offered by the old Hollywood studio system. In what ways do today's global or transnational corporations both conform to and refute this model?

REFERENCES AND FURTHER READING

Adorno, Max. *The Culture Industry: Selected Essays on Mass Culture*. Ed. and introduction J. M. Bernstein. London: Routledge, 1991.

Arnold, Matthew. *Culture and Anarchy*. London: Cambridge University Press, 1960.

Hardt, Michael, and Antonio Negri. *Empire*. Cambridge, MA: Harvard University Press, 2000.

Horkheimer, Max, and Theodor W. Adorno. *Dialectic of Enlightenment*. Trans. John Cumming. New York: Continuum, 2000.

Jameson, Frederic. *Postmodernism or the Cultural Logic of Late Capitalism*. Durham, NC: Duke University Press, 1990.

Slater, Phil. *Origin and Significance of the Frankfurt School: A Marxist Perspective*. London: Routledge & Kegan Paul, 1977.

The Culture Industry: Enlightenment as Mass Deception

The *sociological* theory that the loss of the support of objectively established religion, the dissolution of the last remnants of precapitalism, together with technological and social differentiation or specialization, have led to cultural chaos is disproved every day; for culture now impresses the same stamp on everything. Films, radio and magazines make up a system which is uniform as a whole and in every part. Even the aesthetic activities of political opposites are one in their enthusiastic obedience to the rhythm of the iron system. The decorative industrial management buildings and exhibition centres in authoritarian countries are much the same as anywhere else. The huge gleaming towers that shoot up everywhere are outward signs of the ingenious planning of international concerns, toward which the unleashed entrepreneurial system (whose monuments are a mass of gloomy houses and business premises in grimy, spiritless cities) was already hastening.

Even now the older houses just outside the concrete city centres look like slums, and the new bungalows on the outskirts are at one with the flimsy structures of world fairs in their praise of technical progress and their built-in demand to be discarded after a short while like empty food cans. Yet the city housing projects designed to perpetuate the individual as a supposedly independent unit in a small hygienic dwelling make him all the more subservient to his adversary—the absolute power of capitalism. Because the inhabitants, as producers and as consumers, are drawn into the centre in search of work and pleasure, all the living units crystallize into well-organized complexes. The striking unity of microcosm and macrocosm presents men with a model of their culture: the false identity of the general and the particular. Under monopoly all mass culture is identical, and the lines of its artificial framework begin to show through. The people at the top are no longer so interested in concealing monopoly: as its violence becomes more open, so its power grows. Movies and radio need no longer pretend to be art. The truth that they are just business is made into an ideology in order to justify the rubbish they deliberately produce. They call themselves industries; and when their director's incomes are published, any doubt about the social utility of the finished products is removed.

Interested parties explain the culture industry in technological terms. It is alleged that because millions participate in it, certain reproduction processes are necessary that inevitably require identical needs in innumerable places to be satisfied with identical goods. The technical contrast between the few production centres and the large number of widely dispersed consumption points is said to demand organization and planning by management. Furthermore, it is claimed that standards were based in the first place on consumers' needs, and for that reason were accepted with so little resistance. The result is the circle of manipulation and retroactive need in which the unity of the system grows ever stronger. No mention is made of the fact that the basis on which technology acquires power over society is the power of those whose economic hold over society is greatest. A technological rationale is the rationale of domination itself. It is the coercive nature of society alienated from itself. Automobiles, bombs, and movies keep the whole thing together until their levelling element shows its strength in the very wrong which it furthered. It has made the technology of the culture industry no more than the achievement of standardization and mass production, sacrificing whatever involved a distinction between the logic of the work and that of the social system. This is the result not of a law of movement in technology as such but of its function in today's economy. The need which might resist central control has already been suppressed by the control of the individual consciousness. The step from the telephone to the radio has clearly distinguished the roles. The former still allowed the subscriber to play the role of subject, and was liberal. The latter is democratic: it turns all participants into listeners and authoritatively subjects them to broadcast programmes which are all exactly the same. No machinery of rejoinder has been devised, and private broadcasters are denied any freedom. They are confined to the apocryphal field of the 'amateur,' and also have to accept organization from above. But any trace of spontaneity from the public in official broadcasting is controlled and absorbed by talent scouts, studio competitions and official programmes of every kind selected by professionals. Talented performers belong to the industry long before it displays them; otherwise they would not be so eager to fit in. The attitude of the public, which ostensibly and actually favours the system of the culture industry, is a part of the system and not an excuse for it. If one branch of art follows the same formula as one with a very different medium and content; if the dramatic intrigue of broadcast soap operas becomes no more than useful material for showing how to master technical problems at both ends of the scale of musical experience—real jazz or a cheap imitation; or if a movement from a Beethoven symphony is crudely 'adapted' for a film soundtrack in the same way as a Tolstoy novel is garbled in a film script: then the claim that this is done to satisfy the spontaneous wishes of the public is no more than hot air. We are closer to the facts if we explain these phenomena as inherent in the technical and personnel apparatus which, down to its last cog, itself forms part of the economic mechanism of selection. In addition there is the agreement—or at least the determination—of all executive authorities not to produce or sanction anything that in any way differs from their own rules, their own ideas about consumers, or above all themselves.

In our age the objective social tendency is incarnate in the hidden subjective purposes of company directors, the foremost among whom are in the most powerful sectors of industry—steel, petroleum, electricity, and chemicals. Culture monopolies are weak and dependent in comparison. They cannot afford to neglect their appeasement of the real holders of power if their sphere of activity in mass society (a sphere producing a specific type of commodity which anyhow is still too closely bound up with easygoing liberalism and Jewish intellectuals) is not to undergo a series of purges. The dependence of the most powerful broadcasting company on the electrical industry, or of the motion picture industry on the banks, is characteristic of the whole sphere, whose individual branches are themselves economically interwoven. All are in such close contact that the extreme concentration of mental forces allows demarcation lines between different firms and technical branches to be ignored. The ruthless unity in the culture industry is evidence of what will happen in politics. Market differentiations such as those of A and B films, or of stories in magazines in different price ranges, depend not so much on subject matter as on classifying, organizing, and labelling consumers. Something is provided for all so that none may escape; the distinctions are emphasized and extended. The public is catered for with a hierarchical range of mass-produced products of varying quality, thus advancing the rule of complete quantification. Everybody must behave (as if spontaneously) in accordance with his previous determined and indexed level, and choose the category of mass product turned out for his type. Consumers appear as statistics on research organization charts, and are divided by income groups into red, green, and blue areas; the technique is that used for any type of propaganda.

How formalized the procedure is can be seen when the mechanically differentiated products prove to be all alike in the end. That the difference between the Chrysler range and General Motors products is basically illusory strikes every child with a keen interest in varieties. What connoisseurs discuss as good or bad points serve only to perpetuate the semblance of competition and range of choice. The same applies to the Warner Brothers and Metro Goldwyn Mayer productions. But even the differences between the more expensive and cheaper models put out by the same firm steadily diminish: for automobiles, there are such differences as the number of cylinders, cubic capacity, details of patented gadgets; and for films there are the number of stars, the extravagant use of technology, labour, and equipment, and the introduction of the latest psychological formulas. The universal criterion of merit is the amount of 'conspicuous production' of blatant cash investment. The varying budgets in the culture industry do not bear the slightest relation to factual values, to the meaning of the products themselves. Even the technical media are relentlessly forced into uniformity. Television aims at a synthesis of radio and film, and is held up only because the interested parties have not yet reached agreement, but its consequences will be quite enormous and promise to intensify the impoverishment of aesthetic matter so drastically, that by tomorrow the thinly veiled identity of all industrial culture products can come triumphantly out into the open, derisively fulfilling the Wagnerian dream of the *Gesamtkunstwerk*—the fusion of all the arts in one work. The alliance of word, image, and music is all the more perfect than in *Tristan* because the sensuous elements which all approvingly reflect the surface of social reality are in principle embodied in the same technical process, the unity of which becomes its distinctive content. This process integrates all the elements of the production, from the novel (shaped with an eye to the film) to the last sound effect. It is the triumph of invested capital, whose title as absolute master is etched deep into the hearts of the dispossessed in the employment line; it is the meaningful content of every film, whatever plot the production team may have selected.

The whole world is made to pass through the filter of the culture industry. The old experience of the movie-goer, who sees the world outside as an extension of the film he has just left (because the latter is intent upon reproducing the world of everyday perceptions), is now the producer's guideline. The more intensely and flawlessly his techniques duplicate empirical objects, the easier it is today for the illusion to prevail that the outside world is the straightforward continuation of that presented on the screen. This purpose has been furthered by mechanical reproduction since the lightning takeover by the sound film.

[Real life is becoming indistinguishable from the movies.]The sound film, far surpassing the theatre of illusion,[leaves no room for imagination or reflection on the part of the audience, who are unable to respond within the structure of the film, yet deviate from its precise detail without losing the thread of the *story;* hence the film forces its victims to equate it directly with reality.]The stunting of the mass-media consumer's powers of imagination and spontaneity does not have to be traced back to any psychological mechanisms; he must ascribe the loss of those attributes to the objective nature of the products themselves, especially to the most characteristic of them, the sound film. They are so designed that quickness, powers of observation, and experience are undeniably needed to apprehend them at all; yet sustained thought is out of the question if the spectator is not to miss the relentless rush of facts. Even though the effort required for his response is semi-automatic, no scope is left for the imagination. Those who are so absorbed by the world of the movie—by its images, gestures, and words—that they are unable to supply what really makes it a world, do not have to dwell on particular points of its mechanics during a screening. All the other films and products of the entertainment industry which they have seen have taught them what to expect; they react automatically. The might of industrial society is lodged in men's minds. The entertainments manufacturers know that their products will be consumed with alertness even when the customer is distraught, for each of them is a model of the huge economic machinery which has always sustained the masses, whether at work or at leisure—which is akin to work. From every sound film and every broadcast programme the social effect can be inferred which is exclusive to none but is shared by all alike. The culture industry as a whole has moulded men as a type unfailingly reproduced in every product. All the agents of this process, from the producer to the women's clubs, take good care that the simple reproduction of this mental state is not nuanced or extended in any way.

The art historians and guardians of culture who complain of the extinction in the West of a basic style-determining power are wrong. The stereotyped appropriation of everything, even the inchoate, for the purposes of mechanical reproduction surpasses the rigour and general currency of any 'real style,' in the sense in which cultural *cognoscenti* celebrate the organic precapitalist past. No Palestrina could be more of a purist in eliminating every unprepared and unresolved discord than the jazz arranger in suppressing any development which does not conform to the jargon. When jazzing up Mozart he changes him not only when he is too serious or too difficult but when he harmonizes the melody in a different way, perhaps more simply, than is customary now. No medieval builder can have scrutinized the subjects for church windows and sculptures more suspiciously than the studio hierarchy scrutinizes a work by Balzac or Hugo before finally approving it. No medieval theologian could have determined the degree of the torment to be suffered by the damned in accordance with the *ordo* of divine love more meticulously than the producers of shoddy epics calculate the torture to be undergone by the hero or the exact point to which the leading lady's hemline shall be raised. The explicit and implicit, exoteric and esoteric catalogue of the forbidden and tolerated is so extensive that it not only defines the area of freedom but is all-powerful inside it. Everything down to the last detail is shaped accordingly. Like its counterpart, avant-garde art, the entertainment industry determines its own language, down to its very syntax and vocabulary, by the use of anathema. The constant pressure to produce new effects (which must conform to the old pattern) serves merely as another rule to increase the power of the conventions when any single effect threatens to slip through the net. Every detail is so firmly stamped with sameness that nothing can appear which is not marked at birth, or does not meet with approval at first sight. And the star performers, whether they produce or reproduce, use this jargon as freely and fluently and with as much gusto as if it were the very language which it silenced long ago. Such is the ideal of what is natural in this field of activity, and its influence becomes all the more powerful, the more technique is perfected and diminishes the tension between the finished product and everyday life. The paradox of this routine, which is essentially travesty, can be detected and is often predominant in everything that the culture industry turns out. A jazz musician who is playing a piece of serious music, one of Beethoven's simplest minuets, syncopates it involuntarily and will smile superciliously when asked to follow the normal divisions of the beat. This is the 'nature' which, complicated by the ever-present and extravagant demands of the specific medium, constitutes the new style and is a 'system of non-culture, to which one might even concede a certain "unity of style" if it really made any sense to speak of stylized barbarity.'

The universal imposition of this stylized mode can even go beyond what is quasi-officially sanctioned or forbidden; today a hit song is more readily forgiven for not observing the 32 beats or the compass of the ninth than for containing even the most clandestine melodic or harmonic detail which does not conform to the idiom. Whenever

Orson Welles offends against the tricks of the trade, he is forgiven because his departures from the norm are regarded as calculated mutations which serve all the more strongly to confirm the validity of the system. The constraint of the technically conditioned idiom which stars and directors have to produce as 'nature' so that the people can appropriate it, extends to such fine nuances that they almost attain the subtlety of the devices of an avant-garde work as against those of truth. The rare capacity minutely to fulfil the obligations of the natural idiom in all branches of the culture industry becomes the criterion of efficiency. What and how they say it must be measurable by everyday language, as in logical positivism. The producers are experts. The idiom demands an astounding productive power, which it absorbs and squanders. In a diabolical way it has overreached the culturally conservative distinction between genuine and artificial style. A style might be called artificial which is imposed from without on the refractory impulses of a form. But in the culture industry every element of the subject matter has its origin in the same apparatus as that jargon whose stamp it bears. The quarrels in which the artistic experts become involved with sponsor and censor about a lie going beyond the bounds of credibility are evidence not so much of an inner aesthetic tension as of a divergence of interests. The reputation of the specialist, in which a last remnant of objective independence sometimes finds refuge, conflicts with the business politics of the church, or the concern which is manufacturing the cultural commodity. But the thing itself has been essentially objectified and made viable before the established authorities began to argue about it. Even before Zanuck acquired her, St Bernadette was regarded by her latter-day hagiographer as brilliant propaganda for all interested parties. That is what became of the emotions of the character. Hence the style of the culture industry, which no longer has to test itself against any refractory material, is also the negation of style. The reconciliation of the general and particular, of the rule and the specific demands of the subject matter, the achievement of which alone gives essential, meaningful content to style, is futile because there has ceased to be the slightest tension between opposite poles: these concordant extremes are dismally identical; the general can replace the particular, and vice versa.

Nevertheless, this caricature of style does not amount to something beyond the genuine style of the past. In the culture industry the notion of genuine style is seen to be the aesthetic equivalent of domination. Style considered as mere aesthetic regularity is a romantic dream of the past. The unity of style not only of the Christian Middle Ages but of the Renaissance expresses in each case the different structure of social power, and not the obscure experience of the oppressed in which the general was enclosed. The great artists were never those who embodied a wholly flawless and perfect style, but those who used style as a way of hardening themselves against the chaotic expression of suffering, as a negative truth. The style of their works gave what was expressed that force without which life flows away unheard. Those very art forms which are known as classical, such as Mozart's music, contain objective trends which represent something different to the style which they incarnate. As late as Schöenberg and Picasso, the great artists have retained a mistrust of style, and at crucial points have subordinated it to the logic of the matter. What Dadaists and Expressionists called the untruth of style as such triumphs today in the sung jargon of a crooner, in the carefully contrived elegance of a film star, and even in the admirable expertise of a photograph of a peasant's squalid hut. Style represents a promise in every work of art. That which is expressed is subsumed through style into the dominant forms of generality, into the language of music, painting, or words, in the hope that it will be reconciled thus with the idea of true generality. This promise held out by the work of art that it will create truth by lending new shape to the conventional social forms is as necessary as it is hypocritical. It unconditionally posits the real forms of life as it is by suggesting that fulfilment lies in their aesthetic derivatives. To this extent the claim of art is always ideology too. However, only in this confrontation with tradition of which style is the record can art express suffering. That factor in a work of art which enables it to transcend reality certainly cannot be detached from style; but it does not consist of the harmony actually realized, of any doubtful unity of form and content, within and without, of individual and society; it is to be found in those features in which discrepancy appears; in the necessary failure of the passionate striving for identity. Instead of exposing itself to this failure in which the style of the great work of art has always achieved self-negation, the inferior work has always relied on its similarity with others—on a surrogate identity.

In the culture industry this imitation finally becomes absolute. Having ceased to be anything but style, it reveals the latter's secret: obedience to the social hierarchy. Today aesthetic barbarity completes what has threatened the creations of the spirit since they were gathered together as culture and neutralized. To speak of culture was always contrary to culture. Culture as a common denominator already contains in embryo that schematization and process of cataloguing and classification which bring culture within the sphere of administration. And it is precisely the industrialized, the consequent, subsumption which entirely accords with this notion of culture. By subordinating in the same way and to the same end all areas of intellectual creation, by occupying men's senses from the time they leave the factory in the evening to the time they clock in again the next morning with matter that bears the impress of the labour process they themselves have to sustain throughout the day, this subsumption mockingly satisfies the concept of a unified culture which the philosophers of personality contrasted with mass culture.

The culture industry perpetually cheats its consumers of what it perpetually promises. The promissory note which, with its plots and staging, it draws on pleasure is endlessly prolonged; the promise, which is actually all the spectacle consists of, is illusory: all it actually confirms is that the real point will never be reached, that the diner must be satisfied with the menu. In front of the appetite stimulated by all those brilliant names and images there is finally set no more than a commendation of the depressing everyday world it sought to escape. Of course works of art were not sexual exhibitions either. However, by representing deprivation as negative, they retracted, as it were, the prostitution of the impulse and rescued by mediation what was denied. The secret of aesthetic sublimation is its representation of fulfilment as a broken promise. The culture industry does not sublimate; it represses. By repeatedly exposing the objects of desire, breasts in a clinging sweater or the naked torso of the athletic hero, it only stimulates the unsublimated forepleasure which habitual deprivation has long since reduced to a masochistic semblance. There is no erotic situation which, while insinuating and exciting, does not fail to indicate unmistakably that things can never go that far. The Hays Office [the film censor of the time] merely confirms the ritual of Tantalus that the culture industry has established anyway. Works of art are ascetic and unashamed; the culture industry is pornographic and prudish. Love is downgraded to romance. And, after the descent, much is permitted; even licence as a marketable speciality has its quota bearing the trade description 'daring.' The mass production of the sexual automatically achieves its repression. Because of his ubiquity, the film star with whom one is meant to fall in love is from the outset a copy of himself. Every tenor voice comes to sound like a Caruso record, and the 'natural' faces of Texas girls are like the successful models by whom Hollywood has type-cast them. The mechanical reproduction of beauty, which reactionary cultural fanaticism wholeheartedly serves in its methodical idolization of individuality, leaves no room for that unconscious idolatry which was once essential to beauty. The triumph over beauty is celebrated by humour—the *Schadenfreude* that every successful deprivation calls forth. There is laughter because there is nothing to laugh at. Laughter, whether conciliatory or terrible, always occurs when some fear passes. It indicates liberation either from physical danger or from the grip of logic. Conciliatory laughter is heard as the echo of an escape from power; the wrong kind overcomes fear by capitulating to the forces which are to be feared. It is the echo of power as something inescapable. Fun is a medicinal bath. The pleasure industry never fails to prescribe it. It makes laughter the instrument of the fraud practised on happiness. Moments of happiness are without laughter; only operettas and films portray sex to the accompaniment of resounding laughter. But Baudelaire is as devoid of humour as Hölderlin. In the false society laughter is a disease which has attacked happiness and is drawing it into its worthless totality. To laugh at something is always to deride it, and the life which, according to Bergson, in laughter breaks through the barrier, is actually an invading barbaric life, self-assertion prepared to parade its liberation from any scruple when the social occasion arises. Such a laughing audience is a parody of humanity. Its members are monads, all dedicated to the pleasure of being ready for anything at the expense of everyone else. Their harmony is a caricature of solidarity. What is fiendish about this false laughter is that it is a compelling parody of the best, which is conciliatory. Delight is austere: *res severa verum gaudium.* The monastic theory that not asceticism but the sexual act denotes the renunciation of attainable bliss receives negative confirmation in the gravity of the lover who with foreboding commits his life to the fleeting moment. In the culture industry, jovial denial takes the place of the pain found in ecstasy and in asceticism. The supreme law is that they shall not satisfy their desires at any price; they must laugh and be content with laughter. In every product of the culture industry, the permanent denial imposed by civilization is once again unmistakably demonstrated and inflicted on its victims. To offer and to deprive them of something is one and the same. This is what happens in erotic films. Precisely because it must never take place, everything centres upon copulation. In films it is more strictly forbidden for an illegitimate relationship to be admitted without the parties being punished than for a millionaire's future son-in-law to be active in the labour movement. In contrast to the liberal era, industrialized as well as popular culture may wax indignant at capitalism, but it cannot renounce the threat of castration. This is fundamental. It outlasts the organized acceptance of the uniformed seen in the films which are produced to that end, and in reality. What is decisive today is no longer puritanism, although it still asserts itself in the form of women's organizations, but the necessity inherent in the system not to leave the customer alone, not for a moment to allow him any suspicion that resistance is possible. The principle dictates that he should be shown all his needs as capable of fulfilment, but that those needs should be so predetermined that he feels himself to be the eternal consumer, the object of the culture industry. Not only does it make him believe that the deception it practises is satisfaction, but it goes further and implies that, whatever the state of affairs, he must put up with what is offered. The escape from everyday drudgery which the whole culture industry promises may be compared to the daughter's abduction in the cartoon: the father is holding the ladder in the dark. The paradise offered by the culture industry is the same old drudgery. Both escape and elopement are predesigned to lead back to the starting point. Pleasure promotes the resignation which it ought to help to forget.

Amusement, if released from every restraint, would not only be the antithesis of art but its extreme role. The Mark Twain absurdity with which the American culture industry flirts at times might be a corrective of art. The more seriously the latter regards the incompatibility with life, the more it resembles the seriousness of life, its antithesis; the more effort it devotes to developing wholly from its own formal law, the more effort it demands from the intelligence to neutralize its burden. In some revue films, and especially in the grotesque and the funnies, the possibility of this negation does glimmer for a few moments. But of course it cannot happen. Pure amusement in its consequence, relaxed self-surrender to all kinds of associations and happy nonsense, is cut short by the amusement on the market: instead, it is interrupted by a surrogate overall meaning which the culture industry insists on giving to its products, and yet misuses as a mere pretext for bringing in the stars. Biographies and other simple stories patch the fragments of nonsense into an idiotic plot. We do not have the cap and bells of the jester but the bunch of keys of capitalist reason, which even screens the pleasure of achieving success. Every kiss in the revue film has to contribute to the career of the boxer, or some hit song expert or other whose rise to fame is being glorified. The deception is not that the culture industry supplies amusement but that it ruins the fun by allowing business considerations to involve it in the ideological clichés of a culture in the process of self-liquidation. Ethics and taste cut short unrestrained amusement as 'naïve'—naïveté is thought to be as bad as intellectualism—and even restrict technical possibilities. The culture industry is corrupt; not because it is a sinful Babylon but because it is a cathedral dedicated to elevated pleasure. On all levels, from Hemingway to Emil Ludwig, from Mrs Miniver to the Lone Ranger, from Toscanini to Guy Lombardo, there is untruth in the intellectual content taken ready-made from art and science. The culture industry does retain a trace of something better in those features which bring it close to the circus, in the self-justifying and nonsensical skill of riders, acrobats and clowns, in the 'defence and justification of physical as against intellectual art.' But the refuges of a mindless artistry which represent what is human as opposed to the social mechanism are being relentlessly hunted down by a schematic reason which compels everything to prove its significance and effect. The consequence is that the nonsensical at the bottom disappears as utterly as the sense in works of art at the top.

In the culture industry the individual is an illusion not merely because of the standardization of the means of production. He is tolerated only so long as his complete identification with the generality is unquestioned. Pseudo individuality is rife: from the standardized jazz improvization to the exceptional film star whose hair curls over her eye to demonstrate her originality. What is individual is no more than the generality's power to stamp the accidental detail so firmly that it is accepted as such. The defiant reserve or elegant appearance of the individual on show is mass-produced like Yale locks, whose only difference can be measured in fractions of millimetres. The peculiarity of the self is a monopoly commodity determined by society; it is falsely represented as natural. It is no more than the moustache, the French accent, the deep voice of the woman of the world, the Lubitsch touch: fingerprints on identity cards which are otherwise exactly the same, and into which the lives and faces of every single person are transformed by the power of the generality. Pseudo individuality is the prerequisite for comprehending tragedy and removing its poison: only because individuals have ceased to be themselves and are now merely centres where the general tendencies meet, is it possible to receive them again, whole and entire, into the generality. In this way mass culture discloses the fictitious character of the 'individual' in the bourgeois era, and is merely unjust in boasting on account of this dreary harmony of general and particular. The principle of individuality was always full of contradiction. Individuation has never really been achieved. Self-preservation in the shape of class has kept everyone at the stage of a mere species being. Every bourgeois characteristic, in spite of its deviation and indeed because of it, expressed the same thing: the harshness of the competitive society. The individual who supported society bore its disfiguring mark; seemingly free, he was actually the product of its economic and social apparatus. Power based itself on the prevailing conditions of power when it sought the approval of persons affected by it. As it progressed, bourgeois society did also develop the individual. Against the will of its leaders, technology has changed human beings from children into persons. However, every advance in individuation of this kind took place at the expense of the individuality in whose name it occurred, so that nothing was left but the resolve to pursue one's own particular purpose. The bourgeois whose existence is split into a business and a private life, whose private life is split into keeping up his public image and intimacy, whose intimacy is split into the surly partnership of marriage and the bitter comfort of being quite alone, at odds with himself and everybody else, is already virtually a Nazi, replete both with enthusiasm and abuse; or a modern city-dweller who can now imagine friendship only as a 'social contact': that is, as being in social contact with others with whom he has no inward contact. The only reason why the culture industry can deal so successfully with individuality is that the latter has always reproduced the fragility of society. On the faces of private individuals and movie heroes put together according to the patterns on magazine covers vanishes a pretence in which no one now believes; the popularity of the hero models comes partly from a secret satisfaction that the effort to achieve individuation has at last been replaced by the effort to imitate, which is admittedly more breathless. It is idle to hope that this self-contradictory, disintegrating 'person' will not last for generations, that the system must collapse because of such a psychological split, or that the deceitful substitution of the stereotype for the individual will of itself become unbearable for mankind. Since Shakespeare's *Hamlet,* the unity of the personality has been seen through as a pretence. Synthetically produced physiognomies show that the people of today have already forgotten that there was ever a notion of what human life was. For centuries society has been preparing for Victor Mature and Mickey Rooney. By destroying they come to fulfill.

3 Dick Hebdige, "From Culture to Hegemony," from *Subculture: The Meaning of Style*

EDITORS' INTRODUCTION

The evolution of cultural studies, particularly from the middle of the 19th century to the present—the period that sees the real emergence and phenomenal growth of mass or industrial culture—is nowhere more clearly seen than in the continuing struggle over the meaning of the central concepts of the field. As the study of culture develops, so does terminology, as it is adapted to accommodate new conditions of being, ideas, and understandings. The fact that the word "culture" itself, which meant one thing to Matthew Arnold in the mid-19th century, another thing to F.R. Leavis at the turn of the 20th century, and yet another to Richard Hoggart in the mid-20th century (see the introduction to this volume), remains problematic to this day.

A typical attempt to define the term, in this instance drawn from Peter Brooker's useful *A Concise Glossary of Cultural Theory* begins thus: "An indispensable but multi-accented term with a complex and *still open* [emphasis added] history which in itself expresses the complexity of general human history" (Brooker 50). In *Keywords*, an earlier glossary of central terms for cultural studies, Raymond Williams first asserts and then demonstrates that "culture is one of the two or three most complicated words in the English language...mainly because it has now come to be used for important concepts in several distinct intellectual disciplines and in several distinct and incompatible systems of thought" (Williams 87). Adding the word "popular" to "culture" muddies the waters more, since the word "popular," an ambiguous term itself, has been a flashpoint for critical debates centring on issues of value and power, sometimes demonized, as in Arnold, Leavis, and Adorno and Horkheimer, sometimes celebrated, as when Williams writes with some nostalgia about the working class popular culture within which he grew up, or of a mass culture that he often simultaneously attacked and defended.

At the centre of this debate stand the consumers or users, the subjects of popular culture, and the assessment of what power they have in the face of the juggernaut of culture. Are we merely its dupes, as Adorno and Horkheimer would have it, or do we have the power to resist or even transform it, to use it in unintended ways, or even to create an alternate, counter-, or subculture? How many popular cultures are there in our globalizing world? One, or several billion, or some number in between? Is the power of popular culture in its making, or in its use by its consumers, or is there necessarily always a struggle over power and meaning among the artifact and its makers, its distributors, and its users?

In his 1979 book *Subculture: The Meaning of Style*, from which the following essay is extracted, Dick Hebdige finds that he has to work his way through to a provisional understanding of these questions and ideas to provide a context and launching pad for his own study, in which he attempts to understand the relation between the power of "big culture" and of those who find a cultural space within which to express opposition to hegemony through style and identity. At stake is nothing less than an understanding of the subject, itself a multi-inflected word, or the subjects, of cultural studies, and part of what Hebdige traces, directly and indirectly, is the accumulation and shifting of meanings around that term. In tracing the evolution of our understanding of culture and our relation to it, he moves us from a focus on culture itself, especially what is often referred to as high culture—Arnold's "the best that has been thought and written" and Leavis's "great tradition," seen as repositories of value by which we should have our moral and aesthetic lives formed and against which "low" or popular culture is seen as wanting—to a focus that looks not to make value judgments about varieties of culture but to understand how culture exercises its power over us and what power we have in the ways that we consume and use culture.

In the 1979 volume, Hebdige brings political theory together with semiotics to argue that sub- or countercultures exercise a great deal of power by taking the things and ideas that industrial culture provides them with and using them against the system, as in the ways that punk music (and later rap and hip hop) acted to create a cultural space for working-class or other disaffected youth who felt little connection with an industrialized music industry that seemed to represent interests remote from their own, and to which they had very limited access. This is possible, he argues, partly because the "signs" of culture can be variously read and used, they are polysemous—that is, their meanings are many and are never permanently fixed, are always a site of struggle over signification. Ten years later, in his *Hiding in the Light*, Hebdige was to acknowledge that his earlier reading of subcultures and their power to thumb their noses at hegemony was perhaps overoptimistic. The music industry had appropriated punk music, just as it went on to appropriate and even to produce other counter-hegemonic styles.

Such a process, we might note, is by no means restricted to the music industry. How many former hippies in Canada rolled their eyes or reacted more strongly when they heard Bob Dylan's 1963 archetypal anti-establishment song, "The Times They Are A-Changin'," used in a Bank of Montreal television ad for telephone and e-banking? Rock and Roll anthems are played at Progressive Conservative and Alliance Party conventions, and while the University of Northern British Columbia in Prince George was conceived of as a progressive and "people's" university, they still built it on a hill outside of town. So fine and insidious is the line between hegemony and resistance that even when we try to fall on one side of it, we find ourselves uncomfortably astraddle.

—AG

ISSUES TO CONSIDER WHILE READING

1. How does the physical structure of your university or college and its classrooms reproduce hegemonic (and, therefore, ideological) views of knowledge, power, and value?
2. In what ways and to what degree are universities and colleges subcultures? How has your experience of postsecondary education encouraged you to both resist and reproduce hegemony?

REFERENCES AND FURTHER READING

Althusser, Louis. "Ideology and Ideological State Apparatuses." *Lenin and Philosophy and Other Essays.* Trans. Ben Brewster. London: New Left Books, 1971.

Barthes, Roland. *Image-Music-Text.* Ed. Stephen Heath. London: Collins, 1977.

Brooker, Peter. *A Concise Glossary of Cultural Theory.* London: Arnold, 1999.

Eagleton, Terry. *Ideology: An Introduction.* London: Verso, 1991.

Hebdige, Dick. "Hiding in the Light: Youth Surveillance and Display." *Hiding in the Light: Images and Things.* London: Routledge, 1989. 17–37.

---. *Subculture: The Meaning of Style.* London: Routledge, 1979.

Williams, Raymond. *Keywords.* London: Collins, 1976.

From Culture to Hegemony

CULTURE

Culture: cultivation, tending, in Christian authors, worship; the action or practice of cultivating the soil; tillage, husbandry; the cultivation or rearing of certain animals (e.g. fish); the artificial development of microscopic organisms, organisms so produced; the cultivating or development (of the mind, faculties, manners), improvement or refinement by education and training; the condition of being trained or refined; the intellectual side of civilization; the prosecution or special attention or study of any subject or pursuit. (Oxford English Dictionary)

Culture is a notoriously ambiguous concept as the above definition demonstrates. Refracted through centuries of usage, the word has acquired a number of quite different, often contradictory, meanings. Even as a scientific term, it refers both to a process (artificial development of microscopic organisms) and a product (organisms so produced). More specifically, since the end of the eighteenth century, it has been used by English intellectuals and literary figures to focus critical attention on a whole range of controversial issues. The 'quality of life,' the effects in human terms of mechanization, the division of labour and the creation of mass society have all been discussed within the larger confines of what Raymond Williams has called the 'Culture and Society' debate. It was through this tradition of dissent and criticism that the dream of the 'organic society'— of society as an integrated, meaningful whole—was largely kept alive. The dream had two basic trajectories. One led back to the past and to the feudal ideal of a hierarchically ordered community. Here culture assumed an almost sacred function. Its 'harmonious perfection' was posited against the Wasteland of contemporary life.

The other trajectory, less heavily supported, led towards the future, to a socialist Utopia where the distinction between labour and leisure was to be annulled. Two basic definitions of culture emerged from this tradition, though these were by no means necessarily congruent with the two trajectories outlined above. The first—the one which is probably most familiar to the reader—was essentially classical and conservative. It represented culture as a standard of aesthetic excellence: 'the best that has been thought and said in the world,' and it derived from an appreciation of 'classic' aesthetic form (opera, ballet, drama, literature, art). The second, traced back by Williams to Herder and the eighteenth century was rooted in anthropology. Here the term 'culture' referred to a

> ... particular way of life which expresses certain meanings and values not only in art and learning, but also in institutions and ordinary behaviour. The analysis of culture, from such a definition, is the clarification of the meanings and values implicit and explicit in a particular way of life, a particular culture. (Williams 1958)

This definition obviously had a much broader range. It encompassed, in T.S. Eliot's words,

> ... all the characteristic activities and interests of a people. Derby Day, Henley Regatta, Cowes, the 12th of August, a cup final, the dog races, the pin table, the dartboard, Wensleydale cheese, boiled cabbage cut into sections, beetroot in vinegar, 19th Century Gothic churches, the music of Elgar. . . .

As Williams noted, such a definition could only be supported if a new theoretical initiative was taken. The theory of culture now involved the 'study of relationships between elements in a whole way of life' (Williams 1958). The emphasis shifted from immutable to historical criteria, from fixity to transformation:

> ... an emphasis [which] from studying particular meanings and values seeks not so much to compare these, as a way of establishing a scale, but by studying their modes of change to discover certain general causes or 'trends' by which social and cultural developments as a whole can be better understood. (Williams 1958)

Williams was, then, proposing an altogether broader formulation of the relationships between culture and society, one which through the analysis of 'particular meanings and values' sought to uncover the conceived fundamentals of history; the 'general causes' and broad social 'trends' which lie behind the manifest appearances of an 'everyday life.'

In the early years, when it was being established in the Universities, Cultural Studies sat rather uncomfortably on the fence between these two conflicting definitions—culture as a standard of excellence, culture as a 'whole way of life'—unable to determine which represented the most fruitful line of enquiry. Richard Hoggart and Raymond Williams portrayed working-class culture sympathetically in wistful accounts of pre-scholarship boyhoods (Leeds for Hoggart (1957), a Welsh mining village for Williams (1958)) but their work displayed a strong bias towards literature and literacy and an equally strong moral tone. Hoggart deplored the way in which the traditional working-class community—a community of tried and tested values despite the dour landscape in which it had been set—was being undermined and replaced by a 'Candy Floss World' of thrills and cheap fiction which was somehow bland *and* sleazy. Williams tentatively endorsed the new mass communications but was concerned to establish aesthetic and moral criteria for distinguishing the worthwhile product from the 'trash'; the jazz—a 'real musical form'—and the football—'a wonderful game'—from the 'rape novel, the Sunday strip paper and the latest Tin Pan drool' (Williams 1961). In 1966 Hoggart laid down the basic premises upon which Cultural Studies were based:

First, without appreciating good literature, no one will really understand the nature of society, second, literary critical analysis can be applied to certain social phenomena other than 'academically respectable' literature (for example, the popular arts, mass communications) so as to illuminate their meanings for individuals and their societies. (Hoggart 1966)

The implicit assumption that it still required a literary sensibility to 'read' society with the requisite subtlety, and that the two ideas of culture could be ultimately reconciled was also, paradoxically, to inform the early work of the French writer, Roland Barthes, though here it found validation in a method—semiotics—a way of reading signs (Hawkes 1977).

BARTHES: MYTHS AND SIGNS

Using models derived from the work of the Swiss linguist Ferdinand de Saussure Barthes sought to expose the *arbitrary* nature of cultural phenomena, to uncover the latent meanings of an everyday life which, to all intents and purposes, was 'perfectly natural.' Unlike Hoggart, Barthes was not concerned with distinguishing the good from the bad in modern mass culture, but rather with showing how *all* the apparently spontaneous forms and rituals of contemporary bourgeois societies are subject to a systematic distortion, liable at any moment to be dehistoricized, 'naturalized,' converted into myth:

The whole of France is steeped in this anonymous ideology: our press, our films, our theatre, our pulp literature, our rituals, our Justice, our diplomacy, our conversations, our remarks about the weather, a murder trial, a touching wedding, the cooking we dream of, the garments we wear, everything in everyday life is dependent on the representation which the bourgeoisie *has and makes us have* of the relations between men and the world. (Barthes 1972)

Like Eliot, Barthes's notion of culture extends beyond the library, the opera-house and the theatre to encompass the whole of everyday life. But this everyday life is for Barthes overlaid with a significance which is at once more insidious and more systematically organized. Starting from the premise that 'myth is a type of speech,' Barthes set out in *Mythologies* to examine the normally hidden set of rules, codes and conventions through which meanings particular to specific social groups (i.e. those in power) are rendered universal and 'given' for the whole of society. He found in phenomena as disparate as a wrestling match, a writer on holiday, a tourist guide-book, the same artificial nature, the same ideological core. Each had been exposed to the same prevailing rhetoric (the rhetoric of common sense) and turned into myth, into a mere element in a 'second-order semiological system' (Barthes 1972). (Barthes uses the example of a photograph in *Paris-Match* of a Negro soldier saluting the French flag, which has a first and second order connotation: (1) a gesture of loyalty, but also (2) 'France is a great empire, and all her sons, without colour discrimination, faithfully serve under her flag.')

Barthes application of a method rooted in linguistics to other systems of discourse outside language (fashion, film, food, etc.) opened up completely new possibilities for contemporary cultural studies. It was hoped that the invisible seam between language, experience and reality could be located and prised open through a semiotic analysis of this kind: that the gulf between the alienated intellectual and the 'real' world could be rendered meaningful and, miraculously, at the same time, be made to disappear. Moreover, under Barthes's direction, semiotics promised nothing less than the reconciliation of the two conflicting definitions of culture upon which Cultural Studies was so ambiguously posited—a marriage of moral conviction (in this case, Barthes's Marxist beliefs) and popular themes: the study of a society's total way of life.

This is not to say that semiotics was easily assimilable within the Cultural Studies project. Though Barthes shared the literary preoccupations of Hoggart and Williams, his work introduced a new Marxist 'problematic' which was alien to the British tradition of concerned and largely untheorized 'social commentary.' As a result, the old debate seemed suddenly limited. In E.P. Thompson's words it appeared to reflect the parochial concerns of a group of 'gentlemen amateurs.' Thompson sought to replace Williams's definition of the theory of culture as 'a theory of relations between elements in a whole way of life' with his own more rigorously Marxist formulation: 'the study of relationships in a whole way of *conflict*.' A more analytical framework was required; a new vocabulary had to be learned. As part of this process of theorization, the word 'ideology' came to acquire a much wider range of meanings than had previously been the case. We have seen how Barthes found an 'anonymous ideology' penetrating every possible level of social life, inscribed in the most mundane of rituals, framing the most casual social encounters. But how can ideology be 'anonymous,' and how can it assume such a broad significance? Before we attempt any reading of subcultural style, we must first define the term 'ideology' more precisely.

IDEOLOGY: A *LIVED* RELATION

In *The German Ideology*, Marx shows how the basis of the capitalist economic structure (surplus value, neatly defined by Godelier as 'Profit ... is unpaid work' (Godelier 1970)) is hidden from the consciousness of the agents of production. The failure to see through appearances to the real relations which underlie them does not occur as the direct result of some kind of masking operation consciously carried out by individuals, social groups or institutions. On the contrary, ideology by definition thrives *beneath* consciousness. It is here, at the level of 'normal common sense,' that ideological frames of reference are most firmly sedimented and most effective, because it is here that their ideological nature is more effectively concealed. As Stuart Hall puts it:

> It is precisely its 'spontaneous' quality, its transparency, its 'naturalness,' its refusal to be made to examine the premises on which it is founded, its resistance to change or to correction, its effect of instant recognition, and the closed circle in which it moves which makes common sense, at one and the same time, 'spontaneous,' ideological and *unconscious*. You cannot learn, through common sense, *how things are*: you can only discover *where they fit* into the existing scheme of things. In this way, its very taken-for-grantedness is what establishes it as a medium in which its own premises and presuppositions are being rendered *invisible* by its apparent transparency. (Hall 1977)

Since ideology saturates everyday discourse in the form of common sense, it cannot be bracketed off from everyday life as a self-contained set of 'political opinions' or 'biased views.' Neither can it be reduced to the abstract dimensions of a 'world view' or used in the crude Marxist sense to designate 'false consciousness.' Instead, as Louis Althusser has pointed out:

> . . . ideology has very little to do with 'consciousness'. . . . It is profoundly *unconscious*. . . . Ideology is indeed a system of representation, but in the majority of cases these representations have nothing to do with 'consciousness': they are usually images and occasionally concepts, but it is above all as *structure* that they impose on the vast majority of men, not via their 'consciousness.' They are perceived-accepted-suffered cultural objects and they act functionally on men via a process that escapes them. (Althusser 1969)

Although Althusser is here referring to structures like the family, cultural and political institutions, etc., we can illustrate the point quite simply by taking as our example a physical structure. Most modern institutes of education, despite the apparent neutrality of the materials from which they are constructed (red brick, white tile, etc.) carry within themselves implicit ideological assumptions which are literally structured into the architecture itself. The categorization of knowledge into arts and sciences is reproduced in the faculty system which houses different disciplines in different buildings, and most colleges maintain the traditional divisions by devoting a separate floor to each subject. Moreover, the hierarchical relationship between teacher and taught is inscribed in the very lay-out of the lecture theatre where the seating arrangements—benches rising in tiers before a raised lectern—dictate the flow of information and serve to 'naturalize' professorial authority. Thus, a whole range of decisions about what is and what is not possible within education have been made, however unconsciously, before the content of individual courses is even decided.

These decisions help to set the limits not only on what is taught but on *how* it is taught. Here the buildings literally *reproduce* in concrete terms prevailing (ideological) notions about what education *is* and it is through this process that the educational structure, which can, of course, be altered, is placed beyond question and appears to us as a 'given' (i.e. as immutable). In this case, the frames of our thinking have been translated into actual bricks and mortar.

Social relations and processes are then appropriated by individuals only through the forms in which they are represented to those individuals. These forms are, as we have seen, by no means transparent. They are shrouded in a 'common sense' which simultaneously validates and mystifies them. It is precisely these 'perceived-accepted-suffered cultural objects' which semiotics sets out to 'interrogate' and decipher. All aspects of culture possess a semiotic value, and the most taken-for-granted phenomena can function as signs: as elements in communication systems governed by semantic rules and codes which are not themselves directly apprehended in experience. These signs are, then, as opaque as the social relations which produce them and which they represent. In other words, there is an ideological dimension to every signification.

To uncover the ideological dimension of signs we must first try to disentangle the codes through which meaning is organized. 'Connotative' codes are particularly important. As Stuart Hall has argued, they '... cover the face of social life and render it classifiable, intelligible, meaningful' (Hall 1977). He goes on to describe these codes as 'maps of meaning' which are of necessity the product of selection. They cut across a range of potential meanings, making certain meanings available and ruling others out of court. We tend to live inside these maps as surely as we live in the 'real' world: they 'think' us as much as we 'think' them, and this in itself is quite 'natural.' All human societies *reproduce* themselves in this way through a process of 'naturalization.' It is through this process—a kind of inevitable reflex of all social life—that *particular* sets of social relations, *particular* ways of organizing the world appear to us as if they were universal and timeless. This is what Althusser means when he says that 'ideology has no history' and that ideology in this general sense will always be an 'essential element of every social formation' (Althusser and Balibar 1968).

However, in highly complex societies like ours, which function through a finely tuned graded system of divided (i.e. specialized) labour, the crucial question has to do with which specific ideologies, representing the interests of which specific groups and classes will prevail at any given moment, in any given situation. To deal with this question, we must first consider how power is distributed in our society. That is, we must ask which groups and classes have how much say in defining, ordering and classifying out the social world. For instance, if we pause to reflect for a moment, it should be obvious that access to the means by which ideas are disseminated in our society (i.e. principally the mass media) is *not* the same for all classes. Some groups have more say, more opportunity to make the rules, to organize meaning, while others are less favourably placed, have less power to produce and impose their definitions of the world on the world.

Thus, when we come to look beneath the level of 'ideology-in-general' at the way in which specific ideologies work, how some gain dominance and others remain marginal, we can see that in advanced Western democracies the ideological field is by no means neutral. To return to the 'connotative' codes to which Stuart Hall refers we can see that these 'maps of meaning' are charged with a potentially explosive significance because they are traced and re-traced along the lines laid down by the *dominant* discourses about reality, the *dominant* ideologies. They thus tend to represent, in however obscure and contradictory a fashion, the interests of the *dominant* groups in a society.

To understand this point we should refer to Marx:

> The ideas of the ruling class are in every epoch the ruling ideas, i.e. the class which is the ruling *material* force of society is at the same time its ruling *intellectual* force. The class which has the means of material production at its disposal, has control at the same time over the means of mental production, so that generally speaking, the ideas of those who lack the means of mental production are subject to it. The ruling ideas are nothing more than the ideal expression of the dominant material relationships grasped as ideas; hence of the relationships which make the one class the ruling class, therefore the ideas of its dominance. (Marx and Engels 1970)

This is the basis of Antonio Gramsci's theory of *hegemony* which provides the most adequate account of how dominance is sustained in advanced capitalist societies.

HEGEMONY: THE MOVING EQUILIBRIUM

Society cannot share a common communication system so long as it is split into warring classes.
(Brecht, A Short Organum for the Theatre)

The term hegemony refers to a situation in which a provisional alliance of certain social groups exert 'total social authority' over other subordinate groups, not simply by coercion or by the direct imposition of ruling ideas, but by 'winning and shaping consent so that the power of the dominant classes appears both legitimate and natural' (Hall 1977). Hegemony can only be maintained so long as the dominant classes 'succeed in framing all competing definitions within their range' (Hall 1977), so that subordinate groups are, if not controlled, then at least contained within an ideological space which does not seem at all 'ideological': which appears instead to be permanent and 'natural,' to lie outside history, to be beyond particular interests.

This is how, according to Barthes, 'mythology' performs its vital function of naturalization and normalization and it is in his book *Mythologies* that Barthes demonstrates most forcefully the full extension of these normalized forms and meanings. However, Gramsci adds the important proviso that hegemonic power, precisely *because* it requires the consent of the dominated majority, can never be permanently exercised by the same alliance of 'class fractions.' As has been pointed out, 'Hegemony ... is not universal and "given" to the continuing rule of a particular class. It has to be won, reproduced, sustained. Hegemony is, as Gramsci said, a "moving equilibrium" containing relations of forces favourable or unfavourable to this or that tendency' (Hall and Jefferson 1976).

In the same way, forms cannot be permanently normalized. They can always be deconstructed, demystified, by a 'mythologist' like Barthes. Moreover commodities can be symbolically 'repossessed' in everyday life, and endowed with implicitly oppositional meanings, by the very groups who originally produced them. The symbiosis in which ideology and social order, production and reproduction, are linked is then neither fixed nor guaranteed. It can be prised open. The consensus can be fractured, challenged, overruled, and resistance to the groups in dominance cannot always be lightly dismissed or automatically incorporated. Although, as Lefebvre has written, we live in a society where '... objects in practice become signs and signs objects and a second nature takes the place of the first—the initial layer of perceptible reality' (Lefebvre 1971), there are, as he goes on to affirm, always 'objections and contradictions which hinder the closing of the circuit' between sign and object, production and reproduction.

We can now return to the meaning of youth subcultures, for the emergence of such groups has signalled in a spectacular fashion the breakdown of consensus in the post-war period. It is precisely objections and contradictions of the kind which Lefebvre has described that find expression in subculture. However, the challenge to hegemony which subcultures represent is not issued directly by them. Rather it is expressed obliquely, in style. The objections are lodged, the contradictions displayed (and 'magically resolved') at the profoundly superficial level of appearances: that is at the level of signs. For the sign-community, the community of myth-consumers, is not a uniform body. As Volosinov has written, it is cut through by class:

> Class does not coincide with the sign community, i.e. with the totality of users of the same set of signs of ideological communication. Thus various different class-

es will use one and the same language. As a result, differently oriented accents intersect in every ideological sign. Sign becomes the arena of the class struggle. (Volosinov 1973)

The struggle between different discourses, different definitions and meanings within ideology is therefore always, at the same time, a struggle within signification: a struggle for possession of the sign which extends to even the most mundane areas of everyday life. 'Humble objects' can be magically appropriated; 'stolen' by subordinate groups and made to carry 'select' meanings: meanings which express, in code, a form of resistance to the order which guarantees their continued subordination.

Style in subculture is, then, pregnant with significance. Its transformations go 'against nature,' interrupting the process of 'normalization.' As such, they are gestures, movements towards a speech which offends the 'silent majority,' which challenges the principle of unity and cohesion, which contradicts the myth of consensus. Our task becomes, like Barthes's, to discern the hidden messages inscribed in code on the glossy surfaces of style, to trace them out as 'maps of meaning' which obscurely re-present the very contradictions they are designed to resolve or conceal.

REFERENCES

Althusser, L. *For Marx.* London: Allen Lane, 1969.

Barthes, R. *Mythologies.* London: Jonathan Cape, 1972.

Brecht, Berthold. *A Short Organum for the Theatre.* 1949. *Brecht on Theatre.* Ed. and trans. John Willett. London: Methuen, 1978.

Godelier, M. "Structure and Contradiction in 'Capital.'" *Structuralism: A Reader.* Ed. M. Lane. London: Jonathan Cape, 1970. 112–23.

Gramsci, Antonio. *Selections from Cultural Writings.* Ed. D. Forgacs and G. Nowell-Smith. London: Lawrence and Wishart, 1985.

Hall, S. "Culture, the Media and the 'Ideological Effect.'" *Mass Communication and Society.* Ed. J. Curran, M. Gurevitch, and J. Woollacott. London: Edward Arnold, 1977. 315–48.

Hall, S., and Jefferson, T., eds. *Resistance through Rituals: Youth Subcultures in Post-War Britain.* London: Hutchinson, 1976.

Hawkes, Terrence. *Structuralism and Semiotics.* London: Routledge, 1977.

Hoggart, R. *The Uses of Literacy.* Harmondsworth: Penguin, 1957.

---. "Literature and Society." *The American Scholar* 35 (1966): 277–89.

Lefebvre, H. *Everyday Life in the Modern World.* Allen Lane: London, 1971.

Marx, K., and F. Engels. *The German Ideology.* London: Lawrence and Wishart, 1970.

Thompson, E. P. *The Making of the English Working Class.* Harmondsworth: Penguin, 1968.

Volosinov, V. N. *Marxism and the Philosophy of Language.* London: Seminar Press, 1973.

Williams, R. *Culture and Society: 1780–1950.* Harmondsworth: Penguin, 1958.

---. *The Long Revolution.* Harmondsworth: Penguin, 1961.

4   Walter Benjamin, "The Work of Art in the Age of Mechanical Reproduction"

EDITORS' INTRODUCTION

Perhaps no theoretical writing is more cited, indeed, more reproduced, in readers such as this one, as Walter Benjamin's seminal "The Work of Art in the Age of Mechanical Reproduction." Its centrality for the study of contemporary and popular culture cannot be overemphasized. Benjamin's work has provided the beginning point for any number of readings of popular culture that analyze how the material aspects of production (the technologies in and by which the cultural object is created and marketed) affect the reception, interpretation, and, ultimately, the meaning of culture. Benjamin's text at once offers an acute analysis of his own contemporary context, which saw the rise of technologies of mass production, and seems uncannily to predict our own era of the mass commodification, replication, and simulation of culture. Indeed, Benjamin's work presages a great number of the themes of contemporary cultural theory. Without his groundbreaking work, the cultural analyses of Jean Baudrillard, Roland Barthes, or Paul Virilio—analyses bearing the imprint of Benjamin's interest in the materiality of the cultural object—would be impossible.

A critical entry point into this essay is the fact that it was published in 1936, three years after Benjamin was forced into exile by the Nazi regime in Germany. This fact explains what may seem an oddity in the essay: that it opens and closes with analyses of Fascism. These passages seem out of place only at first glance, however. As Benjamin's essay proceeds, it becomes clear that both technology—the ostensible focus of his analysis—and Fascism have a specific relation to the masses. Fascism is a political system that seeks to harness the energy of the masses (think of the torch-lit rallies of the Nazi Party) in much the same way as mass, or technologically produced, art can do. Benjamin, who is quite clear in his appreciation for both the masses and technology, is anxious to distinguish between the quality of mass responses to the *Führer* and, for instance, the film. As Benjamin suggests, the response to the film is (ideally) one that places the audience in a position of critical power; the response to the spectacle of Fascism is (ideally) one that places the audience in a position of awed passivity. And, as unlikely a beginning for a discussion of technology as this preamble may seem, this dialectic of passivity and critical activity, politicized as it is by the Marxist Benjamin, is precisely where his analysis of the reproduction of art begins.

Benjamin suggests that the new technologies of mechanical reproduction—he thinks primarily of photography and film—have changed our responses to the art object. Prior to the advent of these new technologies in the 19th century, the art object—the painting or, more specifically for Benjamin, the sculpture—had a uniqueness to it, what Benjamin calls an "aura." By aura Benjamin means a sense of an awed distance between the art object and the spectator. In fact, Benjamin maintains (with very little historical evidence, we might add) that the art object was originally a "cult" object that served ritualized purposes. In these rituals, the art object was mediated to the passive spectator by an elite priestly caste and, thus, worshipped at a distance. With mechanical reproduction, the means by which the art object could be duplicated endlessly on film, the uniqueness of the object, its singular location in time and space, is destroyed. Moreover, when the object becomes immediately available to all, the need for ritual, with its attendant elitist structures and hierarchies, is gone:

> Secondly, technical reproduction can put the copy of the original into situations that would be out of reach for the original itself. Above all, it enables the original to meet the beholder halfway, be it in the form of a photograph or a phonograph record. The cathedral leaves its locale to be received in the studio of a lover of art; the choral production, performed in an auditorium or in the open air, resounds in the drawing room. (79)

It is clear that Benjamin envisions a revolutionary role for mechanical reproduction, a specifically political revolution. Mechanical reproduction, by destroying the aura of the work of art, by removing it from its original "presence in time and space" (78), liberates art for the mass. When what Benjamin calls the "authenticity" of the work of art disappears (and by "authenticity" he seems to be combining the notions of "aura" and "originality"), the work offers itself more easily for mass consumption: "But the instant the criterion of authenticity ceases to be applicable to artistic production, the total function of art is reversed. Instead of being based on ritual, it begins to be based on another practice—politics" (81).

The implications for the role of the mass in its new relation to a technologized culture are enormous. Benjamin, perhaps inevitably romanticizing the mass, suggests that film—and his essay is largely a theorizing of the rhetoric of film—compels the audience into a position of active critical involvement in the proceedings. In words sounding very much like Benjamin's contemporary and fellow Marxist, dramatist Bertold Brecht, Benjamin writes that film puts the public "in the position of the critic" (Benjamin 240). This position is facilitated first by film rendering new what is mundanely familiar; film, in other words, alienates the quotidian and forces the audience to see anew what it has always taken for granted. As such, and this suggestion is a crucial subtext to Benjamin's essay, film has an *educative* role to play in culture: it teaches us how to see. In typically modernist language (one recalls the language of Ibsen or Marinetti), Benjamin celebrates the destructive powers of film:

> Our taverns and our metropolitan streets, our offices and furnished homes, our railroad stations and our factories appeared to us to have us locked up hopelessly. Then came the film and burst this prison-world asunder by the dynamite of the tenth of a second, so that now, in the midst of its far-flung ruins and debris, we calmly and adventurously go traveling. (83)

Having rendered the world new, the particularities of film technology also reveal what could not have been seen before: "With the close-up, space expands; with slow motion, movement is extended…a different nature opens itself to the camera than opens to the naked eye" (Benjamin 236). Because the film can be endlessly replayed, stopped, reversed, and analyzed again (what would Benjamin have made of DVD technology?), nuances of experience are revealed. The eye of the film camera, prosthetically extending the critical eye of the spectator, reveals hidden, *unconscious* truths. Benjamin's language is explicitly, and sublimely, psychoanalytic: "The camera introduces us to an unconscious optics as does psychoanalysis to unconscious impulses" (83). It is here, in the analysis of the conflation of the material and psychoanalytical power of the camera, of technology as both political tool of revolution and psychological means to unseen truth, that Benjamin's essay reaches its point of maximum critical density and importance: technology is the means by which the masses are liberated from the illusions of the everyday.

—JB

ISSUES TO CONSIDER WHILE READING

1. One of Benjamin's central points is that Fascism—the spectacle of Nazism—was at some level an aesthetic movement (indeed, the recent film *Max*, starring John Cusack, makes precisely this point). Discuss the idea that politics has an aesthetic aspect; is this true in contemporary Canadian politics?

2. What can be made of the idea that the reproductive possibilities of contemporary technology destroys the "aura" of art? How do you understand the term "aura"? If Benjamin is correct in his analysis of the destruction of the aura, what has taken its place?

REFERENCES AND FURTHER READING

Barthes, Roland. *Mythologies*. New York: Hill and Wang, 1994.

Benjamin, Walter. "The Work of Art in the Age of Mechanical Reproduction." *Illuminations: Essays and Reflections*. Ed. Hannah Arendt. New York: Schocken, 1988.

Brecht, Bertold. "A Short Organum for the Theater." *Brecht on Theatre, the Development of an Aesthetic*. Trans. John Willet. New York: Hill and Wang, 1964. 179–205.

Virilio, Paul. *Open Sky*. London: Verso, 1997.

Zizek, Slavoj. *Enjoy Your Symptom! Jacques Lacan in Hollywood and Out*. 2nd ed. New York: Routledge, 2001.

The Work of Art in the Age of Mechanical Reproduction

"Our fine arts were developed, their types and uses were established, in times very different from the present, by men whose power of action upon things was insignificant in comparison with ours. But the amazing growth of our techniques, the adaptability and precision they have attained, the ideas and habits they are creating, make it a certainty that profound changes are impending in the ancient craft of the Beautiful. In all the arts there is a physical component which can no longer be considered or treated as it used to be, which cannot

remain unaffected by our modern knowledge and power. For the last twenty years neither matter nor space nor time has been what it was from time immemorial. We must expect great innovations to transform the entire technique of the arts, thereby affecting artistic invention itself and perhaps even bringing about an amazing change in our very notion of art."*

—Paul Valéry, PIÈCES SUR L'ART, "La Conquète de l'ubiquité," Paris

PREFACE

When Marx undertook his critique of the capitalistic mode of production, this mode was in its infancy. Marx directed his efforts in such a way as to give them prognostic value. He went back to the basic conditions underlying capitalistic production and through his presentation showed what could be expected of capitalism in the future. The result was that one could expect it not only to exploit the proletariat with increasing intensity, but ultimately to create conditions which would make it possible to abolish capitalism itself.

The transformation of the superstructure, which takes place far more slowly than that of the substructure, has taken more that half a century to manifest in all areas of culture the change in the conditions of production. Only today can it be indicated what form this has taken. Certain prognostic requirements should be met by these statements. However, theses about the art of the proletariat after its assumption of power or about the art of a classless society would have less bearing on these demands than theses about the developmental tendencies of art under present conditions of production. Their dialectic is no less noticeable in the superstructure than in the economy. It would therefore be wrong to underestimate the value of such theses as a weapon. They brush aside a number of outmoded concepts, such as creativity and genius, eternal value and mystery—concepts whose uncontrolled (and at present almost uncontrollable) application would lead to a processing of data in the Fascist sense. The concepts which are introduced into the theory of art in what follows differ from the more familiar terms in that they are completely useless for the purposes of Fascism. They are, on the other hand, useful for the formulation of revolutionary demands in the politics of art.

In principle a work of art has always been reproducible. Manmade artifacts could always be imitated by men. Replicas were made by pupils in practice of their craft, by masters for diffusing their works, and, finally, by third parties in the pursuit of gain. Mechanical reproduction of a work of art, however, represents something new. Historically, it advanced intermittently and in leaps at long intervals, but with accelerated intensity. The Greeks knew only two procedures of technically reproducing works of art: founding and stamping. Bronzes, terra cottas, and coins were the only art works which they could produce in quantity. All others were unique and could not be mechanically reproduced. With the woodcut graphic art became mechanically reproducible for the first time, long before script became reproducible by print. The enormous changes which printing, the mechanical reproduction of writing, has brought about in literature are a familiar story. However, within the phenomenon which we are here examining from

---

* Quoted from Paul Valéry, *Aesthetics*, "The Conquest of Ubiquity," translated by Ralph Manheim, p. 225. Pantheon Books, Bollingen Series, New York, 1964.

the perspective of world history, print is merely a special, though particularly important, case. During the Middles Ages engraving and etching were added to the woodcut; at the beginning of the nineteenth century lithography made its appearance.

With lithography the technique of reproduction reached an essentially new age. This much more direct process was distinguished by the tracing of the design on a stone rather than its incision on a block of wood or its etching on a copper plate and permitted graphic art for the first time to put its products on the market, not only in large numbers as hitherto, but also in daily changing forms. Lithography enabled graphic art to illustrate everyday life, and it began to keep pace with printing. But only a few decades after its invention, lithography was surpassed by photography. For the first time in the process of pictorial reproduction, photography freed the hand of the most important artistic function which henceforth devolved only upon the eye looking into a lens. Since the eye perceives more swiftly than the hand can draw, the process of pictorial reproduction was accelerated so enormously that it could keep pace with speech. A film operator shooting a scene in the studio captures the images at the speed of an actor's speech. Just as lithography virtually implied the illustrated newspaper, so did photography foreshadow the sound film. The technical reproduction of sound was tackled at the end of the last century. These convergent endeavors made predictable a situation which Paul Valéry pointed up in this sentence: "Just as water, gas, and electricity are brought into our houses from far off to satisfy our needs in response to a minimal effort, so we shall be supplied with visual or auditory images, which will appear and disappear at a simple movement of the hand, hardly more than a sign" (*op. cit.*, p. 216). Around 1900 technical reproduction had reached a standard that not only permitted it to reproduce all transmitted works of art and thus to cause the most profound change in their impact upon the public; it also had captured a place of its own among the artistic processes. For the study of this standard nothing is more revealing than the nature of the repercussions that these two different manifestations—the reproduction of works of art and the art of the film—have had on art in its traditional form.

Even the most perfect reproduction of a work of art is lacking in one element: its presence in time and space, its unique existence at the place where it happens to be. This unique existence of the work of art determined the history to which it was subject throughout the time of its existence. This includes the changes which it may have suffered in physical condition over the years as well as the various changes in its ownership[1] the analyses which it is impossible to perform on a reproduction; changes of ownership are subject to a tradition which must be traced from the situation of the original.

The presence of the original is the prerequisite to the concept of authenticity. Chemical analyses of the patina of a bronze can help to establish this, as does the proof that a given manuscript of the Middle Ages stems from an archive of the fifteenth century. The whole sphere of authenticity is outside technical—and, of course, not only technical—reproducibility.[2] Confronted with its manual reproduction, which was usually branded as a forgery, the original preserved all its authority; not so *vis à vis* technical reproduction. The reason is twofold. First, process reproduction is more independent of the original than manual reproduction. For example, in photography, process reproduction can bring out those aspects of the original that are unattainable to the naked eye yet accessible to the lens, which is adjustable and chooses its angle at will. And photographic reproduction, with the aid of certain processes, such as enlargement or slow motion, can capture images which escape natural vision. Secondly, technical reproduction can put the copy of the original into situations which would be out of reach for the original itself. Above all, it enables the original to meet the beholder halfway, be it in the form of a photograph or a phonograph record. The cathedral leaves its locale to be received in the studio of a lover of art; the choral production, performed in an auditorium or in the open air, resounds in the drawing room.

The situations into which the product of a mechanical reproduction can be brought may not touch the actual work of art, yet the quality of its presence is always depreciated. This holds not only for the art work but also, for instance, for a landscape which passes in review before the spectator in a movie. In the case of the art object, a most sensitive nucleus—namely, its authenticity—is interfered with whereas no natural object is vulnerable on that score. The authenticity of a thing is the essence of all that is transmissible from its beginning, ranging from its substantive duration to its testimony to the history which it has experienced. Since the historical testimony rests on the authenticity, the former, too, is jeopardized by reproduction when the substantive duration ceases to matter. And what is really jeopardized when the historical testimony is affected is the authority of the object.[3]

One might subsume the eliminated element in the term "aura" and go on to say: that which withers in the age of mechanical reproduction is the aura of the work of art. This is a symptomatic process whose significance points beyond the realm of art. One might generalize by saying: the technique of reproduction detaches the reproduced object from the domain of tradition. By making many reproductions it substitutes a plurality of copies for a unique existence. And in permitting the reproduction to meet the beholder or listener in his own particular situation, it reactivates the object reproduced. These two processes lead to a tremendous shattering of tradition which is the obverse of the contemporary crisis and renewal of mankind. Both processes are intimately connected with the contemporary mass movements. Their most powerful agent is the film. Its social significance, particularly in its most positive form, is inconceivable without its destructive, cathartic aspect, that is, the liquidation of the traditional value of the cultural heritage. This phenomenon is most palpable in the great historical films. It extends to ever new positions. In 1927 Abel Gance exclaimed enthusiastically: "Shakespeare, Rembrandt, Beethoven will make films ... all legends, all mythologies and all myths, all founders of religion, and the very religions ... await their exposed resurrection, and the heroes crowd each other at the gate."* Presumably without intending it, he issued an invitation to a far-reaching liquidation.

During long periods of history, the mode of human sense perception changes with humanity's entire mode of existence. The manner in which human sense perception is organized, the medium in which it is accomplished, is determined not only by nature but by historical circumstances as well. The fifth century, with its great shifts of population,

---

*Abel Gance, "Le Temps de l'image est venu," *L'Art cinematographique*, Vol. 2, pp. 94 f, Paris, 1927.

saw the birth of the late Roman art industry and the Vienna Genesis, and there developed not only an art different from that of antiquity but also a new kind of perception. The scholars of the Viennese school, Riegl and Wickhoff, who resisted the weight of classical tradition under which these later art forms had been buried, were the first to draw conclusions from them concerning the organization of perception at the time. However far-reaching their insight, these scholars limited themselves to showing the significant, formal hallmark which characterized perception in late Roman times. They did not attempt—and perhaps, saw no way—to show the social transformations expressed by these changes of perception. The conditions for an analogous insight are more favorable in the present. And if changes in the medium of contemporary perception can be comprehended as decay of the aura, it is possible to show its social causes.

The concept of aura which was proposed above with reference to historical objects may usefully be illustrated with reference to the aura of natural ones. We define the aura of the latter as the unique phenomenon of a distance, however close it may be. If, while resting on a summer afternoon, you follow with your eyes a mountain range on the horizon or a branch which casts its shadow over you, you experience the aura of those mountains, of that branch. This image makes it easy to comprehend the social bases of the contemporary decay of the aura. It rests on two circumstances, both of which are related to the increasing significance of the masses in contemporary life. Namely, the desire of contemporary masses to bring things "close" spatially and humanly, which is just as ardent as their bent toward overcoming the uniqueness of every reality by accepting its reproduction.[4] Every day the urge grows stronger to get hold of an object at a very close range by way of its likeness, its reproduction. Unmistakably, reproduction as offered by picture magazines and newsreels differs from the image seen by the unarmed eye. Uniqueness and permanence are as closely linked in the latter as are transitoriness and reproducibility in the former. To pry an object from its shell, to destroy its aura, is the mark of a perception whose "sense of the universal equality of things" has increased to such a degree that it extracts it even from a unique object by means of reproduction. Thus is manifested in the field of perception what in the theoretical sphere is noticeable in the increasing importance of statistics. The adjustment of reality to the masses and of the masses to reality is a process of unlimited scope, as much for thinking as for perception.

The uniqueness of a work of art is inseparable from its being imbedded in the fabric of tradition. This tradition itself is thoroughly alive and extremely changeable. An ancient statue of Venus, for example, stood in a different traditional context with the Greeks, who made it an object of veneration, than with the clerics of the Middle Ages, who viewed it as an ominous idol. Both of them, however, were equally confronted with its uniqueness, that is, its aura. Originally the contextual integration of art in tradition found its expression in the cult. We know that the earliest art works originated in the service of a ritual—first the magical, then the religious kind. It is significant that the existence of the work of art with reference to its aura is never entirely separated from its ritual function.[5] In other words, the unique value of the "authentic" work of art has its basis in ritual, the location of its original use value. This ritualistic basis, however remote, is still recognizable as a secularized ritual even in the most profane forms of the cult of beauty.[6] The secular cult of beauty, developed during the Renaissance and prevailing for three centuries, clearly showed that ritualistic basis in its decline and the first deep crisis which befell it. With the advent of the first truly revolutionary means of reproduction, photography, simultaneously with the rise of socialism, art sensed the approaching crisis which has become evident a century later. At the time, art reacted with the doctrine of *l'art pour l'art*, that is, with a theology of art. This gave rise to what might be called a negative theology in the form of the idea of "pure" art, which not only denied any social function of art but also any categorizing by subject matter. (In poetry, Mallarmé was the first to take this position.)

An analysis of art in the age of mechanical reproduction must do justice to these relationships, for they lead us to an all-important insight: for the first time in world history, mechanical reproduction emancipates the work of art from its parasitical dependence on ritual. To an ever greater degree the work of art reproduced becomes the work of art designed for reproducibility.[7] From a photographic negative, for example, one can make any number of prints; to ask for the "authentic" print makes no sense. But the instant the criterion of authenticity ceases to be applicable to artistic production, the total function of art is reversed. Instead of being based on ritual, it begins to be based on another practice—politics.

…The shooting of a film, especially of a sound film, affords a spectacle unimaginable anywhere at any time before this. It presents a process in which it is impossible to assign to a spectator a viewpoint which would exclude from the actual scene such extraneous accessories as camera equipment, lighting machinery, staff assistants, etc.—unless his eye were on a line parallel with the lens. This circumstance, more than any other, renders superficial and insignificant any possible similarity between a scene in the studio and one on the stage. In the theater one is well aware of the place from which the play cannot immediately be detected as illusionary. There is no such place for the movie scene that is being shot. Its illusionary nature is that of the second degree, the result of cutting. That is to say, in the studio, the mechanical equipment has penetrated so deeply into reality that its pure aspect freed from the foreign substance of equipment is the result of a special procedure, namely, the shooting by the specially adjusted camera and the mounting of the shot together with other similar ones. The equipment-free aspect of reality here has become the height of artifice; the sight of immediate reality has become an orchid in the land of technology.

Even more revealing is the comparison of these circumstances, which differ so much from those of the theater, with the situation in painting. Here the question is: How does the cameraman compare with the painter? To answer this we take recourse to an analogy with a surgical operation. The surgeon represents the polar opposite of the magician. The magician heals a sick person by the laying on of hands; the surgeon cuts into the patient's body. The magician maintains the natural distance between the patient and himself; though he reduces it very slightly by the laying on of hands, he greatly increases it by virtue of his authority. The surgeon does exactly the reverse; he greatly diminishes the distance between himself and the patient by penetrating into the patient's body and increases it but little by the caution with which his hand moves among the organs. In short, in contrast to the magician—who is still hidden in the medical practitioner—the surgeon at the decisive moment abstains from facing the patient man to man; rather, it is through the operation that he penetrates into him.

Magician and surgeon compare to painter and cameraman. The painter maintains in his work a natural distance from reality, the cameraman penetrates deeply into its web.[8] There is a tremendous difference between the pictures they obtain. That of the painter is a total one, that of the cameraman consists of multiple fragments which are assembled under a new law. Thus, for contemporary man the representation of reality by the film is incomparably more significant than that of the painter, since it offers, precisely because of the thoroughgoing permeation of reality with mechanical equipment, an aspect of reality which is free of all equipment. And that is what one is entitled to ask from a work of art.

Mechanical reproduction of art changes the reaction of the masses toward art. The reactionary attitude toward a Picasso painting changes into the progressive reaction toward a Chaplin movie. The progressive reaction is characterized by the direct, intimate fusion of visual and emotional enjoyment with the orientation of the expert. Such fusion is of great social significance. The greater the decrease in the social significance of an art form, the sharper the distinction between criticism and enjoyment by the public. The conventional is uncritically enjoyed, and the truly new is criticized with aversion. With regard to the screen, the critical and the receptive attitudes of the public coincide. The decisive reason for this is that individual reactions are predetermined by the mass audience response they are about to produce, and this is nowhere more pronounced than in the film. The moment these responses become manifest they control each other. Again, the comparison with painting is fruitful. A painting has always had an excellent chance to be viewed by one person or by a few. The simultaneous contemplation of paintings by a large public, such as developed in the nineteenth century, is an early symptom of the crisis of painting, a crisis which was by no means occasioned exclusively by photography but rather in a relatively independent manner by the appeal of art works to the masses.

Painting simply is in no position to present an object for simultaneous collective experience, as it was possible for architecture at all times, for the epic poem in the past, and for the movie today. Although this circumstance in itself should not lead one to conclusions about the social role of painting, it does constitute a serious threat as soon as painting, under special conditions and, as it were, against its nature, is confronted directly by the masses. In the churches and monasteries of the Middle Ages and at the princely courts up to the end of the eighteenth century, a collective reception of paintings did not occur simultaneously, but by graduated and hierarchized mediation. The change that has come about is an expression of the particular conflict in which painting was implicated by the mechanical reproducibility of paintings. Although paintings began to be publicly exhibited in galleries and salons, there was no way for the masses to organize and control themselves in their reception.[9] Thus the same public which responds in a progressive manner toward a grotesque film is bound to respond in a reactionary manner to surrealism.

The characteristics of the film lie not only in the manner in which man presents himself to the mechanical equipment but also in the manner in which, by means of this apparatus, man can represent his environment. A glance at occupational psychology illustrates the testing capacity of the equipment. Psychoanalysis illustrates it in a different perspective. The film has enriched our field of perception with methods which can be illustrated by those of Freudian theory. Fifty years ago, a slip of the tongue passed more or less unnoticed. Only exceptionally may such a slip have revealed dimensions of depth in a conversation which had seemed to be taking its course on the surface. Since the *Psychopathology of Everyday Life* things have changed. This book isolated and made analyzable things which had heretofore floated along unnoticed in the broad stream of perception. For the entire spectrum of optical, and now also acoustical, perception the film has brought about a similar deepening of apperception. It is only an obverse of this fact that behavior items shown in a movie can be analyzed much more precisely and from more points of view than those presented on paintings or on the stage. As compared with painting, filmed behavior lends itself more readily to analysis because of its incomparably more precise statements of the situation. In comparison with the stage scene, the filmed behavior item lends itself more readily to analysis because it can be isolated more easily. This circumstance derives its chief importance from its tendency to promote the mutual penetration of art and science. Actually, of a screened behavior item which is neatly brought out in a certain situation, like a muscle of a body, it is difficult to say which is more fascinating, its artistic value or its value for science. To demonstrate the identity of the artistic and scientific uses of photography which heretofore usually were separated will be one of the revolutionary functions of the film.[10]

By close-ups of the things around us, by focusing on hidden details of familiar objects, by exploring commonplace milieus under the ingenious guidance of the camera, the film, on the one hand, extends our comprehension of the necessities which rule our lives; on the other hand, it manages to assure us of an immense and unexpected field of action. Our taverns and our metropolitan streets, our offices and furnished rooms, our railroad stations and our factories appeared to have us locked up hopelessly. Then came the film and burst this prison-world asunder by the dynamite of the tenth of a second, so that now, in the midst of its far-flung ruins and debris, we calmly and adventurously go traveling. With the close-up, space expands; with slow motion, movement is extended. The enlargement of a snapshot does not simply render more precise what in any case was visible, though unclear: it reveals entirely new structural formations of the subject. So, too, slow motion not only presents familiar qualities of movement but reveals in them entirely unknown ones "which, far from looking like retarded rapid movements, give the effect of singularly gliding, floating, supernatural motions."* Evidently, a different nature opens itself to the camera than opens to the naked eye—if only because an unconsciously penetrated space is substituted for a space consciously explored by man. Even if one has a general knowledge of the way people walk, one knows nothing of a person's posture during the fractional second of a stride. The act of reaching for a lighter or a spoon is familiar routine, yet we hardly know what really goes on between hand and metal, not to mention how this fluctuates with our moods. Here the camera intervenes with the resources of its lowerings and liftings, its interruptions and isolations, its extensions and accelerations, its enlargements and reductions. The camera introduces us to unconscious optics as does psychoanalysis to unconscious impulses.

---

*Rudolf Arnheim, loc. cit., p. 138.

EPILOGUE

…The growing proletarianization of modern man and the increasing formation of masses are two aspects of the same process. Fascism attempts to organize the newly created proletarian masses without affecting the property structure which the masses strive to eliminate. Fascism sees its salvation in giving these masses not their right, but instead a chance to express themselves.[11] The masses have a right to change property relations; Fascism seeks to give them an expression while preserving property. The logical result of Fascism is the introduction of aesthetics into political life. The violation of the masses, whom Fascism, with its *Führer* cult, forces to their knees, has its counterpart in the violation of an apparatus which is pressed into the production of ritual values.

All efforts to render politics aesthetic culminate in one thing: war. War and war only can set a goal for mass movements on the largest scale while respecting the traditional property system. This is the political formula for the situation. The technological formula may be stated as follows: Only war makes it possible to mobilize all of today's technical resources while maintaining the property system. It goes without saying that the Fascist apotheosis of war does not employ such arguments. Still, Marinetti says in his manifesto on the Ethiopian colonial war: "For twenty-seven years we Futurists have rebelled against the branding of war as antiaesthetic…. Accordingly we state: … War is beautiful because it establishes man's dominion over the subjugated machinery by means of gas masks, terrifying megaphones, flame throwers, and small tanks. War is beautiful because it initiates the dreamt-of metalization of the human body. War is beautiful because it enriches a flowering meadow with the fiery orchids of machine guns. War is beautiful because it combines the gunfire, the cannonades, the cease-fire, the scents, and the stench of putrefaction into a symphony. Was is beautiful because it creates new architecture, like that of the big tanks, the geometrical formation flights, the smoke spirals from burning villages, and many others…. Poets and artists of Futurism! … remember these principles of an aesthetics of war so that your struggle for a new literature and a new graphic art … may be illuminated by them!"

This manifesto has the virtue of clarity. Its formulations deserve to be accepted by dialecticians. To the latter, the aesthetics of today's war appears as follows: If the natural utilization of productive forces is impeded by the property system, the increase in technical devices, in speed, and in the sources of energy will press for an unnatural utilization, and this is found in war. The destructiveness of war furnishes proof that society has not been mature enough to incorporate technology as its organ, that technology has not been sufficiently developed to cope with the elemental forces of society. The horrible features of imperialistic warfare are attributable to the discrepancy between the tremendous means of production and their inadequate utilization in the process of production—in other words, to unemployment and the lack of markets. Imperialistic war is a rebellion of technology which collects, in the form of "human material," the claims to which society has denied its natural material. Instead of draining rivers, society directs a human stream into a bed of trenches; instead of dropping seeds from airplanes, it drops incendiary bombs over cities; and through gas warfare the aura is abolished in a new way.

"*Fiat ars—pereat mundus,*" says Fascism, and, as Marinetti admits, expects war to supply the artistic gratification of a sense perception that has been changed in technology. This is evidently the consummation of "*l'art pour l'art.*" Mankind, which in Homer's time was an object of contemplation for the Olympian gods, now is one for itself. Its self-alienation has reached such a degree that it can experience its own destruction as an aesthetic pleasure of the first order. This is the situation of politics which Fascism is rendering aesthetic. Communism responds by politicizing art.

NOTES

1. Of course, the history of a work of art encompasses more than this. The history of the "Mona Lisa," for instance, encompasses the kind of number of its copies made in the 17th, 18th, and 19th centuries.

2. Precisely because authenticity is not reproducible, the intensive penetration of certain (mechanical) processes of reproduction was instrumental in differentiating and grading authenticity. To develop such differentiations was an important function of the trade in works of art. The invention of the woodcut may be said to have struck at the root of the quality of autheticity even before its late flowering. To be sure, at the time of its origin a medieval picture of the Madonna could not yet be said to be "authentic." It became "authentic" only during the succeeding centuries and perhaps most strikingly so during the last one.

3. The poorest provincial staging of *Faust* is superior to a Faust film in that, ideally, it competes with the first performance at Weimar. Before the screen it is unprofitable to remember traditional contents which might come to mind before the stage—for instance, that Goethe's friend Johann Heinrich Merck is hidden in Mephisto, and the like.

4. To satisfy the human interest of the masses may mean to have one's social function removed from the field of vision. Nothing guarantees that a portraitist of today, when painting a famous surgeon at the breakfast table in the midst of his family, depicts his social function more precisely than a painter of the 17th century who portrayed his medical doctors as representing this profession, like Rembrandt in his "Anatomy Lesson."

5. The definition of the aura as a "unique phenomenon of a distance however close it may be" represents nothing but the formulation of the cult value of the work of art in categories of space and time perception. Distance is the opposite of closeness. The essentially distant object is the unapproachable one. Unapproachability is indeed a major quality of the cult image. True to its nature, it remains "distant, however close it may be." The closeness which one may gain from its subject matter does not impair the distance which it retains in its appearance.

6. To the extent to which the cult value of the painting is secularized the ideas of its fundamental uniqueness lose distinctness. In the imagination of the beholder the uniqueness of the phenomena which hold sway in the cult image is more and more displaced by the empirical uniqueness of the creator or of his creative achievement. To be sure, never completely so; the concept of authenticity always transcends mere genuineness. (This is particularly apparent in the collector who always retains some traces of the fetishist and who, by owning the work of art, shares in its ritual power.) Nevertheless, the function of the concept of authenticity remains determinate in the evaluation of art; with the secularization of art, authenticity displaces the cult value of the work.

7. In the case of films, mechanical reproduction is not, as with literature and painting, an external condition for mass distribution. Mechanical reproduction is inherent in the very technique of film production. This technique not only permits in the most direct way but virtually causes mass distribution. It enforces distribution because the production of a film is so expensive that an individual who, for instance, might afford to buy a painting no longer can afford to buy a film. In 1927 it was calculated that a major film, in order to pay its way, had to

reach an audience of nine million. With the sound film, to be sure, a setback in its international distribution occurred at first: audiences became limited by language barriers. This coincided with the Fascist emphasis on national interests. It is more important to focus on this connection with Fascism than on this setback, which was soon minimized by synchronization. The simultaneity of both phenomena is attributable to the Depression. The same disturbances which, on a larger scale, led to an attempt to maintain the existing property structure by sheer force led the endangered film capital to speed up the development of the sound film. The introduction of the sound film brought about a temporary relief, not only because it again brought the masses into the theaters but also because it merged new capital from the electrical industry with that of the film industry. Thus, viewed from the outside, the sound film promoted national interests, but seen from the inside it helped to internationalize film production even more than previously.

8. The boldness of the cameraman is indeed comparable to that of the surgeon. Luc Durtain lists among specific technical sleights of hand those "which are required in surgery in the case of certain difficult operations. I choose as an example a case from oto-rhinolaryngology; ... the so-called endonasal perspective prodcedure; or I refer to the acrobatic tricks of larynx surgery which have to be performed following the reversed picture in the laryngoscope. I might also speak of ear surgery which suggests the precision work of watchmakers. What range of the most subtle muscular acrobatics is required from the man who wants to repair or save the human body! We have only to think of the couching of a cataract where there is virtually a debate of steel with nearly fluid tissue, or of the major abdominal operations (laparotomy)." – Luc Durtain, *op. cit*

9. This mode of observation may seem crude, but as the great theoretician Leonardo has shown, crude modes of observation may at times be usefully adduced. Leonardo compares painting and music as follows: "Painting is superior to music because, unlike unfortunate music, it does not have to die as soon as it is born ... Music which is consumed in the very act of its birth is inferior to painting which the use of varnish has rendered eternal." (Trattato I, 29.)

10. Renaissance painting offers a revealing analogy to this situation. The incomparable development of this art and its significance rested not least on the integration of a number of new sciences, or at least of new scientific data. Renaissance painting made use of anatomy and perspective, of mathematics, metereology, and chromatology. Valèry writes: "What could be further from us than the strange claim of a Leonardo to whom painting was a supreme goal and the ultimate demonstration of knowledge? Leonardo was convinced that painting demanded universal knowledge, and he did not even shrink from a theorectical analysis which to us is stunning because of its very depth and precision ...." –Paul Valèry, *Pièces sur l'art*, "Autour de Corot," Paris, p. 191.

11. One technical feature is significant here, especially with regard to newsreels, the propagandist importance of which can hardly be overestimated. Mass reproduction is aided especially by the reproduction of masses. In big parades and monster rallies, in sports events, and in war, all of which nowadays are captured by camera and sound recording, the masses are brought face to face with themselves. This process, whose significance need not be stressed, is intimately connected with the development of the techniques of reproduction and photography. Mass movements are usually discerned more clearly by a camera than by the naked eye. A bird's-eye view best captures gatherings of hundreds of thousands. And even though such a view may be as accessible to the human eye as it is to the camera, the image received by the eye cannot be enlarged the way a negative is enlarged. This means that mass movements, including war, constitute a form of human behavior which particularly favors mechanical equipment.

Marshall McLuhan, "The Gadget Lover: Narcissus as Narcosis," from *Understanding Media: The Extensions of Man*

EDITORS' INTRODUCTION

In 1964, Canadian media theorist Marshall McLuhan published *Understanding Media: The Extensions of Man.* This text, massively influential in its time, has given us such seminal ideas as "the medium is the message," "hot and cold media," and "the global village." McLuhan's work is vital in that it compels us to step back from the apparently "given" nature of technology (technology is everywhere and rapidly becomes a "natural" part of our various work and home environments) and forces us to see the extent to which technology alters our relations with our culture, environment, and, crucially, our own bodies.

Further, McLuhan's work is prescient in its analysis of how various media seem to reduce drastically our general sense of time and space limits. His phrase "the global village," for instance, refers to the idea that the media collapse any meaningful definition of what may be called temporal and spatial geography; we can now watch, as the world did in 1991 and in 2003, wars occurring in "real time," and we can communicate instantly (and again in "real time") with people anywhere on the globe. McLuhan's work is, thus, vital because he compels us to confront the fact that media—television, radio, print, film—may alter the very ways in which we conceive of our experiences of reality.

If time and space are categories that have meaningful effects on the way we think about ourselves, media, McLuhan argues, are changing the ways we can conceive of ourselves. Indeed, it is crucial to pay careful attention to the often overlooked subtitle of *Understanding Media:* "The Extensions of Man." One of the reasons that McLuhan's work is beginning to attract the attention of a new generation of cultural theorists is that his work does consider that media—and technology, generally—were doing something specific to the *body* itself. McLuhan's idea of the "extension" of the human is not a casual metaphor for the way in which technology allows us to do previously unimagined things. In "The Gadget Lover," for instance, McLuhan theorizes that while humankind has always been fascinated with the idea of extending (and, thus, perhaps losing) itself through various means, modernity places such stress on the body that extending itself becomes a kind of survival mechanism. Using such deliberately polemical phrases as "autoamputation" or "self-amputation" to describe how various media extend (and replace) the body, McLuhan posits technology as essentially prosthetic: "The principle of self-amputation as an immediate relief of strain on the central nervous system applies very readily to the origin of the media of communication from speech to computer" (90). Indeed, in a phrase that seems to anticipate the cybernetic speculations of William Gibson or Phillip K. Dick, McLuhan writes: "With the arrival of electric technology, man extended, or set outside himself, a live model of the central nervous system" (90).

It was perhaps inevitable, thus, that at the point that a model of man was created and placed outside us, it would set itself up as a simulacrum, *replacing* us. McLuhan ultimately suggests that technology, precisely as it functions as a surrogate or simulacrum of humankind, will always place us in a servile position: "By continuously embracing technologies, we relate to them as servomechanisms" (92). Perhaps the most important phrase in this text—as a phrase that anticipates a great deal of contemporary theoretical work on the body (one thinks immediately of Deleuze and Guattari)—occurs as McLuhan speculates on the changes wrought on the body by technology: "Man becomes, as it were, the sex organs of the machine world" (92). McLuhan's point, polemically stated, is that our bodies begin to serve purposes not entirely our own. More precisely, our machines—we did after all create them—begin to assert claims on our own bodies, modifying them to suit machinic purposes.

McLuhan's essay is largely theoretical: he does not assert, for instance, precisely *how* technology modifies the body or how, precisely, we become the sex organs of the machine. Part of the force of McLuhan's theorizing lies precisely in its suggestiveness. And certainly this suggestiveness becomes the basis for a great number of contemporary analyses of technology which can specifically theorize technology not available to McLuhan (and thus extend his own analysis).

The work of Paul Virilio, for instance, is absolutely indebted to McLuhan's notion of "the extensions of man." In *Open Sky,* a postmodernist version of the modernist *Understanding Media,* Virilio speaks about how Internet technology and virtual reality devices initiate an "automation of perception" (Virilio 19), an idea that simply extends McLuhan's notion of the "displacement of perception" (92) that arises when our technology thinks for us. Thus, McLuhan's work ultimately becomes a crucial theoretical base from which to understand the centrality of technology in the contemporary world.

—JB

ISSUES TO CONSIDER WHILE READING

1. At some level, McLuhan's work operates as a polemic; that is, there is a rhetorical force to his work that may simply be present in order to provoke thought. How do you read McLuhan's language in this short essay?
2. Using McLuhan's ideas as a guide, give some consideration to the central idea that technology alters our relation to the external world. To what extent does his central claim make sense?

REFERENCES AND FURTHER READING

Baudrillard, Jean. *Simulacra and Simulations.* New York: Semiotext(e), 1983.

Deleuze, Gilles, and Felix Guattari. *Anti-Oedipus: Capitalism and Schizophrenia.* Minneapolis: University of Minnesota Press, 1983.

Virilio, Paul. *Open Sky.* London, Verso: 1997.

The Gadget Lover: Narcissus as Narcosis

NARCISSUS AS NARCOSIS

The Greek myth of Narcissus is directly concerned with a fact of human experience, as the word *Narcissus* indicates. It is from the Greek word *narcosis*, or numbness. The youth Narcissus mistook his own reflection in the water for another person. This extension of himself by mirror numbed his perceptions until he became the servomechanism of his own extended or repeated image. The nymph Echo tried to win his love with fragments of his own speech, but in vain. He was numb. He had adapted to his extension of himself and had become a closed system.

Now the point of this myth is the fact that men at once become fascinated by any extension of themselves in any material other than themselves. There have been cynics who insisted that men fall deepest in love with women who give them back their own image. Be that as it may, the wisdom of the Narcissus myth does not convey any idea that Narcissus fell in love with anything he regarded as himself. Obviously he would have had very different feelings about the image had he known it was an extension or repetition of himself. It is, perhaps, indicative of the bias of our intensely technological and, therefore, narcotic culture that we have long interpreted the Narcissus story to mean that he fell in love with himself, that he imagined the reflection to be Narcissus!

Physiologically there are abundant reasons for an extension of ourselves involving us in a state of numbness. Medical researchers like Hans Selye and Adolphe Jonas hold that all extensions of ourselves, in sickness or in health, are attempts to maintain equilibrium. Any extension of ourselves they regard as "autoamputation," and they find that the autoamputative power or strategy is resorted to by the body when the perceptual power cannot locate or avoid the cause of irritation. Our language has many expressions that indicate this self-amputation that is imposed by various pressures. We speak of "wanting to jump out of my skin" or of "going out of my mind," being "driven batty" or "flipping my lid." And we often create artificial situations that rival the irritations and stresses of real life under controlled conditions of sport and play.

While it was no part of the intentions of Jonas and Selye to provide an explanation of human invention and technology, they have given us a theory of disease (discomfort) that goes far to explain why man is impelled to extend various parts of his body by a kind of autoamputation. In the physical stress of superstimulation of various kinds, the central nervous system acts to protect itself by a strategy of amputation or isolation of the offending organ, sense, or function. Thus, the stimulus to new invention is the stress of acceleration of pace and increase of load. For example, in the case of the wheel as an extension of the foot, the pressure of new burdens resulting from the acceleration of exchange by written and monetary media was the immediate occasion of the extension of "amputation" of this function from our bodies. The wheel as a counter-irritant to increased burdens, in turn, brings about a new intensity of action by its amplification of a separate or isolated function (the feet in rotation). Such amplification is bearable by the nervous system only through numbness or blocking of perception. This is the sense of the Narcissus myth. The young man's image is a self-amputation or extension induced by irritating pressures. As a counter-irritant, the image produces a generalized numbness or shock that declines recognition. Self-amputation forbids self-recognition.

The principle of self-amputation as an immediate relief of strain on the central nervous system applies very readily to the origin of the media of communication from speech to computer.

Physiologically, the central nervous system, that electric network that coordinates the various media of our senses, plays the chief role. Whatever threatens its function must be contained, localized, or cut off, even to the total removal of the offending organ. The function of the body, as a group of sustaining and protective organs for the central nervous system, is to act as buffers against sudden variations of stimulus in the physical and social environment. Sudden social failure or shame is a shock that some may "take to heart" or that may cause muscular disturbance in general, signaling for the person to withdraw from the threatening situation.

Therapy, whether physical or social, is a counter-irritant that aids in that equilibrium of the physical organs which protect the central nervous system. Whereas pleasure is a counter-irritant (e.g., sports, entertainment, and alcohol), comfort is the removal of irritants. Both pleasure and comfort are strategies of equilibrium for the central nervous system.

With the arrival of electric technology, man extended, or set outside himself, a live model of the central nervous system itself. To the degree that this is so, it is a development that suggests a desperate and suicidal autoamputation, as if the central nervous system could no longer depend on the physical organs to be protective buffers against the slings and arrows of outrageous mechanism. It could well be that the successive mechanization of the various physical organs since the invention of printing have made too violent and superstimulated a social experiment for the central nervous system to endure.

In relation to that only too plausible cause of such development, we can return to the Narcissus theme. For if Narcissus is numbed by his self-amputated image, there is a very good reason for the numbness. There is a close parallel of response between the patterns of physical and psychic trauma or shock. A person suddenly deprived of loved ones and a person who drops a few feet unexpectedly will both register shock. Both the loss of family and a physical fall are extreme instances of amputations of the self. Shock induces a generalized numbness or an increased threshold to all types of perception. The victim seems immune to pain or sense.

Battle shock created by violent noise has been adapted for dental use in the device known as *audiac*. The patient puts on headphones and turns a dial raising the noise level to the point that he feels no pain from the drill. The selection of a *single* sense for intense stimulus, or of a single extended, isolated, or "amputated" sense in technology, is in part the reason for the numbing effect that technology as such has on its makers and users. For the central nervous system rallies a response of general numbness to the challenge of specialized irritation.

The person who falls suddenly experiences immunity to all pain or sensory stimuli because the central nervous system has to be protected from any intense thrust of sensation. Only gradually does he regain normal sensitivity to sights and sounds, at which time he may begin to tremble and perspire and to react as he would have done if the central nervous system had been prepared in advance for the fall that occurred unexpectedly.

Depending on which sense or faculty is extended technologically, or "autoamputated," the "closure" or equilibrium-seeking among the other senses is fairly predictable. It is with the senses as it is with color. Sensation is always 100 per cent sensation, and a color is always 100 per cent color. But the ratio among the components in the sensation or the color can differ infinitely. Yet if sound, for example, is intensified, touch and taste and sight are affected at once. The effect of radio on literate or visual man was to reawaken his tribal memories, and the effect of sound added to motion pictures was to diminish the role of mime, tactility, and kinesthesis. Similarly, when nomadic man turned to sedentary and specialist ways, the senses specialized too. The development of writing and the visual organization of life made possible the discovery of individualism, introspection and so on.

Any invention or technology is an extension or self-amputation of our physical bodies, and such extension also demands new ratios or new equilibriums among the other organs and extensions of the body. There is, for example, no way of refusing to comply with the new sense ratios or sense "closure" evoked by the TV image. But the effect of the entry of the TV image will vary from culture to culture in accordance with the existing sense ratios in each culture. In audile-tactile Europe TV has intensified the visual sense, spurring them toward American styles of packaging and dressing. In America, the intensely visual culture, TV has opened the doors of audile-tactile perception to the non-visual world of spoken languages and food and the plastic arts. As an extension and expediter of the sense life, any medium at once affects the entire field of the senses, as the Psalmist explained long ago in the 115th Psalm:

> Their idols are silver and gold,
> The work of men's hands.
> They have mouths, but they speak not;
> Eyes they have, but they see not;
> They have ears, but they hear not;
> Noses have they, but they smell not;
> They have hands, but they handle not;
> Feet have they, but they walk not;
> Neither speak they through their throat.
> They that make them shall be like unto them;
> Yea, every one that trusteth in them.

The concept of "idol" for the Hebrew Psalmist is much like that of Narcissus for the Greek mythmaker. And the Psalmist insists that the *beholding* of idols, or the use of technology, conforms men to them. "They that make them shall be like unto them." This is a simple fact of sense "closure." The poet Blake developed the Psalmist's ideas into an entire theory of communication and social change. It is in his long poem *Jerusalem* that he explains why men have become what they have beheld. What they have, says Blake, is "the spectre of the Reasoning Power in Man" that has become fragmented and "separated from Imagination and enclosing itself as in steel." Blake, in a word, sees man as fragmented by his technologies. But he insists that these technologies are self-amputations of our own organs. When so amputated, each organ becomes a closed system of great new intensity that hurls man into "martyrdoms and wars." Moreover, Blake announces as his theme in Jerusalem the organs of perception:

> If Perceptive Organs vary, Objects of Perception seem to vary:
> If Perceptive Organs close, their Objects seem to close also.

To behold, use or perceive any extension of ourselves in technological form is necessarily to embrace it. To listen to radio or to read the printed page is to accept these extensions of ourselves into our personal system and to undergo the "closure" or displacement of perception that follows automatically. It is this continuous embrace of our own technology in daily use that puts us in the Narcissus role of subliminal awareness and numbness in relation to these images of ourselves. By continuously embracing technologies, we relate ourselves to them as servomechanisms. That is why we must, to use them at all, serve these objects, these extension of ourselves, as gods or minor religions. An Indian is the servomechanism of his canoe, as the cowboy of his horse or the executive of his clock.

Physiologically, man in the normal use of technology (or his variously extended body) is perpetually modified by it and in turn finds ever new ways of modifying his technology. Man becomes, as it were, the sex organs of the machine world, as the bee of the plant world, enabling it to fecundate and to evolve ever new forms. The machine world reciprocates man's love by expediting his wishes and desires, namely, in providing him with wealth. One of the merits of motivation research has been the revelation of man's sex relation to the motorcar.

Socially, it is the accumulation of group pressure and irritations that prompt invention and innovation as counter-irritants. War and the fear of war have always been considered the main incentives to technological extension of our bodies. Indeed, Lewis Mumford, in his *The City in History,* considers the walled city itself an extension of our skins, as much as housing and clothing. More even than the preparation for war, the aftermath of invasion is a rich technological period; because the subject culture has to adjust all its sense ratios to accommodate the impact of the invading culture. It is from such intensive hybrid exchange and strife of ideas and forms that the greatest social energies are released, and from which arise the greatest technologies. Buckminster Fuller estimates that since 1910 the governments of the world have spent 3 1/2 trillion dollars on airplanes. That is 62 times the existing gold supply of the world.

The principle of numbness comes into play with electric technology, as with any other. We have to numb our central nervous system when it is extended and exposed, or we will die. Thus the age of anxiety and of electric media is also the age of the unconscious and of apathy. But it is strikingly the age of consciousness and of the unconscious, in addition. With our central nervous system strategically numbed, the tasks of conscious awareness and order are transferred to the physical life of man, so that for the first time he has become aware of technology as an extension of his physical body. Apparently this could not have happened before the electric age gave us the means of instant, total field-awareness. With such awareness, the subliminal life, private and social, has been hoicked up into full view, with the result that we have "social consciousness" presented to us as a cause of guilt-feelings. Existentialism offers a philosophy of structures, rather than categories, and of total social involvement instead of the bourgeois spirit of individual separateness or points of view. In the electric age we wear all mankind as our skin.

6 Jean Baudrillard, "The Precession of Simulacra"

EDITORS' INTRODUCTION

Jean Baudrillard's "The Precession of Simulacra" is a central document for cultural studies. Published in 1981 in *Simulacra and Simulation*, Baudrillard's essay provides a model for thinking about what constitutes the "real" in contemporary culture. Indeed, Baudrillard's central (and polemical) point is that a singular notion of what constitutes the real is no longer tenable in a (postmodern) culture that multiplies or refracts the real into a plurality of reflections or simulacra: instead of the real we have its simulation; instead of truth we have its simulacrum. The very idea of accurate representation is lost precisely as everything becomes its own representation. This process of substation and effacement realigns our conception of what constitutes the "real." If the relation between reality and its image was once one of priority (i.e., reality came before its image; the image was a secondary reflection of what was "out there"), the simulacrum entirely negates this relationship of priority (indeed, it effaces the entire *notion* of priority) by removing the grounds by which we can identify the real in the first place. Who is to say, Baudrillard asks, which version of (political, ideological, national) reality is correct? The simulacrum radically relativizes all value, and all grounds of value, by removing the ability and perhaps the desire for any particular constituency to authorize and make claim to the real.

The concept of the simulacrum, as Baudrillard explains it, develops with the evolution of Western culture's understanding of the function of the "image." According to Baudrillard, the image—representational power; the power to represent reality as such—has developed through four historical phases (the fourth of these phases presumably corresponds to the postmodern period):

Such would be the successive phases of the image:

it is the reflection of a profound reality;
it masks and denatures a profound reality;
it masks the *absence* of a profound reality;
it has no relation to any reality whatsoever: it is its own pure simulacrum. (98)

According to Baudrillard's schema, we inhabit (or we did in the 1980s) an epoch in which we can no longer determine (or perhaps *wish* to determine) what is real from what is false because the very distinction has been deconstructed: "It is no longer a question of imitation, nor duplication, nor even of parody. It is a question of substituting the signs of the real for the real" (96). The simulacrum, therefore, is the concrete sign of the loss of representational power.

A central feature of Baudrillard's argument is his distinction between dissimulation and simulation. He draws out this distinction by comparing one who dissimulates or feigns an illness to one who simulates that illness. The dissimulating patient simply pretends to be ill. Simulation, on the other hand, will actually produce symptoms of the illness and, as such, breaks down the distinction between "true" and "false," between the "real" and the "imaginary." Baudrillard's purpose in his essay is to draw attention to the manner in which postmodern culture is suffused by simulation to the extent that we begin to take the sign of the thing as representing the thing itself. This process, what Baudrillard refers to as the making of the hyperreal, obliterates any notion of differential value: as everything becomes an image, the ability to locate the real as a ground for understanding images *as* images is irretrievably lost. In semiotic terms, the simulacrum is a signifier without a signified, a symptom of an illness which cannot be identified as such. Thus, in his (in)famous analysis of Disneyland, Baudrillard is able to suggest that the theme park operates to draw the "objective profile of America" (Baudrillard, *Precession* 12): it offers itself as the perfect, illusory vision of the idea of "America." As such, and through a strange reversal, the hyperreal "values" of Disneyland work to disguise the fact that they do, in fact, truly represent America: "Disneyland exists in order to hide that it is the "real" country, all of "real America that *is* Disneyland" (Baudrillard, *Precession* 12).

Baudrillard is often figured, mistakenly, as a spokesperson for the postmodern, as one who celebrates (after Nietzsche) the refraction of the real, of truth, into its reflections. This is a misreading of the tone of Baudrillard's writing and the tenor of his arguments, which, although wryly playful, express a deep nostalgia for an integrated, singular understanding of the real. As he writes in "The Precession of Simulacra": "None of our societies knows how to manage its mourning for the real, for power, for the social itself, which is implicated in this same breakdown" (Baudrillard 46). The collapse of the working image into hyperreal simulacra represents a *real* threat to the social order, to the possibility of rational intellectual exchange.

The influence of Baudrillard's "The Precession of Simulacra" has been profound. It has found its way into the work of literary critics, political scientists, philosophers, and film theorists. The essay is invariably the beginning point of a great number of essays analyzing perhaps the most scrutinized science fiction film of the 1980s, *Blade Runner*, a film which offers itself as a practical analysis of the simulacrum. *The Matrix*, certainly one of the most influential films of the 1990s, makes numerous references to "The Precession of the Simulacra" and does actually feature a central character (Morpheus) quoting the text: "Welcome to the desert of the real." Baudrillard's work, in its uncanny anticipation of the proliferation of the media, of virtual reality, of the collapse of fiction and reality (as in the so-called "Reality TV" craze of the early 2000s), will continue to serve as a beginning point in any analysis which would wish to understand the nature of the "real" in contemporary culture.

—JB

ISSUES TO CONSIDER WHILE READING

1. Is it possible to suggest that the simulacrum is such a central feature of contemporary culture that we no longer are able to perceive the extent to which culture is already its own substitute? A casual glance at animated series, such as *The Simpsons*, *South Park*, and even *King of the Hill*, will demonstrate how parodies of culture seem to be the norm in contemporary entertainment. How much force do Baudrillard's arguments have in the culture of 2004?

2. Discuss the idea that behind Baudrillard's analysis of the simulacrum is an ethical critique of contemporary culture. If the simulacrum replaces the real, if the real is irrevocably lost in its murderous image, how can we resist the "logic" of the simulacrum?

REFERENCES AND FURTHER READING

Baudrillard, Jean. *The Perfect Crime*. Trans. Chris Turner. London: Verso, 1995.

---. "The Precession of Simulacra." *Simulacra and Simulation*. Trans. Sheila Faria Glaser. Ann Arbor, Michigan: The University of Michigan Press, 1994.

---. *The Transparency of Evil: Essays on Extreme Phenomena*. London: Verso, 1990.

Bukatman, Scott. *Terminal Identity: The Virtual Subject in Postmodern Science Fiction*. Durham: Duke University Press, 1993.

Kellner, Douglas. *Jean Baudrillard: From Marxism to Postmodernism and Beyond*. Stanford University Press, 1990.

Zizek, Slavoj. *Welcome to the Desert of the Real*. London: Verso, 2002.

The Precession of Simulacra

The simulacrum is never what hides the truth—it is truth that hides the fact that there is none. The simulacrum is true.

—Ecclesiastes

If once we were able to view the Borges fable in which the cartographers of the Empire draw up a map so detailed that it ends up covering the territory exactly (the decline of the Empire witnesses the fraying of this map, little by little, and its fall into ruins, though some shreds are still discernible in the deserts—the metaphysical beauty of this ruined abstraction testifying to a pride equal to the Empire and rotting like a carcass, returning to the substance of the soil, a bit as the double ends by being confused with the real through aging)—as the most beautiful allegory of simulation, this fable has now come full circle for us, and possesses nothing but the discrete charm of second-order simulacra.

Today abstraction is no longer that of the map, the double, the mirror, or the concept. Simulation is no longer that of a territory, a referential being, or a substance. It is the generation by models of a real without origin or reality: a hyperreal. The territory no longer precedes the map, nor does it survive it. It is nevertheless the map that precedes the territory—*precession of simulacra*—that engenders the territory, and if one must return to the fable, today it is the territory whose shreds slowly rot across the extent of the map. It is the real, and not the map, whose vestiges persist here and there in the deserts that are no longer those of the Empire, but ours. *The desert of the real itself.*

In fact, even inverted, Borges's fable is unusable. Only the allegory of the Empire, perhaps, remains. Because it is with this same imperialism that present-day simulators attempt to make the real, all of the real, coincide with their models of simulation. But it is no longer a question of either maps or territories. Something has disappeared: the sovereign difference, between one and the other, that constituted the charm of abstraction.

Because it is difference that constitutes the poetry of the map and the charm of the territory, the magic of the concept and the charm of the real. This imaginary of representation, which simultaneously culminates in and is engulfed by the cartographer's mad project of the ideal coextensivity of map and territory, disappears in the simulation whose operation is nuclear and genetic, no longer at all specular or discursive. It is all of metaphysics that is lost. No more mirror of being and appearance, of the real and its concept. No more imaginary coextensivity: it is genetic miniaturization that is the dimension of simulation. The real is produced from miniaturized cells, matrices, and memory banks, models of control—and it can be reproduced an indefinite number of times from these. It no longer needs to be rational, because it no longer measures itself against either an ideal or negative instance. It is no longer anything but operational. In fact, it is no longer really the real, because no imaginary envelops it anymore. It is hyperreal, produced from a radiating synthesis of combinatory models in a hyperspace without atmosphere.

By crossing into a space whose curvature is no longer that of the real, nor that of truth, the era of simulation is inaugurated by a liquidation of all referentials—worse: with their artificial resurrection in the systems of signs, a material more malleable than meaning, in that it lends itself to all systems of equivalences, to all binary oppositions to all combinatory algebra. It is no longer a question of imitation, nor duplication, nor even parody. It is a question of substituting the signs of the real for the real, that is to say of an operation of deterring every real process via its operational double, a programmatic, metastable, perfectly descriptive machine that offers all the signs of the real and short-circuits all its vicissitudes. Never again will the real have the chance to produce itself—such is the vital function of the model in a system of death, or rather of anticipated resurrection, that no longer even gives the event of death a chance. A hyperreal henceforth sheltered from the imaginary, and from any distinction between the real and the imaginary, leaving room only for the orbital recurrence of models and for the simulated generation of differences.

THE DIVINE IRREFERENCE OF IMAGES

To dissimulate is to pretend not to have what one has. To simulate is to feign to have what one doesn't have. One implies a presence, the other an absence. But it is more complicated than that because simulating is not pretending: "Whoever fakes an illness can simply stay in bed and make everyone believe he is ill. Whoever simulates an illness produces in himself some of the symptoms" (Littré). Therefore, pretending, or dissimulating, leaves the principle of reality intact: the difference is always clear, it is simply masked, whereas simulation threatens the difference between the "true" and the "false," the "real" and the "imaginary." Is the simulator sick or not, given that he produces "true" symptoms? Objectively one cannot treat him as being either ill or not ill. Psychosomatics evolves in a dubious manner at the borders of the principle of illness. As to psychoanalysis, it transfers the symptom of the organic order to the unconscious order: the latter is new and taken for "real" more real than the other—but why would simulation be at the gates of the unconscious? Why couldn't the "work" of the unconscious be "produced" in the same way as any old symptom of classical medicine? Dreams already are.

Certainly, the psychiatrist purports that "for every form of mental alienation there is a particular order in the succession of symptoms of which the simulator is ignorant and in the absence of which the psychiatrist would not be deceived." This (which dates from 1865) in order to safeguard the principle of a truth at all costs and to escape the interrogation posed by simulation—the knowledge that truth, reference, objective cause have ceased to exist. Now what can medicine do with what floats on either side of illness, on either side of health, with the duplication of illness in a discourse that is no longer either true or false? What can psychoanalysis do with the duplication of the discourse of the unconscious in the discourse of simulation that can never again be unmasked, since it is not false either?

What can the army do about simulators? Traditionally it unmasks them and punishes them, according to a clear principle of identification. Today it can discharge a very good simulator as exactly equivalent to a "real" homosexual, a heart patient, or a madman. Even military psychology draws back from Cartesian certainties and hesitates to make the distinction between true and false, between the "produced" and the authentic symptom. "If he is this good at acting crazy, it's because he is." Nor is military psychology mistaken in this regard: in this sense, all crazy people simulate, and this lack of distinction is the worst kind of subversion. It is against this lack of distinction that classical reason armed itself in all its categories. But it is what today again outflanks them, submerging the principle of truth.

Beyond medicine and the army, favored terrains of simulation, the question returns to religion and the simulation of divinity: "I forbade that there be any simulacra in the temples because the divinity that animates nature can never be represented." Indeed it can be. But what becomes of the divinity when it reveals itself in icons, when it is multiplied in simulacra? Does it remain the supreme power that is simply incarnated in images as a visible theology? Or does it volatilize itself in the simulacra that, alone, deploy their power and pomp of fascination—the visible machinery of icons substituted for the pure and intelligible Idea of God? This is precisely what was feared by iconoclasts, whose millennial quarrel is still with us today. This is precisely because they predicted this omnipotence of simulacra, the faculty simulacra have of effacing God from the conscience of man, and the destructive, annihilating truth that they allow to appear—that deep down God never existed, that only the simulacrum ever existed, even that God himself was never anything but his own simulacrum—from this came their urge to destroy the images. If they could have believed that these images only obfuscated or masked the Platonic Idea of God, there would have been no reason to destroy them. One can live with the idea of distorted truth. But their metaphysical despair came from the idea that the image didn't conceal anything at all, and that these images were in essence not images, such as an original model would have made them, but perfect simulacra, forever radiant with their own fascination. Thus this death of the divine referential must be exorcised at all costs.

One can see that the iconclasts, whom one accuses of disdaining and negating images, were those who accorded them their true value, in contrast to the iconolaters who only saw reflections in them and were content to venerate a filigree God. On the other hand, one can say that the icon worshipers were the most modern minds, the most adventurous, because, in the guise of having God become apparent in the mirror of images, they were already enacting his death and his disappearance in the epiphany of his representations (which, perhaps, they already knew no longer represented anything, that they were purely a game, but that it was therein the great game lay—knowing also that it is dangerous to unmask images, since they dissimulate the fact that there is nothing behind them).

This was the approach of the Jesuits, who founded their politics on the virtual disappearance of God and on the worldly and specular manipulation of consciences—the evanescence of God in the epiphany of power—the end of transcendence, which now only serves as an alibi for a strategy altogether free of influences and signs. Behind the baroqueness of images hides the éminence grise of politics.

This way the stake will always have been the murderous power of images, murderers of the real, murderers of their own model, as the Byzantine icons could be those of divine identity. To this murderous power is opposed that of representations as a dialectical power, the visible and intelligible mediation of the Real. All Western faith and good faith became engaged in this wager on representation: that a sign could refer to the depth of meaning, that a sign could be exchanged for meaning and that something could guarantee this exchange—God of course. But what if God himself can be simulated, that is to say can be reduced to the signs that constitute faith? Then the whole system becomes weightless, it is no longer itself anything but a gigantic simulacrum—not unreal, but a simulacrum, that is to say never exchanged for the real, but exchanged for itself, in an uninterrupted circuit without reference or circumference.

Such is simulation, insofar as it is opposed to representation. Representation stems from the principle of the equivalence of the sign and of the real (even if this equivalence is utopian, it is a fundamental axiom). Simulation, on the contrary, stems from the utopia of the principle of equivalence, *from the radical negation of the sign as value,* from the sign as the reversion and death sentence of every reference. Whereas representation attempts to absorb simulation by interpreting it as a false representation, simulation envelops the whole edifice of representation itself as a simulacrum.

Such would be the successive phases of the image:

it is the reflection of a profound reality;
it masks and denatures a profound reality;
it masks the *absence* of a profound reality;
it has no relation to any reality whatsoever: it is its own pure simulacrum.

In the first case, the image is a *good* appearance—representation is of the sacramental order. In the second, it is an evil appearance—it is of the order of maleficence. In the third, it plays at being an appearance—it is of the order of sorcery. In the fourth, it is no longer of the order of appearances, but of simulation.

The transition from signs that dissimulate something to signs that dissimulate that there is nothing marks a decisive turning point. The first reflects a theology of truth and secrecy (to which the notion of ideology still belongs). The second inaugurates the era of simulacra and of simulation, in which there is no longer a God to recognize his own, no longer a Last Judgement to separate the false from the true, the real from its artificial resurrection, as everything is already dead and resurrected in advance.

When the real is no longer what it was, nostalgia assumes its full meaning. There is a plethora of myths of origin and of signs of reality—a plethora of truth, of secondary objectivity, and authenticity. Escalation of the true, of lived experience, resurrection of the figurative where the object and substance have disappeared. Panic-stricken production of the real and of the referential, parallel to and greater than the panic of material production: this is how simulation appears in the phase that concerns us—a strategy of the real, of the neoreal and the hyperreal that everywhere is the double of a strategy of deterrence.

POLITICAL INCANTATION

Watergate. The same scenario as in Disneyland (effect of the imaginary concealing that reality no more exists outside than inside the limits of the artificial perimeter): here the scandal effect hiding that there is no difference between the facts and their denunciation (identical methods on the part of the CIA and of the *Washington Post* journalists). Same operation, tending to regenerate through scandal a moral and political principle, through the imaginary, a sinking reality principle.

The denunciation of scandal is always an homage to the law. And Watergate in particular succeeded in imposing the idea that Watergate *was* a scandal—in the sense it was a prodigious operation of intoxication. A large dose of political morality reinjected on a world scale. One could say along with Bourdieu: "The essence of every relation of force is to dissimulate itself as such as to acquire all its force only because it dissimulates itself as such," understood as follows: capital, immoral and without scruples, can only function behind a moral superstructure, and whoever revives this public morality (through indignation, denunciation, etc.) works spontaneously for the order of capital. This is what the journalists of the *Washington Post* did.

But this would be nothing but the formula of ideology, and when Bourdieu states it, he takes the "relation of force" for the *truth* of capitalist domination, and he himself *denounces* this relation of force as a *scandal*—he is thus in the same deterministic and moralistic position as the *Washington Post* journalists are. He does the same work of purging and reviving moral order, an order of truth in which the veritable symbolic violence of the social order is engendered, well beyond all the relations of force, which are only its shifting and indifferent configuration in the moral and political consciences of men.

All that capital asks of us is to receive it as rational *or* to combat it in the name of rationality, to receive it as moral *or* to combat it in the name of morality. Because *these are the same,* which *can be thought of in another way:* formerly one worked to dissimulate scandal—today one works to conceal that there is none.

Watergate is not a scandal, this is what must be said at all costs, because it is what everyone is busy concealing, this dissimulation masking a strengthening of morality, of a moral panic as one approaches the primitive (*mise en*) *scéne* of capital: its instantaneous cruelty, its incomprehensible ferocity, its fundamental immorality—that is what is scandalous, unacceptable to the system of moral and economic equivalence that is the axiom of leftist thought, from the theories of the Enlightenment up to Communism. One imputes this thinking to the contract of capital, but it doesn't give a damn—it is a monstrous unprincipled enterprise, nothing more. It is "enlightened" thought that seeks to control it by imposing rules on it. And all the recrimination that replaces revolutionary thought today comes back to incriminate capital for not following the rules of the game. "Power is unjust, its justice is a class justice, capital exploits us, etc."—as if capital were linked by a contract to the society it rules. It is the Left that holds out the mirror of equivalence to capital hoping that it will comply, comply with this phantasmagoria of the social contract and fulfill its obligations to the whole of society (by the same token, no need for revolution: it suffices that capital accommodate itself to the rational formula of exchange).

Capital, in fact, was never linked by a contract to the society that it dominates. It is a sorcery of social relations, it is a *challenge to society,* and it must be responded to as such. It is not a scandal to be denounced according to moral or economic rationality, but a challenge to take up according to symbolic law.

Paul Rutherford, "Made in America: The Problem of Mass Culture in Canada"

EDITORS' INTRODUCTION

The title of Paul Rutherford's essay (originally published in 1993) appears to tell the whole story: the "problem" of mass culture in Canada is that the vast majority of it is not home grown but made in America. That the majority of our mass culture is American is unarguable: turn on your TV, tune in your radio, or open your newspaper to the movie listings. True, you may just catch Peter Mansbridge or the Barenaked Ladies or see an ad for an Atom Egoyan feature, but they tend to be exceptions that prove the rule. Our almost inevitable cry of "Hey! They're Canadian!" confirms just how used we are to watching American TV, listening to American music, and choosing from among American movies. That the predominance of American mass culture in Canada is necessarily a "problem," however, is a more vexed issue, and it is the one that Rutherford considers in the following pages.

As Rutherford observes, the "problem" of American mass culture arises only within the context of the twin concepts of Canadian nationalism and Canadian identity, concepts that have always been somewhat unstable. "The country has never fit the ideal model [of nationalism]," Rutherford writes; "there has always loomed some outside empire, whether centred in London, the Vatican, or Washington, to restrict the country's sovereignty; ...and the derivative or dependent character of our social or literary or even audio-visual life has been a bitter pill for any devout nationalist to swallow" (103). Most cultural critics would agree that concepts like national identity are largely imaginary; that is, while the notion of a distinct national identity certainly has force and meaning for many, it is, for the most part, produced and reproduced through symbolic means: a flag, a sense of a common history disseminated in the schools, and, importantly, a shared set of cultural objects, practices, and representations.

The "problem" for Canada, then, is that it shares its border—its extremely porous border, as Rutherford points out—with the world's most powerful producer and distributor of cultural objects, practices, and representations, the United States, a country whose mass culture has, to a large extent, become "ours." Entrepreneurs may worry about American domination of the market; nationalists worry about American domination of the imagination. Canadians eat at McDonald's, shop at The Gap, watch the Super Bowl, see Hollywood movies, and read American bestsellers—and are apparently happy to do so. But surely, such a steady diet of American mass culture must have a compromising effect on a sense of distinct national identity, mustn't it?

While the pressures of globalization are making the above concern more common throughout the world, Rutherford demonstrates that it has been a *Canadian* concern almost from Confederation. Assuming the necessarily deleterious effects of the "American example," successive Canadian governments have attempted to prevent, without success, the flow of American mass culture northward and to promote, with only marginal success, the growth of a distinctly Canadian mass culture. Rutherford further demonstrates that such cultural protectionism has been primarily championed by the country's elites and that its results (the establishment of largely "high-culture" institutions, such as the National Film Board and the Canada Council) have been of little interest to the bulk of Canadians who wish to be able to continue reading American magazines, listening to American music, and shopping at American chain stores. We Canadians love American mass culture, apparently, almost as much as we love rolling our eyes at Canadian attempts to imitate it. Does this mean that we are becoming less Canadian? More American?

Rutherford suggests not, and indeed, as recent as 1999, an overwhelming 90 percent of respondents to a *Maclean's*/CBC poll declared that Canada was a distinct society (cited in Wallace 55). One may legitimately worry about the foundation of such a show of confidence, however; when asked to come up with a word that best described the Canadian character, respondents to the poll floundered: the most popular choice, at only 12 percent, was "friendly" (Wallace 55). Rutherford, too, may have an unfounded confidence in the insignificance of things he calls "merely commodities" (112). Nevertheless, "Made in America" makes for fascinating, if somewhat dismal reading—dismal inasmuch as it reveals the extent to which our national questions have not changed over the past 137 years. But, maybe in this case, the questions are more important than the answers.

—CM

ISSUES TO CONSIDER WHILE READING

1. Many writers have joked that the defining characteristic of Canadian identity is worrying about Canadian identity, but Rutherford suggests that most Canadians are not worried about it at all. Should they be?
2. Despite his title, Rutherford concludes that the predominance of American mass culture in Canada is not a problem. Is he too optimistic? Is there anything his argument fails to take into consideration?
3. Near the end of his essay, Rutherford describes three mythic images of Canada. What is the function of these myths? How are they produced?

REFERENCES AND FURTHER READING

Flaherty, David H., and Frank E. Manning, eds. *The Beaver Bites Back? American Popular Culture in Canada.* Montreal and Kingston: McGill-Queen's University Press, 1993.

Van Luven, Lynne, and Priscilla L. Walton, eds. *Pop Can: Popular Culture in Canada.* Scarborough: Prentice-Hall Allyn and Bacon, 1999.

Wallace, Bruce. "What Makes a Canadian?" *Canadian Communications: Issues in Contemporary Media and Culture.* Second ed. Ed. Bohdan Szuchewycz and Jeannette Sloniowski. Toronto: Pearson Education, 2002. 55–58. Originally published in *Maclean's* 112.51 (20 December 1999. 32).

Made in America: The Problem of Mass Culture in Canada

The doctrine of nationalism has bedevilled intellectual discourse in Canada. The country has never fit the ideal model: there has always loomed some outside empire, whether centred in London, the Vatican, or Washington, to restrict the country's sovereignty; the persistence of the "two solitudes," French and English, has made a mockery of efforts to build a pan-Canadian nationality; and the derivative or dependent character of our social or literary or even audio-visual life has been a bitter pill for any devout nationalist to swallow. Unfortunately, nationalist thinking has usually prevailed in debates about culture. My purpose here is to reflect upon the cultural experience of Canada during the past hundred years or so and, along the way, to dispel several myths about what it all means.

…Underpinning the political nationality launched in 1867 was a social ideology that expressed the values of the bourgeois mainstream in British North America. "Our scheme is to establish a government," said George Brown during the Confederation debates, "that will endeavour to maintain liberty, justice, and Christianity [sic] throughout the land."[1] That reference to Christianity, "la principe de notre force" and "the chief cornerstone" of our civilization, would have sparked in contemporaries a recognition of a much wider range of presumptions about the proper society, presumptions that might best be described as the Victorian ethos.[2] Before and after Confederation, both francophone and Anglophone newspapers urged the virtues of a community organized around a series of moral authorities and disciplines: the churches and religion, the family and marriage, the workplace and the work ethic, the school and education, the courts and the rule of law, political parties and partisan loyalties. People were expected to abide by an increasingly rigid code of behaviour which segregated sexes, emphasized self-improvement and class harmony, and embodied a puritanical distrust of pleasure. Although such dreams were never altogether realized in practice—late nineteenth-century Canada was in many ways an "Un-Victorian society"—the ethos imparted to Canada an image as a purer and better country (often portrayed as a young if rather stern maiden) than its big neighbour to the south (which was depicted as an older, leaner, slightly seedy male).[3] Indeed what struck many Canadians when they looked at American society was its disorder, its corruption, its worship of Mammon—in a word, its lack of an effective moral authority.

The ideology was sufficient to justify efforts to protect Canada against the ill effects of the American example and American ideas. One reason that Egerton Ryerson, Ontario's long-time schoolmaster, insisted on taking control of Ontario's textbooks and library books was to rid the state's chief cultural agency, the public schools, of American reading material.[4] A section of the Customs Act, reaffirmed in the famous National Policy Tariff of 1879, prohibited the entry of indecent and treasonous matter, and over time the Customs Department would create what amounted to a Canadian index of forbidden works. A prohibition on the importation, sale, or possession of alcohol in the Northwest Territories was imposed in 1875 to prevent the arrival of the American whisky-trader and, more generally, the lifestyle of the American west.[5] A purpose of the many sabbatarian laws, which culminated in the Lord's Day Act of 1906, was to block the emergence of something journalists like to call "the American Sunday," apparently a day of unhindered licence when bars and theatres stayed open, sporting events were scheduled, streetcars operated, and commerce thrived.

None of this moral protectionism, however, served to prevent the northward spread of the developing mass culture of the United States. Indeed, Canadian elites sometimes welcomed aspects of that culture. Consider the case of tourism: the respected citizens who promoted Quebec City's first winter carnival in 1894 were intent on attracting American visitors by presenting their community as the home of a happy family, set in a pre-industrialized past, where people could escape their daily cares.[6] Likewise, the CPR and other entrepreneurs marketed the country's unspoiled wilderness, its majestic mountains, the awesome Niagara Falls, and beautiful lakes and streams for the pleasure of the sportsman and the tourist alike. Even before the close of the century, then, tourism and travel literature were applying particular images to Canadian places and scenes, if not to the country as a whole.

The most powerful agent of Americanization was the daily press—which was something of a paradox, since it was the workings of the press that created a community of discourse across Canada. The self-styled people's journals that appeared in the late nineteenth century, dailies like the Montreal *Star*, the Toronto *Telegram*, or later Montreal's *La Presse*, were modelled upon the American journals of sensation, human interest, and crusades like James Bennett's *Herald* or Joseph Pulitzer's *World* in New York, although the Canadian version of yellow journalism remained comparatively mild by American standards.[7] By the 1880s and 1890s, newspapers were full of ads for American patent medicines and brand-name goods; just as important, the advertising copy of Canadian products or department stores employed the same style of "Tall Talk" and reason-why argument prevalent in American cities.

Nearly all dailies, even high-quality papers like the Toronto *Globe* or the Montreal *Gazette*, took much of their world news from American papers or news agencies and often subscribed to American syndication services which supplied feature material, humour and fiction, even sermons. According to a survey taken in 1895, thirty-three papers subscribed to the United Press Service and fourteen to the rival Associated Press.[8] The result, said an unhappy *Le Monde* in 1892, was that "le plus petit incident" occurring in the United States was telegraphed across the dominion while important news from Europe was always slighted.[9] Such a concern led the Toronto *Telegram* and the Montreal *Star*, assisted by a modest grant from the federal government, to organize a Canadian Associated Press in 1903 to furnish a summary of news from London directly to Canadian clients. Yet when the Canadian Press news agency was organized after 1907, its chief role was initially to act as a holding company for the Canadian rights to the Associated Press's world copy.[10]

The situation was no less complicated when attention shifted to other kinds of leisure and literary material. There was no tradition of Canadian play-writing to speak of, and most theatres depended on foreign touring companies, mostly American. British and American magazines had always found a ready audience in middle-class homes in English Canada, so when home-grown periodicals like the *Canadian Magazine* or *Maclean's* entered the picture they found that outsiders already occupied their market; in

1912 it was estimated that sales of British magazines and newspapers stood at $77,000, and sales of their American rivals at $880,000.[11] Book publishers made their money by offering British and American reprints rather than original Canadian works, because that practice suited bourgeois tastes.[12] A survey of lists of two hundred bestsellers in English between 1899 and 1919 counted 44 per cent by American authors, 36 per cent by Britishers, and 21 per cent by Canadians.[13] A number of English-Canadian authors like Charles Gordon (writing as Ralph Connor), Gilbert Parker, Stephen Leacock, and Margaret Saunders won large Canadian audiences and some international fame by writing moralistic adventures, historical romances, humour, and animal stories. Their reputation in Britain and the United States was the first evidence of a successful adaptation by a group of Canadians to the tastes of Anglophone readers elsewhere.

…What was especially striking, in sports and much else, was that the taste for things American was greatest among the young and the masses. Many an editor over the years worried about the impact upon impressionable young minds of "pernicious literature"— dime novels, adventure and humour stories, illustrated magazines, all from down south. The American-style people's journals caught on first with clerks, factory workers, domestics, and the like, some of whom had never before been regular newspaper readers. The records of mechanic's institutes and public libraries (many of which were assisted by the generosity of the American millionaire Andrew Carnegie) indicated a definite popular taste for escapist novels, much to the disgust of moralists….

In short, the building of a Victorian Canada was very much an elite cause, though undeniably the ethos had many champions among urban professionals and businessmen as well as in the farm homes of rural Canada. The rougher elements of society preferred an entertainment that was imported from the United States or that imitated American ways.

"The conclusion to which all the converging lines of evidence unmistakably point is that the Americans and the English-speaking Canadians have been welded into one people," wrote the American Samuel E. Moffett in 1907, in a Ph.D thesis first entitled *The Emancipation of Canada*, later *The Americanization of Canada*. "The English-speaking Canadians protest that they will never become Americans—they are already Americans without knowing it."[14] Moffett was right, up to a point: a continental outlook was in the making. The mythology of individualism, the belief in "home, sweet home," the image of the evil city—these and many other notions were shared by people living on both sides of the border. Yet even he recognized that Canadian leaders and newspapers were devoted to their British dominion and hostile to absorption into the flawed republic. Besides, in French Canada the persistence of a traditional cast of mind and the powerful influence of Catholicism buttressed a separate and distinct sense of nationality. Nearly as important, at least in English Canada, was the presence of the British counterweight: …[i]t was not surprising that the Conservative opposition won a spectacular victory in 1911, in part by warning voters that the reciprocity agreement sponsored by Sir Wilfrid Laurier's Liberals would swiftly lead to the absorption of Canada by the United States. This merely reaffirmed the fact that Canadians were the other Americans.

In retrospect, the 1920s were a turning-point in cultural history. Especially in the cities, Canadians became wedded to the idea that a continuous supply of American entertainment and sports was their birthright. In part that was because of the decline or disappearance of any countervailing forces to American influences. But the chief cause was actually Canada's porous border: there was an extraordinary increase in the pace and scope of that American penetration which had always been an aspect of the Canadian experience. Provincial governments speeded the arrival of the so-called car culture by pouring money into highway development to attract the Yankee tourist, even though rural voters were none too pleased by the invasion of the automobile—two to four million American cars were coming each year by the end of the 1920s.[15]

...The most important agencies of Americanization, however, were the old and new media of mass communications.... The circulation of American magazines had reached some 50 million copies by 1926: four years later *Pictorial Review, McCall's, True Story,* and *Saturday Evening Post* (which called itself, with some exaggeration, "Canada's leading magazine") had over 100,000 Canadian sales per issue.[16] But while some Canadian magazines survived, a Canadian movie industry did not. When the Hollywood moguls took control of production, distribution, and exhibition right after the war, the few Canadian interests, such as the producer Ernest Shipman or the Allen chain of cinemas, were replaced or swallowed up, as were independents throughout the continent. People in ever-increasing numbers watched the Hollywood product: there were over 100 million paid admissions by 1930, making movie stars like Mary Pickford, Douglas Fairbanks, or Tom Mix Canada's stars as well (Pickford, America's sweetheart, happened to be Toronto-born).

And it appeared that radio, the most recent of the new media, would go the same way, since the development of private radio was extremely slow by comparison with the explosive growth in the United States, where the NBC and CBS networks were already supplying enriched programming. It was estimated that 80 per cent of the programs Canadians listened to at the end of the 1920s were American.[17] Three of the country's most important radio stations—CKAC (Montreal), CFRB (Toronto), and CKGW (Toronto)—became affiliates of American networks in 1929.[18] That enabled CKGW to bring in NBC's highly successful *Amos 'n' Andy,* which had already proved as popular with Canadian audiences as with American. All of this foreshadowed an American takeover of the airwaves.

...The chief American agency was Hollywood, which during the 1920s marketed a large number of "northerns," portraying Canada as a great, often snowy wilderness, where wolves, halfbreeds, whites, and Mounties fought each other and nature, where the unspoiled environment held out the hope of moral regeneration. Even the state played its part, through tourist advertisements, scenic films, and promotions designed to attract resource capital. It was fitting that the Canada pavilion at the famous "World of Tomorrow" World's Fair in New York in 1939 presented an impression of Canada as a largely unpopulated place full of scenic wonders and infinite resources.[19] It all suggested a land without a past, but with a glorious future.

That kind of imagery may have disturbed some observers. Much more worrisome, though, was the fact that the mass culture of America posed a severe challenge to the Victorian ethos which gave an additional definition to the dominion.... Simply put, mass culture rejected some of its core values (like self-restraint), transmuted others (like home, sweet home), and incorporated another group (like femininity or individualism). And it absorbed elements of pre-existing subcultures that had been outside the mainstream, whether regional (southern country music), ethnic (black ragtime), proletarian (rough sports), or youth (experimentation) to fashion a new, ersatz brew that appealed to every-man and everywoman, and most especially to the middle classes.

…Little wonder that the onslaught of mass culture upset moralists, nationalists, and those who would soon be called highbrows in Canada. Indeed, many a critic belonged to all of these camps. The hold of traditionalism on the country's intelligentsia was extraordinary, not just in the 1920s but for the next generation as well, and their views were often echoed by church and women's groups, in the daily press, and by home-grown magazines. "How can a generation fed on movies and bred on motors understand Wordsworth?" asked the academic Archibald MacMechan.[20]

…Increasingly, critics had begun to wrap themselves in the flag and argue the merits of cultural sovereignty. The danger for Canada no longer lay in annexation, Archibald MacMechan warned in 1920, but "in a spiritual bondage—the subjugation of the Canadian nation's mind and soul to the mind and soul of the United States."[21] Avoiding this imminent peril required that the state either privilege or establish media that would express and nourish Canada's soul. That was not easy to do. Proposals for a yearly quota requiring that perhaps 20 per cent of the films displayed should be British were impractical, partly because of industry opposition but also because there were not enough British movies and those that were available often did not appeal to audiences. In 1931 the Conservative government imposed special duties on American magazines with many ads or full of fiction or comics (in a word, lowbrow). Circulation figures published some years later indicated that the leading Canadian periodicals gained while their American rivals lost; even so, the duties disappeared after the Liberals returned to power in 1935. The lasting achievements were the establishment of public radio in 1932, the Canadian Broadcasting Corporation in 1936, and the National Film Board in 1939, which gave the state tools to realize some of the goals of cultural nationalism.

In fact, the record of these state agencies of culture was mixed. Under the masterly direction of John Grierson, the British documentary filmmaker, the NFB excelled as a source of wartime propaganda which reached millions because it was able to use regular cinemas and to establish non-theatrical circuits to show the product. But that did not threaten the dominance of Hollywood, and after the war the significance of the NFB quickly waned.

The CBC, by contrast, did become an instrument of mass entertainment, or rather two different kinds of entertainment, because it was divided into French and English services, which prevented public radio from ever realizing early hopes that it would build a pan-Canadian consciousness. The French service managed to exploit the existing tradition of popular literature in Quebec to produce some extraordinarily successful radioromans about life in Quebec's past and present. The English service had more success with its hockey broadcasts, which finally made hockey Canada's national sport and the announcer Foster Hewitt a household name, and with its radio plays, notably Andrew Allan's *Stage* series, which featured adapted and original plays by Canadians and won a large enough audience to become the national theatre of English Canada. Yet often the biggest draws on the CBC schedule were the American imports, carried to please listeners and wean them away from American stations. Thus in the February 1950 ratings sweepstakes the top two radio programs on CBL-Toronto were *The Bob Hope Show* and *Fibber McGee and Molly*, followed at some distance by a similar Canadian offering, *The Wayne and Shuster Show*.[22]

The CBC's importance in radio also waned after the war because independent private stations grew in number and power, and so in reach; they offered Canadians a steady diet of recorded American music as well as comedy and drama. But the CBC excelled as a producer of educational broadcasts, opinion forums, and high-quality programming (notably *Wednesday Night*), which earned it kudos from highbrows, though these offerings hardly constituted a counterweight to American imports.

The reality was that Canadian audiences, and especially anglophone audiences, by and large preferred the imported American entertainment even to home-grown imitations, never mind to high-quality material. That did not make them into Americans, however. A survey of opinion carried out by H.F. Angus and other researchers during the mid-1930s indicated that the images of American life flooding Canada often upset Canadians and convinced them of the superiority of their own country. Americans were seen as excitable, even "childlike," "money-mad," lawless, "more corrupt" and "less moral," boastful, and "less cultured," although they were given credit for being "daring and enterprising" or generous. By contrast, Canadians appeared more honourable, law-abiding, and conservative, and their society "quieter, slower in tempo and saner in quality."[23] Public opinion polls during and after the war indicated a similar desire to remain separate: true, in 1943 21 per cent of respondents did feel Canada ought to join the United States, but that figure had fallen to 10 per cent in 1952, where it would remain throughout the 1950s.[24] Put another way, the onslaught of mass culture had not yet destroyed the Victorian imprint on the Canadian identity.

No one should have been surprised that the famous post-war "culture probe," the Massey Commission, worried about "the very present danger of permanent dependence" on "a single alien source." Nor that it espoused an elitist definition of culture ("that part of education which enriches the mind and refines the taste") and evinced a disdain for the vulgarity and the materialism it found all too common on the air and in print.[25] The Massey Commission was born out of "the revolt of the highbrows" against the rule of commerce and the influence of mass culture. A loose coalition of arts, letters, musical, and academic groups took up a crusade to civilize Canada and, in the process, to assert their own significance as a cultural elite. Vincent Massey, the man chosen to head the commission, had already published a tract entitled *On Being Canadian* (1948), wherein he proclaimed the need for the Canadian people to recognize the claims of the arts and crafts, high culture, and the academy, and for the state to sponsor the growth of high culture. He was joined by three academics and one lonely engineer, placing the ivory tower in command. Their 1951 report, both lengthy (517 pages) and literate (opening with a quote from St. Augustine), became the new bible for the cultural nationalists.

Things would change, though not always as the commissioners had hoped. The next fifteen years witnessed the apparent victory of a mature and homogeneous mass culture over the separate identities of class, region, and rural life across the whole of North America. Sports, advertising, and above all entertainment offered a much needed solace to North Americans in a world of insecurity and complexity by propagating, as Roland Marchand has chronicled, "compensating, vicarious adventures in potency and dominion" for a mass of anxious consumers.[26] Canada was no exception: more leisure and more money broke down the old barriers to permissiveness, though it did take time. Beginning in the early 1950s, liquor laws slowly eased across English Canada, Sunday sports and Sunday newspapers became common, and the courts, the customs officials, and the movie censors proved increasingly lenient in their standards of acceptability. The discovery of teenagers set loose a youth cult with its own music, style of dress, codes of behaviour, products, and heroes: when *Love Me Tender*, Elvis Presley's first film, opened in Toronto in 1956, adolescents broke through the cinema's doors, knocked over police and ushers, smashed two mirrors, tore down Elvis posters, and "used lipstick to scribble 'I Love You' on his publicity stills."[27] A shopping madness swept over the land: total retail sales rose from $5.8 billion in 1946 to $16.5 billion in 1960, which brought into being that new focus of urban life, the shopping plaza—and, briefly in 1968, a venue for a "pop" style of politics because of the newcomer Trudeau, dubbed Pierre de la Plaza.[28]

…The victory of the mass culture soon proved illusory. Even in the United States the waning enthusiasm for television, the birth of the counterculture, the feminist assault on advertising and entertainment, and eventually a neo-conservative reaffirmation of "old values" represented something of a reaction against the images and authority of mass culture. In Canada the sense of the country as a distinct public entity, with its own brand of law, politics, and governance and a civic ethic, had survived the new wave of Americanization. Indeed, at the end of the 1960s the country seemed afire with competing brands of nationalisms: Pierre Trudeau's biculturalism, René Lévesque's separatism, the anti-Americanism of the leftist Waffle element in the NDP, a renewed cultural chauvinism, plus a variety of amalgams and variations….

…One of the signs of a distinct civic ethic was the emergence of the politics of culture as an important dimension of public life, much more vital in Canada than in the United States. The Massey report legitimized the belief that the state must become a major player in the cultural life of the country. Over the course of the next generation the federal government steadily expanded its activities into more and more realms of mass communications, sports, recreation, and leisure activities. It endeavoured to mastermind the development of television (a striking contrast with the neglect of radio in the 1920s), initially relying on CBC-TV, but after 1958 creating a complicated mix of private and public services purportedly wedded to a common purpose through the workings of the Canadian content regulations and a semi-autonomous regulatory agency.

The CBC remained the government's main cultural instrument. Its expenditures grew from $10 million a year in 1949–50 to almost $1.4 billion in 1990–91 (of which the government contributed nearly $1 billion).[29] The government established the Canada Council in 1957 to fund "the production of works in the arts, humanities, and social sciences"; the council and other special programs and related agencies became central to the continued health and welfare of the arts and academe in Canada.[30] In the early 1960s the state moved forcefully into amateur sports, motivated by a cult of fitness as well as the pursuit of national unity and glory, for world sports had become a new arena of national competition. In 1965 it amended the Income Tax Act to block foreign ownership of newspapers and periodicals. Similar restrictions extended in 1976 to broadcasting, although the government stayed away from regulating the content of print, evidence of the continued homage paid to the notion of a free press.

In 1968 the government created the Canadian Film Development Corporation (now Telefilm Canada) to promote a feature film industry that might finally challenge

Hollywood's control. In 1970 the Canadian Radio-television Commission, as it was then known, required that 30 per cent of all music played on AM radio be Canadian; the intention was to promote a record industry and a home-grown style of popular music. The provinces (and even well-off municipalities) soon got into the act, with the establishment of arts councils, educational TV, publishing grants, and the like. In short, the scope of the state's cultural policies far exceeded the wildest dreams of the Massey Commission by the time activity slowed down in the mid-1970s.

What has all this state activity actually achieved? Fortunately, the new interest of the state coincided with a burgeoning arts movement. Massey's goal of civilizing the country was realized, and one should thank the Canada Council (along with business patrons) for acting as "midwife" to "the upsurge of the arts" that occurred after 1960.[31] Further, the state worked to nourish a cultural elite of authors, artists, performers, producers, and the like, centred in Montreal and Toronto, who took on the neverending task of interpreting and defending the Canadian experience. The flowering of the novel in English Canada, the excitement of the Quebec theatre, and the booming interest in native and Inuit art are evidence that not all of the doleful effects of mass culture have been realized: the "bad" does not necessarily drive out the "good." Canada does have a "literature," or maybe two "literatures".... However distinct, this literature by and large falls into the category of elite culture, consumed much more by the highly literate than by ordinary people.

The achievements in the realm of the popular arts were not as spectacular because they were already overwhelmingly American, especially in English-speaking Canada. In the 1950s and 1960s managers and producers at CBC-TV hoped that they would be able to offer a complete service, including "something distinctive in the entertainment field" to Canadian viewers.[32] The age-old disdain for the popular arts had finally lost its force. In 1960 the president of the CBC, Alphonse Ouimet, declared that "Canadian culture embraces everything from sled-dog races to symphony orchestras, from comedy to opera, from good talks to jazz."[33]

Yet in reality only Radio-Canada, as before, had much permanent success in this endeavour: it was able to design a collection of téléromans, the first being the famous *La Famille Plouffe*, which drew upon the distinctive traditions and stereotypes in the popular culture of Quebec. In Toronto, by contrast, the TV experiment soon floundered, after some brief success with variety programming, because of limited talent and resources. Many an Anglo-Canadian artist left the country once his or her accomplishments brought job offers from elsewhere: the film director and producer Norman Jewison was only one in a long line of CBC producers who found "happiness" in Hollywood. In addition, CBC-TV had to carry American imports in choice locations on the prime-time schedule, and in greater numbers than in the radio days, to satisfy viewers and to generate the advertising revenues necessary to finance its home-grown programming. The launching of independent private television in 1960 did not bring about the promised development of a made-in-Canada entertainment; instead, it merely increased the amount of air time given over to American imports in order to guarantee profits. That was what viewers wanted, even in Quebec, where the independent Channel 10 was able to capture Montrealers by offering dubbed American series.

To put it another way, Canadians generally preferred to watch Hollywood film and TV drama, to listen to imported rock and roll, or to read American genre fiction as their chief source of relaxation. From the late 1960s Canadian homes eagerly embraced cable television because it promised them, in addition to better signal reception, access to a wider range of American programming. The Caplan-Sauvageau task force on broadcasting was disturbed by evidence that even in French Canada audiences, especially young people, were consuming more and more American products (dubbed, imported, or direct) than ever before.[34]

...The great defenders of home-grown entertainment have always been the cultural elite, who have persuaded themselves that Anglo-Canadians would consume more if more was only available. That assertion remains dubious: even if production values in Toronto matched those of Hollywood (and it is amazing how often people claim they can "tell" a Canadian show by its look and feel), the fact that the artistic producers will avoid the clichés and the conventions of Hollywood actually makes their work more difficult and less accessible to an audience in search of relaxation. The taste for Canadian entertainment remains particular—except for the occasional *Anne of Green Gables,* which strikes the fancy of the masses. No wonder assertions that the Canada–U.S. free trade agreement posed a threat to Canada's apparently fragile culture did not provoke much response from the public.

...The strategy of resistance urged by Canada's nationalists is, at bottom, another example of the highbrow disdain for mass culture, reflecting presumptions about television, movies, and literature that would be readily accepted in the homes of American intellectuals and academics.... The rather chilling notion of a "Fortress Canada" which seems to attract some members of the cultural elite does not fit the reality of what has happened, especially since the advent of television: it amounts to a retreat into a past that never was to suit the ambitions and tastes of a small minority of writers and artists.[35]

...Three images of Canada have occurred time and again in our past and retain their force among the intelligentsia and the public even today. The first of these portrays Canada as a peaceable kingdom, devoted to the hallowed goals of peace, order, and good government, a haven of sanity and tolerance in a disturbed world, a country that is less aggressive and more humane than its American neighbour. That image harks back, of course, to the Victorian and British past, although nowadays its apologists usually perceive the country's experience from the perspective of politics: Canadian history becomes a story of prime ministers and premiers, careful compromises, judicial and constitutional wrangles, a benevolent state, and occasionally British regulars and the RCMP to add a bit of spice. Enthusiasts can look forward to a future in which Canada may "serve as a guide to other peoples who are seeking a pathway to the peaceable kingdom!"[36] What is emphasized here is the ideal of citizenship, the loyalty to a particular polity. The sense of self this image propagates has a good deal of residual strength among Canadians: it is worth remembering that the federal election campaign in 1988 was upset when challenger John Turner managed to persuade a number of people that the Canada–U.S. free trade agreement imperilled our social programs and our political sovereignty.

The second image is "Canada as Nature," an inexact phrase that can incorporate related images of the Great North, the land of empty spaces, or wilderness Canada. When it figures at all, the past becomes a story of individuals and groups who have usually conquered or exploited the land. More attention is generally paid to some golden future: the imagery can accommodate the fetish of technology, whereby man has or will overcome nature, as well as the newer dream of ecology, wherein man lives in harmony with nature. Evidence of its appeal is found in various kinds of advertising, notably tourist ads, as well as in public celebrations, particularly Vancouver's Expo 86.

These two images are in many ways complimentary. The literature about the Niagara region available for sale to the tourist, for example, evidences the two mythologies about Canada. Some English-speaking historians of a conservative persuasion have written chronicles of Canada which incorporate elements of both, notably W.L. Morton in *The Canadian Identity*. Each can accommodate the metaphor of the mosaic or the slogan "unity in diversity" (or Joe Clark's "community of communities") in which Canada becomes a home for many different peoples and cultures. The popularity of multiculturalism in official circles has given this metaphor a good deal of currency, particularly in the schools. Perhaps most important, though, the notions of the peaceable kingdom and Canada as Nature present Canada as very un-American or other-American.[37] In this scheme of things the United States becomes a melting-pot, an industrial dynamo, a land of liberty and licence, an imperial power beset by troubles or sins that can induce a certain smugness in Canadians.

The last image, by contrast, is bleak: Canada appears as a victim, a vassal state, a perpetual colony, an imaginary nation or a non-nation. It has a special attraction for the cultural elite: Robert Fulford (himself a member of this elite) has shaken his head over the pessimism of his fellows, over their "distinct sense of failure, expressed as often as possible in the most alarming terms," whatever the proof to the contrary.[38] The dismal mythology of dependence was first constructed by conservatives like Harold Adams Innis, and later picked up by radicals like Dallas Smythe, to justify their hostility towards American influences, especially economic and cultural imperialism. In its milder expressions, such as that articulated by Margaret Atwood some years ago, the image of the victim highlights the theme of survival in Canadian life.[39] At its most extreme, dependency theory leads to the assumption that Canada's national identity is "purely fictional," in the words of Tony Wilden—designed to hide the fact that "we are colonized—historically, economically, socially, politically, and personally."[40] Both versions, though, amount to a call to arms, a demand that Canadians resist a culture made in America and seek their own destiny.

The image of victim or colony, then, is the most logical expression of cultural nationalism on the intellectual scene in Canada. But it is also the least popular of the three images, since it requires Canadians to deny what has long been part of their symbolic and ideological heritage—namely, the popular arts of the United States—if not to treat everything American as an implacable enemy.

Of all of these images and identities, I think that history is on the side of the mythology of the peaceable kingdom, always allowing for the fact that its most enthusiastic apologists substitute wish for reality. That is because the mythology admits, if only by implication, the importance of the public arts and a distinct political culture as the source of lasting definition in Canada. Frank Sinatra and Michael Jackson, Louis L'Amour and Roger Zelazny, *Miami Vice* and *The Cosby Show*, *Fatal Attraction* and *Nightmare on Elm Street*, *Monday Night Football* and Budweiser ads and even Jimmy Swaggart become merely commodities, something we consume the way we do Coke and hot dogs. The commodities have an impact: I recall hearing on *The Journal* some years ago a Montreal policeman declare that many of his colleagues were attracted into the service by images of fast cars and an exciting life served up in Hollywood's crime shows. But mass culture in itself does not pose, and never has posed, a direct threat to the Canadian identity, because consumers have "read" its messages through a special lens made in Canada. Canada is living proof that the doctrine of nationalism does not really explain how things work.

NOTES

1. Canada, *Parliamentary Debates on the Subject of Confederation of the British North American Provinces,* (Quebec 1865) 86.

2. The quoted phrases are taken from *Le Monde,* 20 December 1887, and the *London Advertiser,* 9 October 1893, respectively.

3. P.B. Waite, "Sir Oliver Mowat's Canada: Reflections on an Un-Victorian Society," *Oliver Mowat's Ontario,* ed. Donald Swainson (Toronto 1972) 12–32.

4. Alison Prentice, *The School Promoters: Education and Social Class in Mid-Nineteenth-Century Upper Canada* (Toronto 1977) 53.

5. James Gray, *Booze: The Impact of Whiskey on the Prairie West* (Toronto 1972) 20–37.

6. See Frank Abbott, "Cold Cash and Ice Palaces: The Quebec Winter Carnival of 1894," *Canadian Historical Review* 69 (1988): 167–202.

7. Paul Rutherford, "The People's Press: The Emergence of the New Journalism in Canada, 1869–1899," *Canadian Historical Review* 56 (June 1975): 167–91.

8. Printer and Publisher, August 1895, 1.

9. *Le Monde,* Paris, 28 September 1892.

10. M.E. Nichols, *The Story of the Canadian Press* (Toronto 1938).

11. Mary Vipond, "National Consciousness in English-Speaking Canada in the 1920s: Seven Studies," Ph.D. thesis, University of Toronto, 1974, 394.

12. See George Parker, *The Beginnings of the Book Trade in Canada* (Toronto 1985) which carries the story up to the end of the nineteenth century.

13. Mary Vipond, "Best Sellers in English Canada, 1899–1918: An Overview," *Journal of Canadian Fiction* 24 (1979): 108.

14. Samuel Moffett, *The Americanization of Canada* (New York 1907) 114.

15. This rapid expansion of the "car culture" probably would not have happened otherwise. See Donald Davis, "Dependent Motorization: Canada and the Automobile to the 1930s," *Journal of Canadian Studies* 21 (1986): 106–32.

16. See J.A. Stephenson, "American Periodical Literature," in H.F. Angus, ed., *Canada and Her Great Neighbor: Sociological Surveys of Opinions and Attitudes in Canada Concerning the United States* (Toronto 1938) 152–72, and Mary Vipond, "Canadian Nationalism and the Plight of Canadian Magazines in the 1920s," *Canadian Historical Review* 58 (1977): 43–63.

17. Margaret Prang, "The Origins of Public Broadcasting in Canada," *Canadian Historical Review* 46 (1965): 4.

18. Frank Peers, *The Politics of Canadian Broadcasting 1920–1951* (Toronto 1969) 56–8.

19. Joyce Nelson, *The Colonized Eye: Rethinking the Grierson Legend* (Toronto 1988) 50–1.

20. MacMechan was an English professor at Dalhousie University in Halifax. S.E.D. Shortt, *The Search for an Ideal: Six Canadian Intellectuals and their Convictions in an Age of Transition 1890–1930* (Toronto 1976) 47.

21. MacMechan, "Canada as a Vassal State," *Canadian Historical Review* 1:4 (December 1920): 347.

22. Data from Elliott-Haynes, *Program Report,* February 1950 (available in box no. 6 of the broadcast ratings collection of the Moving Image and Sound Archives, National Archives of Canada, Ottawa).

23. See Angus, *Canada and Her Great Neighbor* 383–449.

24. Cited in Mildred A. Schwartz, *Public Opinion and Canadian Identity* (Scarborough 1967) 74.

25. Canada, Royal Commission on National Development in the Arts, Letters, and Sciences (the Massey Commission), *Report* (Ottawa 1951): 18, 7.

26. Roland Marchand, "Visions of Classlessness, Quests for Dominion: American Popular Culture, 1945–1960," *Reshaping America: Society and Institutions 1945–1960,* ed. Robert H. Brenner and Gary W. Reichard (Columbus, Ohio 1982) 170.

27. Alexander Ross, *The Booming Fifties: 1950–1960* (Toronto 1977) 43. Ross's book has some marvelous stories about the moods of the 1950s, not the least being his chapter on "The Discovery of the Teenager."

28. M.C. Urguhart and K.A.H. Buckley, *Historical Statistics of Canada* (Toronto 1965), series T1-24, 571.

29. *Canada Year-Book 1952–53* (Ottawa 1953), 848; and *Public Accounts of Canada 1990–91,* vol. 3, (Ottawa 1991), iv-104.

30. J.L. Granatstein, *Canada 1957–1967: The Years of Uncertainty and Innovation* (Toronto 1986) 143.

31. George Woodcock, *Strange Bedfellows: The State and the Arts in Canada* (Vancouver 1985) 71.

32. Quotation from the CBC's "Memorandum" to the Royal Commission on Broadcasting (the Fowler Commission) 15.

33. Quoted in *CBC Times,* 23–29 January 1960, 27.

34. *Report of the Task Force on Broadcasting Policy,* 205–56.

35. I am indebted to John Ingham for the phrase "Fortress Canada."

36. Quotation taken from the jacket blurb for William Kilbourn, ed., *Canada: A Guide to the Peaceable Kingdom* (Toronto 1970). There is more of this kind of rhetoric in Kilbourn's own introduction.

37. One of the best examples of this sort of amalgam, full of all manner of cliché, is Pierre Berton's *Why We Act Like Canadians: A Personal Exploration of Our National Character* (Toronto 1987), a 1982 book reprinted for the free trade debate.

38. Fulford was referring to both cultural nationalism and feminism, citing especially the example of Margaret Atwood, Robert Fulford, *Best Seat in the House: Memoirs of a Lucky Man* (Toronto 1988) 187.

39. Margaret Atwood, *Survival: A Thematic Guide to Canadian Literature* (Toronto 1972).

40. Tony Wilden, *The Imaginary Canadian: An Examination for Discovery* (Vancouver 1980) 2.

8   Naomi Klein, "Alt.everything: The Youth Market and the Marketing of Cool," from *No Logo*

Editors' Introduction

"Alt.everything" is taken from Naomi Klein's influential and contentious book, *No Logo: Taking Aim at the Brand Bullies*. Klein, a Canadian journalist, argues against the synthesizing effects of global capitalism via "branding." "Branding" defines the process whereby companies market as opposed to selling products. This process speaks to Marx's logic of commodity fetishism and to the magic of advertising that Raymond Williams describes. Yet "branding" is more than just hypermarketing in these later stages of global capitalism. Corporate logos are now "cultural accessories and lifestyle philosophers" (Klein 16). They define and reflect a whole way of life for the subjects and groups they "brand" within a seemingly inescapable matrix of corporate (and, thus, cultural) identities and identifications. As Klein argues below, branding is about the "colonization not of physical space but of mental space," and "branding's insatiable cultural thirst just creates more marketing. Marketing that thinks it is culture" (118). Marketing, in short, is now the culture that does our thinking for us. In the introduction to her book, Klein states that we understand the world through a "global web of logos and products" that speak the "euphoric marketing rhetoric of the global village, an incredible place where tribespeople in remotest rain forests tap away on laptop computers, Sicilian grandmothers conduct E-business, and 'global teens' share, to borrow a phrase from a Levi's Web site, 'a world-wide style culture'" (Klein xvii). Like the function of style in Adorno and Horkheimer's culture industry, global "style" is now writ large across the globe. It signifies how, for better or for worse, we are all tied together within a vast strategy that manufactures identities by marketing attitudes.

Klein's approach is implicitly Marxist. She exposes underneath the virtual reality of brand logos the often noxious material effects of global capitalism. This exposure is political in that it gives voice to individual and collective agencies otherwise deadened by branding, as it predetermines every aspect of how we think about ourselves. Klein's "is not a book of predictions, but of first-hand observations" (Klein xviii) which locate her analysis firmly in the field of social and critical practice. She speaks for an anticorporate activism that seeks to change not only how we think of corporations but how corporations think about themselves. As Klein says in her conclusion, rather than a "collection of protectionists getting together out of necessity to fight everything and anything global," "connections" between activists around the globe "have formed across national lines" so that "a different agenda has taken hold, one that embraces globalization but seeks to wrest it from the grasp of the multinationals" (Klein 445). She, thus, calls for global citizenship, rather than global consumerism. In an increasingly global community, citizens must demand within the public arena of international governmental regulation that multinationals be compelled to make their "public relations" really count for something, rather than merely act as a tool to divert public attention away from corporate capitalism's more egregious practices.

This argument can seem reductively pro-political and critically oversimplified in its reading of corporate culture as a sphere of increasing homogenization. When one looks on the back cover of Klein's book, one finds a red circle and slash through the corporate logo for Vintage Canada, Klein's publisher. Using "no logo" to bite the hand that feeds, Klein's gesture is tactical and ironic, but not a little disingenuous. Her work is likewise criticized for being unscholarly because she is a columnist and—heresy of heresies—writing outside the academy and, thus, more within than against corporate culture. How can her journalistic gathering of evidence match that of a "real" sociologist or cultural critic? This is precisely why we have included her work, for the kind of theorizing of culture that we are asking you to undertake is not necessarily, or even always desirably, the province of the academy. Klein writes from a vexed position that challenges our own illusions about academic "objectivity" or "purity." And there is no denying the polemical force of Klein's work, not to mention the great influence it has had in cultural, communication, and mass media studies.

Finally, "Alt.everything" speaks to the very population in whom Klein first noted an anticorporate resistance and activism: postsecondary students, our target audience for this anthology. Her emphasis below is the commodification of youth culture through the branding of what is "cool" in order to individuate whole segments of the youth market as consumers for life (a process that Disney perfects in an even younger demographic, as Henry Giroux argues). "Cool" branding turns otherwise "vibrant cultural ideas," such as camp or grunge, into ironic self-reflections on themselves, into "archeological artifacts" (128). Klein's point is that students need to be all too aware of themselves as "cool" artifacts, rather than "cool" individuals—that is, as subjects who matter differently from whatever significance corporate culture dictates to them. More importantly, they "were preoccupied with the inroads private corporations were making into their public schools" (Klein xviii) and, thus, were broadening their concern with "issues of discrimination and identity—race, gender, and sexuality" to consider the "workings of corporate power, labor rights, and a fairly developed analysis of the working of global economy" (Klein xix). This statement itself speaks to the current state of cultural studies, which, in many academic programs across the country, is quickly shifting to a focus on global studies and to an investigation of the pros and cons of culture as a matrix of global phenomena. It also speaks to a particularly Canadian dilemma that we highlight throughout this anthology: what happens when even "camp" or "ironic" versions of one's identity (two aspects of Klein's discussion below)—as when Canada defines itself as the postmodern versions of other selves, American corporate and political culture among them—*become* the real? Perhaps the resistances of the youth culture for and of whom Klein speaks in *No Logo* are the best answer to this question.

—JF

ISSUES TO CONSIDER WHILE READING

1. Adorno and Horkheimer's essay offers a vision of subjects as mere dupes of the culture industry. In what ways is this vision too limited for our understanding of

twenty-first century cultural subjects? In what ways is it accurate? You might want to think of this question in relation to the Naomi Klein excerpt in this volume.

2. When defining the culture industry, Adorno and Horkheimer are thinking of the kind of 'vertically integrated' model of industrial or economic organization offered by the old Hollywood studio system. In what ways do today's global or transnational corporations both conform to and refute this model?

REFERENCES AND FURTHER READING

Appadurai, Arjun, ed. *Modernity at Large: Cultural Dimensions of Globalization.* Minneapolis: University of Minneapolis Press, 1996.

Bauman, Zygmunt. *Globalization: The Human Consequences.* New York: Columbia University Press, 1998.

Giddens, Anthony. *Runaway World: How Globalization Is Reshaping Our Lives.* New York: Routledge, 2000.

Giroux, Henry. *Disturbing Pleasures.* New York: Routledge, 1994.

Hardt, Michael, and Antonio Negri. *Empire.* Cambridge, MA: Harvard University Press, 2000.

Klein, Naomi. *No Logo: Taking Aim at the Brand Bullies.* Toronto: Vintage Canada, 2000.

Robertson, Roland. *Globalization: Social Theory and Global Culture.* London: Sage, 1992.

Alt.everything: The Youth Market and the Marketing of Cool

…I remember the moment when it hit me that my frustrated craving for space wasn't simply a result of the inevitable march of history, but of the fact that commercial co-optation was proceeding at a speed that would have been unimaginable to previous generations. I was watching the television coverage of the controversy surrounding Woodstock '94, the twenty-fifth-anniversary festival of the original Woodstock event. The baby-boomer pundits and aging rock stars postured about how the $2 cans of Woodstock Memorial Pepsi, festival key chains and on-site cash machines betrayed the anticommercial spirit of the original event and, incredibly, whined that the $3 commemorative condoms marked the end of "free love" (as if AIDS had been cooked up as a malicious affront to their nostalgia).

What struck me most was that the debate revolved entirely around the sanctity of the past, with no recognition of present-tense cultural challenges. Despite the fact that the anniversary festival was primarily marketed to teenagers and college students and showcased then-up-and-coming bands like Green Day, not a single commentator explored what this youth-culture "commodification" might mean to the young people who would actually be attending the event. Woodstock promoter John Roberts explained that today's youth are "used to sponsorship. If a kid went to a concert and there wasn't merchandise to buy, he'd probably go out of his mind."[1]

Roberts isn't the only one who holds this view. *Advertising Age* reporter Jeff Jensen goes so far as to make the claim that for today's young people, "Selling out is not only accepted, it's considered hip."[2] To object would be, well, unhip. There is no need to further romanticize the original Woodstock. Among (many) other things, it was also a big-label-backed rock festival, designed to turn a profit. Still, the myth of Woodstock as a sovereign youth-culture state was part of a vast project of generational self-definition—a concept that would have been wholly foreign to those in attendance at Woodstock '94, for whom generational identity had largely been a prepackaged good and for whom the search for self had always been shaped by marketing hype, whether or not they believed it or defined themselves against it. This is a side effect of brand expansion that is far more difficult to track and quantify than the branding of culture and city spaces. This loss of space happens inside the individual; it is a colonization not of physical space but of mental space.

In a climate of youth-marketing feeding frenzy, all culture begins to be created with the frenzy in mind. Much of youth culture becomes suspended in what sociologists Robert Goldman and Stephen Papson call "arrested development," noting that "we have, after all, no idea of what punk or grunge or hip hop as social and cultural movements might look like if they were not mined for their gold . . ."[3]. This "mining" has not gone unnoticed or unopposed. Both the anticorporate cultural journal *The Baffler* and the now-defunct *Might* magazine brilliantly lampooned the desperation and striving of the youth-culture industry in the mid-nineties. Dozens, if not hundreds, of zines and Web sites have been launched and have played no small part in setting the mood for the kind of brand-based attacks that I chronicle in Part IV of this book. For the most part, however, branding's insatiable cultural thirst just creates more marketing. Marketing that thinks it is culture...

Crowd surfer at Woodstock 1994 concert. *Luc Novovitch/CP Picture Archive*

THE YOUTH MARKET SAVES THE DAY

…1992 was the first year since 1975 that the number of teenagers in America increased. Gradually, an idea began to dawn on many in the manufacturing sector and entertainment industries: This was not a time for selling Tide and Snuggy to housewives—it was a time for beaming MTV, Nike, Hilfiger, Microsoft, Netscape and *Wired* to global teens and their overgrown imitators. Their parents might have gone bargain basement, but kids, it turned out, were still willing to pay up to fit in. Through this process, peer pressure emerged as a powerful market force, making the keeping-up-with-the-Joneses consumerism of their suburban parents pale by comparison. As clothing retailer Elise Decoteau said of her teen shoppers, "They run in packs. If you sell to one, you sell to everyone in their class and everyone in their school."[4]

There was just one catch. As the success of branding superstars like Nike had shown, it was not going to be sufficient for companies simply to market their same products to a younger demographic; they needed to fashion brand identities that would resonate with this new culture, if they were going to turn their lackluster products into transcendent meaning machines—as the dictates of branding demanded—they would need to remake themselves in the image of nineties cool: its music, styles and politics.

COOL ENVY: THE BRANDS GO BACK TO SCHOOL

Fueled by the dual promises of branding and the youth market, the corporate sector experienced a burst of creative energy. Cool, alternative, young, hip—whatever you want to call it—was the perfect identity for product-driven companies looking to become transcendent image-based brands. Advertisers, brand managers, music, film and television producers raced back to high school, sucking up to the in-crowd in a frantic effort to isolate and reproduce in TV commercials the precise "attitude" teens and twenty-somethings were driven to consume with their snack foods and pop tunes. And as in high schools everywhere, "Am I cool?" became the deeply dull and all-consuming question of every moment, echoing not only through class and locker rooms, but through the high-powered meetings and conference calls of Corporate High.

The quest for cool is by nature riddled with self-doubt ("Is this cool?" one can hear the legions of teen shoppers nervously quizzing each other. "Do you think this is lame?") Except now the harrowing doubts of adolescence are the billion-dollar questions of our age. The insecurities go round and round the boardroom table, turning ad writers, art directors and CEOs into turbo-powered teenagers, circling in front of their bedroom mirrors trying to look blasé. Do the kids think we're cool? they want to know. Are we trying too hard to be cool, or are we really cool? Do we have attitude? The *right* attitude?

…The companies that are left out of the crowd of successfully hip brands—their sneakers too small, their pant-legs too tapered, their edgy ads insufficiently ironic—now skulk on the margins of society: the corporate nerds. "Coolness is still elusive for us," says Bill Benford, president of L.A. Gear athletic wear,[5] and one half expects him to slash his wrists like some anxious fifteen-year-old unable to face schoolyard exile for another term. No one is safe from this brutal ostracism, as Levi-Strauss learned in 1998. The verdict was merciless: Levi's didn't have superstores like Disney, it didn't have cool ads like The Gap, it didn't have hip-hop credibility like Hilfiger and no one wanted to tattoo its logo on their navel, like Nike. In short, it wasn't cool. It had failed to understand, as its new brand developer Sean Dee diagnosed, that "loose jeans is not a fad, it's a paradigm shift."[6]

Cool, it seems, is the make-or-break quality in 1990s branding. It is the ironic sneer-track of ABC sitcoms and late-night talk shows; it is what sells psychedelic Internet servers, extreme sports gear, ironic watches, mind-blowing fruit juices, kitsch-laden jeans, postmodern sneakers and post-gender colognes. Our "aspirational age," as they say in marketing studies, is about seventeen. This applies equally to the forty-seven-year-old baby boomers scared of losing their cool and the seven-year-olds kick-boxing to the Backstreet Boys.

As the mission of corporate executives becomes to imbue their companies with deep coolness, one can even foresee a time when the mandate of our elected leaders will be "Make the Country Cool." In many ways, that time is already here. Since his election in 1997, England's young prime minister, Tony Blair, has been committed to changing Britain's somewhat dowdy image to "Cool Britannia." After attending a summit with Blair in an art-directed conference room in Canary Wharf, French president Jacques Chirac said, "I'm impressed. It all gives Britain the image of a young, dynamic and modern country." At the G-8 summit in Birmingham, Blair turned the august gathering into a basement rec room get-together, where the leaders watched All Saints music videos and then were led in a round of "All You Need is Love"; no Nintendo games were reported. Blair is a world leader as nation stylist—but will his attempt to "rebrand Britain" really work, or will he be stuck with the old, outdated Brit brand?…

THE CHANGE AGENTS: COOLING THE WATER COOLER

The journey to our current state of world cool almost ended, however, before it really began. Even though by 1993 there was scarcely a fashion, food, beverage or entertainment company that didn't pine for what the youth market promised, many were at a loss as to how to get it. At the time that cool-envy hit, many corporations were in the midst of a hiring freeze, recovering from rounds of layoffs, most of which were executed according to the last-hired-first-fired policies of the late-eighties recession. With far fewer young workers on the payroll and no new ones coming up through the ranks, many corporate executives found themselves in the odd position of barely knowing anyone under thirty years old. In this stunted context, youth itself looked oddly exotic—and information about Xers, Generation Y and twenty-somethings was suddenly a most precious commodity.

Fortunately, a backlog of hungry twenty-somethings were already in the job market. Like good capitalists, many of these young workers saw a market niche: being professionally young. In so many words, they assured would-be bosses that if they were hired, hip, young countercultures would be hand-delivered at the rate of one per week; companies would be so cool, they would get respect in the scenes. They promised the youth demographic, the digital revolution, a beeline into convergence.

And as we now know, when they got the job, these conduits of cool saw no need to transform themselves into clone-ish Company Men. Many can be seen now, roaming the hallways of Fortune 500 corporations dressed like club kids, skateboard in tow. They drop references to all-night raves at the office water cooler ("Memo to the boss: why not fill this thing with ginseng-laced herbal iced tea?"). The CEOs of tomorrow aren't employees, they are, to use a term favored at IBM, "change agents." But are they impostors—scheming "suits" hiding underneath hip-hop snowboarding gear? Not at all. Many of these young workers are the real deal; the true and committed product of the scenes they serve up, and utterly devoted to the transformation of their brands. Like Tom Cruise in *Jerry Maguire,* they stay up late into the night penning manifestos, revolutionary tracts about the need to embrace the new, to flout bureaucracy, to get on the Web or be left behind, to redo the ad campaign with a groovier, grittier feel, to change quicker, be hipper.

And what do the change agent's bosses have to say about all this? They say bring it on, of course. Companies looking to fashion brand identities that will mesh seamlessly with the zeitgeist understand, as Marshall McLuhan wrote, "When a thing is current, it creates currency." The change agents stroke their bosses' middle-aged egos simply by showing up— how out of touch could the boss be with a radical like this on the same intranet system?...

COOL HUNTERS: THE LEGAL STALKERS OF YOUTH CULTURE

While the change agents were getting set to cool the corporate world from the inside out, a new industry of "cool hunters" was promising to cool the companies from the outside in. The major corporate cool consultancies—Sputnik, *The L. Report,* Bureau de Style— were all founded between 1994 and 1996, just in time to present themselves as the brands' personal cool shoppers. The idea was simple: they would search out pockets of cutting-edge lifestyle, capture them on videotape and return to clients like Reebok, Absolut Vodka and Levi's with such bold pronouncements as "Monks are cool."[7] They would advise their clients to use irony in their ad campaigns, to get surreal, to use "viral communications."

In their book *Street Trends,* Sputnik founders Janine Lopiano-Misdom and Joanne De Luca concede that almost anyone can interview a bunch of young people and make generalizations, "but how do you know they are the 'right' ones—have you been in their closets? Trailed their daily routines? Hung out with them socially? . . . Are they the core consumers, or the mainstream followers?"[8] Unlike the market researchers who use focus groups and one-way glass to watch kids as if they were overgrown lab rats, Sputnik is "one of them"—it is in with the in-crowd.

Of course all this has to be taken with a grain of salt. Cool hunters and their corporate clients are locked in a slightly S/M, symbiotic dance: the clients are desperate to believe in a just-beyond-their-reach well of untapped cool, and the hunters, in order to make their advice more valuable, exaggerate the crisis of credibility the brands face. On the off chance of Brand X becoming the next Nike, however, many corporations have been more than willing to pay up. And so, armed with their change agents and their cool hunters, the superbrands became the perennial teenage followers, trailing the scent of cool wherever it led.

In 1974, Norman Mailer described the paint sprayed by urban graffiti artists as artillery fired in a war between the street and the establishment. "You hit your name and maybe something in the whole scheme of the system gives a death rattle. For now your name is over their name . . . your presence is on their Presence, your alias hangs over their scene."[9] Twenty-five years later, a complete inversion of this relationship has taken place. Gathering tips from the graffiti artists of old, the superbrands have tagged everyone— including the graffiti writers themselves. No space has been left unbranded.

HIP-HOP BLOWS UP THE BRANDS

…Over the past decade, young black men in American inner cities have been the market most aggressively mined by the brandmasters as a source of borrowed "meaning" and identity. This was the key to the success of Nike and Tommy Hilfiger, both of which were catapulted to brand superstardom in no small part by poor kids who incorporated Nike and Hilfiger into hip-hop style at the very moment when rap was being thrust into the expanding youth-culture limelight by MTV and *Vibe* (the first mass-market hip-hop magazine, founded in 1992). "The hip-hop nation," write Lopiano-Misdom and De Luca in *Street Trends,* is "the first to embrace a designer or a major label, they make that label 'big concept' fashion. Or, in their words, they 'blow it up.'"[10]

Designers like Stussy, Hilfiger, Polo, DKNY and Nike have refused to crack down on the pirating of their logos for T-shirts and baseball hats in the inner cities and several of them have clearly backed away from serious attempts to curb rampant shoplifting. By now the big brands know that profits from logowear do not just flow from the purchase of the garment but also from people seeing your logo on "the right people," as Pepe Jeans' Phil Spur judiciously puts it. The truth is that the "got to be cool" rhetoric of the global brands is, more often than not, an indirect way of saying "got to be black." Just as the history of cool in America is really (as many have argued) a history of African-American culture—from jazz and blues to rock and roll to rap—for many of the superbrands, cool hunting simply means black-culture hunting. Which is why the cool hunters' first stop was the basketball courts of America's poorest neighborhoods.

The latest chapter in mainstream America's gold rush to poverty began in 1986, when rappers Run-DMC breathed new life into Adidas products with their hit single "My Adidas," a homage to their favorite brand. Already, the wildly popular rap trio had hordes of fans copying their signature style of gold medallions, black-and-white Adidas tracksuits and low-cut Adidas sneakers, worn without laces. "We've been wearing them all our lives," Darryl McDaniels (aka DMC) said of his Adidas shoes at the time.[11] That was fine for a time, but after a while it occurred to Russell Simmons, the president of Run-DMC's label Def Jam Records, that the boys should be getting paid for the promotion they were giving to Adidas. He approached the German shoe company about kicking in some money for the act's 1987 Together Forever tour. Adidas executives were skeptical about being associated with rap music, which at that time was alternately dismissed as a passing fad or vilified as an incitement to riot. To help change their minds, Simmons took a couple of Adidas bigwigs to a Run-DMC show. Christopher Vaughn describes the event in *Black Enterprise:* "At a crucial moment, while the rap group was performing the song ["My Adidas"], one of the members yelled out, 'Okay, everybody in the house, rock your Adidas!'—and three thousand pairs of sneakers shot in the air. The Adidas executives couldn't reach for their checkbooks fast enough."[12] By the time of the annual Atlanta sports-shoe Super Show that year, Adidas had unveiled its new line of Run-DMC shoes: the Super Star and the Ultra Star—"designed to be worn without laces."[13]

Since "My Adidas," nothing in inner-city branding has been left up to chance. Major record labels like BMG now hire "street crews" of urban black youth to talk up hip-hop albums in their communities and to go out on guerrilla-style postering and sticker missions. The L.A.-based Steven Rifkind Company bills itself as a marketing firm "specializing in building word-of-mouth in urban areas and inner cities."[14] Rifkind is CEO of the rap label Loud Records, and companies like Nike pay him hundreds of thousands of dollars to find out how to make their brands cool with trend-setting black youth.

So focused is Nike on borrowing style, attitude and imagery from black urban youth that the company has its own word for the practice: *bro-ing*. That's when Nike marketers and designers bring their prototypes to inner-city neighborhoods in New York, Philadelphia or Chicago and say, "Hey, bro, check out the shoes," to gauge the reaction to new styles and to build up a buzz. In an interview with journalist Josh Feit, Nike designer Aaron Cooper described his bro-ing conversion in Harlem: "We go to the playground, and we dump the shoes out. It's unbelievable. The kids go nuts. That's when you realize the importance of Nike. Having kids tell you Nike is the number one thing in their life—number two is their girlfriend."[15] Nike has even succeeded in branding the basketball courts where it goes bro-ing through its philanthropic wing, P.L.A.Y (Participate in the Lives of Youth). P.L.A.Y sponsors inner-city sports programs in exchange for high swoosh visibility, including giant swooshes at the center of resurfaced urban basketball courts. In tonier parts of the city, that kind of thing would be called an ad and the space would come at a price, but on this side of the tracks, Nike pays nothing, and files the cost under charity.

TOMMY HILFIGER: TO THE GHETTO AND BACK AGAIN

Tommy Hilfiger, even more than Nike or Adidas, has turned the harnessing of ghetto cool into a mass-marketing science. Hilfiger forged a formula that has since been imitated by Polo, Nautica, Munsingwear (thanks to Puff Daddy's fondness for the penguin logo) and several other clothing companies looking for a short cut to making it at the suburban mall with inner-city attitude.

Like a depoliticized, hyper-patriotic Benetton, Hilfiger ads are a tangle of Cape Cod multiculturalism: scrubbed black faces lounging with their windswept white brothers and sisters in that great country club in the sky, and always against the backdrop of a billowing American flag. "By respecting one another we can reach all cultures and communities," the company says. "We promote . . . the concept of living the American dream."[16] But the hard facts of Tommy's interracial financial success have less to do with finding common ground between cultures than with the power and mythology embedded in America's deep racial segregation.

Tommy Hilfiger started off squarely as white-preppy wear in the tradition of Ralph Lauren and Lacoste. But the designer soon realized that his clothes also had a peculiar cachet in the inner cities, where the hip-hop philosophy of "living large" saw poor and working-class kids acquiring status in the ghetto by adopting the gear and accoutrements of prohibitively costly leisure activities, such as skiing, golfing, even boating. Perhaps to better position his brand within this urban fantasy, Hilfiger began to associate his clothes more consciously with these sports, shooting ads at yacht clubs, beaches and other nautical locales. At the same time, the clothes themselves were redesigned to appeal more directly to the hip-hop aesthetic. Cultural theorist Paul Smith describes the shift as "bolder colors, bigger and baggier styles, more hoods and cords, and more prominence for logos and the Hilfiger name."[17] He also plied rap artists like Snoop Dogg with free clothes and, walking the tightrope between the yacht and the ghetto, launched a line of Tommy Hilfiger beepers.

Once Tommy was firmly established as a ghetto thing, the real selling could begin—not just to the comparatively small market of poor inner-city youth but to the much larger market of middle-class white and Asian kids who mimic black style in everything from lingo to sports to music. Company sales reached $847 million in 1998—up from a paltry $53 million in 1991 when Hilfiger was still, as Smith puts it, "Young Republican clothing." Like so much of cool hunting, Hilfiger's marketing journey feeds off the alienation at the heart of America's race relations: selling white youth on their fetishization of black style, and black youth on their fetishization of white wealth.

INDIE INC.

Offering *Fortune* magazine readers advice on how to market to teenage girls, reporter Nina Munk writes that "you have to pretend that they're running things. . . . Pretend you still have to be discovered. Pretend the girls are in charge."[18] Being a huge corporation might sell on Wall Street, but as the brands soon learned on their cool hunt, "indie" was the pitch on Cool Street. Many corporations were unfazed by this shift, coming out with faux indie brands like Politix cigarettes from Moonlight Tobacco (courtesy of Philip Morris), Dave's Cigarettes from Dave's Tobacco Company (Philip Morris again), Old Navy's mock army surplus (The Gap) and OK Cola (Coke).

In an attempt to cash in on the indie marketing craze, even Coke itself, the most recognizable brand name on earth, has tried to go underground. Fearing that it was too establishment for brand-conscious teens, the company launched an ad campaign in Wisconsin that declared Coke the "Unofficial State Drink." The campaign included radio spots that were allegedly broadcast from a pirate radio station called EKOC: Coke backward. Not to be outdone, Gap-owned Old Navy actually did launch its own pirate radio station to promote its brand—a micro-band transmitter that could only be picked up in the immediate vicinity of one of its Chicago billboards.[19] And in 1999, when Levi's decided it was high time to recoup its lost cool, it also went indie, launching Red Line jeans (no mention of Levi's anywhere) and K-1 Khakis (no mention of Levi's or Dockers).

IRONIC CONSUMPTION: NO DECONSTRUCTION REQUIRED

But Levi's may have, once again, missed a "paradigm shift." It hasn't taken long for these attempts to seriously pitch the most generic of mass-produced products as punk-rock lifestyle choices to elicit sneers from those ever-elusive, trend-setting cool kids, many of whom had already moved beyond indie by the time the brands caught on. Instead, they were now finding ways to express their disdain for mass culture not by opting out of it but by abandoning themselves to it entirely—but with a sly ironic twist. They were watching *Melrose Place*, eating surf 'n' turf in revolving restaurants, singing Frank Sinatra in karaoke bars and sipping girly drinks in tikki bars, acts that were rendered hip and daring because, well, *they* were the ones doing them. Not only were they making a subversive statement about a culture they could not physically escape, they were rejecting the doctrinaire puritanism of seventies feminism, the earnestness of the sixties quest for authenticity and the "literal" readings of so many cultural critics. Welcome to ironic consumption. The editors of the zine *Hermenaut* articulated the recipe:

Following the late ethnologist Michel de Certeau, we prefer to concentrate our attention on the independent use of mass culture products, a use which, like the ruses of camouflaged fish and insects, may not "overthrow the system," but which keeps us intact and autonomous within that system, which may be the best for which we can hope. . . . Going to Disney World to drop acid and goof on Mickey isn't revolutionary; going to Disney World in full knowledge of how ridiculous and evil it all is and still having a great innocent time, in some almost unconscious, even psychotic way, is something else altogether. This is what de Certeau describes as "the art of being in-between," and this is the only path of true freedom in today's culture. Let us, then, be in-between. Let us revel in Baywatch, Joe Camel, *Wired* magazine, and even glossy books about the society of spectacle [touché], but let's never succumb to the glamorous allure of these things.[20]

In this complicated context, for brands to be truly cool, they need to layer this uncool-equals-cool aesthetic of the ironic viewer onto their pitch: they need to self-mock, talk back to themselves while they are talking, be used and new simultaneously. And after the brands and their cool hunters had tagged all the available fringe culture, it seemed only natural to fill up that narrow little strip of unmarketed brain space occupied by irony with pre-planned knowing smirks, someone else's couch commentary and even a running simulation of the viewer's thought patterns. "The New Trash brands," remarks writer Nick Compton of kitsch lifestyle companies like Diesel, "offer inverted commas big enough to live, love and laugh within."[21]

Pop Up Videos, the VH1 show that adorns music videos with snarky thought bubbles, may be the endgame of this kind of commercial irony. It grabs the punchline before anyone else can get to it, making social commentary—even idle sneering—if not redundant then barely worth the expense of energy.

Irony's cozy, protected, self-referential niche is a much better fit than attempts to earnestly pass off fruit drinks as underground rock bands or sneakers as gangsta rappers. In fact, for brands in search of cool new identities, irony and camp have become so all-purpose that they even work after the fact, it turns out that the so-bad-it's-good marketing spin can be deployed to resuscitate hopelessly uncool brands and failed cultural products. Six months after the movie *Showgirls* flopped in the theaters, for instance, MGM got wind that the sexploitation flick was doing okay on video, and not just as a quasi-respectable porno, it seemed that groups of trendy twenty-somethings were throwing *Showgirls* irony parties, laughing sardonically at the implausibly poor screenplay and shrieking with horror at the aerobic sexual encounters. Not content to pocket the video returns, MGM decided to relaunch the movie in the theaters as the next *Rocky Horror Picture Show.* This time around, the newspaper ads made no pretense that anyone had seriously admired the film. Instead, they quoted from the abysmal reviews, and declared *Showgirls* an "instant camp classic" and "a rich sleazy kitsch-fest." The studio even hired a troupe of drag queens for the New York screenings to holler at the crowd with bullhorns during particularly egregious cinematic moments. . . .

SELL OR BE SOLD

After almost a decade of the branding frenzy, cool hunting has become an internal contradiction: the hunters must rarefy youth "microcultures" by claiming that only full-time hunters have the know-how to unearth them—or else why hire cool hunters at all? Sputnik warns its clients that if the cool trend is "visible in your neighborhood or crowding your nearest mall, the learning is over, it's too late. . . . You need to get down with the streets, to be in the trenches every day."[22] And yet this is demonstrably false; so-called street fashions—many of them planted by brandmasters like Nike and Hilfiger from day one—reach the ballooning industry of glossy youth-culture magazines and video stations without a heartbeat's delay. And if there is one thing virtually every young person now knows, it's that street style and youth culture are infinitely marketable commodities.

Besides, even if there was a lost indigenous tribe of cool a few years back, rest assured that it no longer exists. It turns out that the prevailing legalized forms of youth stalking are only the tip of the iceberg: the Sputnik vision for the future of hip marketing is for companies to hire armies of Sputnik spawns—young "street promoters," "Net promoters" and "street distributors" who will hype brands one-on-one on the street, in the clubs and on-line. "Use the magic of peer-to-peer distribution—it worked in the freestyle sport cultures, mainly because the promoters were their friends. . . . Street promoting will survive as the only true means of personally 'spreading the word.'"[23] So all arrows point to more jobs for the ballooning industry of "street snitches," certified representatives of their demographic who will happily become walking infomercials for Nike, Reebok and Levi's.

By fall 1998, it had already started to happen with the Korean car manufacturer Daewoo hiring two thousand college students on two hundred campuses to talk up the cars to their friends. Similarly, Anheuser-Busch keeps troops of U.S. college frat boys and "Bud Girls" on its payroll to promote Budweiser beer at campus parties and bars.[24] The vision is both horrifying and hilarious: a world of glorified diary trespassers and professional eavesdroppers, part of a spy-vs.-spy corporate-fueled youth culture stalking itself, whose members will videotape one another's haircuts and chat about their corporate keepers' cool new products in their grassroots newsgroups.

GETTING OVER IT

...As we will see later on, the sheer voracity of the corporate cool hunt did much to provoke the rise of brand-based activism: through adbusting, computer hacking and spontaneous illegal street parties, young people all over the world are aggressively reclaiming space from the corporate world, "unbranding" it, guerrilla-style. But the effectiveness of the cool hunt also set the stage for anticorporate activism in another way: inadvertently, it exposed the impotence of almost all other forms of political resistance *except* anticorporate resistance, one cutting-edge marketing trend at a time.

When the youth-culture feeding frenzy began in the early nineties, many of us who were young at the time saw ourselves as victims of a predatory marketing machine that co-opted our identities, our styles and our ideas and turned them into brand food. Nothing was immune: not punk, not hip-hop, not fetish, not techno—not even campus feminism or multiculturalism. Few of us asked, at least not right away, why it was that these scenes and ideas were proving so packageable, so unthreatening—and so profitable.

Many of us had been certain we were doing something subversive and rebellious but . . . what was it again?

In retrospect, a central problem was the mostly unquestioned assumption that just because a scene or style is different (that is, new and not yet mainstream), it necessarily exists in opposition to the mainstream, rather than simply sitting unthreateningly on its margins. Many of us assumed that "alternative"—music that was hard to listen to, styles that were hard to look at—was also anticommercial, even socialist. In *Hype!*, a documentary about how the discovery of "the Seattle sound" transformed a do-it-yourself hard-core scene into an international youth-culture-content factory, Pearl Jam's Eddie Vedder makes a rather moving speech about the emptiness of the "alternative" breakthrough of which his band was so emblematic:

> If all of this influence that this part of the country has and this musical scene has—if it doesn't do anything with it, that would be the tragedy. If it doesn't do anything with it like make some kind of change or make some kind of difference, this group of people who feel this certain way, who think these sorts of things that the underdogs we've all met and lived with think— if they finally get to the forefront and nothing comes out of it, that would be the tragedy.[25]

But that tragedy has already happened, and Vedder's inability to spit out what he was actually trying to say had more than a little to do with it. When the world's cameras were turned on Seattle, all we got were a few anti-establishment fuck-yous, a handful of overdoses and Kurt Cobain's suicide. We also got the decade's most spectacular "sellout"— Courtney Love's awe-inspiring sail from junkie punk queen to high-fashion cover girl in a span of two years. It seemed Courtney had been playing dress-up all along. What was revealing was how little it mattered. Did Love betray some karmic debt she owed to smudged eyeliner? To not caring about anything and shooting up? To being surly to the press? Don't you need to buy in to something earnestly before you can sell it out cynically?

Seattle imploded precisely because no one wanted to answer questions like those, and yet in the case of Cobain, and even Vedder, many in its scene possessed a genuine, if malleable, disdain for the trappings of commercialism. What was "sold out" in Seattle, and in every other subculture that has had the misfortune of being spotlighted by the cool hunters, was some pure idea about doing it yourself, about independent labels versus the big corporations, about not buying in to the capitalist machine. But few in that scene bothered to articulate these ideas out loud, and Seattle—long dead and forgotten as anything but a rather derivative fad—now serves as a cautionary tale about why so little opposition to the theft of cultural space took place in the early to mid-nineties. Trapped in the headlights of irony and carrying too much pop-culture baggage, not one of its antiheroes could commit to a single, solid political position.

A similar challenge is now being faced by all those ironic consumers out there—a cultural suit of armor many of us are loath to critique because it lets us feel smug while watching limitless amounts of bad TV. Unfortunately, it's tough to hold on to that subtle state of De Certeau's "in-betweenness" when the eight-hundred-pound culture industry gorilla wants to sit next to us on the couch and tag along on our ironic trips to the mall. That art of being in-between, of being ironic, or camp, which Susan Sontag so brilliantly illuminated in her 1964 essay "Notes on Camp," is based on an essential cliquiness, a club of people who get the aesthetic puns. "To talk about camp is therefore to betray it,"[26] she acknowledges at the beginning of the essay, selecting the format of enumerated notes rather than a narrative so as to tread more lightly on her subject, one that could easily have been trampled with too heavy an approach.

Since the publication of Sontag's piece, camp has been quantified, measured, weighed, focus-grouped and test-marketed. To say it has been betrayed, as Sontag had feared, is an understatement of colossal dimensions. What's left is little more than a vaguely sarcastic way to eat Pizza Pops. Camp cannot exist in an ironic commercial culture in which no one is fully participating and everyone is an outsider inside their clothes, because, as Sontag writes, "in naive, or pure, Camp, the essential element is seriousness, a seriousness that fails."[27]

Much of the early camp culture that Sontag describes involved using an act of imagination to make the marginal—even the despised—glamorous and fabulous. Drag queens, for instance, took their forced exile and turned it into a ball, with all the trappings of the Hollywood balls to which they would never be invited. The same can even be said of Andy Warhol. The man who took the world on a camping trip was a refugee from bigoted small-town America; the Factory became his sovereign state. Sontag proposed camp as a defense mechanism against the banality, ugliness and overearnestness of mass culture. "Camp is the modern dandyism. Camp is the answer to the problem: how to be a dandy in the age of mass culture."[28] Only now, some thirty-five years later, we are faced with the vastly more difficult question, How to be truly critical in an age of mass camp?

Or perhaps it is not that difficult. Yes, the cool hunters reduce vibrant cultural ideas to the status of archeological artifacts, and drain away whatever meaning they once held for the people who lived with them—but this has always been the case. It's a cinch to co-opt a style; and it has been done many times before, on a much grander scale than the minor takeover of drag and grunge. Bauhaus modernism, for example, had its roots in the imaginings of a socialist utopia free of garish adornment, but it was almost immediately appropriated as the relatively inexpensive architecture of choice for the glass-and-steel skyscrapers of corporate America.

On the other hand, though style-based movements are stripped of their original meanings time and time again, the effect of this culture vulturing on more politically grounded movements is often so ludicrous that the most sensible reaction is just to laugh it off. The spring 1998 Prada collection, for instance, borrowed heavily from the struggle of the labor movement. As "supershopper" Karen von Hahn reported from Milan, "The collection, a sort of Maoist/Soviet-worker chic full of witty period references, was shown in a Prada-blue room in the Prada family palazzo to an exclusive few." She adds, "After the show, the small yet ardent group of devotees tossed back champagne cocktails and canapes while urbane jazz played in the background."[29] Mao and Lenin also make an appearance on a Spring 1999 handbag from Red or Dead. Yet despite these clear co-optations of the class struggle, one hardly expects the labor movements of the world to toss in the towel in a huff, give up on their demands for decent working conditions and labor standards worldwide because Mao is suddenly the It Boy in Milan. Neither are union members everywhere accepting wage rollbacks because Pizza Hut aired a commercial in which the boss delivers pizzas to a picket line and all anti-management animosity is abandoned in favor of free food.

...It may seem cold comfort, but now that we know advertising is an extreme sport and CEOs are the new rock stars, it's worth remembering that extreme sports are not political movements and rock, despite its historic claims to the contrary, is not revolution. In fact, to determine whether a movement genuinely challenges the structures of economic and political power, one need only measure how affected it is by the goings-on in the fashion and advertising industries. If, even after being singled out as the latest fad, it continues as if nothing had happened, it's a good bet it is a real movement, if it spawns an industry of speculation about whether movement X has lost its "edge," perhaps its adherents should be looking for a sharper utensil. And as we will soon see, that is exactly what many young activists are in the process of doing.

NOTES

1. "Woodstock at 25,"editorial, *San Francisco Chronicle,* 14 Aug. 1994: 1.
2. "Hits replace jingles on TV Commercials," *The Globe and Mail,* 29 Nov. 1997.
3. Robert Goldman, and Stephen Papson, *Sign Wars: The Cluttered Landscape of Advertising* (New York: Guilford Press, 1996) 43.
4. *Greater Baton Rouge Business Report* 28 June 1994: 30. Decoteau is co-owner of the store Serape in Baton Rouge.
5. *USA Today* 4 Sept. 1996.
6. "Levi's Blues," *New York Times Magazine* 21 Mar. 1998.
7. Robert Sullivan, "Style Stalker," *Vogue* Nov. 1997: 182, 187–88.
8. Janine Lopiano-Misdom, and Joanne De Luca, *Street Trends: How Today's Alternative Youth Cultures are Creating Tomorrow's Mainstream Markets* (New York: HarperCollins Business, 1997) 11.
9. Norman Mailer, "The Faith of Graffiti," *Esquire* May 1974: 77.
10. Lopiano-Misdom, and De Luca, *Street Trends,* 37.
11. Erica Lowe, "Good Rap? Bad Rap? Run-DMC Pushes Rhyme, Not Crime," *San Diego Union-Tribune* 18 June 1987: E-13.
12. Christopher Vaughn, "Simmons Rush for Profits," *Black Enterprise* Dec. 1992: 67.
13. Lisa Williams, "Smaller Athletic Firms Pleased at Super Show; Shoe industry Trade Show," *Footwear News* 16 February 1987:2.
14. *Advertising Age,* 28 October 1996.
15. Josh Feit, "The Nike Psyche," *Willamette Week* 28 May 1997.
16. *Tommy Hilfiger 1997 Annual Report.*
17. Paul Smith, "Tommy Hilfiger in the Age of Mass Customization," in *No Sweat: Fashion, Free Trade, and the Rights of Garment Workers,* ed. Andrew Ross (New York: Verso, 1997) 253.
18. Nina Munk, "Girl Power," *Fortune* 8 Dec. 1997: 137.
19. "Old Navy Anchors Micro-Radio Billboard," *Chicago Sun-Times* 28 July 1998.

20. Editorial, *Hermenaut #10: Popular Culture,* 1995.
21. Nick Compton, "Who Are the Plastic Palace People?" *Face* June 1996: 114–15.
22. Lopiano-Misdom, and De Luca, *Street Trends,* 8–9.
23. Ibid., 110.
24. James Hibberd, "Bar Hopping with the Bud Girls," *Salon* 1 Feb. 1999.
25. Doug Pray, *Hype!,* 1996.
26. Susan Sontag, "Notes on Camp," *Against Interpretation,* ed. Susan Sontag (New York: Anchor Books, 1986) 275.
27. lbid., 283.
28. Ibid., 288.
29. *The Globe and Mail* 22 Nov. 1997.

Unit II *Popular Forms*

INTRODUCTION

INTRODUCTION

> Let Us Make You Fat.
> 50¢ Box Free.
> We Want to Prove at Our Own Expense
> That It Is No Longer Necessary to Be Thin.

So reads the headline of a 1915 advertisement for something called "Sargol." Beneath this—to us—rather surprising copy, and taking up the most part of the ad itself, is a black-and-white illustration. In the foreground, a generously proportioned couple enjoying a day at the beach whisper gleefully and conspiratorially with smug satisfaction, gesturing to a shamefaced and meagre pair behind them. "Gee!" the caption reads, "Look at that pair of skinny scarecrows! Why don't they try Sargol?" Perhaps the only thing more surprising about this ad than the shock of difference is the accompanying shock of familiarity. We may today share few of the presumed health and beauty ideals of the ad's original 1915 audience, but the appeal being made here is still recognizable enough: just imagine a new and better you—and, of course, as a means of doing so, buy yourself some Sargol as quick as you can. The promise that Sargol holds out, the appeal it makes, seems simple and straightforward; however, the success of that appeal is dependent on a not-so-simple response on the part of the ad's readers.

Like most advertisements, the Sargol ad invites potential consumers to put themselves in the picture, but let us think for a moment about precisely where in the picture they are asked to place themselves. First, it seems clear that those who may be actually moved to purchase Sargol must see themselves in, must identify with, the "skinny scarecrows" and their shameful, cringe-inducing thinness—"Gosh, maybe *I* should try Sargol." But potential buyers can only reach the conclusion that their thinness is shameful and cringe inducing if they also simultaneously want to be, *can imagine themselves as,* the couple in the foreground who possess the kind of robust fleshiness that gives one confidence at the beach. In other words, the Sargol advertisement invites, and depends on, a kind of double response from readers, a double response of identification and escape; that is, readers are offered both a position with which they might immediately identify *and* the opportunity to imaginatively escape that position in a fantasy of re-identification, a fantasy here facilitated by the promised transformative properties of Sargol ("we offer to put 10, 15, yes, 30 pounds of good, solid 'stay there' flesh on your bones") and the representation of their effects.

The essays collected in this section of the reader do not consider advertising and its blandishments (see Williams in the following section), but they do examine those popular forms most closely associated with ideas of identification and, especially, escape: paperback fiction, popular music, film, and television—the popular forms often designated by the term "entertainment."

To many, the escape or points of imaginary identification offered by popular entertainment appear to be either innocently amusing or even therapeutic. After a long day, we like to relax in front of the TV; we like to "lose ourselves" in a good book; we sing along with sad songs when we are depressed; we go to movies to forget about the gas bill, the essay that is due, or whatever other pressures and obligations make up our day-to-day routine. According to romance authors Linda Barlow and Jayne Ann Krentz (Krentz is better known as "Amanda Quick"), for example, the point of their popular fictions is precisely to create an "alternative world" to which "the romance reader yields herself" in order to have "a certain intensity of experience" that is rarely found in everyday life (Barlow and Krentz 745). For this reason, they suggest, romance writers employ a lush, heightened language to transport their readers from the real world into the fantasy world of romance. Barlow and Krentz demonstrate what they mean by taking the back cover blurb from Krentz's novel *Seduction* and rewriting it in "ordinary" language; both the original and the rewrite are given here:

Original:

Townsfolk called him devil. For dark and enigmatic Julian, Earl of Ravenwood, was a man with a legendary temper and a first wife whose mysterious death would not be forgotten. Some said the beautiful Lady Ravenwood had drowned herself in the black, murky waters of Ravenwood Pond. Others whispered of foul play and the devil's wrath.

Now country-bred Sophy Dorring is about to become Ravenwood's new bride. Drawn to his masculine strength and the glitter of desire that burned in his emerald eyes, the tawny-haired lass had her own reasons for agreeing to a marriage of convenience… Sophy Dorring intended to teach the devil to love.

Rewrite:

His acquaintances regard Julian, the Earl of Ravenwood, as neurotic. He's an odd character with a belligerent temperament, whose first wife drowned in the family swimming pool. Some believe she committed suicide, others think he murdered her.

Sophy Dorring, an unsophisticated young woman, is engaged to Julian. Strongly attracted to him, she overcomes her initial reluctance to marry and sets her own agenda for their relationship: to help her husband get in touch with his emotions. (Barlow and Krentz 744, 751)

The first version is certainly more colourful and engaging—even if one engages with it in only an ironic, campy way. Barlow and Krentz, who are not ironic, argue that the ordinary language of the second version sacrifices the element of fantasy and, as such, "is worthless to the romance novelist" and, one assumes, the romance reader (Barlow and Krentz 75). Mundane description offers the reader no escape from the world the reader already knows; she would not be moved to "yield" herself to an "alternative world." Such elements as frenetic action and swelling music perform a similar function in film, offering audiences an exciting but organized sensory experience.

Of course, those who study popular entertainment, rather than those who, like Barlow and Krentz, produce it, are less interested in what the right mix of ingredients is for a successful fantasy, and more interested in precisely what it might mean to "yield" oneself to an "alternative world" and imaginary identity. From one point of view, best represented in this volume by Adorno and Horkheimer's essay on "The Culture Industry" (Unit I), there is nothing innocent or merely relaxing about escapist entertainment and the imaginary identifications it encourages. Indeed, in this view, sometimes called the *manipulationist* view or mass culture critique, entertainment is more imprisoning than escapist and all identity and identifications become imaginary.

In manipulationist theory, popular entertainment is understood as a force of ideological and social control; manufactured by the few for consumption by the many, popular forms of entertainment are seen as instilling and reinforcing false beliefs. They are part of a system so totalizing that the dissatisfactions produced by life in a capitalist commodity culture can be "escaped" only through the consumption of more commodities. This view, however, in which "escape" is no escape at all, is limited by its tendency to view the audience of entertainment in the same light it attributes to a cynical culture industry: as a passive, undifferentiated mass. The unreasonable assumption here is that whatever messages entertainment producers put into their products, they will be automatically fixed in the minds of their unthinking audiences. Oddly, despite their more benign understanding of escapist fantasy, even Linda Barlow and Jayne Ann Krentz seem to share this assumption. "Romance readers," they write, "have a keyed-in response to certain words and phrases" and have "the same responses each time they come upon such phrases" (Barlow and Krentz 748).

From an opposite point of view, what Simon During calls "cultural populism" (During 17) and which is best represented in the writings of John Fiske, the escape that popular entertainment affords is neither benignly innocent nor cynically illusory but potentially politically productive. Rejecting the top-down model of manipulationist theory as incapable of explaining why audiences enthusiastically embrace some entertainments and just as enthusiastically reject others, Fiske emphasizes the power of the audience in making the meaning of what it reads or hears or sees. For Fiske, the power of the entertainment industries, all-encompassing in manipulationist theory, ceases the moment its products are consumed by an audience:

> What is distributed is not completed, finished goods, but the resources of everyday life, the raw material from which popular culture constitutes itself. …At the point of sale the commodity exhausts its role in the distribution economy, but begins its work in the cultural. Detached from the strategies of capitalism, its work for the bosses completed, it becomes a resource for the culture of everyday life. (Fiske 35)

Audiences take these resources and use them in selective, original, and even, according to Fiske, subversive ways, connecting with those textual elements that are relevant to their own lives and ignoring those that are not. For example, many episodes of *The Simpsons* make much of Homer's lack of interest in and schemes to evade the responsibility of his boring job at the power plant. A purely textual analysis of these episodes would likely note that despite Homer's rebellious behaviour, the shows generally end with Homer being reminded of his duties to his family and being repositioned as a conventional father and worker, thus neutralizing rebellion and making the texts essentially conservative. Fiske, however, would probably argue that many television viewers, particularly those who are dissatisfied with their jobs, are likely to respond strongly to Homer's shirking and all but ignore the normalizing and moralizing conclusions to the episodes, reading the episodes, then, as rejections of industrialized labour.

"For a text to be popular," Fiske writes, "it must 'utter' what its readers wish to say, and must allow those readers to participate in their choice of its utterance…as they construct and discover its points of pertinence in their social situation" (Fiske 146). In this version of identification and escape, audiences identify only with those textual moments and elements that strike them as having relevance to their own experiences; what they escape is the power of the entertainment industries and of the text to impose meaning as a closed structure. Cultural populism is certainly cheerier than manipulationist theory, but it suffers from too rigid a distinction between cultural text and cultural experience. As Elizabeth Traube notes, although "actual processes of text reception are not unilaterally controlled by textual structures, they are never entirely autonomous of them. Indeed, one type of experience that spectators bring to any viewing involves their prior encounters with other texts, through which they acquire a practical mastery in following textual cues" (Traube 5). One need not deny the power of mass cultural forms to influence and shape experience in order to posit an active audience just as one need not deny the ability of an audience to create meaning in order to see mass cultural forms as influential.

The following essays attempt to keep both the producers and the consumers of popular forms always in sight. They examine the ways in which such factors as gender, nationality, and sexuality, for example, affect production and consumption as well as the dynamic between the two—and, in the case of Joyrich's essay, even the ways in which production and consumption get talked about. Although these essays grant popular forms neither the deterministic power of manipulationist theory nor the necessarily liberating power of cultural populism, they do take entertainment seriously, considering—or, perhaps, entertaining—the ways in which escape and identification can be imagined, re-imagined, and unimagined.

—CM

REFERENCES AND FURTHER READING

Barlow, Linda, and Jayne Ann Krentz. "Beneath the Surface: The Hidden Codes of Romance." *Popular Fiction.* Ed. Gary Hoppenstand. New York: Longman, 1998. 744–753.

Carroll, Noel. *A Philosophy of Mass Art.* New York: Oxford University Press, 1998.

During, Simon. "Introduction." *The Cultural Studies Reader.* Ed. Simon During. New York: Routledge, 1993. 1–25.

Fiske, John. *Understanding Popular Culture.* London: Routledge, 1991.

Traube, Elizabeth G. *Dreaming Identities.* Boulder: Westview, 1992.

Janice Radway, "Romance and the Work of Fantasy: Struggles over Feminine Sexuality and Subjectivity at Century's End"

EDITORS' INTRODUCTION

In literary and cultural studies, the term *romance* has two distinct meanings: on the one hand, *romance* refers to the much-admired chivalric tales of the European Middle Ages, stories of brave, questing knights facing marvellous challenges. On the other hand, with the adjective *popular* in front of it, *romance* designates the critically despised, mass-produced, formulaic "drivel" about love, consumed largely by women. Of all the types of popular category fiction, romance is probably the most universally scorned. Lacking the presumable political significance of the spy-thriller, the possible foresight of science fiction, and even the assumed intellectual challenge of a mystery clue-puzzle, category romances tend to be dismissed out of hand as pure, escapist fantasy of the lowest order. In "Romance and the Work of Fantasy" (1994), Janice Radway revisits some of the conclusions of her now-classic study *Reading the Romance* (1984) and argues that the fantasy of popular romance needs to be taken seriously as a primary cultural site where the possibilities of feminine subjectivity and of feminism are rehearsed.

Although stories of love and marriage have long been associated with the pleasures and concerns of women, the potential effect of these stories on women became the object of intense scrutiny in the early 1970s, when a sudden increase in the production and consumption of category romances coincided with a reinvigorated women's movement. In this context, as Radway points out, the fantasy of popular romance seemed to constitute a double challenge and was attacked by those on the political right and the political left. For conservatives, the proliferation of paperback romances and the imagined insatiability of romance readers indicated yet another deleterious effect of the supposed sexual revolution of the 1960s on respectable femininity; for feminists, the constant fantasizing about "Mr. Right," on which popular romance is predicated, seemed like a step backward. Radway notes that these early critiques were marked by a distinct anxiety about the dangers of fantasy and by the urge to discipline women's behaviour: "these commentators not only rebuked romance readers for neglecting their real tasks—whether cleaning the house and tending the children or challenging the patriarchy—but also laid down a moral vision about what women ought to be doing with their lives" (140). Romance readers were, thus, characterized as cultural dupes, too enthralled by fantasy—and banal fantasy at that—to know what was good for them.

Radway's *Reading the Romance* was one of the first scholarly studies to treat popular romance and its readers seriously and respectfully. Although it includes textual analysis and an analysis of the publishing industry, *Reading the Romance* is primarily an ethnographic investigation of a group of women readers of romance fiction in a Midwestern

American town that Radway calls "Smithton." Initially, Radway expected the Smithton readers to explain to her which narrative elements of romance fiction they found most pleasurable and meaningful; what she discovered instead was a repeated insistence on the pleasures of "the *act of romance reading* rather than on the meaning of the romance" (Radway 87; original emphasis). The Smithton women repeatedly characterized the act of picking up a book as an "escape" from the pressures and tensions of unending domestic routine.

While the stories that popular romance tends to tell seem like nothing more than advertisements for patriarchy and the *status quo,* the Smithton women saw the act of reading romances as relatively combative: picking up a book enabled them to refuse temporarily the constant demand that they take care of others' needs and to do something for their own pleasure. Radway concluded that

> when the act of romance reading is viewed as it is by the readers themselves, from within a belief system that accepts as given the institutions of heterosexuality and monogamous marriage, it can be conceived as an activity of mild protest and longing for reform necessitated by those institutions' failure to satisfy the emotional needs of women. Reading therefore functions for them as an act of recognition and contestation whereby that failure is first admitted and then partially reversed. (Radway 213)

In other words, by not immediately dismissing popular romance as "garbage," Radway discovered that romance reading could have value—if only as a means of coping with the constraints and disappointments of patriarchal institutions by briefly indulging in the fantasy of an idealized version of those institutions.

Despite her attempt to claim the romance for feminism, as Radway admits in the essay reprinted here, her study was still motivated by the sexist assumption that someone ought to worry about the effects of popular romance on women and by the belief that actual social change would obviate the need for escapist fantasy. In "Romance and the Work of Fantasy," Radway complicates the notion of the "escape" that fantasy provides by tracing the ways in which the fantasy of popular romance has changed in response to feminism and by insisting that fantasy can have an impact on actual social conditions. Radway suggests that the changes in the genre, some of which are contradictory, indicate "the struggle to rethink and to rearticulate feminine subjectivity" (143), to imagine new characters and new relationships. Further, arguing that fantasy is central to the process of subject construction and reconstruction, Radway concludes that it is a mistake to assume that the fantasized subject positions and relations of popular romance remain sealed off from the actual lives of the readers. Popular romance, that is, can enable women—at least middle-class, heterosexual women—to envision relationships in which intimacy does not entail the loss of autonomy and identity.

Although the claims that Radway makes for popular romance are actually quite mild, many critics remain reluctant to see anything positive in the genre at all, citing the formulaic nature of the stories and seeing in industry leader Harlequin the realization of Adorno and Horkheimer's conception of the culture industry. Located in Toronto and owned by publishing giant Torstar Corporation, Harlequin, according to its own statistics, sells 160 million romance novels annually to over 50 million readers;

that accounts for one in every six mass-market paperbacks sold in North America (**www.eharlequin.com**). These statistics suggest that popular romance's tales of love and desire should be taken seriously—and not simply because of Adorno and Horkheimer's fears of standardization. As Catherine Belsey notes, "Desire, even when it is profoundly conventional, is at the same time the location of a resistance to convention. It demonstrates that people want something more" (Belsey 7).

—CM

ISSUES TO CONSIDER WHILE READING

1. Radway does not, at any point, challenge the idea that popular romances are a "women's genre." Should—or could—such a notion be challenged? What is at stake in the gendering of popular genres?
2. Why do some genres of popular entertainment get labelled as "escapist"? What kinds of genres usually get this label? Why does Radway reject the idea of simple escape?
3. Radway's essay focuses on romance novels. Do her observations apply to popular romance in other media, such as film or music?

REFERENCES AND FURTHER READING

Belsey, Catherine. *Desire: Love Stories in Western Culture*. Oxford: Blackwell, 1994.

Kaler, Anne K., and Rosemary E. Johnson-Kurek, eds. *Romantic Conventions*. Bowling Green: Bowling Green State University Popular Press, 1999.

Modleski, Tania. *Loving with a Vengeance: Mass-Produced Fantasies for Women*. Hamdon, CT: Archon, 1982.

Pearce, Lynne, and Gina Wisker, eds. *Fatal Attractions: Re-scripting Romance in Contemporary Literature and Film*. Sterling, VA: Pluto Press, 1998.

Radford, Jean, ed. *The Progress of Romance: The Politics of Popular Fiction*. London: Routledge and Kegan Paul, 1986

Radway, Janice A. *Reading the Romance: Women, Patriarchy, and Popular Literature*. Chapel Hill: University of North Carolina Press, 1984.

Romance and the Work of Fantasy: Struggles over Feminine Sexuality and Subjectivity at Century's End

The March 1989 issue of *Romance Writers Report*, the official publication of the Romance Writers of America, is entitled "Beat the Press: Countering Negative Publicity with a Positive Image."[1] No fewer than thirteen different articles in this issue provide concrete advice to the magazine's readers on how to counter the stereotyped image of the romance writer as someone who needs "bubble baths, provocative negligées, and wine to 'get in the mood' to write a love scene."[2] The editors note in their introduction to the section that "some of the horror stories about how romance writers are treated by the media may make you smile, grimace, tear out your hair, or let out a primal scream. Bear with us," they advise reasonably, "keep reading and you may find some specific suggestions for dealing—gently, but firmly and professionally—with the idiots."[3]

This issue of *Romance Writers Report* is important not simply because it constitutes a powerful and coherent defense of the genre by its writers, sometimes in the terms of feminist discourse, but also because it urges us to see that the romance is now, and has been at least for the last fifteen years, a principal site for the struggle over feminine subjectivity and sexuality and, I would argue, over feminism as well.

What I intend in this chapter, therefore, is to review the nature of the struggles that have been conducted at this site and to show that just as feminist discourse about the romance has changed dramatically in a short time, so too has the romance changed as writers have resisted the efforts of the publishing industry to fix the form in the hope of generating predictable profits. Writers have responded instead both to their culture's habitual tendency to dismiss their efforts and to changing attitudes about women and their roles by playing significantly with the fantasy at the heart of their genre. Romance writers have learned to protest in terms like Ann Maxwell's that "romances aren't an inferior form of fiction best suited to beginners and bimbos." They also have seemed to gain confidence in their efforts to claim sexuality for women and to imagine it in a less linear, less goal-directed way, organized now not genitally but polymorphously in elaborated and extended fashion.[4] Equally significant, they have also attempted to imagine a feminine subjectivity that might support such an active sexuality.

My own book, *Reading the Romance,* was only one intervention in this complex and ongoing struggle to redefine feminine subjectivity and sexuality. My objective was to place the romance with respect not only to the discourses of patriarchy but also to those of feminism. Although I tried very hard not to dismiss the activities of the Smithton women and made an effort to understand the act of romance reading as a positive response to the conditions of everyday life, my account unwittingly repeated the sexist assumption that has warranted a large portion of the commentary on the romance. I was still motivated, that is, by the assumption that someone ought to worry responsibly about the effect of fantasy on women readers. …At some level, then, my analysis remains related to those endless newspaper stories about the rising popularity of the genre that began inevitably in the 1970s and early 1980s with a passage of supposedly "lush" and "lurid" prose juxtaposed without commentary to the rational, clear analysis of the knowing, authoritative investigator.

This first volley in the battle over female sexuality waged at the site of the romance was occasioned by the sudden increase in the genre's popularity in the early 1970s. Indeed, the sheer ubiquity of the commentaries and their tone of moral outrage might have led an uninformed observer to conclude that the romance constituted some wholly new threat to the integrity of women. In fact, romance even then had enjoyed a long history and had been closely associated with the interests and pleasures of women. What made the genre newly threatening in the 1970s was that it had developed its narrative in a more openly and explicitly sexual way and that it appeared simultaneously with a revivified women's movement. The romance thus constituted a double challenge. On the one hand, to a traditionally patriarchal culture, it appeared as threatening evidence of the impact of the so-called sexual revolution of the 1960s upon respectable women. There was thus an underlying uneasiness about the insatiability of romance readers (whether for the books themselves or for the sexual excitement they represented) that explained the level of vituperation heaped upon everyone connected with the genre. In an article in the *Village Voice,* for instance, Walter Kendrick referred not only to romance readers "chirping for more" from "frighteningly prolific" romance writers but went on to observe that the romance was itself "escapist, masturbatory, [and] exploitative." He continued, "It's a typical mass-produced American product, catering to a public so dull and timid that even when it dreams, it can conceive only what it's dreamt before."[5]

On the other hand, to feminists like Ann Douglas, the romance constituted evidence of a backlash against the women's movement. "Popular culture is out to get the so-called liberated woman," she wrote. "Mass culture increasingly specializes in dominance games, fantasies in which women lose and men win. It is important that such fantasies are popular among women as well as among men, and that they are fantasies." She argued that the extraordinary disjuncture between their lives and those fantasies ought to "provoke…serious concern for their women readers."[6]

Policing, it seems to me, was the real work enacted by conservative, leftist, and early feminist critiques of romances and their readers. Whatever the distinct differences among these discourses and their political projects, all were built on the distinction between a cold-blooded, pragmatic, and rational realism and a seductive, illusionary fantasy life that could lead to complacency if not to a wholly relished decadence. Anxiety about the dangers of fantasizing underwrote this urge to discipline: these commentators not only rebuked romance readers for neglecting their real tasks—whether cleaning the house and tending the children or challenging the patriarchy—but also laid down a moral vision about what women ought to be doing with their lives. The stern disapproval of these first early critiques evokes the authoritarian and adult disapproval of the parent for the silly, self-indulgent games of the pleasure-seeking child. The move perpetuates what Allon White has called "the social reproduction of seriousness," a set of practices (carried out principally in the institution of the school) that serves to underwrite the familiar oppositions between the serious and the frivolous, the rational and the sentimental, the public and the private.[7] All of these, of course, can be seen as variations of a conceptual division central to post-Enlightenment bourgeois thought, that between the real and the unreal, the latter coded always as fictional, chimerical, or imaginary and therefore without efficacious impact on the real world. By relying on this familiar conceptual armature, the early critics of the romance located it within the domain of the non-serious and therefore constructed the reading of it as a fantastic, entirely suspect escape.

When placed in the context of these early efforts to cope with the burgeoning evidence that many women led active fantasy lives outside the approved norms and conventions, Tania Modleski's [critical study] *Loving with a Vengeance* and my own *Reading the Romance* take on the appearance of transitional events in the struggle over the genre. Both books in fact share a desire to take romances and romance readers seriously—without automatic scorn and derision for their ongoing interest in a fantastic portrayal of heterosexual romance. They thus demonstrate a certain distance from the jeremiads of Kendrick and Douglas by elaborately demonstrating that the fantasy of romance is closely connected with the social and material conditions of women's lives in a patriarchal culture. Modleski noted, in fact, that it was an important part of her project "to show that the so-called masochism pervading these texts is a 'cover' for anxieties, desires and wishes which if openly expressed would challenge the psychological and social order of things." She went on to observe that "for that very reason, of course, they must be kept hidden; the texts, after arousing them must...work to neutralize them."[8] Although her interest in and knowledge of psychoanalysis led her to attribute powerful and positive effects to the fantasies embedded in romances and soap operas and she thus came very close to rethinking the opposition between fantasy and the real, she ultimately continued to privilege a separate order of things where "true" feminist change would have to occur. In concluding her argument about soap operas, for instance, where I believe she was at her most radical, she challenged the opposition only to reinstate it in the end:

> It is important to recognize that soap opera allays *real* anxieties, satisfies *real* needs and desires, even while it may distort them. The fantasy of community is not only a real desire [as opposed to the 'false' ones mass culture is always accused of trumping up], it is a salutary one. As feminists, we have a responsibility to devise ways of meeting those needs that are more creative, honest, and interesting than the ones mass culture has supplied....[9]

What is projected here is a vision of a world where utopian fantasy might stop...where fullness and equality would be achieved definitively. Itself a utopian vision, this one works by imagining that others would no longer need *their* fantasies.

The final passage of my book is little different from this one, repeating as it does this same desire to see the need for the romance wiped out.... Once again, a romance commentator had registered her discomfort with fantasy and insisted on devaluing it by seeing it only as a symptom of problems in the real world. I will shortly argue that this attitude towards fantasy has changed significantly in the academic feminist community and that, when taken further, might provide the basis for a new politics of the romance that could ally feminist critics with romance writers and readers in the project of defending daydreams like the romance as a space where important critical and utopian work gets done.

To return to the struggle, however, it should be noted that romance writers and their editors neither ceased producing the genre nor remained unaware or unaffected by the seemingly endless dismissals of it. Indeed, during the late 1970s and early 1980s, romance production boomed as news of Harlequin Enterprise's success with the publication of these novels in a series format made its way through the publishing industry. In the midst of consolidation and further incorporation, the industry was itself looking for ways to use profits from paperback houses to subsidize the less financially remunerative production of hardback houses that had been grouped together within single corporate conglomerates. The romance looked like a particularly attractive proposition to these new corporate entities because the audience appeared to be readily identifiable and thus could be surveyed for its preferences and because sales could be predicted with a fair degree of accuracy. This sort of reasoning led Simon and Schuster, owned by Gulf and Western, to create Silhouette romances in 1980 that then began to challenge Harlequin for domination of the field. Within three years, sixteen more series had been introduced, and by 1985 40 per cent of all mass market paperback books published in the United States were romances.[10] In that same year, the genre boasted 20 million readers and chalked up a half-billion dollars in sales.[11]

The expansion of romance publishing could not have occurred, of course, if editors and publishers had not been able to identify and even to create many more romance writers. The fact is, however, they were able to do this with very little effort. As more and more women chanced to pick up one of these books at the local mall bookstore or at the supermarket, many of them were moved either by the experience of reading itself or by the increasing publicity about the successes of favourite writers like Janet Dailey and Kathleen Woodiwiss to try their own hands at plotting out such a story. The editors assisted by creating house guidelines capable of advising the novice on appropriate characters, tone, and goals for such stories. A cottage industry developed as a consequence, aided by the proliferation of home computers. The production end of this industry was simultaneously matched by the equally vital development of an advisory apparatus designed to serve romance readers. Since virtually no "respectable" magazine or newspaper ever reviewed category romances, committed readers found it increasingly difficult to make choices about what to read when faced with a steadily growing list of titles every month. In response to this felt need, many amateur newsletters and a few more professionally produced magazines appeared with the express purpose of reviewing romance fiction.

These developments soon triggered efforts to organize this largely amateur industry, a move that was fuelled by the desires of writers to share their experiences and their problems and by the needs of editors to provide a stable supply of adequately conceived and written stories. These desires were first institutionally coordinated and articulated in 1981 when the Romance Writers of America organization was founded in Houston, Texas, by two writers with the help of several prominent editors in the industry. The organization immediately began to publish a newsletter and to organize an annual professional conference. ...[The newsletter] soon developed into a bimonthly professional magazine complete with current marketing information, advice about how to deal with agents and editors, and material on how to integrate a writing career with home and family responsibilities.

Many of these new romance writers in fact clearly conceived of their decision to write as the act of embarking on a professional career. This conceptual move was deeply affected, I believe, by popular media discourses on the middle-class women's movement and by gradually changing attitudes about the acceptability of work for married women. Feminism, it seems to me, first made its way into romances through the career aspirations of the middle-class writers of the genre. Evidence for this can be found in a range of places. In the December 1981 issue of *Romance Report* (the initial title of the organization newsletter), the editors included a short article on an academic study that claimed romances were "moving 'feminist' messages to women who never read a Friedan, Steinem or Greer treatise on the role of women."[12] The headline "Romance Survey—Finally! A Survey in Our Favor" graphically portrayed the editors' sense of embattlement with those who were dismissing both them and their work. The article not only publicly and approvingly linked the romance to feminism but also went on to praise Carol Thurston's claim that paperback historical romances portrayed androgynous heroes and heroines, challenged the value of the macho male, and made new suggestions about women's possibilities. The editors of the publication, at least, were not constructing themselves as traditionalists or conservatives defined simply in opposition to "women's libbers" or "feminists." Nor were they claiming, as they had previously, that all they were writing were harmless escape stories. Rather, they constructed themselves as women actively participating in social change by narrating pleasurable fantasies about newly imagined individuals and relationships. Like their academic sisters, romance writers also seemed to be sensing that fantasies had validity—that they too could be real and thus might have an impact on other aspects of daily life.

...What we should note here is that just as romance writers and their critics were struggling over the right to define what feminine subjectivity and sexuality would look like, so too were they beginning to struggle over the appropriate way to define and to live out feminism. We will see shortly that the stories romance writers penned in response to their understanding of at least some versions of feminism (those that had been caricatured in the media) attempted to refute the assumption that the search for independence among women implied both distaste for men and little need or desire for intimacy. Their project, it would seem, was to construct a feminist position for white, middle-class, heterosexual women that would manage to envision for them autonomy and success as well as intimacy, relationality, and the opportunity for a restorative, limited dependence upon a man.

...Recent developments in romance writing and reading suggest, in fact, that the processes of reconceptualization have...been proceeding apace. The changes produced in the genre are contradictory, which indicates that the struggle to rethink and to rearticulate feminine subjectivity and sexuality goes on. Some of the most important changes in the genre have been extensively chronicled by Carol Thurston in *The Romance Revolution: Erotic Novels for Women and the Quest for a New Sexual Identity*. Although Thurston does not employ a psychoanalytic perspective to make sense of the appearance of thousands of sexually explicit series romances in the 1980s, she does concern herself with changing portrayals of female sexuality. She argues in fact that these new romances "mark the first appearance of a large and coherent body of sexual literature for women, providing the opportunity to learn to use sexual fantasy and to explore an aspect of their identities that patriarchal society has long denied women."[13]

In general, Thurston claims that these stories are progressive, even feminist, because they attempt to imagine a more active, highly elaborated version of feminine sexuality in which the entire body is eroticized and even conversation is libidinally charged. She, too, claims the romance for feminism, although she also makes clear throughout her account that she will have nothing to do with a feminism that she believes sacrifices intimacy and relationality to female autonomy and independence. The language and tone of the following passage give some indication, I think, of how earlier versions of feminist discourses have been received by some women. Thurston herself, like some romance readers and writers, apparently fears that feminism implies not only loneliness but the adoption of a threatening male-identified subjectivity:

> Contrary to the voices of doom warning that romance novels are the opiate of the female masses, operating both to subvert the women's movement and to condemn addictees to a derivative, vicariously experienced life, these tales of female becoming appear to have played the role of unsung and often maligned heroine to the feminist movement's macho and often sadistic hero reaching millions of women most feminist writing, whether fiction or nonfiction, has not.[14]

Clearly this fear of becoming wrongly gendered seems to overpower Thurston's syntax and larger argument…. My own reading of romances written between 1980 and 1989 suggests that a similar anxiety about gender construction is widespread in the culture and that a need to think through the sources of and solutions to this anxiety has underwritten the plot structures of many recent entries in the genre. In fact, as Thurston herself has demonstrated, the basic conflict motivating the romance has changed substantially since the early 1970s. Where previously an innocent, virginal, and lower-classed heroine had to be awakened to her sexuality by an aristocratic, powerful, and experienced hero, now, more often than not, a career woman must learn that she can combine her much-prized independence with both sexual and emotional intimacy. The question the new erotic romance addresses is less one of how a girl becomes a traditional woman than how to think of autonomy and relationality together within a single adult individual. A passage quoted by Thurston from Maureen Bronson's *Tender Verdict* is illustrative: "Anna Provo thought of her limitations. She believed she was inadequate outside of anything but law. Who wanted a woman who wouldn't have children? Who could deal with her hot temper, her single-mindedness about her family and career? It was unreasonable to expect anyone to tolerate her lack of maternal instincts, her busy schedule."[15] The hero of the story, of course, effectively persuades Anna Provo that indeed she can be loved, that even feminist women relish the care and attention of a man. This sort of story suggests that women will not be ungendered by assuming positions of agency and relative power in the public sphere but rather will be able to combine that subject position with the more traditional one of passive object to male attention.

Lest I leave the impression, however, that all such romances give greater weight to the desires represented by traditional femininity and indulge in detailed self-doubt by women about adopting newer roles, I should note that it is equally common to come across sentiments like these quoted by Thurston from Moeth Allison's *Love Everlasting:* "How dare he call her hysterical. How dare he imply she wasn't a whole woman if she didn't marry him. It was an insulting proposal that sounded as if she were some poor stupid slob who'd made a hash of things and needed a man to take care of her."[16] The emotional weight of passages like this one pushes the other way. As much as the new romance heroines are overwhelmed to discover the joys of intimacy, so do they passionately cling to their independence, often extracting from the heroes lengthy assurances that their men will be happiest if the heroines continue to pursue their career objectives.

The intensity of both sorts of passages suggests that feminism has profoundly unsettled accepted thinking about gender construction at century's end and necessitated myriad efforts to rethink it—if still always within the parameters of an unquestioned heterosexuality. Indeed, I see great ambivalence at the heart of recent romances as the genre's writers attempt to think through the apparent contradiction between a more active and autonomous feminine identity and traditional assumptions that relationality and connectedness are not only woman's work but woman's desire as well. What we see in recent romances, I think, is evidence of a halting, exploratory, often contradictory effort to reconstitute gender.

…I am suggesting, then, that if the contemporary popular romance is any indication, feminist discourses from the 1960s to the 1980s have had a significant impact on white middle-class women. Not only have those discourses combined with other material and social developments to move such women increasingly into the paid labour force and to begin to change child-rearing practices, but they have also profoundly affected women's strategies for self-representation and self-construction. They seem to have created both the desire for and the possibility of imagining new subject positions for women, positions that differ substantially from that fixed single positionality finally secured and offered to the reader by the conventional ending of the pre-1970s genre. Recent romances suggest that women are not limited to dreaming only what they have dreamed before, as Walter Kindrick claimed, but are, in their fantasies, attempting to move even more freely back and forth between the subject positions of the desiring subject and the desired object and, even more radically, exploring the possibility of coding those positions not solely complementarily but equivalently and alternatively as potentially masculine and feminine. This move seems not insignificant to me. In fact its effects could be cumulative, perhaps even transformative in the long run.

NOTES

1. *Romance Writers Report* 9 (Mar. 1989): 2.
2. Anne Bushyhead, "The Ten Interview Questions You *Don't* Want to Be Asked—And How to Answer Them," *Romance Writers Report* (Mar. 1989): 23.
3. *Romance Writers Report* (Mar. 1989): 18.
4. Ann Maxwell, "Writing And Defending—Popular Fiction," *Romance Writers Report* (Mar. 1989): 26.
5. Walter Kendrick, "Falling in Love with Love," *Voice Literary Supplement* (3 Aug. 1982): 34.
6. Ann Douglas, "Soft-Porn Culture," *New Republic* (30 Aug. 1980): 28.
7. Allon White, "The Dismal Sacred Word: Academic Language and the Social Reproduction of Seriousness," *LTP: Journal of Literature, Teaching, Politics*, 2 (1983): 4–15.
8. Tania Modleski, *Loving With a Vengeance: Mass-Produced Fantasies for Women* (Hamden, Conn.: Archon Books, 1982) 30.
9. Ibid.,108–9.
10. Carol Thurston, *The Romance Revolution: Erotic Novels for Women and the Quest for a New Sexual Identity* (Urbana: University of Illinois Press, 1987) 63–4.
11. Ibid., 16.
12. "Romance Survey—Finally! A Survey in Our Favor," *Romance Report* 1:5 (Dec. 1981):19.
13. Thurston, *The Romance Revolution*, 88.
14. Ibid., 88.
15. Ibid., 97.
16. Ibid.

10   Minelle Mahtani and Scott Salmon, "Site Reading? Globalization, Identity, and the Consumption of Place in Popular Music"

EDITORS' INTRODUCTION

Popular music is connected to our sense of ourselves—and to our expression of that sense—in more obvious and direct ways than many other cultural commodities. We assume, for example, that our CD collections have the power to reveal something about who we are in a way that our choice of toothpaste does not, and we use music to mark occasions that are important to us: couples getting married, for instance, often choose a "Wedding Song" precisely as a means of giving social expression to private feelings. Of course, the choice of any cultural commodity can be bound up with our sense of ourselves: even something as seemingly impersonal as a washing machine may be chosen because we believe it signifies a particular "lifestyle" (see the essay by Williams in this volume).

But music is a special case. The powerful discourse of authenticity that surrounds the music industry (Björk is a "real" artist, whereas the Spice Girls were not; grunge started out "real," but then it "sold out") makes our consumption of popular music more complex than our consumption of washing machines. First, although—or perhaps because—a language of authenticity operates so powerfully in relation to popular music, we may paradoxically become aware of consciously constructing a specific conception of ourselves by professing allegiance to one particular style or genre of music, rather than another. Second, since, as Anthony DeCurtis puts it, "[p]opular art is supposed to be popular, after all" (DeCurtis 33), our consumption of popular music contributes to a sense, not just of personal identity but of communal identity.

In the essay reprinted here, Minelle Mahtani and Scott Salmon examine how fans use popular music to construct a specific kind of personal *and* communal identity: national identity. Using the example of the Canadian band The Tragically Hip, Mahtani and Scott trace how The Hip's fans have used the band's music to articulate a strong sense of Canadianness within the context of a music industry that has increasingly "gone global."

The term *globalization* has different meanings in different contexts, but all these meanings stem from the developments in media, information, and communication technologies that have created, if not a literally global, at least a broadly transnational connectivity enabling networks of capital, production, and distribution to cross national and cultural boundaries. Some critics of globalization—of *cultural* globalization—use the term synonymously with cultural imperialism. Such critics argue that we are not creating anything that might be called a global culture; rather, a few, select cultural industries are achieving a global reach and, while the financing and distribution may be transnational, the products are mostly American. American music, American films, and American television networks like CNN dominate the global marketplace, quashing opportunities for local, indigenous expression. Other critics argue that the establishment of a global marketplace has led only to the creation of such bland, eminently marketable commodities as The Spice Girls or The Backstreet Boys, groups notable principally for their qualities of facelessness and placelessless. In both cases, cultural globalization is understood to mean a process of cultural homogenization.

Still other critics—Mahtani and Salmon among them—suggest that the forces of globalization can have a positive effect, stimulating local production and localized means of consumption. According to Mahtani and Salmon, the "impossibility of defining any real sense of a global identity in popular music means that local practices and musical idiosyncrasies are increasingly important, not just in terms of providing an expression for notions of national musical identity but as agents of the 'repatriation of difference' which adapt homogenized global musical forms" (149). In other words, the "global" and the "local" need to be understood as interacting elements, rather than as opposed and separate ones; despite the existence of transnational recording companies that encourage the production of a widely marketable global sound, distinct and local musical forms continue to evolve, often as a reaction to globalizing forces, reworking homogenized sounds to invest them with a discrete sense of place.

The ability to evoke "a strong sense of place and national identity" in a popular format is what Mahtani and Salmon see as the reason behind the success of The Tragically Hip (155). In "Site Reading?" they discuss the production and consumption of a "sense of place" through comments from The Tragically Hip and, more particularly, from their fans. The fans Mahtani and Salmon quote characterize The Hip repeatedly as essentially Canadian and suggest that in listening to the band's music and attending their concerts, they feel that they are participating in an expression of nationalism and patriotism.

To some, the fans cited here may seem to have a rather romanticized and naïve sense of what constitutes Canadian national identity: the maple leaf and Hockey Night in Canada. It is a naiveté that is to some extent shared by Mahtani and Salmon who appear to see in the music of The Tragically Hip a more respectable, "authentic" version of the nationalism expressed in the now-famous "I AM CANADIAN" beer commercial featuring an average "Joe" who explains, passionately, why Canadians are different from Americans. As Erin Manning has pointed out, the "I AM CANADIAN" commercial "attests to the fact that, within the Canadian popular imagination, Canadian nationalism is [only] to be celebrated. Nationalism…is not a serious political concern. Rather, nationalism continues to be defined as benign, entertaining, innocent, and seamless. Nationalism is a cultural given, one to be coupled with drinking beer and watching hockey" (Manning 9). While Mahtani and Salmon acknowledge that the issue of national identity is a vexed one, particularly in Canada, they do not question these fans' definitions of Canadianness or what it means to anchor one's sense of national identity in commodified forms. Still, "Site Reading?" is an interesting and useful look at how people might make use of popular culture, rather than be used by it.

—CM

ISSUES TO CONSIDER WHILE READING

1. How do you account for the language of authenticity that surrounds popular music but not other cultural commodities, not even other popular arts like movies or television?
2. Can you think of examples of popular culture that seem distinctly Canadian? What makes them so?

REFERENCES AND FURTHER READING

Berland, J. "Locating Listening: Technological Space, Popular Music, and Canadian Mediations." *The Place of Music.* Ed. Andrew Leyshon, David Matless, and George Revill. New York: Guilford Press, 1998. 129–150.

DeCurtis, Anthony. "Lost in the Supermarket: Myth and Commerce in the Music Business." *Stars Don't Stand Still in the Sky: Music and Myth.* Ed. Karen Kelly and Evelyn McDonnell. Introduction by Greil Marcus. New York: New York University Press, 1999. 30–35.

During, Simon. "Popular Culture on a Global Scale: A Challenge for Cultural Studies?" *Critical Inquiry* 23 (Summer 1997): 808–833.

Manning, Erin. "I AM CANADIAN: Identity, Territory, and the Canadian National Landscape." *Event and Theory* 4.4 (2000). *Project Muse.* <http://muse.jhu.edu/journals/>.

Van Eltern, Mel. "U.S. Cultural Imperialism Today: Only a Chimera?" *SAIS Review* 23.2 (Summer-Fall 2003): 169–188.

Site Reading? Globalization, Identity, and the Consumption of Place in Popular Music

If someone were to ask me what it meant to be Canadian, I would sit them down in a big comfy chair with a Canadian brew in one hand and a hockey stick in the other, play a Hip CD and watch them experience one of the most intellectual and musically talented ensembles produced this side of the border.　　　　　　　　　　　(a fan of The Tragically Hip)[1]

National identity is notoriously hard to define. It is at once an intensely unique and personal experience and, at the same time, a collective entity that is constantly being re-negotiated, contested, re-defined and re-imagined in relation to changing conditions. For the young Canadian quoted above, the experience of national identity is inextricably bound up with the consumption of the music of a particular local rock band, The Tragically Hip. As a multi-cultural society in an increasingly interconnected world, contemporary Canada is grappling with issues of identity and nationhood, striving to maintain an international identity while simultaneously attempting to reconcile major internal conflict over the very nature of that identity (Taylor, 1993). Perhaps better than anything else, popular music exemplifies this new post-colonial context and the conflicts within it, for the very malleability of music makes possible local appropriations and alterations, resulting in all kinds of syncretisms and hybridities. In the Canadian context, the music of The Tragically Hip has provided a vehicle for the expression and assertion of national identity among many of their fans. In this chapter we examine the music of The Hip as a site for the intersection of globalizing forces and local cultures.

Like many other fields, cultural studies has recently been infused with the discourse of globalization. Unfortunately, as elsewhere in the social sciences, the concept remains opaque, contested and subject to a variety of often competing interpretations. Typically, however, the globalization narrative refers to a process involving the transcending of national borders and the internationalization of the production and consumption of commodities (Walters, 1995). In the cultural realm attention has thus been focused on the processes of transculturation, the interchange of cultural elements and the breaking down of distinctive cultural identities, and the loss of national sovereignty (see Bird et al., 1993; Featherstone, 1990).

These themes have been echoed in the literature on popular music; writers have focused on the impacts of commercialization, suggesting they have led to a process of cultural homogenization associated with conditions of placelessness and timelessness (e.g. Adorno, 1992; Meyrowitz, 1985; Wallis and Malm, 1984). For many this equates to a process of "cultural imperialism" whereby local forms of musical expression in societies around the world are being replaced by mass-produced and mass-marketed western (American) ones, or being diluted into a cheap imitation of western pop. More recently, Tomlinson has argued that by the end of the 1980s, the term "imperialism" needed to be replaced by "globalization," indicating a far more disorganized, random process involving "interconnection and interdependence of all global areas which happens in a far less purposeful way" and which "weaken[s] the cultural coherence of all individual nation states, including the economically powerful ones—the 'imperialist powers' of previous eras" (Tomlinson, 1991, pp. 175, 178). This means that while the cultural and social identities of small nations are still dominated by the larger forces of information technology, these forces operate in a remote global sphere where notions of identity cannot be articulated (Mitchell, 1996, p. 50).

In this chapter we contest this reading of the globalization of popular music. We focus on the relationship between globalization, popular music, and the expression of national identity. We argue that the cultural homogeneity interpretation is a misconception of the process of globalization as it has unfolded in the music industry, and is based on a static and rigid opposition of the spheres of the "global" and the "local." The notion of impending homogenization rests on a reductionist understanding of the creative and reflexive nature of the production and consumption of popular music. Drawing on a geographic perspective, we argue that the growing ascendance of globalizing processes actually accentuates the importance of localized processes of consumption and the identification with place as represented through unique musical forms. While we acknowledge that many musical groups have taken advantage of the internationalization of the music industry, deliberately marketing themselves within the global context (e.g. "The Spice Girls" and "The Backstreet Boys"), many other "local" bands, like The Tragically Hip, have capitalized instead on the importance of inserting their own place-based, hybridized sense of national identity into their singing and song writing styles.

The impossibility of defining any real sense of a global identity in popular music means that local practices and musical idiosyncrasies are increasingly important, not just in terms of providing expression for notions of national musical identity but as agents of the "repatriation of difference" which adapt homogenized global musical forms into "heterogeneous dialogues of national sovereignty" (Appadurai, 1990, p. 16). Global musical forms may well be (mis)interpreted in creative and idiosyncratic ways in different localities which invest them with new significance. The reception of local musicians in local contexts is even more idiosyncratic, involving an insider field of reference and interpretation that is often more impenetrable to the outsider. Despite the existence of globalizing forces, distinctive musical forms and differentiated identities have evolved in distinct "local musical spaces."

MUSICAL FUTURES: GLOBALIZATION AND HOMOGENEITY OR A REASSERTION OF THE LOCAL?

In the conclusion to their book *Big Sounds from Small Peoples,* Wallis and Malm (1984) suggest two possible future directions for the ongoing process of globalization and transculturation in music: the interaction of global and local musical cultures will increase to the extent that more and more musical features will become common to an increasing range of musical cultures, and global homogeneity will ensue; or, a variety of different types of music from different cultural contexts and musical cultures will emerge, adapting traditional musical forms to new environments (Wallis and Malm, 1984, pp. 323–4). Since the mid-1980s a number of writers have considered the impact of globalization on the music industry, variously emphasizing either the internationalization of the musical production industry or the consequences of globalization for the process of music consumption (e.g. Burnett, 1996; Kong, 1997; Lovering 1998; Negus 1992; Shuker, 1994).

In the sphere of production, the focus on globalization emphasizes the increasing internationalization of music production and trade accompanying the rise of transnational corporations (TNCs) (Burnett, 1996; Negus, 1992; Suker, 1994). Yet a closer inspection of the reality behind this representation reveals a pattern of investment that is still significantly less than global. An ongoing process of global restructuring over the past decade has actually resulted in the increasing concentration of the industry as a whole. On the eve of the millennium, the "global" music industry remains remarkably concentrated both in terms of control and sales (Leyshon, et al., 1998; Negus, 1992).

In 1992 the music industry generated around $36 billion from the sale of recorded music worldwide, yet over three-quarters of this went to a handful of TNCs (Negus, 1992). Following a series of international mergers in the early 1990s, the music industry was dominated by just five corporations headquartered in Europe, the U.S., and Japan.[2] This process of concentration is not limited to music. All five of these TNCs are currently positioning themselves for the anticipated overlap of global integration of the personal computer, telephone, and video into a single product (Askoy and Robins, 1992). Although these corporations are undoubtedly searching the globe for new or as yet untapped markets, over seventy percent of world record sales are generated in just five national markets. The music industry is undoubtedly globalizing, but its current pattern of ownership and sales remains remarkably concentrated.

According to a number of observers, "globalization" has also transformed the processes of consumption. Once again, interpretations of the consequences vary but the recurring motifs are those of homogeneity and placelessness. Perhaps the most well cited reading is that of Theodore Adorno (1976; 1992), who represents a gloomy vision of the future where globalization simply accelerates the widespread commercialization and commodification of cultural expression, leading to homogenization and uniformity dominated by the lowest common denominator. For Negus (1992), the increasingly global production and consumption of popular music in the 1990s is "defined by the North

Atlantic Anglo-American cultural movements of sounds and images and European, USA and Japanese dominance of financial capital and hardware" (1992, p. 14). This new "global cultural imperialism" is a "true melange of disparate components drawn from everywhere and nowhere, borne upon the modern chariots of global telecommunications systems" (Smith, 1990, p. 177).

However, we believe the processes of globalization are more complex than many of these accounts allow. In particular, the spheres of the "local" and the "global" are more intertwined than these studies lead us to believe. In the realm of commercial production, the globalization of the music industry clearly involves a qualitative—global—reorganization which has involved the concentration of capital in a small number of key corporations and the centralization of production and control within a relatively small number of global sites (Leyshon, et al., 1998; Lovering, 1998; Negus, 1992). However, while these companies certainly have a "global reach," the industry as a whole still exhibits strong tendencies towards localization. This suggests that the global/local interplay embodied in the recent restructuring of the music industry might be better conceptualized as a set of combined processes within which the tendencies of globalization and localization coexist. In a similar way it is possible to see that in the sphere of consumption "globalization" implies a complex re-combination of cultural forms in different places. Far from producing a single homogeneous cultural space, we believe globalization has in fact heightened "localization" of musical tastes and the appreciation of musical diversity (cf. Featherstone,1993; Harvey, 1989)

Recent marketing trends within the music industry have certainly encouraged the production of a "global sound" which sells equally across national and international cultural boundaries. This, for Adorno and others, suggests a future of global uniformity where local differences are flattened beneath the dominance of a bad Western pop universal. It is also possible that particular rock bands have achieved worldwide success by downplaying their national or local styles in favour of standardized and homogenized production or "look." Indeed, artists such as Madonna, Mariah Carey, Michael Jackson, and the Rolling Stones may have become virtually placeless as their product ceaselessly circulates the globe via performance or replication. The consequence of these developments, in the eyes of some observers, is a situation where the sense of collective memory, context and sense of place is effectively erased in favour of a predictable, monolithic global culture (Meyrowitz, 1985; Smith, 1990).

Whatever the judgmental nature of these predictions,[3] they are based on a passive and rather limited conception of processes of cultural production and consumption. It is surely possible to package sound and image and diffuse this product through global media and entertainment networks. It is a challenge of quite a different order to ensure that such products have the capacity to move and inspire audiences, with their own national, ethnic, and personal tastes, to purchase them. In other words, to paraphrase Smith (1990, p. 179), these sounds and images do not descend upon mute (or deaf!) and passive populations on whose tabula rasa they inscribe themselves. If the global sound is to survive and flourish as part of the repertoire of any national culture, it must be successfully integrated with existing tastes. The major music corporations may indeed strive to produce and market a seamless global sound but that fact alone does not guarantee that we will consume it or that, even if we do, it will constitute the majority of our musical diet.[4]

PLACE, POPULAR MUSIC, AND NATIONAL IDENTITY

The experience of pop music is an experience of placing: in responding to a song, we are drawn, haphazardly, into affective and emotional alliances with the performers and with the performers' other fans. (Frith, 1988, p. 139)

The narratives of globalization have called into question our traditional conception of the nation. Indeed, in the last decade, many cultural theorists have declared that the nation, rather than a "real" category, is an invention (Eisenstein, 1996, p. 43). Stuart Hall insists that the "relationship between a national-cultural identity and a nation-state is now beginning…to disappear" (1986, p. 46). Mohanty further declares that "the nation-state is no longer an appropriate socioeconomic unit for analysis" (1991, p.2). Yet the experience of popular music suggests such declarations are misleading. Despite the global reach of transnational recording companies, the landscape of popular music is characterized by the continued existence of alternative spaces of production and resistance. These sites reflect local forms of cultural expression and give rise to "local sounds"—however intangible—produced in particular localities and specific to certain contexts.

Cultural geographers have recently begun to explore these connections between place, nation, and popular music (see Leyshon, et al., eds., 1998; Kong, 1997). Halfacree and Kitchen (1996), for example, discuss the evolution of "Manchester sounds" emanating from the United Kingdom. Outlining geography's role in forging a specific distinctiveness to the city's independent music scene, they suggest that postmodern "neo-tribes" (see Maffesoli, 1989) are produced when fragments of popular music are formed and sustained through specific geographical contexts. Although the authors are careful to explain that popular music does not "spring unproblematically…from place and should not be over-romanticized," they emphasize the need for an analytical approach sensitive to the constitutive role of place in the production of musical forms (Halfacree and Kitchen, 1996, p. 54).

In a similar way, Lovering (1998) suggests that "local music spaces" can be thought of as territories in which a "community of musical taste," identifiable to its participants, emerges and is sustained, reproduced and disseminated through a place-based network of creation, production and consumption (1998, p. 47). In this way distinctive "soundscapes" are formed, nurtured and diffused. These soundscapes can be interpreted as both the product and expression of place-based identities. As is now well documented, rock and roll developed out of styles nurtured in local music spaces in black, and subsequently white, communities mobilized by local entrepreneurs. Likewise, the British pop invasion of the 1960s emerged from a local music space, as did ska, reggae and punk. The subsequent diffusion of these styles and their imitation and adaptation in other music spaces gave rise to the development of distinct recognizable—and commodified—genres. For the listener, these musical forms create an embodied but imaginary space that mediates our feelings, dreams, desires—our internal space—with the social, external space (Berland, 1998, p. 131). In this way music gives us a sense of place, sometimes in connection with coherent spaces, sometimes in their stead. The production—and consumption—of musical forms is thus an expression of place and identity. This reflexivity is vibrant and unpredictable.

CONSIDERING THE NATIONAL CONTEXT: THE CASE OF CANADA

Living in the shadow of a dominant neighbour, questions of national identity and distinctiveness understandably loom large in the Canadian consciousness (Hutcheon, 1991). But anxiety over national identity is more pronounced in Canada than in many post-colonial countries. This is clearly reflected in the case of the music industry by a public discourse that positions it within the political problematic of Canada itself. Far from "disappearing" or being the passive recipient of global forces, the Canadian nation-state has been active in shaping the context in which music is produced and consumed. In the early 1930s the Canadian Parliament, following popular public sentiment, decreed that communication technologies were a central element for the development of national identity and that their content should therefore be qualitatively different than that produced by American commerce. Canada's national broadcasting system was developed with the mandate to "create national community, to resist foreign hegemony, and to advance public interest in contradistinction to commercial (American) media" (Berland, 1998, p. 136) As a result of this official demarcation of a marginalized national space, the Canadian media and arts have been infused with anxiety about cultural and economic sovereignty.

This was particularly pronounced in the case of the music industry, largely through its connection with radio. As Straw (1993) argues, the bond between music and listeners became inextricably linked to government cultural policy. Government agencies currently defend "Canadian culture" through a complex combination of protective regulations, such as Canadian content quotas for broadcasters, and financial subsidy for recording and publishing, such as those supporting recording projects by local musicians. However, as Berland (1998) points out, the results of this policy have effectively served the interests of multinational capital. The quota system has become so arcane and complex that its effectiveness in promoting truly indigenous product is questionable[5] and the subsidies for recording are strongly shaped by the demands of commercial airplay and export potential. As a result, state intervention

> assists the Canadian music industry to export recordings by deepening and extending the means whereby internal manufacture complements and serves the international industry. By seeking to reconcile citizenship and consumption in a mutual enterprise of privatization and delocalisation, the state demonstrates its complicity in the ongoing capitalization of national space. *(Berland, 1998, p. 137)*

Somewhat surprisingly, Canadians, rather than Americans, rank as the second highest (following the Dutch) music consumers in the world, as measured in per capita expenditure on recorded music (Berland, 1998, pp. 135–6). However, only a small fraction of this revenue is reinvested in Canadian music. Indeed, Berland (1998) asserts that the interest of global corporations in Canadian music is largely restricted to the recording of "global sounds" (such as those of Alanis Morrissette or Shania Twain) that can be marketed across the continent (Berland, 1998, p. 136). As a result, smaller Canadian recording companies produce most Canadian content recordings, bearing the creative and economic risks of making music within the country. However, because the record distribution networks are also owned and controlled by global corporations, most Canadian records manufactured and sold within Canada are actually made from imported master tapes. Given the economies of scale involved, it costs approximately ten times more to produce an indigenous product than to import a similar product from the United States (Berland, 1998; Straw, 1993). This situation is further complicated by the "particularities of the Canadian situation" (see Straw, 1993, p. 58). The geographical expanse of Canada and the existence of two distinct linguistic communities and identities have encouraged the development of distribution operations that are either regional in scope or directed towards dispersed international markets. Thus, despite the existence of Canadian content quota regulations for radio, a recording artist usually needs to succeed in the US to be heard in Canada. In the Canadian context of music production, most bands succeed outside of Canada before they "make it big" in their own country.

In the next section, we will examine the ways in which The Tragically Hip confound this scenario. We deliberately avoid providing exhaustive examination of song lyrics,[6] choosing instead to offer comments from band members concerning their musical intentions and comments from fans, who "read" The Tragically Hip through a particular framework of "quintessential" Canadianness.[7] Rather than treat their audience as a passive, uninscribed mass of individuals (i.e. the traditional mass culture critique), we show how fans evoke a sense of nationalism and patriotism through their interpretation of the music of The Tragically Hip, reflecting the "seductive pleasure of belonging...in nations" (George, 1996, p. 200).

THE TRAGICALLY HIP

The Tragically Hip formed in Kingston, Ontario, Canada in 1983.[8] Since that time the band has carved out a loyal and steady following in Canada, graduating from underground clubs to become one of the major acts in Canada. The Tragically Hip have achieved widespread acclaim for their ability to wed gritty rock to impressionistic lyrics, penned primarily by their charismatic lead singer, Gordon Downie. Earning a reputation as exciting performers, their shows now consistently sell out throughout the country to the extent that these "legendary live performers are—easily—the biggest Canadian concert draw today" (Ohler, 1996). This massive national success has prompted numerous Canadian music critics to ask, "What's behind our country's love affair with these five shop-worn, Joe-Everyman guys from Kingston, Ont?" (Ohler, 1996). Local fans and industry insiders attribute it to a combination of many factors, including Downie's manic and hypnotizing stage presence and his richly geographical lyrics. Downie's songs are described as "oblique, often esoteric, but never short of poetic" (Ohler, 1996).[9] However, although critics and fans laud the band's live performances and Downie's lyrics, most attribute The Tragically Hip's national following to their status as the quintessential Canadian band.

The band is currently signed to a multinational recording company and has achieved unprecedented sales figures in Canada,[10] but have yet to replicate this success in the United States. Despite the fact that The Tragically Hip tour regularly in the US, the band seems reluctant to compromise their performance for commercial acceptance in the US or for the "global" legitimacy such success would bring at home in Canada. As Gordon Downie told *Musician* magazine:

You see the road to Los Angeles littered with the corpses of bands seeking American acceptance, as if that would make you a legitimate success story back home. The lesson is that it's pointless to do anything differently to attract the American audience.   *(quoted in Rubiner, 1997)*

Ironically, given this refusal to bend to commercial pressure, the band has been dubbed "Canada's Rolling Stones," in large part because of the identifiably Canadian content in the lyrics of their songs. It is this aspect of the band's popularity that we explore below.

THE PRODUCTION OF PLACE: PERFORMING THE NATION?

The lyrics of The Tragically Hip songs are peppered with local references and imagery of an identifiably Canadian flavour. Their musical style has repeatedly been described as distinctively Canadian, "raw and melodic…straight-ahead yet also strange and strangely inviting, just like the country and the people that it portrays in its songs" (Muretich, 1996a). To the outsider, the identifiably Canadian nature of this sound may be somewhat ephemeral, but lyrically the band has a distinctly local flavour. Evoking a strong sense of place and national identity, contemporary and historical references abound. These range from well-known Canadian places and popular landmarks to regional cuisine and semi-sacred national iconography (canoes, maple leafs and hockey among them). Over the course of several albums, Downie has also ventured into social criticism, addressing a variety of controversial Canadian topics in his songwriting ranging from a highly controversial wrongful murder conviction to the Canadian Broadcasting Corporation.

The sense of place evoked in the songs of The Tragically Hip is, however, often one tinged with an atmosphere of nostalgia. A number of Downie's more place-specific songs present narratives of collective loss, recalling times past and landmark events in Canadian history. The song "Fifty-Mission Cap" (1992), for example, recalls local mythology concerning the mysterious disappearance of a former hockey player and national icon, as well as the Toronto Maple Leaf's landmark Stanley Cup hockey victories. The emergence of a local particularity is explored and mutated in the recovery of a new, national, heritage that remains fluid and flexible. Referring to a collective memory and sense of place, The Tragically Hip contributes to a new re-reading of the past and understanding of Canadian history within a contemporary context. Such representations of national history provide a way to emphasize the local, while continuing to promote Canadian identity in a new, distinctive format which fans obviously find appealing. In working through some of these complicated issues of identity, Downie explores global issues within a local context. The band's sound and style also reveal a search for identity which reconciles various forces, reinterpreting the Canadian tradition of folk singer-songwriters and giving voice to poetic Canadian images. Although Downie is the first to admit that his work is influenced by transcultural elements, a sense of the local remains strong in his performance, where distinctive local contexts are key in creating a sense of place. As guitarist Rob Baker observes, "Every album we've done has reflected who we are and where we come from. We're Canadians who live in a border town in the shadow of the big neighbour" (quoted in Doole, 1991).

THE HIP FANS: THE CONSUMPTION OF NATIONAL IDENTITY?

The Tragically Hip's loyal Canadian following enthusiastically embraces the identifiably national aspects of the band's recordings and live performances. Given the accessible and democratic nature of the Internet, much of this is represented in websites created by fans to celebrate and share their enthusiasm for the band and its music.[11] At the time of writing there were well over a hundred websites devoted exclusively to The Tragically Hip (most of which appear to be based in Canada).[12] Many of these explicitly celebrate the band's Canadian roots and the sense of national identity they represent for their audience. One website, for example, has been created for "all the Hip fans who want to know what Canadian References are in the Hip songs."[13] This site contains a lengthy list of the specifically Canadian references made in the band's lyrics which, in turn, leads to links which explain their significance in further detail. Apart from a number of specific Canadian geographical locations the list also includes a number of (only) locally famous events, such as the 1972 Summit Hockey Series between Canada and Russia, the 1998 ice storm in Eastern Canada and Quebec, Highway 401 and Bobby Orr (a famous Canadian hockey player—who played his professional career in the US). Visitors are also invited to cast their vote for the "most Canadian" Tragically Hip song. Another interesting site in this genre is that of The Tragically Hip Roadtrip Club, established by a group of fans who "visit various places that the Hip have wrote about [sic] or have special meaning about them in relation to The Tragically Hip." At the time of writing all the locations listed on this site were in Canada.[14]

Websites like these illustrate that, for many fans, appreciation of The Tragically Hip centres on the band's ability to evoke a popular and accessible representation of Canadian identity. This is manifest in the band's distinctively Canadian image, not least of which is the reference to local place names and "Canadiana" in their songs. Arguably, for many young Canadians these signifiers resonate more eloquently than many more traditional symbols of nationalism (such as the flag or coat of arms). Indeed, many fans tend to equate The Tragically Hip with an essential, if somewhat ephemeral, "Canadianness." "A big part of the Tragically Hip's appeal is that they're Canadian, they're homegrown...they speak to the Canadian in me" (quoted in Muretich, 1996b). Music critics compare the group with historical Canadian popular icons:

> Just like Hockey Night in Canada and Don Cherry, The Tragically Hip have always been there. The band also reflects our image of ourselves as down-to-earth yet intelligent, from its practical attire to its concerts.   (*Muretich, 1996b*)

REPATRIATING THE GLOBAL? THE TRAGICALLY HIP'S INTERPRETATION

Clearly many of The Tragically Hip's fans are attracted by the sense of identification the band's music stirs in them, fuelled by Downie's tendency to employ specific Canadian references in his lyrics. However, band members themselves insist that they do not intentionally stress nationalism in their music. According to guitarist Rob Baker:

I think there's a certain Canadian content in the songs which stirs Canadians up and doesn't have the same effect on American audiences…[O]ur doing that is a reaction to those bands from 15 years ago that were singing about going to high school in Hollywood. It just seemed natural to sing about what you know, your hometown. But we never considered it nationalism when we were doing it. It was just being honest. *(quoted in Ostroff, 1999)*

While fans and music critics in Canada equate The Tragically Hip with a certain reading of Canadian identity, band members' own reading of nationalism suggests a less static and far more fluid conception which is informed by a sense of global context. For lead singer/lyricist Downie, questions of personal identity, motivated primarily by his interest in exploring who he was and where he came from, inspired his articulation of these subjects in his songwriting. In an interview in 1996 he responded to a question from a fan concerning the band's tendency to evoke a strong sense of patriotism in their fans:

We've never tried consciously to elicit a patriotic response from our fans, nor have we tried to embody that in our lyrics…Over the years, we have written some songs that refer to Canadian events specifically, and others that reflect our response as Canadians to other themes and issues, because of who we are and how we've been raised. If some of our fans can only identify with us on a nationalistic level, instead of a musical one, then I think that reflects more on them than it does on us. Travelling abroad as much as we do has led us to appreciate where we live and who we are and I think our work reflects that; but we have definitely learned that there is no one distinct Canadian voice.[15]

Indeed, it would be unjust to claim that The Tragically Hip's lyrics deal exclusively with Canadian places and events. In scanning for Canadian references on their album "Day for Night" (1994), for example, out of a total of fourteen songs, only three make explicit reference to a Canadian place, event or moment in history. There are also references to other places and times, including El Paso, war-time Russia and coastal France. Elsewhere, the band has dedicated entire songs to places as diverse as Vienna, New Orleans and Chagrin Falls, Ohio. Nevertheless, these allusions tend to be either forgotten or ignored by the fans. Despite the band's attempts to introduce or "repatriate" global themes within their music, their fans' appreciation seems to centre on the band's Canadianness and their ability to evoke a particular experience or sense of what it means to be Canadian.

There are also indications that the band is not entirely comfortable with their role as national symbols or the response that their performances elicit from Canadian fans. Downie recalled one particularly uncomfortable situation which brought this contradiction, between the band's conception of themselves and their audience's reception, into sharp focus:

The closest I've come to feeling entirely strange about what I do was in Europe. We were attracting a lot of Canadians, mostly students abroad. In Scotland, these two guys came out, decked out in Canadian flags, Canadian sweatshirts, Bluejays caps. That's just not what we're about. Nationalism in the textbook definition is a chauvinistic belief. *(quoted in Littlejohn, 1993, p. 13)*

In turn, in acknowledging that many fans identify with them as sonic symbols of nationalism, Downie also recognizes that The Tragically Hip's music is being consumed in a particularized way by their fans. Although the band freely admits that their music is strongly influenced by their appreciation of place, it is the fans themselves who focus on issues of nationalism and patriotism. Downie insists that because of the band's experience of the global, their understanding of nationalism and the local is altered and mutated accordingly. Their own hybrid forms of identity are expressed in their musical performances, which demonstrate how, in the context of a shifting and changing world where borders and boundaries are effortlessly crossed, their comprehension of the local and differentiated expression of hybrid identities becomes even more appealing.

CONCLUSION

In this chapter we have addressed various consequences of the "globalization" of music. In contrast to some of the rather blanket claims made in many recent accounts we believe that, while certainly international in scope, the music industry is, in several crucial respects, still significantly less than truly global. As a result, we have argued that the processes of globalization within the music industry are vastly more complex than many recent accounts allow.

A more appropriate view of the current changes transforming the music industry, we suggest, might be one that viewed the processes of globalization and localization as coexisting in a complex re-articulation of both production and consumption. Thus, in contrast to the dismal prediction of a light of homogeneity and dullness, we argue that "globalization" has in fact heightened the localization of musical tastes and the appreciation of musical diversity.

The realm of popular music provides a forum for artists to proclaim their various fluid and flexible national hybridized identities through the commodification of creative performance. It does not seem to us that a growing global awareness has brought about the demise of local particularisms in popular music. In fact, the influence of the global has a significant impact upon the ways in which the local and the national are interpreted and, in turn, produced through musical performances. Local particularisms are therefore not simply mute or submerged—rather they are asserted and negotiated through new musical forms.

We examined the way the music of Canadian artists, The Tragically Hip, has been interpreted by their fans as embodying a sense of Canadian identity and nationalism. This reading allows for a closer scrutiny of the connections between the production and consumption of place-based lyrics and images in The Hip's music. In the process of cultural consumption, fans may appropriate popular music as symbols of nationhood and national identity. Some suggest that the growing significance of place in the midst of globalizing forces has been interpreted as a desire for stability and security of identity in the middle of an era of turbulence and change (Massey, 1993, p. 236). We have argued here that a sense of identity is being produced, interpreted and transformed in the reflexive creation of music, where live and recorded performances are interpreted and consumed in unpredictable and often localized ways. In the case of The Tragically Hip, the reception of the band's music in the Canadian context was driven by the idiosyncratic interpretation of local fans who "read" the band almost exclusively through the lens of national identity. Indeed, as we have demonstrated, this took place somewhat independently of the band members' own intentions for their music, in that the fans largely resisted or ignored their attempt to repatriate global themes into the music. In large part this process is conducted through the collective act of creative production and adaptation in particular local musical spaces.

NOTES

1. This quote was taken from Lauren Small's review of a concert by The Tragically Hip which took place in Ottawa on February 8, 1999. The review is reproduced at: http://www.canoe.ca/TragicallyHip/ottawa2_2.html

2. These corporations include Warner's Music International, US; Bertlesmann Music Group (BMG), Germany; Polygram International Group, the Netherlands; EMI-Virgin, Great Britain; and Sony Music Entertainment, Japan.

3. It must be noted here that there is certainly an element of elitism in some of these accounts. Despite the slick corporate nature of much of the "global sound" it does not compromise our argument to acknowledge that some of it is of very high quality, which may account, at least in part, for a good measure of its popularity.

4. Lovering (1998) quotes one industry observer struck by the irony that, "at a time when the music business has become more international…musical taste is increasingly parochial. The American charts are dominated by indigenous genres such as rap and grunge, Germany is awash with trash metal bands, Britain has Britpop" (1998, p. 46). These impressions are borne out of sales figures that point to changing geographies of consumption within the music industry. Artists from the US accounted for 45% of global sales in the mid-1980s, but for only 35% by the mid-1990s, and during the mid-1980s, non-American artists surpassed American artists in sales volume within the European market. Similarly, the share of world market enjoyed by British artists is falling, from 20% in 1989 to 15% in 1993, and sales of English language pop music declined sharply relative to local language artists in Germany, Italy and France among other countries (all figures cited in Lovering, 1998, p. 47).

5. A recent example is the song "American Woman," released by African-American recording artist Lenny Kravitz through a multinational recording label, which was deemed "Canadian" under the current quota system because the original version (of which Kravitz's version is a cover) was co-written by Canadian singer-songwriter Burton Cummings.

6. Apart from our desire to emphasize the creative dialectic of consumption and production, the band's chief lyricist has expressly stated: "I'm not too comfortable with the lyrics being separated from the music. I'm not a poet, I'm a lyric writer, and I just want to make them fit or sound right" (quoted in Doole, 1991).

7. Clearly this interpretation does not extend to all Tragically Hip fans or even all Canadian fans, but is nevertheless a distinctive characteristic of their following in Canada.

8. Current band members include: Robert Baker, guitar; Gordon Downie, vocals; Johnny Fay, drums; Paul Langlois, guitar, vocals; and Gordon Sinclair, bass, vocals.

9. Downie's enigmatic lyrics range from the sombre in the song "Inevitability of Death" (1994) where he sings, "But I thought you beat the death of inevitability to death just a little bit/ I thought you beat the inevitability of death to death just a little bit," to the tongue-in-cheek humour of the line, "Your imagination's having puppies" in "Something On" (1999).

10. By 1995, combined sales of The Hip catalogue had passed the 2.5 million mark: one for every 10 people in Canada.

11. Obviously, not all Hip followers have created web sites but this is one tangible—and relatively accessible—expression of fan sentiment.

12. At the time of writing the majority of these sites could be accessed from The Tragically Hip Webring located at: http://www.webring.org/egi-bin/webring?ring=hipring)

13. This site can be found at: http://www.angelfire.com/on/canadianhip/

14. This site can be found at: http://members.home.net/noodles2/tth_club

15. A transcript of this interview can be found at "The fans interview The Hip": http://www.canoe.ca/HipLetter/hip_letter1html

REFERENCES

Adorno, T. *Introduction to the Sociology of Music.* New York: Seabury Press, 1976.

---. *Quasi Una Fantasia.* Trans. R. Livingstone. London: Verso, 1992.

Appadurai, A. "Disjuncture and Difference in the Global Cultural Economy." *Public Culture* 2 (1990): 1–24.

Askoy, A., and K. Robins. "Hollywood for the 21st Century: Global Competition for Critical Mass in Image Markets." *Cambridge Journal of Economics* 16 (1992): 1–22.

Berland, J. "Locating Listening: Technological Space, Popular Music and Canadian Mediations." *The Place of Music.* Ed. A. Leyshon, D. Matless and G. Revill. New York: Guilford, 1988. 129–50.

Bird, J., B. Curtis, T. Putnam, G. Robertson, and L. Tickner, eds. *Mapping the Futures.* London: Routledge, 1993.

Burnett, R. *The Global Jukebox: The International Music Industry.* London: Routledge, 1996.

Doole, K. "A road apple a day…" *HMV Magazine* June 1991: l.

Eisenstein, Z. *Hatreds: Racialized and Sexualized Conflicts in the 21st Century.* London: Routledge, 1996.

Featherstone, M., ed. *Global Culture: Nationalism, Globalization and Modernity.* London: Sage, 1990.

---. "Global and Local Cultures." *Mapping the Future.* Ed. J. Bird, B. Curtis, T. Putnam, G. Robertson, and L. Tickner. London: Routledge, 1993. 169–87.

Frith, S. *Music for Pleasure.* New York: Routledge, 1988.

George, R. *The Politics of Home.* Cambridge: Cambridge University Press, 1996.

Halfacree, K., and R. Kitchen. " 'Madchester Rave On': Placing the Fragments of Popular Music." *Area* 28 (1996): 47–55.

Hall, S. "On Postmodernism and Articulation: An Interview with Stuart Hall." *Journal of Communication Inquiry* 10 (1986): 45–60.

Harvey, D. *The Condition of Postmodernity: An Inquiry into the Origins of Cultural Change.* Oxford: Basil Blackwell, 1989.

Hutcheon, L. *Splitting Images: Contemporary Canadian Ironies.* Toronto: Oxford University Press, 1991.

Kong, L. "Popular Music in a Transactional World: The Construction of Local Identities in Singapore." *Asia Pacific Viewpoint* (1997): 19–36.

Leyshon, A., D. Matless, G. Revill, eds. *The Place of Music.* New York: Guilford, 1998.

---. "Introduction Music, Space and the Production of Place." *The Place of Music.* Ed. A. Leyshon, D. Matless and G. Revill. New York: Guilford, 1998. 1–30.

Littlejohn, M. "Locked in the Trunk of Gord Downie's Mind: The Tragically Hip Store." *HMV Magazine* June 1993: 12–14.

Lovering, J. "The Global Music Industry: Contradictions in the Commodification of the Sublime." *The Place of Music.* Ed. A. Leyshon, D. Matless, and G. Revill. New York: Guilford, 1998. 31–56.

Maffesoli, M. "The Sociology of Everyday Life (Epistemological Elements)." *Current Sociology* 37 (1989): 1–16.

Massey, D. "A Global Sense of Place." *Studying Cultures.* Ed. A. Gray and J. McGuigan. London: Edward Arnold, 1993. 232–40

Meyrowitz, J. *No Sense of Place.* Oxford: Oxford University Press, 1985.

Mitchell, T. *Popular Music and Local Identity.* Leicester: Leicester University Press, 1996.

Mohanty, C. "Cartographies of Struggle: Third World Women and the Politics of Feminism." *Third World Women and the Politics of Feminism.* Ed. C. Mohanty, A. Russo, and L. Torres. Bloomington: Indiana University Press, 1991. 1–51.

Muretich, J. "Tragically Hip: Band Draws the Line at Dome." *The Calgary Herald* 16 Nov. 1996a: B8.

---. "When it Comes to Hip, these Fans Know Passion," *The Calgary Herald* 15 Nov. 1996b: C1.

Negus, K. *Producing Pop: Culture and Conflict in the Popular Music Industry.* London: Longman, 1992.

Ohler, S. "Why Do We Think The Hip are So Hip? Maybe Because They're Ours." *The Edmonton Journal* 12 Nov. 1996: A1.

Ostroff, J. "Small Steps for Canadian Band." *Ottawa Sun* 17 Jan. 1999: B3.

Rubiner, J. "The Tragically Hip." *Contemporary Musicians* 18 (1997) <http://members.tripod.com~ljt/ hipbios.html>.

Shuker, R. *Understanding Popular Music.* London: Routledge, 1994.

Smith, A. "Towards a Global Culture?" *Theory, Culture and Society* 7 (1990): 171–91.

Straw, W. "The English Canadian Recording Industry Since 1970." *Rock and Popular Music: Politics, Policies and Institutions.* Ed. T. Bennett, S. Frith, L. Grossberg, J. Shepherd, and G. Turner. London: Routledge, 1993. 52–65.

Taylor, C. *Reconciling the Solitudes: Essays on Canadian Federalism and Nationalism.* Montreal and Kingston: McGill-Queen's University Press, 1993.

Tomlinson, J. *Cultural Imperialism.* London: Pinter, 1991.

Wallis, R., and K. Malm *Big Sounds from Small Peoples.* London: Constable, 1984.

Walters, M. *Globalization.* London: Routledge, 1995.

11 Lynne Joyrich, "Good Reception? Television, Gender, and the Critical View"

EDITORS' INTRODUCTION

Despite the many events and innovations of the past fifty or sixty years, most cultural commentators refer to the last half of the 20th century as "The Age of Television." Of course, television predates the 1950s and, obviously, is still going strong, but it was in the last five decades of the 20th century that television managed to permeate every corner of the private and the public sphere and become the most massive of all mass media. In 1948, one household in one hundred in North America had a television set; by 1960, nine out of 10 households had acquired a TV. In North America today, television ownership is almost universal, and many households have more than one set. Television has become thoroughly woven into the fabric of our everyday lives, and its ubiquity is perhaps matched only by the ubiquity of commentary upon it. Parents, teachers, politicians, and academics have all had something to say about what television is and what it does.

In this excerpt from "Good Reception? Television, Gender, and the Critical View," Lynne Joyrich examines this commentary, from early concerns about the effects of the new medium on "impressionable" minds and "genuine" culture to more recent discussions of TV as the postmodern medium *par excellence*. Instead of analyzing television itself, Joyrich analyzes the ways in which television is talked about and written about, and she offers a compelling argument that many discussions of television have been structured by an unacknowledged hierarchy of gender, one that dismisses the medium as feminizing and its viewers as feminized.

As Joyrich notes, television has frequently been disparaged for its disorderly aesthetic, what Raymond Williams in *Television: Technology and Cultural Form* (1974) called television's "flow." Unlike books, plays, films, or concerts, for example, which can be experienced and evaluated as relatively discrete events or texts, television offers its viewers a continuous sequence, or a set of alternative continuous sequences, of images and narratives: commercials and trailers for upcoming programmes are integrated into programmes that flow into yet more programmes, trailers, and commercials. According to Williams, our traditional methods of describing and analyzing cultural texts and objects are confounded by television's characteristic flow:

> It would be like trying to describe having read two plays, three newspapers, three or four magazines, on the same day one has been to a variety show and a lecture and a football match. And yet in another way it is not like that at all, for though the items may be various, the television experience has in some important ways unified them. (Williams 95)

It is possible to talk about individual programmes as isolated units—reviewers do so, for example, usually ignoring the commercials—but our experience of television is rarely so neatly ordered. Even those of us who have no desire to channel-surf will, in the course of an evening's viewing, see a surprising array of items brought together: international political news turns into a shampoo commercial which turns into a game show which turns into a clip from a crime drama and so on. Williams suggests that most of us tend to recognize that our experience of TV is quite different from our experience of other media: while we speak of reading a *specific* book or seeing a *specific* film, "we speak of 'watching television,' …picking on the general rather than the specific experience" (Williams 89).

For many commentators, television's seemingly aimless flow is seen as either reflective of its viewers or as somehow "infecting" them: "because the conditions of TV spectatorship are incompatible with classical notions of aesthetic contemplation and instruction," Joyrich writes, "some critics are led to think of the viewers themselves as the problem: the typical viewer is imagined as passive, lazy, vulgar, or stupid—a bored housewife or lethargic child" (165).

Early critics of television saw in the medium yet another means by which an industrialized mass culture might substitute homogenized, trivial formulae that required no thought for a more robust, genuine culture. Such a mass culture, it was argued, could create only a viewer who was at once overstimulated and yet passive, concerned only with comfort, consumption, and gratification (think of poor flabby, flaccid, emasculated Homer Simpson, for example). That is, television creates a banal, effeminate culture sapped of its virility. By the 1960s, cultural critiques of television gave way to social science studies of television's effects. Although these studies were not overtly concerned with a high versus low culture opposition, Joyrich points out that "undergirding the concern with television effects is the notion that the 'junk' viewers are fed … has the power to transform them into either hypnotized and glassy-eyed zombies or, conversely, hyperstimulated automatons incited to violence and/or consumer frenzy" (169). Most frequently, these studies focused specifically on women and children as the "targets" of television programmes, but all viewers were characterized as passively receptive, infants suckling at the Boob Tube.

More recently, television's fragmented and unresolved narratives (think of all the sitcom characters who "forget" what happened last week) and its hybrid forms (what precisely is a "reality *show*"?) have been associated with postmodernism and its disruption of binary categories and traditional (masculine) logic. While this association may seem like a relatively positive account of the supposedly feminine nature of television, Joyrich remains sceptical. Clearly, television viewing is intrinsically neither a feminine nor a masculine activity; the idea that television is somehow feminine and feminizing is a socially constituted one, one that Joyrich ultimately connects, not with passive infantilism or with the subversion of binary logic, but with the promotion of consumer capitalism. To dismiss—or even celebrate—television as feminine is, according to Joyrich, to misunderstand the ways in which this powerful medium addresses us, and thus identifies us, as consumers.

"Good Reception?" is a good example of what we can call "meta-criticism," writing that subjects criticism to the same kind of analysis usually brought to such other cultural texts as films or novels. Readers may wish to review the articles by Adorno and Horkheimer and Baudrillard before reading Joyrich's essay.

—CM

ISSUES TO CONSIDER WHILE READING

1. Why do you think that television viewing has come to be seen as a particularly lazy and passive occupation? If I sit all evening reading a book, I probably will not get called a "Couch Potato," but if I sit all evening watching TV, I might. Why is that? What does this tell you about a presumed hierarchy of cultural activities and values?
2. Explain what Joyrich means when she says that "[i]t comes as no surprise that a medium which has been seen as "feminine" is also a medium which is intimately tied to consumerism."
3. If you were asked to analyze a television "text," which would you choose? A single episode of a programme? With or without commercials? All the episodes in a series? Everything you saw in one sitting? What would be the implications of your choice?
4. Some critics argue that such technologies as VCRs and DVRs are changing the way we watch television, enabling us to disrupt and rearrange television's flow and, therefore, to become more active viewers. Others suggest that we are just becoming different kinds of consumers. What do you think?

REFERENCES AND FURTHER READING

Casey, Bernadette, et al., eds. *Television Studies: The Key Concepts*. New York: Routledge, 2002.

Joyrich, Lynne. *Re-viewing Reception: Television, Gender, and Postmodern Culture*. Bloomington: Indiana University Press, 1996.

McCarthy, Anna. *Ambient Television: Visual Culture and Public Space*. Durham: Duke University Press, 2001.

Parks, Lisa, and Shanti Kumar, eds. *Planet TV: A Global Television Reader*. New York: New York University Press, 2003.

Spigel, Lynn. *Make Room for TV: Television and the Family Ideal in Postwar America*. Chicago: University of Chicago Press, 1992.

Williams, Raymond. *Television: Technology and Cultural Form*. New York: Schoken Books, 1974.

Warhol, Robyn R. *Having a Good Cry: Effeminate Feelings and Pop-Culture Forms*. Columbus: Ohio State University Press, 2003.

Good Reception? Television, Gender, and the Critical View

THE TREATMENT OF TELEVISION

In an article discussing American viewing habits and the popular reception of TV in the mid-1980s, a journalist for *TV Guide* unwittingly summed up the state of television studies during this embattled era:

> Like death and taxes, there are two things that are certain about television audiences. One, they'll complain that a lot of the programs are trivial and/or stupid, and two, they'll spend more and more time watching them. (Hickey 40)

This statement is interesting in several respects. Not only does the author discuss television by way of an analogy to death and money, hinting at television's relationship to the economy as well as the supposed passivity of its viewers, but he points out what is both known and yet strangely disavowed in much contemporary criticism: the enormous significance of television for American culture. Despite the fact that television receives a tremendous amount of popular interest, serious attention to television is still frequently treated with condescending amusement (if not scorn), and TV criticism is relegated to the margins of film or communication studies if, indeed, it enters into academia at all. Outside of a handful of television scholars, few intellectuals want to admit that they watch TV, and even "quality" television shows are devalued in comparison to the more respected arts of theatre, literature, and even film.

Yet many criticisms of television have little to do with actual analyses of television programs—instead, it is often the technology, economy, or audience that is the hidden target of attacks. Since recent information technology has created the market, forms, and practices of media culture, a reaction against the ways in which this technology is organized is often conflated with a rejection of "mass art" itself. This rejection is rarely offered on behalf of the "masses" who bear its name: anxieties and defenses surrounding the reorganization of capital, consumer culture, and class divisions are evident within the debates over "high" and "low" forms. Television quite clearly breaks down the traditional relation between textual production and an educated cultural elite who appreciates the finished product (the art object).[1] Further, because the conditions of TV spectatorship are incompatible with classical notions of aesthetic contemplation and instruction, some critics are led to think of the viewers themselves as the problem: the typical viewer is imagined as passive, lazy, vulgar, or stupid—a bored housewife or lethargic child. Behind many critiques of the medium as exploitative, sensational, trivial, and inane lies an unacknowledged disdain for an audience that is deemed infantile and feminine.

Nonetheless, as the recent increase of television scholars indicates, television demands to be studied and analyzed in detail. Not only has it transformed the social, political, and economic organization of our society, TV has begun to alter our very ways of seeing and knowing. Framed by the discourses of television, contemporary formations of knowledge, identity, and reality have shifted in ways that radically alter the epistemological, aesthetic, and ideological space of American culture. Clearly, this has serious consequences for all aspects of our society—including (but not limited to) constructions of sexual difference. In analyzing the specific place of television in American culture, this question of sexual difference arises with an urgency. While, as noted above, the evaluative standards by which TV is decried are perhaps most centrally defined by divisions of class (assumptions concerning taste, value, critical judgment, and so on), it is precisely because class is already an avowed referent of the attempts to map out a high vs. low cultural distinction that it is crucial to recognize the way in which this distinction is also marked by a difference, that of gender, no less significant yet further veiled. As I argue, the inscription of gender, though often masked, is key to the reception of television—the positioning of the TV viewer as well as television's critical reception—and crucial to the industry's own strategies of production and distribution. Historically, mass culture has often been figured as feminine and denigrated for its supposed threat to the stability of the (masculine) dominant order of high art. Though television is clearly fundamental to the maintenance of contemporary American society, it too has been figured as feminine and thus has been slighted by popular and academic critics alike.

...Rather than disparaging U.S. television for its disordered aesthetic, its narratives for their lack of development and resolution, and its viewers for their effeminate and infantile passivity, we need to understand how television constructs the relations between the audience, text, and culture in new and significant ways. ...Why, for example, are the distinctive narrative strategies of TV belittled in ways that implicate a presumed female audience? What *are* the relations between the specific textual flow of TV (often dismissed as disordered and fragmented in comparison to other cultural forms), the position constructed for the spectator, and the familial, sexual, and economic structures of our society? By tracing the terms in which television has been figured in popular and critical discourse as somehow "feminine" and then considering some of the ways in which TV has both employed and defended itself against the "threat" of a feminized world, the tensions in constructing a sexed and commodified viewer might be exposed...

THE EMERGENCE OF A CRITICAL DISCOURSE ON TELEVISION

Many of the strands of recent American television criticism were inaugurated by the popular culture debates that spanned the decades from the 1930s to the 1960s, reaching their peak in the 1950s. For instance, in his famous 1953 essay, "A Theory of Mass Culture," Dwight MacDonald laid out the arguments that continue to influence much cultural analysis. In this article, MacDonald describes mass culture as a parasite, a "cancerous growth" that feeds on both high and folk cultures as it substitutes standardized and predigested formulae in place of "genuine art" (59, 61). Although mass art theorists often disagreed on the historical or political roots of this "problem," such critics as Clement Greenberg, Ernest van den Haag, Jose Ortega y Gasset, and many others agreed with MacDonald in the conclusion that the mass media promote a "debased, trivial culture" by exploiting our aesthetic and intellectual needs (72). Basing their critiques on traditional standards of aesthetic value, these theorists could only reject the popular culture that is incompatible with such standards. This is clear in the case of television. Lacking the individual expression and personal vision of a unique author or artist, and perhaps more importantly, lacking even a unified and bounded aesthetic object, television texts necessarily defy the terms of a humanist aesthetic discourse.

Unacknowledged in the criticism that came out of the "Great Debate" is the fact that these accepted norms reflect not simply aesthetic values, but ontological, epistemological, and ethical concerns as well; furthermore, these concerns were often articulated across the lines of cultural, class, and sexual difference(s). Claiming that it is art's responsibility to instruct, uplift, unify, and order, both liberal and conservative critics assumed the universality of such criteria as well as the clear and agreed-upon meaning of these rules. Within much of the debate, artistic quality was described as a property which is both timeless and inherent (excellence simply exists in the work to be contemplated) rather than recognized as a socially determined category. That is, aesthetic worth was considered both self-evident and self-realizing: a work's value is immanent to its existence alone. Mass culture, on the other hand, is based upon exchange. By levelling traditional standards and making all works comparable through the medium of money, the mass media dismantle the very categories of analysis brought to bear upon them by their critics.

Collapsing the standards of traditional criticism, television cannot be adequately analyzed in these terms. Although MacDonald remained loyal to traditional aesthetic models, he did suggest television's power to subvert these norms:

> Mass Culture is a dynamic revolutionary force, breaking down the old barriers of class, tradition, taste, and dissolving all cultural distinctions. It mixes and scrambles everything together, producing what might be called homogenized culture…. It thus destroys all values, since value judgements imply discrimination. (62)

Indeed, a culture so "mixed and scrambled" is, for MacDonald, no culture at all. MacDonald equates the "difference" of mass art—its position outside of traditional cultural and aesthetic categories—with the vacuum of no difference whatsoever, the charge of a lack of distinction.

Within his framework (as well as that of several other critics), this absence of form, the "nothing to see" of mass culture, is intimately tied to the notion of a female public and a feminized media: MacDonald defines mass culture as "a tepid, flaccid, Middlebrow Culture that threatens to engulf everything in its spreading ooze" (63–64). The aesthetic disorder he discerns in mass culture is therefore related to a particular spectator position. Remarking on the masses' lack of "cultural equipment," MacDonald associates mass culture with a childish, weak, and impotent viewer, condemning the media for encouraging overstimulation yet passivity, infantile regression, sentimentalism, and what he calls "Momism" (66). Yet MacDonald fails to analyze the significance of his own critical terms. Trapped within the very discursive formations that television dismantles, MacDonald cannot address the specificity of mass-mediated texts and their consumption, let alone the implications of his critique for theories of gender and culture. Rather than trying fit mass art into an already disintegrating canon, what is needed is a theory of representation that includes an analysis of the place of gender within cultural production and reception.

Offering the promise of such a theory, Marxist critics, most notably those of the Frankfurt School, also participated in the popular culture debates. By examining the relations between industrial rationalization, social consciousness, and mass culture, theorists T.W. Adorno, Max Horkheimer, and Herbert Marcuse outlined a sophisticated theory of the mass media in terms of ideological hegemony. Yet despite a political framework which offered possibilities for a complex analysis of gender and class relations, the position detailed by members of the Frankfurt School was still largely determined by traditional notions of aesthetic value which again were often figured in gendered terms…

The rise of the mass media under capitalism is shown to signify the triumph of instrumentalization and commodification over the nonpracticality, play, and negativity inherent in true art, particularly in modernist experimentation. According to the Frankfurt theorists, the mass media lose the independent critical potential of artistic texts as they are restructured along the lines of efficiency and rationalization. Lacking the immanent value of art, media products are reduced to commodities having value only as they can be used to attain consumer satisfaction. Through this promise of fulfillment, mass culture successfully channels desire into a commodity structure, manipulates our sense of needs, homogenizes pleasure, and freezes our critical capacities; like a drug that keeps its audience happy but immobilized, mass culture acts as a seductive but illusory sedative. Exemplifying this process, television has been described by Adorno (borrowing a phrase from Leo Lowenthal) as "psychoanalysis in reverse"—rather than revealing and clarifying our desires, TV exploits and mystifies them in order to further ensnare us in its power. Individual resistance is destroyed as all viewers become consumers fused into conformity, exhibiting en masse a passive acceptance of the status quo.

Yet such regrets over the death of the autonomous individual at the hands of consumer culture fail to question the ways in which "the individual" described is always already presumed to be male. Thus, Adorno too associates the rise of mass culture and the death of a virile and authorial modernism with the threat of femininity and infantilization. In his essay "Television and the Patterns of Mass Culture," he claims that the TV viewer has become "other-directed" rather than attuned to inner conflicts (477) and that with television, the "longing for 'feeling on safe ground'—reflecting an infantile need for protection, rather than his desire for a thrill—is catered to" (476). Rather than the masculine spectator stimulated by the negativity inherent in modernist art, television creates an effeminate viewer, passive and gullible, in need of comfort and support. Within this discourse, TV's mystification becomes almost a castration.

DISCOURSES OF SOCIAL SCIENCE

The concern expressed by Marxist theorists over television's power of mystification and indoctrination was taken up by American social scientists, although they moved away from the Frankfurt School's emphasis on critical social theory. Turning from the interrogation of social and cultural processes—what Paul Lazarsfeld termed "cultural criticism"—to what was known as "administrative research," mainstream television studies aligned itself with communications research in the pursuit of empirical data and in the application of such data to a cultural model.

Two general areas of research took shape: there were initial attempts to determine the persuasive power and effects of television, followed by audience and use-based studies of the needs gratified by television viewing. Each of these models relied upon quantitative content analysis in order to gauge exactly what TV involved: the manifest material of television's output was monitored to determine either how the content of TV's messages affected the audience or how individual audience members made use of these messages in order to actively fulfill their needs (for information, aesthetic experience, stability, reassurance, contact with others, leisure, or escape). Much of this research was valuable, particularly the work that called attention to the limited representations of subordinated groups, demonstrating that the media produce particular constructions of the world rather then "measuring up" to a presupposed reality. Nonetheless, these empirical studies as well as their bases in content analysis tended to be narrowly conceived, and they could not adequately address the question of television's relation to American culture...

For one, these studies isolate abstract variables from the overall viewing experience, disregarding the complexity of television's relation to American culture as a whole, the processes by which behaviors, attitudes, and identities (including those of sexual and/or familial positions) are constructed and assumed, and the multiple contexts in which television (as well as gender) is experienced. Rather than investigating practices of viewing and the ways in which these might intersect with other practices and interpretive frames, most empirical studies maintain an image derived from communications research of an individual viewer in one-to-one contact with a message sender... Furthermore, while the content of the message is quantified and counted, there is no explanation of the particular ways in which this "content" is structured and composed; a specious distinction between "form" and "content" is both presupposed and reinforced.

Despite the value of empirical research, conceptualizing projects in this way actually impeded the analysis of television's meanings as cultural constructs.... Instead, the viewer is often portrayed as a test subject who is summarily "injected" with an overt message which then either takes effect or fails—the reason why some effects research has been characterized as the "hypodermic needle model" of media influence. In the popular and scientific imaginations, this needle is certainly not a sanitized one: what the viewer is pricked with is considered neither pure nor healthy. As both Jane Root and David Morley have pointed out, undergirding the concern with television effects is the notion that the "junk" that viewers are fed (or, to reiterate the more alarmist image of media "addiction," injected) has the power to transform them into either hypnotized and glassy-eyed zombies or, conversely, hyperstimulated automatons incited to violence and/or consumer frenzy (Root 720; Morley 16). Yet both the narcoticized dupes and their counterparts, the overactive hotheads in the supermarkets and the streets, are always *other* viewers: effects research tends to demonstrate a patronizing concern for groups posed as more vulnerable than "us."

Not surprisingly, these "others," the subjects of studies on media effects, are frequently women and children, precisely those populations who most lack access to control over both television production and its reception (the selection of what, when, and how to watch, determined by what Morley, following Sean Cubitt, calls "the politics of the living room" [Morley 37; Cubitt 48]). Therefore, although empirical research moved away from cultural critique in its depiction of a viewer isolated from all other social stimuli, the discourse of social science maintained mass culture criticism's denigrating image of its audience. Even if the viewer was considered to be, at least potentially, one of "us" (not, that is, one of the already powerless "others"), he was figured as nonetheless still in danger of TV's feminizing and infantilizing influence.

In a widely cited study on the harmful effects of television on the American character, for example, Dr. Eugene David Glynn produced some extraordinary generalizations.[2] Remarking upon the "structure inherent in the very medium of television" itself, he warns us of TV's chief dangers: the creation of receptive, smothered, and conformist men in whom "the passive dependent oral character traits [have] become fixed" (179). After listing cases of mental illness that correspond to these problems (illnesses that are, in his opinion, easily incited by television's power), Glynn notes that such are "the traits which children, exposed to television from childhood (infancy, really!), and all through their character forming years, may be expected to develop" (177). He continues:

> [These traits] all demonstrate quite clearly the special set of needs television satisfies, needs centering around the wish for someone to care, to nurse, to give comfort and solace.... These infantile longings can be satisfied only symbolically, and how readily the television set fills in. Warmth, sound, constancy, availability, a steady giving without ever a demand in return, the encouragement to complete passive surrender and envelopment—all this and active fantasy besides. Watching

these adults, one is deeply impressed by their acting out with the television set of their unconscious longing to be infants in mother's lap. (178)

Reinforcing enormous but unexamined cultural assumptions—assumptions concerning the nature of TV's effects as well as the value of qualities culturally coded as feminine—even such "clinical" research promotes the image of an "unmanly" viewer, passive and helpless before the onslaught of TV…

HISTORY/AUTHORITY/REALITY

Historical analyses of television have attempted to provide a more nuanced view, exposing the fallacies in many of the assumptions plaguing empirical research. From early work by Erik Barnouw, Todd Gitlin, and Raymond Williams to more recent work by (among many others) William Boddy and Lynn Spigel, historical scholarship has demonstrated that far from being a neutral instrument or transparent conduit of information, television…has been organized in particular ways, with particular intentions, and with particular effects on the television "message." The social relations of ownership and control behind this "neutral" medium very much define what is presented on TV, how it is presented and received, and therefore, what "reality" is produced. The reality then has important consequences for the representation of gender as well as the specific uses and meanings surrounding TV. Yet histories of television are not immune from the gendered rhetoric that plagues other commentary and analysis—a point apparent even from the title of Barnouw's well-known book, *Tube of Plenty,* which, like much scholarship, implies that television functions as a maternal substitute, offering its own comforting abundance. In fact, some "historical" analyses of mass culture have contributed to, rather than mitigated, the misconceptions surrounding the supposed feminization of American culture under the mass media's sway, and while these arguments now seem outdated and sorely lacking in substantiation, their presumptions nonetheless set the terms that continue to haunt popular and critical accounts of TV…[3]

…More recent work within television and cultural studies has both explicitly and implicitly subjected these claims to interrogation, investigating the complex relations between audience, industry, and text, between televisual and other social meanings and practices.[4] Yet in the arena of popular judgment, the terms and values of the early mass culture debates seem to have had a surprising longevity, and the gendered rhetoric of traditional standards of evaluation are apt to go unchallenged. Television may still be condemned for its failure to conform to accepted criteria of art or slightly modified criteria of "positive" media images, for its inability to rise above what is posed as its sentimentality, triviality, and disordered flow to provide viewers with unified, ordered visions yielding, at best, genuine insight or, at least, informative portrayals of reality…

NEW CULTURAL CONFIGURATIONS, NEW DISCURSIVE FRAMEWORKS

The reception of television is further complicated by its privileged place within debates on (mediatized) postmodernism. Many of the perspectives I've discussed are based on a traditional set of assumptions concerning the nature of art, reality, and communication and therefore exhibit a nostalgic faith in the possibility of "authentic" expression. Television, however, is often seen as a sign—perhaps *the* sign—of the futility of such longings, as the mark of the encroachment of the "hyperreal" into all aspects of daily existence…[5]

Focusing on the changing economic, ideological, and cultural practices produced by the mass media and by information society as a whole, [many] theorists propose that such new cultural configurations produce and demand new discursive and critical frameworks… In postindustrial America, television, video games, and computer networks make up our imaginary and symbolic systems, and as the narratives and conceptual frames that construct our experiences and our society change, so too must the discourses of criticism applied to these fictions. This demands a shift in the critical analyses applied to television and other media.

Though writing in the context of both modernism and the mass culture debates, Marxist critic Walter Benjamin prefigured many of the concerns of postmodern theory in his contribution to the Frankfurt School's critique, providing an analysis which began to revise aesthetic standards of evaluation in the light of the technological and cultural changes of the twentieth century. In his essay "The Work of Art in the Age of Mechanical Reproduction," Benjamin explains that though in principle a work of art has always been reproducible, the rise of technical means of reproduction and mass marketing has caused a profound change in the meaning and impact of aesthetic production. With the multiplications of mass art and the media, the aesthetic object loses it unique presence and thus its claim to autonomous existence, historical testimony, and cultural tradition. Because "the presence of the original is the prerequisite to the concept of authenticity," writes Benjamin, "the whole sphere of authenticity is outside technical—and of course, not only technical—reproducibility" (220). As the concept of authenticity loses meaning, an entire set of traditional concepts and values surrounding art, as well as reality, collapses.

This collapse is further theorized by Jean Baudrillard in his musings on "hyperreality." Moving from Benjamin's analysis of mechanical reproduction to a discussion of today's characteristic forms—electronic and computer simulation—Baudrillard explains that the existential hierarchy of production and reproduction has at last reversed its claims. Not only are objects and texts reproduced, but their very production is governed by the demands of reproducibility; the media have become merely a set of codes and operations applied to models which have no independent life, which exist as pure simulacra—"copies" without originals.

With the breakdown of the binary opposition *original/copy* comes the breakdown of other polarities and, according to Baudrillard, the subversion of binary thought entirely. For as mass culture abolishes notions of authenticity and high technology blurs the boundaries separating science and art and man and machine, firm distinctions between true and false, reality and fabrication, fiction and nonfiction (distinctions which, of course, are always slippery and tenuous no matter how anxiously defended) become even further threatened… Our reality, he claims, becomes as mobile as the media upon which it is based, making it impossible to define an instance of control: "For manipulation is a floating causality where positivity and negativity engender and overlap with one another, where there is no longer any active or passive…, a system where linear continuity and dialectical polarity no longer exist, in a field *unhinged by simulation*" (*Simulations* 30–31).

Within this field of media-infused reality, television ceases to stand out as a theatrical or spectacular form, becoming instead much more banal. In Baudrillard's vision— one perhaps borne out by the camcorder boom and the ensuing explosion of "reality shows" (whose very designation indicated the conflation of previously opposing poles)—we can no longer resolutely distinguish between seeing and being seen. Given this assessment, he questions modes of media analysis which are based upon these customary oppositions.... Baudrillard thus cautions against any description of TV based on "the perspective, deterministic mode, the 'active,' critical mode, the analytic mode—the distinction between cause and effect, between active and passive, between subject and object, between ends and means" (55). Television scrambles these categories and makes us all both active and passive, subject and object.

Certainly, the material divisions defining television production and consumption continue to exist; despite Baudrillard's idealist vision, the institutional structure of the broadcasting industry has hardly been "unhinged." Yet as his statements demonstrate, "television" as a signifier within popular and critical discourse has come to suggest something quite different, demanding an analysis that can come to terms with the cultural reconfiguration that TV represents and through which it is, in turn, represented. Earlier criticism had evaluated television (and other cultural forms) on the basis of the binary terms noted above, prioritizing one pole (truth on the side of the active subject) and relegating the other to a position of low esteem (the passive object, often figured as feminine and duplicitous). According to this theory, however, TV scholars must admit that we are all tainted by the "otherness" of the subordinate position—television viewers (and television critics) are refused the security and unity of the traditional (masculine) subject, possessor of the active gaze and master of history and reference...

TELEVISION AND THE "FEMININE" VIEWER–CONSUMER

Yet simply because television has been associated in both the popular and critical imagination with femininity is no reason for feminist theorists to embrace TV uncritically (if, indeed, at all). The common-sense understanding of female identification in terms of empathy, proximity, or "woman's intuition," as well as theoretical attempts to define "the feminine" in terms of a breakdown in classical logic (as that which escapes binary oppositions), are also discursive and cultural constructions of femininity on par with the assumed feminization of the TV audience. This "feminization" is thus not a natural occurrence, but a socially constituted one—and one that is beneficial to the dominant socio-economic structures of the United States in general and the TV industry specifically—even if it alludes to a subjectivity seen by some critics as descriptive of women's position in culture. Although TV's confusion of oppositional categories and apparent neglect of classical form may provide some possibilities for a radical intervention, television as it is currently organized gears its specific textuality and viewer/text engagement toward a goal quite consonant with capitalist patriarchy—the encouragement of consumption.

It comes as no surprise that a medium which has been seen as "feminine" is also a medium which is intimately tied to consumerism. Not only do we "consume" television texts themselves, we are encouraged to consume the products advertised as well as the "lifestyle" images promoted by both. The "feminization" of the TV viewer thus relates to women's role as primary consumer in our society as much (or more so) as it is derived from the particular dynamics of television spectatorship (which, of course, need not be coded as either feminine or masculine outside of cultural mappings that stake out such positions). For the television industry, the construction of the viewer as consumer is certainly of much greater import than any gender connotations attached to that status; institutionally, that is, the connection between consumerism and femininity may be purely instrumental if it is acknowledged at all. Given the economic imperatives of late capitalism, broadcasters and advertisers are first and foremost concerned with increasing ratings and sales rather than with promoting particular social and sexual relations, but it is impossible (and I believe counterproductive) to map causality in any unilateral direction. TV producers may be trying to reach "consumers" more than they are trying to address "feminine" (or "feminized") viewers, but they assume that the heaviest consumers are most likely to be women on the basis of historical, social, and ideological constructions that mass culture (including television) has itself enforced.

While the material conditions linking femininity and consumerism are then historically determined, the discursive connections are mutually sustaining. Indeed, the very lack of distance involved in TV spectatorship that has led to the tropes I've discussed also yields the psychology of the perfect consumer: an overidentification with the image, or as Benjamin writes, "the desire…to bring things 'closer'…the urge…to get hold of an object at very close range that is symptomatic of mass (consumer) culture" (223). The instability that television evokes and plays upon—an instability fostered by the dissolution of traditional categories, the breakdown of polar logic, the abolition of a fixed referent, and the subversion of unified subjectivity—is thus related to its promotion of consumption. The role of consumer is the sole identity that remains stable in this field of fluid signs; left anxious, bored, or distracted by the continuous barrage of messages, images, and positions, the television viewer may cling to consumption as the only certain value.

In fact, among the open-ended texts of much American television, the commercials notably stand out as offering clear resolution: while prime-time characters and situations never progress (the same faults are exposed in new comical situations each week; no lesson is ever learned), and soap operas stifle any hope for closure, the commercials give us minidramas in which progress, knowledge, and resolution are possible—merely through a simple purchase. Assuredly, not all television commercials work by providing punctuation in precisely this way: some, indeed, mimic the continuing narrative forms of the surrounding television texts (the Energizer bunny that, since 1989, "keeps going and going," or even more indebted to the soap opera which it "interrupts," the ongoing saga of the romantic couple in the Taster's Choice coffee ads initiated in 1990). Yet these commercials employ such clever narrative strategies in order to stand out from the rest of television's flow, therefore also supplying a type of punctuation, one which depends on presenting themselves as exceptions to the rule.

But perhaps these cases are not quite so exceptional after all; U.S. television is so intertwined with consumerism that the relation of programming to advertising goes well beyond the obvious role of the TV show as frame for the commercial and enticement for a particular (commodified) way of life. Some current television forms collapse the distinctions between product, text, and ad entirely; the unambiguously named "infomercial" clearly signals the interpenetration of information technologies and commercial interests. Music videos provide another example of such hybridization (one that has been further mixed into a number of television programs and genres): videos can be described as texts which are commercials for themselves. In both their consumer appeal and their address to an audience of youths, a viewer who is not yet considered a man, music videos are in many ways exemplary, occupying a privileged space in both television history and the "televisual imaginary."[6] As such they demonstrate the gender contradictions that may arise in a medium that is considered "feminine" by many critics but is itself committed to appealing to the public at large. The combination of genres and modes of address employed by the infomercial (particularly those that attempt to appeal equally to men and women) reveals similar pressures.[7]

Of course, these very contradictions—the multitude of differences within what's been dismissed at television's vast sea of indifference—prevents us from selecting any one case as *the* representative one. Nonetheless, some texts seem to me to be particularly instructive in considering television's relationship to discourses of gender (both on TV and about it). As I stated above, it is my belief that the forms most disparaged by cultural critics are frequently the most revealing; while one can't quite claim that they're "characteristic" of television and its specific textual economy (since this economy is distinguished precisely by its lack of unified and stable terms), they certainly adhere most closely to the image of a feminized and/or consumption-driven viewer...

NOTES

1. However, the division between "high" and "low" forms is reinscribed within TV itself in the division between daytime and prime-time programming and between shows marketed as "quality" programming versus television's regular fare.

2. My discussion of this work is indebted to Horace Newcomb's critique of Glynn's sweeping generalizations and the way he makes television "both cause and effect, stimulus and response" (see Newcomb, *TV* 10–12).

3. See, for example, Gilbert Seldes, "The People and the Arts"; and Ann Douglas, *The Feminization of American Culture*.

4. Obviously, I cannot provide an exhaustive list of recent work within television studies here. But some of the primary anthologies of theoretical work on television are Bennett, Boyd-Bowman, Mercer, and Woolacott; Drummond and Paterson; Kaplan, *Regarding Television*; MacCabe, *High Theory/Low Culture*; Mellencamp, *Logics*; Modleski, *Studies*; Newcomb, *Television*; Sieter et al.; and Spigel and Mann...

5. This term (and my description of it) comes from Jean Baudrillard, *Simulations*....

6. Much work on postmodernism and television has focused on music videos. See, for example, Kaplan, *Rocking*; Wollen; and the essays in *Journal of Communication Inquiry* 10.1, a special issue on music video....

7. See Mimi White, *Tele-Advising*, for some brief but insightful comments on the generic hybridity of the infomercial (a combination of home shopping, the talk show, entertainment news, and educational programming) and the way in which it is structured like a "typical" program with advertising interruptions (for price and ordering information) despite its overall commercial function (181).

REFERENCES

Adorno, Theodor W. "Television and the Patterns of Mass Culture." Rosenberg and White 474–88.

Barnouw, Erik. *Tube of Plenty: The Evolution of American Television.* New York: Oxford University Press, 1990.

Baudrillard, Jean. *Simulations.* Tran. Paul Foss, Paul Patton, and Philip Beitchman. New York: Semiotext(e), 1983.

Benjamin, Walter. *Illuminations.* Ed. Hannah Arendt. Trans. Harry Zohn. New York: Schocken, 1969.

Bennett, Tony, Susan Boyd-Bowman, Colin Mercer, and Janet Woolacott, eds. *Popular Television and Film: A Reader.* London: BFI, 1981.

Boddy, William. *Fifties Television: The Industry and its Critics.* Urbana: University of Illinois Press, 1990.

Cubitt, Sean. "Top of the Pops: The Politics of the Living Room." Masterman, 46–48.

Douglas, Ann. *The Feminization of American Culture.* New York: Avon, 1977.

Drummond, Phillip, and Richard Paterson, eds. *Television in Transition: Papers from the First International Television Studies Conference.* London: BFI, 1986.

Gitlin, Todd, ed. *Watching Television.* New York: Pantheon Books, 1986.

Glynn, Eugene David, M.D. "Television and the American Character—A Psychiatrist Looks at Television." *Television's Impact on American Culture.* Ed. William Y. Elliot. East Lansing: Michigan State University Press, 1956. 175–85.

Hickey, Neil. "A Look at What the Neilson Figures Reveal about America's Television Habits." *TV Guide* 7 Dec. 1985: 40.

Horkheimer, Max, and Theodor W. Adorno. *The Dialectic of Enlightenment.* Trans. John Cumming. New York: Continuum, 1987.

Kaplan, E. Ann, ed. *Regarding Television: Critical Approaches: An Anthology.* Frederick, MD: University Publications of America, 1983.

Lazarsfeld, Paul. "Remarks on Administrative and Critical Communications Research." *Studies in Philosophy and Social Science* 9 (1941): 2–16.

MacCabe, Colin, ed. *High Theory/Low Culture: Analyzing Popular Television and Film.* New York: St. Martin's, 1986.

MacDonald, Dwight. "A Theory of Mass Culture." Rosenberg and White, 59–73.

Masterman, Len, ed. *Television Mythologies: Stars, Shows, and Signs.* London: Comedia, 1984.

Mellencamp, Patricia, ed. *Logics of Television: Essays in Cultural Criticism.* Bloomington: Indiana University Press, 1990.

Modleski, Tania, ed. *Studies in Entertainment: Critical Approaches to Mass Culture.* Bloomington: Indiana University Press, 1986.

Morley, David. "Changing Pardigms in Audience Studies." *Remote Control: Television, Audiences, and Cultural Power.* Ed. Ellen Seiter, Hans Borchers, Gabrielle Kreutzner, and Eva-Maria Warth. New York: Routledge, 1989. 16–43.

---. *Family Television: Cultural Power and Domestic Leisure.* London: Comedia, 1986.

Newcomb, Horace, ed. *Television: The Critical View.* New York: Oxford University Press, 1994.

---. *TV: The Most Popular Art.* Garden City, NY: Anchor/Doubleday, 1974.

Root, Jane. *Open the Box.* London: Comedia, 1986.

Rosenberg, Bernard, and David Manning White, eds. *Mass Culture: The Popular Arts in America.* New York: Free, 1957.

Seldes, Gilbert. "The People and the Arts." Rosenberg and White, 74–97.

Spigel, Lynn, and Denise Mann, eds. *Private Screenings: Television and the Female Consumer.* Minneapolis: University of Minnesota Press, 1992.

White, Mimi. *Tele-Advising: Therapeutic Discourse in American Television.* Chapel Hill: University of North Carolina Press, 1992.

Williams, Raymond. *Television: Technology and Cultural Form.* New York: Schocken, 1974.

Wollen, Peter. "Ways of Thinking About Music Video (and Postmodernism)." *Critical Quarterly* 28.1–2 (1986): 167–70.

Cecily Devereux, "'Canadian Classic' and 'Commodity Export': The Nationalism of 'Our' *Anne of Green Gables*"

EDITORS' INTRODUCTION

As Cecily Devereux points out when she sticks her multi-tined fork into *Anne of Green Gables* and the cultural phenomena and artefacts that have sprung up around the book and its title character, Anne Shirley "has accrued considerable currency" (180) as a symbol of "Canadianness" and as a valuable national (and international) commodity. In the Royal Canadian Mint's 1994 catalogue, she adds, the most expensive item was "a twenty-two-karat gold coin commemorating Anne…with a face value of $200 but selling for $399.95" (180). We might ask, as Devereux does, where this added value comes from and to what degree and in what way it might be a function of or related to nationalism and national identity within a global context. Her argument raises and addresses a number of issues that are central in cultural studies and provides some observations that we may find a little surprising.

Among the things that she makes clear in her article is that examining a cultural icon from a solely national perspective, even when that icon is as much a national treasure as we hold Anne to be, may provide only a lopsided picture. So would merely examining *Anne* as a Canadian literary classic. It/she has a circulation in our and other national cultures and a range of uses that are independent of the book. We do not have to have read the book, any more than we have to have actually seen a moose or a beaver in the wild, to feel that the figure is "ours," a part of Canadian identity, as impossible as that may be to finally define. Ideologically, when we see Anne as Canadian, we are accepting certain things about Canadianness that, through interpellation, inform our positions as national subjects. The term interpellation, introduced by French Marxist philosopher Louis Althusser, refers to the abstract and complex process by which a human subject is positioned in relation to ideology. Necessarily it seems, as we see elsewhere in this book (such as the reading by Hebdige), who or what does the interpellation remains vague, as does the related answer to what constitutes hegemony. Whatever the process and whatever or whomever its agents, it seems clear that parts of Canada's ideological set of values and attributes are encoded in *Anne*/Anne.

Despite its apparent Canadianness, however, Devereux demonstrates that *Anne* circulates as a marker of national identity elsewhere, particularly in the United States and Japan. Between its initial 1908 publication in the United States and 1942 when it was first published in Canada, there were 68 American, 27 British, and a number of Australian printings of the book, as well as American film versions of *Anne* that, in the 1919 silent version, for instance, relocated the story in the United States, complete with a skunk (not native to Prince Edward Island), an American flag, and a discourse on American identity that serves as "a point of interpellation for American girlhood" (184). How could this be? Is this another case of Canada selling its cultural birthright, as when the Royal

Canadian Mounted Police (RCMP) in the 1990s temporarily licensed the Disney Corporation as the sole purveyors of the image of the Mountie?

Devereux points to some of the answers to this question in discussing Anne's hybrid nature, neither entirely local nor global, as it functions as both an imaginative resource for the formation of new identities and as a nationalist narrative *per se*. Other explanations for the phenomenon may well lie in the differences in the way we consume and use or reproduce texts in popular culture as opposed to the way we read literary classics. In *Understanding Popular Culture*, for instance, John Fiske argues that we read the texts of popular culture discontinuously, treating them not as sacred objects to be revered in their organic wholeness but, rather, that we make raids on meaning, picking and choosing those meanings that give us a form of pleasure or suit our particular subject positions and reproducing in our own practices those parts of the narrative that appeal to us. And while we may see *Anne*/Anne as ideologically encoded in ways that are peculiarly Canadian, we should remember that while encoding in some ways limits decoding, the two processes are not identical. Consumers of *Anne*, whether of the book, the films, the television series (as well as spin-offs of *Anne of Avonlea*), or the other artefacts of the Anne industry, will use them according to their own lights and to confirm their own ideological positions, whether dominant-hegemonic, negotiated, or oppositional, or Canadian, American, British, Swedish, Australian, or Japanese.

—AG

ISSUES TO CONSIDER WHILE READING

1. In the age of globalization, is there such a thing as a national, racial, or ethnic identity that is not to some degree hybridized? Is there anything that is exclusively Canadian?
2. In Canada, multiculturalism is often cited as a key element of national policy and identity. What does this say about the way Canadian subjects negotiate individual and national identity? What might such a policy claim for the country, and what does it obscure?

REFERENCES AND FURTHER READING

Althusser, Louis. "Ideology and Ideological State Apparatuses." *Lenin and Philosophy and Other Essays*. Trans. Ben Brewster. London: New Left Books, 1971.

Barthes, Roland. *S/Z*. London: Jonathan Cape, 1975.

Featherstone, Mike, ed. *Global Culture: Nationalism, Globalization and Modernity*. London: Sage, 1990.

Fiske, John. "Popular Texts." *Understanding Popular Culture*. London: Unwin Hyman, 1989.

"Canadian Classic" and "Commodity Export": The Nationalism of "Our" *Anne of Green Gables*

In 1924, in the influential early work of national literary cartography called *Highways of Canadian Literature*, J.D. Logand and Donald French suggested that Lucy Maud Montgomery's 1908 novel, *Anne of Green Gables*, was already "a book which may be confidently labelled a 'Canadian classic'" (300). That is, less than 20 years after its first publication (in the United States and Britain), and nearly 20 years before it would actually be published *in* Canada, it had already achieved national "classic" status. French and Logan's observation is important not because their "confiden[ce]" has been so abundantly justified by *Anne*'s enduring appeal, but because it suggestively embeds the novel in a discourse of national self-representation. As a national "classic," *Anne* is a crucial part of the nation's literary history (works that, in 1924, could be seen to be both "good" *and* Canadian, or internationally respectable *and* nationally relevant).

Anne is also, perhaps more significantly, a discursive site for what can be understood in ideological terms as the interpellation of national identity: "we" read *Anne* as part of being "Canadian"; "we" recognize in *Anne* signs of "our" shared "Canadianness," and in that process recognize (or constitute) ourselves as national subjects. Because these terms are ideological they are not necessarily articulated or even apparent, but circulate in representations of the national community as identifying claims: Anne is "our Anne" (Brooymans); she is part of "us." The attributes of this community identity are largely indeterminate (they are a national "essence," and they are also the shared "values" that underpin nationalism). But they are none the less encoded in the text whose value is compounded as it continues to rise in popularity and to be more and more firmly embedded in the discourse of "Canadianness."

At the beginning of the twenty-first century, *Anne of Green Gables* is a Canadian classic. Indeed, it is one of the best-selling English-Canadian novels ever, remaining in print and broadly popular since its first publication in 1908 in the United States and Britain.[1] Montgomery records in her journal receiving the first edition in the mail on 20 June 1908; on 30 June she notes that the novel had already gone into a second printing (*Selected Journals* I 335). According to the *Preliminary Bibliography* of Lucy Maud Montgomery by Ruth Weber Russell, D.W. Russell and Rea Wilmshurst, in the first two years alone, the American edition was printed 16 times; by 1942, it had been printed 68 times (2).[2] The first Canadian edition, issued by Ryerson in 1942, ran to 13 printings before being re-issued in 1964 (Russell et al. 1). In the year 2000, without ever having gone out of print, *Anne* was available in five Canadian editions, along with related birthday books, cookbooks, storybooks and daybooks (*Canadian Books in Print* 634–35). The multiple editions and unbroken print history of *Anne* affirm what is well known—that the novel has maintained a solid base of readership in Canada since it was first published.

In the past two decades, however, and in particular since 1985 when both the first volume of Montgomery's *Selected Journals,* edited by Mary Rubio and Elizabeth Waterson, and the first Sullivan Entertainment telefilm adaptations of *Anne* appeared, it (she?) has entered into a new phase of popularity. This new popularity is marked in part by the proliferation of editions of the novel. It is also, and arguably, made even more obvious by the proliferation of supplementary products that do not, for the most part, reproduce the text itself, but which rely on visual representations of the heroine. The birthday and cookbooks are one kind of product; but recent studies of the novel's appeal have enumerated amongst the Anne artefacts currently for sale "Anne dolls and girl-sized souvenir wigs with red braids" (Gerson 50), plates, fridge magnets, a "wristwatch with a silhouette of Anne's profile on its face ... buttons, calendars, mouse pads, Green Gables tea and preserves" (Lynes 16). The Anne of Green Gables Licensing Authority, established in 1994 (and itself a sign of the rise in her popularity and the need to regulate the distribution and use specifically of her *image*), has also approved Anne potting soil, seeds, maple syrup, tea sets, prints and posters, rugs, curtains, pins, hair accessories, lollipops, Christmas balls, puzzles, furniture, aprons, sculptures, house signs, stained-glass windows, soap, cookies, chocolates and potato chips. This Anne-related merchandise is sold not only in Prince Edward Island (PEI), but across Canada: one can hardly enter a gift or souvenir shop anywhere in the nation without encountering an Anne item.

It is in this context that Montgomery's heroine has emerged as what English Canada's two national newspapers, *The Globe and Mail* and the *National Post,* like to call a "national icon," as Theodore Sheckels puts it, "right up there, with the moose, the beaver, the Mountie, and the Habs" (189). Her national icon status is in part an effect of the book as a Canadian classic; but it also related to the image as an identifiable and identificatory motif. (We do not need to read the book to recognize the heroine: recognition of her and what she represents is visual.) Thus, although Anne was not on the official shortlist of the images favoured in 2000 to appear on the new Canadian paper money, she *was* subsequently put on an unofficial list published in *The Globe and Mail* (Flahive). Anne clearly has accrued considerable currency, not only as an instantly recognizable symbol of "Canadianness," but as a valuable national cultural *commodity*, circulating in national commerce, like the beaver on a Canadian nickel, and crucially, marketable like Mounties (whose image could be sold wholesale to Disney). Carole Gerson has astutely observed that the "material value of Montgomery's book to Canada as a whole is ... emblematize[d by the 1994 issue of] a twenty-two-karat gold coin commemorating Anne ... [w]ith a face value of $200 but selling for $399.95 ... the most expensive item in the [Royal Canadian] Mint's Christmas brochure" (50). Her value is her national recognizability and what her image encodes for national self-recognition (Anne is part of "us"); it is also an index of her commercial success.

It should not be surprising that Anne was "the most expensive item" in the Royal Canadian Mint's 1994 catalogue: what has built up around her over the last century is an immense and rapidly growing industry from which, Gerson notes, many "publishers and marketers," as well as the tourist economy of Prince Edward Island, "realize sizable profits" (50). It is well known that thousands of tourists visit PEI each year to see the land of Anne and to visit the spots fictionalized in the novels. In their 1996 study of Canadian popular culture, Geoff Pevere and Greig Dymond write that,

> Each year, the tiny province of Prince Edward Island, population 130,000, draws 700,000 tourists largely on Anne's allure alone. Approximately 120,000 of these visitors venture to Province House in Charlottetown, where the Canadian Confederation was devised in 1864, but three times as many go to Cavendish, where Anne Shirley was devised in 1905. (13)[3]

It is in this context—what Irene Gammel and Elizabeth Epperly have called "cultural tourism" (199)—that Anne Shirley has become not only a major national icon, but what *The Globe and Mail* characterized as "our biggest cult commodity export" (Everett-Green). That is, the novel and the heroine have a perceptible constituency outside Canada.

Although, as Douglas Baldwin shows in his charting of the rising numbers of tourists to Cavendish (124), this extra-national community has been expanding since 1985, it is not a new phenomenon. Since its publication, *Anne of Green Gables* has had a long history of remarkable success outside Canada. I have already drawn attention to the numbers tabulated by Russell et al. (68 printings by 1942). Gerson, in her 1999 analysis of what she calls "the triangle of author, publisher and fictional character," cites Mary Rubio's observation that "the book had earned Montgomery over $22,000 for more than 300,000 copies by ... 1919" (Gerson 49); she also draws attention to a mid-century study of American bestsellers (*Golden Multitudes* by Frank Mott), which notes that *Anne* had sold between 800,000 and 900,000 copies by 1947 (Gerson 49). Other historians of the book publishing industry in the United States suggest that, by 1966, *Anne* "had sold over a million copies, as well as a number of standard sets" (Madison 530). Given the inclusion of these statistics in studies that are concerned with American publishing and book marketing, these numbers, even in light of the distribution of American editions to Canada prior to the 1942 Ryerson *Anne*, attest to a solid base of readership in the US, the readers that Montgomery referred to in her journal shortly after the first publication of the novel as "the great American public" (*Selected Journals* I 348), implying that they were a significant part of that first readership.[4] The current American market for the novel reinforces this: in the year 2000, *Books in Print* lists 45 versions of *Anne of Green Gables* for sale in the US, along with one study guide and 16 Anne-related "book" items such as diaries and cookbooks.

In Britain, as in the US, *Anne* has had a steady popularity since its publication in 1908 by Pitman. The first British *Anne* was followed by an edition by Harrap in 1925 which, according to the Russell et al. bibliography, was reprinted 27 times before being replaced by a new Harrap edition in 1943, itself reprinted 26 times by 1980. In 2000, Britain's *Whitakers Books in Print* had 22 *Anne of Green Gables* citations. Most were editions of the novel and a few were related texts: a libretto, a "Film and TV Tie-in," an audiotape set and a pop-up dollhouse distributed by Key Porter Canada, all indications of a sturdy British market for *Anne* and for Anne-related products. Russell et al. also show that the novel has been in print consistently in Australia since 1924: the bibliography notes five Australian editions, the most recent of which in 1986 (Angus and Robertson's of 1934) had been reprinted twice in the 1940s, and re-issued twice by 1982 (1).

The immense appeal of *Anne of Green Gables* outside Canada has not, however, been limited to English readers. The 1986 bibliography enumerates many of the translations of the novel that begin to appear as early as 1909, the year after the first publication, when *Anne* was translated into Swedish. Many of these translations are still in print. In Japan, the first translation in 1952 by Hanako Muraoka has gone into numerous editions, and at least 10 other translations have been produced since.[5] The phenomenal success of Anne in Japan is by now well known, and several commentators in the past decade have drawn attention to the widespread appeal of the Anne books and the character in

Japanese culture, as well as to the rising popularity of PEI as a destination for Japanese tourists. According to Douglas Baldwin, between 1986 and 1991, the number of Japanese tourists to PEI rose from 1,180 to an estimated 15,000 (124). In the past decade and a half, moreover, Sullivan Entertainment's Anne-based films have been widely distributed. "After turning *Anne* and *Avonlea* into the highest rated Canadian TV miniseries ever, attracting more than five million nightly viewers at peak," *The Globe and Mail* reported in 1999 that

> Sullivan managed to win global rights to their properties and sell these proudly Canadian shows all over the world. The company became the poster child for Canadian-content television, that rare producer whose shows are proudly nationalistic, popular both here and abroad. Its profit margins are unheard of in the Canadian entertainment business.... (Saunders and MacDonald)

This report also notes that "Sullivan has published more than 50 novels and photo-illustrated storybooks base on *Anne* [and other series]"; the company has also "licensed more than 50 products in Japan ... based on characters in its *Anne of Green Gables* productions" (C5). Recently, their loosely Montgomery-based *Road to Avonlea* series was reported to be enjoying a wave of popularity in Iran (York).

Anne's longstanding and extensive extra-national appeal raises a number of questions. How does an English-Canadian "national icon" also function as "our biggest cult commodity export"? How, to put it another way, does a text which is best understood in the vocabulary or iconography of twentieth-century English-Canadian nationalism signify in other national and nationalist discourses? That is, if it works first to interpellate English-Canadian subjects through ideological recognition in the context of what Benedict Anderson characterized as the "limited and sovereign" community of the nation, how do we explain its appeal in other national contexts? Pevere and Dymond have suggested that "Anne Shirley ... has become the closest any literary equivalent can get to Mickey Mouse" (13): for them, this proximity is a matter of Anne's being, like Disney's mouse, almost globally recognizable and extremely profitable through an immense range of merchandise and visual commodifications (there is, after all, now an Anne watch). But their analogy invites another line of questioning to do with the aligned iconic status of Anne and the mouse: that is, if Anne Shirley is "right up there" with Canadian national symbols such as Mounties and beavers, Mickey Mouse is indisputably an American image. Is it, then, Mickey Mouse's "Americanness" that underpins his appeal? And is it similarly Anne's "Canadianness," the thing that has led to her functioning as a national icon, that explains her cultural value outside Canada?

The history of *Anne* in the US suggests that it is not. Although early reviews of the novel, which appeared in a range of American papers including *New York Times Saturday Review of Books* and the *American Library Association Booklist,* do make note of the Canadian location,[6] by 1919, the first American film adaptation, a silent film directed by William Desmond Taylor, appears to have stripped the story of its cultural specifics. Montgomery writes in her journal in 1920 of having seen

> *Anne* on the screen at the Regent [in Toronto]. It was a pretty little play well photographed but I think if I hadn't already known it was from my book, that I would never have recognized it. The landscape and folks were "New England," never P.E.

Island.... A skunk and an American flag were introduced—both equally unknown in P.E. Island. I could have shrieked with rage over the latter. Such crass, blatant Yankeeism! (*Selected Journals* II 373)

These two images—a skunk and the American flag—may well be because the film rights to *Anne* were sold by her first American publisher: she notes immediately after this comment on the film that "the play [film] has had an enormous success and [she would not] get a cent from it!" (*Selected Journals* II 373). Page reportedly sold the film rights, after Montgomery's contract for partnership in the profits had ended, for $40,000, of which Montgomery should have had half (*Selected Journals* II 358). Her real objection to the film, however, is clearly to what she calls the "crass ... Yankeeism" that has re-made *Anne* as an American nationalist story, or, in other words, to the apparent appropriation of a regionally and nationally specific story for American cultural self-representation. "Crass ... Yankeeism" here signifies a Barnum-esque opportunism for profit, but it also references a nationalism *against* which at least one element of English-Canadian identity politics must be situated. The Molson brewery's recent and widely discussed "Rant" television advertisement for Canadian lager beer (aired 2000), in which Canadian "Joe's" Canadianness is represented as "not-Americanness," returns to a politics that was especially emphatic at the beginning of the twentieth century. At that time the question of annexation was circulating widely, and Anglo-imperialist and other anti-annexation actions bitterly opposed what W.T. Stead characterized as the definitive "trend of the twentieth century," "the Americanization of the world" (Stead).

The 1919 film is the first major attempt to respond commercially to the popularity of *Anne of Green Gables*. Although Page began by giving Montgomery an unusually small percentage of the book's royalties, and held her to a demanding contract for sequels, the real Anne "market," arguably, is established when an image of Anne is visually re-presented on screen, and her story is culturally re-contextualized to exploit her appeal to a non-Canadian market. This re-contextualizing would be compellingly reinforced when the second American film adaptation of *Anne* appeared only 15 years later, in 1934. Theodore Sheckels has argued that this version, a talking picture directed by Walter Nicholls Jr., was the first film process of de-naturalizing Anne. Sheckels suggests that the 1934 film "reflect[s]" American and not Canadian culture, and ultimately effects what he calls "the Americanization of a Canadian icon." The story, he notes, is significantly changed; characters and events are adapted to accommodate a more overt love story between Anne Shirley and Gilbert Blythe (Sheckels 184–85). Montgomery commented after watching it that she "liked it well enough [but t]he whole picture was so entirely different from *my* vision of the scenes and the people that it did not seem *my* book at all. It was just a pleasant, well-directed play by somebody else" (*Selected Journals* III 326)—and, we might add, set somewhere else, to "reflect," as Sheckels puts it, another cultural context and thus to position the story in relation to another ideology of nation. Montgomery's comment is revealing in its suggestion of her own alienation from the story: she becomes an outsider, not only as the author whose work has been altered for an audience in another locale, but as a viewer who sees in the film only signs of difference.

There is of course a long tradition of adapting Canadian fiction for American audiences by relocating it to the US, something that has jarred when the national context has, as in the case of *Anne of Green Gables*, considerable relevance to the story. But what is compellingly indicated by the Hollywood naturalization of Anne should not be surprising: the novel was an American best-seller, and it maintains a growing readership in the US. It regularly figures in studies of American fiction for children, where it is often linked with such American "girl" books as Louisa May Alcott's *Little Women* (1868), Kate Douglas Wiggin's *Rebecca of Sunnybrook Farm* (1903) and Gene Stratton-Porter's *A Girl of the Limberlost* (1909). Eve Kornfield and Susan Jackson have discussed Montgomery's novel within this kind of framework in an article on what they call "the female *Bildungsroman* in nineteenth-century America": they locate Anne in a continuum of American girls' books that present their nationally identified readers with options for growth and self-realization, albeit within a domestic ideology of gendered "duty." *Anne*'s "Canadianness," so fundamental to the heroine's function as sign of nation and the novel's function as a site for identity formation, does not figure in Kornfield and Jackson's discussion: Anne is loosely and largely "American," a girl who is understood to be geographically "new world," and ideologically republican. Her and her narrative's embedding in the ideas of early twentieth-century English-Canadian nationalism is crucially obscured by their inclusion with, and in relation to, American narratives. *This* Anne is not "our Anne" at all, but "*their* Anne."

The configuration of Anne as an "American" girl is important as an index of the novel's functioning in American culture as well as Canadian, not, perhaps, as a national icon, but none the less within the nationalizing discourse of gender and identity that is produced in the American "girl" books which Kornfield and Jackson discuss. An impulse comparable to their classifying of American "girl" books is evident in Anne Scott MacLeod's 1984 study of what she terms the "Caddie Woodlawn syndrome" (a reference to the pioneer child heroine of Carol Ryrie Brink's 1935 novel of the Wisconsin frontier in the 1860s) and in K.L. Poe's article, in *Nancy Drew and Company: Culture, Gender, and Girls' Series*, a 1997 collection edited by Sherrie A. Inness, in which she argues that

> Although many of the residents of Avonlea speak disparagingly of "Yankees," they actually have more in common with them than with their own English and Scottish forebears. Hence, the series has less to do with the English tradition of girls' fiction and is often accepted as part of the American cannon of children's literature, in spite of its Canadian origin. (16)[7]

It is evident that Anne, despite her location in PEI and despite her rise to the status of national icon in English Canada, is also a part of American literary history and American "girl culture," a point of interpellation for American girlhood. This value in American cultures of gender and national identity has been made especially evident in the proliferation of Anne-related personal web sites, in which readers of Anne, many in the US, write of their first reading of the novel as a moment of self-recognition and coming-of-age. Anne, many American readers suggest on the web, is "like" them.

The same kind of self-recognition and, implicitly, national identification has been made regarding the book's popularity in Japan, although with different ramifications. According to Linda Ghan, Japanese women readers find that

Anne is refreshing. Not only does she have dreams which she, through her own "gambateing" [fighting], manages to realize, but—even better—she is not perfect. She is not an ideal. She gets into scraps and scrapes. (80)

"She is [the] alter ego of Japanese women" who, Ghan suggests, historically "have had limited dreams in Japan" and who are "about 20 years behind Canada on consciousness of women's rights and women's issues" (80).

This argument is given by a number of critics with some variations, but on the same basic principle of Anne's appealing "individualism" in what is presented as a homogeneously restrictive culture (Baldwin, Stoffman, Trillin).[8] But it is clear that in Japan, as in the US, Anne has taken on a new and other identity, beyond the book, and well beyond her "Canadianness." The image of Anne which Judy Stoffman presents in an article on *Akage no An,* or Anne of red hair, in Japanese popular culture, both from comic books and a 1979 animated film series, must also be situated in relation to other familiar figures of Japanese comic books and animation such as, for instance, Sailor Moon, one of the most widely distributed Japanese animation heroines of the 1990s.

The pop-cult *An* that Stoffman delineates is thus best understood not within cultural tourism or within a putative westernizing impulse or urge, such as Ghan implies, to promote the advancement of women in non-western cultures, but something culturally specific in converting what is extra-national to a local signification. Yoshiko Akamatsu has suggested that Anne of Green Gables is "a symbol who links Canadian and Japanese cultures" (211), and it *is* her "Canadianness" that underlies her appeal in Japan. But it is also possible to argue that *Akage no An* has a particular value in Japan as a *local* "cult commodity," functioning, as she does in the US, within a local economy and within a limited and sovereign community, with reference not to her "Canadianness," but only, in this instance, to her "Japaneseness." *An,* Yuko Katsura has suggested to Douglas Baldwin, is a "protagonist who ha[s] all the virtues which Japanese children should possess" (127). This notion of her function as a model for Japanese children is reinforced by the inclusion of Montgomery's writing and some Anne-related material in Japanese English textbooks (Akamatsu 210–11), and in the observation that "the novel appeared [for two decades] on the annual list of books recommended by the Ministry of Health and Welfare, a list that carries weight with librarians and educators" (Stoffman 60). In Japan, as in the US, *Anne* has a life of its own, embedded in nationalist discourses that are not English-Canadian, and generating a range of new culturally specific representations.

D.P. Martinez, in her introduction to a 1998 study of Japanese popular culture, points to "the way in which new or imported forms of mass culture [are 'domesticated,'] often acquir[ing] a *do,* or specific 'way'" (11). *Anne of Green Gables,* arguably, has been "domesticated" in a range of cultural contexts, becoming in the process not so much international as globalized, her local specificity and original nationalism transposed and re-shaped in every location, her function as icon and value as commodity shifting endlessly between cultural and economic, local and global. The current provisional global Anne-product which is getting so much critical and media attention is what Imre Szeman suggests characterizes the "relationship between global culture and local identities—a hybrid character ... neither fully global nor local [which may] provide the imaginative resources for the creation of new identities" (12). *Anne of Green Gables,* at the beginning of the twenty-first century, is at that intersection. It may not be possible to see the globalization of Anne in terms of Mickey Mouse's imperialism or the kind of cultural colonization of Disney "worlds" and "lands"; but we might consider it to be undermining a core myth of cultural globalization: the notion that national "commodity exports" move intact across cultures, taking their national iconic status with them. *Anne* is popular in other national and nationalist context not because it is Canadian, but because it is itself a nationalist narrative....

NOTES

1. Most commentators on *Anne* have made this point. Baldwin cites an interesting statistic that "Anne Shirley is the best known fictional character in Canadian history, and *Anne of Green Gables* has been read by more people than any other Canadian book" (123). He notes that, "In a 1991 survey of 1,628 Canadians across Canada, 69 per cent of English Canadians identified the author of *Anne of Green Gables*." *Journal of Canadian Studies* (n.3 131).

2. Russell et al. enumerates the Page printings to 1942 (2).

3. Baldwin notes that 285,000 people visited Cavendish in 1991 (123).

4. Montgomery is referring to a request by Page for a recent photograph of herself: she writes of her reluctance to make the trip to Charlottetown in March to have the portrait taken, and indicates that she only goes because of Page's urgent request "that the great American public ... see [her] face" (*Selected Journals I* 348).

5. According to the 1986 bibliography, *Anne* was translated into Swedish in 1909, Dutch in 1910, Polish in 1912 (still in print in 1980), Danish and Norwegian in 1918, Finnish in 1920, French in 1925, Icelandic in 1933, Hebrew in 1951 and Japanese in 1952 (this translation by Hanako Muraoka has gone into numerous editions, and has been joined by at least 10 other translations). A Slovak translation appeared in what was Czechoslovakia in 1959. *Anne* was translated into Spanish in 1962, Korean in 1963, Portuguese in 1972, Turkish in 1979 and Italian in 1980. In 2001, two versions of a (1991) German translation by Imelda Erckenbrecht (*Ann auf Green Gables*) are available. This list is not complete, but does provide a sense of the tremendous appeal of *Anne* outside Canada.

6. A selection of these reviews is reproduced in *The Annotated Anne* (483–89).

7. Poe cites Elaine Showalter's argument that "rather than contesting the myth of the American spirit, American women saw their own writing as its true incarnation ... Montgomery's creation of a protagonist that embodied that spirit helped to create a new, feminine version of that myth" (17).

8. Robinson suggests that her individualism is also fundamental to the book's popularity in Canada and to its construction of English-Canadian identity (Gammel and Epperly 19).

REFERENCES

Akamatsu, Yoshiko. "Japanese Readings of *Anne of Green Gables*." *L.M. Montgomery and Canadian Culture*. Ed. Irene Gammel and Elizabeth Epperly. Toronto: University of Toronto Press, 1999. 201–12.

Anderson, Benedict. *Imagined Communities: Reflections on the Origin and Spread of Nationalism*. London: Verso, 1983.

Baldwin, Douglas. "L.M. Montgomery's *Anne of Green Gables*: The Japanese Connection." *Journal of Canadian Studies* 28.3 (1993): 123–33.

Berger, Carl. *The Sense of Power: Studies in the Ideas of English-Canadian Imperialism, 1867–1914.* Toronto: University of Toronto Press, 1970.

Brooymans, Hanneke. "Did our Anne of Green Gables Nurture Gay Fantasies?" *Edmonton Journal* (26 May 2000): A3.

Everett-Gree, Robert. "Glenn Gould, Growth Industry." *The Globe and Mail* 18 Sept. 1999: C5.

Flahive, Gerry. "Lend Me a Wayne and Shuster till Payday." *The Globe and Mail* 17 May 2000: A15.

Gerson, Carole. "'Dragged at Anne's Chariot Wheels': The Triangle of Author, Publisher, and Fictional Character." *L.M. Montgomery and Canadian Culture.* Ed. Irene Gammel and Elizabeth Epperly. Toronto: University of Toronto Press, 1999. 49–63.

Ghan, Linda. "Snapshots—Me and Anne: An Album." *Canadian Children's Literature* 91/92.4 (1998): 78–82.

Goldie, Terry. *Fearand Temptation: The Image of the Indigene in Canadian, Australian, and New Zealand Literatures.* Kingston and Montreal: McGill-Queen's University Press, 1989.

Kornfield, Eve, and Susan Jackson. "The Female Bildungsroman in Nineteenth-Century America: Parameters of a Vision." *Journal of American Culture* 10.4 (1987): 69–75.

Lynes, Jeannette. "Consumable Avonlea: The Commodification of the Green Gables Mythology." *Canadian Children's Literature* 91/92.4 (1998): 7–21.

MacLeod, Anne Scott. "The Caddie Woodlawn Syndrome: American Girlhood in the Nineteenth Century." *A Century of Childhood: 1820–1920.* Ed. Mary Lynn Stevens Heininger. Rochester NY: Margaret Woodbury Strong Museum, 1984. 97–119.

Madison, Charles A. *Book Publishing in America.* New York: McGraw-Hill, 1966.

Martinez, D.P., ed. *The Worlds of Japanese Popular Culture: Gender, Shifting Boundaries, and Global Culture.* Cambridge and New York: Cambridge University Press, 1998.

Montgomery, L.M. *The Annotated Anne of Green Gables.* Ed. Wendy E. Barry, Margaret Anne Doody, and Mary E. Doody-Jones. Oxford and New York: Oxford University Press, 1997.

---. *Anne of Green Gables.* 1908. Toronto: McClelland-Bantam, n.d.

---. *Selected Journals. Vol I. 1890–1910.* Ed. Mary Rubio and Elizabeth Waterston. Toronto: Oxford University Press, 1985.

---. *Selected Journals. Vol II. 1910–1921.* Ed. Mary Rubio and Elizabeth Waterston. Toronto: Oxford University Press, 1987.

---. *Selected Journals. Vol III. 1921–1929.* Ed. Mary Rubio and Elizabeth Waterston. Toronto: Oxford University Press, 1992.

Palmer, Howard. *Patterns of Prejudice: A History of Nativisms in Alberta.* Toronto: McClelland & Stewart, 1982.

Pevere, Geoff, and Greig Dymond. *Mondo Canuck: A Canadian Pop Culture Odyssey.* Scarborough: Prentice-Hall, 1996.

Rubio, Mary Henley. "L.M. Montgomery: Scottish-Presbyterian Agency in Canadian Culture." *L.M. Montgomery and Canadian Culture.* Ed. Irene Gammel and Elizabeth Epperly. Toronto: University of Toronto Press, 1999. 106–19.

Russell, R.W., D.W. Russell, and Rea Wilmshurst. *Lucy Maud Montgomery: A Preliminary Bibliography.* Waterloo: University of Waterloo Library, 1986.

Saunders, Doug, and Gail Macdonald. "Anne's Scary Stepparents." *The Globe and Mail* 16 Oct. 1999: C1+.

Sheckels, Theodore F. "Anne in Hollywood: The Americanization of a Canadian Icon." *L.M. Montgomery and Canadian Culture*. Ed. Irene Gammel and Elizabeth Epperly. Toronto: University of Toronto Press, 1999. 183–91.

Stead, W.T. *The Americanization of the World*. New York and London: Horace Markley, 1901.

Stoffman, Judy. "Anne in Japanese Popular Culture." *Canadian Children's Literature* 91/92.4 (1998): 53–63.

York, Geoffrey. "On Iranian TV, Avonea Rules." *The Globe and Mail* 4 Mar. 2000: A1+.

Szeman, Imre. "Globalization." *Encyclopaedia of Postcolonial Studies*. Ed. John Hawley. Westport, CT: Greenwood, 2001.

Trillin, Calvin. "Anne of Red Hair: What Do the Japanese See in *Anne of Green Gables*?" *L.M. Montgomery and Canadian Culture*. Ed. Irene Gammel and Elizabeth Epperly. Toronto: University of Toronto Press, 1999. 213–21.

York, Geoffrey. "On Iranian TV, Avonea Rules." *The Globe and Mail* 4 Mar. 2000: A1+.

Laura Marks, "Packaged for Export, Contents under Pressure: Canadian Film and Video in a U.S. Context"

EDITORS' INTRODUCTION

One way of looking at what it means to be Canadian is to look at how others see us, especially when they mostly meet us through our cultural products. That is what Laura Marks (now Dena Wosk Professor in Art and Culture Studies at Simon Fraser University, although she was a film programmer in Rochester, NY, when she wrote this piece) does when she examines what Canadian film and video look like to Americans. It is also what CBC's ubiquitous pet Newfoundlander, Rick Mercer, does when he presents his sharply satiric and very revealing segments of "Talking to Americans." Out of a pervasive ignorance of things Canadian, Americans, even Harvard professors, readily agree to add their names to the petition asking Prime Minister "Jean Poutine" to stop the "Saskatchewan seal hunt." Although we should acknowledge that the ridiculous question is framed by Mercer and comes from our sense of ourselves in the first place, and apart from the fact that it is fun to say "Saskatchewan" and "poutine," what do you suppose we look like to Americans when their chief cultural imports from Canada that register with them as Canadian are comedians, news anchors, hockey players, a circus, and Celine Dion. How, for instance, do Jim Carrey, Mike Myers, Shania Twain, and Avril Lavigne register as "Canadian" in the American popular imagination?

When Americans take notice of us at all, it seems, we look familiar, but a little "off," somehow blurred. On the basis of what Laura Marks argues here, a line of argument broadly supported in other works in the field, including the essays by Cecily Devereux and Paul Rutherford in this collection, that "blur" might be an apt metaphor. Canadian national identity, Marks and others argue, never stands still long enough for us to get a good look at it. It is a product of all of the performances of Canadianness at any given moment, and that moment is the single frame of a motion picture, rather than a discrete snapshot that constitutes an act of definition. Just as the theorist Mikhail Bakhtin argues that the meaning of language is "unfinalizable," so many analysts of Canadian identity argue that the meaning of the sign "Canadian" is unfixed or, at least, rooted in multiplicity (think about all of our hyphenated Canadian identities) and open ended.

In contrast to myths central to the American identity, we are not the "melting pot" reflected in the motto "*e pluribus unum*" (of the many, one), suggesting both the pressure and compression of national identity. We are instead a cultural mosaic, a picture made of separate parts, a much self-heralded multicultural state where Toronto is hailed as the most multicultural city in the world with Vancouver and Montreal not far behind, and our motto is "*ad mare usque ad mare*" (the Latin carries the sense of "from one sea all the way to the other"), giving a sense of distance, spaciousness, wiggle room.

Closely related to this reading of Canada as a performative nation is the argument, notably made by experimental film-maker and professor Bruce Elder and referred to in

Marks' essay, that we are a postmodern nation, with whatever that entails (see the discussion of postmodernism in the introduction to this text). Do we demonstrate "incredulity in the face of metanarratives" about our history or identity? Do we almost always define ourselves as a nation allusively, self-consciously, through negative or positive references and comparisons to others? Do we see ourselves as a pastiche of styles? And, perhaps most importantly for our purposes here is this question: Is there strong and broad evidence in Canadian cultural products that could lead us to draw particular conclusions about that imaginary community or essence that is "Canada"?

—AG

ISSUES TO CONSIDER WHILE READING

Radio and television broadcasters in Canada have to meet certain Canadian content standards, but despite incentives to film production offered by several levels of government, film exhibitors have no obligation to show any Canadian films. To what extent should culture be protected? Should it be on the free trade table?

REFERENCES AND FURTHER READING

Bhabha, Homi, K. "DissemiNation." *Salman Rushdie and the Third World: Myths of the Nation.* Ed. Timothy Brennan. New York: St. Martin's, 1987.

Dorland, Michael, ed. *The Cultural Industries in Canada: Problems, Policies and Prospects.* Toronto: James Lorimer, 1996.

Elder, Bruce. "The Cinema We Need." *Canadian Forum* Feb. 1985. Rpt. in *Documents in Canadian Film.* Ed. Douglas Featherling. Peterborough: Broadview Press, 1988. 260–71.

Harcourt, Peter. "Roads Not Taken, Avenues Not Explored: Confessions of an Unconscious Canonizer." *Take One* (Summer 1995): 20–26.

Packaged for Export, Contents under Pressure: Canadian Film and Video in a U.S. Context

"It looks the same, there's just something a little bit...off," is what Americans say when visiting English-speaking Canada. What happens, I want to ask, when a Canadian image is presented in an American context? How do Canadian independent filmmakers cope with the representation of Canadian national identity? And how can media construct or demolish national identity? I want to suggest that when viewing artifacts of English-speaking Canada involves this little-bit-offness, it might be considered as an agent of political intervention. Aware that their work will be viewed in the culturally colonizing context of American exhibition, distribution and other support structures, Canadian media workers sometimes present images of Canada that both champion and dispute the notion of Canadian identity. By playing both sides of the coin, these artists are thus able to simultaneously assert and redefine national and local identities. At the same time, Canadian film/videomakers cross to and from the U.S. for recognition and support, and in these border crossings can also be seen to enact another aspect of their critical practice.

I want to look both at how Canadian independent filmmaking is perceived in the U.S. and how independent media represent Canada, with an eye to how these disguised and diffident packages of Canadian culture may become volatile in their reception in the U.S. This exploration is necessarily somewhat personal, because as a dual citizen of the U.S. and Canada I both identify with and fetishize Canadian nationality and find that my insider-outsider relationship to Canada has informed an ongoing obsession with the breakdown of national borders and cultural boundaries.

The notion of Canadian national identity gets part of its resilience from the fact that "Canada" is a term that does not stagger under the burden of signification that "America" does, especially within the popular culture that permeates both countries. "Canada" has a more expansive quality, it is more open to interpretation and redefinition. Thus, it is easier, in a way, for Canadian filmmakers to make a mark on, or a dent in, the national identity. In addition, this uneasiness with the notion of uniform national identity makes Canadians good at interrogating U.S. national identity: better than Americans are doing it themselves.

Rather than attempt a survey, I've drawn selectively on work from English-speaking Canada, drawing on a series of interviews with Canadian film/videomakers who have had instructive experiences on both sides of the border: Helen Lee, John Greyson, Ardele Lister and Sara Diamond. It will not focus on work that represents Canada in terms of what (to outsiders as well as Canadians) is exotic about it, but at work that might "pass" as American. Canadian philosopher Robert Schwartzwald writes, "as in the United States the temptation has been to advance a national identity through the symbols of communities and peoples marginalized along the way, especially the continent's original peoples."[1] This temptation to specularize Canada in terms of its visibly exotic people must be avoided, largely because what this does is allow white power centres to continue to function invisibly. Within Canada this invisibility functions to disguise power; but outside Canada it can work to subvert other invisible powers, Trojan Horse style. Canadian film, seen in the United States can trouble the viewer's consciousness of American cultural and political centrality.

White Dawn, a short video by Kim Tomczak and Lisa Steele, speculates about how this little-bit-offness would look if the relations of cultural imperialism were reversed. It asks, what if all the American movies, TV shows, books and magazines got switched overnight for something that looked almost the same ... but not quite? "It was like a dream I couldn't wake up from," says the narrator who has awakened in this doppelganger universe. "Everything was just ... off." The narrator (a male figure with a female voice-over) realizes that s/he is in Canada. As books by Farley Mowat, Margaret Atwood and Robertson Davies wave across the screen, s/he complains: "these people are so dominating. They've made things, I don't know, so *familiar*. How come I know so much about Newfoundland and Toronto?" Even with "American content" rules and stiff import taxes, dismally tiny proportions of "American" music, books, magazines and music make it onto local markets. Through this simple reversal, the tape suggests a way of turning the tables on the U.S. cultural hegemony in order to supplant what is well known to U.S. viewers with something just a little bit different, and watch the productive confusion that results.

I got the run-around trying to rent *White Dawn* for a video series in Rochester, N.Y. recently because its U.S. distributor had stopped carrying it. This little problem is typical of the way Canadian independent media is viewed, or more accurately not viewed, in the United States. Canadian access to exhibition and distribution in the U.S. is abysmal, and this is perpetuated by patronizing American attitudes toward Canadian independents. Americans in the independent media scene tend to believe Canadian filmmakers are overfunded. A rare article on Canadian filmmaking in *American Film* in 1990, "They Always Get Their Film," conveys this and other misconceptions in its title-page spread that reads: "The Canadian government has sired [sic] a national cinema, but can a film industry survive when every taxpayer is a producer?"[2] The title, with its outlaw, Wild West reference, spreads over a production still in which samurai on horseback ride into a Rocky Mountains panorama: the connotations being that Canada is simultaneously vast wilderness, multicultural paradise and a place where the most outlandish funding proposals are nurtured to fruition.

While Winikoff's article supports the idea that government funding allows Canadian film to be more artful and complex than Hollywood product, it falls back on the notion that government funding impedes filmmakers from world-class achievement. "While a handful of those with international clout, like Norman Jewison and David Cronenberg, can make truly independent films, the vast majority—including those who've already taken home some major awards—are subsidized by the government." Winikoff's assumption is that commercial success is the result of individuals' ability to rise to the top. He ignores the fact that the industry is structured to ensure that virtually only Hollywood films make it into distribution and that independent production is seen as a training ground for Hollywood talent. American individualism is the lens through which this writer sees Canadian filmmakers as "making it" or not. At the same time, contradictorily, he seems to recognize that the (mythical) self-made filmmaker of the U.S. model somehow fails to achieve the aesthetically and intellectually rigorous standard upheld by the subsidized Canadians.

Not only is the perception that Canadian media workers are rolling in lucre false, as we well know; it is also misleading to concentrate on the economics of production, in which it is true that—ignoring for the moment the economics of distribution that favour Americans in practically every way—Canadians do fare somewhat better than U.S. producers *if* they are willing to work within government funding guidelines. Of course, Hollywood utterly monopolizes the fare at the Cineplexes on both sides of the border, meaning that Canadian feature films do not have much theatrical exposure within Canada, let alone outside. While U.S. independents have a plausible chance of having their work shown on public television, this opportunity is lacking for Canadians. But the exposure given to Canadian film by an article such as Winikoff's (who is a "Bronx-born ... sometime playwright now living in Vancouver") perpetuates the notion that a free-market competition exists for filmmakers irrespective of national base.

Meanwhile, the advertising surrounding Winikoff's article in *American Film* is for Canadian film-production unions—the International Alliance of Theatrical Stage Employees (IATSE), the Association of Canadian Film Craftspeople, and the British Columbia Council of Film Unions. Americans reading this article most likely have their eyes on Canada as a site for their own productions. Funnily enough, the background still of samurai riding into the sunset is from a film by Japanese director Haruki Kadokawa—evidence that the attraction to Canada for readers of this magazine may be more to Canada as raw material than to Canada as cultural site or cultural innovator. A sidebar article, "Luring Cameras to Kamloops," describes the joys of filming in B.C., Alberta (for westerns), and Toronto (for that urban look, at a fraction of the price). I don't want to make too much of this, but this combination of articles for American readers perpetuates the notion that Canadian film production is nurtured into somnolence, and that Canadian filmmaking is only interesting once it stands free of the crutch of government funding, but that Canada is pristine ground for American exploration! The subversive power of slight differences doesn't seem to amount to much when American movies shot in Canada go to pains to efface the difference. Filmmaker John Greyson jokes that whenever you see garbage on the street in Toronto, you know it's a "New York" film shoot.

What, then, is a more constructive notion of Canadian film that might be appropriate for export? A number of theorists and artists have argued that Canadian culture tends to be postmodern by virtue of its formation of a national identity in terms of its sense of otherness. In his 1985 manifesto, "The Cinema We Need," Bruce Elder argues that Canadian cinema is predisposed to be postmodernistic cinema.[3] According to Elder, Canadian culture and philosophy never abandoned a premodern epistemology, one in which there persisted an intimate connection between humans and nature, rather than a radical separation. The epistemology kept us concerned with content, with narrative, with tangible links to the world around us. His thesis seems to be drawn from the sturdy old observation that Canadians have had to carve out a living in the inhospitable wilderness and hence have an intimacy with and respect for nature. So when the postmodern era rolled around, Canadian culture was in a position to embrace the otherness at its core because it never really left it.[4]

Elder's argument places Canadian (formalist, experimental) cinema nicely in the position of vanguard. However, he can only do this by perpetuating the frozen-North image that has ceased to define Canada, except for the most uninformed outsiders. While conceptually, according to this argument, Canada nicely occupies the position of postmodern subject, it is only by virtue of being the "other" of a movement incubated somewhere else—Paris and L.A., not Vancouver, Toronto or Montreal. Elder's is a form of provincial postmodernism which does not accept that Canadians produce postmodernism, but only that Canada *is* postmodern. If we agree with Elder's argument, postmodernism would seem to inhere in Canadian culture not by choice but naturally, to bleed from our veins like maple sap. Geoff Pevere, an upstart on the Canadian film criticism scene when he joined the dialogue around Elder's essay, argued as much when he criticized Elder's imperious neglect of the role of the viewer in constructing the political efficacy of a film. Elder's manifesto, Pevere rails in proper in-your-face-cross-generational fashion, promulgates "a view that seeks to establish a hierarchy of knowledge and privilege that exploits mystification as a necessary means of maintaining an imbalance of power between the exalted few that produce and comprehend art and the greater masses who do not. And, while we're at it, just what the fuck is 'art' anyway?"[5]

I would not go so far as Pevere in rejecting Elder's arguments for their aesthetic absolutism. I would, however, argue that Canadian cultures cannot be understood as postmodern without seeing the degree to which they are also postcolonial. Elder was right that the most successful works of independent Canadian cinema today are predisposed to a certain decentring quality. But this is not an effect of having to huddle against the raging north winds, at least not primarily. Rather, its cause is Canada's volatility in terms of cultural composition. The inherent otherness that Elder and others describe as making Canadian national identity more volatile, more prone to redefinition, is directly connected to the flow of new populations and subsequent processes of (second- and third-generation) hybridization. The "constants" of Canadian identity are as insubstantial as the cups of milky tea that are a postcolonial convention. Nevertheless, this latter motif impressed me profoundly as an adolescent immigrant from the States, discovering that her schoolmates, whose parents spoke Bengali, Chinese, Polish, or with a thick Scottish or Jamaican accent, all shared the custom of Red Rose and digestive biscuits in our identical Mississauga tract homes. It took me a while to realize that these lingering marks of empire were the constants of our shared culture, and that cultural imperialism indeed continued to play itself out in some of my friends' lives in decidedly less cozy ways.

Ultimately Pevere does fish the baby of Canadian subjectivity out of the bath water of formalist obfuscation, in a 1987 article in the U.S. magazine *The Independent*. Here Pevere's argument is reminiscent of Elder's emphasis on the Canadian as postmodern, focusing on the quality of alienation in Canadian independent cinema.[6] This quality showed up in many works such as Atom Egoyan's *Next of Kin* (1984) and *Family Viewing* (1987), Patricia Gruben's *Low Visibility* (1984) and Bachar Chbib's *Evixion* (1987). "They demonstrate a critical awareness of how this exposure to the cultural products of an alien culture must necessarily lead to the chronic alienation from their own cultural context," Pevere writes. "In other words, what this generation has achieved, and what simultaneously binds them to, and distinguishes them from, their predecessors, is a level of active autocriticism of their inherited condition of cultural disaffection."[7]

This question of disaffection which is seen by Pevere and others as defining Canadian cultural practice, provides a structure for Ardele Lister's *See Under Canada Nationalism*, a tape that subtly deals with the notion that Canada is structured around a lack. I have a suspicion that *See Under* will always be seen as a work-in-progress, since its object, getting Canadians to define their nation, remains quite elusive. The tape is structured around a list of "Canadian" qualities that Lister uses to survey a variety of opinions and observations. Lister's interviewees are incapable of the windy generalizations of their American counterparts in her tape *Behold the Promised Land*. Instead, their terms are low-key and relative: "nice," "friendly," "not overly aggressive," "not as harsh as the U.S." Found footage is used in a manner which is similarly self-deprecating; the voice-over accompanying a shot of bathers splashing in Georgian Bay asserts: "Canada was covered in ice for 20,000 years but has warmed up almost completely." The film, a '60s promotional film called *Helicopter Canada*, begins with the sound of yodeling. Yodeling? It is as though Canada can only image itself by association with other national traditions: and this in a film promoting tourism in Canada! Lister muses in the tape that "maybe Canada is one of the first postmodern countries. There's no metanarrative, or as Yeats said, the centre will not hold." Ironically enough, despite the difficult time her interviewees have with making generalizations about Canada, they come up with quite concrete reasons to like their country, reasons such as gun control and socialized medicine.

Pevere's article captures a quality predominant in film works of the past decade. However, I would argue that the preoccupations of Canadian independent cinema, and the political agendas they support, have already shifted—as have the theoretical concerns with semiotics, psychoanalysis and feminism in film and media studies that Pevere rightly points out were ascendant "when this bunch [of filmmakers] would've been hitting the books." Now, it seems, as a result of work done in the last decade, the hot issues concern less a generalized alienation than an affirmation of local specificity. A useful maxim of '80s theory which still remains strong suggests that one cannot speak for others but may only represent one's own experience with any intimate authority. Many contemporary Canadian independent films define Canada precisely in terms of what it is not, focusing on regional or ethnic identity or local politics rather than by appealing to a generalized alienation. Most Canadian film/videomakers I have spoken to identify with a particular community before they identify their work as Canadian. Being part of a feminist, or Asian, or rural, Queer or other specific experience gives one an identity more pressing than the abstractions of nationality. In many cases, this identity informs membership in a transnational community that threatens the coherence of national identity. This enables their work to dispute the identities imposed at national and international levels. What I want to argue is that Canada is more flexible with regard to such differences, indeed is even constituted by them. Canadian films, when they deal with national identity at all, *perform* it: there's a self-consciousness of the distance between the national symbols and one's personal and community experience. This is all to the good for the image of Canadian filmmaking, I believe, to the degree that the national image cannot be upheld as a pedagogy, a grand narrative, but is viable as performance.

The former is "the process of identity constituted by historical sedimentation," the latter is "the loss of identity in the signifying process of cultural identification."[8] A pedagogy of national identity insists in large terms, from above, on the existence of things that pull a nation together—flag, national anthem, common history. The other register in which national identity is (de)constructed is the performative level, in which individuals' daily actions elaborate, undermine, and redefine the grand narratives put in place by the pedagogical. The performative, dependent upon the "performances" of millions of individual actors, appears to be the means by which a nation's identity can get derailed or redirected. These two registers of national identity, top-down and bottom-up, work together like a scarf that's being knitted from one end and unraveled from the other. In one direction, the national identity is put in place by national holidays like Thanksgiving; in the other, it is reconstructed by the actual stuff people choose to put on their table.

Using Homi K. Bhabha's categories, I think it is possible to look at nation as differentially defined more in terms of the pedagogical or the performative. A nation with a well-defined national identity, such as the United States, is constantly involved in pedagogy, containing the disunity of its people in the unity of grand national narratives. By contrast, I would argue that the performative level of narrating national identity is more characteristic of Canadian self-definition, in which the nation as a whole is ill-defined precisely to the degree that groups within it are developing their own identities. Pedagogy situates the people of a nation as objects, receivers; the performative constitutes them more as subjects intervening in the definition of a nation. In short, the difference that makes Canada is in the details.

Relatedly, Schwartzwald refers to the notion of becoming as a seductive way to characterize Canadian national identity.[9] The centre (of power, of cultural identity) is continually dissolved by the margins, by what it is becoming. And to the degree that in Canada the centre has never been fixed, except in terms of *what* it is becoming, national identity is fluid and volatile indeed. But it must be asked how much this volatility is the main thing going on, and how much it is a convenient screen for more stable powers. Transnational powers, for example.

Schwartzwald, a Canadian living and teaching in the States, suggests that two things characterize Canadian culture: simple envy, and the concomitant notion of "purity of origins," namely that Canadians, by virtue of being at the periphery of power of the United States, are innocent and free of evil (an attitude that Lister's interviewees seem to support.) Both define Canadian culture in terms of a cycle of dependency. Schwartzwald argues that the way to get out of this relation is "neither by copying the discourses of others, nor by revaluing what is said but devalued within a discourse, but by excavating that which is repressed by relations of dominance.[10] In order to justify distinguishing ourselves from the homogeneous, apparently universal condition that the United States has created for itself (the hegemonic idea that the U.S. occupies such a universal position that it is not necessary to point to it), we have to justify our attachment to specific traditions. This is not "a simple rejection of universality... rather, it takes the form of an acceptance of the 'other' precisely in his difference, a defence of plural traditions, ethnicities and communities, that has been called a 'philosophical federalism.'"[11] The point is that particularity is what *defines* Canada, not in a contingent but in an absolute way.

Interestingly, the notion of Canadian identity as becoming which Schwartzwald pursues shows up in one of the most generous and productive readings of Elder's manifesto. Michael Dorland, who edited some of the Elder exchange in *Cinema Canada,* contrasts the angst about the disappearing subject fashionable in American cinema with "Canadian art [which] (as I read Elder) is a manifestation of the appearing subject-object as the dialectic between person, place and mind. His is a realism in which Canada is not a perpetual becoming or vanishing, but an integer."[12] Canadian identity understood as a ratio between disintegrating and coming into existence is an apt metaphor for the process of national self-creation. It offers a way for individual actions to be seen as part of the construction of nation. While it is easy to flirt with disintegration when you know you're at the stable centre—as is the tendency with American cultural production—when disappearance is a real risk, the acts by which identity is constructed take on more significance. The notion of Canada as becoming however avoids some of the negative construction of Canada as lacking and decentred that these approaches loosely associated with postmodernism tend to share. Instead it ties into the much more productive idea of national identity as performed, an idea outlined above.

In addition to this difference between Canadian and American concepts of postmodern identity, there are somewhat more tangible reasons for Canadian disinterest in the wholesale disappearance of the subject, which came up in a conversation I had with videomaker Sara Diamond. Diamond points out (in an argument similar to Elder's) that the Baudrillardian influence still prevalent among U.S. video artists never took off in Canadian work. Baudrillard seems to have filled a gap for artists and theorists who want to critique the power of the image but have no faith in their ability to influence change. Hence the plethora, especially in the 1980s, of work by U.S. artists dealing with media appropriation and the illusory quality of representation. "Canadians relation to media culture is different," says Diamond. "There have been public TV and public radio here for longer than in the U.S. We've been able to use and to trust the image a little more. Maybe Canadians have been less willing to buy into the notion that media constructs reality totally and insisted on placing media in an instrumental relationship to other forms of resistance."

In contrast, within Canada, Marxist traditions have continued to carry weight among artists. Because Marxist approaches have always had some currency in this country, while they were killed off for some time in the U.S., Canadian media work has been able to evolve formally while maintaining an interest in social content. As well, because media representation has not been so utterly bound up with consumer culture as it has in the U.S. there seems to be less despair that the image is irrevocably corrupted. The more integral relation of art to social content in Canadian video work, Diamond suggests, has to do both with intellectual traditions and with the material circumstances of media production in Canada. Consequently, there is a more integral relation of art to social content in Canadian video work.

Diamond's argument points to how it may be possible for artists such as those I describe here to continue to work politically while also interrogating representation rather than having to choose one of the divergent paths of art or activism that seem to characterize much independent video work in the States. "The division of labour between documentary, community-based work, and video art is very marked in the U.S. whereas they have never been completely separate in Canada...People who did work like this in the States would have been marginalized—such as Martha Rosler, whose work would be typical here." Only recently, Diamond notes, have U.S. artists begun to collapse those categories, in work on AIDS and postcolonial issues. Diamond's comments suggest that the hot new American video work has unacknowledged debt to ongoing explorations by Canadians.

...Lister's *See Under Canada Nationalism* and its companion tape on American identity, *Behold the Promised Land* (1991) embody the difference between the broad-brushed rhetoric of American nationalism and the tentative demarcations of Canadianness. In *Behold the Promised Land*, Americans interviewed at Fourth of July picnics unselfconsciously mouth slogans about their national identity, such as the Brooklyn girl who defines the Fourth of July as "about independence. (Lister asks off-camera, 'Independence from what?') Benjamin Franklin and the government got together and signed a peace treaty ('With who?') with Abraham Lincoln ... and that meant the slaves were free." Other Independence Day celebrants denounce welfare, extol Americans' freedom to work their way to the top, talk about defending their country, and otherwise have no trouble occupying the space created by nationalist rhetoric. Lister makes this alliance clear with footage culled from '50s educational films, which for all their Cold War hyperbole, reflect an attitude that is still alive and well among her contemporary interviewees.

These two tapes' different modes of expression correspond neatly to Bhabha's two ways of constructing national identity: the pedagogical and the performative. In Bhabha's pedagogy-performance model, can the little performances that constitute Canada insinuate themselves into the massive national fiction that constitutes the United States? And if such a subversion is possible, what politics does it serve? Bhabha argues that the difference at the level of performance might, instead of being assimilated and neutralized, disrupt the commonsense nature of the performative. Lister's "Freedom from what?," for example, is a performative response that undermines the national pedagogy. That "little bit off" quality of Canadian images, seen from a U.S. perspective, is the detail that makes it possible to question the whole. The works I have been discussing perform the subversion of American identity by insinuating their differences into the national pedagogy of the U.S. Greyson's work, for example, which I will discuss in more detail below, is barely noticeable as Canadian, yet it is chock-full of references to specific locations in Toronto and Orillia, figures in Canadian media history from Claude Jutra to Barbara Frum and specific Canadian products (like the white-chocolate mousse cake from Dufflet's Bakery on Queen Street in Toronto, featured in *The Making of "Monsters"*).

Given the superficial similarity between English-speaking Canadian media and U.S. media, it seems possible that a Canadian performative, as it "intervenes or insinuates itself *in-the-place-of*,"[13] could disrupt the American pedagogy. Within Canada, needless to say, middle-class urban dwellers of Anglo-Saxon extraction occupy the power centre. But placed next to the more absolutely powerful—namely, the same sort of people in urban centres in the States—Canada's bland powerful can trouble that absoluteness.

Many Canadian filmmakers are not as sanguine as I am about the subversive potential of Canadian identity in American contexts. Greyson, for example, says that "Americans have an amazing tendency to assimilate Canadian work to American experience. It's perceived as out-of-state work; I'd say we're seen as Midwestern. Canada doesn't exist as a national entity to the U.S. It's perceived as regionally other, not nationally other." Yet Greyson's own work, by placing the locations and events of southern Ontario at the centre as though they were universal, does seem to unsettle the complacency of U.S. work that assumes to speak from the centre. Throughout his career Greyson's films have been aggressively local. They simply assume that viewer will care about bathroom raids in Orillia (*Urinal*), docudramas on CBC (*The Making of "Monsters"*), or exhibits at the "Toronto Natural History Museum" (*Zero Patience*). Greyson talks about "the authority of the local," the ability of small towns and obscure events to take on a mythic quality through their representation in literature or film. Specific, possibly obscure references have the ability to destabilize the fictive centre that New York independent filmmakers, no less than Hollywood, promote.

Greyson's new feature film, *Zero Patience* (1993) will probably be the film that propels Greyson to international acclaim, and so it is interesting to look at how the local, mostly Toronto, references that structure *Zero Patience*, operate without explanation or apology. The Canadian elements of the film are in part necessary, such as the fact the so-called Patient Zero was a French Canadian, and in part gratuitous, such as the ubiquitous references to the Canadian synchronized swimming team on the radio news. Greyson plays knowingly with the conjunction of sexual and cultural othering in the character of Patient Zero: and defaming the Quebecois is one motivation of the Toronto bureaucrats who take an interest in him. Its principal character is the nineteenth century Orientalist traveller and scholar Sir Richard Burton, miraculously still alive and working as chief taxidermist at the Toronto Natural History Museum.

As in Greyson's previous work, constant references to the Canadian and Toronto contexts privilege a viewer's own local knowledge and slightly estrange non-Canadians.

Zero Patience also advertises the Toronto media community in which Greyson's work is so embedded, and this does so on the level of in-jokes. In a musical sequence about the dispute over causes of AIDS other than HIV (Greyson's ability to couch complex issues in the form of the musical number transcends the Gilbert and Sullivanesque), the "bloodstream" is played by members of this community, such as former NAC (National Action Committee) president Judy Rebick, gay activist videomakers Andy Fabo and Michael Balser, and Lisa Steele's daughter Larue Peoples—all floating amid red and white balloons in an indoor swimming pool. While the significance of these people will probably be lost on a non-Canadian, even non-Toronto audience, I think structuring the film around a specific, local community and local knowledges gives it a sort of cognitive density. The point of local authority is not to fetishize local peculiarities but to allow them to multiply until they create a texture of (un)familiarity.

Independent filmmaking in the U.S. is so heavily based on New York (and to a lesser degree San Francisco, Los Angeles and Chicago) that in film and video the experience of these places come to stand for "the city," and life in general. Partly this is a result of simple budget constraints on film- and videomakers (often students) living in these communities. Lacking means to travel or to stage environments, independent filmmakers make do with the city at hand: Central Park stands in for other expanses of trees and grass; tiny, crummy apartments stand in for "home"; and urban buildings festooned with posters and razor wire become the backdrop for all manner of not necessarily urban subjects. Thus New York (and to a lesser extent, other big cities) gains a hegemony on representation. Images of this city become naturalized, so that even when a work is not necessarily set in New York, the city's quite idiosyncratic qualities become the common denominator. Films made in New York end up being films about New York. The result, as Greyson points out, is that work that does not share these characteristics looks strange, hard to place, "out of state." The culture in which independents produce also has a particular, well-known cast in New York. Ideas of how artists look, what they eat, what they do for jobs, etc., are naturalized in the weird and brutal environment of this town, producing wardrobe anxiety for all of us who work in the area of independent media in North America.

Canadian filmmakers are highly aware that "international" recognition really means making it in New York. As Greyson says, "Everybody's great goal is always to rush down to New York and have a great success there. I think the title of Serge Guilbaut's book says it all, *How New York Stole the Idea of Modern Art.* I think it's really accurate on how cultural imperialism exports itself.... New York is brilliant at bringing the players from the periphery and constituting them in the centre, then sending them back out to the periphery."

...The battle of representation between Canadian and U.S. films (a battle probably only perceived as such from the Canadian side) is really more a battle between Toronto, Montreal and New York. Although Toronto is loathed as the highly funded, brain-draining centre of cultural production within English-speaking Canada, it is those qualities that give Toronto filmmaking a wedge in the image culture generated around New York. One hegemonic urban centre's images cannot be supplanted by those of a small town, rural area or mid-sized city, but another hegemonic urban centre has a fighting chance.

The fact that Lister was an "illegal alien" underscores the fact of American protectionism that ultimately blocks Canadians' sense of dual identity. Canadians feel we share American cultural identity, but if we try to move on it by working or living in the U.S., we learn that it's not transferable. Insofar as Canada fits into the American imaginary at all, the dynamic is quite different. To try to tease out that difference, let me indulge in one more dual citizen anecdote, which is funny because two events hinge on the same spoken word. An American friend of mine in Rochester knew me for about a year before I came out to her as a Canadian. She exclaimed, "I knew you were too funky to be just American!" About a year later, a Canadian acquaintance who also lives in Rochester found out I was Canadian too. She protested, "But you're too funky to be Canadian!"

While my friend's observations may not have proved beyond the shadow of a doubt that I am "funky," they do provoke speculation on how this elusive quality is perceived as part of national identity by Americans and Canadians. My American friend had a notion of American identity as something firmly held together from on high that didn't have room for such qualities as funkiness, which she perceived as nonconformist. My Canadian friend thought funkiness denoted a strong will, a quality that is part of the pedagogy of American identity. The moral, I suppose, is that there is no symmetry between two nations when one affirms its identity in a constant reenactment of national pedagogy, while the other constantly reworks its national definition at the micro-level; but if people think you are funky you can get by anywhere.

Michael Dorland argues that the discussion matters deeply because "now, more than ever before, it devolves upon the Canadian cultural project (as manifested by the Canadian artistic and intellectual imagination) to bear the entire burden of not only reviving, but enlarging what is left of the sense of Canadian difference." It will have become obvious that this is not my project here: I have been more interested to use the notion of Canadianness to reveal American not-sameness—the non-identity of "America" with its own narrative. Ultimately, the concern of this article has been not to defend a national identity but to suggest that the U.S. hegemony on national representation is a fragile construction, which Canadian cultural production is in a privileged position of being able to unbalance. Canadian culture need not, and probably should not, have this project as its primary goal. But the very ingredient that expresses Canadian diffidence, the performative quality of a Canadian culture, catalyzes on contact the slow disintegration of the U.S. national narrative.

NOTES

1. Robert Schwartzwald, "an/other Canada. another Canada? other Canadas," *The Massachusetts Review* (Spring–Summer) 1990: 12.

2. Kenneth Winikoff, "They Always Get Their Film," *American Film* (July 1990): 26–30, 44–5.

3. Bruce Elder, "The Cinema We Need," *The Canadian Forum* (February 1985); rpt. in *Documents in Canadian Film*, Ed. Douglas Fetherling (Peterborough: Broadview Press, 1988) 260–71.

4. This thesis, so popular among theorists of Canadian identity, sounds awfully similar to psychoanalytic theories of female identity. Girl children, because they identify with their mother, are never able to separate completely and form a coherent identity. Canada, according to such an argument, cannot enter modern culture because it cleaves to the Nature at the foundation of its identity.

5. Geoff Pevere, "The Rites (and Wrongs) of the Elder or The Cinema We Got: The Critics We Need," *Documents in Canadian Film*: 328.

6. Geoff Pevere, "An Outsider's Aesthetic: Contemporary Independent Film in Canada," *The Independent* (June 1987): 13–18.

7. Ibid., p. 15.

8. Homi K. Bhabha, "DissemiNation," *Salman Rushdie and the Third World: Myths of the Nation*, ed. Timothy Brennan (New York: St. Martin's Press, 1987) 304.

9. Schwartzwald, p. 24.

10. Ibid., p 37.

11. Ibid., p 42.

12. Michael Dorland, "The Shadow of Canadian Cinema: Bruce Elder's Immodest Proposal," *Documents in Canadian Film*, 322.

13. Bhabha, p. 305.

Unit III *Cultural Sites and Material Culture*

INTRODUCTION

INTRODUCTION

One of the most productive outcomes of the advent of cultural studies and its emphasis on cultural materialism is that it has expanded our view of what artefacts of the cultural sphere around us we can legitimately turn our critical attention toward. It is not that we had never seen these artefacts before; we had just never seen them with the kind of critical intensity that we do now. Ever since Gutenberg's invention of movable type in the 15th century we have lived in what Marshall McCluhan calls the "Gutenberg Galaxy," in which the swift and mass dissemination of information has transformed the public sphere in which we live. This transformation has, in turn, transformed the circulation of knowledge—what we *do* with the information that we have. Gutenberg's invention becomes a kind of metaphor for an ur-cultural machine which generates all kinds of "discourse networks" (to use a phrase coined by Friedrich Kittler) for the mass reproduction of commodities, both material and immaterial.

The logic behind the quick and efficient production of books is not so different from the logic that informs Ford's auto assembly line, the transatlantic telegraph, steam-powered locomotion, the telephone, the television, and the Internet. Our point about all of these phenomena is that they all produce commodities of one kind or another: the assembly line produces cars, whereas the Internet produces information, but *both* are commodities because, to borrow Marx's terms, they both have a use value and an exchange value. They are not just inert objects; they are objects that gain their identities by virtue of how they are used, exchanged, circulated—by virtue of how they *mean*—in the sphere of what we have come to call in this anthology "culture." Another way of saying this is to say that material culture is not *just* material.

Cultural studies teaches us, then, that while Gutenberg's invention enabled the wider dissemination of the Bible, linguistic sign systems are not the only way to read the sphere of culture. In many ways, our education system still makes the linguistic signage of books the pre-eminent source of knowledge. It is no small irony that the medium we have chosen to tell *you* about this fact is the book you are reading at this very moment. In books, we quite frequently encounter discussion *about* material culture—architecture, sporting events, toys—but we still learn to read these material artefacts *through* the text. The following articles, although words on pages, ask us to consider these artefacts on their own terms as *texts* for us to read, just as we would read a book. But they also ask us to consider these artefacts as cultural *sites* where material culture is *produced*, not only as a series of material artefacts or commodities (as in the production of cars on an assembly line or the creation of a Web page to disseminate knowledge) but also as the production of the site itself, within which these objects come into being through the subjects who make, use, and interact with them.

In his discussion of the West Edmonton Mall, Rob Shields speaks of social spatialization, which is a way of expanding on Henri Lefebvre's notion of the "production of space." Space, as Karen Dubinsky argues below, is "socially constructed." We have to think of the types of space that we create and that are created for us: geographical, psychological, virtual, political, architectural, social, environmental. Even the space of an apparently entirely natural setting, such as Jasper National Park, is one that we produce through our perceptions of it. First of all, this space is distinguished from spaces around it by virtue of its being designated a "park" (as opposed to simply a place where nature exists) that is "national" (rather than provincial or corporate or under the jurisdiction of some other controlling body). This designation, in turn, mobilizes a whole series of distinctions that condition how we think of this space: the federal government that protects/manages "natural" spaces; the T-shirts or postcards of the park we buy in Jasper to send to others; the contentious history of the building of Canada's national rail system, of industry, and of tourism that both brought us closer to and compromised the environmental integrity of natural spaces, such as the Rocky Mountains.

The world we live in, then, is the creation of what Dubinsky, quoting Shields, calls a series of "imaginary geographies" associated with "particular values, historical events and feelings" (239). This is also to say that, just as our bodies are neither just bodies nor entirely "our own" (as we shall see in the next section of articles), no space is "natural." An opera house is not just a place where people gather to enjoy operas performed. It evokes not only the production of the opera but the production of an elaborate series of cultural and social distinctions and hierarchies—of subjects moving in and through the space of the opera house, of their reactions to the production itself, of their desire to *be seen* at the opera or perhaps just to enjoy hearing the singing, and of the fact that the house is state owned, rather than privately owned. All of these factors contribute to the *production* of the opera house as a cultural *site* or space, rather than just an inert building in which people go to enjoy operas performed. Think of the elaborate imaginary geography that is Disneyworld. Think of the complex production of social, cultural, or political meanings at an event like the Olympics.

By looking at material culture as a cultural site, we are asking you to consider culture as something that is not an object fixed in time and space but, again, produced by its evolution through time and space and by its interaction with a variety of social forces and ideologies. How do we read something that is not fixed in space and time? In our discussion of semiotics in the general introduction to this volume (see also Dick Hebdige's article), we asked you to entertain the idea of texts as sign systems or semiotic fields of meaning. This section of readings asks you to expand this idea to consider all aspects of culture as part of semiotic fields. We only have space to discuss a few examples of these fields in the following articles, but we hope that these examples will give you a sense of how all of culture can be read as fields that indicate the interplay of various personal and public desires, beliefs, and ideologies within a social arena.

This is also to say that this arena only "makes sense" because there are subjects within it to make sense of it, to interact with it. But we can carry this thought further: subjects made this arena in the first place and made the discourse networks or modes of industrial or technological production that inform how subjects are then, in turn, *made by* these networks. We need to consider further, that is, how this sphere of culture that subjects *make*, in turn, *produces* the subjects who made it—how much they control and are controlled by this sphere.

In the first instance, then, this section addresses certain artefacts of culture: the magazine or print ads, the commodities they advertise, the shopping mall that both advertises and sells commodities, the Barbie dolls that are sold to little girls to play with, the otherwise 'natural' site that advertises itself as a tourist attraction. But we can already see, just by reading, how we have described these artefacts even in this last list that it is not just the artefact alone we are talking about, as we have already suggested. We cannot consider the artefact without considering its mode of production; and this production is not just about how the artefact was made as a material artefact but is informed by a whole host of material practices that manifest how the artefact is both produced *and* consumed. Moreover, when we say "produced," we do not just mean the way that Barbie dolls are plastic poured into metal moulds; we also mean how they are produced in culture: how the dolls are "packaged," both in boxes for sale but also through advertising and public relations and the myths generated by these processes, for the consumers to whom they are sold.

We can see, then, how "production" shades over into "consumption," which, again, does not mean simply the purchase of a commodity. The word "consume" is interesting here because it evokes how a product gets used, how a Barbie doll is played with by a little girl in Greenwich, USA, or by a little girl in Johannesburg, South Africa, or how a set of Martha Stewart Everyday bath towels purchased by a housewife in Salt Lake City, Utah, or by a gay accountant in Calgary, Alberta, signifies the cultural cachet that comes with owning Martha Stewart products (or, rather, the cachet that Martha Stewart Inc. advertises to its consumers to get them to buy into the Martha Stewart ideology of how an elegant and tastefully appointed household is a "good" household).

We see here already at work the tension between what Martha Stewart Inc. or Mattel "sells" to its consumers, which is to say the ideologies it wants its consumers to "consume" or "buy into," and the ways in which the product is used or "bought into" by these users. To understand this tension we also have to consider how the above critical description itself "uses" the ideas of Barbie or Martha Stewart in its own way, that is, according to its own biases. Why would it always be a "little girl" playing with Barbie? Why not a little boy? Why do we distinguish boys from girls at all, let alone then refer to them as "little"? Would we always assume this girl or boy would be "straight"? Why use the stereotype of a "housewife" or "gay man" when we think of consumers who might purchase bath towels or worry about which bath towels to purchase? The idea of consumption, then, intimates how products are used, but it also suggests how products are consumed, that is to say "digested" and "internalized" by those that "consume" them, and how we, in turn, accept this consumption as natural or given when, in fact, it is anything but. How products are sold is, as Williams argues in his article in this section, a "magic system" that, to borrow Marx's phrase, "fetishizes" commodities for their illusory but no-less-powerful properties that accrue to those who possess—or want to possess—these commodities. Both Williams and Auerbach show us how this magic does not happen magically, however. But neither does consumption happen magically. People can internalize meanings in countless different ways. They can buy into them wholesale; they can transgress, subvert, or ignore entirely what they are "reading." As Stuart Hall reminds us, how culture is *de*coded can be very different from how it is *en*coded.

We need to see the Barbie doll, then, not on its own, but as part of the practice of its being sold in shopping malls. We need to see the cultural identities it is selling, just as we need to see those that the shopping mall arranges for our consumption on a broader scale or those the magazine advertisement sells. And in turn, we need to see the ad or the mall, not just as a mechanism facilitating the work of capitalism, of buying and selling, but as the world of culture. A shopping mall is *also* a tourist destination and a place for young people to loiter; a magazine ad can be a work of art or a piece of toilet paper. Marx shows us that the shift from use value to exchange value is one of the primary sites where capitalism exerts its hegemonic influence. But there are other ways to view how artefacts are used and exchanged, and this process of use and exchange takes place through a history and in a shifting space that is not just the three-dimensional moment of its appearance.

This is also to say that we are all producers *and* consumers of *meanings* and that to consume meanings is also to produce other meanings. As John Fiske argues, there are on the one hand "centralizing, disciplinary, hegemonic, massifying, commodifying" (Fiske 28) forces at work in culture, usually stemming from the economic needs and demands of "culture industries," which are "perfectly in line with the disciplinary and ideological requirements of the existing social order" (Fiske 28). But Fiske continues:

> Opposing these forces, however, are the cultural needs of the people, this shifting matrix of social allegiances that transgress categories of the individual, or class or gender or race or any category that is stable within the social order. These popular forces transform the cultural commodity into a cultural resource, pluralize the meanings and pleasures it offers, evade or resist its disciplinary efforts, fracture is homogeneity and coherence, raid or poach upon its terrain. (Fiske 28)

Two things can be emphasized here: the idea of culture as a commodity that turns into a "cultural resource" for those who interact with it and the idea of this resource as constituting a "terrain," rather than a thing or object. This terrain can be anywhere within the world of culture, which means that any cultural site is, by virtue of its usage by and interaction with subjects, a *popular* site of meaning for the production and consumption of meaning. This site can be as local as the way in which girls play with Barbie dolls or a one-page advertisement in a magazine for Bacardi rum, or it can be as global as the Internet.

Michel de Certeau speaks of the "culture of everyday life" defined not by the subjects in culture or the object with which these subjects interact but by the interaction *between* subjects and objects. In this arena of social activity, the material culture of the objects themselves is frequently taken as natural or given. We might be trained to think objectively and critically about the kind of knowledge presented to us in books, in films, or even on television, but we are less accustomed to thinking as critically about the bus we are riding on, the classroom we are sitting in, the wrappers out of which we are eating our french fries. What codes and values do these artefacts offer for our decoding? So, by just reading the book you are currently reading, you are adopting a vital but at the same time somewhat isolated and isolating stance of critical and cultural intervention. You might also consider where this particular book fits within other writings on its subject. You might reflect upon the organization of books on the shelves in the library or upon the way in which libraries themselves organize knowledge and, thus, train us as subjects to enter into and interact with the world around us. You might consider what role the library plays within the institutional setting of the university. If you are reading at this moment in the classroom, you might lift your head to wonder why the lecture room is designed as a box, rather than a circle, why it is arranged with rows of seats sloped downward from the back of the room toward the front of the room, where the lecturer stands as an authority figure disseminating certain kinds of knowledge to you in a particular fashion. What if all the seats in the room were turned toward the back of the room? How would this change things? How might you talk about, study, or be critical of the process or site of cultural production that is the classroom? How might you consider the classroom's place within the university itself? How might you consider where the field you are studying fits within the university? If you are studying Popular Culture, the chances are someone sees your doing this as having less cultural or educational use value than if you were taking a course in Business Management.

Material culture is not just a series of commodities in front of us; it is all around us, in process, in flux. We are immersed in it. We need to think of material culture's embodied nature because we as bodies exist in such close proximity to it. We can, thus, think of Raymond Williams's "Advertising: The Magic System" as offering a kind of archetypal example of how simple material products are turned into magical semiotic fields of meaning—fields of consumer dreams. But Williams also shows us this process itself has a complex history which demonstrates how commodities do not just show up full-blown from the manufacturers who make them and the advertisers and promoters who frame them in such a way as to make them more desirable and, thus, to manage their identities—and the identities of those who purchase them. (Note that the producers and consumers are not *just* from the sphere of capitalism itself, even though capitalism impinges at some point upon all cultural activity.)

Jeffrey Auerbach's article on a Bacardi rum advertisement, Karen Dubinsky's on honeymooning and tourism at Niagara Falls, and Ann duCille's on Barbie dolls then offer ways of reading these various "artefacts" of culture as having a complex and shifting history that is written by the ways in which these artefacts are both produced and consumed in time and space, by various people at various times, informed by various ideological forces—gender, sexuality, race, economics, politics, nationalism, ethnicity, to name only a few—that magically attempt to manage and control this process. Just as the pages printed in uniform fashion on Gutenberg's invention were meant magically to manifest the Word of God for a much wider public sphere learning to read for the first time, the mass production of Barbie dolls, shopping malls, or tourist destinations magically manifest certain identities we are meant to assume naturally, as if without question. But the difference between how a 15th-century audience was trained *to read* the Bible and how it learned to read "on its own" (witness Martin Luther and the Protestant Reformation) were often two widely discrepant activities. The following readings are themselves, then, examples of the "popular artefacts" that emerge from *this* reading process.

—JF

REFERENCES AND FURTHER READING

Barthes, Roland. "The World of Wrestling." *Mythologies*. London: Paladin, 1973.

de Certeau, Michel. *The Practice of Everyday Life*. Berkeley: University of California Press, 1984.

Foucault, Michel. "Space, Knowledge and Power." *The Foucault Reader*. Ed. Paul Rabinow. London: Peregrine, 1987.

Kittler, Friedrich. *Discourse Networks: 1800/1900*. Trans. Michael Metteer and Chris Cullens. Stanford, CA: Stanford University Press, 1990.

Lefebvre, Henri. *The Production of Space*. Trans. Donald Nicholson-Smith. Oxford and Cambridge, Mass.: Blackwell, 1991.

Shields, Rob. *Places on the Margin: Alternative Geographies of Modernity*. London: Routledge Chapman Hall, 1991.

14 Raymond Williams, "Advertising: The Magic System"

EDITORS' INTRODUCTION

Such is the power and reach of advertising that most North Americans can correctly identify over a thousand corporate logos but cannot name the species of seven native plants in their own environment. That fact alone suggests that in the early 21st century, our "natural" landscape, the forms with and within which we live, is the one we have created through culture in its largest sense, with the corporate culture of free enterprise capitalism front and centre among its creators.

And what do we know of that corporate culture that figures so largely in hegemony? A great deal of what we know about both the corporation itself (for instance, who runs it and how it is run) and its products is brought to us via Advertising and its 20th century clone, Publicity, ably backed by their attendant pollsters and spin doctors. As Raymond Williams neatly sums it up in his essay, "Advertising was developed to sell goods, in a particular kind of economy. Publicity was developed to sell persons, in a particular kind of culture" (220), and as both the economy and the culture evolve, so do advertising and publicity. Today, the two are inseparable, held together by the billions of dollars that bind the sports, film, music, and television industry stars—themselves the products of the publicity machines of the culture industry—to products. Even acclaimed film directors who otherwise might be seen as persistently critical of hegemonic culture, notably including American Spike Lee and Canadian Denis Arcand, lend their talents to the shooting of television commercials. The annual launch of very expensive new ad campaigns during the Super Bowl broadcast is as much a part of the pregame media hype as the game itself. Even the cost of producing the ads, the amounts paid to their stars, and the cost of airing the ads become part of the hype. In the year 2001, StatsCan figures show that stand-alone advertising agencies in Canada billed their clients $5.9 billion dollars for creating and placing advertising and publicity. Even that lofty figure does not include the many billions more spent by marketing, advertising, and publicity departments in large companies; the cost of the actual production of ads by large and small production companies and publishers; or the cost of putting those ads on the air, in newspapers, on billboards, or in your mailbox. Pretty much wherever we turn and pretty much whatever we turn on, advertising is in our face. We might even want to argue that it is the face of popular culture itself: it knits us in and it knits us out, it tells us how we should look and feel and what we need to be and do and have in order to lead fulfilling lives.

There is no doubt that Williams's subject is one that any consideration of our popular culture should take a very careful look at. An important pioneer in the field of cultural studies, Williams originally wrote this piece for his 1961 book *The Long Revolution* but only published it, as an essay, in his 1980 *Problems in Materialism and Culture*. Like many of the originators of a particularly British strand of cultural studies, Williams comes at his subject from the political left, taking his leads from Marxist and socialist critiques of entrepreneurial capitalism. In his account, advertising develops from a minor process of drawing "specific attention" (212) and providing "information" (212) which he traces over a long period of our history, to the major "institutionalized system of commercial information and persuasion" (212) that it has become in the last hundred years. It is inextricably tied to the development, organization, and reproduction of modern capitalism. And just as Marx argues that capitalism makes its products "fetishes" that conceal their origins in labour and exploitation, Williams argues that advertising, in the service of that capitalism, works a kind of magic on commodities: it transforms them into signifiers of the desirable; it ties them to our bodies, our emotions, and our senses.

While, from today's perspective, we may be skeptical about the grand sweep and the methodology of the historical narrative that comprises the first half of Williams' essay, and the world seems to have turned even farther away from the kind of state socialism and state control of markets that the second half of the essay implicitly and explicitly espouses, yet there remains a great deal to learn from the materials he assembles and a great deal to think about in his analysis of them. Central to his argument and his methodology is the idea of the magic in advertising. Taking Marx's notion of the fetish and extending it by substituting the term "magic," he focuses on it not only as a masking device and a building block of false consciousness but also suggests that we pay attention to the process of creating that magic, to the nature of the value(s) that magic adds, and to the ideology it promotes. He argues that the stories our advertising tells, the ways it chooses to tell them, and the ideologies that these stories advance, do a great deal to reproduce the specific form of political and economic hegemony that is dominant in a particular place and period. In a materialist culture, he observes, we are clearly not materialist enough, or the products themselves would be enough to satisfy us without the value-added magical properties advertising assigns to them. Interestingly, as we follow Williams' historical narrative and the statistical tables he provides, we can observe how many of these magic bullets are aimed at our bodies and that the more dubious the value of the product, the bigger is the magic bullet. Here, we might want to think about the rise of the now ubiquitous infomercial and the Home Shopping Channel.

Williams also wants us to think about the relation of specific forms of advertising to particular forms or expressions of culture and ideology. While he focuses almost entirely on the British scene, we might want to compare Canadian advertising styles and ideology with those of other nations. In advertising on television, for instance, we could note a national predilection for narrative ads that are tied to the work we do. Exemplary are those of the iconic Tim Horton's chain, where the consumption of coffee and lunch is always figured as a break from work, or in the stories that another national icon, the Canadian Tire chain, tells us, particularly in such examples as the unusually long-running and nostalgic ad in which the presumably hard-working farmer dad buys his young son the red bicycle he covets in the Canadian Tire catalogue. Interesting in this ad, and strongly supporting Williams's argument, is the fact that you could buy neither that red bicycle nor parts for the father's truck at today's Canadian Tire. Clearly, they are not really selling products directly in this ad: they are selling families, nostalgia, and national identity.

In contrast, while we tend to tell stories that evoke warm feelings, the British and the Australians often rely on humour (although of markedly different types), and the Japanese use a kind of assault advertising that features a good deal of animation, frequently involving insects. American TV ads are particularly interesting as they tend to feature a combination of rapid montage editing—ironically, borrowed from early Soviet films—where the juxtaposition of image A (say, a car) and image B (an attractive man or woman or both) produces idea C (the right car will make you sexy, desirable, and fulfilled), with a great deal of camera movement. As Alfred Hitchcock so tellingly observed in conversation with fellow filmmaker Francois Truffaut, "A moving camera is an emotional camera." Movement produces energy and an emotional surge, which are thus associated with the product we are being told we need in order to lead satisfying lives. Magic, indeed!

—AG

ISSUES TO CONSIDER WHILE READING

1. While Minister of Culture in the Chretien government, Sheila Copps aired the Molson "I Am Canadian" ad to a group of Americans to demonstrate Canadianness. Was this an apt strategy? Why?
2. Broadcasters typically aim for continuity among the programs they show, the ads shown during that program, and the consumers of the program. How, in both style and content, is that aim reflected in the programs you regularly watch?

REFERENCES AND FURTHER READING

Ewen, S. *Captains of Consciousness: Advertising and the Social Roots of Consumer Culture*. New York: McGraw-Hill, 1976.

Featherstone, Mike. *Consumer Culture and Postmodernism*. London: Sage, 1991.

Fiske, John. *Television Culture*. London: Methuen, 1987.

Grossberg, Lawrence, Ellen Wartela, and D. Charles Whitney. *Media Making: Mass Media in a Popular Culture*. Thousand Oaks, CA: Sage, 1998.

Jhally, Sut. *The Codes of Advertising: Fetishism and the Political Economy of Meaning in the Consumer Economy*. New York: St. Martins, 1987.

Lunt, Peter K., and Sonia Livingstone. *Mass Consumption and Personal Identity*. Buckingham: The Open University Press, 1992.

Miller, Daniel. *A Theory of Shopping*. Ithaca, NY: Cornell University Press, 1999.

Ohmann, Richard. *Selling Culture: Magazines, Markets and Class*. New York: Verso, 1996.

Twitchell, James. *AdCult USA: The Triumph of Advertising in American Culture*. NY: Columbia University Press, 1996.

Williams, Raymond. *Problems in Materialism and Culture*. London: Verso, 1980.

Advertising: The Magic System

HISTORY

It is customary to begin even the shortest account of the history of advertising by recalling the three thousand year old papyrus from Thebes, offering a reward for a runaway slave, and to go on to such recollections as the crier in the streets of Athens, the paintings of gladiators, with sentences urging attendance at their combats, in ruined Pompeii, and the fly-bills on the pillar of the Forum in Rome. This pleasant little ritual can be quickly performed, and as quickly forgotten: it is, of course, altogether too modest. If by advertising we mean what was meant by Shakespeare and the translators of the Authorized Version [the King James Version of the Bible]—the processes of taking or giving notice of something—it is as old as human society, and some pleasant recollections from the Stone Age could be quite easily devised.

The real business of the historian of advertising is more difficult: to trace the development from processes of specific attention and information to an institutionalized system of commercial information and persuasion; to relate this to changes in society and in the economy; and to trace changes in method in the context of changing organizations and intentions.

The spreading of information, by the crier or by handwritten and printed broadsheets, is known from all periods of English history. The first signs of anything more organized come in the seventeenth century, with the development of newsbooks, mercuries and newspapers. Already certain places, such as St. Paul's in London, were recognized as centres for the posting of specific bills, and an extension of such posting to the new publications was a natural development. The material of such advertisements ranged from offers and wants in personal service, notices of the publications of books, and details of runaway servants, apprentices, horses and dogs, to announcements of new commodities available at particular shops, enthusiastic announcements of remedies and specifics, and notices of the public showing of monsters, prodigies and freaks. While the majority were the simple, basically factual and specific notices we now call 'classified,' there were also direct recommendations, as here, from 1658:

> That excellent, and by all Physicians, approved China drink, called by the Chineans Tcha, by other nations *Tay* alias *Tee,* is sold at the Sultaness Head Cophee-House in Sweeting's Rents, by the Royal Exchange, London.

Mention of the physicians begins that process of extension from the conventional recommendations of books as 'excellent' or 'admirable' and the conventional adjectives which soon became part of the noun, in a given context (as in my native village, every dance is a Grand Dance). The most extravagant early extensions were in the field of medicines, and it was noted in 1652, of the writers of copy in newsbooks:

> There is never a mountebank who, either by professing of chymistry or any other art drains money from the people of the nation but these arch-cheats have a share in the booty—because the fellow cannot lye sufficiently himself he gets one of these to do't for him.

...With the major growth of newspapers, from the 1690s, the volume of advertisements notably increased. The great majority of them were still of the specific 'classified' kind, and were grouped in regular sections of the paper or magazine. Ordinary household goods were rarely advertised; people knew where to get these. But, apart from the wants and the runaways, new things, from the latest book or play to new kinds of luxury or 'cosmatick' made their way through these columns. By and large, it was still only in the pseudo-medical and toilet advertisements that persuasion methods were evident. The announcements were conventionally printed, and there was hardly any illustration. Devices of emphasis—the hand, the asterisk, the NB—can be found, and sailing announcements had small woodcuts of a ship, runaway notices similar cuts of a man looking back over his shoulder. But, in the early eighteenth century, these conventional figures became too numerous, and most newspapers banned them. The manufacturer of a 'Spring Truss' who illustrated his device, had few early imitators.

A more general tendency was noted by [Samuel] Johnson in 1758:

> Advertisements are now so numerous that they are very negligently perused, and it is therefore become necessary to gain attention by magnificence of promises and by eloquence sometimes sublime and sometimes pathetick. Promise, large promise, is the soul of an advertisement. I remember a washball that had a quality truly wonderful—it gave *an exquisite edge to the razor!* The trade of advertising is now so near perfection that it is not easy to propose any improvement.

This is one of the earliest of 'gone about as far as they can go' conclusions on advertisers, but Johnson, after all, was sane. Within the situation he knew, of newspapers directed to a small public largely centred on coffee-houses, the natural range was from private notices (of service wanted and offered, of things lost, found, offered and needed) through shopkeepers' information (of actual goods in their possession) to puffs for occasional and marginal products. In this last kind, and within the techniques open to them, the puffmen had indeed used, intensively, all the traditional forms of persuasion, and of cheating and lying. The mountebank and the huckster had got into print, and while the majority of advertisements remained straightforward, the influence of this particular group was on its way to giving 'advertising' a more specialized meaning.

DEVELOPMENT

There is no doubt that the Industrial Revolution, and the associated revolution in communications, fundamentally changed the nature of advertising. But the change was not simple, and must be understood in specific relation to particular developments. It is not true, for example, that with the coming of factory production large-scale advertising became economically necessary. By the 1850s, a century after Johnson's comment, and with Britain already an industrial nation, the advertising pages of the newspapers, whether *The Times* or the *News of the World*, were still basically similar to those in eighteenth-century journals, except that there were more of them, that they were more closely printed, and that there were certain exclusions (lists of whores, for example, were no longer advertised in the *Morning Post*).

…Yet still in the 1850s advertising was mainly of a classified kind, in specified parts of the publication. It was still widely felt, in many kinds of trade, that (as a local newspaper summarized the argument in 1859)

> it is not *respectable*. Advertising is resorted to for the purposes of introducing inferior articles into the market.

Rejecting this argument, the newspaper *(The Eastbourne Gazette and Fashionable Intelligencer)* continued:

> Competition is the soul of business, and what fairer or more legitimate means of competition can be adopted than the availing oneself of a channel to recommend goods to the public notice which is open to all? Advertising is an open, fair, legitimate and respectable means of competition; bearing upon its face the impress of free-trade, and of as much advantage to the consumer as the producer.

The interesting thing is not so much the nature of this argument, but that, in 1859, it still had to be put quite this way. Of course the article concluded by drawing attention to the paper's own advertising rates, but even then, to get the feel of the whole situation, we have to look at the advertisements flanking the article. Not only are they all from local tradesmen, but their tone is still eighteenth-century, as for example:

To all who pay cash and can appreciate
GOOD AND FINE TEAS
CHARLES LEA

Begs most respectfully to solicit a trial of his present stock which has been selected with the greatest care, and paid for before being cleared from the Bonded warehouses in London…

In all papers, this was still the usual tone, but, as in the eighteenth century, one class of product attracted different methods. Probably the first nationally advertised product was Warren's Shoe Blacking, closely followed by Rowland's Macassar Oil (which produced the counter-offensive of the antimacassar), Spencer's Chinese Liquid Hair Dye, and Morison's Universal Pill. In this familiar field, as in the eighteenth century, the new advertising was effectively shaped, while for selling cheap books the practice of including puffs in announcements was widely extended. Warren's Shoe Blacking had a drawing of a cat spitting at its own reflection, and hack verses were widely used.

…The manner runs back to that of the eighteenth-century hucksters and mountebanks, but what is new is its scale. The crowned heads of Europe were being signed up for testimonials (the Tsar of all the Russias took and recommended Revalenta Arabica, while the Balm of Syriacum, a 'sovereign remedy for both bodily and mental decay,' was advertised as used in Queen Victoria's household). Holloway, of course a 'Professor,' spent £5,000 a year, in the 1840s, spreading his Universal Ointment, and in 1855 exceeded £30,000.

Moreover, with the newspaper public still limited, the puffmen were going on the streets. Fly-posting, on every available space, was now a large and organized trade, though made hazardous by rival gangs (paste for your own, blacking for the others). It was necessary in 1837 to pass a London act prohibiting posting without the owner's consent (it proved extremely difficult to enforce). In 1862 came the United Kingdom Bill-posters Association, with an organized system of special hoardings, which had become steadily more necessary as the flood of paste swelled. Handbills ('throwaways') were distributed in the streets of Victorian London with extraordinary intensity of coverage; in some areas a walk down one street would collect as many as two hundred different leaflets. Advertising vans and vehicles of all sorts, such as the seven-foot lath-and-plaster Hat in the Strand, on which Carlyle commented, crowded the streets until 1853, when they were forbidden. Hundreds of casual labourers were sent out with placards and sandwich boards, and again in 1853 had to be officially removed from pavement [sidewalk] to gutter. Thus the streets of Victorian London bore increasingly upon their face 'the impress of free trade,' yet still, with such methods largely reserved to the sellers of pills, adornments and sensational literature, the basic relation between advertising and production had only partly changed. Carlyle said of the hatter, whose 'whole industry is turned to *persuade* us that he has made' better hats, that 'the quack has become God.' But as yet, on the whole, it was only the quack.

...As for products mainly advertised, the way was still led by the makers of pills, soaps and similar articles. Beecham's and Pears are important by reason of their introduction of the catch-phrase on a really large scale; 'Worth a Guinea a Box' and 'Good morning! Have you used Pears' soap?' passed into everyday language. Behind this familiar vanguard came two heavily advertised classes: the patent food, which belongs technically to this period, and which by the end of the century had made Bovril, Hovis, Nestlé, Cadbury, Fry and Kellogg into 'household names'; and new inventions of a more serious kind, such as the sewing-machine, the camera, bicycle and the typewriter. If we add the new department-stores, towards the end of the century, we have the effective range of general advertising in the period, and need only note that in method the patent foods followed the patent medicines, while the new appliances varied between genuine information and the now familiar technique of slogan and association.

The pressure on newspapers to adapt to techniques drawn from the poster began to be successful from the 1880s. The change came first in the illustrated magazines, with a crop of purity nudes and similar figures; the Borax nude, for example, dispelling Disease and Decay; girls delighted by cigarettes or soap or shampoos. The poster industry, with its organized hoardings, was able from 1867 to use large lithographs. And Pears introduced the 'Bubbles' poster in 1887. A mail-order catalogue used the first colour advertisement, of a rug. Slowly, a familiar world was forming, and in the first years of the new century came the coloured electric sign. The newspapers, with Northcliffe's *Daily Mail* in the lead, dropped their columns rule, and allowed large type and illustrations. It was noted in 1897 that 'the *Times* itself' was permitting 'advertisements in type which only three years ago would have been considered fit only for the street hoardings,' while the front page of the *Daily Mail* already held rows of drawings of rather bashful women in combinations [long underwear]. Courtesy, Service and Integrity, as part of the same process, acquired the dignity of large-type abstractions. The draper, the grocer, and their suppliers had followed the quack.

TRANSFORMATION

The strange fact is, looking back, that the great bulk of products of the early stages of the factory system had been sold without extensive advertising, which had grown up mainly in relation to fringe products and novelties. Such advertising as there was, of basic articles, was mainly by shopkeepers, drawing attention to the quality and competitive pricing of the goods they stocked. In this comparatively simple phase of competition, large-scale advertising and brand-naming of goods were necessary only at the margin, or in genuinely new things. The real signs of change began to appear in the 1880s and 1890s, though they can only be correctly interpreted when seen in the light of the fully developed 'new' advertising of the period between the wars.

The formation of modern advertising has to be traced, essentially, to certain characteristics of the new 'monopoly' (corporate) capitalism, first clearly evident in this same period of the end and turn of the nineteenth century. The Great Depression which in general dominated the period from 1875 to the middle 1890s (though broken by occasional recoveries and local strengths) marked the turning point between two modes of industrial organization and two basically different approaches to distribution. After the Depression, and its big falls in prices, there was a more general and growing fear of productive capacity, a marked tendency to reorganize industrial ownership into larger units and combines, and a growing desire, by different methods, to organize and where possible control the market. Among the means of achieving the latter purposes, advertising on a new scale, and applied to an increasing range of products, took an important place.

Modern advertising, that is to say, belongs to the system of market-control which, at its full development, includes the growth of tariffs and privileged areas, cartel-quotas, trade campaigns, price-fixing by manufacturers, and that form of economic imperialism which assured certain markets overseas by political control of their territories. There was a concerted expansion of export advertising, and at home the biggest advertising campaign yet seen accompanied the merger of several tobacco companies into the Imperial Tobacco Company, to resist American competition. In 1901, a 'fabulous sum' was offered for the entire eight pages of *The Star*, by a British tobacco advertiser, and when this was refused four pages were taken, a 'world's record,' to print 'the most costly, colossal and convincing advertisement ever used in the evening newspaper the world o'er.' Since the American firms retaliated, with larger advertisements of their own, the campaign was both heavy and prolonged. This can be taken as the first major example of a new advertising situation.

That this period of fundamental change in the economy is the key to the emergence of full-scale modern advertising is shown also by radical changes within the organization of advertising itself. From the eighteenth century, certain shops had been recognized as collecting agencies for advertisements, on behalf of newspapers. In the nineteenth century, this system (which still holds today for some classified advertisements) was extended to the buying of space by individual agents, who then sold it to advertisers. With the growth in the volume of advertising, this kind of space-selling, and then a more developed system of space-brokerage, led to a growth of importance in the agencies, which still, however, were virtual agents of the Press, or at most intermediaries. Gradually, and with increasing emphasis from the 1880s, the agencies began to change their functions, offering advice and service to manufacturers, though still having space to sell for the newspapers. By the turn of the century, the modern system had emerged: newspapers had their own advertising managers, who advanced quite rapidly in status from junior employees to important executives, while the agencies stopped selling space, and went over to serving and advising manufacturers, and booking space after a campaign had been agreed. In 1900 the Advertisers Protection Society, later the Incorporated Society of British Advertisers, was formed: partly to defend advertising against such attacks as those of SCAPA [Society for Checking Abuses of Public Advertising—founded 1898], partly to bring pressure on newspapers to publish their sales figures, so that campaigns could be properly planned. Northcliffe, after initial hesitations about advertising (he had wanted to run *Answers* without it), came to realize its possibilities as a new basis for financing newspapers. He published his sales figures, challenged his rivals to do the same, and in effect created the modern structure of the Press as an industry, in close relation to the new advertising. In 1917, the Association of British Advertising Agents was founded, and in 1931, with the founding of the Audit Bureau of Circulations, publishing audited net sales, the basic structure was complete.

It is in this same period that we hear first, with any emphasis, of advertising as a profession, a public service, and a necessary part of the economy. A further aspect of the reorganization was a more conscious and serious attention to the 'psychology of advertising.' As it neared the centre of the economy, it began staking its claims to be not only a profession, but an art and a science.

The half-century between 1880 and 1930, then, saw the full development of an organized system of commercial information and persuasion, as part of the modern distributive system in conditions of large-scale capitalism. Although extended to new kinds of product, advertising drew, in its methods, on its own history and experience. There is an obvious continuity between the methods used to sell pills and washballs in the eighteenth century ('promise, large promise, a quality truly wonderful') and the methods used in the twentieth century to sell anything from a drink to a political party. In this sense, it is true to say that all commerce has followed the quack. But if we look at advertising before, say, 1914, its comparative crudeness is immediately evident. The 'most costly, colossal and convincing advertisement' of 1901 shows two badly-drawn men in tails, clinking port glasses between announcements that the cigarettes are five a penny, and the slogan (The Englishman's Toast—Don't be gulled by Yankee bluff, support John Bull with every puff') is in minute type by comparison with 'Most Costly' and 'Advertisement.' Play on fear of illness was of course normal, as it had been throughout quack advertising, and there were simple promises of attractiveness and reputation if particular products were used. But true 'psychological' advertising is very little in evidence before the First War, and where it is its techniques, both in appeal and in draughtsmanship and layout, are crude. Appropriately enough, perhaps, it was in the war itself, when now not a market but a nation had to be controlled and organized, yet in democratic conditions and without some of the older compulsions, that new kinds of persuasion were developed and applied. Where the badly-drawn men with their port and gaspers belong to an old world, such a poster as 'Daddy, what did you do in the Great War?' belongs to the new. The drawing is careful and detailed: the curtains, the armchair, the grim numb face of the father, the little girl on his knee pointing to her open picture-book, the boy at his feet intent on his toy-soldiers. Alongside the traditional appeals to patriotism lay this kind of entry into basic personal relationships and anxieties. Another poster managed to suggest that a man who would let down his country would also let down his sweetheart or his wife.

Slowly, after the war, advertising turned from the simple proclamation and reiteration, with simple associations, or the earlier respectable trade, and prepared to develop, for all kinds of product, the old methods of the quack and the new methods of psychological warfare. The turn was not even yet complete, but the tendencies, from the twenties, were evident. Another method of organizing the market, through consumer credit, had to be popularized, and in the process changed from the 'never-never,' which was not at all respectable, to the primly respectable 'hire-purchase' and the positively respectable 'consumer credit.' By 1933, a husband had lost his wife because he had failed to take this 'easy way' of providing a home for her. Meanwhile, Body Odour, Iron Starvation, Night Starvation, Listlessness and similar disabilities menaced not only personal health, but jobs, marriages and social success.

These developments, of course, produced a new wave of criticism of advertising, and, in particular, ridicule of its confident absurdities. In part this was met by a now standard formula: 'one still hears criticism of advertising, but it is not realized how much has been done, within the profession, to improve it' (for example, a code of ethics, in 1924, pledging the industry, *inter alia* 'to tell the advertising story simply and without exaggeration and to avoid even a tendency to mislead.' If advertisers write such pledges, who then writes the advertisements?). The 'super-sensitive faddists' were rediscovered, and the 'enemies of free enterprise.' Proposals by Huxley, Russell, Leavis, Thompson and others, that children should be trained to study advertisements critically, were described, in a book called *The Ethics of Advertising*, as amounting to 'cynical manipulation of the infant mind.'

But the most significant reply to the mood of critical scepticism was in the advertisements themselves: the development of a knowing, sophisticated, humorous advertising, which acknowledged the scepticism and made claims either casual and offhand or so ludicrously exaggerated as to include the critical response (for example, the Guinness advertisements, written by Dorothy Sayers, later a critic of advertising).[1] Thus it became possible to 'know all the arguments' against advertising, and yet accept or write pieces of charming or amusing copy.

One sustained special attack, on an obviously vulnerable point, was in the field of patent medicines. A vast amount of misleading and dangerous advertising of this kind had been repeatedly exposed, and eventually, by Acts of 1939 and 1941, and by a Code of Standards in 1950, the advertisement of cures for certain specified diseases, and a range of misleading devices, was banned. This was a considerable step forward, in a limited field, and the Advertising Association was among its sponsors. If we remember the history of advertising, and how the sellers of ordinary products learned from the quack methods that are still in use in less obviously dangerous fields, the change is significant. It is like nothing so much as the newly-crowned Henry the Fifth dismissing Falstaff with contempt. Advertising had come to power, at the centre of the economy, and it had to get rid of the disreputable friends of its youth: it now both wanted and needed to be respectable.

ADVERTISING IN POWER

Of the coming to power there was now no question. Estimates of expenditure in the inter-war years vary considerably, but the lowest figure, for direct advertising in a single year, is £85,000,000 and the highest £200,000,000. Newspapers derived half their income from advertising, and almost every industry and service, outside the old professions, advertised extensively. With this kind of weight behind it, advertising was and knew itself to be a solid sector of the establishment.

Some figures from 1935 are interesting, showing advertising expenditure as a proportion of sales:

Proprietary medicines	29.4%
Toilet goods	21.3%
Soaps, polishes, etc.	14.1%
Tobacco	9.3%
Petrol and oil	8.2%
Cereals, jams, biscuits	5.9%
Sweets	3.2%
Beer	1.8%
Boots and Shoes	1.0%
Flour	0.5%

The industry's connections with its origins are evident: the three leading categories are those which pioneered advertising of the modern kind. But more significant, perhaps, is that such ordinary things as boots, shoes and flour should be in the table at all. This, indeed, is the new economy, deriving not so much from the factory system and the growth of communications, as from an advanced system of capitalist production, distribution, and market control.

Alongside the development of new kinds of appeal came new media. Apart from such frills as sky-writing, there was commercial radio, not yet established in Britain (though the pressure was there) but begun elsewhere in the 1920s and beamed to Britain from the 1930s. Commercial television, in the 1950s, got through fairly easily. Among new methods, in this growth, are the product jingle, begun in commercial radio and now reaching classic status, and the open alliance between advertisers and apparently independent journalists and broadcasters. To build a reputation as an honest reporter, and then use it either openly to recommend a product or to write or speak about it alongside an advertisement for it, as in the evening paper 'special supplements,' became commonplace. And what was wrong? After all, the crowned heads of Europe, and many of our own Ladies, had been selling pills and soaps for years. The extension to political advertising, whether direct or by pressure-groups, also belongs, in its extensive phase, to this period of establishment; in the 1950s it has been running at a very high rate indeed.

The only check, in fact, to this rapidly expanding industry was during the last war, though this was only partial and temporary, and the years since the war, and especially the 1950s, have brought a further spectacular expansion. It is ironic to look back at a book published in wartime, by one of the best writers on advertising, Denys Thompson, and read this:

> A second reason for these extensive extracts is that advertising as we know it may be dispensed with, after the war. We are getting on very well with a greatly diminished volume of commercial advertising in wartime, and it is difficult to envisage a return to the 1919–1939 conditions in which publicity proliferated.

Mr Thompson, like Dr Johnson two centuries earlier, is a sane man, but it is never safe to conclude that puffing has reached its maximum distension. The history, rightly read, points to a further major growth, and to more new methods. The highly organized field of market study, motivation research, retained sociologists and psychologists, is extremely formidable, and no doubt has many surprises in store for us. Talent of quite new kinds is hired with increasing ease. And there is one significant development which must be noted in conclusion: the extension of organized publicity.

'Public Relations'

Advertising was developed to sell goods, in a particular kind of economy. Publicity has been developed to sell persons, in a particular kind of culture. The methods are often basically similar: the arranged incident, the 'mention,' the advice on branding, packaging, and a good 'selling line.' I remember being told by a man I knew at university (he had previously explained how useful, to his profession as an advertiser, had been his training in the practical criticism of advertisements) that advertisements you book and paid for were really old stuff; the real thing was what got through ordinary news. This seems to happen now with goods: 'product centenaries,' for example. But with persons it is even more extensive. It began in entertainment, particularly with film actors, and it is still in this field that it does most of its work. It is very difficult to pin down, because the borderline between the item or photograph picked up in the ordinary course of journalism and broadcasting, and the similar item or photograph that has been arranged and paid for, either directly or through special hospitality by a publicity agent, is obviously difficult to draw. Enough stories get through, and are even boasted about, to indicate that the paid practice is extensive, though payment, except to the agent, is usually in hospitality (if that word can be used) or in kind. Certainly, readers of newspapers should be aware that the 'personality' items, presented as ordinary news stories or gossip, will often have been paid for, in one way or another, in a system that makes straightforward advertising, by comparison, look respectable. Nor is this confined to what is called 'show business'; it has certainly entered literature, and it has probably entered politics.

The extension is natural, in a society where selling, by any effective means, has become a primary ethic. The spectacular growth of advertising, and then its extension to apparently independent reporting, has behind it not a mere pressure-group, as in the days of the quacks, but the whole impetus of a society. It can then be agreed that we have come a long way from the papyrus of the runaway slave and the shouts of the town-crier: that what we have to look at is an organized and extending system, at the centre of our national life.

THE SYSTEM

In the last hundred years, then, advertising has developed from the simple announcements of shopkeepers and the persuasive arts of a few marginal dealers into a major part of capitalist business organization. This is important enough, but the place of advertising in society goes far beyond this commercial context. It is increasingly the source of finance for a whole range of general communication, to the extent that in 1960 our majority television service and almost all our newspapers and periodicals could not exist without it. Further, in the last forty years and now at an increasing rate, it has passed the frontier of the selling of goods and services and has become involved with the teaching of social and personal values; it is also rapidly entering the world of politics. Advertising is also, in a sense, the official art of modern capitalist society: it is what 'we' put up in 'our' streets and use to fill up to half of 'our' newspapers and magazines: and it commands the services of perhaps the largest body of organized writers and artists, with their attendant managers and advisers, in the whole society. Since this is the actual social status of advertising, we shall only understand it with any adequacy if we can develop a kind of total analysis in which the economic, social and cultural facts are visibly related. We may then also find, taking advertising as a major form of modern social communication, that we can understand our society itself in new ways.

It is often said that our society is too materialist, and that advertising reflects this. We are in the phase of a relatively rapid distribution of what are called 'consumer goods,' and advertising, with its emphasis on 'bringing the good things of life,' is taken as central for this reason. But it seems to me that in this respect our society is quite evidently not materialist enough, and that this, paradoxically, is the result of a failure in social meanings, values, and ideals.

It is impossible to look at modern advertising without realizing that the material object being sold is never enough: this indeed is the crucial cultural quality of its modern forms. If we were sensibly materialist, in that part of our living in which we use things, we should find most advertising to be of insane irrelevance. Beer would be enough for us, without the additional promise that in drinking it we show ourselves to be manly, young in heart, or neighbourly. A washing-machine would be a useful machine to wash clothes, rather than an indication that we are forward looking or an object of envy to our neighbours. But if these associations sell beer and washing-machines, as some of the evidence suggests, it is clear that we have a cultural pattern in which the objects are not enough but must be validated, if only in fantasy, by association with social and personal meanings which in a different cultural pattern might be more directly available. The short description of the pattern we have is *magic*: a highly organized and professional system of magical inducements and satisfactions, functionally very similar to magical systems in simpler societies, but rather strangely coexistent with a highly developed scientific technology.

This contradiction is of the greatest importance in any analysis of modern capitalist society. The coming of large-scale industrial production necessarily raised critical problems of social organization, which in many fields we are still struggling to solve. In the production of goods for personal use, the critical problem posed by the factory of advanced machines was that of the organization of the market. The modern factory requires not only smooth and steady distributive channels (without which it would suffocate under its own product) but also definite indications of demand without which the expensive process of capitalization and equipment would be too great a risk. The historical choice posed by the development of industrial production is between different forms of organization and planning in the society to which it is central. In our own century, the choice has been and remains between some form of socialism and a new form of capitalism. In Britain, since the 1890s and with rapidly continuing emphasis, we have had the new capitalism, based on a series of devices for organizing and ensuring the market. Modern advertising, taking on its distinctive features in just this economic phase, is one of the most important of these devices, and it is perfectly true to say that modern capitalism could not function without it.

Yet the essence of capitalism is that the basic means of production are not socially but privately owned, and that decisions about production are therefore in the hands of a group occupying a minority position in the society and in no way directly responsible to it. Obviously, since the capitalist wishes to be successful, he is influenced in his decisions about production by what other members of the society need. But he is influenced also by considerations of industrial convenience and likely profit, and his decisions tend to be a balance of these varying factors. The challenge of socialism, still very powerful elsewhere but in Britain deeply confused by political immaturities and errors, is essentially that decisions about production should be in the hands of the society as a whole, in the sense that control of the means of production is made part of the general system of decision which the society as a whole creates. The conflict between capitalism and socialism is now commonly seen in terms of a competition in productive efficiency, and we need not doubt that much of our future history, on a world scale, will be determined by the results of this competition. Yet the conflict is really much deeper than this, and is also a conflict between different approaches to and forms of socialism. The fundamental choice that emerges, in the problems set to us by modern industrial production, is between man as consumer and man as user. The system of organized magic which is modern advertising is primarily important as a functional obscuring of this choice.

NOTE

1. Dorothy L. Sayers, after working in the advertising industry, went on to become a highly successful and critically esteemed mystery novelist and an Oxford University professor of medieval French literature. Among her Lord Peter Wimsey novels is *Murder Must Advertise* (1933), which contains an excellent and humorous representation and critique of advertising in the period. (Ed's. Note)

15   Jeffrey Auerbach, "Art, Advertising, and the Legacy of Empire"

EDITORS' INTRODUCTION

Jeffrey Auerbach's "Art, Advertising, and the Legacy of Empire" should be read in conjunction with the pieces by Williams and duCille. Using a 1997 Mount Gay Barbados Rum ad, Auerbach analyzes what ideologies advertising exploits to sustain the magic of commodity fetishism described by Williams. One of these ideologies is the long history of colonialism which has sustained the power of the same patriarchal capitalism duCille sees at work behind Barbie's multicultural facade. Auerbach suggests how capitalism— which ostensibly promotes a free-market economy that allows its subjects the right to self-determination, and to profit from it—has never really moved past its origins in 19th-century British imperialism. We are just New Victorians subjected to, and by, the same ideologies our ancestors set in motion over two hundred years ago.

Note how Auerbach's semiotic analysis of advertising's visual field decodes the ad's signifiers in order to subvert the ad agency's intentions. The ad innocuously equates drinking rum with hedonistic pleasure. But the ad's caption, "The Primitive Spirit Refined," betrays how the intended meaning of signifiers mutates in a variety of competing meanings. These meanings suggest the "production, consumption, and commercialization of commodities" (225) used by Britain to sell to its citizens the inhospitable colonies—to sell the Empire back to itself. This propaganda worked two ways: to entice people to the colonies but also to ensure the white man's supremacy over indigenous cultures that threatened Britain's imperial project.

The Empire implemented this self-selling through five tropes: exoticization, racialization, sexualization, commodificaion, and civilization. The first three point to how the Empire refashioned the colonial Other in order to profit from this refashioning—that is, in terms of profiting from the commodities exploited and then exported from the colonies by the Empire, to sell at home in the domestic marketplace. This economy was especially important by the 1920s, when "Britain's industrial dominance was being challenged, and at a time of increasing protectionism around the world" (232). (One recalls that one of America's cures for its citizens after the traumatic effects of 9/11 was to "shop" their way out of this trauma, at whatever cost.) This commodification served the Empire's ultimate goal of "civilizing" the uncivilized in order to bring what the Empire could not at first control under the purview of a capitalist hegemony.

Auerbach's history of how advertising commodifies the culture it advertises echoes advertising's history of self-management in Williams's article. In both cases, advertising subsumes racial, sexual, gendered, or national differences within the normalized, homogeneous, standardized, and dominant identity of capitalism itself. As Auerbach notes, "It is no longer the empire itself that is being sold, but rather the commodities the empire produced" (226). So, "the commodification of empire" gives way to the "imperialization of commodities" (227). Auerbach's longer sections on racialization and sexualization especially make clear that the body, specifically the female body, carries the burden of this transition.

One can contemplate how the British imperialization of the colonies has given way to an imperialization of the commodity, the cultural power of which now belongs primarily to the United States, a former colony of the Empire before it became an imperial power itself. Auerbach's analysis raises provocative questions: What differences in the Americas did Britain erase to sustain its own imperial identity, and how has the United States itself repeated these erasures to sustain *its* empire of capitalism? Where does Canada, a country confederated in the Victorian period but without radically divorcing itself from the Empire, now stand in relation to the United States, both former colonies? Canada is both the colony Britain "commodified" to its own ends—just as the United States sometimes commodifies Canada, in turn—*and* an identity unto itself.

—JF

ISSUES TO CONSIDER WHILE READING

1. Auerbach analyzes five ideological strategies at work in the Barbados Rum advertisement: exoticization, racialization, sexualization, commodification, and civilization. Choose another magazine advertisement (or an advertisement of any kind), and analyze what ideological strategies (perhaps the same as Auerbach's, perhaps different) inform this advertisement. What kinds of histories inform these strategies? Is their origin national? political? economic? religious?
2. To what extent do other cultural "imperialisms" inform the construction of Canadian identities in Canadian popular culture? Can these identities be said in any way to constitute their own form of Canadian cultural imperialism?

FURTHER READING

Bhabha, Homi K. *The Location of Culture*. New York: Routledge, 1994.

Gates, Henry Louis, Jr. "Writing 'Race' and the Difference It Makes." *"Race," Writing, and Difference*. Chicago: University of Chicago Press, 1986. 1–20.

Hyam, Ronald. *Empire and Sexuality*. Manchester: Manchester University Press, 1992.

Pieterse, Jan Nederveen. *White on Black: Images of Africa and Blacks in Western Popular Culture*. New Haven: Yale University Press, 1992.

Williams, Raymond. *The Long Revolution*. Harmondsworth: Penguin, 1961.

Art, Advertising, and the Legacy of Empire

"The Primitive Spirit Refined," a 1997 advertisement for Mount Gay Barbados Rum created by Blum/Herbstreith, depicts a dark-skinned woman in a revealing yellow bikini, reclining in a rowboat with two muscular white men and a light-skinned woman who stands behind them. The image can be effectively divided into two parts: a black half, in the foreground, where the one darker-skinned woman sits by herself; and a white half, where the three lighter-skinned people are grouped together in a pyramid. The two women are clearly looking at each other, but is the white woman smiling confidently? knowingly? warily? And what is meant by the title? Does it refer to the black woman who is the "primitive spirit" and needs to be "refined"; to the white threesome partying in Barbados, drinking rum, whose "primitive spirits" need to be "refined"; or to the two men, whose "primitive spirits"—their lust for the women (or perhaps for each other)—need to be "refined"? Or, does it refer simply to the rum itself, suggesting that it is of such a high quality that it can be characterized as refined?

It is now a truism to assert that the consequences of colonialism have been long-lasting and far-reaching. But this advertisement is an example *par excellence* of just how pervasive that influence has been, especially in popular culture, because it incorporates and perpetuates the primary tropes through which British artists represented their empire visually during the nineteenth century. It employs a geographic space that is commonly regarded as a vacation spot or island paradise, thus continuing the nineteenth-century tradition of representing the far-flung regions of the British empire as Edenic lands, places of leisure and dreams, not work. By positing a polar opposition between blacks and whites, it sustains the well-established practice of British men and women contrasting their light skin with the darker-skinned people that they encountered during their journeys throughout the world. It extends a long tradition of British artists depicting non-white women as sexual objects. It is an advertisement for a product, and the production, consumption, and commercialization of commodities were essential components of British imperialism. And finally, its title invokes what was referred to in the nineteenth century as Britain's "civilizing mission," its self-proclaimed goal of "civilizing" the so-called "primitive" people it encountered.

The development of these five tropes—exoticization,

Blum/Herbstreith. The Primitive Spirit Refined (1997). *Reprinted by permission of Alan Blum, Blue Elephant (formerly Blum Herbstreith).*

racialization, sexualization, commodification, and civilization—took place historically as a form of propaganda, a way to advertise the empire, necessary to persuade people to populate otherwise inhospitable places and to justify political and economic rule. Popular literature by writers such as Rider Haggard and Rudyard Kipling notwithstanding, there is considerable evidence to suggest that the empire was a boring, disappointing place. When Thomas Manning finally reached Lhasa (which would later serve as the inspiration for Shangri-La in James Hilton's *Lost Horizon)* in 1811, he complained that there was "nothing striking, nothing pleasing in its appearance" (Markham 256). Nearly a century later and on another continent, Mary Kingsley described life in the African forest as "the most awful life in death imaginable. It is like being shut up in a library, whose books you cannot read, all the while tormented, terrified, and bored" (Kingsley 33). Even the Marquess of Hastings, who became Governor-General and Commander-in-Chief in India in 1814, groused that "The situation of a Governor-General . . . is one of the most laborious that can be conceived," and he, like so many others in that country, found the heat so oppressive as to be almost unbearable (Rawdon-Hastings 28, 39). These are but a few examples of the hardships experienced by those nineteenth-century Britons who traveled overseas to the empire. Whether as explorers, settlers, governors, soldiers, or wives, life in the empire was, for many, dangerous, disappointing, and disheartening.

Because of this, a massive propaganda campaign developed, some of it overt (such as the posters and pamphlets urging men and women to colonize North America or South Africa), most of it covert. While John MacKenzie has ably documented the extent of imperial propaganda during the late-nineteenth and twentieth centuries, very little scholarly attention has been devoted to the earlier period, before the age of High Imperialism.[1] And yet, as the above examples suggest, enormous efforts were needed in order to justify the expense and to overcome the hardships associated with imperial expansion. Instrumental in this process were the contributions of professional artists such as William Hodges and Benjamin West, whose works were commissioned by agents (and agencies) of the British state to promote and publicize the empire through spectacularly lavish, heroic paintings that were not only hung in public galleries and official government buildings such as India House, but could be popularized by engravers and published in mass-circulating newspapers, broadsheets, and illustrated weeklies. These visual images portrayed the many and diverse regions of the empire as Edenic paradises, cornucopias of natural riches, empty lands available for settlement. Where indigenous people were represented, as will be discussed below, they were figured either as noble savages or degenerate heathens, in neither case a threat, and frequently, at least as far as missionaries were concerned, an impetus, to British colonization.

What this modern rum advertisement reveals is the legacy of this process, a legacy that continues to influence the way we see the world, in magazines such as *National Geographic,* in commercial shops such as Banana Republic, and in journalistic and travel writing. But although the form has remained largely the same, what is being advertized has in fact changed. It is no longer the empire itself that is being sold, but rather the commodities the empire produced. Whereas the development of the five tropes outlined above eventually commodified the empire, ironically what is left in the postcolonial world are only the commodities themselves, imperialized; that is, sold through the tropes and devices of imperial art. This article charts, therefore, a transformation, from the commodification of empire to the imperialization of commodities. "The Primitive Spirit Refined" thus represents what Renata Rosaldo has called "imperialist nostalgia": mourning the passing of what we ourselves have destroyed, making racial domination appear innocent and pure (68–69). The nineteenth-century empires have long since disappeared, but the structures that maintained them live on. This advertisement demonstrates that the visual imagery of colonialism has and continues to influence representations on both sides of the Atlantic, not just in Britain but in the United States as well.

To begin with the obvious, the setting is the Barbados, the long-time British colony which through the use of slave-labor became a leading producer of sugar and rum. Thus the very location of the advertisement invokes the history of the British empire, though sanitized so as to conceal the deleterious consequences such as exploitation and environmental degradation associated with global commodity capitalism. The advertisement also draws on the picturesque tradition of turning newly-discovered or distant lands into exotic paradises. The picturesque was a literary and artistic aesthetic that developed during the second half of the eighteenth century.[2] Based on the work of Claude Lorrain and Nicholas Poussin, the picturesque first found its English statement in William Gilpin's essays and his drawings of the English Lake District, and took as its starting point the idea that nature was imperfect and needed to be organized when it was painted. Claude and his followers—theorists such as Payne Knight and Uvedale Price, and artists such as William Hodges and the Daniells (Thomas, William, and Samuel) who carried the picturesque aesthetic overseas—developed formulas for composing pictures which were based upon certain rules of classical proportion. For example, "Oaitepeha (Tautira) Bay, Tahiti," also called "Tahiti Revisited" (c. 1776), by William Hodges, the draftsman on Cook's second voyage to the Pacific in 1773–5, demonstrates the artist's use of a picturesque framework that includes a detailed and darkened foreground, verdant hills positioned as side screens, and a river winding through the deep-toned central distances, carrying the viewer's eye toward the rugged, hazy, mountainous background.

Hodges's painting, however, as Bernard Smith has pointed out, complicates the picturesque tradition by replacing conventional classical motives with others more typical of Tahiti: plantations of bread-fruit and coconut palms have substituted for cypresses and olive trees, and the precipitous peaks of the mountains have supplanted the rolling hills of the Italian countryside (64). Hodges has captured tropical light and flavor, but within a formulaic classical setting, thus making the familiar unfamiliar, and the unfamiliar familiar. Additionally, the introduction of two Tahitian women prominently in the foreground, bathing in the river, one with exotic tattoos, has transformed the landscape into a sensual— even sexual—paradise. Into this picture, which is, as befitting the picturesque tradition, still very much concerned with the landscape and its beauty, Hodges has interwoven several well-established elements of the island-paradise theme: the life free of moral restraints, suggested by the beauty of the nude bathing girls; and, the exoticism and paganism of foreign lands, suggested by the mysterious statue towering over them.

The Mount Gay Barbados Rum advertisement replicates many of these picturesque elements, despite the lack of any discernable landscape. Structurally, the photograph incorporates a darkened foreground, a richly colored central distance, and a hazy horizon. In this case, though, people, not mountains, serve as side screens, channeling the viewer's eye toward the center of the image. And, the faded, worn, rowboat not only provides the sort of detail characteristic of the picturesque, a modern-day ruin, but also suggests a certain kind of "rusticity," according to James France, Brand Manager of Mount Gay Barbados Rum for Remy Amerique, the product's American distributor. France indicated in an interview, moreover, that by emphasizing the beauty of the Caribbean (he mentioned specifically the aqua-colored water), "The Primitive Spirit Refined" was very much about "escapism," another characteristically picturesque element as well as an important component of many imperial adventures.

In fact, the absence of landscape is critical to the success of this advertisement, as the "otherness" of the Barbados, its identifying characteristics, have been eliminated, to be replaced by an ideal otherness. As Judith Williamson has noted in an essay on advertising, femininity, and colonization, advertisements for suntan lotion, make-up, and perfume frequently employ imaginary islands which serve to represent an "other" place and culture without having to recognize any real place or culture. As she puts it, "What is taken away in reality, then, is re-presented in image and ideology so that *it stands for itself* after it has actually ceased to exist" (112). Thus in a typically picturesque manner, the Mount Gay Barbados Rum advertisement appears to depict a particular place when in fact it is invoking an idealized, fantasized state of mind and being. By doing so, it eliminates both difference and danger.

The second way in which the Mount Gay Barbados Rum advertisement incorporates the techniques of British imperial art is that in nineteenth-century images of the British empire, blacks and whites were almost always depicted as opposites, defining each other through their mutual and seemingly intractable differences. In H. F. C. Darell's lithograph, "Interview at Block Drift" (1852) of a meeting between Col. Hare, the British Lieutenant Governor, and the chief of the Xhosa (against whom the British skirmished for most of the first half of the nineteenth century), the British are arranged on one side, the Africans on the other. The British are clothed, whereas the Africans are only half-covered; Darell has portrayed the British as civilized and refined, the Africans as primitive. The Africans are subservient, all but one being seated, whereas the British are standing. And, while both sides have troops supporting them, the British soldiers are mounted on horses, and closer to their principals, and hence in the dominant position.[3] Darell's drawing functions, therefore, as a "manichean allegory," to use Abdul JanMohamed's term, an allegorized set of oppositions not just between black and white, but by extension between good and evil, superiority and inferiority, civilized and savage, self and other, subject and object, and, as we shall see, intelligence and emotion, rationality and sensuality. It bolsters, and even lays the foundations of, "the putative superiority of the European and the supposed inferiority of the native" in the colonialist context (82).

The awkward and ambiguous gaze between the two women in the Mount Gay Barbados Rum advertisement solidifies their uneven racial positions. Because the viewer sees the black woman's expression only as it is reflected, mirror-like, in the face of the white woman, the black woman has literally been effaced. She lacks an identity separate from that of the white woman. In this image, the black woman can see herself only as the white woman sees her; she lacks ego, an independent sense of self that does not need validation. Moreover, although the darker-skinned woman in the foreground appears larger, in fact her female counterpart is standing over her, almost impossibly so, perhaps on the prow of the rowboat. These two tools, self-reflection and surveillance, were essential to and even constructed the colonial relationship (Lutz and Collins 187–216; Pratt 143).

Race is, as Henry Louis Gates, Jr. has written, "a trope of ultimate, irreducible difference between cultures, linguistic groups, or adherents of specific belief systems which—more often than not—also have fundamentally opposed economic interests." This trope is particularly dangerous because it "pretends to be an objective term of classification" (5). This opposition between white and black is part of a much broader process of Western identity formation. Recent studies have demonstrated that identities—national, racial, ethnic, individual—are rarely if ever formed in a vacuum. They are contingent and relational, formed referentially in comparison and frequently in opposition to other identities. By exposing or describing the "other"—typically darker-skinned people—writers and artists help clarify what they believe are essential features in themselves. The Mount Gay Barbados Rum advertisement, then, serves as a locus for its target audience—the group of young, white, (and presumably American) vacationers—to define themselves against the black (presumably Caribbean) woman. Once the Barbados has been constructed as an exotic resort populated by "blacks," a place to drink and relax, a Third World theme park known for the production of raw material and commodities, America becomes a place of work, capitalist enterprise, and urban industry, peopled by "whites." While the advertisement's purpose is clearly to sell a product, it is also selling a way of life, reinforced by the small type that exhorts the viewer to leave behind the corporate world of dress ties and social mingling and instead "appreciate the kinship of sand."

Not only were darker-skinned people portrayed as the opposite of the lighter-skinned British; they were also gendered and sexualized. Men of color were frequently feminized, making them seem less threatening, as in George French Angas's portrait of a Zulu dancer with smooth features, a heart-shaped face, delicate arms and legs, and a pendulous belly reminiscent of a pregnant woman. Women, as in the Mount Gay Barbados Rum advertisement, were often turned into attractive and exotic sex objects. This was true in Egypt, where David Roberts drew Nubian Women, one of whom is topless and carries on her head a jug, a symbol of virginity and sexuality; and it was true in South Africa, where in "Fuller's Hloek" T. W. Bowler and W. R. Thompson implied that no matter where they went, British men would find seductive, beautiful, half-naked women, standing by the river.

In his *History of Sexuality,* Michel Foucault identified the "hystericization of women's bodies" as one of the great strategic unities that have informed the Western discourse of sex since the eighteenth century (103–4). For Foucault, "hystericization" is the process whereby the feminine body is "thoroughly saturated with sexuality" in such a way as to define a set of specifically feminine biological and moral responsibilities such as fertility and devotion to family. Within such a system of representation, the woman is constituted as her body, and her body as her sexual nature. Of course Foucault is less concerned here with the female body per se than with the manner in which the body is constructed as an erotic sign within the discourse of sexuality, and therefore his notion of a rhetorically constructed body can be used to explain a parallel discursive strain which represents the colonized world—and those that comprise it—as female, producing what David Spurr has termed "the eroticization of the colonized" (170). This analogy can be extended to encompass ideas about the fertility of land.

The emphasis on female nudity in imperial art also conforms to Euro-American myths about black women's sexuality. Black women have been consistently portrayed in Western art and science as being excessively (and accessibly) sexual in nature. According to Sander Gilman (1985), lack of modesty in dress has also historically marked black women as uncivilized. Scholars though, have given short shrift to the many images of darker-skinned women that emphasize their beauty and femininity, focusing instead on the denigration of black women though their sexualization and masculinization. Saartjie Baartman, the Hottentot Venus, is the best-known and most oft-cited example (Gilman, 1986), but one might also point to George French Angas's "Zulu Woman with Children" (1849) in which the woman has muscular arms and is able to carry great weight. She is also portrayed as having large, udder-like breasts, symbolizing not virginal promiscuity and seductiveness, but maternal fecundity. Homi Bhabha has shown there to be a manichean duality that characterized Western representations of the Other, vacillating between the angelic and the demonic in such a way as to create an Other that is so extreme as to be neither human nor historical (although it needs to be pointed out that this same duality has also been present in Western art, notably in depictions of the Virgin Mary and Mary Magdalene). Western attitudes toward non-Western sexuality (whether African or "Oriental") have been especially ambivalent, on the one hand idealizing and eroticizing, on the other hand rejecting and condemning, as the Other is simultaneously sexualized and declared taboo.

Breasts especially were central to the selling and conquest of empire, just as they are featured—in fact, barely concealed—in the Mount Gay Barbados Rum advertisement. In the early pages of Rider Haggard's *King Solomon's Mines,* for example, Alan Quartermain produces a map of the route to the diamond mines of Kukuanaland, somewhere in southern Africa. It is a copy of the original, which was drawn in 1590 by a Portugese trader, Jose da Silvestre, as he lay dying of hunger on the "nipple" of a mountain with two peaks named Sheba's Breasts. When inverted, this map, which Ann McClintock has convincingly shown to be "explicitly sexualized" (3), reveals a diagram of the female body, but truncated, so that the only parts drawn along the route to "mouth of [the] treasure cave" are those that denote female sexuality. When Quartermain finally reaches Sheba's Breasts, he compares them to "overpowering volcanoes" that "took [his] breath away" (Haggard 86). As Marilyn Yalom has demonstrated, though with almost no discussion of the imperial sphere, the breast has indeed been fetishized, objectified, eroticized, politicized, and commercialized in modem Western culture.

All of which lends credence to Ronald Hyam's thesis that many British men left their homeland for the empire because Victorian standards of morality were so strict, and because the opportunities for sexual adventure were much greater overseas. If so, then the images discussed here became, in effect, propaganda—or perhaps even pornography—on behalf of the empire, luring men overseas with the promise of sexual adventure. Although exact figures are difficult to compile, the evidence suggests that those who peopled the empire were overwhelmingly young, single, and male, although increasingly less so by the late-nineteenth century. For example, six times more men than women emigrated to the Chesapeake in the 1630s, and although the number of women increased after 1650, men continued to outnumber women in the colony by a ratio of nearly three to one throughout the rest of the century (Horn 182). A similar pattern existed in the

Carolinas, where about 70 percent of settlers between 1670–1680 were men (Weir 391). And Robert Hughes found that only 14 per cent of those who were transported to Australia between 1788–1852 were women (244). Not surprisingly, the Mount Gay Barbados Rum advertisement, according to Claire Jordan, International Brand Manager for Mount Gay Rum, was targeted to the white, "sophisticated," "professional managerial male," aged 25–49, and it was largely for this reason that the advertisement appeared in *Sports Illustrated, Golf Digest,* and *Playboy.* In short, the so-called target audience and the strategy employed, for both imperial art and for the Mount Gay Barbados Rum advertisement, were the same, despite being separated by a century and a continent.

It is also possible, of course, to interpret the sexual undertones of this advertisement as suggestive of homosocial or even homoerotic attachment. The "primitive spirit" that needs to be "refined" may refer less to the men's lust for the two women than their lust for each other, or at least their desire for male affection and companionship. Part of the sexual freedom of the empire was the ability to pursue one's desires, whether hetero- or homosexual; Rhodes, Burton, and Lawrence are only the most famous examples. Certainly the homosocial element is present in male adventure stories such as Kipling's "The Man Who Would Be King," in which Dravot and Carnahan sign a virtual marriage contract foreswearing women and alcohol, and pledging to stand by each other in times of trouble, as well as *King Solomon's Mines,* in which Sheba's Breasts figuratively castrate Quartermain, leaving him "impotent" (85). As Quartermain put it rather dismissively, "Women are women, all the world over, whatever their color" (246). The white woman's statement in the advertisement, then, may refer less to her female counterpart and the relationship between them, than to the relationship between them and the two men, who seem not even to notice the two women, but are instead sitting together, gazing off in an entirely different direction.

Fourth, the Mount Gay Barbados Rum advertisement continues a long history of commodifying the British Empire, from the imperial displays at the Great Exhibition, to the famous Pears' Soap advertisements of the late-nineteenth century, to the Empire Marketing Board of the 1920s. Certainly one of the most important functions of the British Empire, and one of the imperatives underlying its expansion, was to supply British men and women with luxury goods. As Thomas Richards discerned, commodities were "convenient vehicle[s] for expanding the Empire's sphere of influence" (151). Luxuries such as tea from China, coffee from Arabia, tobacco from America, opium from Bengal, and sugar from the West Indies were originally intended for the rich, but soon appealed to all levels of society. Sugar became the most valuable of these novelties because it was the key ingredient in so many other products, including jam, candy, tea, and of course rum, which quickly replaced beer as the beverage of choice on long sea voyages because it kept better, took up less space, and could be mixed with lemon juice to combat scurvy. So important was sugar that in 1763, at the end of the Seven Years' War, France ceded to Britain all of Canada rather than the tiny island of Guadeloupe in the Caribbean, one of the "sugar islands."

Rarely was the link between commodities and empire clearer than in the poster advertising campaign of the Empire Marketing Board. The Board was established by the British government in 1926, and according to Stephen Constantine was "an attempt to consolidate imperialist ideas and an imperial world view as part of the popular culture of the British people" (1). It is often regarded as one of the first "propaganda" ministries. One of its most important and influential projects was a poster-based advertising campaign that sought to foster economic and commercial links between Britain and its colonies by urging men and women to "Buy Empire Goods from Home and Overseas" and to "Buy Empire Every Day," whether it was tea from Ceylon (now Sri Lanka) or salmon from Canada. There was a fairly widespread perception in the 1920s that the British economy was in poor health. Britain's industrial dominance was being challenged, and at a time of increasing protectionism around the world, it looked to colonial suppliers and markets.

But by the 1920s the imperatives behind imperial art had changed from what they had been a century earlier: the idea was to emphasize development and extractable resources, rather than pristine, untouched lands, and women were no longer depicted as sex objects, but as "primitive" laborers, in some cases barely even human, as in E. McKnight Kauffer's poster titled simply, "Cocoa" (1927). What is striking about the Mount Gay Barbados Rum advertisement is that it conjoins the eighteenth-century exotic island (and islander) motif with the late-nineteenth- and early-twentieth-century reification of commodities to promote its product through a multitude of devices.

Finally, the caption to the Mount Gay Barbados Rum advertisement clearly harkens back to the British view of the peoples of their empire as uncivilized, taking it as their mission to "civilize" them. In an 1879 cartoon from the humor magazine *Punch* called "A Lesson," a teacher, John Bull, the male personification of Great Britain, is punishing and humiliating a student by making him write "Despise not your enemy" on the blackboard, teaching the Zulu warrior the virtues of moderation and subservience. The image refers to the Zulu Wars which raged for most of the third quarter of the 19th century. The immediate prompt for this cartoon was the capturing by the Zulus of a British army camp, which resulted in the deaths of over 500 British soldiers. Before leaving the camp the Zulu warriors stripped and disemboweled their victims, and stole hundreds of rifles. Whereas John Bull is fully dressed, from his shirt collar to his heavy boots, much of the Zulu's body is exposed; he lacks clothing, marking him, for British viewers, as savage and uncivilized. He is portrayed as a child—in contrast to John Bull, whose balding head suggests that he is old and wise; his hair and skirt give the Zulu a feminine appearance, thus emasculating him as well; and, his hairy, barrel-chest and distended stomach, suggest that he is lower down on the evolutionary scale and closer to the apes than the Englishman.

To be sure, the caption to the Mount Gay Barbados Rum advertisement offers a number of possible meanings. There is, of course, the literal reading, offered by James France, that "primitive spirit" refers to the product (the rum, a "spirit") and "refined" refers both to the way it has been processed ("refined" or "distilled") and to the character of the brand (Mount Gay). But the refinement of raw materials into commodities suitable for resale is hardly a neutral process. It was, rather, the foundation of the British imperial system, and thus even if France's interpretation is correct, it carries with it a number of resonances that link back to the nineteenth century empire. More provocatively, though, within the context of the tradition of British imperial art outlined above, it seems clear that even if only subconsciously, "primitive spirit" refers to the black woman who needs to be "refined." But either way, this contemporary advertisement invokes the visual history of the British Empire at a number of different levels, which may in fact help to explain its effectiveness, suggesting that the very visual tropes that helped to sell the empire in the nineteenth century became normalized during the course of the twentieth.

This analysis, then, suggests a number of general conclusions. First, imperialism was as much a cultural project as a military endeavor, and thus scholars need to look not only at battles and treaties and international rivalries, but at the ways men and women thought about and represented their empires, especially visually. Imperialism is constructed as much in the mind as it is a physical reality. Second, imperialism was not something that happened exclusively on the imperial frontier (whether Africa, the Caribbean, or the American West); it also occurred "at home," in the minds and on the canvasses of artists. Third, gender and race are critical to any understanding of imperialism. Even though it was men who manned the merchant ships and wielded the rifles of colonial armies, men who owned and oversaw the mines and slave plantations, and men who engineered the global flows of capital, women, usually half-naked, served as the lure to get those men overseas. As for race, it should be clear that the "white people" saw themselves as fundamentally different from and superior to those they encountered overseas, and that these imagined racial differences in turn became justifications for continued imperialism.

Finally, it needs to be emphasized that imperialism was, and continues to be, a supra-national phenomenon. Scholars such as Winthrop Jordan and Jan Nederveen Pieterse have long argued for the links between European and American attitudes toward race, and scholars of the picturesque, most recently Stephen Daniels, have articulated the links between European and American visions of the landscape. It has been suggested here that this line of analysis be extended to issues of tourism and commodity capitalism as well. This advertisement makes clear that the exercise of power is subtle and long-lasting, and that the images and visual tropes of nineteenth-century British imperialism linger on and continue to inform current ways of thinking and representing the world.

NOTES

1. One exception is late-sixteenth and early-seventeenth century America. See Peter C. Mancall, ed. *Envisioning America: English Plans for the Colonization of North America, 1580–1640*. Boston: Bedford Books, 1995; David Quinn, *North America from Earliest Discovery to First Settlements* (New York: Harper and Row, 1975). For a suggestive analysis of early-nineteenth-century French imperial art, see Todd Porterfield, *The Allure of Empire: Art in the Service of French Imperialism 1798–1836* (Princeton: Princeton University Press, 1998).

2. The discussion of the picturesque offered here is not intended to suggest that it was in any way, or at any time, a stable, unified, or unitary aesthetic. Although Christopher Hussey in *The Picturesque: Studies in a Point of View* (London: F. Cass, 1927) established the picturesque as an "interregnum between classic and romantic art" (4), there were debates about what it was at the time, as there have been ever since. See Stephan Copley and Peter Garside, eds., *The Politics of the Picturesque* (Cambridge: Cambridge University Press, 1994); Kim Ian Michasiw, "Nine Revisionist Theses on the Picturesque." In *Representations, Vol.* 38, 76–100. 1992; Malcolm Andrews, *The Search for the Picturesque* (Stanford: Stanford University Press, 1989).

3. It is worth noting that the African chief in the middle has noticeably lighter skin than the other Xhosa, is clothed like a Greco-Roman hero, and classically posed. He is not a savage, but someone with whom the British can do business. Darell thus is differentiating between the chief, whom he perceives to be of a higher class, and his tribesmen; the chief is a go-between, an intermediary step on the imagined evolutionary ladder.

REFERENCES

"A Lesson." *Punch* 76 (1879): 91.

Angas, George French. *The Kafirs Illustrated.* London: J. Hogarth, 1849.

Bhabha, Homi K. "The Other Question." *Screen* 24 (1983): 18–36.

Bowler, T. W., and W. R. Thompson. *The Kaffir Wars and the British Settlers in South Africa.* London: Day & Son, 1865.

Constantine, Stephen. *Buy & Build: The Advertising Posters of the Empire Marketing Board.* London: HMSO, 1986.

Daniels, Stephen. *Fields of Vision: Landscape Imagery and National Identity in England and the United States.* Princeton, NJ: Princeton University Press, 1993.

Darell, H. F. C. *China, India, Cape of Good Hope and Vicinity.* London: Day & Sons, 1852.

Foucault, Michel. *The History of Sexuality.* Vol. 1. New York: Random House, 1978.

France, James. Personal interview. 15 May 1998.

Gates, Henry Louis, Jr. "Writing 'Race' and the Difference It Makes." *"Race," Writing, and Difference.* Chicago: University of Chicago Press. 1986. 1–20.

Gilman, Sander. "Black Bodies, White Bodies: Toward an Iconography of Female Sexuality in Late Nineteenth-Century Art, Medicine, and Literature." *"Race," Writing, and Difference.* Ed. Henry Louis Gate, Jr. Chicago: University of Chicago Press, 1986. 223–61.

---. *Difference and Pathology: Stereotypes of Sexuality, Race, and Madness.* Ithaca: Cornell University Press, 1985.

Haggard, H. Rider. *King Solomon's Mines.* Oxford: Oxford University Press, 1989.

Horn, James. "Tobacco Colonies: The Shaping of English Society in the Seventeenth-Century Chesapeake." *The Oxford History of the British Empire.* Vol. 1. Ed. Nicholas Canny. Oxford: Oxford University Press, 1998. 170–92.

Hughes, Robert. *The Fatal Shore.* New York: Random House, 1986.

Hyam, Ronald. *Empire and Sexuality.* Manchester: Manchester University Press, 1992.

JanMohamed, Abdul R. "The Economy of Manichean Allegory: The Function of Racial Difference in Colonialist Literature." *"Race," Writing, and Difference.* Ed. Henry Louis Gates, Jr. Chicago: University of Chicago Press, 1986. 78–106.

Jordan, Claire. Personal interview. 11 May 1998.

Jordan, Winthrop D. *White over Black. American Attitudes toward the Negro, 1550-1812.* Chapel Hill: University of North Carolina Press, 1968.

Kingsley, Mary. *Travels in West Africa.* London: Everyman, 1993.

Lutz, Catherine A., and Jane L. Collins. *Reading National Geographic.* Chicago: University of Chicago Press, 1993.

MacKenzie, John M. *Propaganda and Empire: The Manipulation of British Public Opinion 1880–1960.* Manchester: Manchester University Press, 1984.

Markham, Clements, ed. *Narratives of the Mission of George Bogle to Tibet, and of the Journey of Thomas Manning to Lhasa.* London: Trübner and Company, 1876.

McClintock, Anne. *Imperial Leather: Race, Gender and Sexuality in the Colonial Contest.* New York: Routledge, 1995.

Pieterse, Jan Nederveen. *White on Black: Images of Africa and Blacks in Western Popular Culture.* New Haven: Yale University Press, 1992.

Pratt, Mary Louise. "Scratches on the Face of the Country; or, What Mr. Barrow Saw in the Land of the Bushmen." *"Race," Writing, and Difference.* Ed. Henry Louis Gates, Jr. Chicago: University of Chicago Press, 1986. 138–62.

Rawdon-Hastings, Francis. *The Private Journal of the Marquess of Hastings.* 2 vols. Ed. Marchioness of Bute. London: Saunders and Otley, 1858.

Richards, Thomas. *The Commodity Culture of Victorian England: Advertising and Spectacle, 1851–1914.* Stanford: Stanford University Press, 1990.

Smith, Bernard. *European Vision and the South Pacific.* 2nd ed. New Haven: Yale University Press, 1985.

Spurr, David. *The Rhetoric of Empire: Colonial Discourse in Journalism, Travel Writing, and Imperial Administration.* Durham: Duke University Press, 1993.

Weil, Robert M. "'Shaftesbury's Darling': British Settlement in The Carolinas at the Close of the Seventeenth Century." *The Oxford History of the British Empire.* Vol. I. Ed. Nicholas Canny. Oxford: Oxford University Press, 1998. 375–97.

Williamson, Judith. "Woman Is an Island: Femininity and Colonization." *Studies in Entertainment: Critical Approaches to Mass Culture.* Ed. Tania Moleski. Bloomington: Indiana University Press, 1986. 99–118.

Yalom, Marilyn. *A History of the Breast.* New York: Knopf, 1997.

16 Karen Dubinsky, from *The Second Greatest Disappointment: Honeymooning and Tourism at Niagara Falls*

EDITORS' INTRODUCTION

With the possible exceptions of dedicatedly ironic "post-tourists," it is as likely as not that most of you reading this would prefer to go over Niagara Falls in a barrel than to go there for your honeymoons. Nevertheless, for well over a hundred years, from the 1830s to the 1960s, Niagara Falls was not simply *a* honeymoon destination but *the* "Honeymoon Capital of the World." In this excerpt from *The Second Greatest Disappointment: Honeymooning and Tourism at Niagara Falls*, Karen Dubinsky considers how such an unlikely association—the association of millions of gallons of falling water with the inauguration of wedded bliss—came about. The title of Dubinsky's book—taken from the common paraphrase of Oscar Wilde's comment on the Falls after his visit in 1882 ("Every American bride is taken there, and the sight of the stupendous waterfall must be one of the earliest, if not the keenest, disappointments in American married life")—is an indication that, even in its heyday, the linkage of waterfalls and newlyweds was seen as unlikely. But it is also an indication that it was popularly taken for granted.

Interestingly, the evolution of the modern, North American concept of the honeymoon and the development of Niagara Falls as a tourist destination occurred at the same time. In the early 19th century, wealthy newlyweds (you needed to be wealthy to afford to travel) went on "wedding tours," often accompanied by family members. The purpose of the wedding tour, which eventually became a middle-class custom as well, was to visit still more family members who had been unable to attend the wedding itself. "Rather than a moment of romantic seclusion for two people," Dubinsky notes, "the wedding tour affirmed the bonds between the new couple and their family, community, and wider social network" (Dubinsky 22). The custom of the private honeymoon, an occasion for removed intimacy, became common only after mid-century. Also by mid-century, the construction of railroads, of the Erie and Welland Canals, and of bridges connecting the United States and Canada not only made Niagara Falls easier to get to, but the establishment of fine hotels with stunning views of the Falls themselves had made the spot a popular resort for North Americans who could afford to travel.

But this temporal coincidence—the emergence of the private honeymoon and of Niagara Falls as a popular tourist destination—is not sufficient to account for the place becoming "The Honeymoon Capital of the World." To answer the question of how this came about, Dubinsky turns to geographer Rob Shields's idea of "imaginary geographies," the imagined association of particular places with particular ideas and values: New York City is "exciting and never sleeps," Paris is "for lovers," Toronto—for a big city—is "clean and safe." How *do* such associations come about? It is tempting to say that, in most cases, it is likely a matter of clever advertising, but one of the things that Dubinsky demonstrates in her book is that the cultural association of Niagara Falls with honeymoons predates any entrepreneurial "hard sell"; indeed, in this case, the selling of Niagara Falls specifically as a honeymoon destination is something that occurs only in the last 30 or so years of its status as such. Something else drew literally millions of newlywed couples to this spot.

Dubinsky finds the answer in the ways legions of travellers described their experience of seeing the waterfall. She canvasses the quite voluminous record—verbal and visual—of 19th-century descriptions of Niagara Falls, descriptions by the famous, infamous, obscure, and even anonymous, noting the recurring use of gendered imagery. "Travellers speak about the waterfall," she writes, "as though it were female and invest it with dangerous, alluring, and quite sexual powers" (Dubinsky 4). The cumulative effect of these descriptions, she suggests, was a fairly widespread cultural association of the place with ideas of forbidden romantic pleasures making it seem an ideal spot for the private honeymoon.

The process by which tourist destinations become popular is complex and, to some extent, irrational. Why one particular waterfall, or city, or island and not others? *The Second Greatest Disappointment* proposes that this process has less to do with where people are actually going than with where they *imagine* they are going. Thus, while tourism is often characterized as an opportunity to experience "difference"—different lands, different people, different weather—the ways in which that "difference" is imagined actually tells us about ourselves.

—CM

ISSUES TO CONSIDER WHILE READING

1. In this section of her book, Dubinsky focuses on the cultural construction of Niagara Falls, but her book is equally about the cultural construction of heterosexuality and marriage and their accompanying rituals (she calls Niagara Falls "the greatest theme park of heterosexuality" [3]). What is the cultural purpose of supposedly "private" rituals, such as the honeymoon?

2. Think about your own "imaginary geographies." What preconceptions do you have about places you have never been to? Think of somewhere you want to go: where did that desire come from?

3. People sometimes make a distinction between travel and tourism. Many university and college students, for example, say that they want to travel after graduation; they do not say that they want to become tourists. Sometimes, the distinction is made along the lines of high culture/low culture: the educated elites travel; the ignorant masses are tourists. Are such distinctions viable? What purpose do they serve?

REFERENCES AND FURTHER READING

Dubinsky, Karen. *The Second Greatest Disappointment: Honeymooning and Tourism at Niagara Falls.* New Brunswick, NJ: Rutgers University Press, 1999.

Krotz, Larry. *Tourists: How Our Fastest Growing Industry is Changing the World.* London: Faber, 1997.

McGreevy, Patrick. *Imagining Niagara: The Making and Meaning of Niagara Falls.* Amherst: University of Massachusetts Press, 1994.

Shields, Rob. *Places on the Margin: Alternative Geographies of Modernity.* London: Routledge, 1991.

Turner, Louis, and John Ash. *The Golden Hordes: International Tourism and the Pleasure Periphery.* London: Constable, 1975.

Urry, John. *The Tourist Gaze: Leisure and Travel in Contemporary Society.* London: Sage, 1990.

The Second Greatest Disappointment: Honeymooning and Tourism at Niagara Falls

…Nineteenth-century honeymooners had a peculiar relationship to their culture; they were, for a moment at least, decided oddities and outsiders. Social conservatives voiced their firm disapproval for the ritual, doctors and sex experts thought honeymooners should be given dire warnings and then, for a period, banished, and pornographic writers delighted in mocking social convention by exposing the main premise of the institution: entry into heterosexual culture. Yet honeymooning couples do not completely exist outside conventional geographic markers, for one such location, Niagara Falls, has been privileged as a honeymoon site par excellence for the past two centuries. Indeed, Niagara Falls was the first and, for a long time, the only honeymoon resort in the world.

The association of Niagara Falls with honeymoons is almost as old as tourism at the Falls itself, dating from the early nineteenth century. The legend, now a staple of Niagara Falls tourist promotion and local history, that the first honeymooners were the U.S. statesman Aaron Burr's daughter Theodosia and her husband, who visited in 1801, or Napoleon Bonaparte's brother Jerome and his wife, who came in 1803, has been challenged by historian Elizabeth McKinsey, who dates the origins of what she calls the "honeymoon craze" at Niagara to the late 1830s. Scattered references to honeymooners crop up in travellers' writings of the 1830s and 1840s. That era also saw perhaps the first Niagara honeymoon reference in popular culture, a celebrated 1841 ditty called, simply, "Niagara Falls." Its first verse goes:

> Oh the lovers come a thousand miles,
> They leave their home and mother
> Yet when they reach Niagara Falls,
> They only see each other.[1]

Visitors seemed to take honeymooners for granted as part of the Niagara landscape, but while newlyweds probably felt conspicuous, no one paid them much attention. During her stay in 1864, English visitor Frances Monck simply noted the presence of "several bridal couples" at her hotel. She also wrote approvingly that "they look very loving." Occasionally the presence of newlyweds provided another reference point for visiting Europeans to distinguish themselves—for good or ill—from North Americans.

Captain William Butler, visiting from England in the 1870s, commented tersely that he saw several "newlywed couples conducting themselves in that demonstrative manner characteristic of such people in the New World."[2]

Niagara's fame as a honeymoon resort was, then, taken in stride by visitors through the nineteenth century, yet the first obvious hard sell of the region to honeymooners did not occur until almost one hundred years later. The honeymoon, like travel itself, was long a luxury, not an item of mass consumption, and so it was not really advertised or promoted in the nineteenth or early twentieth centuries. There were faint attempts at marketing the Niagara Falls honeymoon in the 1920s, such as specific references to honeymooners in general tourist promotion. These were piecemeal measures, hardly an ad campaign, particularly when contrasted with the real selling of Niagara as a honeymoon haven—including the creation of honeymoon certificates, honeymoon hotels, and other promotional devices—that would begin during World War II. Why, then, did huge numbers of honeymooning couples "vote with their feet" and visit the Falls in the nineteenth century, without being directly encouraged by anyone?

This raises the question of how certain sites become designated as popular places to visit, as well as of how particular places become invested with specific qualities. Consider, for example, the British seaside, a popular tourist destination for several centuries. Seaside resorts were popular because they were close to cities and towns and relatively easy to get to. But this was not the only reason that British holidaymakers flocked to seaside towns. They were also attracted to the sea because of its supposed health-giving properties. Later, in Britain as elsewhere, people began to think of the sun, not the sea, as healthy and rejuvenating, though in recent decades the depleting ozone layer has been changing this phenomenon as well.

In Canada nature tourism became popular in the nineteenth century and was, like trips to the British seaside, based on the notion that the woods provided a pure and nourishing environment. Throughout the early part of the twentieth century, the Ontario government, for example, sold the province, and especially the North, as a place of health, rest, and transformation. A "rest cure in a canoe," as *Rod and Gun in Canada* dubbed it in 1909, was just the thing to cure the ailments of white-collar urbanites.

Places are more than simply locations; the spatial is also socially constructed, and places can mean different things at different times. Social divisions are often spoken of in spatial terms—the "wrong side of the tracks," for example. Like individuals, places can become labelled: Paris is romantic, New York is scary, Canada is boring.... This combination of social divisions and spatial metaphors becomes incorporated into what geographer Rob Shields calls "imaginary geographies," so much so that certain sites become associated with "particular values, historical events and feelings."[3] Tourist promoters can take these associations of places with values, events, and feelings and create successful enterprises from them. But these efforts have their limits....

For Niagara Falls to become a popular honeymoon spot—especially in the absence of massive promotion—there must have been something there to begin with. The answer to this puzzle—honeymoon popularity a century or so before honeymoon promotion— lies in how romance, sex, and danger were incorporated in the imaginary geographies of nineteenth-century Niagara Falls visitors.

The tourist industry began in Niagara Falls immediately after the War of 1812. The first tourist entrepreneur was William Forsyth, an American from Buffalo, who in 1822 built the first hotel, the six-storey Pavilion, on the Canadian side. He promptly fenced in his property, so that only paying hotel guests could view the Falls from his vantage point. The first hotel on the U.S. side, Parkhurst Whitney's Eagle Hotel, also dates from this era. The opening of the Erie Canal in 1825 brought more visitors, as did the opening of the Welland Canal in 1832 followed by construction of railroads and bridges linking the two countries during the 1840s and 1850s.

...By the 1840s Thomas Cook was whisking hundreds of English tourists around on the world's first package tours. That decade too saw the launch of the first Atlantic steamship service, and Niagara Falls was hosting more than 40,000 visitors per year. Until the American Civil War, the Falls were especially popular for the Southern U.S. aristocracy, whose members wished to escape the summer heat on the plantation by attending the Niagara "Season." The grandest hotels in the area were built in the 1830s: Canada's Clifton House, "an abode of almost unparalleled gaiety," built by Monty Chrysler in 1833, and the U.S. Cataract House (also owned by Parkhurst Whitney). Each featured balconies and verandas with spectacular views, as well as gardens, billiard rooms, baths, and nightly balls and parties. The Clifton House even kept a pack of hounds should guests decide to venture out for an afternoon of sporting. In its fine dining room the hotel employed French and German waiters to act as interpreters for European guests. Many more fine hotels opened their doors in the 1850s and 1860s, most of them owned by the Falls Company, a consortium of seven men who took over much of the land adjacent to the waterfall.

In this period everyone who could afford it went to Niagara, often as part of the Northern Tour, the American equivalent of the European Grand Tour. Other stops in North America included Boston and Quebec City. Visits to scenic attractions became important cultural currency for the U.S. upper classes. In the same way that an earlier generation regarded visits to the great cities of Europe as a central component of good breeding, early nineteenth-century Americans learned that the consumption of scenery closer to home demonstrated their gentility.[4] While the occasional early visitor claimed Niagara as "the great centre of attraction to all persons of every class," its upper-class aura held until at least the end of the American Civil War, which, according to a guidebook published towards the end of the century, cut off the summer pleasures of the Falls' "remunerative southern patronage."[5]

The waterfall was the main attraction, but always with plenty of sidelines. Two of the most popular attractions, both instituted in the 1830s, were (and remain) the U.S. side's Cave of the Winds and the Canadian side's Table Rock tours, in both of which people could walk through the Falls, buffeted by wind and water, and view them from "inside." Another popular attraction, the *Maid of the Mist* steamer (named after a fake "Indian legend" of virgin sacrifice), began its journeys to the base of the waterfall in 1840. Thomas Barnett's museum of "rare and exotic" curiosities (such as deformed animals and Indian and Chinese handicrafts) opened in 1827, and the villages on both sides of the Falls boasted bathing places, billiard rooms, bowling alleys, and public gardens. ...Battlefields were also an important part of the early tourist experience. Travellers would hire guides who claimed to have been survivors of the War of 1812 and be taken to Lundy's Lane, to the monument to English war hero General Isaac Brock (constructed in 1824), and to other famous war sites.

Entrepreneurs also found creative ways of embellishing the waterfall itself. The first major tourist gathering occurred in 1827, when hotel owner William Forsyth had condemned a schooner filled with live animals to go over the Falls. Some fifteen thousand people (many of whom would have paid Forsyth and other landowners for the privilege of watching the event from their properties) gathered for the spectacle. Feats of human daring were also important (and massively advertised) audience builders. Daredevil Sam Patch jumped over the Falls in 1829, and the most famous Niagara Falls stunt artist, the great "Blondin," performed his high-wire act over the Falls in 1859, repeating it the next year for another huge and appreciative audience, including the visiting Prince of Wales. Other tightrope walkers followed Blondin's lead, including an Italian woman, Maria Spelterini, who dazzled crowds in 1876 with her costume—a scarlet tunic, green bodice, and flesh-coloured tights—and her added twist: her feet were encased in peach baskets as she made her way across the wire.

High-wire acts were eclipsed by the "barrel craze," beginning in 1886 (by which time Niagara was already passé for the prestigious holiday-goer). The first person who successfully went over the Falls in a barrel was a woman, a widowed school teacher named Annie Taylor, who plunged over in 1901 (and has ever since been the subject of misogynist lampooning in Niagara Falls tourist history).

Niagara Falls was also sold in the popular and high culture of the period. As McKinsey's book demonstrates beautifully, Niagara Falls was the most-often painted subject in early American art. The place became the first example of Canadian scenery depicted on a movie screen and was a hugely popular subject for filmmakers and photographers at the turn of the century.[6] It was also the subject of plays and novels as well as some inventive visual spectacles, in the United States and abroad. In New York a popular play, *A Trip to Niagara, or Travellers in America*, took place in front of a moving panorama depicting the scenery between New York City and Niagara. In the 1840s two museums, one in London and P.T. Barnum's American Museum, exhibited scale models of the Falls. The most unusual spectacle toured the United States in the 1850s: a moving "panorama" featuring a thousand-foot-long canvas that took one and a half hours to unroll, with depictions based on two hundred paintings of the Falls.

Niagara Falls became a fashionable and desirable tourist resort in the early and midnineteenth century in part through mass spectacles and promotional gimmicks, but also because as a celebrity itself the Falls was visited by a veritable who's who of nineteenth-century luminaries.[7] In this first period of prestigious tourism, celebrity tourists helped make Niagara a cultural icon. Niagara became famous for being famous, and fame did not—as it would in the twentieth century—render the place boring or passé.

Indeed, fame helped…. Niagara was one of the "canonical sights" of the New World: "What the pyramids are to Egypt…so is Niagara to North America," exclaimed [a] visitor in the 1870s. Another said it "beats Michael Angelo" [sic] for artistry. A guidebook contended that Niagara was to waterfalls as Shakespeare was to poetry.[8]

…The main objective of visitors was quiet contemplation of the waterfalls. To really "do" Niagara, the visitor stayed for a long period of time and watched the Falls in awed silence, from different vantage points and in different lights. "Words are powerless, guides are useless," wrote *London Times* correspondent Nicholas Woods in 1861. "He who wishes to see and feel Niagara must watch it for himself."[9]

We know a lot about what the nineteenth-century traveller felt and thought about Niagara, because a good many of them took the trouble to write down their impressions. In the nineteenth century, travel was a literary activity; the travelling class was also the reading class. Literary celebrities published accounts of their visit to the Falls, as did a host of less famous travel writers, poets, and diarists. Guidebooks and gift books also contained pages and pages of descriptive writings. Charles Dickens is probably the most often cited writer of Niagarana; passages from his travel journal, published in 1842, were quickly repackaged in countless guidebooks, and he continues to be quoted by tourist industry promotional literature to this day.

But the imaginative outpourings of hundreds of other obscure or even anonymous writers also found their way into print. The desire to offer impressions of Niagara was institutionalized by the tourist industry; the proprietors of Table Rock House provided guest books in their sitting room, where people would write a few lines abut their experiences after taking the Table Rock tour under the Falls. At least two anthologies from this album were published as souvenir books in the 1840s and 1850s.

Travellers were determined to "read" the waterfall, and a number of different meanings appear in the writings of nineteenth-century visitors. Travel writing provides a revealing commentary on the place of the narrator—the self—in relation to the surroundings. Many Americans, for example, imagined Niagara as a symbol of their nation. In paintings that depicted bald eagles, stars and stripes, and flag-draped young women standing before the waterfall, Americans—intent on national definition and celebration—appropriated the Falls for the spirit of their young country.[10] Because the Falls were shared by another nation, and the Canadian Horseshoe Falls was the larger and more compelling of the two, this claim was rather complicated to sustain.

The U.S. visitors who commented on the Canadian waterfall often did so jokingly, expressing remorse or envy. Novelist William Howells admitted that he watched the "mighty wall of waters" on the Canadian side "with a jealousy almost as green as themselves," and an anonymous scribbler in the Table Rock album expressed the same sentiment in verse: "My pride was humbled and my boast was small, for England's King has got the fiercest Fall." U.S. President John Quincy Adams turned the history of

As seemingly bewildered Native men look on, Father Louis Hennepin claims the Falls for Christianity in the 1670s. This twenty-foot-wide mural was painted in 1961 by Thomas Hart Benton and hangs in the Visitors Center of the New York Power Authority in Lewiston, N.Y. *Reprinted by permission of the New York Power Authority.*

Canada/U.S. border battles into an act of God. "It is as though," he mused, "Heaven had considered this vast natural phenomenon too great for one nation."[11] Canadian writer Agnes Machar's patriotic delight that "our Canadian falls are the grandest" was a theme taken up by surprisingly few Canadian visitors.[12]

The waterfall also acquired an important religious identity. For many tourists, Niagara had all the trappings of a sacred shrine, a view that achieved official recognition in 1861 when Pope Pius IX established a pilgrim shrine at Niagara Falls. Many referred to the place as a "cathedral," and others suggested it was "where God himself baptizes." "I feel as if I had entered a living temple of the Eternal," wrote one visitor, who invited others to "come and worship at the shrine of Niagara." Irish poet Thomas Moore probably spoke for many when he wrote in a letter to his mother in 1804: "Oh! Bring the atheist here, and he cannot return an atheist!"[13]

Religious sentiment about the Falls helped shape another type of meaning: the moral power of Niagara. Niagara was the setting of several didactic Christian children's books, and the Canadian social purity movement also found Niagara Falls a powerful visual metaphor to illustrate its agenda. The "Mighty Niagara of Souls" was an image used by the Canadian Salvation Army to arouse concern for the plight of countless lost souls— the drunkard, the gambler, the sensualist, the society lady and her "fallen" sister—who were "fast being hurried over the 'Niagara' of life into the whirlpool of eternity."[14]

Nineteenth-century moralists found Niagara Falls a powerful symbol of damnation and destruction because of another long-standing set of meanings evoked by the waterfall: its association with both pleasure and terror. From the first written description of the Falls in 1683 by Father Louis Hennepin, who called it "the most Beautiful, and at the same time most Frightful Cascade in the World," such ambivalence has characterized much writing about Niagara. "The pleasure is exquisite but violent," wrote one visitor in 1821. Yet the lure of Niagara was as potent as its danger. As another early nineteenth-century traveller commented, he could "hardly consent to leave this seemingly dangerous, and enchanting spot."[15]

Despite the voluminous accounts of visits to Niagara Falls, writers again and again expressed the difficulties of describing the experience. "There is no term of our language too high, or idea of our imagination adequately comprehensive, to describe this profound and impressive scene," wrote one anonymous guidebook author.[16] ...One device many writers used to describe the indescribable was to attribute human feelings and emotions to the rushing waters. Some simply compared the waters to humans. "When one has looked at the waters for a certain time one feels certain that the mass is alive," declared a typical visitor in 1873.[17] Isabella Bird described the U.S. rapids: "rolling and struggling down, chafing the sunny islets, as if jealous of their beauty," they then "flung [themselves] upwards, as if infuriated against the sky." She concluded, "There is something very exciting in this view, one cannot help investing Niagara with feelings of human agony and apprehension."[18]

Others were less self-conscious than Bird in their use of human imagery, but no less expansive. The rapids were seen as "a symbol of life and human passion.... The helplessness of its frenzied sweep saddens your heart." These characterizations, varying in mood and emotion, fill volumes of Niagara Falls prose. The rapids "gambol along in a sportive mood," then become "possessed by demons." The mist is like "children of the air," and the "greedy" waters evoke a "sullen majesty," a "haughty grandeur," or "dance and curl in rap-ture." Cliffs "frown," billows are "angry," shores too are "sullen." Novelist Henry James saw the Horseshoe Falls as an exhausted swimmer, "shrieking, sobbing, clasping hands, tossing hair."[19] Others saw the river "telling its tale—at first in broken syllables of foam and flurry, and then…in rushing, flashing sentences and passionate ejaculations." Niagara Falls, declared the Niagara Parks Commission, gave tourists the opportunity to see the "awe inspiring spectacle of nature in one of her turbulent moods."[20]

That last passage indicates another common descriptive device: the waters were not simply personified, they were given a gender, and most of the time this was the female gender. To almost all writers who used gender in their descriptions, Niagara was a woman: the "Queen of the Cataracts," the "Water Bride of Time," the "Daughter of History," and the "Mother of all Cascades." Niagara Falls has always been an icon of femininity.

While incorporating female imagery into their descriptions of Niagara, many writers also projected suitably heterosexual responses, which sometimes took the form of simple flattery, particularly of the "costume" of the waterfall. Niagara "wears a garb that wins from man…wonder, awe, and praise." At "her" base, she would "wrap herself saucily in the rainbow robe" of mist. During the reign of "King Winter," Niagara dons a "coat of crystal" and sparkles like "a gem in the diadem of nature." One particularly poetic writer saw, amidst Niagara's winter scene, trees "bowed down to the earth with their snowy vestments, like so many white nuns doing saintly homage to the genius of the place." Others saw Niagara's mist as a veil, sometimes bridal, at other times ghostlike. Writers also described the electrical illumination of the waterfalls using metaphors of fashion, though not always positively. Lady Mary McDowell Hardy was horrified to see Niagara "dressed up like a transformation scene in a pantomime. It was like putting a tinsel crown and tarlatan skirts on the Venus of Milo."[21]

To many observers Niagara was *like* a woman; others were more literal. British visitor William Russell claimed, "I never looked at it [the waterfall] without fancying I could trace in the outlines the indistinct shape of a woman, with flowing hair and drooping arms, veiled in drapery." The invented tale of the "Maid of the Mist," who went over the waterfall, fuelled many such fantasies. Promoters of Canada Steamship Lines tours to the Falls in 1915 invited tourists to imagine that "instinctively we see the Indian maid in her flower-bedecked canoe approach the apex of the Falls, her body erect, her demeanour courageous." Images of naked "Indian maidens" going over the waterfall adorn postcards, souvenirs, and advertising, as well as "high art," to this day.[22]

The positioning of the waterfall as female and the viewer as male enhanced the pleasure of "doing" Niagara. Not surprisingly, then, sexual imagery abounds in descriptions of the Falls. The spray from the mist was often described as a "kiss." The sound of the water rushing was a "moan." Islands rest on the "bosom" of the waterfall, and the "soft shales" of the cliff "gradually yield before the attack" of the rushing water. The "clinging curves" of water "embrace" the islands, and water "writhes," "gyrates," and "caresses the shore." The whirlpool is "passionate." Some writers recoil from the "mad desire" of the waters. For others, "nowhere else is Nature more tender, constrained, and softly clad." Niagara—"nature unclothed"—was "seductively restless" and "tries to win your heart with her beauty."[23]

Niagara certainly won many hearts. "Like a beautiful and true, an excellent and admirable mistress," wrote George Holley in 1872, "the faithful lover may return to it with ever new delight, ever growing affection."[24] Poets spoke of the "smooth, lustrous, awful, lovely curve of peril…cruel as love, and wild as love's first kiss!" Another evoked the image of Sappho, "that immortal maid—enchantress sweet." One poem published in a 1901 collection illustrates the "exquisite pleasures" of Niagara in no uncertain terms:

> Nymph of Niagara! Sprite of the mist!
> With a wild magic my brow thou hast kissed;
> I am thy slave, and my mistress art thou,
> For thy wild kiss of magic is still on my brow.
> I feel it as first when I knelt before thee
> With thy emerald robe flowing brightly and free
> Fringed with the spray-pearls and floating in mist
> That was my brow with wild magic you kissed.[25]

…Fictional treatments of visits to Niagara also recounted the magnetic sexual lure of the waterfall. Agnes Machar depicts Niagara as the first stop in her story of a holiday journey of several young Canadians. The protagonist, May, is joined at Niagara by her cousin Kate and Kate's cousin Hugh, whom May had not previously met. Young May is initially shy around Hugh, but after their look at the waterfall together (a "curving, quivering sheet of thundering surge…dazzlingly pure in its virgin beauty"), May looks at Hugh in a new light. She feels "much less shy" around him and notices him physically for the first time. She is mesmerized by his "heightened colour" and the "absorbed expression of dark blue eyes." Hugh, it turns out, is also transformed by his view of the Falls. "I never felt," he tells May, "as if I had got so near the state of self-annihilation, the 'Nirvana' we read about." May had "much of the same feelings herself," though she was "too reserved to say it out." …[B]y the end of the trip Hugh proposes marriage, asking May to "travel down the river of life together."[26]

Isabel March, the reluctant honeymooner in William Howell's *Their Wedding Journey*, was similarly transformed by Niagara, though she was ambiguous about her feelings. Howells treats Isabel's determination not to reveal herself as an "evident bride" with gentle humour, particularly because she is one of the countless "evident" newlyweds at Niagara Falls. This parody of Victorian manners comes to a crescendo when Isabel, positioning the waterfall as a sexual male, confesses she cannot contain herself any longer: "I'm tossed upon rapids, and flung from cataract brinks, and dizzied in whirlpools; I'm no longer yours, Basil; I'm most unhappily married to Niagara. Fly with me, save me from my awful lord!"[27]

The waterfall could also—befitting a female of many moods—turn ugly, and many horrified but fascinated visitors commented on the fatal lure of the waters. "As you gaze upon the rush you feel a horrid yearning in your heart to plunge in and join the mad whirl and see the mystery out," declared one. Some suggested scientific explanations for the experience, positing that the sight of such a "frightful eminence" caused a rush of blood to the brain, which in turn produced a "partial derangement."[28] Yet most others relied less on science than common discourses of feminine sexuality, depicting the waterfall as an alluring and enchanting female, bewitching and sometimes entrapping legions of male suitors.

…The fatal attraction of the waters was promoted and celebrated as an integral part of the Niagara experience. Stories of babies accidentally swept over the Falls as their mothers looked on helplessly, construction workers falling off bridges, "weak-minded" souls (usually female) who jumped from the cliffs, and intoxicated men (usually Native people) going over in canoes abound in guidebooks, and these tales obviously enhanced perceptions of the area's dangers. …The most popular accident story in the nineteenth century was the tale of Charles Addington and Antoinette DeForest. The two were picnicking with their families, who lived in Buffalo, on Luna Island in June 1849. Addington, aged twenty-two, playfully grabbed DeForest, aged eight, and pretended to throw her in the current. Antoinette fell in, and Charles jumped in after her. The two went over the falls and did not survive. This most "melancholy of all Niagara tragedies" was recounted in guidebooks and travel writing over the next fifty years, but how it was told varied markedly. Few guidebooks reported the ages of the two victims. Most told this as a story of two lovers who went over the falls "locked in each other's arms."[29]

…I am not arguing that guidebooks, tourist promoters, or travel writers should be reprimanded for sloppy research. Rather, I am suggesting that the relationship between self and other, which is fundamental to travel and to travel writing, is often more revealing about self. At Niagara, the gendered, sexualized descriptive imagery, fatal attraction of the waters, and tales of death and destruction, as well as invented stories of romance and tragedy, were all of a piece and helped create a romantic, sexual, and frightening image of Niagara Falls. Such imagery helped fix an image of the Falls as a place of forbidden pleasures: just the spot for a Victorian honeymoon.

…Many people have speculated about why Niagara Falls became associated with the honeymoon, and the question has provoked an endless series of jokes, witticisms, and bon mots. …The answer does not lie in mimicry. Niagara could not have sustained its reputation as "Honeymoon Capital of the World" for two centuries because a handful of famous newlyweds turned up in the 1830s. Nor does another popular answer—falling water creates negative ions, which cheer people up and make them think about sex—get us very far.

Niagara Falls undoubtedly did make visitor after visitor think about sex, but the creation of the place as a honeymoon mecca was a complex process that brought together several strands: its reputation as an elite tourist resort; its proximity to a large, concentrated population; changing mores about the honeymoon itself in nineteenth-century social and family life; cultural depictions of Niagara as an icon of beauty, which were more likely than not expressed in terms of gender and heterosexual attraction; and the forbidden pleasures of sexuality, romance, and danger that countless travellers experienced while gazing at, or playing with, the waterfalls.

NOTES

1. Quoted in Elizabeth McKinsey, *Niagara Falls: Icon of the American Sublime* (Cambridge: Cambridge University Press, 1985) 180. McKinsey includes all five verses.

2. Frances E. Monck, *My Canadian Leaves: An Account of a Visit to Canada in 1864-1865* (London: Richard Bentley, 1891) 161. Captain William Butler, *The Great Lone Land* (London: Sampson, 1872) 25.

3. Rob Shields, *Places on the Margin: Alternative Geographies of Modernity* (London: Routledge, 1991) 11, 29.

4. Dona Brown, *Inventing New England: Regional Tourism in the Nineteenth Century* (Washington: Smithsonian Institute Press, 1995) 15–40.

5. Isabella Bird, *The Englishwoman in America.* (London, 1856) 217; rpt. Toronto: University of Toronto Press, 1966. *Niagara Falls: Nature's Greatest Wonder,* 22. Buffalo: Matthews and Northrup, n.d., c.1890.

6. McKinsey. *Niagara Falls,* 2, 29. On Niagara in Canadian photography and film, see Patricia Pierce, ed., *Canada: The Missing Years* (Don Mills, ON: Stoddart, 1985) and Peter Morris, *Embattled Shadows: A History of Canadian Cinema, 1895–1939.* (Montreal and Kingston: McGill-Queen's University Press, 1992) 8–9.

7. The roster of nineteenth-century celebrity visitors is impressive, and includes: Charles Dickens, Frances Trollope, Anthony Trollope, Abraham Lincoln, Rupert Brook, Oscar Wilde, Nathaniel Hawthorne, Mark Twain, Anna Jameson, Daniel Webster, Harriet Martineau, Margaret Fuller, H.G. Wells, Sarah Bernhardt, Jenny Lind, Henry James, Harriet Beecher Stowe, William Morris, and Walt Whitman.

8. Butler, *The Great Lone Land,* 25; Henry Jones, *Portraits of Plenty* (Boston: Houghton Mifflin, 1883) 370; Thursty McQuill, *The Hudson River by Daylight,* 97. n.p., 1875.

9. Nicholas Woods, *The Prince of Wales in Canada and the United States* (London: Bradbury, 1861) quoted in Charles Mason Dow, *Anthology and Bibliography of Niagara Falls,* Vol. 1 (Albany: J.B. Lyon, 1921) 273.

10. McKinsey, *Niagara Falls,* 101.

11. William Howells, "Niagara First and Last." In William Howells et al., ed., *The Niagara Book: A Complete Souvenir of Niagara Falls* (Buffalo: Underhill and Sons, 1893) 9; George Menzies, *Album of Table Rock* (1846); *A Souvenir of Niagara Falls* (Buffalo: Sage, 1864) 1.

12. Agnes Machar, *Down the River to the Sea* (New York: Home Book Co., 1894) 25.

13. Menzies, *Album of Table Rock and Sketches of the Falls* (Buffalo: Thomas and Lathrop, 1856); John Russell, ed., *Memoirs, Journal and Correspondence of Thomas Moore* (London, 1853) 4., quoted in Ralph Greenhill and Thomas Mahoney, *Niagara* (Toronto: University of Toronto Press, 1969).

14. "The Mighty Niagara of Souls," *War Cry,* Nov. 9, 1895, quoted in Mariana Valverde, *The Age of Light, Soap and Water: Moral Reform in English Canada* (Toronto: McClelland and Stewart, 1991) 37.

15. McKinsey, *Niagara Falls,* 11, 39.

16. *Niagara Falls Guide, with Full Instructions to Direct the Traveller* (Buffalo: J. Faxon, 1850) 32.

17. A.R.C. Grant and Caroline Combe. *Lord Rosebery's North American Journal—1873* (London: Sedgewick and Jackson, 1967) 60.

18. Bird, *Englishwoman in America,* 224.

19. George Curtis. *Lotus Eating—A Summer Book* (New York: Harpers, 1852), rpt. in Dow, *Anthology and Bibliography,* 254; Daniel Pidgeon, *An Engineer's Holiday* (London, 1882), quoted in Dow, *Anthology and Bibliography,* 338; Mrs. S.D. Morse, *Greater Niagara* (Niagara Falls, NY: Gazette Printing, 1896) 12.; J. Murray Jordan, *Niagara in Summer and Winter* (Philadelphia, 1904); Peter Conrad, *Imagining America,* (New York: Oxford University Press, 1980) 16.

20. Jones, *Portrait of Plenty,* 365; *The Niagara Parks Commission Welcomes You,* n.d., c.1950.

21. Mary McDowell Hardy, *Between Two Oceans* (London, 1884) in Dow, *Anthology and Bibliography,* 342.

22. William Russell, quoted in Dow, *Anthology and Bibliograhpy,* 318; Canada Steamship Lines, *Niagara to the Sea,* 1915.

23. [This passage is compiled from a variety of the descriptions cited above.]

24. George Holley. *Niagara: Its History, Geology, Incidents and Poetry* (Toronto: Hunter Rose, 1872) 1.

25. Myron Pritchard, ed. *Poetry of Niagara* (Boston: Lothrop Publishing Co., 1901).

26. Agnes Machar, *Down the River*, 12–15, 263.

27. William Howells, *Their Wedding Journey* (Boston: Houghton Mifflin, 1851) 103.

28. Woods, *Prince of Wales*, in Dow *Anthology and Bibliography*, 271; F.H. Johnson, *Every Man His Own Guide at Niagara Falls* (Rochester: Dewey, 1852) 37.

29. *Complete Illustrated Guide to Niagara Falls and Vicinity* (Niagara Falls, NY: Gazette Publishing, c.1880) 31; Bird, *Englishwoman in America*, 225.

17 Rob Shields, "Social Spatialization and the Built Environment: The West Edmonton Mall"

EDITORS' INTRODUCTION

Shopping malls have been around for some time. For the Great Exhibition of 1851, the Crystal Palace, a gigantic glass and steel structure, was built to showcase Britain's capitalist and imperialist might. Or consider the enclosed galleries and arcades of Europe in the later 19th century. But the malls that began appearing in the 1950s (the first, Greenhills, was built in 1956 in Minnesota, also home of the more recent and mammoth Mall of the Americas) are specifically related to the mid-20th-century explosion of the suburbs in the midst of America's post–World War II economic and population boom. People flocked to the country's open spaces from urban centres, a reversal of the exodus from rural areas to the cities that defined much of 19th- and 20th-century economic growth in the United States and Canada.

The suburbs evoked middle-class values that came to define the good life of American democracy after World War II. Returning soldiers supplanted the women who had laboured in the factories of wartime domestic production, and a new ethos of the feminized domestic space versus the masculinized public sphere (not unlike the 19th-century "separate spheres") re-aligned the gender economy. The middle-class home, furnished by consuming mothers and paid for by bread-winning fathers, was increasingly fuelled by the mall's retail lifeblood. Great anxiety also fuelled this consumerist paradise, under threat of nuclear annihilation during the Cold War, for instance, and so the idyll of the suburban home came to epitomize a middle-class stability in need of protection from the outside.

This idea of social insulation is significant for Rob Shields, who starts his article with the idea that malls create an artificial environment that protects consumers from the weather—a characteristically Canadian dilemma, given the location of the West Edmonton Mall. The mall's protective environment, simple as it seems, has virtually transformed how we think of the public space and how it orchestrates the interactions of subjects, especially when the function of the public space is consumption. But the West Edmonton Mall is about more than just capitalism. Like Disneyland, it recreates the world on its own terms, a simulation of reality that is one of the central concerns of many of the essays in this volume. Malls, thus, reconfigure how we think of social space. As Shields notes, our "basically Cartesian understanding and commonsense conceptions of geographical space as a three-dimensional, seamless, and apparently neutral void" (258) has been radically altered by postmodernism and by the reconfiguration of material space as a virtual environment. This virtuality is the result of technology but also of the fact that social space is fundamentally a site in which neither objects nor subjects are mobile and changeable, rather than fixed or stable. The virtuality of social space is more the constellation of social practices (what Pierre Bourdieu calls *habitus*) that define how subjects act and react, define and redefine, manage and are managed by the social conditions of their existence in all its facets—the impact of virtual technologies being only one of these facets.

To understand why Shields treats malls with such theoretical complexity, we need to understand that, as malls have developed according to changes in the marketplace and shifting cultural and social determinants, they have emerged as more than simple retail outlets or community centres (see Morris). The West Edmonton Mall (the WED) is the perfect example of the mall as a shopping pleasure palace-cum-theme park. The WED turns the simple exchange of commodities into a Disneyesque simulation of capitalism's magic and vibrancy, a simulation that William Severini Kowinski discusses in his influential study, *The Malling of America*. For Kowinski, malls are the magic of commodity fetishism writ large. Obscuring the factories where commodities are produced, they fetishize another kind of factory that is the site of their consumption. Malls turn the simple and mundane labour of buying goods (and services) into theatrical experience: consumerism as spectacle with consumers as both spectators *and* actors. Just as Disney theme parks "make fantasies concrete" (Kowinski 51), so do malls take Disney's nostalgic, sentimentalized, and idealized version of a 19th-century streetscape as the model for their own idealized space with, as Kowinski notes, "just the right touch of obvious artificiality to make it permanently extraordinary" (52).

Shields works partly from Kowinski's understanding of how malls *work,* that is, how they construct, orchestrate, and manipulate public spaces and the subjects within them. A recurring figure in Shield's analysis is that of the *flaneur,* first described by the 19th-century poet Charles Baudelaire in "The Painter of Modern Life" as a "passionate spectator." The *flaneur,* like the mall consumer, strolls through the spectacle of modern life, but is detached, unaffected by its spectacle. The *flaneur* appears most powerfully in Shields's analysis to suggest how subcultures, outside the mainstream of middle-class mall culture and thus otherwise denied access to the mall's hegemonic display of cultural values, turn the wandering and mere observation encouraged by the mall environment into a subversion of its ideological manipulations. Mall subject *par excellence,* the *flaneur* is able to suspend his disbelief in the mall's pleasure dome and models for us the position of observer who draws his own conclusions from empirical observation. This observation is important if we are to resist the sheer (but nonetheless coercive) banality of consumerism that malls evoke, despite—or *because of*—their excessive attempt to "wow" us with the artifice of capitalism's spectacle. Shields's articles asks us to think about material culture on our own terms by resisting its strategies for obedient consumerism.

—JF

ISSUES TO CONSIDER WHILE READING

1. Shields's article asks us to consider how malls, through their carefully controlled organization of public space, also organize a space for consumer training, a training that the figure of the *flaneur* subverts. In what ways, if any, do malls create communal spaces for social interactions unaffected by the demands of consumption and consumerism?
2. In what ways are malls like theme parks?

REFERENCES AND FURTHER READING

Auerbach, Jeffrey. *The Great Exhibition of 1851: A Nation on Display*. New Haven, CT: Yale UP, 1999.

Gibian, Peter. "The Art of Being Off-Center. Shopping Center Spaces and the Spectacles of Consumer Culture." *Mass Culture and Everyday Life*. Ed. Peter Gibian. New York: Routledge, 1997. 238–92.

Kowinski, William Severini. *The Malling of America: An Inside Look at the Great Consumer Paradise*. New York: W. Morrow, 1985.

Meyrowitz, Joshua. *No Sense of Place: The Impact of Electronic Media on Social Behaviour*. New York: Oxford University Press, 1985.

Morris, Meaghan. "Things to Do With Shopping Centres." *Grafts: Feminist Cultural Criticism*. Ed. Susan Sheridan. London: Verso, 1988.

Soja, Edward W. *Postmodern Geographies: The Reassertion of Space in Critical Social Theory*. London: Verso, 1989.

Sorkin, Michael, ed. *Variations on a Theme Park: The New American City and the End of Public Space*. New York: Hill and Wang, 1992.

Washburn, Katherine, and John F. Thornton, eds. *Dumbing Down: Essays on the Strip Mining of American Culture*. New York: W. W. Norton and Co., 1996.

Social Spatialization and the Built Environment: The West Edmonton Mall

When you have a space that you have separated from the outside world, and the ability to create your own world inside, governed by your own rules, what you have is the ability to make magic. You've got yourself a house of fantasy.

(W. S. Kowinski, *The Malling of America*)

INTRODUCTION

The West Edmonton Mall, the world's largest, is one example of the continuing mutation of shopping malls in Canada where inclement winter temperatures have given an added boost to developers' ambitions to have them become the new, privatized, centres of the public lives of city dwellers. In this reading, the alterations in the spatial system of public and private places will be linked with the incipient postmodernization of Western urban cultures (Cooke, 1986). Malls, as interventions in the fabric of urban public space, are fragments of broader changes in the system of spatiality and concrete spatial practices at global, national, and local scales. 'Postmodernism' is a symptom of these changes along with the changing crowd practices by which individuals and groups actualize or deflect these new spatial arrangements. The mediated outcome is as much cognitive as it is a system of practices, of *habitus*. While reflecting real power relations, any outcomes are thus full of contradictions, reversals, and accommodations. This phenomenon is often treated through metaphors such as 'space' (Lefebvre, 1981) or 'sociospatial dialectic' (Soja, 1980), terms which have been criticized for their vagueness, lack of empirical content, internal contradictions, and elision of important aspects of spatiality (Gottdiener, 1985; Sayer, 1985). For precision and clarity this sociospatial aggregate of processes, a mode of being, a manner of 'seeing' and way of doing (De Certeau, 1985), is referred to as *social spatialization* (Shields, 1986)[1] in this article.

Benjamin, the Frankfurt School sociologist of culture (see Lash, 1987), assessed the 19th-century arcades of Paris as *the* defining buildings of the 19th century. They concretized a mode of spatial practice, the new commodity trade and the emergence of cross-class patterns of leisure and consumption in the late 19th century. In his *Passagenwerk* (1978), left unfinished when he committed suicide after being captured by the Gestapo, he developed a reading of these sites as allegories of the society and culture which produced them—the *topoi* of social structures and sentiments (1973). In this paper, I treat the West Edmonton Mall as a site of consumer culture and my work is oriented by the precedent of Benjamin's cultural analysis of 19th-century shopping arcades.

CANADIAN URBAN FASHIONS: OF ATRIA, ARCADES, AND GALLERIA

Before we consider the Mall itself, it is worthwhile outlining some of the general conditions of this form of privatized public consumption space. One of the dominant features of Canadian urban production over the last decade has been the proliferation of private-public spaces: atria, arcades, and galleria. The number, concentration, and ostentation of these developments are on a par with those of the United States to the south *(American Institute of Architects' Journal,* 1981), much better known for its urban ambitiousness, and rivals those of the arcade-building spree in Europe in the late 19th century (Geist, 1983). The output of Canadian architects and developers has also expanded abroad, to the extent that Canadian firms now rank both first (Cadillac Fairview Corp.) and second (the Ghermasian brothers' Triple Five Corp. which owns the West Edmonton Mall) amongst the largest developers and owners of public consumption spaces in the United States (Elash and Jenish, 1984). This activity has more recently been extended to Britain with the construction of the Tyneside Centre in Newcastle for a British developer. In Canada the West Edmonton Mall, the 'Madonna Inn' of shopping centres,[2] a shopping mall cum indoor 'Disneyland' completed in 1986, is the world's largest shopping and indoor leisure centre. It illustrates the changing nature of urban public space: the increasingly primary role of privately owned and controlled consumption spaces, and the impacts that the movement of crowds from public streets to indoors can have on spatial norms.

To be a user of a shopping mall such as the West Edmonton Mall entails having quite different expectations, understandings, and spatial competence from, for example, the set of understandings involved in shopping on a British high street. In the high street, there is a much more clearly marked separation between public pavement, where certain types of behaviour and 'crowd practice' are acceptable, and the privately controlled store area where the same behaviour is not. Being in the tightly policed, semiprivate interior of a mall is quite different from being 'on the street.' "No loitering," as the signs in the mall say. Certain types of comportment are expected. The emotions linked with boisterous behaviour are smothered under a flood of continuous, calming, psychologically tested 'music.'

Dawson and Lord (1983, page 110) point out the central role of malls amongst the repertoire of social spaces in Western cities, noting that in malls, "business deals are struck and social relationships made as they are in the street cafés of continental Europe." This observation could be considerably extended if one considers the glass-covered atria with bars, restaurants geared to business lunches, and personal service shops which now form the ground floor of almost every Canadian office block. Further, as is illustrated by the West Edmonton Mall's full-time work force of several thousand and the much larger number of part-time workers, shopping centres could generate considerable employment in the service sector. They represent the working location for a group of ever-increasing size as the restructuring of the labour force in developed countries continues.

The shopping centre and its practices—a new indoor *flânerie* (strolling), the habit of window shopping as much as 'hanging out' or being an onlooker enjoying the crowds—have become established features of contemporary urban life that are evolving in tandem with broader social transformations in Europe and America. *Flânerie* has acquired a less gendered character to become an almost universal diversion amongst new middle-mass consumers (see below). Thus, in the United States, for example, the most frequented public spaces are shopping malls (US Bureau of Statistics, 1980, cited in Dawson and Lord, 1983, page 111). Nonetheless, the major studies of social structure, both in Europe and North America have little to say on such consumption spaces despite their now pivotal position in the lives of several hundred million consumers. Yet within some advanced capitalist societies the shopping centre seems set to become the focus of the community: one can already find doctors, dentists, swimming pools, libraries, and schools in Canadian and US malls....

THE WEST EDMONTON MALL

Calgary has Banff, Vancouver has the ocean and now, thanks to the mall, Edmonton has a world-class tourist attraction (Ed Bleiken, Director, Edmonton Economic Development Authority, interviewed in Bergman and Cohen, 1984, page 20).

These people aren't just hunting for specific items. They are impulse buyers, the *best* kind. They spend more money. . . . They'll come for the Rockies and us (Rubin Stahl, President, West Edmonton Mall, interviewed in Orr, 1985, pp. 26–27).

This project comprises every major tourist attraction in the world. It is the largest, most comprehensive tourist attraction ever built in the *universe*. Now people in this area never need go to New York or Paris or Miami. They can come here. We travelled the world to see where people liked to go. But they couldn't go to everything in one day. So we have put it all under one roof. So now you don't even have to worry if it's raining. (Nader Ghermasian, Owner, Triple Five Corp., interviewed in Orr, 1985, pp. 26–27).

Fantasyland has put us on the map with the Eiffel Tower, Buckingham Palace and the pyramids! (Jill Romanowski, Tourism Director, West Edmonton Mall, interviewed in Walker, 1984, page 53).

The West Edmonton Mall is remarkable for its counterpoint of, in essence, a banal suburban mall with the ecstatic boosterism of local growth coalitions and superlative attractions—the largest this, the biggest that.

We thought if the mall is going to be the world's largest, let's do the world's largest indoor amusement centre and make it a world-class tourist attraction. We're looking for tourists now, and the only way to attract them is with something really different, something *really* awesome (Stahl interviewed in Jenish, 1985, page 85).

Here, architecture has been by-passed in favour of play structures and interior decor which make the statements which the unremarkable suburban exterior does not. In contrast to the concrete and brick exterior, the interior is a bricolage (a makeshift assemblage) of historicist recreations of foreign streetscapes and high-tech fantasy. The plainly commercial style of the building envelope, however, underlines the staged nature of the Mall: only a simulacrum of carnival—a pseudo-experience of a true urban vitality (Lefebvre, 1975). No critical or scholarly research has yet been carried out on the West Edmonton Mall style of mixed amusement and shopping arcade. Partly, this is because the West Edmonton Mall obeys exactly the formula of the North American suburban shopping-mall typology established by the Viennese architect Victor Gruen, at the Southdale Mall in Dina, MN (1956) whose main features were two 'anchor' department stores one at each end of a long 'street' of specialty shops. Thirty years later, the completed West Edmonton Mall measures 4.5 million ft^2, housing 825 stores on a two-level *mile-long* concourse plus a 15-acre indoor funfair.

Of this, the most recent expansion, Phase III, was a $350 million, 2.7 million ft^2 expansion of the original 64-acre, 434-store mall and entertainment centre. This added nearly another 400 more stores. A 2.5-acre indoor lake stocked with dolphins and grandly dubbed the "Deep Sea Adventure" contains many of the most 'hyped' elements of the new mall with four minisubs (a larger fleet than the Canadian navy!) which take tourists on tours of underwater aquaria, and a reproduction 80-ft Spanish galleon anchored in the middle. Additionally there are an 18-hole minigolf course; 40 restaurants, including 4 McDonald's; a 10-acre water park ('the biggest ever' of course); and a 100 000 ft^2, 13-ride carnival midway, or funfair, with a 142-ft triple-loop rollercoaster (also the 'biggest indoor one in the world,' etc.). This expansion of the "Fantasyland" carnival was accomplished with $20 million in tax concessions over 10 years, granted after the owners, the Ghermasian brothers' Triple Five Corp., threatened to stop construction.

Phase III included reproduction streetscapes and facades such as "Europa Boulevard." A skylit arcade vaguely resembles a 19th-century Parisian street of boutiques. Another 'touristique' recreation of New Orleans Bourbon Street is flanked by nightclubs and lined with wrought-iron lamps. At the entrance stand two mechanized fibreglass sculptures, one of a black jazz band, the other of several ladies of the New Orleans night. A 350-room hotel offers a selection of theme rooms directly in the Madonna Inn mould. For example, one is decorated in gala 1950s Hollywood style, featuring bubble machines, and others are done up in Roman, Polynesian, or Inuit fashion. Last, a Pentecostal chapel was opened at the hub of the Mall, described by one commentator as being, "just starboard of the galleon *Santa Maria*" (Harbeck, 1986, page 52).

Nonetheless, the Mall transgresses no social taboos; such things are to be expected in any such attraction. In this sense, its spuriousness is accepted and institutionalized as the values and material culture of the carnival and funfair. It is "'tacky' when anyone can afford it and 'pretentious' when it is dear," and this "pretension and tackiness generate the belief that somewhere, only not right here, not right now, perhaps just over there someplace, in another country, in another life-style, in another social class, perhaps, there is a *genuine* society" (MacCannell, 1976, page 155)....

ANALYSIS: POSTMODERNISM OF THE NORTHERN FRONTIER

Recentring the Frontier

The West Edmonton Mall is a child of its times. It provides a focus for a whole host of observations of the relationship between production, consumption, and the popular imagination. If it is taken on its own terms as what Benjamin called a site of "collective dreaming" and fantasy (1973), it is also a tangible manifestation of relations of production and dominant ideologies. As such, the West Edmonton Mall is a palimpsest both of past practices and of future possibilities and predispositions. It fragments conventional geographical space and historical time with its wild combination of interior settings; evoking disparate times and places while it seeks to impose its own stable order on the ensemble. At the turn of a corner, one is in a simulated 'New Orleans.' Another corner—'Paris.'

If this is a demonstration of the global awareness and interest of North Americans, then this awareness is of the most basic sort. It appears to be organized only according to an acquaintance with the world through mass tourism, the consumption of cheaply produced craft goods from the Third World, and sensationalistic media. One begins to feel as if one were inside a story which switches from place to place and ranges across the centuries in a kind of spatiotemporal haze. Jameson describes a similar vertiginous feeling inside the Bonaventure Hotel in Los Angeles (1984). Liberties are taken with conventional understandings of the consistency and unity of the site expressed architecturally as stylistic coherence and with our sense of the world as an ordered, seamless, network of more or less distant places.

Paradoxically, Dawson and Lord have pointed out that, although disturbing some communities,

> ... increased social interaction can occur in large multi-use shopping centres but the rationale for this is that such centres provide a sense of place for the community. The strength of these centres in new suburban areas lacking any community identity is a notable aspect of contemporary urban society (1983, page 110).

The West Edmonton Mall expands upon this function. It not only promotes a new representation of space and encourages the elaboration of the corresponding spatial practice of *flânerie,* but also constructs what Lefebvre has called a "*space of representation*" (1981), a space in which the social imaginary is opened to new visions. That is, the Mall is a type of 'play space' which encourages its users to abandon what we might, for the sake of argument, call the 'modern rational' conception of the world. By adopting an alternative cosmology they can momentarily suspend their hinterland relationship to the difficult capitalist world of distant, abstract powers and indulge in a collective fantasy which produces the illusion of a different logic of space and a different capital logic. This new 'logic,' and the new 'understanding' which goes with it, involve a transformation of the spatial indices of location and reality which operate as metaconcepts, guiding metaphors, and imbue conceptual categories and symbolic systems with an often unrecognized 'spatial life.' For example, consider the many spatial metaphors expressing social status ("coming from the 'wrong side of town'"), power, time, prestige, order (right versus left), reason, etc. catalogued by Lackoff and Johnson (1979). Whereas the human experience of gravity engenders a separation of up and down (Needham, 1973), dichotomies such as right and left (Durkheim and Mauss, 1963, page 12; Needham, 1973) or here and there (Benveniste, 1966, page 253; Freud, 1976) are more arbitrary and culturally variable bases for classification.

The Mall presents an allegorical rejection of the geographic world of distant centres in which Edmonton is on the periphery. This order is replaced with the Mall's own internal "hyperreality" (Eco, 1986; Gottdiener, 1986; Jameson, 1984) where "everything looks real, and therefore it is real; in any case the fact that it seems real is real, and the thing is real even if, like Alice in Wonderland it never existed." This is not done with the ethic of "We are giving you the reproduction so that you will want the original," but rather, "We are giving you the reproduction so you will no longer feel any need for the original" (Eco, 1986, pages 16, 19). Commercial copies—signs—of authentic experiences of Paris, New Orleans, and so on, aspire to supplant their referents. What is being asserted at the West Edmonton Mall is a new collective sense of place founded on the notion of having transcended the geographical barrier of distance which has so long kept the provincial capital of Edmonton culturally isolated, not only from the rest of Canada but also from the rest of the world. This displaced sense of place also rests on a denial of locality. The Mall has nothing to do with the real setting or history of Edmonton. There are no fake Rockies, no Indians, and no sculpted ranch hands. One hankers after a fibreglass herd of cattle being driven down the 'Main Street' of the concourse.

As a world view there is no overall unity here. The real-space relations of the globe are replaced by imaginary-space relations. The events of different epochs, cultures, and settings are to be combined in a Disneyland-esque 'pastiche' of scenes. Overarching 'grand narratives' are eschewed in favour of a microrationality: a modest local order fabricated in the face of a disordered world from which a few precious historical mementoes are rescued for this suburban 'Ark'—a galleon, a Parisian Street, a funfair. This cognitive rearrangement of spatial relations amounts to a *local narrative* which is legitimated under the '*local authority*' of the visible, tangible power and everyday influence over the lives of its users that the Mall gives its owners.

This argument is an extension of MacCannell's thesis of "touristic certainty" which describes the cases where tourists, naively misunderstanding the local language, create bizarre explanations or histories of a sight or event through misreadings, pastiche, and collage. This is based on the importing of their experience and a mixture of personal intuition and reasoning into a different cultural context without any guideposts for ascertaining the accuracy of their 'sleuthing.'

The basis of touristic certainty, knowing the truth about a sight, is adapted to a type of society in which social relationships are arbitrary, fleeting and weightless, in which growth and development takes the form of an interplay of differentiations. Within this manifold, the individual is liberated to assemble and destroy realities by manipulating sociocultural elements according to the free play of the imagination (1976, page 141).

At the Mall, the effect is like living in a painting by Magritte where reality and representation merge, or like one of the impossible worlds of Escher. For example, sculptures of prostitutes stand in for real people and roller coaster rides defy gravity. It is a world where Spanish galleons sail up Main Street past Marks and Spencer to put in at "New Orleans," where everything is tame and happy shoppers mingle with smiling dolphins. Even the climate of this Canadian version of paradise is tame. And "everything is here": convenient shopping, convenient global sightseeing. Never a rainy day!

But is this all? Clearly not all the shoppers are happy. Nor are all the users shopping. Some people have not got the message of this spatial medium. Or have they? Perhaps some are more than one step ahead. This question brings us to the problem of the *reception* and *mediation* of the Mall by its users. What practical coping mechanisms are used to 'ward off' the spirits of the West Edmonton Mall? What ironic reversals and hijackings of intended perceptions are being made and how do these dialectically relate to and inflect the modes of spatial practice present? This issue is largely ignored by writers on the built environment, but a consideration of spatial practice will establish its importance in bringing to life any environment. Without this practice—*flânerie* in the case of the West Edmonton Mall—places are dead, designer's maquettes for real sites.

Clearly spatial practices, the habitual routines of "place ballets" (Parkes and Thrift, 1980) are concretized in the built environment and sedimented in the landscape. Such practices 'articulate' the multitudinous possibilities of sites. They are part of the constitution of the qualitative reality of sites as places where certain events and actions are known and expected to take place.

> 'The user of the city takes up fragments . . . to actualize them..' . . . He dooms certain sites to inertia or to decay, and from others he forms 'rare' ('fortuitous') or illegal spatial 'shapes' . . . the walker, in relation to his position, creates a near and a far, a *here* and a *there* . . . indicative of an actual appropriation of space by an 'I' . . . thereby establishing a conjunctive and disjunctive articulation of places" (Barthes, cited in De Certeau, 1985, pages 130–131).

The West Edmonton Mall represents a spatial ensemble which both encourages and requires a specific type of 'crowd practice' for commercial viability (Shields, 1984). The aggregate, wandering consumer crowd of today is complemented by (and is a prerequisite of) the celebratory and festive shopping mall. This type of spatial performance is quite different from the much less commercialized public behaviour of the *boulevardier* or *flâneur* who strolled the 19th-century shopping arcades of Paris, but upon whose model the new Canadian shopping arcades of the 1980s such as the West Edmonton Mall or the Eaton's Centre in Toronto are based.

To capture this dialectical 'production' of ordered space through the articulation of topoi via spatial practices and cognitive metaphors, the term 'social spatialization' is used below. This captures at the same time (1) the sense of an achieved fact of a 'spacing' of classes, moralities, and cultural universes (Bourdieu, 1984)—the commonplace spatial assumptions and daily practices, gestures, body language, and functional and symbolic divisions of the environment that are a powerful and necessary foundation for *habitus* (Bourdieu, 1972) and (2) social structuration (Giddens, 1984).

Postmodernism in a Cold Climate

Transformations of spatial codes and norms have been argued to lie at the heart of an epochal 'postmodern' transformation of Western urban culture (Jameson, 1984). This *bricolage* of historical and spatial contexts wreaks havoc with our cultural sense of collective identity, with the spatial metaphors which mediate and represent the relationship between communities and individuals, and with linear notions of historicity as progress which have lain at the heart of Western thought (Jameson, 1984; Kant, 1968). Changes in spatialization manifest themselves as changes in material culture and social structuration.

Hence, changes in understandings of space together with changes in spatial practice and metaphoric destabilizations of spatial codes constitute changes in individual's *spatiality* and social spatializations. They have 'knock-on' effects in terms of the spatiotemporal balance of epistemology (on this, see Lyotard, 1980). For example, incremental changes in our basically Cartesian understanding and commonsense conceptions of geographical space as a three-dimensional, seamless, and apparently neutral void have led to a relativized conception of geographical space as a socially constructed convention or as a Kantian form of intuition (Kant, 1968). This implies concomitant changes in truth categories and alters the borders separating reason and nonreason. Beyond the construction of shopping malls, there are incremental changes in politics and in judicial decisionmaking (Lyotard, 1979) as old standards of judgment lose their legitimacy and broad-based acceptance. Because of this "generalized incredulity," one is forced into the "art of judgement without standards" (Lyotard, 1984). "How is it possible to envision justice and to act justly in an era that no longer believes in Truth, God, universal emancipation, cause and effect, or History?" (Lindsay, 1984, page 53). Lyotard argues that this gives rise to a new justice in which exclusionary grand narratives give way to the "pagan equality" of multiple narratives, none of which holds any privilege over the others (1977, pages 86–87).

...There is a further consequence of the 'play' with our everyday 'modern' sense of space at the West Edmonton Mall. It interferes with the users' construction of a coherent 'meaning-full' spatial practice according to the conventions of the rational, *legible* spatial arrangements of modernity. Partly because of its sheer size, and partly because of its labyrinthine layout, there is a tendency to lose one's bearings (Jameson, 1984; Moles and Rohmer, 1982). This spatial confusion is heightened by the bricolage of historical settings, throwing off-balance the ordered progression of history. There are no transitional spaces. The Mall appears as a nonrational assemblage held together only by the threads of pedestrian footsteps which link these drifting historical stage sets into a spatial whole (see De Certeau, 1985, page 129). This "spatial illegibility" defies univocal semiotic "readings" (Lefebvre, 1981, pages 124–125; 165) and complicates analysis because the link between the interior sites and sets is an ephemeral spatial 'narrative' or itinerary. It cannot be transcribed as a simple nonqualitative line which elides the modes of being of the person walking (now going, stopping, now wandering, window shopping, passing-by, etc.) (see Barthes, 1970–71, pages 11–13). Thus, on first glance, the analytic gaze finds confusion, the threat of the nonrational, history disordered, and so on. As Jameson (1984) asks, how are we to know *our* place if spatial and temporal coordinates are so jumbled? And, important for the analyst, how are we to chart the whole, relating individual itineraries with group 'mappings' or social spatializations? As both user and reviewer, it is easy to succumb to the fragmentary nature of the Mall either by refusing to look further than the spatial practice of our personal itinerary, or by sketching a one-dimensional narrative which flattens the polyvocality of the mall by reifying it as solely, for example, an unmediated expression of capital. There are many strategies by which people impose their own agendas: evading or rescripting the planned experiences of the mall.

This critique may be levelled at Gottdiener who concentrates his recent analysis of shopping malls on their "instrumental" nature, "the control of crowds to facilitate consumption" (1986, page 296). His situation of malls at the intersection of changes in the spatial arrangement of cities and retailers' ambitions (Gottdiener, 1986, page 292) provides a basis for analysis. However, this must be critically extended. In suburbia, "there are few public places.... Everyday life is structured by the many separations of social living" (1986, pages 290–291). Isolated individuals crave "a certain type of urban ambiance"—the sociability[3] of the ancient town square and the liveliness of the market. Prisoners of the separation of spheres of rationality constitutive of bourgeois identity (Lash, 1986), suburbanites are the further victims of instrumental rationality deployed in the service of the commodity trade cloaked in the robes of social communion. The experience of *communitas* (communion with others in a group) is harnessed for the benefit of consumption. "The function of mall design...is to disguise the exchange relation between producer and consumer...and to present cognitively an integrated facade which facilitates this instrumental purpose by the stimulation of consumer fantasies" (Gottdiener, 1986, page 293).

...Surely the multidimensional nature of the mall as a social artefact exceeds its semiotic and economic functions, so highly stressed in Gottdiener's analysis? The diversity of interaction in a mall is missing. What of the subversion of the 'mall design' and the intended consumer experience? The lesson of the Modern Movement in architecture and planning has been that human life transcends this control.

...This lesson can also be drawn from Benjamin's work which prefigures more recent political economic studies of consumption sites. However, it succeeds in maintaining the presence of the human agents without whom no mall or arcade would exist, and whose spatial practices are necessary preconditions for the success of the malls. It is Benjamin who first characterized the arcade or mall as a concretization of the commodity trade and of an entire social praxis in space. This remains true for the present day. However, the expanded role of the West Edmonton Mall is fulfilled by its crowds in pursuit of novelty (by window shopping) and fantasy (at the funfair) as well as commodities. Widely disparate objects are brought together in the name of nostalgia and memory. This was once only possible in literary fantasies (Said, 1978); on a small scale in interiors; or in the fantastic creations of the rich or eccentric such as the orientalesque Brighton Pavilion, or newspaper baron William Randolph Hearst's California house San Simeon, built out of a collection of imported ruins (for a description, see Eco, 1986). The Mall *is* organized by such speculative and classifying operations. But this is not the limit of the phenomenon. The spatial practice of the users transcends the skeletal figure of the Mall.

Liminality or Carnivalesque

An anthropologist would recognize the interior of the Mall to be a space of *liminality* (that is, a space between social stations) organized around the passage from suburban reality and the new buildings of a 1970s oil-boom town to an environment organized by consumption, nostalgia, and *carnivalesque* abandon (Bakhtin, 1984). The difference between situations of liminality and carnivalesque is that liminality is tightly ritualized. The festival of the carnivalesque represents the inversion or discarding of social codes and hierarchical norms. In liminal situations, participants place themselves under the care of priest-like intermediaries who control the ritual. In carnival, all participants are fully involved as equals, engendering an intense experience of *communitas*. Beaches are thus an example of contemporary liminal zones (areas designated as a social margin). Social codes of appropriate behaviour clearly operate on any beach, hedging in and constraining those on whom the social norms of modesty have temporarily lost their grip. The partial lifting of social taboos on nudity is tightly regulated by the imposition of other, ritualized, normative practices (Goffman, 1963; Turner, 1974; 1979, page 13).

The West Edmonton Mall promises the 'Big Time.' This removes it from the realm of conventional convenience-oriented malls and places it outside of the realm of the mundane and quotidian. It promises a fulfilling fantasy and consumption experience as a break from the humdrum of everyday life. However, it is itself built out of borrowed and artificial attractions which displace genuine attractions and authenticity. The claims and superlatives come crashing into the banal and inauthentic as the Mall extends one problem of contemporary North American life which is increasingly an elaboration of images of reality elsewhere: of adopted poses, identities, and the memorabilia of trips in search of authenticity (MacCannell, 1976, page 155). By definition, "where one is now is not 'where it's at.'"

Even though we are promised a shoppers' paradise and a tourists' Mecca, the Mall by itself provides a fundamentally unsatisfying experience centred only around the amusements of the funfair and *commodity divertissement*—the diversions of novelty consumption items which are often only the objects of consumers' gaze. Window shoppers, the 'tourists' referred to above, outstrip the numbers of real consumers. Although a momentary gratification from this spatial practice of *flânerie* is possible, the promise cannot be delivered. It is *jouissance* (literally 'play,' 'masturbation'), not the 'real thing.' The flattening of new real commodities against fake historical settings betrays a nonchalance for authenticity, despite the *accuracy* of the reconstructions. This hallucination "serves to level the various historical periods and erase the distinction between historical reality and fantasy" (Marin cited in Eco, 1985, page 43). As at Disneyland, the West Edmonton Mall not only presents a set of illusions, but also a set of illusions which are glorified as fantasies, as masterpieces of falsification. What is falsified is our will to buy, which we take as real. Hence the Mall management's claim which echoes the quotation from Kowinski with which this paper opened:

It *is* magic. It brings people in and once they're here they're susceptible to any and every influence" (Rubin Stahl, President, West Edmonton Mall, interviewed in Saroka and Jenish, 1984, page 20).

Taken alone, the success of the mall would be doubtful: there is an ironic and tragic twist to this suburban version of the 'democratization' of joy and consumption. Rather than what would classically have been called a liminal experience which essentially marks a transition in the life cycle or a *rite de passage* (Van Gennep, 1960), this unredemptive experience is a too-noisy, glitzy, and eventually boring, sham. The modern-day *flâneurs* who travel to the West Edmonton Mall simply to stare or vicariously observe and rub shoulders with other twentieth-century *jouisseurs* ultimately achieve little more than their participation as part of the process of one of *the* definitive shopping events of our age.

But, this participation is an apparently important ritual of membership in a certain *consumption community*. There is a strange psychology to this. Merely to be in attendance at the "court of commodities" (Benjamin, 1973) is to claim one's status as a consumer which, under a capitalism which reduces people to their function in an economist equation, is to assert one's *existence* and to be recognized as a person. Being a consumer, with the right to attend these rituals seems to have almost overtaken the importance of being a citizen. In the mind of the consumer, this 'one-dimensional' existence is affirmed just by *being there*: the *possibility* of participating in consumption even if not actually doing so. The West Edmonton Mall provides a place which celebrates and reinforces this consumption community of middle-class and middle-mass shoppers, excluding those who cannot participate in the consumer act (for examples, see Gladstone, 1985). The population within the mall is thus markedly young, fit, and ascribes to middle-class standards. The mall, no more than one public space, has become "mis-recognized"[4] as a *world* (Arendt, 1961, page 210) with consumption legitimated as the heart of *communitas*.

…Malls introduce an unheard-of degree of surveillance, with almost Orwellian overtones, into daily life. Old protest strategies such as the familiar picket line in front of a store become impossible in a shopping mall. The transfer of public space indoors to private quarters means that, unlike the street-life of the European tradition, the surrounding environment in the centre is carefully and consciously managed, unlike its counterpart in the streets of Amsterdam or Marseille which Dawson likens it to.

This has had a dramatic impact on the norms of Canadian youth subcultures. A 'clear space' is needed for group action, for the elaboration and testing of codes of behaviour which are an essential part of socialization, generally rule out the already-domesticated, rule-governed space of the home. Given the winter climate, minimum age restrictions at clubs, and the problem of the lack of social amenities for adolescents in many suburbs, malls have become a preferred venue for under-18s (Shields, 1985). To congregate in such spaces as the West Edmonton Mall requires that one observe bourgeois norms of social docility and conservatism both in dress and action. The displays of 'peacock clothing' or 'punk spectacle' common in the United Kingdom or USA are relegated to just outside the doors of this Mall. Instead, the clothing adopted is a fashion industry edition of punk or gothic style. In Canada, at least, the credo is: One must always look as if one has bought something or is about to buy. Hence their uniform, classless appearance. Also, there are thus no hangouts. The greatest rebellion is the act of sitting down on the floor, ignoring benches, defying the planned environment in a gesture which questions the conventional discourse of space at the Mall. Movement after a few minutes is often essential to avoid the security guards patrolling for loiterers. Hence the initial invisibility of those 'hanging out': the circulating crowds of adolescents have learned the social and spatial practice of *flânerie* rather than spectacle (see also Debord, 1973). This homogeneity masks a different reality. Marks of marginality and group affiliation are transposed to a higher plane, becoming subtler, harder to detect, perhaps repressed.

Although the promoted image is one of freedom, unfettered impulse buying, and liminality, the reality is one of control, new forms of discipline, and surveillance. In Canada, this contradiction has already engendered a series of constitutional challenges to mall-owners' right to bar people selectively, in one case a 60-year-old cripple, from malls on the grounds of loitering. In response, owners have successfully argued that, in Canada, property rights take priority over human rights and freedoms (Gladstone, 1985).

Why patronize such a place? The key to the success of the Mall appears to lie in the manner of appropriation by its users, the *flâneurs*. Popularly, shopping centres have been called "places to see and be seen in," but the comparison to the theatre is not entirely a happy one. The spatial genealogy of the West Edmonton Mall leads back to Bentham's panopticon prison governed by total visual surveillance as much as to the market squares of old. The carnivalization of the Mall by its users provides the only means at hand to balance its "commercial terror" (Shelsky cited in Lefebvre, 1981, page 357). Like Urry's "post-tourist," who knows that mass tourism is a game played for status (1988), the West Edmonton Mall has its "post-shoppers" who, as *flâneurs*, play at being consumers in complex, self-conscious mockery. The entire experience is thus inverted into its ironic mirror image. This tinges the complicitous self-implication and apathy of the *flâneurs* and latter-day shoppers with parody. The effect is to disrupt the pretentiousness of the Mall with its museum relics and respatialization of reality. The users, both young and old, are not just resigned victims, but actively subvert the ambitions of the Mall developers by developing the insulation value of the stance of the jaded, world-weary *flâneur*; asserting their independence in a multitude of ways apart from consuming (Bowlby, 1985). It is *this* practice, as opposed to the only-too-modern centralizing ambitions of the mall builder, which is the heart of postmodern experience of the Mall.

[Editor's Summary: In conclusion, we are presented with a 'split' spatialization, a social schizophrenia. This is composed of an apparent conformism with the Mall as an institutionalized (although irreverent) space of representation and representation of space and the polite docility of practice it demands; and the contrasting erratic, conflicting usages and intentions of its users. These *flâneurs*, 'post-shoppers', exploit the possibilities of the Mall for their own purposes. whether programmed into the building by the architects or not. In the process, they transform and contradict learned theories and sententious discourses on space, as social theorists have learned to their chagrin before.]

NOTES

1. This term finds its genesis in the work and terminology of Foucault who devoted several lectures and papers to this question [1964; 1976; see also his better-known interviews in the journal *Hérodote* (issues 1 and 3, 1976, with responses in issue 5, 1977)].

2. The Madonna Inn near San Luis Obispo, CA, is a popular rendition of opulent extravagance. It consists of a series of what might be called built fantasies on the theme of the sumptuous at a low price. For example, Eco describes the rest rooms as "an immense underground cavern, something like Altamira . . . with Byzantine columns supporting plaster baroque cherubs. The basins are big imitation-mother-of-pearl shells, the urinal is a fireplace carved from the rock.... water comes down from the wall of the hood, in a flushing cascade something like the Caves of the Planet Mongo.... Then there are the bedrooms...each with a different theme...you can have the Prehistoric Room, all cavern and stalactites, the Safari Room and so on (1986, pages 24–25).

3. Sociologically speaking, there are a number of unspecified and counterintuitive notions in this analysis. Gottdiener conflates 'sociability' with 'socialization' and reverses his position on whether or not social organization is composed of hierarchies or rhizomatic networks (1986, page 296). He uses the notion of "deep structure" to underwrite his assertion that changes in social *organization* have caused the phenomenon he calls "metropolitan deconcentration" (1985). The actual dynamics of this linkage, not to mention what is intended by "social organization," need development and specification. Also, he accepts without critique Barthes's dehistoricized notion of the "classic city form" (Gottdiener, 1986, page 290) which has a central focus (for example, a city with a central town square like Ghent in Belgium, Moscow, or the Latin American colonial cities, but not London or even Rome which were always polynodal) which he contrasts with the present "deconcentration."

4. On "mis-recognition" *(méconnaissance)*, see Bourdieu (1984).

REFERENCES

Arendt, H. "The Crisis in Culture: Its Social and Political Significance." *In Between Past and Future.* New York: Viking, 1961.

Barthes, R. "Semiologie et urhanism" *Architecture Aujourd'hui* 153 (1970–1971): 11–13.

Benjamin, W. *Charles Baudelaire: A Lyric Poet in the Era of High Capitalism.* Trans. Q. Hoare. London: New Left Books, 1973.

---. *Das Passagenwerk. Gesamtnelte Schrifien.* Vol. 5. Ed. R. Tiedemann, H. Schweppenhauser. Frankfurt: Surkharnp, 1978.

Benveniste, G. *Problémes de Linguistique Générale.* Vol. 1. Paris: Gallimard, 1966.

Bergman, G., and L. Cohen. "More Ghermazian Ultimatums." *Alberta Report* 9 Sept. 1984: 20.

Boorstein, D. *The Image: A Guide to Pseudo-events in America.* New York: Harper and Row, 1961.

Bowlby, R. *Just Looking: Consumer Culture in Dreiser, Gissing, and Zola.* Andover, Hants: Methuen, 1985.

Cooke, P. "Modernity, Postmodernity and the City. " Paper presented to the BSA Sociology and Environment Study Group, London School of Economics, February; Copy available from the author, Department of Town Planning. Cardiff: University of Wales at Cardiff, 1986.

Dawson, J A., and J.D. Lord. *Shopping Centre Development: Policies and Prospects.* Beckenham, Kent: Croom Helm, 1983.

Debord, G. *Society of the Spectacle.* Detroit: Black and Red, 1973.

De Certeau, M. "Practices of space." *On Signs.* Ed. M. Blonsky. Oxford: Basil Blackwell, 1985. 122–45.

Deleuze, G., and F. Guattari. *The Anti-Oedipus.* Paris: Editions de Minuit, 1976.

Durkheim, E., and M. Mauss. *Primitive Classification*. Chicago, IL: University of Chicago Press, 1963.

Eco, U. *Truths and Transgressions*. New York: Harper and Row, 1985.

---. "A Photograph." *Faith in Fakes*. London: Seeker and Warburg, 1986. 213–7.

Elash, A. and D. Jenish. "Fantasyland's Giant Ambition." *Alberta Report* 11 Oct. 1984: 20–1.

Foucault, M. *The Birth of the Clinic: An Archeology of Medical Perception*. New York: Random House, 1976.

---. "Space, Knowledge and Power." *The Foucault Reader*. Ed. P Rahinow. New York: Random House, 1984. 239–56.

Freud, S. *The Interpretation of Dreams*. Ed. A. Richards. Harmondsworth, Middx: Penguin Books, 1976.

Geist, J. F. *Arcades*. Trans. J. O. Newman, and J. H. Smith. Cambridge, MA: MIT Press, 1983.

Giddens, A. *The Constitution of Society*. Cambridge: Polity Press, 1984.

Gladstone, W., with B. Wallance. "Public Use of Private Space." *Maclean's* 5 Aug. 1985: 49–50.

Goffman, E. *Behaviour in Public Places*. Glencoe, IL: Free Press, 1963.

Gottdiener, N.I. "Recapturing the Center: A Semiotic Analysis of Shopping Mall." *The City and the Sign: An Introduction to Urban Semiotics*. Ed. M. Gottdiener, and A. P. Lagopoulos. New York: Columbia University Press, 1986. 288–302.

Harbeck, W. "The Mission to the Mall." *Western Report* 10 Mar. 1986: 52.

Harvey, D. "Flexible Accumulation Through Urbanization: Reflections on 'Post-Modernism' in the American City." Mimeo. Paper presented at an Urban and Regional Studies Seminar, University of Sussex, May. Copy available from the author, School of Geography. Oxford: University of Oxford, 1987.

Jameson, F. "Postmodernism, or the Cultural Logic of Late Capitalism." *New Left Review* 146 (1984): 53–92.

Jenish, D. "Under the Rug." *Canadian Business* April 1985:84–94.

Kant, I. "Concerning the Ultimate Foundations of the Differentiation of Regions in Space." *Selected Pre-critical Writings*. Ed. G. R. Lucas. Manchester: University of Manchester Press, 1968. xii–xviii.

Kowinski, W. S. *The Mailing of America*. New York: Basic Books, 1982.

Lackoff, G., and M. Johnson. *Metaphors We Live By*. Chicago, IL: University of Chicago Press, 1979.

Lash, S. "Modernity or Modernism? Weber and Contemporary Social Theory." *Max Weber. Rationality and Modernity*. Ed. S. Whimster, and S. Lash. Hemel Hempstead, Herts: Allen and Unwin, 1986. 197–214.

---. "Postmodern Culture: The Eclipse of Aura." *Current Perspectives in Social Theory*. Volume 6. Ed. J. Wilson. London: JAJ Press, 1987. 197–213.

Lefebvre, H. *La Pensée marxiste et la yule*. Paris: Casterman, 1972.

---. *Le Droit a Ia ville*. Paris: Anthropos, 1975.

---. *La Production de l'espace*. 2nd ed.1974. Paris: Anthropos, 1981.

Lindsay, C. "Experiments in postmodern dialogue." *Diacritics* 14 (1984): 3, 52–62.

Lyotard, J-F. *Instructions Palennes*. Paris: Galilee, 1977.

---. *Just Gaming*. Trans. W. Godzich. Manchester: Manchester University Press, 1979.

---. *The Post-Modern Condition.* Trans. G. Bennington, and B. Massumi. Minneapolis, MN: University of Minnesota Press, 1980.

---. "The Differend, the Referent, and the Proper Name." *Diacritics* 14.3 (1984): 4–14.

MacCannell, D. *The Tourist.* London: Macmillan, 1976.

Moles, A., and E. Rohmer. *Labyrinthes du vécu. L'Espace: mati're d'actions.* Paris: Meridiens, 1982.

Needham, R. *Right and Left: Essays on Dual Symbolic Classification.* Chicago: University of Chicago Press, 1973.

Orr, F., with T. Gallagher. "Shopping the Light Fantastic." *Alberta Report* 23 Sept. 1985: 26ff.

Parkes, D.N., and Thrift, N.J. *Times, Spaces and Places: A Chronogeograp/zical Perspective.* Chichester, Sussex: John Wiley, 1980.

Said, E. *Orientalism.* New York: Vintage Books, 1978.

Salter, M. "The Ghermazians' Secrets." *Maclean's* 15 April 1985: 34–5.

Saroka, D., and Jenish, D. "Triple Five's New Fantasy." *Alberta Report* 30 April 1984: 19–21.

Sayer, A. "The Difference that Space Makes." *Social Relations and Spatial Structures.* Ed. D. Gregory, and J. Urry. London: Macmillan, 1985. 49–66.

Shields, R. "The Toronto Eaton's Centre: Ideology and Design." *The Frontenac Review.* Queen's University, Kingston, Ontario, 1984. 45–68.

---. "A Cross-Country Report on Concerns Expressed by Youth in International Youth Year, 1985." Mimeo. Ottawa: Ministry of State for Youth, 1985.

---. "Towards a Theory of Social Spatialization: Henri Lefebvre, the Problem of Space and the Postmodern Hypothesis." MA thesis. Carleton University, 1986.

Soja, E. "The Socio-Spatial Dialectic." *Annals of the Association of American Geographers* 70 (1980): 207–25.

Turner, V. *Dramas, Fields and Metaphors.* Ithaca, NY: Cornell University Press, 1974.

---. *Process, Performance and Pilgrimage.* New Delhi: Concept Publishing, 1979.

Urry, J. "Cultural Change and Contemporary Holiday-Making." Lancaster Regionalism Group. Lancaster: University of Lancaster, 1988.

Van Gennep, A. *The Rites of Passage.* Trans. M. B. Vizedom, and G. L. Caffee. Chicago: University of Chicago Press, 1960.

Walker, R. "Downtown Edmonton Fights for Its Life." *Maclean's* 23 April 1984: 53.

18 Ann duCille, "Dyes and Dolls: Multicultural Barbie and the Merchandizing of Difference"

Ann duCille's essay addresses how material culture forms subjects—in this case black women—by subjecting them to ideologies taken for granted by the dominant culture—in this case the white, male culture. DuCille's use of her own experience of how ideologies have shaped—and misshaped—her views of the social sphere acts as a critical intervention that reshapes its terms. For duCille, ideology literally shapes bodies by shaping thinking about one's body. Her title, thus, tells us how "guys" and "dolls" are typecast through "dyes" and "dolls" not only in terms of gender but also race, sexuality, and class—how culture creates or "casts" us as subjects in terms of how we mark or "dye" ourselves. Like Disney's politics of innocence, Barbie "[does] the dirty work of patriarchy and capitalism in the most insidious way—in the guise of child's play" (269). DuCille debunks Barbie's iconic status, but not without considering her (or rather "its") formidable staying power. Barbie enjoys phenomenal success, despite shifts in racial or sexual codes. Her increasingly multicultural facade suppresses cultural differences that reveal, in turn, long-standing racial and gender stereotypes.

How does a piece of plastic commodify the gender and race of bodies according to larger national and cultural idealisms? In "The Anthropometry of Barbie," Alan Swedlund and Jacqueline Urla examine shifts in body types in 20th-century anthropometrical research conducted by the American army after World War II. This anthropometry produced ideal male and female body standards against which to measure citizens physically, hygienically, and behaviourally—and thus socially and culturally. This fact is telling enough once one uncovers the racist, sexist, and nationalist prescriptions assumed by this body typing. More disturbing, however, is the extent to which Barbie, Ken, and their various (re)incarnations model a virtually unrealizable physical standard that is, ironically, its own deviance from the reality of existing bodies. We are asked to "normalize" this "deviance" on our own terms by submitting our biological development to an impossible conformity. What is rather abnormal becomes normal as a way of marginalizing other "abnormalities" that do not meet this standard: black women's bodies, homosexual bodies, other ethnic or sexual bodies.

Barbie's unattainable ideal creates a vicious circle of consumption, duCille suggests, because it ensures that women will more conspicuously buy things in order *to* attain this ideal: "I can dream myself into Barbie's perfect world, so long as I dream myself in her image" (277):

> What is fascinating, . . . what both invites and resists theorizing, is not the lump of molded plastic that is Barbie, but the imaginary life that is not—that is *our* invention. Barbie as a cultural artifact may be able to tell us more about ourselves and our society—more about society's attitudes toward *its* women—than anything we might say about the doll her- or, rather, *itself.* (276)

Here, the essay addresses the power of both *fantasy*—make-believe and illusion—and *ph*antasy—a subject's or culture's drive to seek out its desires in objects we invest with incredible power and esteem. As duCille writes, "If Barbie is a monster, she is our monster, our ideal" (276). Like Mary Shelley's monster, she is sutured from our dreams and desires to produce a prototypical subject brought to life by the god-like power of our projections.

DuCille's final point is that dying Barbie black has less to do with Mattel's sensitivity to cultural difference than with the "merchandizing of difference." Casting the dye is about using ideologies *of* race, gender, and sexuality to mould consumers in particular ways, to sell back to them a particular vision of themselves. DuCille, paraphrasing David Rieff, writes that our "newly globalized consumer economy [is] multi-culturalism's silent partner" (274). One can think of Auerbach's account of the Empire's marketing of cultural differences in the 19th century and ask: How have things changed? duCille's auto-critical essay asks us to undertake our own anthropometry: how do our own bodies conform, or not, to various ideas of race, sexuality, or class imposing their own impossible ideals on us? "Cultural difference," Swedlund and Urla note, "is reduced to surface variations in skin tone and costumes that can be exchanged at will," so that "difference" becomes "sameness, as ethnicity is tamed to conform to a restricted range of feminine beauty" (Swedlund and Urla 405)—or masculine beauty, depending on which doll one is playing with. As duCille notes in comparing her story to the fantasy of a Barbie World (to paraphrase the popular Aqua song), this vision has little to do with reality—although, as she notes ominously at the end of the article, apparently it does. Barbie's beauty, to borrow Naomi Woolf's phrase, may be a "beauty *myth*," but a persistent one. DuCille asks us to ask: "Why?"

—JF

ISSUES TO CONSIDER WHILE READING

1. In what ways can duCille's notion of the "merchandizing of cultural difference" be applied to the commodification of other groups otherwise marginalized or 'othered' by dominant culture?
2. What other artefacts of popular culture are informed by the intersection of race and gender that duCille critiques? What arenas of popular culture allow for a more productive expression of racial subjectivities?

REFERENCES AND FURTHER READING

Barthel, Diane. *Putting on Appearances: Gender and Advertising.* Philadelphia: Temple University Press, 1988.

Gates, Henry Louis. "Writing 'Race' and the Difference It Makes." *"Race," Writing, and Difference.* Chicago: University of Chicago Press, 1986. 1–20.

Haraway, Donna. "A Cyborg Manifesto: Science, Technology and Socialist-Feminism in the Late Twentieth Century." *Simians, Cyborgs, and Women: The Reinvention of Nature.* London: Free Association Books, 1991.

Jacobus, Mary, Evelyn Fox Keller, and Sally Shuttleworth, eds. *Body/Politics: Women and the Discourses of Science.* New York: Routledge, 1990.

Morrison, Toni. *The Bluest Eye*. New York: Plume Book, 1994.

Swedlund, Alan, and Jacqueline Urla. "The Anthropometry of Barbie." *Deviant Bodies: Critical Perspectives on Difference in Science and Popular Culture*. Ed. Jennifer Terry and Jacqueline Urla. Bloomington: Indiana University Press.

Woolf, Naomi. *The Beauty Myth: How Images of Beauty Are Used against Women*. New York: William Morrow, 1991.

Dyes and Dolls: Multicultural Barbie and the Merchandizing of Difference

…As suggested by my title, I am going to use the figure of multicultural Barbie to talk about the commodification of race and gender difference. I wanted to back into the present topic, however, into what I have to say about Barbie as a gendered, racialized icon of contemporary commodity culture, by reaching into the past—into the admittedly contested terrain of the personal—to evoke the ideological work of child's play. More than simple instruments of pleasure and amusement, toys and games play crucial roles in helping children determine what is valuable in and around them. Dolls in particular invite children to replicate them, to imagine themselves in their dolls' images. What does it mean, then, when little girls are given dolls to play with that in no way resemble them? What did it mean for me that I was nowhere in the toys I played with?

…Many of the major toy manufacturers have taken on a global perspective, a kind of nearsightednesss that constructs this whole new world as small and cultural difference as consumable. Perhaps nowhere is this universalizing myopia more conspicuous than in the production, marketing, and consumption of Barbie dolls. By Mattel's reckoning, Barbie enjoys 100 percent brand name recognition among girls ages three to ten, ninety-six percent of whom own at least one doll, with most owning an average of eight. Five years ago, as Barbie turned thirty, *Newsweek* noted that nearly 500 million Barbies had been sold, along with 200 million G.I. Joes—'enough for every man, woman, and child in the United States and Europe' (Kantrowitz 59–60). Those figures have increased dramatically in the past five years, bringing the current worldwide Barbie population to 800 million. In 1992 alone, $1 billion worth of Barbies and accessories were sold. Last year, Barbie dolls sold at an average of one million per week, with overall sales exceeding the $1 billion all-time high set the year before. As the Boston *Globe* reported on the occasion of Barbie's thirty-fifth birthday on March 9, 1994, nearly two Barbie dolls are sold every second somewhere in the world; about fifty percent of the dolls sold are purchased here in the United States (Dembner 16).

The current Barbie boom may be in part the result of new, multiculturally oriented developments both in the dolls and in their marketing. In the fall of 1990, Mattel, Inc. announced a new marketing strategy to boost its sales: the corporation would 'go ethnic' in its advertising by launching an ad campaign for the black and Hispanic versions of the already popular doll. Despite the existence of Black, Asian, and Latina Barbies, prior to the fall of 1990 Mattel's print and TV ads featured only white dolls. In what *Newsweek* described as an attempt to capitalize on ethnic spending power, Mattel began placing ads for multicultural Barbies in such Afrocentric publications as *Essence* magazine and on such Latin-oriented shows as 'Pepe Plata' after market research revealed that most black and Hispanic consumers were unaware of the company's ethnic dolls. This targeted advertising was a smart move, according to the industry analysts cited by *Newsweek,* because 'Hispanics buy about $170 billion worth of goods each year, [and] blacks spend even more.' Indeed, sales of black Barbie dolls reportedly doubled in the year following this new ethnically-oriented ad campaign.[1] But determined to present itself as politically correct as well as financially savvy, Mattel was quick to point out that ethnic audiences, who are now able to purchase dolls who look like them, also have profited from the corporation's new marketing priorities. Barbie is a role model for all of her owners, according to product manager Deborah Mitchell, herself an African American. 'Barbie allows little girls to dream,' she asserted—to which the *Newsweek* reporter added (seemingly without irony): 'now, ethnic Barbie lovers will be able to dream in their own image' (Berkwitz 48).

Dream in their own image? The *Newsweek* columnist inadvertently put his finger on precisely what is so troubling to many parents, feminist scholars, and cultural critics about Barbie and dolls like her. Such toys invite, inspire, and even demand a potentially damaging process not simply of imagining but of interpellation. When little girls fantasize themselves into the conspicuous consumption, glamor, perfection, and, some have argued, anorexia of Barbie's world, it is rarely, if ever, 'in their own image that they dream.'[2] Regardless of what color dyes the dolls are dipped in or what costumes they are adorned with, the image they present is of the same mythically thin, long-legged, luxuriously-haired, buxom beauty. And while Mattel and other toy manufacturers may claim to have the best interests of ethnic audiences in mind in peddling their integrated wares, one does not have to be a cynic to suggest that profit remains the motivating factor behind this merchandising of difference.[3]

Far from simply playing with the sixty or so dolls I have acquired in the past year, then, I take them very seriously. In fact, I regard Barbie and similar dolls as Louis Althusser might have regarded them: as objects that do the dirty work of patriarchy and capitalism in the most insidious of ways—in the guise of child's play. But, as feminists have protested almost from the moment she hit the market, Barbie is not simply a child's toy or just a teenage fashion doll; she is an icon—perhaps *the* icon—of true white womanhood and femininity, a symbol of the far from innocent ideological stuff of which the (Miss) American dream and other mystiques of race and gender are made.

Invented by Ruth Handler, one of the founders of Mattel, and named after her daughter, Barbie dolls have been a very real force in the toy market since Mattel first introduced them at the American Toy Fair in 1959. In fact, despite the skepticism of toy store buyers—who at the time were primarily men—the first shipment of a half million dolls and a million costumes were sold out immediately (Larcen A7). The first Barbies, which were modeled after a sexy German doll and comic strip character named Lilli, were all white, but in 1967 Mattel premiered a black version of the doll called 'Colored Francie.' 'Colored Francie,' like white 'Francie Fairchild' introduced the year before, was supposed to be Barbie's 'MOD'ern' younger cousin. As a white doll modeled and marketed in the image of Hollywood's Gidget, white Francie had been an international sensation, but Colored Francie was not destined to duplicate her prototype's success. Although the 'black is beautiful' theme of both the civil rights and black power movements may have suggested a ready market for a beautiful black doll, Colored Francie in fact did not sell well.

Evelyn Burkhalter, owner, operator, and curator of the Barbie Hall of Fame in Palo Alto, California—home to 16,000 Barbie dolls—attributes Colored Francie's commercial failure to the racial climate of the times. Doll purchasing patterns, it seems, reflected the same resistance to integration that was felt elsewhere in the nation. In her implied family ties to white Barbie, Colored Francie suggested more than simple integration. She implied miscegenation: a make-believe mixing of races that may have jeopardized the doll's real market value. Cynthia Roberts, author of *Barbie: Thirty Years of America's Doll* (1989), maintains that Colored Francie flopped because of her straight hair and Caucasian features (44), which seemingly were less acceptable then than now. No doubt Mattel's decision to call its first black Barbie 'Colored Francie' also contributed to the doll's demise. The use of the out-moded, even racist term 'colored' in the midst of civil rights and black power activism suggested that while Francie might be 'MOD'ern,' Mattel was still in the dark(y) ages. In any case, neither black nor white audiences bought the idea of Barbie's colored relations, and Mattel promptly took the doll off the market, replacing her with a black doll called Christie in 1968.

While a number of other black dolls appeared throughout the late sixties and seventies—including the Julia doll, modeled after the TV character played by black singer and actor Diahann Carroll—it was not until 1980 that Mattel introduced black dolls that were called Barbie like their white counterparts. Today, Barbie dolls come in a virtual rainbow coalition of colors, races, ethnicities, and nationalities—most of which look remarkably like the prototypical white Barbie, modified only by a dash of color and a change of costume. It is these would-be multicultural 'dolls of the world'—Jamaican Barbie, Nigerian and Kenyan Barbie, et cetera, et cetera, et cetera—that interest me. For me these dolls are at once a symbol and a symptom of what multiculturalism has become at the hands of contemporary commodity culture: an easy and immensely profitable way off the hook of Eurocentrism that gives us the face of cultural diversity without the particulars of racial difference.

If I could line up across the page the ninety 'different' colors, cultures, and other incarnations in which Barbie currently exists, the fact of her unrelenting sameness (or at least similarity) would become immediately apparent. Even two dolls might do the trick: 'My First Barbie' in white and 'My First Barbie' in black, for example, or white 'Western Fun Barbie' and black 'Western Fun Barbie.' Except for their dye jobs, the dolls are identical: the same body, size, shape, and apparel. Or perhaps I should say *nearly* identical because in some instances—with black and Asian dolls in particular—coloring and other subtle changes (stereotypically slanted eyes in the Asian dolls, thicker lips in the black dolls) suggest differently coded facial features.

In other instances, when Barbie moves across cultural as opposed to racial lines, it is costume rather than color that distinguishes one ethnic group or nation from another. Nigeria and Jamaica, for instance, are represented by the same basic brown body, dolled-up in different native garbs—or Mattel's interpretation thereof.[4] With other costume changes, this generic black body becomes Western Fun Barbie or Marine Barbie or Desert

Storm Barbie, and even Presidential Candidate Barbie, who, by the way, comes with a Nancy Regan-red taking-care-of-business suit as well as a red, white, and blue inaugural ball gown. Much the same is true of the generic Asian doll—sometimes called Kira—who reappears in a variety of different dress-defined ethnicities. In other words, where Barbie is concerned, clothes not only make the woman, they make the racial and/or cultural difference.

Such difference is marked as well by the cultural history and language lessons that accompany each doll in Mattel's international collection. The back of Jamaican Barbie's box tells us, for example, 'How-you-du (Hello) from the land of Jamaica, a tropical paradise known for its exotic fruit, sugar cane, breathtaking beaches, and reggae beat!' The box goes on to explain that most Jamaicans have ancestors from Africa. Therefore, 'even though our official language is English, we speak patois, a kind of "*Jamaica Talk*," filled with English and African words.' The lesson ends with a brief glossary (eight words) and a few more examples of the 'Jamaica Talk,' complete with translations: "A hope yu wi come-a Jamaica! (I hope you will come to Jamaica!); and 'Teck care a yusself, mi fren! (Take care of yourself, my friend!)' A nice idea, I suppose, but for me these quick-and-dirty ethnographies only enhance the extent to which these would-be multicultural dolls treat race and ethnic difference like collectibles, contributing more to commodity culture than to the intercultural awareness they claim to inspire.

Is the current fascination with the black or colored body—especially the female body—a contemporary version of the primitivism of the 1920s? Is multiculturalism to postmodernism what primitivism was to modernism? It was while on my way to a round table discussion on precisely this question that I bought my first black Barbie dolls in March 1993. As carbon copies of an already problematic original, these colorized Mattel toys seemed to me the perfect tools with which to illustrate the point I wanted to make about the collapse of multiculturalism into an easy pluralism that simply adds what it constructs as the Other without upsetting the fundamental precepts and paradigms of Western culture or, in the case of Mattel, without changing the mold.

Not entirely immune to such critiques, Mattel sought expert advice from black parents and early childhood specialists in the development and marketing of its newest line of black Barbie dolls. Chief among the expert witnesses was clinical psychologist Darlene Powell Hopson, who co-authored with her husband Derek S. Hopson a study of realism and child development entitled *Different and Wonderful: Raising Black Children in a Race-Conscious Society* (1990). As part of their research for the book, the Hopsons repeated a ground-breaking study conducted by black psychologists Kenneth and Mamie Clark in the 1940s.

The Clarks used black and white dolls to demonstrate the negative effects of racism and segregation on black children. When given a choice between a white doll and a black doll, nearly 70 percent of the black children in the study chose the white doll. The Clarks' findings became an important factor in *Brown v. the Board of Education* in 1954. More recently, some scholars have called into question not necessarily the Clarks' findings but their interpretation: the assumption that, in the realm of make-believe, a black child's choosing a white doll necessarily reflects a negative self concept.[5] For the Hopsons, however, the Clarks' research remains compelling. In 1985 they repeated the Clarks' doll test and found that an alarming 65 percent of the black children in their sample chose a white doll over a black one. Moreover 76 percent of the children interviewed said that the black dolls 'looked bad' to them (Hopsons xix).

In addition to the clinical uses they make of dolls in their experiments, the Hopsons also give considerable attention to what they call 'doll play' in their book, specifically, mentioning Barbie. 'If your daughter likes "Barbie" dolls, by all means get her Barbie,' they advise black parents. 'But also choose Black characters from the Barbie world. *You do not want your child to grow up thinking that only White dolls, and by extension White people, are attractive and nice*' (Hopsons 127, emphasis in the original). (Note that 'Barbie,' unmodified in the preceding passage, seems to mean *white* Barbie dolls.) The Hopsons suggest that parents should not only provide their children with black and other ethnic dolls but that they should get involved in their children's doll play. 'Help them dress and groom the dolls while you compliment them both,' they advise, offering the following suggested routine: '"This is a beautiful doll. It looks just like you. Look at her hair. It's just like yours. Did you know your nose is as pretty as your doll's?"' (119) They also suggest that parents use 'complimentary words such as *lovely, pretty or nice* so that [the] child will learn to associate them with his or her own image' (124).

Certainly it is important to help children feel good about themselves. One might argue, however, that the 'just like you' simile and the beautiful doll imagery so central to these suggestions for what the Hopsons call positive play runs the risk of transmitting to the child a colorized version of the same old beauty myth. Like Barbie dolls themselves, they make beauty—and by implication worth—a matter of physical characteristics.

In spite of their own good intentions, the Hopsons, in linking play with 'beautiful' dolls to positive self-imaging, echoed Mattel's own marketing campaign. It is not surprising, then, that the Hopsons' findings and the interventional strategies they designed for using dolls to instil ethnic pride caught the attention of Mattel. In 1990 Darlene Hopson was asked to consult with the corporation's product manager Deborah Mitchell and designer Kitty Black-Perkins—both African Americans—in the development of a new line of 'realistically sculpted' black fashion dolls. Hopson agreed and about a year later Shani and her friends Asha and Nichelle became the newest members of Barbie's ever-expanding family.

…Shani and her friends are the most authentic black female thing the mainstream toy market has yet produced. 'Tomorrow's African American woman' (an appellation which, as Lisa Jones has noted, both riffs and one-ups *Essence*'s "Today's Black Woman') has broader hips, fuller lips, and a broader nose, according to product manager Deborah Mitchell. Principal designer Kitty Black-Perkins, who has dressed black Barbies since their birth in 1980, adds that the Shani dolls are also distinguished by their unique, culturally-specific clothes in 'spice tones [and] ethnic fabrics,' rather than 'fantasy colors like pink or lavender' (as quoted by Jones 36)—evidently the colors of the faint of skin.

The notion that fuller lips, broader noses, wider hips, and higher derrieres somehow make the Shani dolls more realistically African American raises many difficult questions about the authenticity, truth, and the ever-problematic categories of the real and the symbolic, the typical and the stereotypical. Just what are we saying when we claim that a doll does or does not 'look black'? How does black look? What would it take to make a doll look authentically African American? What preconceived, prescriptive ideals of legitimate blackness are inscribed in such claims of authenticity? How can doll manufacturers or any other image makers—the film industry, for example—attend to cultural, racial, and phenotypical differences without merely engaging the same simplistic big-lips/broad-hips stereotypes that make so many of us—blacks in particular—grit our (pearly white) teeth? What would it take to produce a line of dolls that more fully reflects the wide variety of sizes, shapes, colors, hair styles, occupations, abilities, and disabilities that African Americans—like all people—come in? In other words: what price difference?

If such specificity—such ethnic 'authenticity'—were possible to achieve in a doll, its purchase price, I suspect, would be much higher than a profit-driven corporation like Mattel would be willing to pay. Let me again invoke Shani to prove my point. On the one hand, Mattel was concerned enough about producing an ethnically correct black doll to seek the advice of black image specialists such as Darlene Hopson in the development and marketing of the Shani line. Ultimately, however, the company was not willing to follow the advice of such experts where doing so would cost the corporation more than the price of additional dyes and ethnic fabrics.

For example, Hopson reportedly argued not just for gradations in skin tones in the Shani dolls but also for variations in body type and length and styles of hair—for an Afro here or an asymmetrical cut there. But, while Mattel acknowledged both the legitimacy and the ubiquity of such arguments, profit motive mediated against the very realism the corporation set out to achieve in these dolls. 'To be truly realistic, one [Shani doll] should have shorter hair,' Deborah Mitchell confessed to Lisa Jones. 'But little girls of all races love hair play. We added more texture. But we can't change the fact that long combable hair is still a key seller' (Jones 36).

Mitchell, of course, has a point. It is after all the taste of the consumers that is inscribed in Barbie's long, combable hair. In the process of my own archival research—poking around in the dusty aisles of Toys R Us—I encountered a black teenage girl in search, like me, of the latest black Barbie. During the impromptu interview that ensued, my subject confessed to me in gory, graphic details the many Barbie murders and mutilations she had committed over the years. 'It's the hair,' she said emphatically several times. 'The hair, that hair; I want it. I want it.' Her words recalled my own torturous childhood struggles with the straightening combs, curling irons, and relaxers that bi-weekly transformed my wooly, 'just like a sponge' kinks into what the white kids at school marveled at as my 'Cleopatra [read straight] hair.' During one of those bi-weekly sessions with my mother and the straightening comb, I was foolish enough to say out loud what I had wished for a long time: that I had straight hair like the white girls at school. I still remember my mother's hurt, her sense of her daughter's racial heresy. Mitchell and Mattel indeed have a point. The difficult truth just may be that part of Shani's and black Barbie's attraction for little black girls in particular is the escape from their own often shorter, harder to comb hair that these dolls' lengthy straight locks represent.

Barbie's svelte figure, like her long combable hair, became Shani's body type as well. And, here, too marketability seems to have overruled professed attempts to capture the 'unique facial features' and the 'special style and beauty of the African American people.' Even the reported subtle changes that are supposed to signify Shani's black difference—her much-remarked broader hips and elevated buttocks, for example—are little more than optical illusions, according to anthropologists Jacqueline Urla and Alan Swedlund of the University of Massachusetts at Amherst. Urla and Swedlund, who have been studying the anthropometry—the body measurements—of Barbie for some time, argue that, while Shani's hips may appear to be wider, they are actually smaller in both circumference and breadth than those of other Barbie dolls. It is essential, after all, that all the dolls be able to share the same clothes, thus making any dramatic alteration in body type unlikely. The effect of a higher buttocks is achieved, Urla and Swedlund maintain, by changing the angle of the doll's back. In other words, the Shani doll's buttocks may appear stereotypically higher, but she is not really dimensionally different from all the other eleven-and-a-half-inch fashion dolls.[6]

Lisa Jones concludes her *Village Voice* article on Barbie by noting that the women behind Shani—black women like Hopson and Mitchell—want the doll to be more than just a Barbie in blackface. While Hopson, in particular, certainly hoped for—shall I say—*different* difference she nevertheless maintains that the Shani dolls demonstrate 'social consciousness on Mattel's part' (Jones 36). British fashion designer and Barbie aficionado extraordinaire BillyBoy made a similar point in praising Mattel for integrating Barbie's family with first Colored Francie and then Christie in the late 1960s (BillyBoy 82). After nearly thirty years, I think we can forgive Mattel its Colored Francie faux pas and perhaps even applaud the attempt. But if Shani (who came out in a new scantily clad Soul Train edition in 1993) stands as Mattel's best effort to 'go ethnic,' as it were—to corner the contemporary mainstream market in 'realistically sculpted' black dolls that 'bring to life' the 'special style and beauty of the African-American people'—she stands on shaky ground.

And yet it may not be fair to single out Mattel as an example of what seems to be a national if not international phenomenon. Racial difference, like ethnic Barbie, is a hot commodity, and it isn't only Mattel who is making money. In the words of David Rieff, a contributing editor of *Harper's Magazine*:

> Everything is commodifiable, even Afrocentrism (there is money being made on all the Kinte [*sic*] cloth and Kwanza [*sic*] paraphernalia that are the rage among certain segments of the black community, and not only the black community), bilingualism (currently the hottest growth market in publishing is Spanish-language children's books), and the other 'multicultural' tendencies in American society that conservatives fear so desperately. (*Harper's,* August 1993).

Rieff goes so far as to call this newly globalized consumer economy multiculturalism's silent partner. I want to be careful in expressing my own concerns about the relationship between multiculturalism and the conspicuous consumption of difference, however, lest my critique appear complicit with that of the conservatives to whom Rieff refers, who fear the possibilities of a truly transformative social, cultural, and economic order, which I in fact would welcome.

All cultural commodities are not created equal. It seems to me that however profitable their production may be for the publishing industry, Spanish-language children's books serve a useful, educational function for their target audiences. On the other hand, even taking into account the argument that black girls need black dolls to play with, I have a difficult time locating the redeeming social value in Mattel's little plastic women, even—or perhaps, especially—when they are tinted brown and decorated in Kente cloth and Kufi hats, as the new Soul Train Shani dolls are....

THE BODY POLITIC(S) OF BARBIE

...In focusing thus far on the mechandising of racial, perhaps more so than gender difference, I do not mean to imply that racial and gender identities are divisible, even in dolls. Nor, in observing that most if not all of Mattel's 'dolls of the world' look remarkably like what the company calls the 'traditional, blond, blue-eyed Barbie,' do I mean to suggest that the seemingly endless recapitulation of the white prototype is the only way in which these dolls are problematic. In fact, the most alarming thing about Barbie may well be the extent to which she functions as what M.G. Lord calls a teaching tool for femininity, whatever her race or ethnicity. Lord, the author of *Forever Barbie: The Unauthorized Biography of a Real Doll* (1995), describes Barbie as a 'space-age fertility icon. She looks like a modern woman, but she's a very primitive totem of female power' (Dembner 1).

Barbie has long had the eye and ire of feminists, who, for the most part, have reviled her as another manifestation of the damaging myths of female beauty and the feminine body that patriarchy perpetuates through such vehicles as popular and commodity culture. A counternarrative also exists, however, one in which Barbie is not an empty-headed, material girl bimbo, for whom math class is tough, but a feminist heroine, who has been first in war (a soldier who served in the Gulf, she has worn the colors of her country as well as the United Colors of Benetton), first in peace (she held her own summit in 1990 and she's a long-time friend of UNICEF, who 'loves all the children of the world'), and always in the hearts of her country (Americans buy her at the rate of one doll every second). While time does not allow me to reiterate or to assess here all the known critiques and defenses of Barbie, I do want to discuss briefly some of the gender ideals that I think are encoded in and transmitted by this larger-than-life little woman and what Barbie's escalating popularity says about contemporary American culture.

In *Touching Liberty: Abolition, Feminism, and the Politics of the Body* (1993), Karen Sanchez-Eppler argues that all dols are intended to teach little girls about domesticity (133). If such tutelage is Barbie's not so secret mission, her methodology is far more complex and contradictory than that of the Betsy Wetsy and Tiny Tears baby dolls I played with thirty-five years ago. Those dolls invoked and evoked the maternal, as they and the baby bottles and diapers with which they were packaged invited us to nestle, nurse, and nurture. Barbie's curvaceous, big-busted, almost fully female body, on the other hand, summons not the maternal but the sexual, not the nurturant mother but the sensuous woman. As Mel McCombie has argued, rather than rehearsing parenting, as a baby doll does, Barbie's adult body encourages children to dress and redress a fashion doll that yields lessons about sexuality, comsumption, and teenage life (3). Put another way, we might say that Barbie is literally and figuratively a titillating toy.

Bodacious as they may be, however, Barbie's firm plastic breasts have no nipples, nothing that might offend, nothing that might suggest her own pleasure. And if her protruding plastic mounds signify a simmering sensuality, what are we to make of her missing genitalia? McCombie suggests that Barbie's genital ambiguity can be read as an 'homage to "good taste"' and as a 'reflection of the regnant mores for teenage girls—to be both sexy and adult yet remain virginal' (4). I agree that her body invites such readings, but it also seems to me that there is nothing ambiguous about Barbie's crotch. It's missing in inaction. While male dolls like Ken and Jamal have bumps 'down there' and in some instances simulated underwear etched into plastic, most Barbies come neither with drawers nor with even a hint of anything that needs covering, even as 'it' is already covered or erased. As an icon of idealized femininity, then, Barbie is locked into a never-never land in which she must be always already sexual without the possibility of sex. Conspicuously sensual on top but definitively nonsexual below, her plastic body indeed has inscribed within it the very contradictory, whore/madonna message with which patriarchy taunts and even traumatizes young women in particular.

This kind of speculation about Barbie's breasts has led the doll's creator, Ruth Handler, to chide adults for their nasty minds. 'In my opinion people make too much of breasts,' Handler has complained. 'They are just part of the body' (BillyBoy 26). Mrs. Handler has a point (or maybe two). I feel more than just a little ridiculous myself as I sit here contemplating the body parts and sex life of a piece of plastic. What is fascinating, however, what I think is worth studying, what both invites and resists theorizing, is not the lump of molded plastic that is Barbie, but the imaginary life that is not—this is *our* invention. Barbie as a cultural artifact may be able to tell us more about ourselves and our society—more about society's attitudes toward *its* women—than anything we might say about the doll her- or, rather, *itself*.

…Jacqueline Urla and Alan Swedlund maintain that Barbie's body type constructs the bodies of other women as deviant and perpetuates an impossible standard of beauty. Attempting to live up to the Barbie ideal, others argue, fosters eating and shopping disorders in teenage girls—nightmares instead of dreams. BillyBoy, one of Barbie's more ardent supporters, defends his heroine against such charges by insisting that there is nothing abnormal about the proportions of Barbie's body. Rather, he asserts, 'she has the ideal that Western culture has insisted upon since the 1920s: long legs, long arms, small waist, high round bosom, and long neck' (22). The irony is that BillyBoy may be right. 'Unrealistic' or not, Barbie's weight and measurements (which if proportionate to those of a woman 5'6" tall would be something like 110 pounds and a top heavy 39-18-33) are not much different from those of beauty queens to whom Bert Parks used to sing 'Here she is, Miss America. Here she is, our ideal.'[7] If Barbie is a monster, she is our monster, our ideal.

But is Barbie bad? Someone asked me the other day if a black doll that looks like a white doll isn't better than no black doll at all. I must admit that I have no ready answer for this and a number of other questions posed by my own critique. Although, as I acknowledged in the beginning, the dolls I played with as a child were white, I still remember the first time I saw a black doll. To me, she was the most beautiful thing I had ever seen; I wanted her desperately, and I was never again satisfied with white Betsy Wetsy and blond, blue-eyed Patty Play Pal. She was something else, something *Other*, like me, and that, I imagine, was the source of her charm and my desire.

If I did not consciously note my own absence in the toys I played with, that absence, I suspect, had a profound effect on me nevertheless. We have only to read Toni Morrison's chilling take *The Bluest Eye* to see the effect of the white beauty myth on the black child. And while they were by no means as dire for me as for Morrison's character Pecola Breedlove, I was not exempt from the consequence of growing up black in a white world that barely acknowledged my existence. I grew up believing I was ugly: my kinky hair, my big hips, the gap between my teeth. I have spent half my life smiling with my hand over my mouth to hide that gap, a habit I only began to get over in graduate school when a couple of Nigerian men told me that in their culture, where my body type is prized much more than Barbie's, such gaps are a sign of great beauty. I wonder what it would have meant for me as a child to see a black doll—or any doll—with big hips and a gap between her two front teeth.

Today, for $24.99, Mattel reaches halfway around the world and gives little girls black like me—Nigerian Barbie to play with. Through the wonders of plastic, dyes, and mass production, the company brings into the homes of African American children a Nigerian that I as a young child did not even know existed. The problem is that Mattel's Nigeria does not exist either. The would-be ethnic dolls of the world Mattel sells, like their 'traditional, blond, blue-eyed' all-American girl prototype, have no gaps, no big ears, no chubby thighs or other 'imperfections.' For a modest price, I can dream myself into Barbie's perfect world, so long as I dream myself in her image. It may be a small world, a whole new world, but there is still no place for me as *me* in it.

This, then, is my final doll story. Groucho Marx said that he wouldn't want to belong to a club that would have him as a member. In the same vein, I am not so sure that most of us would want to buy a doll that 'looked like us.' Indeed efforts to produce and market such truer-to-life dolls have not met with much commercial success. Cultural critics like me can throw stones at her all we want, but part of Barbie's infinite appeal is her very perfection, the extent to which she is both product and purveyor of the dominant white Western ideal of beauty.

And what of black beauty? If Colored Francie failed thirty years ago in part because of her Caucasian features, what are we to make of the current popularity and commercial success of Black Barbie and Shani, straight hair and all? Have we progressed to a point where 'difference' makes no difference? Or have we regressed to such a degree that 'difference' is only conceivable as similarity—as mediated text that no matter what its dye job ultimately must be readable as white. Listen to our language: we '*tolerate* difference'; we practice 'racial tolerance.' Through the compound fractures of interpellation and universalization, the Other is reproduced not in her own image but in ours. If we have gotten away from 'Us' and 'Them,' it may be only because Them R Us.

Is Barbie bad? Barbie is just a piece of plastic, but what she says about the economic base of our society—what she suggests about gender and race in our world—ain't good.

NOTES

1. Mattel introduced the Shani doll—a black, Barbie-like doll—in 1991, which also may have contributed to the rise in sales, particularly since the company engaged the services of a PR firm that specializes in targeting ethnic audiences.

2. Of course, the notion of 'dreaming in one's own image' is always problematic since dreams, by definition, engage something other than the 'real.'

3. Olmec Toys, a black-owned company headed by an African American woman named Yla Eason, markets a line of black and Latina Barbie-like dolls called the Imani Collection. Billed on their boxes as 'African American Princesses' and 'Latin American Fantasy,' these dolls are also presented as having been designed with the self images of black children in mind. 'We've got one thing in mind with all our products,' the blurbs on the Imani boxes read: 'Let's build

self-esteem. Our children gain a sense of self importance through toys. So we make them look like them.' Given their obvious resemblance to Barbie dolls—their long, straight hair and pencil-thin plastic bodies—Imani dolls look no more 'like them,' like 'real' black children, than their prototype. Eason, who we are told was devastated by her son's announcement that he couldn't be a super-hero because he wasn't white, may indeed want to give black children toys to play with that 'look like them.' Yet, in order to compete in a market long dominated by Mattel and Hasbro, her company, it seems, has little choice but to conform to the Barbie mold.

4. After many calls to the Jamaican Embassy in Washington, D.C. and to various organizations in Jamaica, I have determined that Jamaican Barbie's costume—a floor-length granny-style dress with apron and headrag—bears some resemblance to what is considered the island's traditional folk costume. I am still left wondering about the decision-making process, however: why the doll representing Jamaica is figured as a maid, while the doll representing Great Britain, for example, is presented as a lady—a blonde, blue-eyed Barbie doll dressed in a fancy riding habit with boots and hat.

5. See among others Morris Rosenburg's books *Concerning the Self* (1979) and *Society and the Adolescent Self-Image* (1989) and William E. Cross's *Shades of Black: Diversity in African American Identity* (1991), all of which challenge the Clarks' findings. Cross argues, for example, that the Clarks confounded or conflated two different issues: attitude toward race in general and attitude toward the self in particular. How one feels about race is not necessarily an index of one's self-esteem.

6. Urla and Swedlund's findings are reported in an essay entitled, 'The Anthropometry of Barbie: Unsettling Ideals of the Feminine Body in Popular Culture,' in *Deviant Bodies*, eds. Jennifer Terry and Jacqueline Urla (Bloomington: Indiana University Press), 1995.

7. In response to criticism from feminists in particular, the Miss America Pageant has attempted to transform itself from a beauty contest to a talent competition, whose real aim is to give college scholarships to smart, talented women (who just happen to look good in bathing suits and evening gowns). As part of its effort to appear more concerned with a woman's IQ than with her bra size, the Pageant did away with its longstanding practice of broadcasting the chest, waist, and hip measurements, as well as the height and weight, of each contestant.

REFERENCES

Berkwitz, David N. "Finally, Barbie Dolls Ads Go Ethnic." *Newsweek* 13 Aug. 1990: 48.

BillyBoy. *Barbie: Her Life and Times*. New York: Crown, 1987.

Cross, William E., Jr. *Shades of Black: Diversity in African American Identity*. Philadelphia: Temple University Press, 1991.

Dembner, Alice. "Thirty-five and Still a Doll." *Boston Globe* 9 Mar. 1994: 1, 16.

Hopson, Darlene Powell, and Derek S. Hopson. *Different and Wonderful: Raising Black Children in a Race-Conscious Society*. New York: Simon & Schuster, 1990.

Jones, Lisa. "A Doll is Born." *Village Voice* 26 Mar. 1991: 36.

Kantrowitz, Barbara. "Hot Date: Barbie and G.I. Joe." *Newsweek* 20 Feb. 1989: 59–60.

Larcen, Donna. "Barbie Bond Doesn't Diminish with Age." *Hartford Current* 17 Aug. 1993: A6–7.

Lorde, M.G. *Forever Barbie: The Unauthorized Biography of a Real Doll*. New York: William Morrow, 1994.

McCombie, Mel. "Barbie: Toys Are Us." Unpublished paper.

Roberts, Cynthia. *Barbie: Thirty Years of America's Doll.* Chicago: Contemporary Books, 1989.

Rosenberg, Morris. *Concerning the Self.* New York: Basic Books, 1979.

---. *Society and the Adolescent Self-Image.* Middletown, CT: Wesleyan University Press, 1989.

Sanchez-Eppler, Karen. *Touching Liberty: Abolition, Feminism, and the Politics of the Body.* Berkeley: University of California Press, 1993.

Stewart, Julia. *African Names.* New York: Carol, 1993.

Urla, Jacqueline, and Alan Swedlund. "The Anthropometry of Barbie: Unsettling Ideals of the Feminine in Popular Culture." *Deviant Bodies.* Ed. Jennifer Terry and Jacqueline Urla. Bloomington: Indiana University Press, 1995.

Unit IV   *Reading the Body in Popular Culture*

INTRODUCTION

INTRODUCTION

Popular and academic interest in the body is a central feature of contemporary culture. Even a casual scan of recent academic publications will reveal that the body has become a central point of interest for theorists and critics from disciplines as diverse as sociology, history, economics, and literary studies. These disciplines are interested in how the body, or the idea of the body, is constructed out of a confluence of issues relating to power, language, and historical forces. The body, or "body issues," is also a central obsession for contemporary culture generally. We often hear about how the representation of the female body on television, in film, and in magazines works to shape our understandings of the accepted "definitions" of the female form. More specifically, it becomes clear that the popular representation of the body also raises issues of power and ideology: Why is one narrow—and increasingly narrowing—image of the body the accepted "norm" in popular and contemporary culture? Who has the power to represent the human form? To what extent is an understanding of the body being dictated by the ideological desires of the Hollywood system?

A major question, and one that this section of *Cultural Subjects* works to answer, is this: Why is the body a point of interest in contemporary culture in the first place? The purpose of the following section is to explore how the body is represented in those popular genres and forms seemingly most focused on the body: horror, science fiction, and cyberculture. Each of these popular forms focuses resolutely on the body, exploring it as a point of departure, to the point of obsession. One thinks, for instance, of the *Terminator* film series: Arnold Schwarzenegger's body is the site of primary fascination, but actress Linda Hamilton's body works as crucial counterpoint. Her body's conspicuous development from conventionally "feminine" to intimidatingly muscled is a critical subtext of the films. Or, one might call to mind the television series *The X-Files*, specifically those episodes not following the alien conspiracy arc: more often than not, these episodes focus on some "freakish" aspect of the body, from psychopathic killers whose metamorphic bodies awake to feed every 33 years, to uncanny half-man, half-worm creatures inhabiting and feeding off the waste products of the contemporary city. As a good gothic text, *The X-Files* explores the extreme boundaries of our understanding of what constitutes the "human." One might, finally, think of how certain examples of online culture, for instance online shooter games, offer themselves as spaces where the real body is left behind in favour of its fantasy replacement. Online culture generally, and online gaming specifically, is a space of radical transformation of the limitations of the (real) body.

A general theoretical reading of these texts, one that is explored fully in what follows, is that they represent various ways in which the body is understood in contemporary culture. A corollary idea is this: contemporary culture has reached the point where the body, under threat from technological, biological, and scientific developments—and thus subject to radical transformations from within and without—is becoming increasingly difficult to "read." Popular culture, thus, offers itself as an extended interpretation of the various representations, the various "texts," of the body.

READING THE BODY

Popular culture is fascinated by the body. More specifically, popular culture is a location where specific fascinations and anxieties about the body are played out. As we track through the history of popular film and fiction and as we pass through various examples of online culture (gaming, chat rooms, Multi-User Dungeons), we can see the degree to which contemporary culture seems to be working out evolving relations to and understandings of the human body. Popular culture explores the boundaries, limitations, and possibilities of the body, as well as, crucially, staging fantasies of its excruciating violation and erasure. By so doing, contemporary popular culture suggests that the human subject is primarily to be defined as a *bodily* subject: subjectivity, the self's comprehension of itself, is represented and understood through the body. Ultimately, the (popular) cultural subject is a bodily subject.

How do we account for this obsession with the body in contemporary popular culture? A likely, and often suggested, beginning is the public perception of and fascination with science and technology in the 1940s and 1950s. Certainly, the advent of militarized nuclear power and its demonstrated effects in Hiroshima and Nagasaki in 1945 can be directly linked to a huge number of Hollywood films in the 1950s, all of which explore, overtly or through thinly disguised allegory, the horrific consequences of science and technology on the environment and the human body. The conjunction of the growth of nuclear (and other) technology with the perception of the Soviet Empire as an imminent threat produced some of the most memorable science fiction films of the 1950s.

The consciousness of the threat—and promise—posed by science and technology is not, of course, new. Mary Shelley's *Frankenstein* (1818), with its various Hollywood (mis)interpretations, is the *locus classicus* of the idea that science—the pursuit of knowledge without ethical restraint—will inevitably create harm. Victor Frankenstein's need to plumb the depths of nature; to seek nature out in her hiding place is an expression of the orthodox scientific desire to know the world despite the consequences. And certainly one reading of the creature—and its monstrous body—is as a representation of the uncanny, perhaps unconscious, element at work in the pursuit of knowledge: it stands as the *embodiment* of the destructive energies inherent in Frankenstein's unnatural meddling with natural processes. And, of course, one of the enduring fascinations—and anxieties—of Shelley's novel is the question of the precise nature of the monster that Victor produces. Seemingly an amalgamation of a variety of separate human body parts (and quite possibly animal parts), the body of the creature is a perfect emblem of Freud's notion of the uncanny. At once familiar and repulsively unfamiliar (as are the giant creatures and people represented in the nuclear paranoia films of the 1950s), the creature's body defies explanation and, perhaps, representation.

It is here, in the examination of scientific and technological pressures—pressures that are translated and sublimated in contemporary popular culture into expressions of anxieties about a variety of *external* threats to the body—that the fragile importance and centrality of the body is highlighted. The body is the location of knowledge. More precisely, it is through the body, "in" the body, that we identify ourselves and know the world. By focusing so relentlessly on the body, popular culture suggests that subjectivity—the self's identification of itself *as* a self—is primarily an experience of the body. Moreover, the various representations of the body—as victim, as locus of anxiety and desire, as apotheosis and sublimation of the corporeal (as in various films exploring the fascination with technological simulations of the human)—figure the body as a screen onto which culturally constructed notions of identity are projected and reflected. The body on the screen, in other words, represents the culture's understanding of itself. What happens, horror and science fiction works ask, when the body is violated by external threats to the point where it becomes unrecognizable and unreadable? Or to the point where it becomes the Other to itself?

These questions are the beginning point of any number of crucial Hollywood films: *The Invasion of the Body Snatchers* (1950, dir. Don Siegel; 1978, dir. Philip Kaufman; 1993, [*Body Snatchers*] dir. Abel Ferrara); *Night of the Living Dead* (1968, dir. George Romero); *Rosemary's Baby* (1968, dir. Roman Polanski); *The Exorcist* (1973, dir. William Friedkin); *Alien* (1979, dir. Ridley Scott). The question also allows us to move freely through various genres and cultural expressions in contemporary culture, from horror, to science fiction, to cyberculture. Each of these cultural expressions must come to terms with the body as a site of fascination and desire and as a possible location of violation. It is possible even to suggest that fascination and violation are inseparable in these genres: fascination (of both the film and its viewer) becomes violation precisely as violating the body becomes the pretext or, in the case of the slasher films of especially the 1980s, the point of departure for the film.

Certainly, a perusal of some of the classic postmodernist horror films of the past decades reveals that the body is the precise location of desire, fascination, and anxiety. *Rosemary's Baby*, which nominally presents itself as a film "about" demonic possession of the vulnerable female body, can easily be read as an examination of the more prosaic, if not sometimes more pathological, horrors of the bodily invasion, the bodily changes, that occur in pregnancy and delivery. The verité banality of the couple's relationship, Mia Farrow's character's prosaic maternal concerns, and the immediately recognizable social context of the film (an upper-middle-class New York apartment complex) accentuate, in a darkly humorous way, the demonic themes which are almost excessive to the film's requirements, those of exploring the anxieties of bodily transformation in pregnancy. And yet, Polanski requires his audience to recognize the equation he is drawing between demonic possession and pregnancy: Mia Farrow's body simply becomes the pretext, the location, for the working out of this unsettling logic.

In *The Exorcist* a similar *frisson* occurs when the "naturalism" in the film's exploration of all-too-recognizable guilt is met with the baroque grotesqueries of demonic possession. *The Exorcist* is an acute examination of a variety of familial guilt: Chris MacNeil struggles to raise a daughter without a male presence; Father Karras's guilt over his neglect of his dying mother is an important counterpoint to the anxiety being played out in Regan's household. As Friedkin's exploration of these guilts suggest, this is clearly a film about more than Satanic influence in the world. Regan's body becomes the locus and expression of the varieties of guilt attending these characters: Regan, to put it differently, is the objective (bodily) correlative of the guilt felt by both the priest and the mother and, as the film suggests, these kinds of guilt can have lethal consequences.

In both these films, it becomes clear that the horror genre requires an objective, corporeal representation of oftentimes submerged, but nevertheless present, themes. The horror film, with its excessive display of the body, is one example of what film critic Linda Williams in "Film Bodies" calls the "body genre": these are films that put the body on overt display as on object of fascination and violation. We think of Regan's body being flagrantly tortured in *The Exorcist*; the various violations of the body that occur in slasher films, such as the *Nightmare on Elm Street* series; the grotesque transformations of the scientist's body in Cronenberg's *The Fly* (1986); and the sublime representation of the flayed body in *The Silence of the Lambs*. Moreover, the body operates, as suggested above, as the site of larger cultural issues: fear, guilt, and anxiety. One of the reasons these films still hold our attention is precisely that the body is multiply encoded, perhaps even *excessively* encoded. It can—indeed, it must—be read in a number of ways, as a reflection of the plurality of the requirements of the film, the character, and the viewer: the body is read as a location where external supernatural threats are realized *even as* the body comes to be read as a site where naturalistic, more recognizably human expressions of anxiety are projected.

Crucially, in horror, the body is quite obviously there. In science fiction and in cyberspace, something else happens to the body. In *Terminal Identity*, Scott Bukatman analyzes the representation of the self in postmodern science fiction. His beginning point is the suggestion that the body, the material human body, is the hidden point of fascination in science fiction: "*The body* has long been the repressed content in science fiction, as the genre obsessively substitutes the rational for the corporeal, and the technological for the organic" (Bukatman 19). Horror films bring the body to the foreground, enjoying the spectacle of its violation. In science fiction, Bukatman argues, the body takes a back seat to the spectacle of technology. One thinks here of the eerie, almost inhuman spectacle of technology in *2001: A Space Odyssey* (1968, dir. Stanley Kubrick)—those mesmerizing, almost fetishistic shots of spinning space stations, the clear fascination with the technology of the interior of the spacecraft (the spinning walkways offering themselves as echoes of the spinning space stations), and, of course, the perfectly disembodied, purely technologized Hal. Bukatman's Freudian metaphor, however, indicates that precisely because the body is the repressed content of science fiction, it will, like all things repressed, make its presence felt, sometimes with a vengeance.

If science fiction has technology as its primary point of (fetishistic) interest, we must notice how some key films of the last decades explore the anxious relations between technology and the corporeal subject, between science's advances and the body's fears. Certainly, *Blade Runner* (1981, dir. Ridley Scott) offers the viewer the spectacle of a technologized, albeit distopic, near future. The film's opening panorama makes clear the spectacular nature of what is to follow. But the same shot, with the watching eye (of, presumably, Deckard) suggests in its visual pun (Eye/I) that identity, represented as located *in* the body (as implanted memories) and revealed *by* the body (as in the Voight-Kampf test that "reads" the eye to reveal potential replicants), will be the film's primary focus. The proliferation of simulacra, of technology that can mimic, if not simulate to a crucial fault, the physicalities of the human subject (to be "more human than human," as the Frankensteinian Tyrell puts it), suggests that the film's point of fascination and fear is the idea that the human can be *almost* perfectly—and thus uncannily—replicated.

Ridley Scott's *Alien* is, perhaps, the best example of science fiction film's obsession with the corporeal. We must notice, however, that one of the film's particular brilliances is its hybrid nature: this is a horror film masquerading as science fiction; it is a slasher film set in a haunted spacecraft. The hybridity of the film allows Scott to merge the crucial points of interest of these genres and exploit their particular energies. Thus, while the requisite emphasis on technology is in place, the underpinning anxiety of the film is precisely the question of the body, *human and technological*, under siege. John Hurt's character's body is the film's primary—and most memorable—point of departure, not only because of the spectacularly gruesome nature of his "birthing" scene but also because his body has become the point of entry for the violation of the body of the ship itself and, consequently (and ineluctably), the bodies of the crew. *Alien* is a film unremitting in its exploration of the anxieties of the violation of boundaries, of the violation of points of exclusion and definition. The ship's "body" defines the limits and boundaries of the human culture now being attacked; the body of the human, now under siege by a parasitical entity, is threatened with nullification or, more horribly, with becoming merely a host for the creature: as a host, the human loses its primary sense of self as a *singular* self to become a pretext for the creature. The infamous scene, lovingly filmed, of Ripley undressing under the undetected gaze of the creature (and, of course, the viewer) at the film's close, makes clear Scott's theme: the vulnerable human body is under constant external—but soon to be internalized—threat.

In horror and science fiction films, the body, as a site of desire and violation, is represented ultimately as a kind of liability, always open to the desiring gaze of the (psychopathic, alien, supernatural) Other, the gaze that is always potentially harmful. William Gibson, in his now classic *Neuromancer*, makes explicit the idea that the physical body is something to be transcended (or repressed) precisely because of its limitations. Early in the novel, his hero Case emerges from cyberspace: "For Case, who'd lived for the bodiless exultation of cyberspace, it was the Fall. In the bars he'd frequented as a cowboy hotshot, the elite stance involved a certain relaxed contempt for the flesh. The body was meat. Case fell into the prison of his own flesh"(Gibson 6). Cyberspace, defined in *Neuromancer* as "a consensual hallucination experienced daily by billions of legitimate operators"

(Gibson 51), represents freedom from the constraints of the body. In certain Multi-User Dungeons, chatrooms, and online games, cyberspace represents freedom from the constraints of *bodily identity*. If the body is an identifying marker of gender, race, and class, cyberspace—whose centre is everywhere and whose circumference is a utopian nowhere—represents, perhaps, a fully democratic (or democratizing) space where subjects are judged solely on the basis of fabricated projections of the self. Cyberspace, thus, is a space of the liberating death of the (actual) body.

The (real and virtual) body playing the online video game, for instance, is the site of both liberation and anxiety. Part of the logic of the game suggests that the player is potentially unlimited in her capacity for both violence and survival. In the enormously popular role-playing action game *Quake II*, modifications of which proliferate on the Web, the shooter is able to configure her body according to taste and fantasy; she is able to choose her "skin," (her appearance in terms of skin tone and marking), her gender, her physical capabilities (armour, weapon, running speed, and shooting accuracy). The game, thus, gives the impression of what may be termed "subjective creation," the ability to construct a (fantasy) projection of the self. It is this body—mechanized, altered, marked, en-gendered—that enters the cyberworld of the "Deathmatch," that site, where players outfitted in their various bodies, engage in potentially unlimited battles to the "death."

The virtual cyberbody (the body used to play) is a confluence of machine and flesh; the actual playing subject is a cyborg in the sense that she "interfaces" with the computer to enter cyberspace. The cyborg, as Donna Haraway reminds us, is the site of a potential liberatory politics, displacing, as it does, traditional paradigms of understanding the subject. It is, however, not difficult to see that the radically outfitted (almost prophylactic) cyberbody speaks to a cultural anxiety over the limits and boundaries of the body (and community) subjected to increasing threats from disease, from actual violence, and from the encroachments of technology itself. The cyberbody, thus, is the perfect location for exploring bodily and technological anxiety as the millennium unfolds. The cyberbody is played out in a space that is both private and public (is both me and the Other to me) and which, thus, attempts to transcend the limitations of corporeal and culturally inscribed spaces. The cybercommunity in the Deathmatch is the expression of community "at a distance": contact that is no contact, with bodies that are no-bodies, in a space that is no-space, where death, crucially, becomes only a minor inconvenience to be erased as your body resurrects, endlessly. The presentation of cyberspace as a "location" of freedom, of pure democracy, is, of course, one of the tantalizing illusions of cyberspace and the Internet, one of its central points of fascination that must be interrogated. Moreover, the removal of the signs of the body that precedes the entry into cyberspace (what Haraway calls the process of turning the human into the "cyborg") results in a very limited kind of freedom. Like Mikhail Bakhtin's idea of the carnival, cyberspace is a space of temporary freedom from bodily restraints and normative values: this temporary freedom works, in fact, to reify the very thing—the body—being escaped precisely by virtue of facilitating, so seductively, its removal.

At some level, thus, popular culture needs the body—or, to be more precise, finds it difficult to effect its total erasure. This is true for reasons both prosaic and theoretically more complicated. In popular film, especially, a point of identification is always required by the audience: a completely disembodied film—a film without the human subject—is unlikely to succeed financially, critically, or emotionally. More interestingly, as mentioned earlier, it seems that a common structural principle of the horror and science fiction films is to present the human subject as the embodiment of the films' larger thematic concerns and requirements: in other words, horror and science fiction films need the body if only to fantasize about its total eradication. A related, perhaps structurally inverse, principle is at work in certain examples of online culture: these (potentially) utopian sites present themselves as spaces of freedom from the often limiting experience of the everyday.

Specifically, these sites present themselves as opportunities *virtually* to leave the body. But it is this word, *virtual*, that has a double resonance: the online universe is virtual in the sense that it is a simulated escape; it is virtual, however, in the sense that is cannot ever fully replace the "real." The symbolic energy of the online space is derived from the fact that the virtual body is ultimately a sign of the return to the corporeal real. In horror, science fiction, and various examples of cyberculture, the body is an inescapable point of origin and return. How the body is articulated and represented—how it is read—is the subject of the essays that follow in this unit.

—JB

ISSUES TO CONSIDER WHILE READING

1. Do you agree with the idea, proposed it seems by a great deal of contemporary theory, that the body is the initial, if not paramount, site of knowledge? If not, how do we account for popular culture's obsessive interest in the body? What, in your reading, does the body really represent in popular culture?
2. One of the suggestions offered in this introduction is that the horror film very often seems to be addressing generalized cultural anxieties, rather than individual concerns. This reading, therefore, suggests that films must be understood in a particular, if fluid, constellation of cultural desires. How can this understanding of the polysemic nature of the horror film be used to read popular culture generally?

REFERENCES AND FURTHER READING

Bakhin, Mikhail. *Rabelais and His World*. Bloomington: Indiana University Press, 1984.

Bukatman, Scott. "Terminal Flesh." *Terminal Identity: The Virtual Subject in Postmodern Science Fiction*. Durham, NC: Duke University Press, 1993.

de Certeau, Michel. *The Practice of Everyday Life*. Berkeley, CA: University of California Press, 1984.

Freud, Sigmund. "The Uncanny." *The Standard Edition of the Complete Psychological Works of Sigmund Freud*. Trans. J. Stracey. Vol. 17. London: Hogarth Press and the Institute of Psychoanalysis, 1974. 219–56. 24 vols.

Gibson, William. *Neuromancer*. New York: Ace Books, 1984.

Williams, Linda. "Film Bodies: Gender, Genre, and Excess." *Film Quarterly* 44.4 (1991): 2–13.

19 Linda Mizejewski, "Action Bodies in Futurist Spaces: Bodybuilder Stardom as Special Effect"

EDITORS' INTRODUCTION

In this article, Linda Mizejewski offers an energetic analysis of the spectacular—and spectacularized—male body in science fiction films. Her analysis of the bodies of Arnold Schwarzenegger, Jean-Claude Van Damme, Sylvester Stallone, and Wesley Snipes seeks to discover why the male "super-body" (298) has become such a point of fascination in Hollywood. Mizejewski suggests that we are drawn to the spectacular male body because it embodies our fascinations with "the impossible" and "the unnatural," staples, in fact, of science fiction, at least since Mary Shelley's *Frankenstein* (another text, incidentally, featuring a spectacular male body). Underpinning these fascinations, however, is a deeper compulsion to stage the body that ultimately becomes a projection of contemporary anxieties and desires. Because these films specifically spectacularize the male body (through special effects, lighting, camera angles), the male body veers into a kind of "precariousness as a posture or a fiction" (Mizejewski 154), where "masculinity itself is at stake ultimately as a special effect" (Mizejewski 154).

Mizejewski's analysis is based on her study of three science fiction films: *Total Recall* (1990); *Timecop* (1994); and *Demolition Man* (1993). Each of these films features a hypermasculinized male protagonist (or antagonist in the case of Snipes' Demolition Man) in contexts that reveal the extent to which the masculine is defined by the limits of the body. Mizejewski reads Verhoeven's *Total Recall* as an explicit celebration of masculine autonomy and self-definition embodied in Quaid/Schwarzenegger (it is impossible to separate their identities: Schwarzenegger is always Schwarzenegger in whatever role he plays). Quaid/Schwarzenegger, as a prototypical (action) hero, seeks to discover his true identity: the film, like all quest narratives, is "about" the male hero's recognition of himself. Placed in counterpoint to the hero's autonomy, however, is the sense that Quaid/Schwarzenegger's identity is, in fact, under constant threat: Quaid/Schwarzenegger's body is revealed to house two identities; his memories—and, thus, his sense of subjectivity—are revealed to be a complete fabrication.

Similar anxieties about the status of the masculine play out in *Timecop* and *Demolition Man*. These films seek also to efface the threats posed to the supermale—by the racial or sexual Other—by asserting the pre-emptive authority of white heterosexuality. *Timecop*'s plot, in fact, is motivated by the hero's desire to rescue his wife from a past in which she and his unborn son are killed. Mizejewski's analysis of the means by which Walker/Van Damme will eventually find his wife suggests a fundamental conjunction between the special effect and the spectacular body (itself, Mizejewski argues, a special effect as a result of years of bodybuilding). While *Timecop* has all the trappings of a typical science fiction film (technology proliferates, time itself is transversed), an object of equal fascination is Walker/Van Damme's body which, as Mizejewski demonstrates (in an analysis of a painful-looking but astonishing sequence in which Van Damme performs a remarkable split on a kitchen counter) is crucial for the resolution of the plot: he must perform as a spectacularly capable body in order to rescue his wife from the villains in the past. *Demolition Man*, which features Sylvester Stallone and Wesley Snipes, works out tensions surrounding the hypermasculinized body: in this case, the male body is under threat from another hypermasculinized male, who, as it happens, is black. The film, thus, explores a complex trajectory of parody and anxiety: while the film is filled with tongue-in-cheek references to past action films—thus, perhaps, poking fun at them—it is also filled with laudatory images of the body as the only possible means of re-establishing racial, political, and sexual balance. Spartan/Stallone's eventual victory over the energetically evil and stereotypically "black" Phoenix/Snipes stands as an emblem of the reassertion of white, masculine power. But the film also threatens to open up into campy displays of homosexual enjoyment as the antagonist's spectacular (and often effects-driven) acts of violence, which should reassert order, are read as a kind of homosexual bonding. The very things—the body, the special effects—that should place the masculine body in an undisputed position of power are those that inevitably threaten to display its "weakness."

Mizejewski's article is a fine example of deconstructive film criticism. Her major premise is that films have a manifest and a latent content. On the one hand, these films seem to celebrate, rather unproblematically, the power (and glory) of the hypermasculine body: it is the body that resolves the ideological tensions in the science fiction film. On the other hand, the films can be read as displaying a latent anxiety about their first premises, an anxiety that may contradict the manifest content: perhaps the male body is *not* enough to restore the order of things. The strength of Mizejewski's article is that she gives a concrete reading of these forces (they are racial and gendered), and she reads the technology of filmmaking *itself* as being a crucial component in the film's seeming undermining of its own first premises.

—JB

ISSUES TO CONSIDER WHILE READING

1. Mizejewski's essay is premised on the idea that films can be read as being essentially at odds with themselves; that is, there is a meaning that a film seems to wish to communicate and a meaning it may not wish to communicate but inevitably does. To what extent does this kind of observation about popular culture make sense generally? That is, is it possible to impute this kind of complexity to all forms of popular culture?

2. Can we read Mizejewski's analysis into the representation of the female body as it becomes, perhaps, hypermasculinized? We may think of the body of Linda Hamilton in *Terminator 2* as a starting point for discussion. Do similar issues of anxiety and desire play out on the body of the spectacularized female body?

REFERENCES AND FURTHER READING

Cohan, Steven, and Ina Rae Hark, eds. *Screening the Male: Exploring Masculinities in Hollywood Cinema*. London: Routledge, 1993.

Meyer, Moe, ed. *The Politics and Poetics of Camp*. London: Routledge, 1994.

Mizejewski, Linda. "Action Bodies in Futurist Spaces: Bodybuilder Stardom as Special Effect." *Alien Zone II: The Spaces of Science Fiction Cinema*. London: Verso, 1999.

Tasker, Yvonne. *Spectacular Bodies: Gender, Genre, and the Action Cinema*. London: Routledge, 1993.

Willis, Sharon. *High Contrast: Race and Gender in Contemporary Hollywood Film*. Durham: Duke University Press, 1997.

Action Bodies in Futurist Spaces: Bodybuilder Stardom as Special Effect

...The hero of *Total Recall*, construction worker Douglas Quaid (Arnold Schwarzenegger) begins his adventure—or psychosis—at Rekall, Inc., a memory-implantation business where a person can buy recollections of a remarkable or adventurous vacation, even another identity for the trip. The Rekall sales clerk suggests that all vacations are tediously alike because 'no matter where you go, there you are.' In a sense, this comment sums up how Schwarzenegger's coding as a star operates in any film: no matter what the narrative, there it is—the spectacle of the incredible body that calls attention to itself. In an interview, the director of *Total Recall* has commented on the cause-and-effect relationship of the films' narrative and the Schwarzenegger body. 'He has this kind of physique that is bigger than life, isn't it?' said Verhoeven, explaining that, after the casting, 'we had to rewrite the script completely.'[1] This is a clue about the contradiction between *Total Recall*'s postmodern concept of character and its far more traditional, coherent characterization coded by the Schwarzenegger body itself.

In the course of this film, Quaid faces a video image of his body in a previous identity, utilizes a hologram body that can be riddled with bullets for a fake death, and passes through a detector screen that projects his body as a skeleton. In addition to these tactics that foreground the question of the body itself—how it is represented, where it is located, how it materializes—the film's narrative revolves around the question of who in fact is inside this body, which is actually that of the double character Houser/Quaid as played by Schwarzenegger. The adventure/schizophrenia is made possible by Rekall's futuristic memory-reprogramming technology, which creates virtually 'new' subjects inside the same physique. As Robert Miklitsch points out, this technology slyly alludes to and reifies the technology of cinema itself, and the power of cinematic fantasy.[2] Thus the plotline, already haunted by the double status of hero and villain in the same body, may also be understood as a vivid Hollywood dream about its own medium. In the interview in which he discusses the certainties or determining effects of casting Schwarzenegger, Paul Verhoeven describes the doubleness of the adventure/dream as the use of 'the principle of uncertainty, Heisenberg's principle.... That means, of course, that there are different realities possible at the same moment. What I wanted to do in *Total Recall* is to do a movie where both levels are true.'[3]

Such self-reflexive, postmodern strategies of narrative and character typically challenge and decentre concepts of the self: what, after all, constitutes the subject if its ways of knowing, its stories, its fantasies and desires, do not match or are not aligned with a knowable body, mind, gender? Yet this crisis—or positing—of a postmodern subject which should take us 'beyond gender' is constituted in *Total Recall* precisely as a gender-related crisis: specifically, around the anatomy of the male body and the threat of its dissolution into the feminized and the maternal. While classic notions of narrative and character are questioned and even foregrounded as illusion in this film, the text repeatedly valorizes and posits as triumphant a particular male body as an essentially autonomous and unified entity despite its constant encounters with its own ghostly, feminine, maternal, treacherous Others.

The Schwarzenegger physique operates as one of the films' iconographic features: moreover, as a construct of bodybuilding technologies, it can be understood as a special effect, 'bigger than life,' as startling as the film's hologram battle-scene or its wall-size television set. In its massive inperishability, the Schwarzenegger body survives whole and sound despite being punched, mauled, crunched, stabbed, shot, thrown, or kicked in every key scene. These physical blows include punches and kicks to the crotch, with the double implication that the masculinity of this body is as indestructible as its triceps or biceps. Because Quaid/Houser has been programmed with a microchip implant, cyborg-style, Claudia Springer aligns this body and character with the 'invincible armored cyborgs' evident in the *Terminator* films as well as in *RoboCop* (Verhoeven, 1987) and *RoboCop 2* (Irvin Kershner, 1990). In *Total Recall,* she says, the hero's fragmented 'psychological instability has no visual signifier; he is undeniably present and solid as a rock as played by Arnold Schwarzenegger.'[4]

While the Schwarzenegger physique is indeed a constant signifier in *Total Recall,* the film renders visual representations of the split subject by means of two special effects that are remarkable for their relationship to the star physique. They not only produce two amazing illusions and spectacles but also serve to emphasize the specialness of the massive/masculine/muscular Schwarzenegger body as another, parallel amazing spectacle, 'solid as a rock.' These special effects are the female cyborg and the stunning 'interior' scene of 'recall' which takes us into Quaid's memory.

The female cyborg is a high-tech version of a very old 'special effect'—cross-dressing—and it occurs when Quaid hides inside a female robotic form in order to get through passport control on Mars.[5] At the crucial moment of 'passing,' the shell or disguise inexplicably begins to malfunction and then explodes, revealing Quaid inside, and suggesting that the huge Schwarzenegger body simply cannot be contained by the feminine masquerade. The visual dynamics also clearly represent the male giving birth to himself through the machine of his own construction—certainly a metonymic reference to Schwarzenegger's real-life bodybuilding.

The storyline reinforces this trajectory of male birth, for 'Quaid' is himself a construct of the evil colonial agency: in a later scene, Quaid actually comes face to face with a videotape of his 'parents': the agency chief Cohaagen and Quaid's former self, Houser. Thus the postmodern strategy here, the play with split subjectivity or the multiply constructed self, is a particularly masculinist one, envisioning self-creation as the male-constructed self. The play of identity and fictionality is suspiciously linked to the video image of two male parents smiling back at their son. The absence of the mother is openly flaunted in this scene. When told there is someone (his 'real' or former self) who wants to meet him, Quaid says sarcastically, "Who is it this time? My mother?'

Curiously enough, had this narrative followed the Oedipal path it originally invokes—the man in search of who he has been—the key identification would indeed be recognition of the mother: the ultimate 'recall' would acknowledge the mother's body. 'Total recall' would be nothing less than the emergence of the entire subconscious, the acknowledgement of a sexual biology in which there is actually a woman (as opposed to the male triad Quaid-Houser-Cohaagen), and acknowledgement of the symbolic merging with the mother. But the trajectory recoils from this recollection: the fantasy of *Total Recall* seems to be the possibility of male self-reproduction, of never having been part of a woman's body at all. This is the memory that can be totally repressed in an action film centred on the Schwarzenegger body, a text in which 'a man is defined by his actions,' as Quaid is told by the guru—underground leader Kuato. Kuato serves as the hypnotist who triggers the second special effect, which may be contextualized within the question of coherent male identity: a dazzling continuous shot that take us 'into' Quaid's memory and 'into' the interior of the planet.[6] The shot begins as a close-up of Quaid's forehead, dissolving to one of the walls of the Mars interior. Within this space, the camera/memory recovers the visual presence of the three men, Cohaagen and two henchmen, repeating the image of the all-male family.

However, Kuato's agency in this recall is a threatening reminder of boundary transgression through symbiosis. The product of a peculiar Martian mutation, Kuato is an embryo-like creature contained within the body of another man, who must go into a brief 'labour' to produce the miniature guru (both child and adult, sexed and sexless) from the space of his abdomen. As an astonishing special effect himself, Kuato as feminized man and as a visual representation of symbiosis is a shocking reminder that every male body as hard-edged as Quaid's was once merged with a woman's—though Kuato's male parent in one sense disavows female maternity altogether. The contrast with the Quaid body is also important: Kuato as a special effect is a gooey, grotesque and helpless figure of merger and symbiosis in contrast to the specialness and power of Quaid's body and its own 'impossible' strength.

To begin the journey/hypnosis, Kuato asks Quaid to hold both his hands; and while the close-up of Quaid's forehead is the entrance to the continuous shot beginning the sequence, the exit is a dissolve into the iris of Kuato's eye, suggesting a particular symbolic connection. If in fact a *man* is defined by his actions rather than by interior exploration or 'recall,' then this sequence may signify the danger the text otherwise seeks to disavow— the feminization of Quaid/Houser/Schwarzenegger, which is always the threat posed by the male bodybuilder on display.[7]

Yet my argument here is that the threat to the male body in *Total Recall* is not feminization as castration, effeminacy or homosexuality, but the transgression of autonomy and coherence as represented in symbiosis, the pre-Oedipal merging in which gendered identity is lost. The threat is the threat of becoming, of process, of the possibility that the body is not separate and stable, but could at any moment turn into or merge with something else. Maternity as the site of mutation and merger is the sight from which this particular action-hero turns away in total recoil.

Critics often comment on the special effect as the hallmark of science-fiction cinema, but special effects are also crucial in the action/adventure genre. The technology of the composite matte shot, for example, used to create space-station attacks, is also used to enable breathtaking escapes for Indiana Jones—that is, to construct physical feats of a superlative, indestructible body. In science-fiction, special effects create amazing, impossible machines and amazing, impossible bodies: monstrous organisms such as Kuato, 'invincible armored cyborgs' such as those in the *Terminator* and *Robocop* films; but also—in conjunction with the action genre—a Douglas Quaid in *Total Recall* or a John Spartan in *Demolition Man* who can outleap explosions and bullets. The difference is the extent to which these technologies call attention to themselves, announcing themselves as 'special' or effacing themselves as 'natural.' The spectacular male body amplified through special effects—the muscular body rolling deftly out of the collapsing building—evokes a different level of marvel and disavowal (belief and disbelief) than does the marvel of Kuato or of Martian landscapes.

Bodybuilder stardom, the network of references to real ability and performance, creates an especially resonant signifier in science fiction, investing its otherwise unbelievable worlds with a powerful material and cultural urgency. The spectacular physical performance refers to and celebrates the bodybuilder-star's talents and strengths, even as it refers to the hype and the glossy technologies of stardom. As a result, this performance effaces easy differentiations between the levels of reference in the film text: stardom, performance, cinematic technology, and the imaginary universe of the film's fiction. In *Total Recall,* this levelling of effects glamorizes the Schwarzenegger body as both impossible and true, special but credible, a 'solid' anchor for the plotline's twists, doublings and illusions.

Making the distinction between marked and unmarked special effects, Michael Stern argues that in spite of the artifice and technology of *every* cinematic shot, certain special effects in science-fiction cinema—usually the 'ones that enact the possibilities, delights, and terrors of glamorous new technologies'—create the illusion that the textual features around them are 'natural objects.'[8] This distinction and, more importantly, its resulting delineations of nature and artifice, have particular relevance to the male bodybuilder as a signifier in this genre. Beginning with Mary Shelley's *Frankenstein,* science fiction's productive tension between nature and technology has always been specifically gendered. In an early description of this genre, Vivian Sobchak describes its trajectory in what could be a capsule description of *Total Recall:* 'the male desire to break free from biological dependence on the female as Mother and Other, and to mark the male self as separate and autonomous.'[9]

However, the muscular hero/star embodies *both* nature and the 'glamorous technologies' of cinema and bodybuilding. Schwarzenegger performs as Quaid, who, despite the microchip in his head, is construction worker, husband, dreamer—a 'natural' man. But Schwarzenegger also performs his own stardom, which involves at least three obviously 'unnatural' postmodern technologies: the transparent device of celebrity, the self-creation of bodybuilding, and the editing and cinematographic processes which have become cinematic attractions in their own right. As a result, this bivalent body recuperates traditional masculinity as a 'naturally' superior category, but also manifests it in self-consciously artificial, postmodern mechanisms, so that masculinity can be read in ironic, contradictory ways.

Stern claims that science fiction 'foregrounds technology as a special effect—magical, socially ungrounded—while naturalizing the technologies of domination themselves.'[10] Readings of the multiple political agendas of *Total Recall* reveal how slippery the 'technologies of domination' are rendered, through the film's ironic reversals and self-reflexive 'recallings' of its own racist and misogynist traces.[11] The masculine superbody, both identical to and distinct from the 'magical' special effects of this film, renders 'the natural' as an empty signifier, so that questions of ideology (as naturalizations of assumptions and power) become blurred—or are reworked, revised, 'recalled.'

The distinctly maculinist and racially specific inclinations of this body as special effect can be traced in *Timecop* and *Demolition Man*, science-fiction films in which the borderline status for the bodybuilder-hero ensures the survival of the 'natural' or 'human' as white/heterosexual/male. In their respective narratives, the Jean Claude Van Damme character and the Stallone character end their adventures by reasserting biological norms as social/ideological ones: white heterosexuality. In *Demolition Man*, the Stallone character must recuperate physical sexuality itself, which has been forbidden as too dangerous in an age of sexual-contact viruses even more deadly than HIV/AIDS. The film's final scene features the traditional kiss with the female adventure partner, just as corny and possibly camp-ironic as the closure of *Total Recall*, significant here because kissing itself is *verboten* in this dangerous future. In *Timecop*, the closure revisits and corrects history by bringing back to life the hero's pregnant wife who has been killed by the bad guys in one version of the past. The final shot of the film includes the traditional couple's kiss, and also the embrace of their son who, à la *Terminator*, would never have been born if the 'bad' past had persisted. Unlike the closure of *Total Recall*, which wavers between schizoid fantasy and superheroism, the closure of *Timecop* in front of a restored Victorian house (the couple's 'dream' house) has little ironic overtone and instead restates the film's general trajectory about restoration of a traditional past.

Max Walker, the Van Damme character of *Timecop*, rescues his murdered wife and unborn son through the technologies of time travel and his own superior physical swiftness and discipline. While the time travel is marked as constructed and special (with warped screens, fiery spacemobiles and liquid morphing), the impossible physical feats of Walker (constructed through cinematography and editing) are masked as moments of masculine heroics. The significance of this masked technology is suggested in the attempted assassination scene in Walker's apartment, where he is sleeping on the sofa and wearing only gym shorts, the better to exhibit his gleaming torso in the imminent foray. A tracking shot reveals an assemblage of computers, monitors, videoscreens and scanners recognizable as the ordinary machineries of modernity: but here they also promise extraordinary effects, for this is the year 2004, and Walker's job is the policing of time travel. Despite this postmodern occupation and the accumulated whizz-bang equipment, Walker has fallen asleep with one of the homeliest and most familiar technologies of the twentieth century: the home movie, a video recording of his dead wife. Walker/Van Damme as timecop and 'natural' man (half-naked, watching home videos of a beautiful wife) literally embodies a borderline or boundary between these family/familiar, traditional masculine identities and a more disparate identity posed by a plotline in which the self can be split and doubled in various pasts.

The awakening of Walker by the assassins signals a fight scene that has become a set-piece of the genre, juxtaposing high-tech gadgetry and hand-to-hand combat involving knives, muscles, laser and/or traditional artillery, and some version of the martial arts.

Attacked by a whirling, kick-boxing, knife-wielding Oriental, and also by a bureaucratic goon with a death-ray gun, Walker kills both in a ballet of machinery and machismo, finally saving himself from electrocution through a special effect, a fantastic/fantasy leap that lands him in a perfect leg-splaying split (the form that cheerleaders ache to attain) on two kitchen counters. Van Damme's split is real enough, but the leap is accomplished by two matching shots that are impossible to discern on first viewing. In the shot that flaunts the feat's accomplishment, the Van Damme body, laterally suspended in mid-air, divides the screen space. The split also visualizes the position of Walker/Van Damme between actual physical agility (he can perform the perfect acrobatic contortion) and technological artifice (only an editing process could have materialized the speed of his reaction).

Like Houser in *Total Recall,* Walker is later split onscreen to confront a former self in the time-loop gymnastics of the narrative, with its unsettling insinuations about manipulated personal and national histories. The interface of these split selves, as in the Schwarzenegger film, is the powerful male embodiment of performances ambiguously situated between artifice and biology. An acrobatic split is precisely such a performance, entailing the shocking sight of the legs tortured into opposite angles, directing attention to the crotch. And in the long run, the association of this feat with female cheerleading pushes its absurdity: the spectacle of Walker so earnestly and seriously splayed across his kitchen counters is richly readable as camp.

At this moment in the plotline the police arrive in the figure of a black female time-cop, Fielding (Gloria Reuben). Fielding is assigned to be Walker's new partner, and is also an internal affairs watchdog. Not surprisingly, Fielding as foil embodies all the incoherences resisted by the Walker/Van Damme character: she is treacherous, unreliable, and physically vulnerable to the time-travel process easily weathered by Walker. In a film heavily indebted to its predecessors, *Timecop* suggests in the Fielding character a reworking of two racially marked characters from *Total Recall:* Quaid's partner/romantic interest Melina and the treacherous/victimized African-American taxi driver Benny. And, as in *Total Recall,* the racial politics are slippery to the point of unreadability.[12] Is Fletcher's position as timecop a triumph of her own talents or an affirmative-action appointment, the contempt for which we read in a snide remark by the agency director during the time-travel scene? Is her betrayal of Walker a subversive move characterizing her independence within the white power structures, or is it a racist characterization of unreliability? The narrative in some ways positions her sympathetically. As Walker's double, for example, she is similarly aligned with an absent family by means of an oldfashioned technology, a photograph of her parents and her little brother and even her death as part of a 'bad' past that can be rewritten. Although we never see them work as a team again, a scene near the end of the film posits Fielding and Walker as future timecop partners and buddies.

Because the film identifies body as character in this way, Fielding's body (and hence her character) simply does not count as much as the heroic Van Damme body, even though she is supposedly his partner-timecop. Certainly she does not count in the narrative except as a physical foil. After her murder, Walker alone must triumph over the villains and correct the past in order to undo the murder of his wife. The fact that this action also undoes Fielding's murder is presented as an afterthought: Walker (and likewise the audience) is truly surprised to find Fielding alive again at timecop headquarters in 2004.

Moreover, Walker's physical superiority is intrinsic to the accomplishment of this narrative because it operates parallel to other special effects in the climactic battle scene:

his 2004 self returns to his 1994 self and faces it in the same shot; the villain self-destructs (morphs and melts); and the 1994/2004 Walker body enacts superheroic deflections of artillery, falling building pieces, and fiery explosions. These special effects render this battle scene as preposterous as any comic-book cartoon, but the scene is also grounded in more serious references. His pregnant wife is present and endangered, for one thing, and the athleticism of Van Damme as he whirls and kicks to defend her is impressive. This climactic fight occurs on the roofs and grounds of the restored Victorian house, so the entire postmodern time-loop narrative is literally grounded in a middlebrow dream of a perfect house and family. The racial specificity of this dream is suggested by the image of white parents and toddler son in the closing shots, an image displacing Fielding's photograph of her black parents and small brother.

My argument here is that this concluding scenario, with its class and racial inflections, and even its hammy excesses, is a highly constructed Hollywood effect. However, it is composed as an inevitable, recognizable, 'real' scenario coexisting in a future world with time travel, time loops, and multiple selves available in concurrent histories. The Walker character, as constituted by the Van Damme body, functions to efface the state of this Victorian home and family in 2004 as 'special'—that is, artificially and technologically constructed—because his body/character interfaces so seamlessly with the unnatural and even absurd features of this fictive world. Its real-life performative talents extended by cinematic technologies, this body's obvious superiority is also obviously a cartoon or fantasy. Thus its racial constitution, foregrounded by the casting of Fielding, can be dismissed as an artificial surface feature without ideological implications. Likewise, the identities of the anonymous Oriental assassin and the villainous Jewish senator Aaron McComb (Ron Silver) can be attributed to the multicultural randomness of the text rather than to a pattern of enemies as racial or ethnic Others. When we move to the racial double in *Demolition Man,* however, the stakes are raised considerably. For facing John Spartan/Stallone—the white, crazy outsider cop familiar from the *Lethal Weapon* and *Die Hard* series—is no female buddy or mutant taxi driver, but a formidable black enemy who is his physical equal, the psychotic criminal Simon Phoenix played by Wesley Snipes.

As even this much implies, Stallone and Snipes in *Demolition Man* enact parodies of their own super-macho Hollywood stereotypes. As enemies flash-frozen in 1996 and thawed in the year 2032, their characters are retrieved not only from the lawless, primitive last decades of the twentieth century, but also from the films of those decades. In addition to the joke about President Schwarzenegger, characters refer to Rambo, Luke Skywalker, and Jackie Chan movies; a *Lethal Weapon* poster is visible on an office wall. With comic-book names and tongue-in-cheek posturing, the Phoenix and Spartan characters mock the 1990s-style, super-violent bodybuilder action star, but they valorize this star and style as well. Scene after thrilling scene of muscle, carnage, car chases and explosions confirm the entertainment value of this venue. The plotline twist carries these characters from contemporary action (the historical era and the genre) to science fiction and a brave new future; the term is never used, but the satirical target is obviously 'political correctness.'

As Lenina explains, 'anything that's bad for you' in this dystopia has been banned: tobacco, alcohol, drugs, violence, physical sex, contact sports, spicy food and 'uneducational toys.' A 'verbal morality code' prohibits vulgar language, which is overheard and punished by the all-seeing state machinery, so Spartan is issued demerit tickets every time he says 'shit' or 'fuck.' The joke here, besides the comedy of the hulky Stallone being treated like a foul-mouthed schoolchild, is that these terms refer to oldfashioned body functions refashioned in the twenty-first century: sex has been replaced by virtual-reality machines, and toilet paper has been less explicably replaced by 'the three sea shells.' In addition, the mise-en-scene is packed with a multicultural future populace of Los Angeles (a crime-free San Angeles in 2032) whose robes, capes and saris could easily be read as feminine.

An enforced, artificial homogeneity ensures the non-violence of this multicultural paradise. Differences in the citizens' costume and ethnicities are superficial: no matter what people look like, they think the same way and have the same desires. In the 'franchise wars' earlier in the century, Taco Bell won, so now 'all restaurants are Taco Bell,' Lenina tells us. Actual differences of desire (taste) and class have been driven underground, where the starving rebels still look and act like Los Angeles street people and action-movie heroes from 1996: they sweat, they grunt, they use real guns. (They also closely resemble the Martian underground of *Total Recall* and the street-level population of *Blade Runner*.) But they are unable to liberate themselves until two 'real men' come back from 1996 to introduce oldfashioned kick-ass violence and racial and gender difference.

John Spartan is several times referred to as an 'animal,' a 'Neanderthal,' and 'a muscle-bound grotesque'; but he and Phoenix are posited as more human than their future counterparts, so that masculinity is again naturalized in comparison to the special-effect gadgetry of the nightmare future. Masculine gender stereotypes are validated through satirical humour. Seeking to tone down his machismo, the state machinery has secretly encoded Spartan with sewing and knitting skills, and he impulsively whips up a sweater when he comes across some needles and yarn. After Spartan shocks the police with his foul language, Lenina explains to them that talking dirty 'used to be a bonding device for insecure heterosexual males.' With the latter comment, *Demolition Man* makes the familiar move (from *Lethal Weapon* and recent James Bond films, for example) of citing its own macho excessiveness, joking about it, and then enacting it with a cleaner conscience.

In contrast, the racial dynamic, the triumph of the white cop over the black thug, is positioned more precariously within the comic-book superheroics, with more variable potential readings. The script contains no references to racism as a bonding device for insecure whites, but the film's visual depictions of 'Neanderthal' white cop and 'super-bad' black criminal can be read as a demystifying joke, sanctioning the dynamic as a send-up of stereotypes. 'Real' difference bursts upon the hyper-clean surface of San Angeles with Simon Phoenix's rap irreverence, punky dyed-blonde hair, and politically incorrect body, sculpted into muscles not needed in the non-violent future. Thus his menacing gangsta excesses are delivered with a big wink towards the audience—although the wink, and even the target audience, are conveniently ambiguous.[13] For example, when Phoenix finds machine guns and Uzis displayed as museum pieces, he smashes the pristine glass exhibit cases and restores the use value of the guns by blowing away the white guards and police. The possible spectatorial pleasures of this sequence range from the subversive (a gleeful rampage against white uptight museum culture) to the racist (a gleeful rampage demonstrating primitive blackness). Phoenix himself is destined eventually to be electrocuted, incinerated and detonated by the white cop, who escapes the same explosion, gets the girl, redeems the future, and liberates the repressed underground. Given the film's self-referential humour, this clichéd resolution may be read as a snide reminder that white Hollywood is in charge of creating these future worlds, where even in science fiction the black dude does not get a break. But the film can also be read as an in-your-face triumph over politically correct agendas, plotlines and representations.

However, perhaps the most suggestive reading of this film's relationship between body politics and racial politics is offered in the credit sequence early in the film. The racial tensions of *Demolition Man* are clearly invoked in its remarkable opening scenes, which introduce the characters and conflicts as contemporary referents. The establishing shots show buildings on fire in a 1996 Los Angeles, alluding to the openings of *Blade Runner* and *Terminator*, and also to Los Angeles's tense history of fiery racial incidents, including the riots after the Rodney King decision in 1992, the year before the film was released.

Given this racial allusion, I want to emphasize the figuring of the Stallone super-body as conduit to and bond with the disavowing satire of multiculturalism that follows. The tone of the film switches to comic-book punchiness only after it shifts to its 2032 scene, the transition being nude shots of Stallone over which we see the credits. These shots reveal the John Spartan character frozen in a blue liquid, composing an erotic and aestheticized visualization of the famous Stallone physique. His body is literally the bridge between a contemporary scene of racial violence and a science-fiction future which 'fixes' the racism and the violence through satire and self-referential irony. Super-muscular, frozen, poised for action but floating in passive self-exhibition, the Stallone body as channel here is the bodybuilder/science-fiction device *par excellence*, in that the entire plotline rests on its collusion with a fictive technology (flash-frozen and revived nearly four decades later) and its star status (authentically powerful but also hyped). This is also a body destined to meet its match, its equally gorgeous black Other. 'I've been dreaming about killing you for forty years,' Phoenix tells him in the future. Dreaming of each other, Spartan and Phoenix are bonded together in a passion that crosses genres and decades in Hollywood's version of Los Angeles and San Angeles.

I am suggesting, of course, that *Demolition Man*'s excessive representations of gender and race—the two 'naturally different' super-bodies within an 'unnatural' future world— also expose and offer the multiple *sexual* readings of these super-bodies. The over-the-top male iconicity also functions within the recent cinematic history of black-white buddy films and their homoerotic overtones.[14] In *Demolition Man*, the implications are spelled out by Lenina's malapropisms that garble twentieth-century clichés: she gushes that Phoenix has 'matched his meet' in Spartan, who really 'licked his ass.' 'Let's go blow this guy,' she cheers. Spartan rolls his eyes and corrects her: '*met* his match, *kicked* his ass, blow him *away.*' Too late. The slips of the tongue register the unspoken or the unspeakable.

The self-consciousness of bodybuilder stardom in *Demolition Man*—the title itself poised between parody and a more earnest flexing of muscle—raises a wider question about the uses of the male body in science-fiction cinema and its subsequent camp appeal. The in-the-know campness of this film ranges from its broad satire (advertising jingles from the twentieth century are now pop tunes) to more subtle allusions: the future police chief is costumed and made to look like Erich von Stroheim, 'The Man You Love to Hate,' in Griffith's *Hearts of the World* (1918); and the virtual-sex scene is borrowed from Roger Vadim's *Barbarella* (1968). However, the nuances of the male posing and flexing, beginning with Stallone's provocative, frozen nudity, also suggest camp's queer, more radical, dimensions and politics.[15] After all, my argument in this chapter has been that science fiction's bodybuilder star, as a special effect, destabilizes binary concepts of 'nature' and 'the unnatural' already contended in this genre. Given queer theory's positing of masculinity as performance, science fiction visualizes masculinity as an even more fantastic illusion and special effect.

The founding text of science fiction, Mary Shelley's *Frankenstein*, illustrates how these radical underminings of category have always hovered around the genre's 'built' male body. The category at stake is often described as human nature itself, but the embodiment of this crisis or anxiety is male/masculine. J.P. Telotte points out that in such films as *Blade Runner, Robocop* and *Total Recall,* the 'image of a generally empty human nature is 'a generally *masculine* empty nature' (stress in original). Telotte's analyses of bodily representation in science-fiction cinema emphasize the tensions between surface and depth, between the private body and the body on public display as self-aware image. Looking at the two *Terminator* films and their male robotic forms, he discusses the difficulties of reading the body and judging bodies by appearances, noting that 'When the body is all surface, exposed, a visible function, there is little point to motivations or special knowledge ... scant space left for human identity.'[16] Telotte's topic is 'humanity identity' as a site of anxiety in these films, but the conflicts he cites (surface versus depth, private versus public, appearance versus 'special knowledge') also constitute the tropes and contradictions expressed in camp. In camp humour, the artificial cultural definitions of 'nature' beg impersonation, drag, exaggeration and posturing. We can consider Van Damme's 'split' across kitchen counters and Schwarzenegger's burst from the female robot as excessive bodies and outrageous performances with pointedly humorous overtones. The 'emptiness' of the super-built male body as signifier suggests the emptiness of its gendered and sexual identities, but also—for a more radical, queer camp—its infinite plenitude of meanings.[17] What boundaries are evoked or demolished by Stallone's exposed, sculpted body, floating in blue ether? Connecting representations of 1990s masculinity and the science-fiction future, his body is impossible, spectacular, a special effect.

NOTES

1. Chris Shea, and Wade Jennings, "Paul Verhoeven: An Interview," *Post Script* 12.3 (1993): 9.

2. "*Total Recall*: Production, Revolution, Simulation-Alienation Effect," *Camera Obscura* 32 (1993-4): 10.

3. Shea and Jennings, "Paul Verhoeven: An Interview," *Post Script* 12.3 (1993): 18–19.

4. Springer, "Muscular Circuitry," *Genders* 18 (1993): 95.

5. Jonathan Goldberg points out that the cross-dressing "transforms him into a latter-day Divine," and connects the cross-gendering to the plotline's "attempt to suture identities." See Jonathan Goldbert, "Recalling Totalities: The Mirrored Stages of Arnold Schwarzenegger," *Differences: A Journal of Feminist Cultural Studies* 4.1 (1992): 193.

6. Fred Glass comments that female genital space is powerfully suggested in this shot: see "Totally Recalling Arnold: Sex and Violence in the New Bad Future," *Film Quarterly* 44.1 (1990): 8.

7. Yvonne Tasker points out that the action film partially allays this threat of feminization by avoiding pin-up "poses" by the bodybuilder hero and keeping him in constant motion. See Yvonne Tasker, *Spectacular Bodies: Gender, Genre, and the Action Cinema* (London: Routledge, 1993) 77.

8. Michael Stern, "Making Culture into Nature" 1980. *Alien Zone: Cultural Theory and Contemporary Science Fiction Cinema,* ed. Annette Kuln. (London: Verso, 1990) 69.

9. Vivian Sobchack, "The Virginity of Astronauts: Sex and the Science Fiction Film," in ibid., 1985, 108.

10. Stern, "Making Culture into Nature," p. 70.

11. See Goldberg, "Recalling Totalities," 193–6. See also Johanna Schmertz. "On Reading the Politics of *Total Recall*" *Post Script* 12.3. Schmertz argues for "the political polyvalence" of *Total Recall,* even while conceding the film's classic masculine narrative. Robert Miklitsch, however, interprets the film's sexual politics as subservient to its "explicitly revolutionary context." See *'Total Recall'* p. 16.

12. Johanna Schmertz describes the dual liberatory of racist readings of the Benny character in *Total Recall* in "On Reading the Politics of *Total Recall*" p. 38.

13. Discussing similar diverse audiences and readings of *Die Hard,* Sharon Willis in *High Contrast* points out that the Hollywood market "demands such layers of audiences as a prerequisite of a film's success" p. 40.

14. Ibid., 28–31.

15. *Demolition Man,* with its bodybuilder aesthetics, homoerotic overtones, but conservative satire, demonstrates the difficulty of clearly distinguishing a "popular" camp from a more radical queer camp. See Moe Meyer's overview of the politics of this debate in "Introduction: Reclaiming the Discourse of Camp," *The Politics and Poetics of Camp,* ed. Moe Meyer (London and New York: Routledge, 1994).

16. These quotations come, respectively, from 'The Tremulous Public Body: Robots, Change, and the Science Fiction Film,' *Journal of Popular Film and Television* 19.1 (1991):16; and "The Terminator, Terminator 2, and the Exposed Body," *Journal of Popular Film and Television* 20. 2 (1992): 30.

17. See Jonathan Goldberg's analysis of the erotics of the Schwarzenegger body, in "Recalling Totalities" p. 176.

20 Barbara Creed, "Horror and the Monstrous-Feminine: An Imaginary Abjection"

EDITORS' INTRODUCTION

Barbara Creed's essay examines the experience of the horror film from anthropological and psychoanalytical perspectives. Beginning with the idea that all societies have a concept of the monstrous-feminine—an idea of woman as "shocking, terrifying, abject" (303)—Creed moves on to explore the notion that the power of the contemporary horror film, with its proliferating images of the feminine, resides in its representation of the monstrous-feminine. Read through the lens of Julia Kristeva's massively influential work, *Powers of Horror*, a text that placed the concept of the "abject" into wide critical circulation, the horror film becomes the site of an uncomfortable negotiation between culture's fascination with and repulsion by the very notion of the feminine.

All definitions of the abject (or taboo) suggest that the abject, while an object of disgust, is necessary to the foundation of culture: we define ourselves by what we exclude; we are *not*, for example, our waste products. The abject, in other words, defines us in a negative way. Moreover, the abject exerts a kind of fascination precisely because it is so radically "other" to a culture and yet uncannily connected to it: that which is abjected is tabooed, feared, loathed, precisely because it threatens clear definitions: the corpse, for example, is at once recognizable and yet absolutely other; our bodily waste products, to use another example, become things to be loathed as soon as they cross the boundary between being "in" the body and "out" of it. The abject, as Kristeva is careful to point out, is that which crosses and confuses boundaries. Creed takes the notion of the abject further—and, in the process, critiques Kristeva for not going far enough—and suggests that very often the abject, that which is rejected, cursed, or seen as filthy and to be excluded *because* of this filth, is feminine.

Creed's analysis is primarily based on a reading of Ridley Scott's seminal film *Alien* (1979), although she does make passing, and fascinating, references to other crucial horror films throughout her essay. Scott's film is crucial for Creed because it is a "complex representation of the monstrous-feminine in terms of the maternal figure as perceived within a patriarchal ideology" (303). In other words, the film offers itself as an extended fantasy about what constitutes and is constituted by the feminine in contemporary Western culture. Creed argues that the film is massively charged with images (and ideas) of the monstrous-feminine, not simply in the alien itself (which she argues is a fairly obvious image of the vagina-dentata) but in the various ways in which the alien and its behaviour brings to mind notions of the treacherous mother, the mother as the primordial abyss. Moreover, the film's first section—in which the crew of the *Nostromo* explore the abandoned alien craft—is a clear examination of the notion of the "archaic mother" (310), the mother which is threateningly reproductive and generative. The archaic mother, Creed argues, is an abstract idea that is translated into material form in the horror film. It is usually represented as terrifying creatures—massive spiders, oversized sharks, shapeshifting, pulsating, glistening organisms (as in John Carpenter's *The Thing*)—that threaten, to use Creed's own Freudian language, to castrate the (usually male) hero in the film. The archaic mother, thus, is both endlessly generative and uncompromisingly dedicated to destruction. Indeed, the archaic mother primarily signifies death: "the archaic mother is present in all horror films as the blackness of extinction—death" (310). In *Alien*, the abandoned ship is figured both as a site of generation (it contains thousands of "eggs") and as an object to be penetrated and violated by the human crew (they enter the ship through "doors" more than vaguely reminiscent of vaginal openings). The human crew thus enacts the fantasy of violating the feminine and, consequently, stages the monstrous-feminine's revenge for that violation.

One of the most important aspects of Creed's article is the way in which it makes sense of the experience of watching a horror film. One of the great pleasures of watching a horror film—although the word "pleasure" must be understood in a complex way—is precisely the sense that the spectator is threatened by what she sees but that she always will escape intact. What compromises this pleasure, according to Creed, is the negative figuration of the mother that allows this horror/pleasure dialectic to occur in the first place. By staging and re-staging "a constant repudiation of the maternal figure" (315), the horror film ultimately presents itself as a deeply misogynistic genre. Creed argues that the maternal figure, present in horror film to threaten but ultimately to reconstitute the subject, serves to reconstitute the social and symbolic orders, orders themselves based on the suppression and repudiation of the maternal.

—JB

ISSUES TO CONSIDER WHILE READING

1. Does Creed's notion that horror films are essentially misogynistic resonate with your experience of the genre? Certainly, the idea that sexuality—and often female sexuality—is punished in the horror film is indisputable, but is it possible that Creed's reading of the "archaic mother" overstates the facts?
2. Does Creed's article make sense of the desire to see the horror film? Certainly, we must make some sort of intellectual sense of the desire to see pain, horror, and suffering; does this article help explain what Freud calls the scopophilic drive?

REFERENCES AND FURTHER READING

De Lauretis, Teresa. *Alice Doesn't: Feminism, Semiotics, Cinema*. Bloomington: Indiana University Press, 1984.

Bataille, George. "The Notion of Expenditure." *Visions of Excess, Selected Writings, 1927–1939*. Ed. Allan Stoekl. Minneapolis: University of Minnesota Press, 1985. 116–29.

Freud, Sigmund. "Fetishism." *The Standard Edition of the Complete Psychological Works of Sigmund Freud*. Ed. James Strachey. Vol. 21. London: Hogarth Press, 1961. 149–57.

Kristeva, Julia. *Powers of Horror*. Trans. Leon S. Roudiez. New York: Columbia University Press, 1982.

Horror and the Monstrous-Feminine

Mother…isn't quite herself today.   *Norman Bates, PSYCHO*

All human societies have a conception of the monstrous-feminine, of what it is about woman that is shocking, terrifying, horrific, abject. 'Probably no male human being is spared the terrifying shock of threatened castration at the sight of the female genitals,' Freud wrote in his paper, 'Fetishism' in 1927.[1] Joseph Campbell, in his book, *Primitive Mythology*, noted that:

> …there is motif occurring in certain primitive mythologies, as well as in modern surrealist painting and neurotic dream, which is known to folklore as 'the toothed vagina'—the vagina that castrates. And a counterpart, the other way, is the so-called 'phallic mother,' a motif perfectly illustrated in the long fingers and nose of the witch.[2]

Classical mythology also was populated with gendered monsters, many of which were female. The Medusa, with her 'evil eye,' head of writhing serpents and lolling tongue, was queen of the pantheon of female monsters; men unfortunate enough to look at her were turned immediately to stone.

It is not by accident that Freud linked the sight of the Medusa to the equally horrifying sight of the mother's genitals, for the concept of the monstrous-feminine, as constructed within/by patriarchal and heliocentric ideology, is related intimately to the problem of sexual difference and castration. In 1922 he argued that the 'Medusa's head takes the place of a representation of the female genitals';[3] if we accept Freud's interpretation, we can see that the Perseus myth is mediated by a narrative about the *difference* of female sexuality as a difference which is grounded in monstrousness and which invokes castration anxiety in the male spectator. 'The sight of the Medusa's head makes the spectator stiff with terror, turns him to stone.'[4] The irony of this was not lost on Freud, who pointed out that becoming stiff also means having an erection. 'Thus in the original situation it offers consolation to the spectator: he is still in possession of a penis, and the stiffening reassures him of the fact.'[5] One wonders if the experience of horror—of viewing the horror film—causes similar alterations in the body of the male spectator. And what of other phrases that apply to both male and female viewers—phrases such as: 'It scared the shit out of me'; 'It made me feel sick'; 'It gave me the creeps'? What is the relationship between physical states, bodily wastes (even if metaphoric ones) and the horrific—in particular, the monstrous-feminine?

…The science-fiction horror film *Alien* is a complex representation of the monstrous-feminine in terms of the maternal figure as perceived within a patriarchal ideology. She is there in the text's scenarios of the primal scene, of birth and death; she is there in her many guises as the treacherous mother, the oral sadistic mother, the mother as primordial abyss; and she is there in the film's images of blood, of the all-devouring vagina, the toothed vagina, the vagina as Pandora's box; and finally she is there in the chameleon figure of the alien, the monster as fetish-object of and for the mother. But it is the archaic mother, the reproductive/generative mother, who haunts the *mise en scène* of the film's first section, with its emphasis on different representations of the primal scene.

According to Freud, every child either watches its parents in the act of sexual intercourse or has phantasies about that act—phantasies which relate to the problem of origins. Freud left open the question of the cause of the phantasm but suggested that it may initially be aroused by 'an observation of the sexual intercourse of animals.'[6] In his study of 'the Wolf Man,' Freud argued that the child did not initially observe his parents in the act of sexual intercourse but that he witnessed the copulation of animals whose behaviour he then displaced onto his parents. In situations where the child actually witnesses sexual intercourse between its parents, Freud argued that all children arrive at the same conclusion: 'They adopt what may be called a *sadistic view of coition*'[7] If the child perceives the primal scene as a monstrous act—whether in reality or phantasm—it may phantasise animals or mythical creatures as taking part in the scenario. Possibly the many mythological stories in which humans copulate with animals and other creatures (Europa and Zeus, Leda and the Swan) are reworkings of the primal scene narrative. The Sphinx, with her lion's body and woman's face, is an interesting figure in this context. Freud suggested that the Riddle of the Sphinx was probably a distorted version of the great riddle that faces all children—Where do babies come from? An extreme form of the primal phantasm is that of 'observing parental intercourse while one is still an unborn baby in the womb.'[8]

One of the major concerns of the sci-fi horror film (*Alien, The Thing, Invasion of the Body Snatchers, Altered States*) is the reworking of the primal scene in relation to the representation of other forms of copulation and procreation. *Alien* presents various representations of the primal scene. Behind each of these lurks the figure of the archaic mother, that is, the image of the mother in her generative function—the mother as the origin of all life. This archaic figure is somewhat different from the mother of the semiotic chora, posed by Kristeva, in that the latter is the pre-Oedipal mother who exists in relation to the family and the symbolic order. The concept of the parthenogenetic, archaic mother adds another dimension to the maternal figure and presents us with a new way of understanding how patriarchal ideology works to deny the 'difference' of woman in her cinematic representation.

The first birth scene occurs in *Alien* at the beginning, where the camera/spectator explores the inner space of the mother-ship whose life support system is a computer aptly named—'Mother.' This exploratory sequence of the inner body of the 'Mother' culminates with a long tracking shot down one of the corridors which leads to a womb-like chamber where the crew of seven are woken up from their protracted sleep by Mother's voice monitoring a call for help from a nearby planet. The seven astronauts emerge slowly from their sleep pods in what amounts to a re-birthing scene which is marked by a fresh, antiseptic atmosphere. In outer space, birth is a well controlled, clean, painless affair. There is no blood, trauma or terror. This scene could be interpreted as a primal fantasy in which the human subject is born fully developed—even copulation is redundant.

The second representation of the primal scene takes place when three of the crew enter the body of the unknown space-ship through a 'vaginal' opening: the ship is shaped like a horseshoe, its curved sides like two long legs spread apart at the entrance. They travel along a corridor which seems to be made of a combination of inorganic and organic material—as if the inner space of this ship were alive. Compared to the atmosphere of the *Nostromo,* however, this ship is dark, dank and mysterious. A ghostly light glimmers and the sounds of their movements echo throughout the caverns. In the first chamber, the three explorers find a huge alien life form which appears to have been dead for a long time. Its bones are bent outward as if exploded from the inside. One of the trio, Kane, is lowered down a shaft into the gigantic womb-like chamber in which rows of eggs are hatching. Kane approaches one of the eggs; as he touches it with his gloved hand it opens out, revealing a mass of pulsating flesh. Suddenly, the monstrous thing inside leaps up and attaches itself to Kane's helmet, its tail penetrating Kane's mouth in order to fertilise itself inside his stomach. Despite the warnings of Ripley, Kane is taken back on board the *Nostromo* where the alien rapidly completes its gestation processes inside Kane.

This representation of the primal scene recalls Freud's reference to an extreme primal scene fantasy where the subject imagines travelling back inside the womb to watch her/his parents having sexual intercourse, perhaps to watch her/himself being conceived. Here, three astronauts explore the gigantic, cavernous, malevolent womb of the mother. Two members of the group watch the enactment of the primal scene in which Kane is violated in an act of phallic penetration—by the father or phallic mother? Kane himself is guilty of the strongest transgression; he actually peers into the egg/womb in order to investigate its mysteries. In so doing, he becomes a 'part' of the primal scene, taking up the place of the mother, the one who is penetrated, the one who bears the offspring of the union. The primal scene is represented as violent, monstrous (the union is between human and alien), and is mediated by the question of incestuous desire. All re-stagings of the primal scene raise the question of incest, as the beloved parent (usually the mother) is with a rival. The first birth scene, where the astronauts emerge from their sleep pods, could be viewed as a representation of incestuous desire *par excellence:* the father is completely absent; here, the mother is sole parent and sole life-support.

From this forbidden union, the monstrous creature is born. But man, not woman, is the 'mother' and Kane dies in agony as the alien gnaws its way through his stomach. The birth of the alien from Kane's stomach plays on what Freud described as a common misunderstanding that many children have about birth, that is, that the mother is somehow impregnated through the mouth—she may eat a special food—and the baby grows in her stomach from which it is also born. Here, we have a third version of the primal scene.

A further version of the primal scene—almost a convention [9] of the science fiction film—occurs when smaller crafts or bodies are ejected from the mother-ship into outer space; although sometimes the ejected body remains attached to the mother-ship by a long life-line or umbilical cord. This scene is presented in two separate ways: one when Kane's body, wrapped in a white shroud, is ejected from the mother-ship; and the second, when the small space capsule, in which Ripley is trying to escape from the alien, is expelled from the underbelly of the mother-ship. In the former, the 'mother's' body has become hostile; it contains the alien whose one purpose is to kill and devour all of Mother's children. In the latter birth scene the living infant is ejected from the malevolent body of the 'mother' to avoid destruction; in this scenario, the 'mother's' body explodes at the moment of giving birth.

Although the 'mother' as a figure does not appear in these sequences—nor indeed in the entire film—her presence forms a vast backdrop for the enactment of all the events.

She is there in the images of birth, the representations of the primal scene, the womb-like imagery, the long winding tunnels leading to inner chambers, the rows of hatching eggs, the body of the mother-ship, the voice of the life-support system, and the birth of the alien. She is the generative mother, the pre-phallic mother, the being who exists prior to knowledge of the phallus.

In explaining the difficulty he had in uncovering the role of the mother in the early development of infants, Freud complained of the almost 'prehistoric' remoteness of this 'Minoan-Mycenaean' stage:

> Everything in the sphere of this first attachment to the mother seemed to me so difficult to grasp in analysis—so grey with age and shadowy and almost impossible to revivify—that it was as if it had succumbed to an especially inexorable repression.[10]

Just as the Oedipus complex tends to hide the pre-Oedipal phase in Freudian theory, the figure of the father, in the Lacanian re-writing of Freud, obscures the mother-child relationship of the imaginary. In contrast to the maternal figure of the Lacanian imaginary, Kristeva posits another dimension to the mother—she is associated with the pre-verbal or the semiotic and as such tends to disrupt the symbolic order.[11]

I think it is possible to open up the mother-question still further and posit an even more archaic maternal figure, to go back to mythological narratives of the generative, parthenogenetic mother—that ancient archaic figure who gives birth to all living things. She exists in the mythology of all human cultures as the Mother-Goddess who alone created the heavens and earth. In China, she was known as Nu Kwa, in Mexico as Coatlicue, in Greece as Gaia (literally meaning 'earth') and in Sumer as Nammu. In 'Moses and Monotheism,' Freud attempted to account for the historical existence of the great mother-goddesses.

> It is likely that the mother-goddesses originated at the time of the curtailment of the matriarchy, as a compensation for the slight upon the mothers. The male deities appear first as sons beside the great mothers and only later clearly assume the features of father-figures. These male gods of polytheism reflect the conditions during the patriarchal age.[12]

Freud proposed that human society developed through stages from patriarchy to matriarchy and finally back to patriarchy. During the first, primitive people lived in small hordes, each one dominated by a jealous, powerful father who possessed all the females of the group. One day the sons, who had been banished to the outskirts of the group, overthrew the father—whose body they devoured—in order to secure his power and to take his women for themselves. Overcome by guilt, they later attempted to revoke the deed by setting up a totem as a substitute for the father and by renouncing the women whom they had liberated. The sons were forced to give up the women, whom they all wanted to possess, in order to preserve the group which otherwise would have been destroyed as the sons fought amongst themselves. In 'Totem and Taboo,' Freud suggests that here 'the germ of the institution of matriarchy'[13] may have originated. Eventually, however, this new form of social organisation, constructed upon the taboo against murder and incest, was replaced by the re-establishment of a patriarchal order. He pointed out that the sons had:

> ...thus created out of their filial sense of guilt the two fundamental taboos of totemism, which for that very reason inevitably corresponded to the two repressed wishes of the Oedipus complex.[14]

Freud's account of the origins of patriarchal civilisation is generally regarded as mythical. Lévi-Strauss points out that it is 'a fair account not of the beginnings of civilisation, but of its present state' in that it expresses 'in symbolical form an inveterate fantasy'—the desire to murder the father and possess the mother.[15] In her discussion of 'Totem and Taboo,' Kristeva argues that a 'strange slippage' (p. 56) has taken place in that although Freud points out that morality is founded on the taboos of murder and incest his argument concentrates on the first to the virtual exclusion of the latter. Yet, Kristeva argues, the 'woman—or mother—image haunts a large part of that book and keeps shaping its background' (p.57). She poses the question:

> Could the sacred be, whatever its variants, a two-sided formation? One aspect founded by murder and the social bond made up of a murderer's guilt-ridden atonement, with all the projective mechanisms and obsessive rituals that accompany it; and another aspect, like a living, more secret and invisible, non-representable, oriented toward those uncertain spaces of unstable identity, toward the fragility—both threatening and fusional—of the archaic dyad, toward the non-separation of subject/object, on which language has no hold but one woven of fright and repulsion? (pp. 57–8)

From the above, it is clear that the figure of the mother in both the history of human sociality and in the history of the individual subject poses immense problems. Freud attempts to account for the existence of the mother-goddess figure by posing a matriarchal period in historical times while admitting that everything to do with the 'first attachment to the mother' is deeply repressed—'grey with age and shadowy and almost impossible to revivify.' Nowhere does he attempt to specify the nature of this 'matriarchal period' and the implications of this for his own psychoanalytical theory, specifically his theory of the Oedipus complex which, as Lacan points out, 'can only appear in a patriarchal form in the institution of the family.'[16] Kristeva criticises Freud for failing to deal adequately with incest and the mother-question while using the same mystifying language to refer to the mother; the other aspect of the sacred is 'like a lining,' 'secret and invisible,' 'non-representable.' In his re-reading of Freud, Lacan mystifies the figure of women even further: '...the woman is not-all, there is always something with her which eludes discourse.'[17] Further, all three writers conflate the archaic mother with the mother of the dyadic and triadic relationship. They refer to her as a 'shadowy' figure (Freud); as 'non-representable' (Kristeva); as the 'abyss of the female organ from which all life comes forth' (Lacan[18]), then make no clear attempt to distinguish this aspect of the maternal imago from the protective/suffocating mother of the pre-Oedipal or the mother as object of sexual jealousy and desire as she is represented in the Oedipal configuration.

The maternal figure constructed within/by the writings of Freud, Lacan and Kristeva is inevitably the mother of the dyadic or triadic relationship—although the latter figure is more prominent. Even when she is represented as the mother of the imaginary, of the dyadic relationship, she is still constructed as the *pre-Oedipal* mother, that is, as a figure about to 'take up a place' in the symbolic—as a figure always in relation to the father, the representative of the phallus. Without her 'lack,' he cannot signify its opposite—lack of a lack or presence. But if we posit a more archaic dimension to the mother—the mother as originating womb—we can at least begin to talk about the maternal figure as *outside* the patriarchal family constellation. In this context, the mother-goddess narratives can be read as primal-scene narratives in which the mother is the sole parent. She is also the subject, not the object, of narrativity.

For instance in the 'Spider Woman' myth of the North American Indians, there was only the Spider Woman, who spun the universe into existence and then created two daughters from whom all life flowed. She is also the Thought Woman or Wise Woman who knows the secrets of the universe. Within the Oedipus narrative, however, she becomes the Sphinx, who also knows the answers to the secret of life but here her situation has been changed. She is no longer the subject of the narrative; she has become the object of the narrative of the male hero. After he has solved her riddle, she will destroy herself. The Sphinx is an ambiguous figure; she knows the secret of life and is thereby linked to the mother-goddess but her name, which is derived from 'sphincter,' suggests she is the mother of toilet training, the pre-Oedipal mother who must be repudiated by the son so that he can take up his proper place in the symbolic. It is interesting that Oedipus has always been seen to have committed two horrific crimes: patricide and incest. But his encounter with the Sphinx, which leads to her death, suggests he is also responsible for another horrific crime—that of matricide. For the Sphinx, like the Medusa, is a mother-goddess figure; they are both variants of the same mythological mother who gave birth to all life. Lévi-Strauss has argued that a major issue in the Oedipus myth is the problem of whether or not man is born from woman. This myth is also central to *Alien*:

> Although the problem obviously cannot be solved, the Oedipus myth provides a kind of logical tool which relates the original problem—born from one or born from two?—to the derivative problem: born from different or born from same?[19]

The Medusa, whose head, according to Freud, signifies the female genitals in their terrifying aspect, also represents the procreative function of woman. The blood which flows from her severed head gives birth to Pegasus and Chrysaor. Although Neptune is supposed to be the father, the nature of the birth once again suggests the parthenogenetic mother. In *Alice Doesn't*, Teresa de Lauretis argues that:

> … to say that narrative is the production of Oedipus is to say that each reader—male or female—is constrained and defined within the two positions of a sexual difference thus conceived: male-hero-human, on the side of the subject; and female-obstacle-boundary-space, on the other.[20]

If we apply for definition to narratives which deal specifically with the archaic mother—such as the Oedipus and Perseus myths—we can see that the 'obstacle' relates specifically to the question of origins and is an attempt to repudiate the idea of woman as the source of life, woman as sole parent, woman as archaic mother.

In his article, "Fetishism in the Horror Film," Roger Dadoun also refers to this archaic maternal figure. He describes her as:

> …a mother-thing situated beyond good and evil, beyond all organised forms and all events. This is a totalising and oceanic mother, a 'shadowy and deep unity,' evoking in the subject the anxiety of fusion and dissolution; a mother who comes before the discovery of the essential *beánce*, that of the phallus. This mother is nothing but a fantasy inasmuch as she is only ever established as an omnipresent and all-powerful totality, an absolute being, by the very intuition—she has no phallus—that deposes her … (p. 54 of this volume).[21]

Dadoun places emphasis on her 'totalizing, oceanic' presence. I would stress her archaism in relation to her generative powers—the mother who gives birth all by herself, the original parent, the godhead of all fertility and the origin of procreation. What is most interesting about the mythological figure of woman as the source of all life (a role taken over by the male god of monotheistic religions) is that, within patriarchal signifying practices, particularly the horror film, she is reconstructed and represented as a *negative* figure, one associated with the dread of the generative mother seen only as the abyss, the monstrous vagina, the origin of all life threatening to re-absorb what it once birthed. Kristeva also represents her in his negative light:

> Fear of the uncontrollable generative mother repels me from the body; I give up cannibalism because abjection (of the mother) leads me toward respect for the body of the other, my fellow man, my brother. (pp. 78–9)

In this context it is interesting to note that Freud linked the womb to the *unheimlich*, the uncanny:

> It often happens that neurotic men declare that they feel that there is something uncanny about the female genital organs. This *unheimlich* place, however, is the entrance to the former *Heim* [home] of all human beings, to the place where each one of us lived once upon a time and in the beginning. There is a joke saying that 'Love is home-sickness'; and whenever a man dreams of a place or a country and says to himself, while he is still dreaming: 'this place is familiar to me, I've been here before,' we may interpret the place as being his mother's genitals or her body.[22]

Freud also supported, and elaborated upon, Schelling's definition of the uncanny as 'something which ought to have remained hidden but has come to light.'[23] In horror films such as *Alien*, we are given a representation of the female genitals and the womb as uncanny—horrific objects of dread and fascination. Unlike the mythological mother-narratives, here the archaic mother, like the Sphinx and the Medusa, is seen only in a negative light. But the central characteristic of the archaic mother is her total dedication to the generative, procreative principle. She is outside morality and the law. Ash's eulogy to the alien is a description of this mother:

> I admire its purity; a survivor unclouded by conscience, remorse or delusions of morality.

Clearly, it is difficult to separate out completely the figure of the archaic mother, as defined above, from other aspects of the maternal figure—the maternal authority of Kristeva's semiotic, the mother of Lacan's imaginary, the phallic woman, the castrated woman. While the different figures signify quite separate things about the monstrous-feminine, as constructed in the horror film, each one is also only part of the whole—a different aspect of the maternal figure. At times the horrific nature of the monstrous-feminine is totally dependent on the merging together of all aspects of the maternal figure into one—the horrifying image of woman as archaic mother, phallic woman and castrated body represented as a single figure within the horror film. However, the archaic mother is clearly present in two distinct ways in the horror film.

1) The archaic mother—constructed as a negative force—is represented in her phantasmagoric aspects in many horror texts, particularly the sci-fi horror film. We see her as the gaping, cannibalistic bird's mouth in *The Giant Claw*; the terrifying spider of *The Incredible Shrinking Man;* the toothed vagina/womb of *Jaws;* and the fleshy, pulsating, womb of *The Thing* and *Poltergeist.* What is common to all of these images of horror is the voracious maw, the mysterious black hole which signifies female genitalia as a monstrous sign which threatens to give birth to equally horrific offspring as well as threatening to incorporate everything in its path. This is the generative archaic mother, constructed within patriarchal ideology as the primeval 'black hole.' This, of course, is also the hole which is opened up by the absence of the penis; the horrifying sight of the mother's genitals—proof that castration can occur.

However, in the texts cited above, the emphasis is not on castration; rather it is the gestating, all-devouring womb of the archaic mother which generates the horror. Nor are these images of the womb constructed in relation to the penis of the father. Unlike the female genitalia, the womb cannot be constructed as a 'lack' in relation to the penis. The womb is not the site of castration anxiety. Rather, the womb signifies 'fullness' or 'emptiness' but always it is its *own point of reference.* This is why we need to posit a more archaic dimension to the mother. For the concept of the archaic mother allows for a notion of the feminine which does not depend for its definition on a concept of the masculine. The term 'archaic mother' signifies woman as sexual difference. In contrast the maternal figure of the pre-Oedipal is always represented in relation to the penis—the phallic mother who later becomes the castrated mother. Significantly, there is an attempt in *Alien* to appropriate the procreative function of the mother, to represent a man giving birth, to deny the mother as signifier of sexual difference—but here birth can exist only as the other face of death.

2) The archaic mother is present in all horror films as the blackness of extinction—death. The desires and fears invoked by the image of the archaic mother, as a force that threatens to re-incorporate what it once gave birth to, are always there in the horror text—all pervasive, all encompassing—because of the constant presence of death. The desire to return to the original oneness of things, to return to the mother/womb, is primarily a desire for non-differentiation. If, as Georges Bataille[24] argues, life signifies discontinuity and separateness, and death signifies continuity and non-differentiation, then the desire for and attraction of death suggests also a desire to return to the state of original oneness with the mother. As this desire to merge occurs after differentiation, that is after the subject has developed as separate, autonomous self, then it is experienced as a

form of psychic death. In this sense, the confrontation with death as represented in the horror film, gives rise to a terror of self-disintegration, of losing one's self or ego—often represented cinematically by a screen which becomes black, signifying the obliteration of self, the self of the protagonist in the film and the spectator in the cinema. This has important consequences for the positioning of the spectator in the cinema.

One of the most interesting structures operating in the screen-spectator relationship relates to the sight/site of the monstrous within the horror text. In contrast to the conventional viewing structures working within other variants of the classic text, the horror film does not constantly work to suture the spectator into the viewing processes. Instead, an unusual phenomenon arises whereby the suturing processes are momentarily undone while the horrific image on the screen challenges the viewer to run the risk of continuing to look. Here I refer to those moments in the horror film when the spectator, unable to stand the images of horror unfolding before his/her eyes, is forced to look away, to not-look, to look anywhere but at the screen. Strategies of identification are temporarily broken, as the spectator is constructed in the place of horror, the place where the sight/site can no longer be endured, the place where pleasure in looking is transformed into pain and the spectator is punished for his/her voyeuristic desires. Perhaps, this should be referred to as a *fifth* look operating alongside the other 'looks' which have been theorised in relation to the screen-spectator relationship.[25]

Confronted by the sight of the monstrous, the viewing subject is put into crisis—boundaries, designed to keep the abject at bay, threaten to disintegrate, collapse. According to Lacan, the self is constituted in a process which he called the 'mirror phase,' in which the child perceives its own body as a unified whole in an image it receives from outside itself. Thus, the concept of identity is a structure which depends on identification with another. Identity is an imaginary construct, formed in a state of alienation, grounded in mis-recognition. Because the self is constructed on an illusion, Lacan argues that it is always in danger of regressing:

> Here we see the ego, in its essential resistance to the elusive process of Becoming, to the variations of Desire. This illusion of unity, in which a human being is always looking forward to self-mastery, entails a constant danger of sliding back again into the chaos from which he started; it hangs over the abyss of a dizzy Assent in which one can perhaps see the very essence of Anxiety.[26]

The horror film puts the viewing subject's sense of a unified self into crisis, specifically in those moments when the image on the screen becomes too threatening or horrific to watch, when the abject threatens to draw the viewing subject to the place 'where meaning collapses,' the place of death. By not-looking, the spectator is able momentarily to withdraw identification from the image on the screen in order to reconstruct the boundary between self and screen and reconstitute the 'self' which is threatened with disintegration. This process of reconstitution of the self is reaffirmed by the conventional ending of the horror narrative in which the monster is usually 'named' and destroyed.[27]

Fear of losing oneself and one's boundaries is made more acute in a society which values boundaries over continuity and separateness over sameness. Given that death is represented in the horror film as a threat to the self's boundaries, symbolised by the threat of the monster, death images are most likely to cause the spectator to look away, to not-look. Because the archaic mother is closely associated with death in its negative aspects, her presence is marked negatively within the project of the horror film. Both signify a monstrous obliteration of the self and both are linked to the demonic. Again, Kristeva presents a negative image of the maternal figure in her relationship to death:

> What is the demoniacal—an inescapable, repulsive, and yet nurtured abomination? The fantasy of an archaic force, on the near side of separation, unconscious, tempting us to the point of losing our differences, our speech, our life; to the point of aphasia, decay, opprobrium, and death? (p. 107)

Alien collapses the image of the threatening archaic mother, signifying woman as 'difference,' into the more recognised figure of the pre-Oedipal mother;[28] this occurs in relation to two images of the monstrous-feminine: the oral-sadistic mother and the phallic mother. Kane's transgressive disturbance of the egg/womb initiates a transformation of its latent aggressivity into an active, phallic enemy. The horror then played out can be read in relation to Kristeva's concept of the semiotic chora. As discussed earlier, Kristeva argues that the maternal body becomes the site of conflicting desires (the semiotic chora). These desires are constantly staged and re-staged in the workings of the horror narrative where the subject is left alone, usually in a strange hostile place, and forced to confront an unnameable terror, the monster. The monster represents both the subject's fears of being alone, of being separate from the mother, and the threat of annihilation—often through re-incorporation. As oral-sadistic mother, the monster threatens to re-absorb the child she once nurtured. Thus, the monster, like the abject, is ambiguous; it both repels and attracts.

In *Alien*, each of the crew members comes face to face with the alien in a scene whose *mise en scène* is coded to suggest a monstrous, malevolent maternal figure. They watch with fascinated horror as the baby alien gnaws its way through Kane's stomach; Dallas, the captain, encounters the alien after he has crawled along the ship's enclosed, womb-like air ducts; and the other three members are cannibalized in a frenzy of blood in scenes which emphasise the alien's huge razor-sharp teeth, signifying the monstrous oral-sadistic mother. Apart from the scene of Kane's death, all the death sequences occur in dimly-lit, enclosed, threatening spaces reminiscent of the giant hatchery where Kane first encounters the pulsating egg. In these death sequences the terror of being abandoned is matched only by the fear of re-incorporation. This scenario, which enacts the conflicting desires at play in the semiotic chora, is staged within the body of the mother-ship, the vessel which the space-travellers initially trust, until 'Mother' herself is revealed as a treacherous figure programmed to sacrifice the lives of the crew in the interests of the Company.

The other face of the monstrous-feminine in *Alien* is the phallic mother. Freud argued that the male child could either accept the threat of castration, thus ending the Oedipus complex, or disavow it. The latter response requires the (male) child to mitigate his horror at the sight of the mother's genitals—proof that castration can occur—with a fetish object which substitutes for her missing penis. For him, she is still the phallic mother, the penis-woman. In 'Medusa's Head' Freud argued that the head with its hair of writhing snakes represented the terrifying genitals of the mother, but that this head also functioned as a fetish object.

The hair upon the Medusa's head is frequently represented in works of art in the form of snakes, and these once again are derived from the castration complex. It is a remarkable fact that, however frightening they may be in themselves, they nevertheless serve actually as a mitigation of horror, for they replace the penis, the absence of which is the cause of horror.[29]

Freud noted that a display of the female genitals makes a woman 'unapproachable and repels all sexual desires.' He refers to the section in Rabelais which relates 'how the Devil took flight when the woman showed him her vulva.'[30] Perseus' solution is to look only at a reflection, a mirror-image of her genitals. As with patriarchal ideology, his shield reflects an 'altered' representation, a vision robbed of its threatening aspects. The full difference of the mother is denied; she is constructed as other, displayed before the gaze of the conquering male hero, then destroyed.[31] The price paid is the destruction of sexual heterogeneity and repression of the maternal signifier. The fetishisation of the mother's genitals could occur in those texts where the maternal figure is represented in her phantasmagoric aspects as the gaping, voracious vagina/womb. Do aspects of these images work to mitigate the horror by offering a substitute for the penis?

Roger Dadoun argues very convincingly that the Dracula variant of the vampire movie seems 'to illustrate the work of what might be called the *fetish function*':

> …against primitive identification with the mother, a phallus; against the anxiety of psychotic collapse, sexuality; against spatio-temporal disorganisation, a ritual—and that completes the construction, on the positive side of fetishism, as it were, of a sexualised phallic object, all the more rigid and impressive for being fragile and threatened. In this object, one may perhaps have the pleasure of recognising a familiar figure of the horror film, Count Dracula. (p. 41 of this volume)

Dadoun argues that the archaic mother exists as a 'non-presence,' and 'must be understood as a very archaic mode of presence' (p. 52). Signs of the archaic mother in the Dracula film are: the small, enclosed village; the pathway through the forest that leads like an umbilical cord to the castle; the central place of enclosure with its winding stairways, spider webs, dark vaults, worm-eaten staircases, dust and damp earth—'elements which all relate back to the *imago* of the bad archaic mother' (p. 53). At the centre of this, Dracula himself materialises. With his black cape, pointed teeth, rigid body—carried 'like an erect phallus'—piercing eyes and 'penetrating look,' he is the fetish form, 'a substitute for the mother's penis' (pp. 54; 55).

> It is clear, however, since the threat comes from the mother's absent phallus, that the principal defence is sex. The vampire, marked and fascinated by the mother's missing penis and identifying with the archaic mother, doesn't have a phallus but becomes one instead. He moves from what he does not have to what he can be, if only an illusion … (p. 57 of this volume)

As he emerges in Dadoun's argument, the Dracula figure is very much acting on behalf of the mother—he desires to be the phallus for the mother. When he is finally penetrated by the stake, his heart 'turns out to be hollow, a gaping wound. This is castration made flesh and blood and absence…' (p.57). However, it is possible that we could theorise fetishism differently by asking: Who is the fetish-object a fetish for? The male or female subject? In general, the fetishist is usually assumed to be male, although Freud did allow that female fetishism was a possibility.[32] The notion of female fetishism is much neglected although it is present in various patriarchal discourses.

In her article, 'Woman-Desire-Image,' Mary Kelly argues that 'it would be a mistake to confine women to the realm of repression, excluding the possibility, for example, of female fetishism':

> When Freud describes castration fears for the woman, this imaginary scenario takes the form of losing her loved objects, especially her children; the child is going to grow up, leave her, reject her, perhaps die. In order to delay, disavow, that separation she has already in a way acknowledged, the woman tends to fetishise the child: by dressing him up, by continuing to feed him no matter how old he gets, or simply by having another 'little one.'[33]

In *The Interpretation of Dreams,* Freud discusses the way in which the doubling of a penis-symbol indicates an attempt to stave off castration anxieties. Juliet Mitchell refers to doubling as a sign of a female castration complex: 'We can see the significance of this for women, as dreams of repeated number of children—"little ones"—are given the same import.'[34] In this context, female fetishism represents an attempt by the female subject to continue to 'have' the phallus, to take up a 'positive' place in relation to the symbolic.

Female fetishism is clearly represented within many horror texts—as instances of patriarchal signifying practices—but only in relation to male fears and anxieties about women and the question: What do women want? (*The Birds, Cat People, Alien, The Thing.*) Women as yet do not speak their own 'fetishist' desires within the popular cinema—if, indeed, women have such desires. The notion of female fetishism is represented in *Alien* in the figure of the monster. The creature is the mother's phallus, attributed to the maternal figure by a phallocentric ideology terrified at the thought that women might desire to have the phallus. The monster as fetish object is not there to meet the desires of the male fetishist, but rather to signify the monstrousness of woman's desire to have the phallus.

In *Alien*, the monstrous creature is constructed as the phallus of the negative mother. The image of the archaic mother—threatening because it signifies woman as difference rather than constructed as opposition—is, once again, collapsed into the figure of the pre-Oedipal mother. By re-locating the figure of woman within an Oedipal scenario, her image can be recuperated and controlled. The womb, even if represented negatively, is a greater threat than the mother's phallus. As phallic mother, woman is again represented as monstrous. What is horrific is the desire to cling to her offspring in order to continue to 'have the phallus.' Her monstrous desire is concretised in the figure of the alien; the creature whose deadly mission is represented as the same as that of the archaic mother—to reincorporate and destroy all life.

If we consider *Alien* in the light of a theory of female fetishism, then the chameleon nature of the alien begins to make sense. Its changing appearance represents a form of doubling or multiplication of the phallus, pointing to the mother's desire to stave off her castration. The alien is the mother's phallus, a fact which is made perfectly clear in the birth scene where the infant alien rises from Kane's stomach and holds itself erect, glaring angrily around the room, before screeching off into the depths of the ship. But the alien is more than a phallus, it is also coded as a toothed vagina, the monstrous-feminine as the cannibalistic mother. A large part of the ideological project of *Alien* is the representation of the maternal fetish object as an 'alien' or foreign shape. This is why the body of the heroine becomes so important at the end of the film.

Much has been written about the final scene, in which Ripley/Sigourney Weaver undresses before the camera, on the grounds that its voyeurism undermines her role as successful heroine. A great deal has also been written about the cat. Why does she rescue the cat and thereby risk her life, and the lives of Parker and Lambert, when she has previously been so careful about quarantine regulations? Again, satisfactory answers to these questions are provided by a phallocentric concept of female fetishism. Compared to the horrific sight of the alien as fetish object of the monstrous-feminine, Ripley's body is pleasurable and reassuring to look at. She signifies the 'acceptable' form and shape of woman. In a sense the monstrousness of woman, represented by Mother as betrayer (the computer/life support system), is controlled through the display of woman as reassuring and pleasurable sign. The image of the cat functions in the same way; it signifies an acceptable, and in this context, a reassuring, fetish object for the 'normal' woman.[35] Thus, Ripley holds the cat to her, stroking it as if it were her 'baby,' her 'little one.' Finally, Ripley enters her sleep pod, assuming a virginal repose. The nightmare is over and we are returned to the opening sequence of the film where birth was a pristine affair. The final sequence works, not only to dispose of the alien, but also to repress the nightmare image of the monstrous-feminine, constructed as a sign of abjection, within the text's patriarchal discourses.

Kristeva's theory of abjection, if viewed as decription rather than prescription, provides a productive hypothesis for an analysis of the monstrous-feminine in the horror film. If we posit a more archaic dimension to the mother, we can see how this figure, as well as Kristeva's maternal authority of the semiotic, are both constructed as figures of abjection within the signifying practices of the horror film. We can see its ideological project as an attempt to shore up the symbolic order by constructing the feminine as an imaginary 'other' which must be repressed and controlled in order to secure and protect the social order. Thus, the horror film stages and re-stages a constant repudiation of the maternal figure.

But the feminine is not *per se* a monstrous sign; rather, it is constructed as such within a patriarchal discourse which reveals a great deal about male desires and fears but tells us nothing about feminine desire in relation to the horrific. When Norman Bates remarked to Marion Crane in *Psycho* that: 'Mother ... isn't quite herself today,' he was dead right. Mother wasn't herself. She was someone else. Her son—Norman.

NOTES

1. Sigmund Freud, "Fetishism," *On Sexuality* Vol. 7 (Harmondsworth: Penguin, Pelican Freud Library, 1981) 354.

2. Joseph Campbell, *The Masks of God: Primitive Mythology* (New York: Penguin, 1969) 73.

3. Sigmund Freud, "Medusa's Head," in James Strachey, ed., *The Standard Edition of the Complete Psychological Works of Sigmund Freud*, vol. 18 (London: Hogarth Press, 1964) 273–74.

4. Ibid., p. 273.

5. Ibid.

6. Sigmund Freud, "From the History of an Infantile Neurosis," *Case Histories II* Vol. 9 (Harmondsworth: Penguin, Pelican Freud Library, 1981) 294.

7. Sigmund Freud, "On the Sexual Theories of Children," *On Sexuality* Vol. 7 (Harmondsworth: Penguin, Pelican Freud Library, 1981) 198.

8. Sigmund Freud, "The Paths to the Formation of Symptons," *Introductory Lectures on Psychoanalysis* Vol. 1 (Harmondsworth: Penguin, Pelican Freud Library, 1981) 417.

9. Daniel Dervin argues that this structure does deserve the status of a convention. For a detailed discussion of the primal scene phantasy in various film genres, see his "Primal Conditions and Conventions: The Genres of Comedy and Science Fiction," *Film/Psychology Review* (Winter-Spring 1980): 115–47.

10. Sigmund Freud, "Female Sexuality," *On Sexuality* Vol. 7 (Harmondsworth: Penguin, Pelican Freud Library, 1981) 373.

11. For a discussion of the relation between "the semiotic" and the Lacanian "imaginary" see Jane Gallop, *Feminism and Psychoanalysis: The Daughter's Seduction* (London: Macmillan Press, 1983) 124–5.

12. Sigmund Freud, "Moses and Monotheism," in James Strachey, ed., *The Standard Edition of the Complete Psychological Works of Sigmund Freud*, vol. 23, p. 83.

13. Sigmund Freud, "Totem and Taboo," *The Origins of Religion* Vol. 13 (Harmondsworth: Penguin, Pelican Freud Library, 1985) 206.

14. Ibid., 205.

15. Lévi-Strauss, quoted in George Bataille, *Death and Sensuality: A Study of Eroticism and the Taboo* (New York: Walker and Company, 1962) 200.

16. Jacques Lacan, *The Language of The Self,* ed. Anthony Wilden (Baltimore: Johns Hopkins Press, 1970) 126.

17. Jacques Lacan, *Le Seminaire XX*, p. 34, translated in Stephen Heath, "Difference," *Screen* 19.3 (Autumn 1978) 59.

18. Jacques Lacan, *Le Seminaire II*, p. 196, translated in Stephen Heath, "Difference," 54.

19. Claude Lévi-Strauss, *Structural Anthropology,* trans. C. Jacobson and B. G. Schoepf (New York: Doubleday, 1976) 212.

20. Teresa de Lauretis, *Alice Doesn't: Feminism, Semiotics, Cinema* (Indiana University Press 1984) 121.

21. Roger Dadoun, "Fetishism in the Horror Film." Page citations are given in brackets in the text and refer to the article as reprinted in this volume.

22. Sigmund Freud, "The Uncanny," *The Standard Edition of the Complete Psychological Works of Sigmund Freud,* vol. 17, ed. James Strachey, p. 245.

23. Ibid., 225.

24. Georges Bataille, *Death and Sensuality: A Study of Eroticism and the Taboo.*

25. For a discussion of cinema and the structures of the 'look' see Paul Willemen, "Letter to John," *Screen* 21.2 (1980): 53–66.

26. Jacques Lacan, "Some Reflections on the Ego," *The International Journal of Psychoanalysis* 24 (1953) 15.

27. For a discussion of the relationship between the female spectator, structures of looking and the horror film, see Linda Williams, "When The Woman Looks," *Revision,* American Film Institute Monograph Series, vol. 3, ed. Mary Anne Doane, Patricia Mellencamp and Linda Williams (Frederick, MI: University Publications of America, 1984).

28. Dadoun refers to a similar process when he speaks of the displacement of the large "omnipresent" into the small "occulted mother" (p. 54).

29. Sigmund Freud, "Medusa's Head," p.105.

30. Ibid., 106.

31. For a fascinating discussion of the place of woman as monster in the Oedipal narrative, see Teresa de Lauretis, *Alice Doesn't,* chapter 5.

32. Sigmund Freud, "An Outline of Psychoanalysis," *The Standard Edition of the Complete Psychoanalytic Works of Sigmund Freud,* vol. 23, ed. James Strachey, p. 202: "This abnormality, which may be counted as one of the perversions is, as is well known, based on the patient (who is *almost always* male) not recognizing the fact that females have no penis…" (my emphasis).

33. Mary Kelly, "Woman-Desire-Image," *Desire* (London: Institute of Contemporary Arts, 1984) 31.

34. Juliet Mitchell, *Psychoanalysis and Feminism* (Harmondsworth: Penguin, 1974) 84.

35. The double bird images of Hitchcock's *The Birds* function in the same way: the love birds signify an "acceptable" fetish, the death birds a fetish of the monstrous woman.

21 Scott Bukatman, from *Terminal Identity: The Virtual Subject in Postmodern Science Fiction*

EDITORS' INTRODUCTION

Scott Bukatman's *Terminal Identity* is an analysis of how human identity—subjectivity—is represented, defined, and problematized in contemporary science fiction. He argues that contemporary culture is fully dependent on the various tropes of science fiction in order to understand itself; simultaneously, however, science fiction works continually to interrogate, even undermine, the idea of what constitutes the human as a subject both mental and corporeal.

To simplify for a moment, Bukatman suggests that an understanding of the subject, as represented in and following from the discourse of science fiction, is constructed in direct relation to the technological matrices which dominate its reality: the televisual and, crucially, the cybernetic. Bukatman's main argument is that the human subject is malleable—indeed, it must adapt to suit, or interface with, the technological structures it has created. At base, thus, Bukatman's main theoretical point of departure is that the human, or the idea of what constitutes the human, is not stable, singular, unique, or naturally occurring but is, rather, a construct that, crucially and perhaps perversely, is created in response to fully artificial (yet human-created) structures. As such, the human, as represented in science fiction at least, becomes increasingly technologized, increasingly resembles the sublime machines it has created. The title of Bukatman's book (borrowed from William Burroughs) indicates the direction of his argument: "humanistic" conceptions of subjectivity seem to come to an end precisely as identity is formed in relation to the computer terminal or television screen.

The excerpt that follows is taken from Chapter 4 of *Terminal Identity*. Entitled "Terminal Flesh," this chapter, at first glance, seems something of a contradiction in Bukatman's analysis, precisely because it is about the phenomenal, fleshly body. Given that the trajectory of his argument suggests a gradual *removal* of the flesh in science fiction, this chapter seems at least out of place; but, as Bukatman correctly observes, the body, despite the fact of its seeming removal, is always the repressed content of science fiction (Bukatman, *Terminal Identity* 19). Bukatman's analysis, moreover, is precisely of the *compromised body*, the body under attack from the alien, often technological, Other. The penetration of the body by alien technologies sets up a radical interrogation of the limits and boundaries of the human. In his analysis of Canadian director David Cronenberg's *The Fly* (1986), a film that sees the body of the scientist-protagonist commingled with aspects of the organic (the fly) and inorganic (teleportation technology), Bukatman writes: "Self and other, human and nonhuman, subject and object all become jumbled and dissolved within a universe increasingly malleable, decentered, and cryptic" (326). It is not difficult to see how the body of the scientist, now human and machine, becomes a grotesque precursor to the fully realized cyborg entities that haunt the screens in the late 1980s and 1990s (*The Terminator, Robocop*).

What is most disturbing about the films of the late 1970s and 1980s is the precise manner in which the alien Other transforms the body of the human. In *The Invasion of the Body Snatchers* (1978), or *The Thing* (1980)—both remakes of classic 1950s films— the alien Other transforms the human body into a simulacrum of itself. The body, thus, becomes fully uncanny: at once familiar and totally alien, the body is impossible to read, to comprehend. In what is Bukatman's finest observation about the body in the hybrid science fiction–horror film, he writes:

> The return of the body could actually be understood as an obsession with the *surface* of the body. While the interior organs are externalized or revealed to the viewer's fascinated gaze, the "depth" of subjectivity continues to be denied. The subject continues to be displaced in horror fiction, while the body is hyperbolized— opened up, as it were—as an infinite set of surfaces. (321)

It is the idea that the "depth" of subjectivity, the depth of human identity, is denied— or reorganized—in science fiction and horror that marks such films as *Alien*, *The Thing*, or *The Fly* as important. Given that science fiction is a genre fascinated by the twinned ideas of technology and the Other (and we have seen how often technology *becomes* the Other), and given the notion that technology is always disruptive and creates a crisis for culture (to quote historian Walter McDougall), it is no surprise that the human subject is the continuing site of this crisis.

What is crucial about *Terminal Identity*, however, is Bukatman's suggestion that an understanding of what constitutes the human subject is fully dependent on an understanding (or, indeed, misunderstanding or misreading) of the human body. The strength of Bukatman's argument derives from the idea that contemporary culture—at least as realized in science fiction and horror—is a fully *corporeal* culture: *subjectivity inheres in the body* even, and especially, as the body is placed under erasure.

—JB

ISSUES TO CONSIDER WHILE READING

1. What are some of the ethical implications of Bukatman's notion that postmodern culture increasingly sees a blurring of the boundaries between the human body and technology?
2. Is it possible to figure the crisis of subjectivity which Bukatman refers to in positive terms? That is, how would one conceptualize the fluidity of the subject in terms that are liberating?

REFERENCES AND FURTHER READING

Bukatman, Scott. *Blade Runner*. London: British Film Institute, 1997.

---. "Terminal Flesh." *Terminal Identity: The Virtual Subject in Postmodern Science Fiction*. Durham, NC: Duke University Press, 1993.

Haraway, Donna. "A Cyborg Manifesto: Science, Technology, and Socialist-Feminism in the Late Twentieth Century." *Simians, Cyborgs, and Women*. New York: Routledge, 1991.

McDougall, Walter. *The Heavens and the Earth: A Political History of the Space Age.* New York: Basic Books, 1985.

Terminal Identity: The Virtual Subject in Postmodern Science Fiction

INTO THE PLASMA POOL

"It's weird and pissed off, whatever it is." — The Thing

The Extrusion of the Flesh

The superimposition of technology on the human is dramatized in all its effects throughout science fiction: this is its function. The computer alone is narrated as a prosthetic extension, as an addictive substance, as a space to enter, as a technological intrusion into human genetic structures, and finally as a replacement for the human in a posthuman world (the computer is *juxtaposed* to the human; it is *superimposed* upon the human, and it ultimately *supersedes* the human). As in performance art, the body becomes the site of exploration, a site in which the implications of postmodern dissolution are inscribed and hypostatized. The body is already an interface between mind and experience; Merleau-Ponty writes of the body as a medium that permits a consciousness of the world. The subject "is [the] body and [the] body is the potentiality of a certain world."[1] The obsessive restaging of the alteration of the body is also a constant refiguring or redefinition of the subject through biotechnological apparatuses.

The cyborg performance art of Stelarc exemplifies these concerns with an explicitly surrealist sense of transgression, and with an immediate emphasis upon the flesh—as paradigmatic a postmodern landscape as cyberspace itself. Stelarc, an Australian performance artist living in Japan, has filmed his bodily interior, amplified its functions, enhanced its abilities, and worked toward "the body's transcendence of all conventional boundaries." As cyberpunk John Shirley has written, "All the signposts direct us to him."[2]

Through the sonic amplification of his bodily functions, Stelarc transforms his body into "an acoustical landscape"—an array of beats, beeps, and gurgles. The subject is replaced into the continuity of biological process, but this fusion is only performed through a symbiosis with electronic technology. Stelarc's more recent work has moved from mapping the body to extending and enhancing its capabilities. "Event for Amplified Body, Laser Eyes, and Third Hand," featured a third hand activated by his abdominal and thigh muscles. His real left arm was "controlled" by the random electrical impulses of a muscle stimulator. Stelarc has bounced laser beams off mirrored contact lenses, "drawing" with the beams that emanate from his eyes.

The Krokers note that Stelarc "makes of his own body its own horizon of sometimes repulsive, sometimes fascinating, possibilities."[3] He has explored and experimented with the "architecture" of the body, treating the body as an environment which needs to be made more adaptable. Shirley quotes Stelarc as stating, "We're at the time now where we have to start redesigning the human body to match the technology we've created...[We] are confronted by the end of the human form as we know it." As Shirley points out, this is strikingly similar to "ideas explored by Bruce Sterling in *Schismatrix* and Samuel Delany in *Nova*."[4]

A concern with biological interface and dissolution pervades not only science fiction, but horror as well. One SF author wrote, "I have recently launched full-tilt into the deep end of Horror, THE coming venue for speculative fiction."[5] Cyberpunks K. W. Jeter and John Shirley have also shifted their attention to splatterpunk horror. Mass-market bookstores have instituted horror fiction sections; horror novels regularly appear on bestseller lists; horror films remain among the most durable of film genres; horror comics, primarily aimed toward an adult and subcultural market, have made their most significant appearance since the 1950s; heavy metal rock is dominated by images derived from horror; and the field is characterized by a dynamic interchange of talents.[6] *LOCUS*, the SF industry newspaper, now includes a section on "Horror/Dark Fantasy."

Just as the anxieties regarding technology and the Other have produced complex responses within science fiction, so the horror genre has produced a wide range of textual strategies, most of which center upon an extensive hyperbolization of the body and its (dys)functions. The works of science fiction that have been considered here have evidenced an increasing "subjectlessness" in their rhetorical effects and strategies. The threats in the horror film to the subject's health and well-being are, perhaps, excessive attempts at a recuperative mission. The task of the horror film might therefore be to rescue the body, and thus the subject, from the vicissitudes of modern urban, cybernetic, and viral existences;[7] in other words, from the interface with those exterior forces that threaten the subject's hegemony. But while horror has become ever more dedicated to an obsessive centering upon the *body* of the subject, this does not necessarily mark a return to the *terms* of the subject. The return of the body could actually be understood as an obsession with the *surface* of the body. While the interior organs are externalized or revealed to the viewer's fascinated gaze, the "depth" of subjectivity continues to be denied. The subject continues to be displaced in horror fiction, while the body is hyperbolized—opened up, as it were—as an infinite set of surfaces (Baudrillard's *fractal subject*).

The concern with defining the limits of the human finds expression in several science fiction/horror films of the 1980s that were organized around the phenomenon of "shapeshifting." The continually metamorphosing Alien in the film of the same name is anticipated and echoed in the return of the human simulacra in *The Invasion of the Body Snatchers* (1978), in the degenerating scientist of *The Fly*, and, perhaps most disturbingly, in the impressively mimetic alien invader of *The Thing*. All these were remakes of earlier works—even *Alien* bears its own gothic association (e.g., James Whale's 1932 *The Old Dark House*). While the originals teased the audience with hints of the hideous transformations that occurred shrouded in fog or perhaps just off-screen, the remakes rewrite the originals by lingering on the lurid biomechanics with an almost affectionate disgust. The elaborate special effects of Rick Baker (*The Thing, Videodrome*), Rob Bottin (*Total Recall* [1990], and Carlo Ribald (*Alien, E.T.* [1982]), emphasizing complex facial reactions and muscular responses, renders the alien body in hyperreal, hyper-biologized terms. The Other, which can look exactly like ourselves, is endowed with the status of pure flesh.

Alien In this context the importance of *Alien* cannot be overemphasized. The film is located at the juncture between science fiction and horror films, and an analysis of its strategies reveals much about the conditions of those genres. *Alien* presents the return of the repressed—the body—to the space of the science fiction film.

One first wants to note the film's extraordinary opening sequence, which presents the revelation of a fully realized world from which people are absent. The space-faring tugboat *Nostromo*, with a vast refinery in tow, cruises past the viewer amidst the silent voids of interplanetary space. The film then cuts to a series of languorous interior tracking shots that reveal the complex detail of empty corridors and control rooms. This introductory maneuver is a significant trope of the science fiction film, restaged in, for example, the African landscapes that open *2001* or the panavision cityscapes of *Blade Runner* or even the cosmic montages (often by astronomical artist Chesley Bonestell) that open such 1950s films as *The War of the Worlds*. Such an evacuation of the human from these richly detailed visions of existence surely complements the pervasive diminution of the human figure that occurs in science fiction set design, epitomized here through the scalar exaggerations of the monstrous *Nostromo*. As in *2001*, the ship is autonomous—a self-sustaining cybernetic organism that simply obviates the need for a human presence.

Suddenly, aboard the *Nostromo*, fluorescent lights flicker to life and the irresistible clatter of computer printouts swamps the soundtrack. A closeup of an activated console reveals the first sign of human habitation—a plastic coffee cup which clutters the surface. This intrusion of a particularly casual, nonrational, and unsystematized version of the human has the effect of separating *Alien* from the pristinely rational spaces and spacemen of *2001*'s earlier odyssey. Interestingly, the cluttered spaces of the *Nostromo* recall most clearly the fateful nuclear bomber of Kubrick's *Dr. Strangelove*, and that film is further evoked during a later crash-landing sequence that recalls the bomber fire through identical near-documentary camerawork and editing. This occasional documentary filmic style, especially when coupled with the improvisational acting styles of the cast, emphasizes a quotidian reality at odds with the deep-space setting. From the outset of *Alien*, then, the future has become exactly like the present.[8]

The iconography of *Alien* is thus largely familiar to viewers of the science fiction film, but the spaceship, the ringed planet, the urban industrialized space represented by this floating factory, the astronauts (whose suits evoke memories of Jules Verne and Captain Nemo), the android, the alien—each of these generic icons is filtered through the heterogeneous referential systems of postmodernity. The coffee cups on the console are the first sign of a space which belies the utopian technologism of most space exploration films. *Alien* uses several designers—Ron Cobb and Chris Foss for the Nostromo, Jean (Moebius) Giraud for the spacesuits, H. R. Giger for the alien and alien vessel, Michael Seymour and Ridley Scott for the overall production design—and the result is a fascinating mismatch of styles. The crew members possess no history and no real psychology—like the android, Ash, they are fully functional simulacra. And, of course, the alien itself is a creature of continual transformation—the very trope of an organic-technological malleability. The viewer is prepared—carefully prepared—for the complex phenomenology of science fiction cinema, with its surfeit of complex spaces all demanding to be read and comprehended.

Like the creature of the title, however, the film has one further metamorphosis to perform. At one very clearly marked point in the narrative, *Alien* definitively shifts its generic dominant from science fiction to horror. From the moment that the embryonic alien bursts forth from Kane's stomach, the carefully elaborated politically and economically credible future epoch with its detailed social hierarchy becomes the merest background to the new narrative task, which is simply to hunt down and kill the alien intruder—the monster. The rationality of computer directives and planetary scans is replaced by the irrational behaviors of frightened crew members hunting, inevitably alone, for the cat. At the same time, the complicated, but readable spaces of the ship succumb to the frantic pulsations of some inexplicably placed strobe lights. In short, a chaos engulfs the film—narratively and stylistically—not simply the chaos of a misplaced coffee cup, but a new and apocalyptic chaos that leads to the destruction of nearly all that we have been.

This disjunction, which might mark the film's failure, can be productively read to understand the film's undeniable significance. Vivian Sobchack has written eloquently about what she calls "the virginity of astronauts" in SF cinema: "More than any other American film genre, then, science fiction denies human eroticism and libido a traditional narrative representation and expression. Sex and the science fiction film is, therefore, a negative topic": "The virginal astronauts of the science fiction film are a sign of penetration and impregnation without biology, without sex, and without the opposite, different, sex. They signify a conquering, potent, masculine and autonomous technology which values production over reproduction, which creates rather than procreates."[9] The splattering "birth" of the alien from the stomach of the male crew member Kane, then, represents the end of such "immaculate conceptions." The denial of sexuality, which is everywhere in the mainstream science fiction cinema, here reaches its limits. This is the return of the repressed, with a vengeance.

If science fiction cinema denies the body, displacing its attention instead onto the cool mechanics of telematic view screens, phallic spaceships, and androgynous androids, then, by contrast, horror is all *about* the body. The threat in the horror film is externalized; it almost always takes a physical form. This is neatly literalized in *Forbidden Planet,* wherein the murderous creatures are "monsters from the id." In the last two decades the horror film has presented a further hyperbole of the body—a meticulous lingering upon the destruction or transformation of the human body (a physicality divorced from any significant subjectivity).

One notes the massive feminization of the body that occurs in contemporary science fiction and horror, best represented in *Alien's* sets as well as its monstrous delivery. This grotesque parody of birth, and the slit that appears on Max Renn's stomach in *Videodrome,* confront the male subject with a proximate organicism at odds with male "rationality," "technologism," and "civilization." The male is positioned at the mercy of a banished biological nature in which not even the body provides that "halo of protection" that Baudrillard once referred to. Thus the hyperbolization of the body must be read as both a confrontation with and a denial of the limits of the rational.[10] Barbara Creed notes a pervasive interest in the maternal body within what she calls the "science fiction horror film." In *Alien,* for example, "virtually all aspects of the *mise-en-scène* are designed to signify the female: womb-like interiors, fallopian tube corridors, small claustrophobic spaces."[11] Sobchack concurs: "Nearly all of Alien's imagery is organic and/or sexual," she writes, "whereas the humans are not—except for Ripley's climactic emergence as female toward the end of the narrative.[12] The importance of the set designs by Swiss painter H. R. Giger cannot be over-emphasized: sections of the film privilege a thoroughly sculptural space of techno-organic corridors, tunnels, and biological designs. The rationalist space of the spaceship becomes an embodied, and specially feminine, space. The extruded organic forms, black fibreglass aesthetic and arrayed irregular, translucent egg-shapes suggest the sculptures of Eva Hesse more than a little, with her latent eroticism now made manifest.

Creed further argues that Alice Jardine's conception of "gynesis," in which the feminine comes to represent the arena over which our master-narratives have lost control, finds extensive figuration in the science fiction film. "[T]he body, particularly the woman's body, has come to signify the unknown, the terrifying, the monstrous."[13] Thus the dissolution of boundaries that seems endemic to the postmodern text is coded onto the body, the body that "becomes woman" through pervasive metamorphoses. It is therefore not surprising that many writings on *Alien* have concentrated upon the sexual anxiety that underlies the film's narrative and design. Although the film presents the viewer with a seeming rarity in this genre, namely a strong and competent female protagonist, it is clear that anxiety about feminism is displaced onto the figure of the alien Other (furthermore, in *Alien*, as in much science fiction, anxiety about *race* is equally predominant and equally inscribed in the design of the monster).

In *The Philosophy of Horror,* Noel Carroll maintains that the two simultaneous responses which define the work of horror are fear and disgust. Following anthropologist Mary Douglas, Carroll notes that we are afraid of and disgusted by the "impure": those things which violate or transgress our fundamental cultural categorizations.[14] When considering the evident metamorphosis of *Alien* from a work of science fiction to one primarily engaged with the structures and stylistics of the horror film, it might be worth asking what interstitial categories are embodied by the alien. For example, although Ash, the android, notes that he "admires its purity," the alien is actually very *im*pure. It is humanoid, but not human. It is simultaneously male and female, as many commentators have noted: "The alien, which is fond of womb-like and vagina-like spaces, is distinctly phallic, and it attacks Ripley, like a fantasy rapist, while she is undressing. But the alien is also equipped with a rather impressive set of vaginal teeth. It is born of eggs, and it continually gives birth to itself."[15] It is at once organic and inorganic, and this dichotomy structures much of the film. The android, Ash, is both organic and inorganic as well, and "his" destruction is marked by the gushing forth of the milky fluids which constitute "his" "blood." The ship on which the alien is found (the product of another alien race) is a masterpiece of organic machinery—a technological space that is also a body. Ash's comments notwithstanding, then, we may admire the alien for its interstitial *im*purity.

The separation of (rational) technology and (slimy) biology is very nearly a structuring principle of the science fiction film, and thus the transgression represented by *Alien*'s alien is unquestionably important. The organic, almost intestinal, spaces of both the alien craft and the corridors of the Nostromo are invaded by a silicon-based life form that blends easily with the pipes and protrusions of human machinery. The blasting steam in the engine room and the condensed water that drips from high ceilings foreshadow the onslaught of fluids that characterize later sections of the film. Kane gives "birth," first with a splatter, and then with a gushing, of blood. The alien's dripping blood corrodes metal on three decks. Ash's milky fluids drench his still-functioning robot body. And in grotesque closeup, the alien's metallic teeth extrude while liquids spray about its mouth. More than anything else, it is this flood of bodily fluids that separates *Alien* from the antiseptic and virginal spaces of the science fiction cinema, so brilliantly epitomized and parodied in *2001*. The pronounced, indeed hyperbolic, transition from science fiction to horror actually marks a profound moment in the history of the genre: *Alien* is the film in which *the body* invades the pristine and sexless rational spaces of the science fiction film. The genre hasn't been the same since.

The Fly The term "body horror" situates the dominant realm of excess in American cinema of the 1980s. "Visions of excess are visions of the body and visions of death," Andrew Haase has noted of Bataille's writings, arguing that his concepts "possess the ability to take us directly to the limits of the body."[16] At a time when the comprehensible sense of continuity represented by history or religion or instrumental reason has given way to the sole remaining continuity of the physical, visible body, these films reveal the anxiety that accompanies this hyperbole of the flesh. The only continuity within these films seems to be the radical *dis*continuity of endless transformation and decay (what will the Thing look like *this* time?). The numberless permutations of which Alien and Thing seem capable repeatedly challenge the rationality of a body that has been the fundament of social and political being.

Thus the body becomes an elaborate fiction; a paraspace represented through the spectacularity of the special effect, presenting the death of the Subject through an obsessive play of simulation, replacement, and degeneration. The recurrent deconstruction of the body actually supports the subject's inviolability as the "place" of the subject shifts from the pure physicality of the body to the mind, the computer, or some other cyborg formation. The shifting experiential spaces described in the last chapters here meet a new uncertainty of bodily definition and subject knowledge through the immixture of 1950s "sci-fi" paranoia about the infiltration of the Other and the growing sense that we have indeed met the Other, and it is us. "I know I'm human," the protagonist of *The Thing* rationalizes, but this has become a hollow, and even a useless, knowledge.

These concerns are also relevant to Cronenberg's *The Fly*. Seth Brundle is a scientist with a teleportation device that he promises will "end all concepts of borders and frontiers, time and space." A subject is encoded as computer data at one point and is decoded at another; the genetic data is the same, but the physical being is newly constructed." ("Is it live or Memorex?" is Brundle's savvy quip.) The dissolution of geographic boundaries yields before the breakdown of genetic and bodily hegemony. Brundle had previously been incapable of grasping the uniqueness of the organic—"the flesh," an explicit reference to Burroughs—and his teleporter was attuned solely to the sterility of the inorganic. His education in the pleasures of the flesh leads to success, but the experiment goes awry due to a random mishap as an errant fly is encoded with Brundle as *part* of Brundle. Following his bizarre transformation, he at first believes the device to have improved him: *"You might think you were the one to teach me about the flesh, but you only know society's straight line about the flesh…I'm talking PENETRATION beyond the veil of the flesh, a deep penetrating dive into the plasma pool!"* The languages of Burroughs and Cronenberg commingle as the "improved" Brundle calls for a transcendence. In his film "the (anti)hero starts out trying to breach the divide between man and machine, self and object," Manohla Dargis points out.[17] While Brundle's euphoria is misplaced, a similar yearning cuts across Cronenberg's body of work (work of the body): a desire for dissolution always accompanied by a fear of the void. Long live the new flesh.

The Brundle-fly ultimately fuses with the metallic transporter itself. Self and other, human and nonhuman, subject and object all become jumbled and dissolved within a universe grown increasingly malleable, decentered, and cryptic. There is no "resistance," "no halo of private protection, not even [one's] own body, to protect [us] anymore" (Baudrillard). Viruses and parasites demonstrate the vulnerability of the body to invasion from without; telepathy and physical projection break down the dichotomy between public and private; subjectivity and temporality collapse; man merges with machine: we have arrived in a zone without borders.

Blood Music   While the xenophobia and technological paranoia of SF and horror overlap, it has fallen to science fiction to narrate—and therefore produce—the human/machine interface in all its potential complexities.[18] Greg Bear's novel *Blood Music,* and his earlier novella of the same name, are highly effective hard-science narratives that perform some significant revisions of familiar 1950s horror film tropes.[19] Like *The Fly,* which it sometimes resembles, *Blood Music* combines the bodily obsession of horror with the technological otherness of science fiction. *Blood Music* is an exemplary narrative of implosion, viral contamination, mutation, organic/technological interface, the disappearance of the body, and the end of the subject. In its two versions, novella and novel, Bear succeeded in condensing a range of concerns that were endemic to SF in the 1980s. Although his other fiction lacks its resonance, *Blood Music* was recognized as a foundational cyberpunk text, despite the hard-SF trappings that remain untainted by any street sensibility.

The tale is set within the nascent biochip (or nanotechnology) industry—"the incorporation of protein molecular circuitry with silicon electronics,"[20] Dr. Vergil Ulam of Genetron has constructed Medically Applicable Biochips—"Microscopic logic circuits. You inject them into the human body, they set up shop where they're told and troubleshoot."[21] Ulam has already injected these, now modified to randomly develop (or evolve), into his own blood stream. Soon the molecules have aggregated into complex microorganisms with their own behaviors, their own societies, and their own agendas. Their complexity is enormous; these organisms exist as almost pure genetic information. The resultant evolution is surprising, as he explains: "Something is happening inside me. They talk to each other with proteins and nucleic acids, through the fluids, through membranes. They tailor something—viruses, maybe—to carry long messages or personality traits or biologic, plasmid-like structures. That makes sense. Those are some of the ways I programmed them. Maybe that's what your machine calls infection—all the new information in my blood. Chatter. Tastes of other individuals. Peers. Superiors. Subordinates"(71). Viral infection marks the pervasive dissolution of the human and the passage to a posthuman order.

Here, then, is an amusing inversion of the premises of Theodore Sturgeon's "Microcosmic God," as the scientist invents a race and becomes a deity, but now is himself transformed by his creations. The new microbodies reconstruct Ulam's body, demonstrating a thorough mastery of their environment. Gradually, they become aware that Ulam is not the universe: "They're trying to understand what space is. That's tough for them. They break distances down into concentrations of chemicals. For them, space is a range of taste intensities.'" The narrator finds Ulam in a bathtub, surrounded by pinkish water that isn't bubble bath: "It's coming from my skin. They're not telling me everything, but I think they're sending out scouts. Hey! Astronauts! Yeah.'" From there it is only a matter of time before the "noocytes" transgress the boundary of the flesh and infect the world. Edward Milligan and his wife, Gail, are the next to dissolve: "They fell quiet and simply reveled in each other's company. What Edward sensed nearby was not the physical form of Gail, not even his own picture of her personality, but something more convincing, with all the grit and detail of reality, but not as he had ever experienced her before... Edward and Gail grew together on the bed, substance passing through clothes, skin joining where they embraced and lips where they touched" (102–3).

Blood Music first seems only another installment of the alien invasion narrative, a paradigm perhaps best represented by *Invasion of the Body Snatchers*. The human is threatened by outside forces that are antithetical to "the human": that is, they are not mammalian; they are "clusters" rather than "individuals"; and they have no emotions (clearly the defining human quality in traditional SF: *never* do humans encounter *more* emotional creatures than themselves). If the only variation here was to substitute an *internal* threat for the more familiar external one, Bear's work would merit attention only as an AIDS-era update of a Cold War theme.[22] What he does, however, is to present the passage beyond the flesh—beyond the human—as a significant and legitimate evolutionary step. The human is not reified as an unchanging and finished product; instead, the work is concerned most exclusively with metamorphosis, transformation, development, and evolution. The characters in *Blood Music* may face the future with trepidation, but they face it.

Like *Videodrome*, *Blood Music* attempts to narrate a passage beyond the body, beyond the flesh, in hyper-bodily terms. Here, for example, is a quintessentially postmodern narration of the disconnection of the body from the world, one reminiscent of Stelarc's audio-body performance pieces:

Truly, you WISH to journey among us, be among us?
— I do.
He stares at the red and green and blue on the VDT. The figures lose all meaning for the moment, as if he is a new born child. Then the screen, the table it rests on, the lavatory curtain beyond and the Walls of the containment chamber are replaced by a silvery null.
Michael Bernard is crossing an interface.
He is encoded.
No longer conscious of all the sensations of being in a body. No more automatic listening and responses to the slide of muscles past one another, the bubbling of fluids in the abdomen, the push and roar of blood and pounding of the heart. He no longer balances, tenses or relaxes. It is like suddenly moving from the city into the heart of a quiet cave. (188)

This is one of the most physical passages in science fiction, reminiscent of Cronenberg not only in its viral intimacy, but also in its simultaneous sense of a transcendence of, and attachment to, the body. It is also emblematic of Delany's paraspace, in the rhetorical heightening which enacts the death of the subject (in science fiction "the subject" is often humanity itself). In its poetic brevity and repetition, the passage even recalls the "death" of HAL in *2001* ("My mind is going. I can feel it").

The noosphere is another dataplane, still another visualization of information circulation and control. On the molecular-cybernetic level, information is again perceptible and malleable. Another scientist is given a tour of a noocyte cluster, a passage through a biological cyberspace:

> [He] stood alone in the noosphere, surrounded by options he hardly knew how to take advantage of. He held his hand out toward the surrounding information. It rippled all around him, waves of light spreading from nadir to zenith. Ranks of information exchanged priorities and his memories stacked up around him like towers of cards, each represented by a line of light.
> The lines cascaded.
> He had been thinking. (204)

The human has become a computer while retaining and even augmenting a biological "nature." The narrative represents, and thus produces, the subject as, indeed, a soft machine. In Shirley's *Eclipse Corona*, languages of electronics and biology collapse onto one another:

> Jerome's chip communicating with his brain via an interface of rhodopsin protein; the ribosomes burrowing neurohumoral transmitters from the brain's blood supply, re-ordering the transmitters so that they carried a programmed pattern of ion releases for transmission across synaptic gaps to the brain's neuronal dendrites; the chip using magnetic resonance holography to collate with brain-stored memories and psychological trends. Declaiming to itself the mythology of the brain; re-enacting on its silicon stage the personal Legends of his subjective world history.[23]

That the brain is like a computer, or even that the brain *is* a computer, finds expression in countless narratives about artificial intelligence, where the brain is figured as only so much programmable software, well-suited for duplication and even simulation. In Rudy Rucker's comic, proto-cyberpunk novel, *Software*, the inventor of the robots ("boppers") is about to receive their "gift of immortality:" "The mind…memories, habits, opinion, skills… is all software. The boppers had extracted Cobb's software and put it in control of this robot body."[24] Rucker, Michael Swanwick, and Bruce Sterling feature the term "wetware" in their writings: "As the cell divided, the bopper software would replicate along with the human DNA wetware. But the final step of building the bopper software into the human wetware had yet to be made."[25] Here is another cyborg term, connoting organicism ("wet") and technology ("ware"). Rucker, a computer programmer as well as a writer, is possessed of an eerie acceptance of the terminal future: "One could legitimately regard the sequence human-bopper-meatbop as a curious but inevitable zigzag in evolution's mighty stream."[26] Rucker's burlesque and distinctly subcultural voice endows these potentially paranoid projections with a kind of loopy charm.

Something intelligent and unsentimental is at work in these novels. Vernor Vinge, the author of "True Names," has praised *Blood Music* for its narration of transcendence. Vinge observed that SF edges up on this moment in which our own models will no longer be applicable, but for obvious reasons this is where the narrative must break down. That Bear actually "illustrates this wonderful/terrifying possibility" of the end of the human, the dissolution of the subject, is remarkable (that diacritical slash in Vinge's writing neatly condenses the ambivalence, multiple meanings, and representational limits of the language of science fiction).[27] Although there is no grand transcendent gesture in Rucker's fictions, these also produce a "remarkable" dissolution of the "natural" human position. "Soon," the narrator of "Blood Music" notes, "there will be no need for centralization."[28]

NOTES

1. Merleau-Ponty, *Phenomenology of Perception*, 106.

2. John Shirley, "Stelarc and the New Reality," *Science Fiction Eye* 1.2 (1987): 59.

3. Kroker and Kroker, 25.

4. Shirley, "Stelarc and the New Reality," 59. Shirley was directed toward Stelarc by people who found his work reminiscent of the "wire dancers" in his novel Eclipse. He astutely notes the "conceptual synchronicity" that cut across media boundaries in the 1980s, "in *Neuromancer*, in *Schismatrix*, in *Eclipse*, in Laurie Anderson and other performance artists, which would seem to indicate a kind of 'steam engine time,' for the recognition of the new, hyper-intimate and all-encompassing phase of man's interaction with technology."

5. Ian Watson, "Introduction to 'Vile Dry Claws of the Toucan," *SEMIOTEXT(E) SF*, ed. Ridy Ricker et al. (New York: Semiotext(e), 1989) 170.

6. Authors Stephen King and Clive Barker have each directed films; Barker, Jeter, and Nancy Collins are extensively involved in comics production and illustration; Neil Gaiman writes comics and novels; and Cronenberg has appeared as an actor in Barker's films.

7. Thanks to Richard Allen for this proposal.

8. William Gibson was also struck by the film's design: "I thought there were germs of stories implicit in the art direction. I always wanted to know more about these guys. Why were they wearing dirty sneakers in this funky spaceship? I think it influenced my prose SF writing because it was the first funked-up dirty kitchen-sink space ship and it made a big impression on me." Sheldon Teitelbaum, "William Gibson's Neuroaliens" *CINEFANTASTIQUE* 22.6 (1922): 12.

9. Vivian Sobchack, "The Virginity of Astronauts: Sex and the Science Fiction Film," *Alien Zone: Cultural Theory and Contemporary Science Fiction Cinema*, ed. Annette Kuhn (London: Verso, 1990) 103 and 108. Klaus Theweleit describes an eerily similar mode operating in writings by Freikorps-men, as women are again banished: "It is men who procreate ... Men create the future." Klaus Theweleit, *Male Fantasies*, trans. S. Conway, E. Carter, and C. Turner (Minneapolis: University of Minnesota, 1978) vol. 2, 88.

10. Of course, in linking the irrational with the position of the feminine, I am describing a dominant construction of femininity which seems to operate beneath these films.

11. Barbara Creed, "Gynesis, Postmodernism, and the Science Fiction Horror Film," *Alien Zone: Cultural Theory and Contemporary Science Fiction Cinema*, ed. Annette Kuhn (New York: Verso, 1990) 215.

12. Sobchack, "The Virginity of Astronauts," 110.

13. Creed, "Gynesis, Postmodernism, and the Science Fiction Horror Film," 216.

14. Noël Carroll, *The Philosophy of Horror, or Paradoxes of the Heart* (New York: Routledge, 1990) 83.

15. Judith Newton, "Femininism and Anxiety in Alien," *Alien Zone: Cultural Theory and Contemporary Science Fiction Cinema*, ed. Annette Kuhn (London: Verso, 1990) 83.

16. Andrew Haase, "Body Shops: The Death of Georges Bataille," *Body Invaders: Panic Sex in America*, ed. Arthur Kroker and Marilouise Kroker (New York: St. Martin's Press, 1987) 140.

17. Manohla Dargis, "Is This the End?" *Village Voice Film Special* 2 June, 1992:16.

18. Michael Crichton's mass-market bestseller *The Terminal Man*, for all its hard-science trappings, is obviously reminiscent not only of Frankenstein (horror or science fiction?) but also of *Psycho* (Hitchcock, 1960): the psychotic's home is distinguished by its notably anachronistic décor, the dénouement occurs in a basement, and, most evidently, the narrative is predicated upon a "split" personality (here split between brain and computer functions).

19. Greg Bear, "Blood Music," *Tangents* (New York: Warner Books, 1989); Greg Bear, *Blood Music* (New York: Ace Books, 1985).

20. John Elkington, *The Gene Factory: Inside the Science and Business of Biotechnology* (New York: Carroll & Graf, 1985) 214. The biochip industry regards genes and computer programs as theoretically identical: both represent encoded information. "One biochip pioneer, Dr. James McAlear of the US firm Gentronix, has suggested that a biochip could be a microprocessor constructed from organic molecules, like the human brain itself." Elkington continues: "He has argued that such molecular computers 'open up the possibility of three-dimensional circuits, increased speeds, reach a million billion elements per cubic centimeter. On this scale, all the memory elements of every computer manufactured to this day could be contained in a cube one centimeter on a side'" (214).

21. Bear, "Blood Music," 13. Most references will be from the novel, but the original novella contains some significant language that was not always retained in the expanded version.

22. The link between these "inhuman" creatures and the American perception of Communists has, of course, been thoroughly analyzed.

23. Shirly, *Eclipse Corona*, 31.

24. Rucker, *Software*, 112.

25. Rudy Rucker, *Wetware* (New York: Avon Books, 1988) 41.

26. Rucker, *Wetware*, 73.

27. Vinge, "True Names," 144.

28. Bear, "Blood Music," 40.

22 Mizuko Ito, "Virtually Embodied: The Reality of Fantasy in a Multi-User Dungeon"

EDITORS' INTRODUCTION

Mizuko Ito's "Virtually Embodied" is an analysis of a specific form of Internet culture, the Multi-User Dungeon (the MUD). The MUD is a text-based virtual world in which "users" act out various combat and role-playing games. The MUD offers itself as the ideal (in all senses of the term) space for the kinds of anthropological, feminist, and sociological analyses Ito works out in her essay, first because the MUD seems to be a space of illusory freedom from the limits and restraints of the physical body and the material world; second, the MUD encourages the user to extend and blur the boundaries of her own subjective sense of self, creating, in turn, new ways of presenting herself to the world.

Ito's analysis draws on Donna Haraway's important "A Cyborg Manifesto" (1985) an essay that, in part, celebrates the blurring of the boundaries between the human and the machine. According to Haraway, the cyborg represents a new kind of subjectivity, a subjectivity arising in the interaction—the interface—between human and machine. Ito analyzes the MUD as a representative location of this kind of interaction and looks to understand how the uncanny pressures of technology transform our notions of the human.

Ito argues that the virtual world is not completely divorced from the materiality of the "real" world, as, she argues, some commentators would suggest. The virtual world, the MUD in particular, is best understood as a confluence of the material and the imaginary, a place, in more concrete terms, where the imaginary is accessible only through the means of (very real) technology, technology that, while increasingly accessible to all, places certain economic restrictions on some. Ito thus emphasizes that an analysis of virtual reality cannot allow the technological means of entering the virtual world to disappear because this technology places very real restrictions on what kinds of virtuality are accessible and by whom. Moreover, Ito's analysis of what she calls the "embodied circumstances of Internet use" (Ito 89) suggests that users do not *enter* virtual worlds free from their cultural contexts and, in turn, cannot *participate* in these worlds without feeling the limitations imposed by these same contexts: the user may feel that the virtual world offers an escape from, for example, the circumstances of gender, race, and class (or even species), but this escape is always more virtual than real. Nevertheless, as Ito is at pains to suggest, the virtual world of the MUD is a staggeringly complex site where social relations, history, and politics, however fantastically realized (one can be a wizard, a peasant, or a warrior, for example), are being "constituted" (335). This is to say that users actively work *against* the sense that what they are participating in is just a game by a "partial bracketing" (336) of "real life" which involves "a stilling of the physical body, and a turning of one's attention to the text on the screen" (336). The ethics of the virtual world, thus, are—like the real player—intimately conjoined to the machine which links the virtual user to the real world where actual ethical pressures apply. What is crucial to note about Ito's analysis of various online cultural practices ("marriage" and "murder") is that the position of the user is one that compels him to maintain constant awareness of his plurality as subject: the virtual world asserts certain ethical pressures—or invites freedom *from* these pressures—but the real world continually asserts its presence claiming partial and, in some instances, total ethical authority.

Ito's article is important for a number of reasons. First, it offers a *practical* analysis of issues that all too often are abstracted into the ether of academic writing. Her interviews with her subjects bring complex issues down to a real—or virtual?—level of immediate clarity. Her interviews, more importantly, indicate that the user of the MUD is a complex subject continually engaged in complex self-analysis. Second, Ito's analysis makes clear—and this is crucial—that the virtual world has far-reaching implications for how our understanding of ethics works—and will continue to work—in an increasingly technologized world. The virtual world, a hybrid reality of machine and humanity, offers itself as a space where the limitations and possibilities of *both* machine and human continually compel us to think through the implications of their joining: Ito's analysis makes clear that ultimately we are all cyborgs at one level or another. Our continual dependence on and enjoyment of the sublime technologies of the computer necessitates, finally, that we subject our cyborg status to a sustained analysis in order that we understand precisely the nature of the relationship between body and machine, between the real and the virtual.

—JB

ISSUES TO CONSIDER WHILE READING

1. Do you think questions of ethics apply in cyberspace? That is, do you think the "action at a distance" of cyberspace is "real"? Is it possible that cyberspace presents a fundamental challenge to conventional understandings of ethics, of ethical action?
2. Do you agree with the idea—offered in concrete terms since McLuhan and Haraway—that our relationship to technology transforms us into cyborgs? The idea would seem to impute a great deal of transformative power to the machine, would seem, in fact, to depend on us actually agreeing to view ourselves as cyborgs. How can we resist—if resistance is needed—the idea of the cyborg?

REFERENCES AND FURTHER READING

Haraway, Donna. "A Cyborg Manifesto: Science, Technology, and Socialist-Feminism in the Late Twentieth-Century." *Simians, Cyborgs, and Women*. New York: Routledge, 1991. 183–202.

Ito, Mizuko. "Virtually Embodied: The Reality of Fantasy in a Multi-User Dungeon." *Internet Culture*. Ed. David Porter. London: Routledge Inc., 1997.

Rheingold, Howard. *The Virtual Community: Homesteading on the Electronic Frontier*. New York: Addison-Wesley, 1993.

Rushkoff, Douglas. *Cyberia: Life in the Trenches of Hyperspace*. San Francisco: Harper, 1994.

Virilio, Paul. *Open Sky*. London: Verso, 1997.

Virtually Embodied: The Reality of Fantasy in a Multi-User Dungeon

MULTI-USER DUNGEONS

MUDs are text-based virtual worlds in which Internet users can create characters in a shared, interactive space. The first MUDs were built in the early 1980s around fantasy role playing themes reminiscent of Dungeons and Dragons games, concretizing heroic fantasy stories into an interactive, social, distributed form. Currently, there are a proliferation of different types of MUDs with different themes, purposes, and operating systems. The MUDs that I study are LPMUDs, which are "traditional" and "mainstream" MUDs in the sense that the are combat and role-playing game oriented, and tend to use medieval images.[1] These combat-oriented MUDs stand in contrast to non-gaming "talker" MUDs or educational or professional MUDs. There are currently hundreds of MUDS running worldwide with tens of thousands of users.

As a player on an LPMUD, what you see on your computer monitor is text that describes the environment and other characters in the environment, as well as the action that you and others perform. Travel through the environment is accomplished with simple commands such as "North," "South," "East," "West," "Up," "Down," "Open Door," etc. Typing the "who" command gives you a list of other participants, and their titles. You can talk to other players in private, or use public chat channels by typing in the desired conversational text. "Soul" commands enable your character to express activity such as smiling, frowning, waving, pouting, blushing, etc.[2]

When first creating a permanent character,[3] you are asked to choose a character name, a gender (usually male or female), and a race (such as elf, dwarf, human, etc.), and begin playing as a first level player. Your character has certain attributes and assets that improve as you accumulate more treasure and kill monsters and other players, and solve quests on the MUD.[4] Gaining experience points, loot, and levels, as well as social recognizability and connections is an extremely time-consuming process, so commitment to a particular character and MUD is solidified as one's character develops. While the first two or three levels might be gained in the first few days of playing, achieving the higher ranks of levels fifteen and above, out of a usual twenty to thirty levels, can take months of very active engagement. A sense of presence and location in the virtual world is strengthened through a progressive customization of social position and material accumulation. Higher-level players construct elaborate residences, costumes, and social cliques. As in any community, in other words, a sense of belonging, identity, and social status requires substantial commitment on the part of its members.

Above players in the MUD hierarchy are wizards, who have gained the highest levels and accomplished all the quests, and are responsible for actually building the MUD environment and administering the MUD. LPMUDs are unabashedly hierarchical. Highest level wizards are often called Gods and, as the name implies, have near absolute power to implement decisions on their MUDs. It is often the idiosyncratic visions of particular wizards that become coded into the MUD environment as concrete, structuring resources. While wizards fully participate in the same social conviviality as the players, their pleasures revolve around authorship and management rather than combat and play. Compared to the gaming structures that govern players, formal parameters for wizard conduct are fewer, being generally limited to some form of peer review and management hierarchy.

While I have not conducted any systematic demographic study of the user base of these worlds,[5] access requires either affiliation with a university; governmental institution; or high-tech corporation or private ownership of a computer with a modem, an Internet account, and a personal phone line. The ability to touch-type is generally a necessity, and if one is to contribute to the actual construction of these worlds, some expertise in computer languages is required. Thus, while the user base of the Internet at large may be increasingly diverse, the *production* of MUD worlds is overwhelmingly dominated by the technologically elite. Running a MUD server will usually require special access to a university or corporate computer system. Thus the fantasy of the MUD environment is a complex interaction between a network of various "real world" material technologies as well as the cultural capital of its users and designers.

MUDder subjectivity is both technologically empowered and highly contingent on local and material conditions. Here, I would like to borrow from Donna Haraway's image of the cyborg that is never whole (Haraway 1991), "compounds of the organic, technical, mythic, textual and political" (Haraway 1992, 42), or what Marilyn Strathern might call circuits of partial connections (Strathern 1991). This cyborg is a techno-organic machine within which the division between the symbolic and the material are blurred in a fluid dance of partially determinate relationality. In what follows, I have attempted some preliminary steps toward such a description of cyborg subjectivity.

FANTASY AND REALITY

In the revised introduction to *Reading the Romance,* Janice Radway describes her focus on the actual reader of romance novels as a response to the dominant analytic tendency for purely text-based studies of literature. In her book, she pursues a reader-based account, based on interviews and questionnaires, of the practices of reading romance novels alongside a textual analysis of their content. In her conclusion, she describes an analytic tension between the textual analysis, which sees the structures of a conservative patriarchy reinscribed in the novels, and the reader-oriented approach, which sees the act of reading as located resistance against oppressive structures of the patriarchal family. Rather than privileging one perspective as more encompassing or correct, she suggests that, by juxtaposing both viewpoints, one can achieve a richer analysis. In Radway's words:

> Had I looked solely at the act of reading as it is understood by the women themselves or, alternately, at the covert significance of the romance's narrative structure, I might have been able to provide one clear-cut, sharp-focus image. In the first case, the image would suggest that the act of romance reading is oppositional because it allows the women to refuse momentarily their self-abnegating social role. In the second, the image would imply that the romance's narrative structure embodies a simple recapitulation and recommendation of patriarchy and its constituent social practices and ideologies. However, by looking at the romance-reading behavior of real women through several lenses, ... this study has consciously chosen to juxtapose multiple views of the complex social interaction between people and texts known as reading (Radway 1991, 210).

Radway takes pains to emphasize the act of romance reading as located opposition, but she also describes a certain ambivalence, suggesting that "when viewed from the vantage point of a feminism that would like to see the women's oppositional impulse lead to real social change, romance reading can also be seen as an activity that could potentially disarm that impulse" (Radway 1991, 213). The analytic tension that Radway describes between the fantasy world of the texts and "real" social contexts is precisely the analytic conundrum that I am attempting to address, and thus provides a prime starting point for my analysis of MUD practices. Like Radway, I have struggled to reconcile the symbolic content of MUDs with the located processes and material conditions of engagement with these worlds, and I find her juxtaposition of fantasy content and readerly practice suggestive. In particular, her attempts to read across the split between text and society, trying to incorporate both into her analysis, are pointers to an analysis that takes both textual and material realities into account. What I find wanting in Radway's treatment, however, is a way of describing the textual worlds of the romance readers as themselves constitutive of "real" social relations, and participation in fantasy as itself a social event to be analyzed in terms not ultimately reducible to a social reality outside the text. While certainly the act of reading involves an isolated person engaging with a text, I am left wondering if these novels, artifacts that migrated translocally, can be seen as comprising an intertextual virtual community. I wonder if one can conceptualize romance reading as a participatory and profoundly social engagement with the broader community, not predicated on physical co-presence. The complex social and economic maneuverings that enable these women to carve out their own time and space to read, and their intense and immersive engagement with these novels, points, for me, to metaphors of travel, extension, and participation rather than merely isolation and escapism.

The MUDs that I study also participate in an analytically perplexing text/society relation in that they involve inert and physically isolated bodies interacting with vividly immersive fantasy texts. The sorts of tropes around violence, conquest, and colonization operating in many of these worlds, as well as in the discourse around the Internet more generally, are rich material for content analyses.[6] But MUDs differ from novels in that they foreground interactivity and travel to alternative domains through an explicitly networked sociality. So instead of focusing on how textual artifacts constructed on the Net circulate through "real" social contexts at large, I would like to examine the inter- and intra-textuality of the Net as itself a social and political context where history, politics, and discourse are being constituted. By insisting on the reality of the virtual I do not intend to reduce social practice to language games, but rather to foreground the inseparability of semiotic and material technologies. In Appadurai's words, I would like to insist on the role of "the imagination as a social practice" (Appadurai 1990, 5), rather than as merely a commentary on, or a reflection of, "real" social relations whose ultimate ground is a singular subjectivity localized by the biological body.

Within MUDs, the tension between textuality and "real" sociality is similar to the relation between the native categories of "real life" and "just a game." Often MUD users (or MUDders, as they call themselves) use the category of "real life" as a denaturalized category, to refer to existence that is not computationally contingent. In other words, as MUDder Howard Hsieh defines it in his MUD dictionary, real life is "the stuff that interrupts your mudding" (Hsieh 1994). The statement, "It's just a game," followed by the injunction, "Get a life," is a claim made occasionally by MUDders in order to chastise somebody who is overly invested in a MUD, or to diffuse the wrath of a colleague who finds their MUD activity reprehensible. So while these categories of "real life" versus "the game" are ubiquitous oppositional categories within MUD conversation, what counts as the real is hotly contested. Both "the game" and "real life" are partial realities that matter (Turkle 1994).

Immersion in the MUD context, whether for purely social or gaming purposes, requires partial bracketing of "real life"—a stilling of the physical body, and a turning of one's attention to the text on the screen. While all MUDders that I have spoken to point to this sensation of immersion, or bracketing, the degree to which and the ways in which the virtual world is considered a reality that matters and that has consequentiality in their lives varies widely. The flavor of the controversy surrounding the reality or real life consequences of MUDs is captured in the following statement in the document of MUD "Frequently Asked Questions," written by Jennifer Smith, and published periodically in the newsgroup rec.games.mud.misc. Question 13 reads,

> Is MUDding a game, or an extension of real life with gamelike qualities? It's up to you. Some jaded cynics like to laugh at idealists who think it's partially for real, but we personally think they're not playing it right. Certainly the hack-'n-slash stuff is only a game, but the social aspects may well be less so (Smith, J. 1994).

So while a vague sentiment exists among MUDders that there are certainly elements of MUDs that are fantastic, silly, trivial, and just for fun, other aspects, most notably the social, have a reality to them that is not easily denied. "Reality," or visible and salient relationships, is a located inflection of consequentiality, not reducible to commonsensical distinctions between fantasy and reality. The case of MUD marriage and romance may furnish some material for illuminating this dynamic.

LIVING THE ROMANCE

Different MUDs institutionalize marriage in different ways, but in the LPMUDs that I study, predictable norms of monogamous heterosexuality are playfully reproduced. One can generally find a chapel, a priest, and heterosexual newlyweds, provided with familiar props such as rings, wedding dresses, and bouquets. Couples might subsequently pool bank accounts, or talk on a special private channel enabled by their wedding rings. They sometimes even adopt other players as their children. It is rare to have things such as sex and pregnancy coded into the MUD system, but Farside, the primary MUD that I play, does have a simple but bizarre concretization of sexuality. To be sexually active, one must first purchase genitalia, after which it will be noted in your character description that you are sexually mature. A simple command will enable you to have sex with another character of the opposite gender, providing that they too are sexually mature, and frequent sexual acts may eventually lead to pregnancy of the female character. After a period of time she will have a child, described by the system as a slave with its mother's attributes and pre-programmed to obey her and follow her around.[7]

These gaming components of marriage and kinship are relatively simple, and are used by MUDders as resources to structure social interaction. While it is possible to "read" this text—this concretization of social relations in virtual environments—as a simple reinscription of hegemonic notions of gender, kinship, and sexuality, to *end* there would be to miss the peculiarities of MUD materiality, reducing MUDs to merely a commentary on or reflection of real life, rather than as an alternative space with its own unique networks of accountability. To read a MUD as a text *about* real life ignores the travel that takes place through the prostheses of networking technologies and the profoundly embodied nature of experience in virtual worlds. One is not "in" real life reading the MUD, one is, as Stone might say, elsewhere (Stone 1991). The elements that I have described are merely the structural elements of the gaming system; the reality, so to speak, of MUDsex and MUDmarriage is a bit more complex.

For example, my partner in real life often eyes me suspiciously as I sit in front of my terminal—"You're not MUDmarried are you?" "Are you having netsex?" We both laugh, and yet I scrupulously avoid MUD romance because of a sort of uncomfortable guilty twinge; clearly a result of his only partially serious questions. My bracketing of the two worlds is apparently incomplete.

By contrast, one of my MUD friends, despite protestations from her jealous real-life mate, is married to a number of different MUDders on different MUDs. Though her real-life mate is also a MUDder, Tenar, or Melissa in real life, refuses to MUDmarry him, or even to have virtual sex with him. She is a powerful and well-liked figure on a number of different MUDs, and no doubt has little trouble in maintaining numerous romantic Internet liaisons. She describes virtual sex as akin to an interactive romance novel. The metaphor is crucial. The fantasy "text" is paramount, the real bodies nonexistent. She explains: "It is how you describe yourself and how you act (on the Internet) that makes up the 'real you.'…real-life persons' looks mean so little to me…." She explains to me, additionally, that the real-life gender of her MUDspouse would be of little concern to her. "You see," she explains to me, "to me there is no real body." What is at stake here is not the immediacy or reality, if you will, of experience on a MUD. Both my friend and I are equally embedded within the MUD environment; we both are effective travelers. What is at stake, rather, is the visibility of certain relationships from our respective points of view. For her, the appeal of the virtual world lies in the relative invisibility of real life consequences and relationships. "Too much reality in virtual reality kills it all."

This is not to say that the virtual body lacks substance. Tenar is a unique, well-developed, and profoundly real partial reembodiment of Melissa. She describes herself as constructing an online description of herself that recalls her svelte eighteen-year-old body. And she tells me, with disarming honesty, "I don't bring Melissa into the game, but I bring Tenar back with me." In other words, Melissa is invisible from the point of view of Tenar, but Melissa sees Tenar as a more positive self image that animates her real life.

Both Melissa and I fully participate in an online social reality that is not reducible to experiences localized by our biological bodies, despite the fact that we have differing senses of accountability in our participation in these partially disjunctive worlds. Farside, for both of us, is a reality that matters. We are each able to occupy unique subject positions within the MUD universe that are related in partial and shifting ways to identities localized by biological bodies.[8]

CRIME, DISCIPLINE, AND ACCOUNTABILITY

In considering the complex couplings and decouplings of MUDders from and between fantasy worlds, virtual identities emerge as extensible and malleable, but also particular, contingent, and embodied through the prosthetic technologies of computers and computer networks. These virtual characters can be seen as alternative reembodiments in a partially disjunctive world, with complex mechanisms for handling connection and accountability that are absolutely contingent on the technosocial apparatuses that produce their effects.

One of the arenas where consequentiality and accountability are hotly contested on combat MUDs is around the social practice of killing other players (pking). Pking is a social practice toward which many MUDders experience a degree of ambivalence. For example, Scott Frank, an anthropologist and a MUDder, sees it as morally reprehensible, and yet, significantly, Frank is a co-founder of a vigilante group on Farside that hunts and kills players that have killed defenseless players, or that have MUD-raped somebody.[9] Other players will use pking only if provoked. For example, they might kill somebody that has stolen some of their loot. Other players enjoy pking "for the thrill of it," and higher level players will often engage in extensive pking battles, as part of the game. Generally, though, it is considered sociopathic behavior for higher level characters to prey on newbies, and many MUDs have rules in place prohibiting this kind of practice.

In a face-to-face interview that I had with Frank, he elucidated the ambivalence around killing and violence, and the complex play between the categories of the virtual ("abstract") and the real.

> MIZUKO ITO: Do you ever have moral positions about violence on MUDs?
>
> SCOTT FRANK: [shakes his head] A MUD is very far removed. Gosh, I sound kind of hypocritical. On the one hand, I'm saying stuff like social skills transfer. But then I'm saying that I don't think violence does. Violence is very, very abstract on a MUD. When you're talking with somebody, and utilizing social skills, you're *really* doing it. When you're fighting a monster, you're not *actually* going out and hitting anything. There are different layers of reality. You're really talking to people. You're not *really* fighting something.
>
> MI: How about pking?
>
> SF: Pking...[shakes head] See, I don't get pking. It's never, ever appealed to me. The thought of ending somebody's...I mean, somebody who's *real*, somebody who has their own thoughts. Of ending that person's extension on a MUD. It's just...It's almost like killing to me I guess. I just don't get it.
>
> MI: So that feels very different to you from killing monsters.
>
> SF: A monster is nothing. A monster is an extension of the game. It's not *real*. A person's *real*.

The "reality" of violence on MUDs is carefully qualified; violent fantasy is neither the same as "real life" violence nor reducible to "just a game." While the non-computational is elided within the category of the real, some of the terms of "real" consequentiality are located squarely within the gaming context. Virtual death only has structural consequences of virtual bodies, and yet it is "real" or more consequential than monster killing because of an identification with biologically based subjectivity. The "reality" of the fantasy character, the extension of MUDder subjectivity, is a result of both intratextual and extratextual connections. It can not be reduced to either. The explicit and implicit rules of MUD practice are based on an acknowledgment of both kinds of relationships.

In terms of machine connectivity, access to the MUD server is enabled by the Internet, and for Farside, as in most combat MUDs, access is open for anyone who has telnet capabilities on the Net and the semiotic technologies necessary for discursive engagement with these worlds. With the right kind of Internet access, one can open multiple connections either to the same MUD or to a number of different MUDs at the same time. There is generally little restriction on the numbers of characters that one can create or the numbers of MUDs that one can be logged on to concurrently. What is restricted, however, is the number of characters that one can run concurrently on a particular combat MUD. Otherwise, a number of virtual characters connected with a particular biological body could collectively gain unfair advantage, ganging together to attack a monster or another player. Dispensable adjunct characters could die sacrificial deaths in order to consolidate experience points and treasure in a single primary character, creating a monstrous collective organism that defies socially acceptable subject categories. In other words, most combat MUDs require multiple characters of a single physically located self to be either spatially or temporally distanced from each other.

While most players abide by this rule, in the case of the occasional rule transgression, virtual bodies are difficult to discipline. The technical capability for multiple self-proliferation sits in uneasy tension with the social more of one body per person. Pakka, the sheriff of Farside, explained to me the difficulties he has had in disciplining characters on MUDs:

> Multiple characters are extremely hard to catch. Something has to set off in your mind—this person, these two are always on together. They call in from the same location. They always run together. You've got to notice that.

Once Pakka catches somebody breaking the rules, punishment is also difficult to enforce. He can banish and delete a particular character on a MUD, but nothing prevents the repeated creation of newbie (new) characters that can hurl a continuous barrage of abuse at the sheriff. For repeat offenders, the entire site has to be banned, which means anyone logging in from that site can no longer get on. This slows but does not stop a "criminal" who has access to multiple computers at a computer lab. In other words, the freedom of travel enabled by multiple concurrent connections makes it extremely difficult to fix a singular subject position to a particular virtual body. The sheriff can strip a character of all possessions and physical strength, but the voice of an adept cybernaut inhabiting an anonymous, unmarked body proves nearly impossible to stifle.

The rule on multiple synchronous characters on a single MUD does not, however, prohibit a range of other intriguing possibilities around multiple virtual identities. Different MUDs provide different pleasures, fantasies, capabilities, and features, and different social positions within MUDs provide opportunities for experiencing different social locations. Some MUDders have confided in me the pleasures and difficulties of gender swapping, and occasionally a story circulates about a chagrined MUDder's discovery of the unexpected biological gender of a MUD intimate. Wizards, who have to act as responsible administrators or coders on their home MUDs, often create player characters on other MUDs to revisit the pleasures of combat and play. Sometimes they will log onto their home MUD just to check out the environment and social scene from the point of view of a low-level player. Generic newbie or guest characters also provide opportunities for anonymous lurking and freedom from a socially marked, recognizable character. Anonymity is one of many possible subject positions on MUDs, and is usually the exception rather than the rule.

MUDder subjectivity, then, is both enabled and policed by sociotechnical structures of extension and control that are distributed through global networks. They are neither disconnected from nor reducible to subjectivity localized by the biological body in a fixed locale, but are concretely reembodied through computational prostheses.

MACHINE EMBODIMENT

In his discussion of computers and digitality, Brian Cantwell Smith argues for a deconstruction of the conceptual boundary between the formal realm of "pure symbols" and the messy world of objects and referents:

> Inside is the pure, clear realm of symbols, abstract, classified, discretely categorized, mathematically modeled. The "semantic" realm, on the contrary, is assumed to be outside—out in the messy "real world."

Instead, Smith insists that:

> [C]omputers participate in their subject matters: they muck around in, create and destroy, change and constitute, to say nothing of represent and reason and store information about, a hundred realms—new realms, some of them, that owe their existence to the very computers that interact with them.

A good example is when you scratch a CD: "a fingernail can leave a wake of devastation hundreds of bits wide," triggering complex recovery schemes to prop up the "digital abstraction" (Smith 1994). The questions that I have been asking in this paper parallel Smith's inquiry in some crucial ways. Where Smith questions whether computer functions are merely symbolic, I question whether online worlds are merely virtual. Or more specifically, I might suggest an understanding of the virtual as the computationally embodied, rather than as the dematerialized.

The questions of machine bodies, and their participation in the construction of online worlds, returns us to the issue of the boundary between the physical and the nonphysical in computers and computer networks. From the point of view of the human user, online worlds provide opportunities for creative bodily forgetting, where the user is plunged into a sort of magical realm of the digital. The machine, in this scenario, is a faithful extension of user agency, its bodily processes rendered invisible to maintain an ideally seamless fantasy abstraction. In the discourses around the Internet, machine bodies are similarly rendered homogeneous and invisible, silent and faithful enactors of a global web of seamless information. What this picture leaves out, and what social and cultural studies of science and technology draw attention to, are heterogeneities, the concreteness, and the local particularities—in short, the materiality—of information.

One of the consequences of online ethnography is that these heterogeneous materialities and localities are excruciatingly difficult to see, since the technically naive ethnographer participates in the same systems of erasure; the guts of my own computer, and the computer that I bounce across to get to Farside, not to mention the physical bodies of other Farsidians, are systematically unavailable to me. And beyond these absences lie the many agents and agencies implicated in the production and maintenance of computers and computer networks—multinational corporations, microelectronics factory workers, and military funding agencies, to name a few. My attempt, here, is to take a few steps toward making some of these absences at least partially visible from the point of view of, and in the terms of, the actual online worlds. This is not to say that these systems of erasure are not powerful and enabling; they are the very basis of our successful couplings with prosthetic devices. What I am suggesting, however, is that while we participate in these empowering worlds, we should also be in some way accountable, or at the very least, appreciative, of the webs of invisible agencies that enable our extensions (Suchman 1994).

Returning to Haraway and Strathern's circuits of partial connections, the figure of the cyborg suggests translocal networks and relations that are never disembodied or deterritorialized into a homogenized global imagination. Thus, for example, unified communities are not imagined through particular mass media texts, but rather lived through negotiating particular locations and relationships within texts that migrate through particular sociotechnical apparatuses. So the seeming immutability and imaginary homogeneity of a particular text is constantly being subverted by the selective positionings of heterogeneous agents that co-construct meaning with the structuring resources of the text. Close attention to technological contingencies will help counteract the tendency to see global informational networks as an unimpeded free flow of information and cultural capital in a purely symbolic realm.

In closing, I would like to underscore the very local computational contingencies that qualify the freedom of MUDder travel with a sad epilogue to my story of Farside. During the period of my engagement with Farside it has shifted locations to a number of different machines around the world. The files that contain all the information about the MUD operating system, the world, and every character reside in the server unless there are backups on other machines, In August, 1994, the machine that Farside was living in experienced a system failure, and all player files and interface elements were lost. There were no backups, and shortly thereafter the university banned MUDs. Farsidians immigrated en masse to, among other MUDs, Kerovnia, a MUD that many Farsidians also had characters on. Marius, the administrator of Farside, would post occasional notes on Kerovnia as to his efforts at reconstructing files, or trying to find a new site. Farsidians waited in helpless distress for some good news. I pined at the loss of my fieldsite, not to mention the character that, for me, was quite an accomplished ninth level. I created a newbie character on Kerovnia, and began conducting interviews with former Farsidians there, happy to see old friends using the same names on a MUD that had many shared elements with Farside.

A few months thereafter, I received a letter from Marius, forwarded through many email boxes around the world that he had tried his best, but had to conclude that all was lost for Farside. I have not had a chance to discuss with many fellow Farsidians about the loss, so I can only speculate as to their reactions. I do recall, however, a number of years ago, when I was a newbie on Farside, there was a MUD called Sushi that was often used as an alternate by Farsidians. Some months later, Sushi, for reasons unknown to me, was shut down. There was a sudden influx of new characters on Farside with the tag "Sushiite" appended to their titles. For a few months, they comprised a highly visible enclave within the Farside social and political scene, a displaced but proud sub-community.

Perhaps Farsidians will similarly rally around an imagined community in a displaced locale, or perhaps they will quietly disperse and assimilate to other worlds, virtual or otherwise. Or perhaps they will reconstruct their world out of fragmentary code and collective memory. Regardless of the outcome, it is clear that Farsidian identity is located not only in the fantasy text, but in the machine architectures and social relations that animated that text. Just as mass media artifacts operate as material structures that enable the articulation of certain subject positions, global networks are concrete sedimentations of particular machines and machine sociality.

Certainly, bits of code mobilized by silicon chips and transported through fiber optics and telephone lines do not have the same materiality as flesh and blood, hunger, and organic pain. And my parallels between diasporic identity politics and Farsidian displacement are not meant as a trivialization of the more weighty consequentiality of organically embodied experience. And yet, as I sit, tightly coupled to my computer keyboard, embedded in semiotic meanderings through my computer monitor, I question any clean separation between human and machine, the social and the technological, the real and the textual. Current trends in technology development and international politics suggest that, increasingly, machine bodies will be the zones of contestation for transnational power brokering. It is hardly the moment to ignore either the materiality or consequentiality of the virtual imagination.

NOTES

1. "LP" are the initials of the developer of this particular MUD operating system.

2. A typical MUD environment and encounter might appear as follows:

    You are near the center of the little village of Dambarsham. To the north, along Kite Row, you can hear laughter and merry-making. East the road continues into the center of Dambarsham. A street named Wildman's Walk is south, from which you can hear a loud "clanking" noise. You quickly come to the conclusion that this is not a quiet little country village. The only peace is to the west, where the road starts to make its way out of Dambarsham. There are four obvious exits: west, north, south, and east.

    -Duke Adinar appears

    -Duke Adinar waves

    >wave

    -You wave

    >say hi Ad

    -You say "hi Ad"

    -Duke Adinar grins mischievously

3. I am using the term "character" here to describe what has elsewhere been called an "avatar" or an "online persona." I use it as an ironic play on mass media and fantasy characters. I will be using "biological" body in a similarly ironic way to describe the non-computational side of MUDder identifications.

4. By typing "score" or "inventory" you can see your current attributes and possessions. For example:

>score

You are Mimi the lowrank ranger (nice).

You have 5276 experience points, 3405 gold coins, 74 hit points (74).

66 spell points.

Wimpy mode.

Age: 13 hours 32 minutes 52 seconds.

Dexterity: 3 Strength: 4 Constitution: 4

Intelligence: 3 Power: 4 Agility: 4

As of now you are level 3.

>inventory

You are carrying:

Cola bottle.

Cloak.

A Hawk (perched on shoulder).

A hawk's quicktyper.

A White Sash (worn).

The Hitch-hikers Guide to the Galaxy.

Mimi's house key.

Permanent invitation to visit Joichi's house.

5. In his 1993 book, Howard Rheingold cites two estimates of the MUD user base in 1992: Richard Bartle, designer of the first MUD, estimates 100,000 users past and present. Pavel Curtis, MUD developer at Xerox PARC, estimates 20,000 active MUDders (Rheingold 1993, 146).

6. See Grey and Driscoll 1992, Stone 1990.

7. Male characters have been known to have sex changes in order to acquire their own slaves.

8. For a discussion of further cases of "constructions and reconstructions of the self" in MUDs, see Turkle 1994.

9. On Farside the command "fuck [character name]" results in an online description of sexual engagement with the person in question. MUDrape in this context refers to an unwanted sexual liaison of this sort, or to a range of more idiosyncratic unsolicited sexual advances.

REFERENCES

Appadurai, Arjun. "Disjuncture and Difference in the Global Culture Economy." *Public Culture* 2.2 (1990): 1–24.

Bambara, Toni Cade. "Reading the Signs, Empowering the Eye: *Daughters of the Dust* and the Black Independent Cinema Movement." *Black American Cinema*. Ed. Manthia Diawara. New York: Routledge, 1993. 118–44.

Bijker, Wiebe E., and John Law, eds. *Shaping Technology/Building Society: Studies in Sociotechnical Change*. 1994.

Bijker, Wiebe E., Thomas P. Hughes, and Trevor Pinch, eds. *The Social Construction of Technological Systems: New Directions in the Sociology and History of Technology*. Cambridge: MIT Press, 1987.

Bobo, Jacqueline. "Reading Through the Text: The Black Woman as Audience." *Black American Cinema*. Ed. Manthia Diawara. New York: Routledge, 1993. 272–287.

Clarke, Adele, and Joan Fujimura, eds. *The Right Tools for the Job: At Work in the Twentieth-Century Life Sciences*. Princeton: Princeton University Press, 1992.

Downey, Gary Lee, Joseph Dumit, and Sarah Williams. "Granting Membership to the Cyborg Image." *The Cyborg Handbook*. Ed. Chris Hables Gray, Heidi Figueroa-Sarriera, and Steven Mentor. New York: Routledge, 1996.

Escobar, Arturo. "Welcome to Cyberia: Notes on the Anthropology of Cyberstructure." *Current Anthropology* 35.3 (1994): 211–32.

Fisher, Scott. "Telepresence: Context and Sense-ability in Digital Worlds." *TechnoCulture Matrix*. Ed. Toshiharu Ito. Tokyo: NTT Publishing Co., 1994. 86–7.

Fujimura, Joan. "On Methods, Ontologies, and Representations in the Sociology of Science: Where Do We Stand?" *Social Organization and Social Progress: Essays in Honor of Anselm Strauss*. Ed. David Maines. New York: Aldine de Gruyter, 1991. 207–48.

Grey, Chris, and Mark Driscoll. "What's Real About Virtual Reality?" *Visual Anthropology Review* 8 (Fall 1992): 39–49.

Gupta, Akhil. "Blurred Boundaries: The Discourse of Corruption, the Culture of Politics, and the Imagined State." *American Ethnologist* 22.2 (1995): 375–402.

Haraway, Donna. "A Cyborg Manifesto: Science, Technology, and Socialist-Feminism in the Late Twentieth Century." 1985. *Simians, Cyborgs, and Women*. New York: Routledge, 1991.127–48.

---. "Situated Knowledges: The Science Question in Feminism and the Privilege of Partial Perspective." 1986. *Simians, Cyborgs, and Women*. New York: Routledge, 1991. 183–202.

Hayles, Katherine. "The Materiality of Informatics." *Configurations* 1 (1992): 147–70.

Helmreich, Stefan. "Anthropology Inside and Outside the Looking-Glass Worlds of Artificial Life." Presented at the workshop Biology, Computers, and Society: At the Intersection of the "Real" and the "Virtual," Stanford University, June 2–4, 1995.

Hess, David. "Introduction: The New Ethnography and the Anthropology of Science and Technology." *Knowledge and Society* 9 (1992): 1–26.

Hsieh, Howard. "Mudders Dictionary." 18 Sept. 1994 <http://rec.games.mud.misc>.

Jasanoff, Shelia, Gerald E. Markle, James C. Petersen, and Trevor Pinch, eds. *Handbook of Science and Technology Studies*. Thousand Oaks: Sage, 1995.

Lynch, Michael, and Steve Woolgar, eds. *Representation in Scientific Practice.* Cambridge: MIT Press, 1988.

Mankekar, Purnima. "National Texts and Gendered Lives: An Ethnography of Television Viewers in a North Indian City." *American Ethnologist* 10.3 (1993): 543–63.

Mickering, Andrew, ed. *Science as Practice and Culture.* Chicago: University of Chicago Press, 1992.

Radway, Janice A. *Reading the Romance: Women, Patriarchy, and Popular Literature.* 1984. Chapel Hill: University of North Carolina Press, 1991.

Rheingold, Howard. *The Virtual Community: Homesteading on the Electronic Frontier.* New York: Addison-Wesley, 1993.

Rushkoff, Douglas. *Cyberia: Life in the Trenches of Hyperspace.* San Francisco: Harper San Francisco, 1994.

Smith, Brian Cantwell. "Coming Apart at the Seams: the Role of Computation in a Successor Metaphysics." Presented at the workshop Biology, Computers, and Society: At the Intersection of the "Real" and the "Virtual," Stanford University, June 2-4, 1994.

Smith, Jennifer. "MUD Frequently Asked Questions." 1 June 1994 <http://rec.games.mud.misc>.

Stone, Allucquere Rosanne. "Will the Real Body Please Stand Up?: Boundary Stories about Virtual Cultures." *Cyberspace: The First Steps.* Ed. Michael Benedikt. Cambridge: MIT Press, 1992. 81–118.

Stenger, Nicole. "Mind Is a Leaking Rainbow." *Cyberspace: The First Steps.* Ed. Michael Benedikt. Cambridge: MIT Press, 1992. 49–58.

Strathern, Marilyn. *Partial Connections.* Savage, Maryland: Rowman and Littlefield, 1991.

Suchman, Lucy. "Working Relations of Technology Production and Use." *Computer Supported Cooperative Work* 2 (1994): 21–39.

Tomas, David. "Old Rituals for New Space: *Rites de Passage* and William Gibson's Cultural Model of Cyberspace." *Cyberspace: The First Steps.* Ed. Michael Benedikt. Cambridge: MIT Press, 1992. 31–48.

Traweek, Sharon. "An Introduction to Cultural and Social Studies of Sciences and Technologies." *Culture, Medicine, and Psychiatry* 17 (1993): 3–25.

Turkle, Sherry. "Constructions and Reconstructions of Self in Virtual Reality: Playing in the MUDs." *Mind, Culture, and Activity* 1.3 (1994): 158–67.

Woolley, Benjamin. *Virtual Worlds: A Journey in Hype and Hyperreality.* Cambridge: Blackwell, 1992.

Glossary

Agency: A term used to discuss the degree to which human subjects or groups can act and exert their will self-consciously to direct social practices and intervene effectively in the course of history. Views of agency vary widely. Generally, liberal humanism sees subjects as largely unified and self-determining, and therefore having considerable power in shaping their own lives as well as a more general social destiny. Anti-humanist, Marxist, and most poststructuralist arguments lead to a near-total denial of agency, since power has little or no source in individual or group decisions. Stuart Hall argues that the human agent is fragmented and decentred, "subjected" by power yet able to act against those powers.

Appropriation: In popular culture, the term refers to the process by which new, usually anti-hegemonic cultural forms (e.g., heavy metal, punk, rap, Afro-American urban ghetto styles in fashion) are incorporated and commodified by the culture industry. This is often read as an indicator of the ability of late capitalism to absorb dissent into itself and turn it around for a profit; however, it is important to remember that resistance continues to circulate and change in form, even as its products are co-opted by a dominant culture.

Capitalism: The world's current dominant economic system, wherein the means of creating and distributing wealth lies within the control of individuals and corporations, rather than within the state or other collective agencies. Within capitalism private enterprise's central aim is to produce profit and the value of goods and labour is determined not by a standard of usefulness or social significance, but by what the market will bear. Central to capitalist ideology and operating within it at the level of the given or "common sense" are beliefs in private property, individual freedom, and unending economic growth.

Code (and Encoding, Decoding): The term "code" in Cultural Studies is derived mainly from Structuralism and Semiotics, where it is argued that all communication systems, from simple gestures to complex literary or filmic narratives, can be understood as operating according to a system of rules and conventions (codes) that are analogous to the primary system of language. Thus, Roland Barthes, in *Image-Music-Text* uses this method to analyze, among other things, music, images, narrative, and fashion. In his analysis of the codes of the visual sign in advertising, for instance, he identifies three messages: the literal message given by the objects in the ad, which is noncoded, the symbolic message, which creates coded ideological and cultural meanings, and the linguistic, made up of the caption and printed text, also coded. Anthropologist Claude Lévi-Strauss used a similar method to analyze myth as encoded in a way that supports and validates the ideological tradition and preferred values of a particular community. Stuart Hall in "Encoding, Decoding" discusses encoding and decoding at the points of production and reception of the television discourse, arguing that they are not symmetrical, and offers a model of the process that argues that readers may, but need not necessarily decode messages according to the preferences encoded in them. In his highly influential essay, he argues that we can also decode in negotiated or oppositional ways.

Colonialism: A term generally used to describe literally the historical and physical process whereby dominant nations or groups have subjugated and controlled less powerful ones. It has also been used metaphorically, as when influential German filmmaker Wim Wenders (*Wings of Desire, The American Friend*) argues that the United States has "colonized the consciousnesses" of people around the world. This latter usage is more generally described as a kind of nonterritorial imperialism. See **Postcolonialism** below.

Commodification: The transformation of any cultural product, action (including labour itself), object, or idea from its use value to its exchange value; that is, into something that can be bought or sold. The culture industry, it is often argued, commodifies a wide variety of cultural forms, with a corresponding loss of authenticity and implicit value.

Commodities: In Marx's *Capital*, capitalism demands the production of an increasing number of commodities, both objects and services, for consumption or exchange by persons other than their producers. "Use value," typically the basis of pre-19th century economic systems where goods were usually exchanged for other goods, is replaced in later capitalism by "exchange value" expressed in monetary terms. This results in a shift to a consumer culture where an almost magical value, Marx's "commodity fetishism," is attributed to objects based not on the labour and material that produced them but on the price that they can command. Raymond Williams in "Advertising: the Magic System" extends Marx's analysis of commodity fetishism to include a consideration of the process whereby commodities acquire magical properties.

Consumerism: While theoretical and analytical work on popular culture in the age of modernism focused largely on cultural products and production, much of such work in the age of postmodernism is concerned with consumption, as demonstrated by Jean Baudrillard in his seminal 1970 work, *La Societé de Consommation*. Emblematized in the "hyperreality" of the shopping mall is the implicit belief that the acquisition of commodities is the best way to address the needs and wants of individuals. These acts of consumption, not only shopping but the consumption of fashion, music, media productions, and even "places," are also seen by Dick Hebdige and others as playing a major role in the formation of personal, gender, and group identities.

Counterculture: Generally, since the 1960s, all groups that oppose the dominant existing social and political order and embrace alternative practices or ways of organizing society. These movements, often now referred to as social movements, can be so diverse as to include hippies; antiglobalization environmentalists; feminist, gay and lesbian, and civil rights groups; anti-war activists; punk rockers; or any group that in one way or another challenges 'authority' and 'common sense' ideology with the intent to change society.

Cultural imperialism: While imperialism *per se* involves the physical conquest and use of the resources of one nation by another, as in the cases of the British and the Roman Empires, cultural imperialism can be seen as an ideological process of infiltration founded on the imperial nation's certainty of its cultural and political superiority at the expense of indigenous cultures. Recent globalization theorists have challenged the notion of cultural imperialism, arguing that the process of global production and consumption is neither simple nor passive.

Cultural Studies: A term referring to both a broad set of subjects for study and a broad set of methodologies for the study of those subjects. Thus, Cultural Studies turns its attention to "texts" including books, magazines, films, television shows, music, advertising, malls, urban design, and automobiles; to "ways of life" or practices, including shopping, fashion, eating, drinking; and to more abstract structures, such as language, beliefs, "common sense" ideologies, and the institutions that surround them. As a set of methodologies, Cultural Studies works across a wide range of disciplines, often combining analytical strategies and methods from literary and film studies, linguistics, anthropology, discourse analysis, sociology, communications, reception and audience studies, demographics, and historical research.

Diegetic, Non-diegetic: Derived from the Greek term for narrative, diegetic elements in visual media are those which originate in the narrative, including dialogue, sound effects understood to be coming from the actions within the narrative, and music whose source is within the narrative. Non-diegetic elements are those which do not originate in the narrative, such as soundtrack music and credits.

Discourse: The term discourse originated in linguistics and literary analysis, but largely through the work of Michel Foucault it has come to be broadly used in Cultural Studies to describe the ways the conventions and habitual usages of written and oral language work with specific structures and institutions to shape social reality at a given historical moment. Particular discursive formations and practices are associated with distinct areas of knowledge and institutions (e.g., science, law, information technology, skateboarding); with intellectual modes (poststructuralism, psychoanalysis); fields of study (film, economics, philosophy); or social groups or occasions (the discourse of politicians, prisoners, funerals, sports broadcasts). Discursive formations are seen to reinforce established subjectivities, and are themselves reinforced by such institutions as law, the media, and education.

Frankfurt School: A group of innovative and highly influential social and cultural theorists who established the Institute for Social Research at the University of Frankfurt in 1923, relocated to New York with the rise of Nazism in the 1930s, and returned to Frankfurt in 1950. Their aim was to set out a "critical theory" of society, although the individual members of the group agreed on no fixed set of ideas and often disagreed with one another. Their work is heavily indebted to, although not entirely wed to, Marxist theory and offers analyses of popular culture that emphasize its means of production and its implicit ideological constraints. Members of the group included Theodor Adorno, Max Horkheimer, Herbert Marcuse, and Erich Fromm. Walter Benjamin also contributed to the Institute's *Journal for Social Research*. One of the group's definitive works, Adorno and Horkheimer's *The Dialectic of Enlightenment* (1947), from which this anthology's "The Culture Industry: Enlightenment as Mass Deception" is taken, sees enlightenment, rationalism, and humanism as complicit with totalitarianism and the controlled societies of late capitalism.

Genre: A type of cultural production characterized by a recognizable set of conventions or practices relating to characters, narratives, and systems of representation. In cultural studies, the term is most often used in analyses of popular genres, such as the western, the musical, the romance, science or detective fiction, soap operas, or news broadcasts, and treats these as coded systems whose structures and practices can be decoded in the same ways as other verbal and visual products of culture. Such a strategy has been used to counter the cultural elitism that sets such works apart from the products of so-called "high" culture and to enter into the debate over the value of various forms of cultural production. The notion of a genre as a pure or discrete form has been challenged by Jacques Derrida, who in "The Law of Genre" argues that while the idea genre functions as a norm to repel impurities, there is also a corresponding law of impurity or "principle of contamination." In *Acts of Literature*, Derrida further argues that "Every text participates in one of several genres, there is no genreless text," which suggests both that all texts function within genres and that genres cannot be absolutely distinguished from one another. Thus, we should consider intertextual relations within and among genres, and mixed modes rather than pure ones. A great deal of contemporary film, television programs, and fiction seems to work in this way, including such works as Ridley Scott's film *Bladerunner* (science fiction, hard-boiled detective fiction, the western, quest romance) and TV's *The Sopranos* (gangster movies, soap opera, epic).

Globalization: Originating in the 1980s in relation to the rise of international companies and the growth of their markets in late 20th century capitalism, seen as a result of economic, political, and technological changes, this contested term has acquired broad cultural currency. On one hand, globalization is seen as having the potential to improve conditions for the world's poorest regions and to create a more unified global society. More commonly, however, globalization is seen as reinforcing hegemony by providing already dominant powers with cheap labour and raw materials mostly in Third World countries while also opening new markets for multinational companies with an associated rise in cultural imperialism and destruction of indigenous cultures in the developing countries. Other positions on globalization challenge the comprehensiveness of the process and consider the relation between the local and global in producing new hybrid cultures.

Habitus: A concept developed by Marcel Mauss and significantly elaborated by Pierre Bourdieu, habitus describes the way in which a variety of environments (home, school, other social institutions) are internalized by individuals to form dispositions toward particular embodied orientations and behaviours affecting activities, including eating, sleeping, walking, having sex, giving birth, and so on. These "body techniques" are products of particular social contexts and are culturally and historically specific, evolving from a family, ethnic, class, and gender habitus that through time structures and restructures the individual. In Bourdieu's account, the habitus is not a fixed or fully determined system but, rather, a basis for endless but limited improvisation, which he compares to the mastery of an instrument in jazz or of the rules of a sport that enable individuals to improvise in response to immediate circumstances.

Hegemony: From the Greek term for "rule" or "leadership," the term enters Cultural Studies through the work of Italian communist philosopher Antonio Gramsci (1891–1937) to denote the ways in which dominant ideologies and groups exercise control over weaker ones in capitalist society. Such dominance is achieved not by force but by gaining consent in such a way that the unequal distribution of power seems legitimate and natural, simply the way things are, ideology generally operating below the level of consciousness. As Terry Eagleton argues, hegemony thus "includes ideology, but is not reducible to it." Hegemony is never total and never entirely stable; rather, it is a shifting equilibrium, a provisional and usually unconscious alliance of the forces in dominance at a particular moment, operating in constant struggle or negotiation with emerging oppositional ideas and subordinate groups. Underlying any understanding of how hegemony operates is Marx's contention in *The Communist Manifesto* that "the ideas of the ruling class are in every epoch the ruling ideas" and, thus, the class that controls material production will also control the realm of ideas and mental production, including culture itself.

Identity: Generally taken to be an individual's unique personality or inner self, the term identity is a concept in crisis in Cultural Studies for several reasons. First, individual identity, once seen as fixed and coherent, has been displaced by doubt and uncertainty as we all assume various identities in response to changing situations and relationships. Second, recent geopolitical events in Eastern Europe and elsewhere have undermined the stability of received identities just as they redrew political and geographic boundaries, and third, globalization has altered individuals' sense of identity as pre- and postmodern societies hybridize resulting in more fluid, less fixed identities. Furthermore, Marxist and psychoanalytical theories see identity as constructed by largely unconscious processes of interpellation and theories of performativity challenge the rigidity of essentialist notions of gender, ethnicity, race, and sexuality.

Identity politics: The strategic assertion of unity among groups defined by such characteristics as race, culture, ethnicity, or sexuality in order to achieve a higher degree of agency. Practitioners of identity politics challenge prevailing power structures by demanding recognition and the extension of majority rights to minority groups.

Ideology: A crucial term whose meaning in Cultural Studies has generated at least as much debate as the meaning of culture itself. In its most general sense, it refers to a set of values and beliefs common to a given society. Typically, these beliefs and values are made to seem natural, common sensical, even universally true, even though they are the products of the particular history or collective activity of that society and may seem arbitrary or false to those who subscribe to a different or competing ideology. (This sense is well expressed in the paradigm that C.J. Geertz offers in his 1973 *The Interpretation of Cultures:* "I have a social philosophy, you have political opinions, he has an ideology.") Ideology, thus, refers to the social and political processes that mask the origins of the beliefs and values that form what Johanna Smith has called "the unexamined ground of our experience." In North American society, for instance, capitalism is generally made to seem the only rational system of economic organization and is seen as historically inevitable. While this is false, ideology works to make such beliefs seem like common sense. American Marxist critic Fredric Jameson sees all thought as ideological and argues that recognition of that central fact, that is, bringing ideology from the unconscious to the conscious level, will enable us to see through and even transcend ideology.

Ideological state apparatuses (ISAs): One of a pair of terms coined by French Marxist Louis Althusser to describe how social structures/organizations ensure that subjects take up the ideology of the state or ruling class. ISAs work indirectly (i.e., through ideology, rather than direct coercion) while repressive state apparatuses (RSAs), particularly the police or the military, explicitly enforce the laws of a culture. ISAs work via interpellation to reinforce hegemonic roles.

Interpellation: In Louis Althusser's theory of ideology, the process that produces subjects in a way that leads them to assume an identity in terms of the dominant ideology of their society or nation. In Althusser's classic illustration of this process, a policeman calls out "'Hey, you there!' One individual (nine times out of 10 the right one) turns round, believing/suspecting/knowing that it is for him." In recognizing the call, the individual is constituted as a particular kind of subject, and subjectivity itself is seen to be always and already a product of ideology. Subsequent work by Stuart Hall and others has demonstrated that the success of interpellation depends on the degree to which individuals recognize and identify with the roles assigned to them by the dominant culture/ideology.

Mass culture: The form of culture available since the advent of mass production and mass distribution, especially those things produced for profit and aimed at a large and diverse audience. Early studies of mass culture, typified by Adorno and Horkheimer's essay in this volume, were almost always critical of mass culture's products, contrasting them with both "high" or "elite" culture (e.g., classical music and literature) and "authentic" folk culture. Currently, some critics argue that mass culture is breaking down as a result of identity politics, market segmentation, and the growing availability of technologies, such as desktop publishing, the Internet, and digital video that allow for the nonindustrial production and dissemination of cultural products.

Media convergence: The horizontal integration of more recent media (e.g., cable and the Internet) with older media forms (e.g., radio, television, film, newspapers, books, magazines) by large corporations (e.g., AOL-Time-Warner), in order to realize greater profits through the pooling of resources.

Multiculturalism: A concept from sociopolitical thought that describes the coexistence of many different cultures or ethnicities in one country. Often, a government policy or national act of definition, as in Canada, the claim of multiculturalism suggests that the nation is characterized by cultural freedom and tolerance of difference. Critics of such claims argue that the policy glosses over real imbalances of power among ethnic groups in the face of the continuing centrality of white ethnic groups, or that the claim that contemporary cultures can be clearly differentiated is itself false since all cultures are already hybrid.

Multinational (corporation): Any firm that extends beyond a single nation's boundaries by operating branches in at least several countries simultaneously.

Myth(ology): In cultural theory, a term borrowed from literary and anthropological studies and elaborated by structural anthropologist Claude Lévi Strauss and semiotician and literary critic Roland Barthes. For Lévi Strauss, myths express universal themes in narratives that follow highly common structures. He concluded that myths were coded according to universal human mental patterns and addressed common human needs. For Barthes, the term is virtually synonymous with ideology and describes how sign systems work to express and justify the dominant beliefs and values of a given society at a given time. Many cultural critics, following Barthes, take as their task the disembedding of these myths to reveal the class and cultural attitudes that shape daily life and that normally operate below the level of consciousness. See also **Interpellation** and **Habitus**.

Nation/Nationalism: As a form of what Benedict Anderson calls an "imagined community" (*Imagined Communities: Reflections on The Origin and Spread of Nationalism*, 1983), the nation exemplifies and participates in the process by which identities that are constructed or imagined through interpellation or other means come to assume the force of nature. Such ideological constructs typically lead to essentialist definitions of national identity, reproduced in and then reinforced by the accounts of the history of the nation, and in its cultural texts, myths, and images. These acts of definition are, in turn, used to distinguish more or less absolutely one nation from another on the basis of geography, language(s), race, ethnicity, politics, or other cultural markers. In this way, nationalism arises out of these distinctions among nations, rather than as a product of a single nation. It may also arise out of the imposition of identity by an imperial power or the rejection of that identity and the assertion of a different one by a nation that comes out from under the yoke of oppression or foreign rule. A great deal of current work in postcolonial studies argues that both individual and national identities are never pure but always hybridized. Although our usual, common-sense way of understanding the relationship between nation and nationalism is to see the nation—a people defined by collective belonging to an extensive community, usually defined in relation to a specific territory—as primary, with nationalism as a frequent, though not inevitable, by-product, recent theories of the development of nations (Anderson, Gellner) suggest that the relationship might best be understood as working the other way around: that is, nations are how the ideological impulse of nationalism is legitimated and given concrete shape.

Patriarchy (Patriarchal): A social system in which men, usually through the figure of the father, hold power in the family and in the social structure. Patriarchy has more recently been used as a term in feminist criticism, where it is often equated with sexism, to describe the total system of gender relations in which male dominance has historically worked to dominate and disempower women and to support systemic inequities in society. The term now seems to have most value as a rallying cry in feminism, rather than as point of analysis. Contemporary critics argue that to analyze patriarchy on its own is to neglect the specific forms it takes under capitalism and through history, the relation between patriarchy and class, the specificities of nation, race, and ethnicity in relation to patriarchy, and the fact of different kinship and family structures in many cultures and societies.

Performativity: A term borrowed from the theatre and performance studies and used to express the constructedness of identity, it is especially used in discussions of sexuality. Developed most extensively in the theory of Judith Butler, performativity refers to the process by which identities are enacted through repeated performance, rather than inherently possessed or inhabited. The idea of performativity works on the premise that such roles as sex and gender are produced within an ideologically determined social script. While it is not possible to throw away the script—to be "oneself" instead of playing one's assigned role—the theory of performativity, by highlighting the tension between the scripted ideal and its embodied performance, offers possibilities for resisting the straitjacket of essentialist and traditionally defined identities.

Postcolonial(ism): Defined historically, the term "postcolonial" refers to the period after the formal retraction of colonial rule in the developing world. This varies considerably, but in the case of the former British colonies, it refers to the period after World War II. From the point of view of cultural theory, postcolonialism refers to the working through of the effects of colonization on a society or culture. It shares with poststructuralism and postmodernism a recognition of difference, rather than homogeneity, an anti-essentialist position on identity and meaning within culture, and often offers a critical perspective on the presumptive superiority of Eurocentric culture. The study of postcolonial culture examines the various mechanisms of colonialism (e.g., political rule, economic exploitation, colonial education systems) and their long-term, imbedded cultural and social implications. While many former colonies are now independent states, postcolonial studies insist on the need to recognize and understand the ways in which its effects persist in the ideologies and the social, cultural, and political life of those states today. Many contemporary postcolonial studies also address concepts of hybridity, imperialism, diasporic communities, the representations of migrancy, notions of race and ethnicity, and the role of the language of colonizers in creating a sense of inferiority among the colonized and a suppression of their indigenous culture.

Posthumanism: A term not to be confused with antihumanism, which involves a rejection of theories about humans promulgated during the period of the Enlightenment and after, without theorizing about what biological or technological destiny may lie beyond the form humans now take. Posthumanism as a philosophy questions concepts that underpin the tradition of humanism, such as identity, agency, subjectivity, consciousness, the soul, the idea of human beings as unique individuals and as a clearly defined, superior life form, and ultimately rejects the autonomy of "the human" in favour of the cyborg—a being defined by a combination of human and machine and/or animal characteristics. Posthumanism has been taken up both by feminists, for whom it represents a way of challenging biologically essentialist views of sex and gender, and by proponents of genetic engineering, who support the idea of designing "better," more powerful humans through technological enhancement. In this sense, the post- in posthumanism seeks to tell us what will come beyond, or after humans.

Postmodernism: A term with variant meanings when applied in different contexts. As a historical period that follows modernism, it generally denotes a phase in Western history that coincides with the information revolution and new forms of economic, social, and cultural life, especially since the appearance in the 1980s of Fredric Jameson's "Postmodernism of the Cultural Logic of Late Capitalism" (1984) and the film *Bladerunner*. When taken to refer to a sensibility, condition, or aesthetic, postmodernism is characterized by self-consciousness, skepticism in the face of grand or totalizing narratives, such as psychoanalysis or Marxism (Francois Lyotard in *The Postmodern Condition*), formal and stylistic borrowing, irony, pastiche, parody, recycling, sampling, and a mixing of high and low cultures. For Jean Baudrillard, postmodernism names the condition of a consumer society where the signifier has become detached from its signified and simulations replace the "real" world. For Fredric Jameson, it refers to a new phase of capitalism, usually referred to as late, or global capitalism, that is radically distinct from capitalism's earlier incarnations. As these variant understandings indicate, the term postmodernism is one of the most vexed in contemporary theory, and we may well do better to speak of postmodernisms, rather than a singular postmodernism.

Pseudo-individualization: As set out by Adorno and Horkheimer, this term refers to the mode of capitalist production wherein virtually identical cultural products are superficially varied to appeal to their consumers' sense of individuality (itself expressed superficially through virtually meaningless style in Adorno and Horkheimer's account), unique taste, and apparent freedom of choice.

Representation: A crucial term for all disciplines, particularly including all forms of Cultural Studies and the social sciences, that are concerned with how meaning is produced and consumed. Positions on representation vary widely, from what Stuart Hall identifies as the "reflective approach," in which representation is taken as reflecting the "true meaning of something as it already exists in the world" to the "intentional approach" in which things mean what the users of signs (e.g., words, images, gestures) intend them to mean, to the view of some poststructuralists who believe in an unreferenced play of signs detached from their signifiers. Seeing all of these positions as flawed, Hall proposes a constructionist approach, where "things don't mean," but "we construct meaning, using representational systems—concepts and signs." This view sees representation as a symbolic practice which gives meaning to the world (*Representation: Cultural Representations and Signifying Systems*, 1997). In all of these accounts, representation is inseparable from the socially specific processes of ideology and mythology and constructs the world in particular ways that have significant bearing on the organization of society.

Semiotics: Part of a move (spearheaded by Ferdinand de Saussure) in linguistic theory away from understanding how languages developed historically, or diachronically, to looking at them as structures at a single moment in time, or synchronically. de Saussure was interested in how the individual elements of language—signs—worked together, according to rules of selection and combination, to produce meaning. A fundamental principle of de Saussure's theory was the premise that the relationship between the two "parts" of a sign—a word (or signifier) and the concept it refers to (the signified)—is not natural but arbitrary, determined by convention.

Sign: The smallest unit (such as a word, image, or sound) of communication to which meaning is attached. In order to be a sign, the unit must meet three criteria: it must possess a physical form, it must refer to something else, and it must do so in a way that is recognizable to others. The sustained and large-scale interconnection of signs facilitates the construction of shared sign systems that enable individuals to communicate with other members of their culture in a comprehensible manner.

Simulacrum: A term having a variety of meanings, from "a material image of a deity," to "something having merely the form of a certain thing without its substance" to "specious imitation." The term is most closely associated with social theorist Jean Baudrillard who in *Simulacra and Simulation* makes clear that we inhabit a particular historical epoch dominated by the simulacrum. According to Baudrillard, the simulacrum has a history with four phases (see introduction to *Simulacrum and Simulation*). The postmodern period is defined by the fourth phase of the simulacrum which erases any discernable distinction between reality and its image. More specifically, this fourth phase is dominated by a culture (largely media driven) that produces images without attempting to ground them in reality. As a signifier without a signified (see *Sign,* above), a symptom of an illness which cannot be identified, the simulacrum proliferates and becomes more real than the reality to which it once was attached. Baudrillard's mandate is to draw attention to the fact that we allow ourselves to have reality—political, ideological, historical—mediated to us by images, rather than confronting the brute force of the real itself.

Stereotypes: A form of representation that reduces people to a few simple, essential characteristics presented as fixed by nature. Stereotyping is predicated on the simplistic notion that an individual's membership within any given social group (based on, for instance, class, gender, race, age, or sexuality) invariably predisposes him or her to possess certain personality characteristics, attitudes, or behaviours.

Structuralism: An analytical approach characterized largely by a shift in focus from interpreting a text in order to unveil its hidden meaning to identifying and interrogating the ways in which meaning is brought into being structurally. Structuralism is a diverse approach encompassing numerous methodologies, connected by this concern with the ways in which the structure of any given text is implicated in the production of its meaning. Although it has been subject to intensive critique (focusing, for example, on its inability to take account of historical change), structuralism's once-radical rejection of the role of relationship and context in determining meaning has been enormously influential in many disciplines.

Subculture: A term that describes groups or communities that deviate or differ from existing social norms. Subcultures are typically conceived of as groups of individuals who come together around shared practices and ideas that are rejected or treated with suspicion by the official, mainstream culture. By creatively expressing their dissatisfaction with existing social norms and practices, subcultures challenge and modify what counts as normal, everyday life. Subcultures are often identified with youth and youth culture in particular.

Index

and homogeneity, 149–50
and music industry, 150–51
and national cultural exports, 185–86
and "repatriation of difference," 147,
    149–50
Globe and Mail, 182
Glynn, Eugene David, 169–70
Godelier, M., 69
Goldiggers, 52
Goldman, Robert, 118
Gordon, Charles, 105
Gottdiener, N.I., 259
Gramsci, Antonio, 71, 72
Great Exhibition of 1851, 249
Greenberg, Clement, 166
Greyson, John, 191, 193, 198–99
Grierson, John, 107
Griffith, D.W., 298
Gruben, Patricia, 194
Gruen, Victor, 254
Grunge, 127
Guibaut, Serge, 199

H
Haag, Ernest van den, 166
Haase, Andrew, 325
Habitus, 249, 251
Haggard, Rider, 226, 230
Hahn, Karen von, 128
Hall, Stuart, 8–9, 69, 71, 72, 152
Hamilton, Linda, 281
Handler, Ruth, 269, 276
Haraway, Donna, 286
Hardy, Lady Mary McDowell, 244
Harlequin, 137
Harrap, 181
Harrington, Lee, 3
Hastings, Marquess of, 226
Hawksmoor, 31
Hearts of the World, 298
Hebdige, Dick, 33, 39, 64–73
Hegemony, 33, 35, 72–73, 210
Heidegger, Martin, 46
Helicopter Canada, 194
Hennepin, Louis, 243
Hermenaut, 124–25
"Hermeneutics of suspicion," 19
Hesse, Eva, 324

Heteronormativity, 26
Hewitt, Foster, 107
Hiding in the Light (Hebdige), 65
Hilfiger. *See* Tommy Hilfiger
Hilton, James, 226
Hip Hop, 122–23
The History of Sexuality (Foucault), 26, 229
Hitchcock, Alfred, 20–21, 211
Hockey, 107
Hodges, William, 226, 227
Hoggart, Richard, 7, 10, 67
Holley, George, 244
Honeymoon, concept of, 238–39
Hopson, Darlene Powell, 271, 272
Hopson, Derek S., 271, 272
Horkheimer, Max, 34, 36, 38, 51–63, 133,
    167
Horror genre
    body in, 283–84, 321–29
    monstrous-feminine, 301–17
Howells, William, 242
How New York Stole the Idea of Modern Art
    (Guibaut), 199
Hsieh, Howard, 335
Hughes, Robert, 231
Human identity, 42–50
    external forces, 42, 44–46
    language and, 45–50
    literature and, 47–49
    psychoanalytic theory, 46
    in science fiction, 318–30
Hutcheon, Linda, 30
Hyam, Ronald, 230
Hype!, 127
Hyperreality, 94, 96, 171–72, 256

I
"I AM CANADIAN" beer commercial, 147,
    183
Identification, imaginary, 131–32
Ideological State apparatuses (ISAs), 24
Ideology
    Althuser and, 23–24
    and common sense, 68–71
    of dominant groups, 71
    hegemony, 33
    and popular culture, 34–35
    and superstructure, 22–23

"Imaginary geographies," 239
"Imagined community," 28
Imperialism
    and civilization, 226, 232–33
    and commodification, 226, 231–32
    and culture, 233
    and exoticization, 225–28
    and globalization, 146–47
    and racialization, 225–26, 228–29
    and sexualization, 226, 229–31
Imperial Tobacco Company, 216
"In-betweenness," 125, 127
The Incredible Shrinking Man, 310
The Independent, 194
"Indie" marketing, 124
Infomercials, 173
Inness, Sherrie A., 184
Innis, Harold Adam, 112
Institute for Social Research. *See* Frankfurt
    School
International Alliance of Theatrical Stage
    Employees (IATSE), 192
Interpellation, 24, 177
The Interpretation of Dreams (Freud), 314
Intertexuality, 31–32
"Interview at Block Drift," 228
*An Introduction to Cultural Theory and
    Popular Culture* (Storey), 34
The Invasion of the Body Snatchers, 283, 304,
    319, 321, 327
Ironic consumption, 124–25, 127–28
Ito, Mizuko, 331–43

J

Jackson, Michael, 151
Jackson, Susan, 184
"Jamaica Talk," 271
Jamal doll, 275–76
James, Henry, 244
Jameson, Fredric, 33, 255, 259
JanMohamed, Abdul, 228
Jardine, Alice, 324
Jaws, 310
Jerusalem (Blake), 91
Jeter, K.W., 321
Jewison, Norman, 110, 192
Johnson, M., 256
Johnson, Samuel, 213

Jonas, Adolphe, 89
Jones, Lisa, 273, 274
Jordan, Claire, 231
Jordan, Winthrop, 233
Joyrich, Lynne, 162–76
Jutra, Claude, 198

K

Kadokawa, Haruki, 193
Kauffer, E. McKnight, 232
Keats, John, 49
Kelly, Mary, 314
Ken doll, 275–76
Kendrick, Walter, 140
Key Porter Canada, 181
Keywords (Williams), 2, 64
King, Stephen, 15
Kingsley, Mary, 226
King Solomon's Mines (Haggard), 230, 231
Kipling, Rudyard, 226, 231
Kitchen, R., 152
Kittler, Friedrich, 203
K-1 Khakis, 124
Klein, Naomi, 40, 115–30
Knight, Payne, 227
Kornfield, Eve, 184
Kowinski, William Severini, 250, 260
Krentz, Jayne Ann, 132–33
Kristeva, Julia, 301, 304, 307, 309, 310, 312
Kroker, Arthur, 320
Kroker, Marilouise, 320
Kubrick, Stanley, 322

L

The L. Report, 121
L.A. Gear, 119
Lacan, Jacques, 17, 307, 310, 311
Lackoff, G., 256
Lacoste, 123
Lang, Fritz, 31
Latent content, 19
Lauretis, Teresa de, 308
Laurier, Sir Wilfrid, 105
Lawrence, D.H., 30
Lazarsfeld, Paul, 168
Leacock, Stephen, 105
Leavis, F.R., 3–5, 64
Leavis, Q.D., 4

Mattel, 268, 269, 270, 271, 273, 274, 277
Maxwell, Ann, 139
McClintock, Ann, 230
McCombie, Mel, 275
McDaniels, Darryl, 122
McDougall, Walter, 319
McKinsey Elizabeth, 238
McLuhan, Marshall, 39, 87–92, 121, 203
Mechanical reproduction, 74–86
    art, 77
    authenticity and, 78–79
    film, 81–83
    of sound, 78
Medusa, 303
Mercer, Rick, 189
Merleau-Ponty, Maurice, 320
Meta-criticism, 163
Metanarratives, 32
Metro Goldwyn Mayer, 56
Metropolis, 31
MGM, 125
Might magazine, 118
Miklitsch, Robert, 290
Miller, J. Hillis, 20
Mitchell, Deborah, 272, 273
Mitchell, Juliet, 314
Mizejewski, Linda, 288–300
Modernist period, 30
Modern Movement, in architecture, 259
Modleski, Tania, 140, 141
Moffet, Samuel E., 105
Mohanty, C., 152
Molson, "Rant" commercial, 147, 183
Monck, Frances, 238
Le Monde (Paris), 104
Mondo Canuck (Pevere and Dymond), 12, 180, 182
Montgomery, Lucy Maud, 179, 181, 182–83
    See also Anne of Green Gables
       (Montgomery)
Montreal Gazette, 104
Montreal Star, 104
Moore, Thomas, 243
Morley, David, 169
Morrison, Toni, 276–77
Morrissette, Alanis, 153
Morton, W.L., 112

"Moses and Monotheism" (Freud), 306
Mother-Goddess, 306, 308
Mount Gay Barbados Rum advertisement, 223–235
Movable type, invention of, 203
Movies
    characteristics of film, 82–83
    uniformity of, 56–57
Multiculturalism, and conspicuous consumption of difference, 273–74
Multi-User Dungeon (MUD), 331–43
Mumford, Lewis, 92
Munsingwear, 123
Muraoka, Hanako, 181
Murder, 20–21
Music, popular
    Canadian industry, 153–54
    corporate concentration, 150–51
    "localization" and diversity, 151, 152, 156–59
    and national identity, 155–56
    production of place
Music videos, 173
Mythologies (Barthes), 18, 68, 72
Myths, structuralism and, 17

N
Nammu, 306
Nancy Drew and Company (Poe), 184
Nation
    American identity, 195, 197
    consumption of national identity, 156–58
    and national identity, 28–30, 152, 189–202
    pedagogical identity, 195
    in popular imagination, 147
    See also Canada
National Film Board (NFB), 107
National Policy Tariff of 1879, 103
National Post, 180
Naturalization, process of, 71
Nature tourism, 238
Nautica, 123
NBC, 106
Neuromancer, 285
New Democratic Party (NDP), 109

Newspapers
    advertising, 212–14
    Americanization of, 104
New York Herald, 104
New York Times Saturday Review of Books, 182
New York Trilogy, 31
New York World, 104
Next of Kin, 194
Niagara Falls, 236–48
    accident stories, 245–46
    attractions, 240–41
    female imagery, 244
    human imagery, 243–44
    "imaginary geographies" and, 239
    and nationalism, 242–43
    religious sentiment, 243
    sexual imagery, 244–45
    tourism, 239–41
    travel writing, 242–45
Nichelle doll, 272
Nicholls, Walter, Jr., 183
Nietzsche, Friedrich, 19
Nightmare on Elm Street series, 284
Night of the Living Dead, 283
Nights at the Circus (Carter), 33
Nike, 120, 122, 123, 126
North-American Cultural Studies, 10
Northern tour, 240
Nu Kwa, 306

O

"Oaitepeha (Tautira) Bay, Tahiti," 227
O'Brien, Susie, 26, 29–30
O'Connor, Flannery, 44
"Ode to a Nightingale" (Keats), 49
Oedipus complex, 307
Oedipus myth, 308
Of Grammatology (Derrida), 20, 48
OK Cola, 124
The Old Dark House, 321
Old Navy, 124
On Being Canadian (Massey), 108
Open Sky (Virilio), 88
Oral-sadistic mother, 312
Other, Otherness
    abjection and, 301
    of Barbados, 228
    dominant ideology and, 28

sexualization of, 226, 229–31
    See also Race
Overdetermination, 23–24

P

Page, 183
Papson, Stephen, 118
Parker, Gilbert, 105
Parody, in postmodernism, 31–32
Passagenwerk (Benjamin), 252
The Passion (Winterson), 33
Pearl Jam, 127
Pedagogical-performative model, 195, 197–98
Peoples, Larue, 199
Pepe Jeans, 122
"Person" *vs.* "human subject," 42–50
Pevere, Geoff, 12, 180, 182, 193, 194, 195
Phallic mother, 312–13, 314
Phantasm, 304
Phantasy, defined, 267
Philip Morris, 124
"Philosophical federalism," 196
The Philosophy of Horror (Carroll), 324
Picturesque tradition, 227–28
Pieterse, Jan Nederveen, 233
Pitman, 181
Pitt, Brad, 52
Pius IX, 243
Poe, K.L., 184
Polanski, Roman, 284
Politix cigarettes, 124
Polo, 122, 123
Popular culture
    "body issues," 281–87
    as consumption, 6
    definitions, 5–6
    as everyday culture, 6
    as folk culture, 5
    as mass culture, 5–6
    study of, 6–12, 67
    See also Culture; Mass culture
Pop Up Videos, 125
Postcolonialism, 29
Poster advertising, 214–15
The Postmodern Condition (Lyotard), 32
Postmodernism, 30–34
Poststructuralism, 19–21

Pound, Ezra, 30, 33
Poussin, Nicholas, 227
Power
    and ideology, 71
    relations of, 38, 39, 59, 64–73
    and subjection, 42
Powers of Horror (Kristeva), 301
Prada, 128
Prague circle, 17
Preliminary Bibliography of Lucy Maud
    Montgomery (Russell et al.), 179, 181
Presley, Elvis, 109
La Presse (Montreal), 104
Price, Uvedale, 227
Primitive Mythology (Campbell), 303
"The Primitive Spirit Refined." *See* Mount
    Gay Barbados Rum advertisement
Problems in Materialism and Culture
    (Williams), 209
Projection, 49
Psycho, 315
Psychoanalysis, 43
    and human identity, 46–47
    monstrous-feminine, 303, 304, 306–7,
      309, 314
Public relations, 220
Puff Daddy, 123

Q
Quake II, 286
Queer Studies, 26

R
Race
    British imperial and, 225–26, 228–29,
      232
    Demolition man, 296–97
    fetishization of white wealth, 123–24
    and identity, 28, 229
    and sexuality, 228–30
    white beauty myth, 276–77
Radio-Canada. *See* Canadian Broadcasting
    Corporation (CBC)
Radway, Janice, 34, 136–45, 334–35
The Raiders of the Lost Ark, 31
Ralph Lauren, 123
Reading the Romance (Radway), 136, 139, 334
Reality shows, 171–72

Rebecca of Sunnybrook Farm (Wiggin), 184
Rebick, Judy, 199
Red Line jeans, 124
Red or Dead, 128
Reifenstal, Leni, 51
"The Resistance to Psychoanalysis" (Freud),
    47
Reuben, Gloria, 295
"Revelation" (O'Connor), 44
Ribald, Carlo, 321
Rich, Adrienne, 26
Richards, Thomas, 231
Rieff, David, 274
Rifkind, Steve. *See* Steven Rifkind Company
Road to Avonlea series, 182
    See also Anne of Green Gables
      (Montgomery)
Roberts, Cynthia, 270
Roberts, David, 229
Roberts, John, 117
Rock and roll
Rod and Gun, 239
Rolling Stones, 151
Romance novels
    dismissal of, 138–41
    and feminine subjectivity, 143–44
    and located opposition, 335
    popularity of, 137–38
    publishing industry, 141–42
    writers, 142
Romance Report, 142
The Romance Revolution (Thurston), 143
Romance Writers Report, 138–39
Romanticism, 48–49
Romeo and Juliet, 45–46
Root, Jane, 169
Rosaldo, Renata, 227
Rosemary's Baby, 283–84
Rosler, Martha, 197
Rousseau, Jean-Jacques, 42, 48
Royle, Nicholas, 39–40, 42–50
Rubio, Mary, 179
Rucker, Rudy, 328
Run-DMC, 122
Russell, D.W., 179, 181
Russell, Ruth Weber, 179, 181
Russell, William, 244
Rutherford, Paul, 40, 101–14

Credits

This page constitutes an extension of the copyright page. We have made every effort to trace the ownership of all copyrighted material and to secure permission from copyright holders. In the event of any question arising as to the use of any material, we will be pleased to make the necessary corrections in future printings. Thanks are due to the following authors, publishers, and agents for permission to use the material indicated.

Unit 1, page 42: "Me," excerpted from *An Introduction to Literature, Criticism, and Theory* by Bennett & Royle. Reprinted by permission of Pearson Education Limited; **51:** "The Culture Industry: Enlightenment as Mass Deception," from *Dialectic of Enlightenment* by Theodor Adorno and Max Horkheimer. Copyright © English translation 1972 by Herder and Herder. Reprinted by permission of The Continuum International Publishing Group; **64:** "From Culture to Hegemony," extracted from: *Subculture: The Meaning of Style* by Dick Hebdige, 1979. Reprinted by permission of Taylor & Francis Books Ltd; **74:** "The Work of Art in the Age of Mechanical Reproduction," excerpted from *Illuminations* by Walter Benjamin, copyright © 1955 by Skhrkamp Verlag, Frankfurt a.M., English translation by Harry Zohn copyright © 1968 and renewed 1996 by Harcourt, Inc., reprinted by permission of Harcourt, Inc; **87:** "The Gadget Lover," from *Understanding Media: The Extensions of Man* by Marshall McLuhan, pp. 41-47, ISBN: 0262631598, 1994. Reprinted by permission of MIT Press; **93:** Excerpt from "The Precession of Simulacra," by Baudrillard and trans. by Glaser, pp. 1-6, 14-15. Reprinted by permission of University of Michigan Press; **101:** Excerpt from "Made in America: The Problem of Mass Culture in Canada," reprinted by permission of McGill-Queen's University Press; **115:** "Alt.Everything: The Youth Market and the Marketing of Cool," extracted from No Logo by Naomi Klein, Vintage Canada Edition, 2000. Copyright © 2000 by Naomi Klein. Reprinted by permission of Alfred A. Knopf Canada.

Unit 2, page 136: Excerpt from "Romance and the Work of Fantasy: Struggles over Feminine Sexuality and Subjectivity at Century's End" reprinted by permission of the author; **146:** "Site Reading? Globalization, Identity, and the Consumption of Place in Popular Music," by Minelle Mahtani and Scott Salmon, in *Popular Culture: Production and Consumption* by C. Lee Harrington and Denise D. Bielby (eds), Chapter 13, pp. 165-176. Reprinted by permission of Blackwell Publishing; **162:** "Good Reception? Television, Gender, and the Critical View" excerpted from *Re-viewing Reception* (Electronic resource) by Lynne Joyrich, pp. 21-42, ISBN: 0585028753, 1996. Reprinted by permission of Indiana University Press; **177:** Excerpt from "'Canadian Classic' and 'Commodity Export': The Nationalism of 'Our' *Anne of Green Gables*," by Cecily Devereux, in *Journal of Canadian Studies*, Vol. 36, No. 1, Spring

2001, pp. 11-25. Reprinted by permission of the Journal of Canadian Studies; **189:** Excerpt from "Packaged For Export, Contents Under Pressure: Canadian Film and Video in a U.S. Context," reprinted by permission of Laura U. Marks.

Unit 3, page 209: "Advertising: The Magic System," excerpted from *Problems in Materialism and Culture* by Raymond Williams. Reprinted by permission of Verso Books; **223:** "Art, Advertising, and the Legacy of Empire" by Jeffrey Auerbach, in *Journal of Popular Culture*, Vol. 35.4, Spring 2002, pp. 1-21. Reprinted by permission of Blackwell Publishing; **236:** Excerpt from "The Second Greatest Disappointment: Honeymooning and Tourism at Niagara Falls," reprinted by permission of Between the Lines Press; **249:** Excerpt from "Social Spatialization and the Built Environment: The West Edmonton Mall," reprinted by permission of Rob Shields; **266:** Excerpt from Ann du Cille, "Dyes and Dolls: Multicultural Barbie and the Merchandizing of Difference" in *Differences: A Journal of Feminist Cultural Studies*, Volume 6, No. 1, pp. 46-68. Copyright, 1994, Indiana University Press. All rights reserved. Used by permission of the publisher.

Unit 4, page 288: Excerpt from "Action Bodies in Futurist Spaces" by Linda Mizejewski, in *Alien Zone 2* by Annette Kuhn, Verso Books, 1999. Reprinted by permission of Verso Books; **301:** Excerpt from "Horror and the Monstrous-Feminine: An Imaginary Abjection," from *Fantasy and the Cinema* by James Donald. Reprinted by permissions of BFI Publishing; **318:** Scott Bukatman, excerpts from *Terminal Identity: The Virtual Subject in Postmodern Science Fiction*, pp. 243-247, 259-272. Copyright, 1993, Duke University Press. All rights reserved. Used by permission of the publisher; **331:** Excerpt from "Virtually Embodied: The Reality of Fantasy in a Multi-User Dungeon," copyright 1997 From *Internet Culture* by David Porter (ed). Reproduced by permission of Routledge/Taylor & Francis Books, Inc.